COMMAND REFERENCE (a-l)

UNIX SVR4.2

Edited by Lynda Feng

UNIX
Press

Published by Prentice-Hall, Inc.
A Simon & Schuster Company
Englewood Cliffs, New Jersey 07632

IMPORTANT NOTE TO USERS

While every effort has been made to ensure the accuracy and completeness of all information in this document, USL assumes no liability to any party for any loss or damage caused by errors or omissions or by statements of any kind in this document, its updates, supplements, or special editions, whether such errors, omissions, or statements result from negligence, accident, or any other cause. USL further assumes no liability arising out of the application or use of any product or system described herein; nor any liability for incidental or consequential damages arising from the use of this document. **USL disclaims all warranties regarding the information contained herein, whether expressed, implied or statutory, including implied warranties of merchantability or fitness for a particular purpose.** USL makes no representation that the interconnection of products in the manner described herein will not infringe on existing or future patent rights, nor do the descriptions contained herein imply the granting of any license to make, use or sell equipment constructed in accordance with this description.

USL reserves the right to make changes to any products herein without further notice.

Certain pages contained in this document, which bear a notice that they are derived from material which is copyright (c) 1990 the Massachusetts Institute of Technology, are based on information contained in MIT's X Windows documentation. The following paragraph applies to those pages in their original form as provided by M.I.T.:

> "Permission to use, copy, modify, and distribute this documentation (*i.e., the original MIT and DEC material*) for any purpose and without fee is hereby granted, provided that the above copyright notice appears in all copies and that both that copyright notice and this permission notice appear in supporting documentation, and that the name of MIT or Digital not be used in advertising or publicity pertaining to distribution of the software without specific, written prior permission. MIT and Digital make no representation about the suitability of the software described herein for any purpose. It is provided 'as is' without expressed or implied warranty."

TRADEMARKS

UNIX is a registered trademark of UNIX System Laboratories, Inc. in the USA and other countries.
WE is a registered trademark of AT&T.
XENIX is a registered trademark of Microsoft Corporation.

10 9 8 7 6 5 4 3 2 1

ISBN 0-13-042599-0

PRENTICE HALL

ORDERING INFORMATION

UNIX® SYSTEM V RELEASE 4.2 DOCUMENTATION

To order single copies of UNIX® SYSTEM V Release 4.2 documentation, please call (515) 284-6761.

ATTENTION DOCUMENTATION MANAGERS AND TRAINING DIRECTORS:

For bulk purchases in excess of 30 copies, please write to:

Corporate Sales Department
PTR Prentice Hall
113 Sylvan Avenue
Englewood Cliffs, N.J. 07632

or

Phone: (201) 592-2863
FAX: (201) 592-2249

ATTENTION GOVERNMENT CUSTOMERS:

For GSA and other pricing information, please call (201) 461-7107.

Prentice-Hall International (UK) Limited, *London*
Prentice-Hall of Australia Pty. Limited, *Sydney*
Prentice-Hall Canada Inc., *Toronto*
Prentice-Hall Hispanoamericana, S.A., *Mexico*
Prentice-Hall of India Private Limited, *New Delhi*
Prentice-Hall of Japan, Inc., *Tokyo*
Simon & Schuster Asia Pte. Ltd., *Singapore*
Editora Prentice-Hall do Brasil, Ltda., *Rio de Janeiro*

Command Reference - Volume I

Introduction

Commands a - l

Permuted Index

Command Reference - Volume II

Introduction

Commands m - z

nm(1) .... print name list of an object file
nohup(1) .... run a command immune to hangups and quits
notify(1) .... notify user of the arrival of new mail
nroff(1) .... (BSD) format documents for display or line-printer
nslookup(1M) .... query name servers interactively
nsquery(1M) .... Remote File Sharing name server query
od(1) .... octal dump
olwm(1) .... Window Manager
pack, pcat, unpack(1) .... compress and expand files
pagesize(1) .... (BSD) display the size of a page of memory
partsize(1M) .... returns the size of the active UNIX System partition
passwd(1) .... change login password and password attributes
paste(1) .... merge same lines of several files or subsequent lines of one file
pathconv(1F) .... search FMLI criteria for filename
pchown(1M) .... change owner of mail files
pciconsvr.ip(1M) .... manages the connection between the personal computer and the host
pcidebug(1M) .... controls log output of the executing DOS server
pcidossvr(1M)
maintains an exclusive dialog with the bridge driver (BRIDGE.DRV) on the personal computer
pcimapsvr.ip(1M) .... listens for broadcasts from the connection server daemons
pciprint(1M) .... sample print program
pcistart(1M) .... starts the PC-Interface daemons on the host
pcistop(1M) .... terminates PC-Interface execution on the host
pcnfsd(1M) .... NFS daemon for PC–NFS user authentication and remote printing
pdiadd(1M) .... add new disk, tape, or SCSI devices to the UNIX System kernel
pdiconfig(1M) .... determine which PDI disk, tape, and SCSI controllers are present
pdimkdev(1M) .... generate device nodes for the Portable Device Interface (PDI) subsystem
pdimkdtab(1M)
.... update the device table entries for the Portable Device Interface (PDI) subsystem
pdirm(1M) .... remove existing disk, tape, or SCSI devices from the UNIX System kernel
pfb2pfa(1) .... convert PostScript Type 1 outline fonts from binary to ASCII
pfmt(1) .... display error message in standard format
pg(1) .... file perusal filter for CRTs
ping(1M) .... send ICMP ECHO_REQUEST packets to network hosts
pkgadd(1M) .... transfer software package or set to the system
pkgask(1M) .... stores answers to a request script
pkgchk(1M) .... check accuracy of installation
pkginfo(1) .... display software package and/or set information
pkgmk(1) .... produce an installable package
pkgparam(1) .... displays package parameter values
pkgproto(1) .... generate a prototype file
pkgrm(1M) .... removes a package or set from the system
pkgtrans(1) .... translate package format

Permuted Index

Introduction

The UNIX System is widely praised for its broad set of flexible commands that give ordinary users far more power than other operating systems. This two-volume book contains a description of every UNIX System command in alphabetical order by command name, including the BSD® and XENIX® System variants. The Command Reference is part of a comprehensive reference set produced by the makers of UNIX System V Release 4 software. The set contains a manual page for every UNIX system interface.

Experienced UNIX system users will find the Command Reference indispensable. Readers who are familiar with another operating system, or any programming language, can rely upon the Command Reference to quickly become conversant with UNIX system commands. Those who are not familiar with any command interfaces should use the Command Reference in conjunction with some introductory tutorial material.

The Command Reference describes the superset of commands available on a fully loaded UNIX system. The most commonly used commands are available on all UNIX systems, but more specialized commands may be part of optionally installable software packages. If you cannot execute a command, first look in the directories where most commands reside to see if it is installed on your system. If you find it, try to execute it by typing the command's full pathname. If you still cannot execute it, verify that you have sufficient privileges to run it.

INTRODUCTION

Finding the Right Page

Reference books are handy when you know what command you are looking for, but less useful when you don't known what particular command to use. In such cases, the index (at the back of the book) can be helpful. Its middle column lists keywords and the manual pages on which they appear. Before you use the index, read the explanation that precedes it.

The SEE ALSO line at the bottom of each manual page cross-references related material, including manual pages in other books in the reference set. The Command Reference only contains commands — as opposed to system calls, file descriptions and so on. All commands are designated by a section number beginning with (1), such as (1), (1M), (1C), and (1F). System calls are designated with (2), libraries with (3), files with (4), miscellaneous pages with a (5), and special files with (7). The table on the inner front cover of this book lists the categories denoted by different section numbers, along with the books in which they are found.

The section 1 commands are further broken down into: (1), (1C), (1F), and (1M). The alphabetic appendages provide a clue about a command's purpose: (1) are general user's commands, (1C) are a subset of the networking commands, (1M) are system administration commands, and (1F) are Forms and Menu Language Interface commands.

When looking for a manual page, you will sometimes encounter multiple manual pages for a single command. For example, two manual pages are required when a UNIX system variant, such as XENIX or BSD, has a like-named command that behaves differently than its UNIX System V Release 4 counterpart. The behavior of such commands on your system depends on whether the XENIX or BSD compatibility software is installed.

Similarly, you may find two or more like-named manual pages for commands that function differently on different file system types. The UNIX system supports several types of file systems, including Veritas, UFS, and S5. (File systems are just methods of organizing data on a disk.) File system commands (such as `df`(1M)) may have some options that are valid for all file system types and other options that are only valid for a particular file system type. In such cases, a generic manual page describes the options that apply to all file system types, and a separate manual page describes options that apply to a particular file system.

In cases where there is more than one manual page for a single command, a top center header on the page indicates the distinction among the like-name pages.

Manual Page Format

All manual page entries use a common format, not all of whose parts always appear:

- The **NAME** section gives the name(s) of the entry and briefly states its purpose.
- The **SYNOPSIS** section summarizes the use of the command, program or function. A few conventions are used:
  - **`Constant width typeface`** strings are literals and are to be typed just as they appear.
  - *Italic* strings usually represent substitutable argument prototypes and functions.
  - Square brackets [ ] around an argument prototype indicate that the argument is optional. When an argument prototype is given as *name* or *file*, it typically refers to a file name.

- Ellipses . . . are used to show that the previous argument prototype may be repeated.
- For commands, an argument beginning with a minus – or plus + sign is often taken to be a flag argument, even if it appears in a position where a file name could appear. Therefore, it is unwise to have files whose names begin with – or +.

- The **DESCRIPTION** section describes the utility.
- The **EXAMPLE** section gives example(s) of usage, where appropriate.
- The **FILES** section gives the file names that are built into the program.
- The **SEE ALSO** section gives pointers to related information. Reference to manual pages with section numbers other than those in this book can be found in other reference manuals, as listed above.
- The **DIAGNOSTICS** section discusses the diagnostic indications that may be produced. Messages that are intended to be self-explanatory are not listed.
- The **NOTES** section gives generally helpful hints about the use of the utility.

NAME

`intro` – introduction to commands and application programs

DESCRIPTION

This section describes, in alphabetical order, commands, including user commands, programming commands and administrative commands.

There are several instances of multiple manual pages with the same name. For example, there are eight manual pages called **`mount`**(1M). In each such case the first of the multiple pages describes the syntax and options of the generic command, that is, those options applicable to all FSTypes (file system types). The succeeding pages describe the functionality of the FSType-specific modules of the command. These pages all display the name of the FSType to which they pertain centered and in parentheses at the top of the page. You should not attempt to call these modules directly - the generic command provides a common interface to all of them. Thus the FSType-specific manual pages should not be viewed as describing distinct commands, but rather as detailing those aspects of a command that are specific to a particular FSType.

Manual Page Command Syntax

Unless otherwise noted, commands described in the **SYNOPSIS** section of a manual page accept options and other arguments according to the following syntax and should be interpreted as explained below.

name [-*option*...] [*cmdarg*...]
where:

[ ]	Surround an *option* or *cmdarg* that is not required.
...	Indicates multiple occurrences of the *option* or *cmdarg*.
name	The name of an executable file.
option	(Always preceded by a "-".) *noargletter*... or, *argletter optarg*[,...]
noargletter	A single letter representing an option without an option-argument. Note that more than one *noargletter* option can be grouped after one "-" (Rule 5, below).
argletter	A single letter representing an option requiring an option-argument.
optarg	An option-argument (character string) satisfying a preceding *argletter*. Note that groups of *optargs* following an *argletter* must be separated by commas, or separated by white space and quoted (Rule 8, below).
cmdarg	Path name (or other command argument) *not* beginning with "-", or "-" by itself indicating the standard input.

Command Syntax Standard: Rules

These command syntax rules are not followed by all current commands, but all new commands will obey them. **`getopts`**(1) should be used by all shell procedures to parse positional parameters and to check for legal options. It supports Rules 3-10 below. The enforcement of the other rules must be done by the command itself.

1. Command names (*name* above) must be between two and nine characters long.
2. Command names must include only lower-case letters and digits.
3. Option names (*option* above) must be one character long.
4. All options must be preceded by "-".
5. Options with no arguments may be grouped after a single "-".
6. The first option-argument (*optarg* above) following an option must be preceded by white space.
7. Option-arguments cannot be optional.
8. Groups of option-arguments following an option must either be separated by commas or separated by white space and quoted (for example, `-o xxx,z,yy` or `-o "xxx z yy"`).
9. All options must precede operands (*cmdarg* above) on the command line.
10. "--" may be used to indicate the end of the options.
11. The order of the options relative to one another should not matter.
12. The relative order of the operands (*cmdarg* above) may affect their significance in ways determined by the command with which they appear.
13. "-" preceded and followed by white space should only be used to mean standard input.

DIAGNOSTICS

Upon termination, each command returns two bytes of status, one supplied by the system and giving the cause for termination, and (in the case of "normal" termination) one supplied by the program [see **wait**(2) and **exit**(2)]. The former byte is 0 for normal termination; the latter is customarily 0 for successful execution and non-zero to indicate troubles such as erroneous parameters, or bad or inaccessible data. It is called variously "exit code", "exit status", or "return code", and is described only where special conventions are involved.

NAME

accept, **reject** – accept or reject print requests

SYNOPSIS

accept *destinations*
reject [**-r** *reason*] *destinations*

DESCRIPTION

accept allows the queuing of print requests for the named *destinations*. A *destination* can be either a printer or a class of printers. Run **lpstat -a** to find the status of *destinations*.

reject prevents queuing of print requests for the named *destinations*. A *destination* can be either a printer or a class of printers. Run **lpstat -a** to find the status of *destinations*.

-r *reason* Assign a *reason* for rejection of requests. This *reason* applies to all *destinations* specified. The *reason* is reported by **lpstat -a**. It may contain supplementary code set characters, as defined in the locale specified in the **LC_CTYPE** environment variable [see **LANG** on **environ**(5)]. If it contains blanks, *reason* must be enclosed in quotes. The default reason is **unknown reason** for existing destinations, and **new destination** for destinations just added to the system but not yet accepting requests.

FILES

/var/spool/lp/*
/usr/lib/locale/*locale***/LC_MESSAGES/uxlp**
language-specific message file [See **LANG** on **environ**(5).]

SEE ALSO

enable(1M), **lpadmin**(1M), **lpsched**(1M)

NAME

acct: **acctdisk**, **acctdusg**, **accton**, **acctwtmp** **closewtmp**, **utmp2wtmp** – overview of accounting and miscellaneous accounting commands

SYNOPSIS

/usr/lib/acct/acctdisk

/usr/lib/acct/acctdusg [**-u** *file*] [**-p** *file*]

/usr/lib/acct/accton [*file*]

/usr/lib/acct/acctwtmp "*reason*"

/usr/lib/acct/closewtmp

/usr/lib/acct/utmp2wtmp

DESCRIPTION

Accounting software is structured as a set of tools (consisting of both C programs and shell procedures) that can be used to build accounting systems. **acctsh**(1M) describes the set of shell procedures built on top of the C programs.

Connect time accounting is handled by various programs that write records into **/var/adm/wtmp**, as described in **utmp**(4). The programs described in **acctcon**(1M) convert this file into session and charging records, which are then summarized by **acctmerg**(1M).

Process accounting is performed by the UNIX system kernel. Upon termination of a process, one record per process is written to a file (normally **/var/adm/pacct**). The programs in **acctprc**(1M) summarize this data for charging purposes; **acctcms**(1M) is used to summarize command usage. Current process data may be examined using **acctcom**(1).

Process accounting and connect time accounting [or any accounting records in the **tacct** format described in **acct**(4)] can be merged and summarized into total accounting records by **acctmerg** [see **tacct** format in **acct**(4)]. **prtacct** [see **acctsh**(1M)] is used to format any or all accounting records.

acctdisk reads lines that contain user ID, login name, and number of disk blocks and converts them to total accounting records that can be merged with other accounting records.

acctdusg reads its standard input (usually from **find / -print**) and computes disk resource consumption (including indirect blocks) by login. If **-u** is given, records consisting of those filenames for which **acctdusg** charges no one are placed in *file* (a potential source for finding users trying to avoid disk charges). If **-p** is given, *file* is the name of the password file. This option is not needed if the password file is **/etc/passwd**. (See **diskusg**(1M) for more details.)

accton alone turns process accounting off. If *file* is given, it must be the name of an existing file, to which the kernel appends process accounting records [see **acct**(2) and **acct**(4)].

acctwtmp writes a **utmp**(4) record to its standard output. The record contains the current time and a string of characters that describe the *reason*. A record type of ACCOUNTING is assigned [see **utmp**(4)]. *reason* must be a string of 11 or fewer characters, numbers, **$**, or spaces. For example, the following are suggestions for use in reboot and shutdown procedures, respectively:

```
acctwtmp "acctg on" >> /var/adm/wtmp
acctwtmp "acctg off" >> /var/adm/wtmp
```

For each user currently logged on, **closewtmp** puts a false **DEAD_PROCESS** record in the **/var/adm/wtmp** file. **runacct** (see **runacct(1M)**) uses this false **DEAD_PROCESS** record so that the connect accounting procedures can track the time used by users logged on before **runacct** was invoked.

For each user currently logged on, **runacct** uses **utmp2wtmp** to create an entry in the file **/var/adm/wtmp**, created by **runacct**. Entries in **/var/adm/wtmp** enable subsequent invocations of **runacct** to account for connect times of users currently logged in.

FILES

/etc/passwd	used for login name to user ID conversions
/usr/lib/acct	holds all accounting commands listed in sub-class 1M of this manual
/var/adm/pacct	current process accounting file
/var/adm/wtmp	login/logoff history file

SEE ALSO

acct(2), **acct**(4), **acctcms**(1M), **acctcom**(1), **acctcon**(1M), **acctmerg**(1M), **acctprc**(1M), **acctsh**(1M), **diskusg**(1M), **fwtmp**(1M), **runacct**(1M), **utmp**(4)

acctcms (1M)

NAME

acctcms – command summary from per-process accounting records

SYNOPSIS

/usr/lib/acct/acctcms [**-a** [**-p**] [**-o**]] [**-c**] [**-j**] [**-n**] [**-s**] [**-t**] *files*

DESCRIPTION

acctcms reads one or more *files*, normally in the form described in **acct**(4). It adds all records for processes that executed identically-named commands, sorts them, and writes them to the standard output, normally using an internal summary format. The options are:

- **-a** Print output in ASCII rather than in the internal summary format. The output includes command name, number of times executed, total kcore-minutes, total CPU minutes, total real minutes, mean size (in K), mean CPU minutes per invocation, "hog factor," characters transferred, and blocks read and written, as in **acctcom**(1). Output is normally sorted by total kcore-minutes.
- **-c** Sort by total CPU time, rather than total kcore-minutes.
- **-j** Combine all commands invoked only once under "***other."
- **-n** Sort by number of command invocations.
- **-s** Any filenames encountered hereafter are already in internal summary format.
- **-t** Process all records as total accounting records. The default internal summary format splits each field into prime and non-prime time parts. This option combines the prime and non-prime time parts into a single field that is the total of both, and provides upward compatibility with old (that is, pre-UNIX System V Release 4.0) style **acctcms** internal summary format records.

The following options may be used only with the **-a** option.

- **-p** Output a prime-time-only command summary.
- **-o** Output a non-prime (offshift) time only command summary.

When **-p** and **-o** are used together, a combination prime and non-prime time report is produced. All the output summaries will be total usage except number of times executed, CPU minutes, and real minutes, which will be split into prime and non-prime.

A typical sequence for performing daily command accounting and for maintaining a running total is:

```
acctcms file ... > today
cp total previoustotal
acctcms -s today previoustotal > total
acctcms -a -s today
```

SEE ALSO

acct(1M), **acct**(2), **acct**(4), **acctcom**(1), **acctcon**(1M), **acctmerg**(1M), **acctprc**(1M), **acctsh**(1M), **fwtmp**(1M), **runacct**(1M), **utmp**(4)

NOTES

Unpredictable output results if `-t` is used on new style internal summary format files, or if it is not used with old style internal summary format files.

acctcom (1)

NAME

acctcom – search and print process accounting file(s)

SYNOPSIS

acctcom [*options*] [*file . . .*]

DESCRIPTION

acctcom reads *file*, the standard input, or /var/adm/pacct, in the form described by acct(4) and writes selected records to the standard output. Each record represents the execution of one process. The output shows the COMMAND NAME, USER, TTYNAME, START TIME, END TIME, REAL (SEC), CPU (SEC), MEAN SIZE (K), and optionally, F (the fork/exec flag: 1 for fork without exec), STAT (the system exit status), HOG FACTOR, KCORE MIN, CPU FACTOR, CHARS TRNSFD, and BLOCKS READ (total blocks read and written).

A # is prefixed to the command name if the command was executed by a privileged user. If a process is not associated with a known terminal, a ? is printed in the TTYNAME field.

If no *files* are specified, and if the standard input is associated with a terminal or /dev/null (as is the case when using & in the shell), /var/adm/pacct is read; otherwise, the standard input is read.

If any *file* arguments are given, they are read in their respective order. Each file is normally read forward, that is, in chronological order by process completion time. The file /var/adm/pacct is usually the current file to be examined; a busy system may need several such files of which all but the current file are found in /var/adm/pacct*incr*.

The *options* are:

-a Show some average statistics about the processes selected. The statistics will be printed after the output records.

-b Read backwards, showing latest commands first. This option has no effect when the standard input is read.

-f Print the fork/exec flag and system exit status columns in the output. The numeric output for this option will be in octal.

-h Instead of mean memory size, show the fraction of total available CPU time consumed by the process during its execution. This "hog factor" is computed as (total CPU time)/(elapsed time).

-i Print columns containing the I/O counts in the output.

-k Instead of memory size, show total kcore-minutes.

-m Show mean core size (the default).

-r Show CPU factor [user-time/(system-time + user-time)].

-t Show separate system and user CPU times.

-v Exclude column headings from the output.

-l *line* Show only processes belonging to terminal **/dev/term/***line*.

-u *user* Show only processes belonging to *user* that may be specified by: a user ID, a login name that is then converted to a user ID, a **#**, which designates only those processes executed by a privileged user, or **?**, which designates only those processes associated with unknown user IDs.

-g *group* Show only processes belonging to *group*. The *group* may be designated by either the group ID or group name.

-s *time* Select processes existing at or after *time*, given in the format *hr* [: *min* [: *sec*]].

-e *time* Select processes existing at or before *time*.

-S *time* Select processes starting at or after *time*.

-E *time* Select processes ending at or before *time*. Using the same *time* for both **-S** and **-E** shows the processes that existed at *time*.

-n *pattern* Show only commands matching *pattern* that may be a regular expression as in **regcmp**(3G), except + means one or more occurrences.

-q Do not print any output records, just print the average statistics as with the **-a** option.

-o *ofile* Copy selected process records in the input data format to *ofile*; suppress printing to standard output.

-H *factor* Show only processes that exceed *factor*, where factor is the "hog factor" as explained in option **-h** above.

-O *sec* Show only processes with CPU system time exceeding *sec* seconds.

-C *sec* Show only processes with total CPU time (system-time + user-time) exceeding *sec* seconds.

-I *chars* Show only processes transferring more characters than the cutoff number given by *chars*.

FILES

/etc/passwd
/var/adm/pacct*incr*
/etc/group

SEE ALSO

acct(1M), **acct**(2), **acct**(4), **acctcms**(1M), **acctcon**(1M), **acctmerg**(1M), **acctprc**(1M), **acctsh**(1M), **fwtmp**(1M), **ps**(1), **regcmp**(3G), **runacct**(1M), **su**(1M), **utmp**(4)

NOTES

acctcom reports only on processes that have terminated; use **ps**(1) for active processes.

If *time* exceeds the present time, then *time* is interpreted as occurring on the previous day.

acctcon (1M)

NAME

acctcon, **acctcon1**, **acctcon2** – connect-time accounting

SYNOPSIS

/usr/lib/acct/acctcon [*options*]

/usr/lib/acct/acctcon1 [*options*]

/usr/lib/acct/acctcon2

DESCRIPTION

acctcon converts a sequence of login/logoff records to total accounting records (see the **tacct** format in **acct(4)**). login/logoff records are read from standard input. The file **/var/adm/wtmp** is usually the source of the login/logoff records, however, because it may contain corrupted records or system date changes, it should first be fixed using **wtmpfix**. The fixed version of file **/var/adm/wtmp** can then be redirected to **acctcon**. The **tacct** records are written to standard output. Here are the options for **acctcon**:

-l *file* — *file* is created to contain a summary of line usage showing line name, number of minutes used, percentage of total elapsed time used, number of sessions charged, number of logins, and number of logoffs. This file helps track line usage, identify bad lines, and find software and hardware oddities. Hangup, termination of **login**(1) and termination of the login shell each generate logoff records, so that the number of logoffs is often three to four times the number of sessions. See **init**(1M) and **utmp**(4).

-o *file* — *file* is filled with an overall record for the accounting period, giving starting time, ending time, number of reboots, and number of date changes.

acctcon is a combination of the programs **acctcon1** and **acctcon2**. **acctcon1** converts login/logoff records, taken from the fixed **/var/adm/wtmp** file, to ASCII output. **acctcon2** reads the ASCII records produced by **acctcon1** and converts them to **tacct** records. **acctcon1** can be used with the –l and –o options, described above, as well as with the following options:

-p — Print input only, showing line name, login name, and time (in both numeric and date/time formats).

-t — **acctcon1** maintains a list of lines on which users are logged in. When it reaches the end of its input, it emits a session record for each line that still appears to be active. It normally assumes that its input is a current file, so that it uses the current time as the ending time for each session still in progress. The **-t** flag causes it to use, instead, the last time found in its input, thus assuring reasonable and repeatable numbers for non-current files.

EXAMPLES

The **acctcon** command is typically used as follows:

```
acctcon -l lineuse -o reboots < tmpwtmp > ctacct
```

The **acctcon1** and **acctcon2** commands are typically used as follows:

```
acctcon1 -l lineuse -o reboots < tmpwtmp | sort +1n +2 > ctmp
acctcon2 < ctmp > ctacct
```

FILES

/var/adm/wtmp

SEE ALSO

acct(1M), acct(2), acct(4), acctcms(1M), acctcom(1), acctmerg(1M), acctprc(1M), acctsh(1M), fwtmp(1M), init(1M), login(1), runacct(1M), utmp(4)

NOTES

The line usage report is confused by date changes. Use **wtmpfix** (see **fwtmp**(1M)), with the **/var/adm/wtmp** file as an argument, to correct this situation.

acctmerg (1M)

NAME

acctmerg – merge or add total accounting files

SYNOPSIS

/usr/lib/acct/acctmerg [**-a**] [**-i**] [**-p**] [**-t**] [**-u**] [**-v**] [*file*] . . .

DESCRIPTION

acctmerg reads its standard input and up to nine additional files, all in the **tacct** format [see **acct**(4)] or an ASCII version thereof. It merges these inputs by adding records whose keys (normally user ID and name) are identical, and expects the inputs to be sorted on those keys. Options are:

- **-a** Produce output in ASCII version of **tacct**.
- **-i** Input files are in ASCII version of **tacct**.
- **-p** Print input with no processing.
- **-t** Produce a single record that totals all input.
- **-u** Summarize by user ID, rather than user ID and name.
- **-v** Produce output in verbose ASCII format, with more precise notation for floating–point numbers.

EXAMPLES

The following sequence is useful for making "repairs" to any file kept in this format:

acctmerg -v <*file1* > *file2*

Edit *file2* as desired . . .

acctmerg -i <*file2* > *file1*

SEE ALSO

acct(1M), **acct**(2), **acctcms**(1M), **acctcom**(1), **acctcon**(1M), **acctprc**(1M), **acctsh**(1M), **fwtmp**(1M), **runacct**(1M), **acct**(4), **utmp**(4)

NAME

acctprc, **acctprc1**, **acctprc2** – process accounting

SYNOPSIS

/usr/lib/acct/acctprc

/usr/lib/acct/acctprc1 [*ctmp*]

/usr/lib/acct/acctprc2

DESCRIPTION

acctprc reads standard input, in the form described by **acct(4)**, and converts it to total accounting records [see the **tacct** record in **acct**(4)]. **acctprc** divides CPU time into prime time and non-prime time and determines mean memory size (in memory segment units). **acctprc** then summarizes the **tacct** records, according to user IDs, and adds login names corresponding to the user IDs. The summarized records are then written to standard output. **acctprc1** reads input in the form described by **acct**(4), adds login names corresponding to user IDs, then writes for each process an ASCII line giving user ID, login name, prime CPU time (tics), non-prime CPU time (tics), and mean memory size (in memory segment units). If *ctmp* is given, it is expected to contain a list of login sessions sorted by user ID and login name. If this file is not supplied, it obtains login names from the password file, just as **acctprc** does. The information in *ctmp* helps it distinguish between different login names sharing the same user ID.

From standard input, **acctprc2** reads records in the form written by **acctprc1**, summarizes them according to user ID and name, then writes the sorted summaries to the standard output as total accounting records.

EXAMPLES

The **acctprc** command is typically used as shown below:

```
acctprc < /var/adm/pacct > ptacct
```

The **acctprc1** and **acctprc2** commands are typically used as shown below:

```
acctprc1 ctmp </var/adm/pacct | acctprc2 >ptacct
```

FILES

/etc/passwd

SEE ALSO

acct(1M), **acct**(2), **acct**(4), **acctcms**(1M), **acctcom**(1), **acctcon**(1M), **acctmerg**(1M), **acctsh**(1M), **cron**(1M), **fwtmp**(1M), **runacct**(1M), **utmp**(4)

NOTES

Although it is possible for **acctprc1** to distinguish among login names that share user IDs for commands run normally, it is difficult to do this for those commands run from **cron**(1M), for example. A more precise conversion can be done using the **acctwtmp** program in **acct**(1M). **acctprc** does not distinguish between users with identical user IDs.

A memory segment of the mean memory size is a unit of measure for the number of bytes in a logical memory segment on a particular processor.

acctsh (1M)

NAME

acctsh: **chargefee**, **ckpacct**, **dodisk**, **lastlogin**, **monacct**, **nulladm**, **prctmp**, **prdaily**, **prtacct**, **runacct**, **shutacct**, **startup**, **turnacct** – shell procedures for accounting

SYNOPSIS

/usr/lib/acct/chargefee *login-name number*

/usr/lib/acct/ckpacct [*blocks*]

/usr/lib/acct/dodisk [-o] [*files* . . .]

/usr/lib/acct/lastlogin

/usr/lib/acct/monacct *number*

/usr/lib/acct/nulladm *file*

/usr/lib/acct/prctmp

/usr/lib/acct/prdaily [**-l**] [**-c**] [*mmdd*]

/usr/lib/acct/prtacct *file* [**"***heading***"**]

/usr/lib/acct/runacct [*mmdd*] [*mmdd state*]

/usr/lib/acct/shutacct [**"***reason***"**]

/usr/lib/acct/startup

/usr/lib/acct/turnacct on | **off** | **switch**

DESCRIPTION

chargefee can be invoked to charge a *number* of units to *login-name*. A record is written to **/var/adm/fee**, to be merged with other accounting records by **runacct**.

ckpacct should be initiated via **cron**(1M) to periodically check the size of **/var/adm/pacct**. If the size exceeds *blocks*, 1000 by default, **turnacct** will be invoked with argument *switch*. If the number of free disk blocks in the **/var** file system falls below 500, **ckpacct** will automatically turn off the collection of process accounting records via the *off* argument to **turnacct**. When at least 500 blocks are restored, the accounting will be activated again on the next invocation of **ckpacct**. This feature is sensitive to the frequency at which **ckpacct** is executed, usually by **cron**.

dodisk should be invoked by **cron** to perform the disk accounting functions. By default, it will use **diskusg**, **bfsdiskusg**, **sfsdiskusg**, **vxdiskusg**, and **ufsdiskusg** [see **diskusg**(1M)] to do disk accounting on the **S5**, **bfs**, **sfs**, **vxfs**, and **ufs** file systems in **/etc/vfstab** and **acctdusg [see acct**(1M)] on other file systems. Note that when **dodisk** uses **/etc/vfstab**, it will skip remote resources. If the **-o** flag is used, it will use **acctdusg** [see **acct**(1M)] to do a slower version of disk accounting by login directory for all file systems. *files* specifies the one or more filesystem names where disk accounting will be done. If *files* are used, disk accounting will be done on these filesystems only. If the **-o** flag is used, *files* should be mount points of mounted filesystems. If the **-o** option is omitted, *files* should be the special file names of mountable filesystems.

`lastlogin` is invoked by `runacct` to update `/var/adm/acct/sum/loginlog`, which shows the last date on which each person logged in.

`monacct` should be invoked once each month or each accounting period. *number* indicates which month or period it is. If *number* is not given, it defaults to the current month (01–12). This default is useful if `monacct` is to executed via `cron`(1M) on the first day of each month. `monacct` creates summary files in `/var/adm/acct/fiscal` and restarts the summary files in `/var/adm/acct/sum`.

`nulladm` creates *file* with mode 664 and ensures that owner and group are `adm`. It is called by various accounting shell procedures.

`prctmp` can be used to print the session record file (normally `/var/adm/acct/nite/ctmp` created by `acctcon1` [see `acctcon`(1M)].

`prdaily` is invoked by `runacct` to format a report of the previous day's accounting data. The report resides in `/var/adm/acct/sum/rprt/mmdd` where *mmdd* is the month and day of the report. The current daily accounting reports may be printed by typing `prdaily`. Previous days' accounting reports can be printed by using the *mmdd* option and specifying the exact report date desired. The `-l` flag prints a report of exceptional usage by login id for the specified date. Previous daily reports are cleaned up and therefore inaccessible after each invocation of `monacct`. The `-c` flag prints a report of exceptional resource usage by command, and may be used on current day's accounting data only.

`prtacct` can be used to format and print any total accounting (`tacct`) file.

`runacct` performs the accumulation of connect, process, fee, and disk accounting on a daily basis. It also creates summaries of command usage. For more information, see `runacct`(1M).

`shutacct` is invoked during a system shutdown to turn process accounting off and append a "reason" record to `/var/adm/wtmp`.

`startup` can be invoked when the system is brought to a multi-user state to turn process accounting on.

`turnacct` is an interface to `accton` [see `acct`(1M)] to turn process accounting `on` or `off`. The `switch` argument moves the current `/var/adm/pacct` to the next free name in `/var/adm/pacct`*incr* (where *incr* is a number starting with `1` and incrementing by one for each additional `pacct` file), then turns accounting back on again. This procedure is called by `ckpacct` and thus can be taken care of by the `cron` and used to keep `pacct` to a reasonable size. `shutacct` uses `turnacct` to stop process accounting. `startup` uses `turnacct` to start process accounting.

FILES

`/var/adm/fee`	accumulator for fees
`/var/adm/pacct`	current file for per-process accounting
`/var/adm/pacct`*incr*	used if `pacct` gets large and during execution of daily accounting procedure
`/var/adm/wtmp`	login/logoff summary

/usr/lib/acct/ptelus.awk	contains the limits for exceptional usage by login ID
/usr/lib/acct/ptecms.awk	contains the limits for exceptional usage by command name
/var/adm/acct/nite	working directory
/usr/lib/acct	holds all accounting commands listed in section 1M of this manual
/var/adm/acct/sum	summary directory contains information for **monacct**
var/adm/acct/fiscal	fiscal reports directory

SEE ALSO

acct(1M), **acct**(2), **acct**(4), **acctcms**(1M), **acctcom**(1), **acctcon**(1M), **acctmerg**(1M), **acctprc**(1M), **cron**(1M), **diskusg**(1M), **fwtmp**(1M), **runacct**(1M), **utmp**(4)

NAME

addbib – (BSD) create or extend a bibliographic database

SYNOPSIS

/usr/ucb/addbib [-a] [-p *promptfile*] *database*

DESCRIPTION

When **addbib** starts up, answering **y** to the initial **Instructions?** prompt yields directions; typing **n** or RETURN skips them. **addbib** then prompts for various bibliographic fields, reads responses from the terminal, and sends output records to *database*. A null response (RETURN) means to leave out that field. A "-" (minus sign) means to go back to the previous field. A trailing backslash allows a field to be continued on the next line. The repeating **Continue?** prompt allows the user either to resume by typing **y** or RETURN, to quit the current session by typing **n** or **q**, or to edit *database* with any system editor (**vi**, **ex**, **ed**).

The following options are available:

-a Suppress prompting for an abstract; asking for an abstract is the default. Abstracts are ended with a CTRL–D.

-p *promptfile*
Use a new prompting skeleton, defined in *promptfile*. This file should contain prompt strings, a TAB, and the key-letters to be written to the *database*.

USAGE

Bibliography Key Letters

The most common key-letters and their meanings are given below. **addbib** insulates you from these key-letters, since it gives you prompts in English, but if you edit the bibliography file later on, you will need to know this information.

%A	Author's name
%B	Book containing article referenced
%C	City (place of publication)
%D	Date of publication
%E	Editor of book containing article referenced
%F	Footnote number or label [supplied by **refer**(1)]
%G	Government order number
%H	Header commentary, printed before reference
%I	Issuer (publisher)
%J	Journal containing article
%K	Keywords to use in locating reference
%L	Label field used by **-k** option of **refer**(1)
%M	Bell Labs Memorandum (undefined)
%N	Number within volume

`%O`	Other commentary, printed at end of reference
`%P`	Page number(s)
`%Q`	Corporate or Foreign Author (unreversed)
`%R`	Report, paper, or thesis (unpublished)
`%S`	Series title
`%T`	Title of article or book
`%V`	Volume number
`%X`	Abstract — used by **roffbib**, not by **refer**
`%Y,Z`	Ignored by **refer**

SEE ALSO

ed(1), **ex**(1), **indxbib**(1), **lookbib**(1), **refer**(1), **roffbib**(1), **sortbib**(1), **vi**(1)

NAME

adduser – create a login for a new user

SYNOPSIS

adduser *login_name name user_ID logdir* **Yes** | **No**

DESCRIPTION

Adduser is used to create a login for a new user. It must be given the following arguments:

login_name This is the name entered by the user when logging in. It can be no longer than eight alphanumeric characters.

name This is the user's full name. It identifies the person to whom the login is assigned. If *name* contains spaces, it must be in quotes.

user_ID This is the numerical user ID that will be associated with the *login_name*. It must be between 100 and 60,000 and must be unique for each user.

logdir This is the user's home directory. It must be a valid directory name and cannot already exist on the system. Typically the user's home directory matches the login name. For example, the home directory for the owner of login name **ams** might be **/usr/ams**.

Yes | **No** If the user will have system administration privileges.

admin (1)

NAME

admin – create and administer SCCS files

SYNOPSIS

admin [**-i**[*name*]] [**-b**] [**-n**] [**-r***rel*] [**-t**[*name*]] [**-f***flag*[*flag-val*]] [**-d***flag*[*flag-val*]] [**-a***login*] [**-e***login*] [**-m**[*mrlist*]] [**-y**[*comment*]] [**-h**] [**-z**] *file* . . .

DESCRIPTION

admin is used to create new SCCS files and change parameters of existing ones. Arguments to **admin**, which may appear in any order, consist of keyletter arguments (that begin with -) and file names (note that SCCS file names (*file*) must begin with the ASCII characters **s.**).

If *file* does not exist, it is created and its parameters are initialized according to the specified keyletter arguments. Parameters not initialized by a keyletter argument are assigned a default value. If *file* does exist, parameters corresponding to specified keyletter arguments are changed, and other parameters are left unchanged.

If *file* is a directory, **admin** behaves as though each file in the directory were specified as *file*, except that non-SCCS files (last component of the path name does not begin with **s.**) and unreadable files are silently ignored.

If *file* is **-**, the standard input is read; each line of the standard input is taken to be the name of an SCCS file to be processed. Again, non-SCCS files and unreadable files are silently ignored.

The keyletter arguments are listed below. Each argument is explained as if only one *file* were to be processed because the effect of each argument applies independently to each *file*.

-i[*name*] The *name* of a file from which the contents for a new SCCS file are to be taken. (If *name* is a binary file, then you must specify the **-b** option.) This contents constitutes the first delta of the file (see **-r** keyletter for delta numbering scheme). If the **-i** keyletter is used, but *name* is omitted, the contents are obtained by reading the standard input until an end-of-file is encountered. If this keyletter is omitted, then the SCCS file is created so that the result of a **get**(1) will be an empty file. Only one SCCS file may be created by an **admin** command on which the **i** keyletter is supplied. Using a single **admin** to create two or more SCCS files requires that they be created empty (no **-i** keyletter). Note that the **-i** keyletter implies the **-n** keyletter. Supplementary code set characters may be used in *name* and in the file itself.

-b encode the contents of *name*, specified to the **-i** option. This keyletter must be used if *name* is a binary file; otherwise, a binary file will not be handled properly by SCCS commands.

-n This keyletter indicates that a new SCCS file is to be created (implied by **-i**).

-r*rel* The *rel*ease into which the initial delta is inserted. This keyletter may be used only if the **-i** keyletter is also used. If the **-r** keyletter is not used, the initial delta is inserted into release 1. The level of the initial delta is always 1 (by default initial deltas are named 1.1).

-t[*name*] The *name* of a file from which descriptive text for the SCCS file is to be taken. If the **-t** keyletter is used and **admin** is creating a new SCCS file (the **-n** and/or **-i** keyletters also used), the descriptive text file name must also be supplied. In the case of existing SCCS files: (1) a **-t** keyletter without a file name causes removal of the descriptive text (if any) that is currently in the SCCS file, and (2) a **-t** keyletter with a file name causes text (if any) in *file* to replace the descriptive text (if any) that is currently in the SCCS file. Supplementary code set characters may be used in *name* and in the file itself.

-f*flag* This keyletter specifies a *flag*, and, possibly, a value for the *flag*, to be placed in the SCCS file. Several **-f** keyletters may be supplied on a single **admin** command line. The allowable *flag*s and their values are:

- **b** Allows use of the **-b** keyletter on a **get** command to create branch deltas.
- **c***ceil* The highest release (that is, ceiling): a number greater than 0 but less than or equal to 9999 that may be retrieved by a **get** command for editing. The default value for an unspecified **c** flag is 9999.
- **f***floor* The lowest release (that is, floor): a number greater than 0 but less than 9999 that may be retrieved by a **get** command for editing. The default value for an unspecified **f** flag is 1.
- **d***SID* The default delta number (SID) to be used by a **get** command.
- **i**[*str*] Causes the **No id keywords (ge6)** message issued by **get** or **delta** to be treated as a fatal error. In the absence of this flag, the message is only a warning. The message is issued if no SCCS identification keywords [see **get**(1)] are found in the text retrieved or stored in the SCCS file. If a value is supplied, the keywords must exactly match the given string. The string must contain a keyword, and no embedded newlines.
- **j** Allows concurrent **get** commands for editing on the same SID of an SCCS file. This flag allows multiple concurrent updates to the same version of the SCCS file.
- **l***list* A *list* of releases to which deltas can no longer be made (**get -e** against one of these "locked" releases fails). *list* has the following syntax:

  <list> ::= *<range>* | *<list>* , *<range>*
  <range> ::= *RELEASE NUMBER* | **a**

  The character **a** in *list* is equivalent to specifying all releases for *file*.
- **n** Causes **delta** to create a null delta in each of those releases (if any) being skipped when a delta is made in a new release (for example, in making delta 5.1 after delta 2.7, releases 3 and 4 are skipped). These null deltas serve as anchor points so that branch deltas may later be created from them. The absence of this flag causes skipped releases to be non-existent in the SCCS

file, preventing branch deltas from being created from them in the future.

q*text* User-definable text substituted for all occurrences of the **%Q%** keyword in SCCS file text retrieved by **get**. Supplementary code set characters may be used in *text*.

m*mod* *mod*ule name of the SCCS file substituted for all occurrences of the **%M%** keyword in SCCS file text retrieved by **get**. If the **m** flag is not specified, the value assigned is the name of the SCCS file with the leading **s.** removed. Supplementary code set characters may be used in the module name *mod*.

t*type* *type* of module in the SCCS file substituted for all occurrences of **%Y%** keyword in SCCS file contents retrieved by **get**.

v[*pgm*]
Causes **delta** to prompt for Modification Request (MR) numbers as the reason for creating a delta. The optional value specifies the name of an MR number validity checking program [see **delta**(1)]. This program will receive as arguments the module name, the value of the type flag (see **t***type* above), and the *mrlist*. (If this flag is set when creating an SCCS file, the **m** keyletter must also be used even if its value is null).

x Causes **get** to create files with execute permissions.

-d*flag* Causes removal (deletion) of the specified *flag* from an SCCS file. The **-d** keyletter may be specified only when processing existing SCCS files. Several **-d** keyletters may be supplied in a single **admin** command. See the **-f** keyletter for allowable *flag* names.

(**l***list* used with **-d** indicates a *list* of releases to be unlocked. See the **-f** keyletter for a description of the **l** flag and the syntax of a *list*.)

-a*login* A login name, or numerical UNIX System group ID, to be added to the list of users who may make deltas (changes) to the SCCS file. A group ID is equivalent to specifying all login names common to that group ID. Several **a** keyletters may be used on a single **admin** command line. As many logins or numerical group IDs as desired may be on the list simultaneously. If the list of users is empty, then anyone may add deltas. If login or group ID is preceded by a **!** they are to be denied permission to make deltas.

-e*login* A login name, or numerical group ID, to be erased from the list of users allowed to make deltas (changes) to the SCCS file. Specifying a group ID is equivalent to specifying all **login** names common to that group ID. Several **-e** keyletters may be used on a single **admin** command line.

-m[*mrlist*] The list of Modification Requests (MR) numbers is inserted into the SCCS file as the reason for creating the initial delta in a manner identical to **delta**. The **v** flag must be set and the MR numbers are validated if the **v** flag has a value (the name of an MR number validation program). Diagnostics will occur if the **v** flag is not set or MR validation fails.

-y[*comment*]
The *comment* text is inserted into the SCCS file as a comment for the initial delta in a manner identical to that of **delta**. Omission of the **-y** keyletter results in a default comment line being inserted.

The **-y** keyletter is valid only if the **-i** and/or **-n** keyletters are specified (that is, a new SCCS file is being created). Supplementary code set characters may be used in *comment*.

-h Causes **admin** to check the structure of the SCCS file [see **sccsfile**(4)], and to compare a newly computed check-sum (the sum of all the characters in the SCCS file except those in the first line) with the check-sum that is stored in the first line of the SCCS file. Appropriate error diagnostics are produced. This keyletter inhibits writing to the file, nullifying the effect of any other keyletters supplied; therefore, it is only meaningful when processing existing files.

-z The SCCS file check-sum is recomputed and stored in the first line of the SCCS file (see **-h**, above). Note that use of this keyletter on a truly corrupted file may prevent future detection of the corruption.

The last component of all SCCS file names must be of the form **s.***file*. New SCCS files are given mode 444 [see **chmod**(1)]. Write permission in the pertinent directory is, of course, required to create a file. All writing done by **admin** is to a temporary **x.***file*, called **x.***file*, [see **get**(1)], created with mode 444 if the **admin** command is creating a new SCCS file, or with the same mode as the SCCS file if it exists. After successful execution of **admin**, the SCCS file is removed (if it exists), and the **x.***file* is renamed with the name of the SCCS file. This renaming process ensures that changes are made to the SCCS file only if no errors occurred.

It is recommended that directories containing SCCS files have mode 755 and that SCCS files themselves have mode 444. The mode of the directories allows only the owner to modify SCCS files contained in the directories. The mode of the SCCS files prevents any modification at all except by SCCS commands.

admin also makes use of a transient lock file (called **z.***file*), which is used to prevent simultaneous updates to the SCCS file by different users. See **get**(1) for further information.

FILES

x.*file* [see **delta**(1)]
z.*file* [see **delta**(1)]
bdiff Program to compute differences between the "gotten" file and the **g.***file* [see **get**(1)].

EXAMPLES

The following example shows how to create an SCCS file, **s.prog.c**, from the contents of a file containing a C language program, **prog.c**.

```
admin -iprog.c s.prog.c
```

An example for a file containing a shell program is similar, except that you should use the **-fx** option , so that **get**(1) will create **file.sh** to be executable.

```
admin -ifile.sh -fx s.file.sh
```

You should include some SCCS information at the top of a file. In the above shell example, to include the file name, the SCCS version number, and the date and time of the last delta, include the following line at the beginning of **file.sh**:

```
#Id: %W%  Last Delta: %G% %U%
```

The above line would be translated by a **get**(1) command as:

#Id: @(#)file.sh   1.8 Last Delta: 4/25/91 17:05:19

SEE ALSO

bdiff(1), **ed**(1), **delta**(1), **get**(1), **help**(1), **prs**(1), **sccsfile**(4), **what**(1)

DIAGNOSTICS

Use the **help** command for explanations.

NOTES

If it is necessary to patch an SCCS file for any reason, the mode may be changed to 644 by the owner allowing use of a text editor. You must run **admin -h** on the edited file to check for corruption followed by an **admin -z** to generate a proper check-sum. Another **admin -h** is recommended to ensure the SCCS file is valid.

NAME

adminrole – display, add, change, delete roles in the TFM database

SYNOPSIS

adminrole [**-n**] [**-a** [*cmd*:*path*[:*priv*[:*priv*. . .]][,. . .]] *role* . . .
adminrole [**-a** [*cmd*:*path*[:*priv*[:*priv*. . .]][,. . .]] *role* . . .
[**-r** *cmd*[:*priv*[:*priv*. . .]][,. . .]] *role* . . .
adminrole [**-d**] *role* . . .
adminrole

DESCRIPTION

The **adminrole** command allows administrators to display, add, change, and delete roles in the Trusted Facility Management database. The TFM database is intended to be used only when the Enhanced Security Utilities are installed and running, and is the vehicle through which unprivileged user processes run privileged commands.

A role contains a list of commands. Each command contains a (possibly empty) list of privileges. The **tfadmin** command will use these privileges to set up its process before it invokes this command for a member of the role. The **adminrole** command has the following options:

-n For every role in the list, create a new role description.

-a Add a command to a role, add the role to the database if it does not already exist.

-r Remove a command from a role or remove privileges from a command within a role.

-d Delete a role.

No options
List the contents of the specified roles.

No Arguments
List the contents of all roles in the database.

The **adminrole** command takes as its arguments the list of roles to which the actions specified by the options applies. The argument to the **-a** or **-r** option is a comma-separated list of command descriptions. For the **-a** option, the command description includes the name of the command to be added, the full path at which the command file resides, and the privilege set, represented by a colon-separated list of privilege names (for example, **mount:/etc/mount:macread:mount**). There is no limit on the length of the path name; however, **/** ("root" or "slash") alone may not be specified.

The command description for the **-r** option is the same as for the **-a** option except that the full path and the separating colon are not given (for example, **mount:macread:mount**). If users in the specified roles get no privilege when they invoke the command, the privilege description may be omitted. The **-n** and **-r** options may not be used together. Doing so will cause an error, since incompatible options have been specified.

If the **-d** is used in an attempt to delete a non-existent role, an error will result.

SEE ALSO

adminuser(1M), **tfadmin**(1M), **intro**(2)

DIAGNOSTICS

This command exits with a 0 if all requested operations succeeded, 1 if any operation failed.

The following diagnostic messages are printed by adminrole:

command name "*cmd*" already exists

role name "*role*" already exists

undefined role name "*role*"

process privilege "*priv*" does not exist in command "*cmd*"

insufficient command specification: "*string*"

full command pathname must be specified

duplicate process privilege: "*priv*"

cannot add role "*role*"

cannot alter role "*role*"

role "*role*" currently being changed, try again later

cannot remove role "*role*"

cannot change command "*cmd*"

full path to TFM database must be specified

undefined command name "*cmd*"

TFM database does not exist

cannot initialize TFM database

improper command name: "*string*"

invalid process privilege: "*string*"

unrecognized privilege number: "*number*"

incompatible options specified

NAME

adminuser – display, add, change, delete administrators in the TFM database.

SYNOPSIS

adminuser [**-n**] [**-o** *role*[,. . .]]
[**-a** *cmd***:***path*[**:***priv*[**:***priv*. . .]][**,**. . .]]
user . . .
adminuser [**-o** *role*[,. . .]
[**-r** *cmd*[**:***priv*[**:***priv*. . .]][**,**. . .]]
[**-a** *cmd***:***path*[**:***priv*[**:***priv*. . .]][**,**. . .]]
user . . .
adminuser [**-d**] *user* . . .
adminuser

DESCRIPTION

The **adminuser** command allows administrators to display, add, change, and delete administrators in the Trusted Facility Management (TFM) database. The TFM database is intended to be used only when the Enhanced Security Utilities are installed and running, and is the vehicle through which unprivileged user processes run privileged commands.

A user definition contains a list of commands. Each command contains a list of privileges. The **tfadmin** command uses these privileges to set up its process before invoking this command for the user. In addition to the command definitions, there is a list of roles available to the user, and a default command specification.

The options to the command are:

-n For every user in the list, create a new user description, and, optionally, create a role list or add a command to that user.

-o Create the specified role list for every user in the list.

-a Add a list of commands to the definitions of a given list of users.

-r Remove the list of commands from the list of users. If the user supplies privileges in the command descriptions, then leave the command but remove the specified privileges.

-d Delete the given list of users.

No options
Print out the capabilities of the given list of users.

No arguments
Print the capabilities of every user in the database.

The **adminuser** command takes as its arguments the list of users to which the actions specified by the options applies. The list of users is a list of user login names. Only administrative users, that is administrators to whom access to privileged commands is to be granted, should be added to the TFM database.

The argument to the **-o** option is a comma-separated list of role names. This list will create a new role list for the specified users, replacing any existing role lists.

The argument to the `-a` or `-r` option is a comma-separated list of command descriptions. For the `-a` option, the command description includes the name of the command to be added, the full path at which the command file resides, and the privilege vector, represented by a colon-separated list of privilege names (for example, `mount:/etc/mount:macread:mount`). There is no limit on the length of the path name; however, / ("root" or "slash") alone may not be specified.

The command description for the `-r` option is the same as for the `-a` option except that the full path and the separating colon are not given (for example, `mount:macread:mount`). If the users get no privileges when they invoke the command, the privilege description may be omitted.

The `-n` and `-r` options may not be used together. If `-n` is specified with `-r`, an error will occur because incompatible options have been specified.

FILES

`/etc/security/tfm/users/*`
`/etc/security/tfm/users/*/default`
`/etc/security/tfm/users/*/roles`
`/etc/security/tfm/users/*/cmds/*`

SEE ALSO

`adminrole`(1M), `tfadmin`(1M), `intro`(2)

DIAGNOSTICS

This command exits with a 0 if all requested operations succeeded, 1 if any operation failed.

The following diagnostic messages are printed by adminuser:

command name "*cmd*" already exists

user "*user*" already exists

undefined user "*user*"

process privilege "*priv*" does not exist in command "*cmd*"

role name "*role*" is not unique

insufficient command specification: "*string*"

duplicate process privilege: "*priv*"

full command pathname must be specified

full path to TFM database must be specified

undefined command name "*cmd*"

cannot read role list for user "*user*"

cannot add user "*user*"

cannot alter user "*user*"

user "*user*" currently being changed, try again later

cannot remove user "*user*"

cannot change command *"cmd"*
cannot change role list for user *"user"*
TFM database does not exist
cannot initialize TFM database
improper command name: *"string"*
invalid process privilege: *"string"*
unrecognized privilege number: *"number"*
incompatible options specified

alpq (1)

NAME

alpq – query the **alp** STREAMS module

SYNOPSIS

alpq

DESCRIPTION

The **alpq** command takes no arguments or options. It presents, on its standard output, a list of the functions currently registered with the **alp** STREAMS module. For information on building and using these functions, see **alp**(7).

The output list contains entries like the following:

```
1  Ucase     (Upper to lower case converter)
```

The first field is a sequence number. The second field is the function's name (by which it may be accessed), and the third field is the function's explanation string.

The **alpq** command works by pushing the **alp** STREAMS module, querying it via **ioctl**(2), and then popping it immediately; its standard input (normally the user's tty) must therefore be a stream.

SEE ALSO

alp(7), **kbd**(7), **kbdcomp**(1M), **kbdload**(1M)

NAME

apropos – (BSD) locate commands by keyword lookup

SYNOPSIS

/usr/ucb/apropos *keyword* . . .

DESCRIPTION

apropos shows which manual pages contain instances of any of the given keywords in their title. Each word is considered separately and the case of letters is ignored. Words which are part of other words are considered; thus, when looking for "compile," **apropos** will find all instances of "compiler" also.

Try

```
apropos password
```

and

```
apropos editor
```

If the line starts "*filename*(*section*) . . . " you can do "**man** *section filename*" to get the documentation for it. Try

```
apropos format
```

and then

```
man 3s printf
```

to get the manual page on the subroutine **printf**.

apropos is actually just the **-k** option to the **man**(1) command.

FILES

/usr/share/man/whatis data base

SEE ALSO

catman(1M), **man**(1), **whatis**(1)

ar(1)

NAME

ar – maintain portable archive or library

SYNOPSIS

ar [-V] -*key* [*arg*] [*posname*] *afile* [*name* . . .]

DESCRIPTION

The **ar** command maintains groups of files combined into a single archive file. Its main use is to create and update library files. However, it can be used for any similar purpose. If an archive is composed of printable files, the entire archive is printable.

When **ar** creates an archive, it creates headers in a format that is portable across all machines. The portable archive format and structure are described in detail in **ar**(4). The archive symbol table [described in **ar**(4)] is used by the link editor **ld** to effect multiple passes over libraries of object files in an efficient manner. An archive symbol table is only created and maintained by **ar** when there is at least one object file in the archive. The archive symbol table is in a specially named file that is always the first file in the archive. This file is never mentioned or accessible to the user. Whenever the **ar** command is used to create or update the contents of such an archive, the symbol table is rebuilt. The **s** argument to *key*, described below, will force the symbol table to be rebuilt.

-V Cause **ar** to print its version number on standard error.

-*key* [*arg*] *key* is formed with one of the following characters: **drqtpmx**. *arg* is formed with one of more of the following letters: **vucls**. An additional single-character argument to *key*, called the positioning character (chosen from one of the following letters: **abi**), can be used with *key* characters **r** and **m**. *key* characters are described below.

posname Archive member name used as a reference point in positioning other files in the archive.

afile Archive file.

name One or more constituent files in the archive file.

The meanings of the *key* characters are as follows:

d Delete the named files from the archive file.

r Replace the named files in the archive file. If the optional argument **u** is used with **r**, then replace only those files with dates of modification later than the named files already in the archive. If an optional positioning character from the set **abi** is used, then the *posname* argument must be present and specifies that new files are to be placed after (**a**) or before (**b** or **i**) *posname*. Otherwise new files are placed at the end.

q Quickly append the named files to the end of the archive file. Optional positioning characters are invalid. The command does not check whether the added members are already in the archive. This option is useful to avoid creating a large archive piece-by-piece.

`t` Print a table of contents of the archive file. If no names are given, all files in the archive are listed. If names are given, only those files are listed.

`p` Print the named files in the archive.

`m` Move the named files to the end of the archive. If an optional positioning character from the set **abi** is used, then the *posname* argument must be present and specifies that new files are to be placed after (`a`) or before (`b` or `i`) *posname*. Otherwise new files are placed at the end.

`x` Extract the named files. If no names are given, all files in the archive are extracted. In neither case does **x** alter the archive file.

The meanings of the other key arguments are as follows:

`v` Give a verbose file-by-file description of the making of a new archive file from the old archive and the constituent files. When used with `t`, give a long listing of all information about the files. When used with **x**, print the name of the file preceding each extraction.

`c` Suppress the message that is produced by default when *afile* is created.

`l` This option is obsolete. It is recognized, but ignored, and will be removed in the next release.

`s` Force the regeneration of the archive symbol table even if **ar**(1) is not invoked with a command which will modify the archive contents. This command is useful to restore the archive symbol table after the **strip**(1) command has been used on the archive.

FILES

/usr/lib/locale/*locale***/LC_MESSAGES/uxar**
language-specific message file [See **LANG** on **environ**(5).]

SEE ALSO

a.out(4), **ar**(4), **ld**(1), **lorder**(1), **strip**(1)

NOTES

If the same file is mentioned twice in an argument list, it may be put in the archive twice.

Since the archiver no longer uses temporary files, the `-l` option is obsolete and will be removed in the next release.

By convention, archives are suffixed with the characters `.a`.

NAME

arch – (BSD) display the architecture of the current host

SYNOPSIS

`/usr/ucb/arch`

DESCRIPTION

The **arch** command displays the architecture of the current host system.

SEE ALSO

mach(1), **uname**(1)

NAME

arp – address resolution display and control

SYNOPSIS

arp *hostname*

arp -a [*unix* [*kmem*]]

arp -d *hostname*

arp -s *hostname ether_address* [**temp**] [**pub**] [**trail**]

arp -f *filename*

DESCRIPTION

The **arp** program displays and modifies the Internet-to-Ethernet address translation tables used by the address resolution protocol [**arp**(7)].

With no flags, the program displays the current ARP entry for *hostname*. The host may be specified by name or by number, using Internet dot notation.

The following options are available:

-a Display all of the current ARP entries by reading the table from the file *kmem* (default **/dev/kmem**) based on the kernel file *unix* (default **/stand/unix**).

-d Delete an entry for the host called *hostname*. This option may only be used by a privileged user.

-s Create an ARP entry for the host called *hostname* with the Ethernet address *ether_address*. The Ethernet address is given as six hexadecimal bytes separated by colons. The entry will be permanent unless the word **temp** is given in the command. If the word **pub** is given, the entry will be published, for instance, this system will respond to ARP requests for *hostname* even though the hostname is not its own. The word **trail** indicates that trailer encapsulations may be sent to this host.

-f Read the file named *filename* and set multiple entries in the ARP tables. Entries in the file should be of the form

hostname ether_address [**temp**] [**pub**] [**trail**]

with argument meanings as given above.

SEE ALSO

arp(7), **ifconfig**(1M)

NAME

as – assembler

SYNOPSIS

as [**-VTm**] [**-Q** *yn*] [**-Y** *key***,***dir*] [**-o** *objfile*] [**-t** *cpu*] *file* . . .

DESCRIPTION

The **as** command produces an object file from the concatenation of the specified assembly language input *files*. At least one source file must be specified, except when the **-V** option is given. The name "**-**" designates the standard input, and may be specified anywhere within the list of files.

The recognized assembly language does not include a general macro processing capability. Instead, **as** provides for optional preprocessing of the input by the **m4** command. [See **m4**(1).]

The following options may be specified in any order:

-V Writes the assembler's packaging, release, and version information on the standard error output. As a special case, the assembler does no other processing if no input files are specified.

-T Accepts input that contains old-style (COFF) directives. Nevertheless, most such directives are still ineffective, as the assembler generates an ELF object file.

-m Sends the input through the **m4** macro processing command prior to assembly. All file operands are passed unmodified to the **m4** command. (By using the "**--**" option-terminator, **m4** options can be preserved and passed through to the **m4** command; see the EXAMPLES section, below.) If present, the predefined macros file, *LIBDIR*/**cm4defs**, will be given to the **m4** command as the initial input file.

-Q *yn* Appends the assembler's release information to the "**.comment**" section of the generated output object file if *yn* is **y**; otherwise (if *yn* is **n** or if no **-Q** option is specified), nothing is added.

-Y *key***,***dir* Changes to *dir* the directory in which to find the files specified by *key*: the **m4** macro processing command (**m**), the predefined macros file (**d**), or both.

-o *objfile* Causes *objfile* to be the name of the generated output object file. If no **-o** is specified, then the output object file is created in the current directory with a name that depends on the specified input files. If an input file with a name that ends with "**.s**" is present, the output file name is formed by replacing the suffix of the first such name with "**.o**"; otherwise, the output file is some variation of "**a.out**".

-t *cpu* Specifies the target processor to be *cpu*, which may be **486** (the default), or **386**.

EXAMPLES

```
as -m -Yd,. -- -DK=7 mydefs sys/file.s
```

will send, in order, **./cm4defs** (if it exists) and **mydefs** and **sys/file.s** through **m4** with the macro **K** predefined to be **7**, assemble the output of **m4**, and generate the ELF object file output in **./file.o**.

FILES

BINDIR/**m4**
LIBDIR/**cm4defs**

SEE ALSO

a.out(4), **cc**(1), **elf**(3E), **ld**(1), **m4**(1), **nm**(1), **strip**(1)

NOTES

The **m4** macro processor is not line-oriented and recognizes many regular identifiers as its keywords (**index** and **len**, for example). Thus, preprocessing compiler-generated assembly language with **m4** requires care.

Whenever possible, you should access the assembler through a compilation system interface program such as **cc**.

NAME

at, **batch** – execute commands at a later time

SYNOPSIS

at [**-f** *script*] [**-m**] *time* [*date*] [**+** *increment*]

at -l [*job* . . .]

at -r *job* . . .

at -d *job*

at -z *job*

at -Z *job*

batch

DESCRIPTION

at and **batch** read commands from standard input to be executed at a later time.

at allows you to specify when the commands should be executed; *date* and *time* are recognized according to the locale specified in the **LC_TIME** environment variable [see **LANG** on **environ**(5)], as described below. Jobs queued with **batch** will execute when system load level permits. **at** may be used with the following options:

-f *script* Reads commands to be executed from the named *script* file.

-m Sends mail to the user after the job has been completed. Mail is sent even if the job does not produce output. Standard output and standard error output are mailed to the user unless redirected elsewhere. **-m** has no effect on jobs which already print to standard output or standard error; the mail message will not be duplicated. The environment variables, current directory, umask, and ulimit are retained when the commands are executed. Open file descriptors, traps, and priority are lost.

-l [*job*] Reports all jobs scheduled for the invoking user, or just the *job*s specified. When invoked by a privileged user, all jobs scheduled are reported.

-r *job* Removes specified *job*s previously scheduled with **at** for the invoking user. When invoked by a privileged user, any *job* previously scheduled with **at** is removed.

-d *job* Displays the contents of the specified *job*.

An unprivileged user is restricted to display information only on jobs that the user owns and that are at the user's level. A user with the appropriate privileges is able to display information about all jobs.

Standard output and standard error output are mailed to the user unless they are redirected elsewhere. The shell environment variables, current directory, umask, and ulimit are retained when the commands are executed. Open file descriptors, traps, and priority are lost.

Users are permitted to use **at** if their name appears in the file **/etc/cron.d/at.allow**. If that file does not exist, the file **/etc/cron.d/at.deny** is checked to determine if the user should be denied access to **at**. If neither file exists, only root is allowed to submit a job. If only **at.deny** exists and is empty, global usage is permitted. The allow/deny files consist of one user name per line. These files can only be modified by a privileged user.

If the **DATEMSK** environment variable is set, it points to a template file that **at** will use to determine the valid *time* and *date* values instead of the values described below. For more information about using **DATEMSK**, see the last paragraph of the DESCRIPTION section.

time may be specified as follows, where *h* is hours and *m* is minutes: *h*, *hh*, *hhmm*, *h*:*m*, *h*:*mm*, *hh*:*m*, *hh*:*mm*. A 24-hour clock is assumed, unless **am** or **pm** is appended to *time*. If **zulu** is appended to *time*, it means Greenwich Mean Time (GMT). *time* can also take on the values: **noon**, **midnight**, and **now**. **at now** responds with the error message **too late**; use **now** with the *increment* argument, such as: **at now + 1 minute**.

An optional *date* may be specified as either a month name followed by a day number (and possibly a year number preceded by a comma) or a day of the week. Month and weekday names used for *date* are recognized according to the locale specified in the **LC_TIME** environment variable [see **LANG** on **environ**(5)]. Both the month name and the day of the week may be spelled out or abbreviated to three characters. Two special "days," **today** and **tomorrow**, are recognized. If no *date* is given, **today** is assumed if the given hour is greater than the current hour and **tomorrow** is assumed if it is less. If the given month is less than the current month (and no year is given), next year is assumed.

The optional *increment* is simply a number suffixed by one of the following: **minutes**, **hours**, **days**, **weeks**, **months**, or **years**. (The singular form is also accepted.) Note that when *increment* is **1 minute**, **at** displays the warning **job may not be executed at the proper time**, because the **cron**(1M) command's smallest unit is the minute; that is, an **at** job entered at 12:01:45 and requested to run in one minute will run at 12:02:00 rather than 12:02:45. The modifier **next** may precede the *increment*; it means "+ 1."

Thus valid commands include:

```
at 0815am Jan 24
at 8:15am Jan 24
at now + 1 day
at now next day
at 5 pm Friday
```

at and **batch** write the job number and schedule time to standard error.

at -r removes jobs previously scheduled by **at** or **batch**. The job number is the number returned to you previously by the **at** or **batch** command. You can also get job numbers by typing **at -l**. You can only remove your own jobs unless you are the privileged user.

If the environment variable **DATEMSK** is set, **at** will use its value as the full path name of a template file containing format strings. The strings consist of field descriptors and text characters and are used to provide a richer set of allowable date formats in different languages by appropriate settings of the environment variable **LC_TIME** [see **LANG** on **environ**(5)]. [See **getdate**(3C) for the allowable list of field descriptors; this list is a subset of the descriptors allowed by **calendar**(1) that are listed on the **date**(1) manual page.] The formats described above for the *time* and *date* arguments, the special names **noon**, **midnight**, **now**, **next**, **today**, **tomorrow**, and the *increment* argument are not recognized when **DATEMSK** is set.

EXAMPLES

The **at** and **batch** commands read from standard input the commands to be executed at a later time. **sh**(1) provides different ways of specifying standard input. Within your commands, it may be useful to redirect standard output.

This sequence can be used at a terminal:

> **batch**
> **sort** *filename* **>** *outfile*
> CTRL-d (hold down 'control' and depress 'd')

This sequence, which shows redirecting standard error to a pipe, is useful in a shell procedure (the sequence of output redirection specifications is significant):

> **batch <<!**
> **sort** *filename* **2>&1 >** *outfile* **| mail** *loginid*
> **!**

To have a job reschedule itself, invoke **at** from within the shell procedure, by including code similar to the following within the shell file:

> **echo "sh** *shellfile***" | at 1900 thursday next week**

The following example shows the possible contents of a template file **AT.TEMPL** in **/var/tmp**.

```
%I %p, the %est of %B of the year %Y run the following job
%I %p, the %end of %B of the year %Y run the following job
%I %p, the %erd of %B of the year %Y run the following job
%I %p, the %eth of %B of the year %Y run the following job
%d/%m/%y
%H:%M:%S
%I:%M%p
```

The following are examples of valid invocations if the environment variable **DATEMSK** is set to **/var/tmp/AT.TEMPL**.

```
at 2 PM, the 3rd of July of the year 2000 run the following job
at 3/4/99
at 10:30:30
at 2:30PM
```

FILES

/etc/cron.d	main cron directory
/etc/cron.d/at.allow	list of allowed users
/etc/cron.d/at.deny	list of denied users
/etc/cron.d/queuedefs	scheduling information
/var/spool/cron/atjobs	spool area
/usr/lib/locale/*locale***/LC_MESSAGES/uxcore**	language-specific message file [See **LANG** on **environ**(5).]

SEE ALSO

atq(1), **atrm**(1), **calendar**(1), **cron**(1M), **crontab**(1), **date**(1), **environ**(5), **getdate**(3C), **kill**(1), **mail**(1), **nice**(1), **ps**(1), **sh**(1), **sort**(1)

NAME

`atq` – display the jobs queued to run at specified times

SYNOPSIS

`atq` [`-c`] [`-n`] [*username* . . .]

DESCRIPTION

`atq` displays the current user's queue of jobs submitted with `at` to be run at a later date. If invoked by a privileged user, `atq` will display all jobs in the queue.

If no options are given, the jobs are displayed in chronological order of execution.

When a privileged user invokes `atq` without specifying *username*, the entire queue is displayed; when a *username* is specified, only those jobs belonging to the named user are displayed.

The `atq` command can be used with the following options:

`-c` Display the queued jobs in the order they were created (that is, the time that the `at` command was given).

`-n` Display only the total number of jobs currently in the queue.

FILES

`/var/spool/cron`
spool area

`/usr/lib/locale/`*locale*`/LC_MESSAGES/uxcore`
language-specific message file [See `LANG` on `environ`(5).]

SEE ALSO

`at`(1), `atrm`(1), `cron`(1M)

NAME

attradmin – attribute map database administration

SYNOPSIS

attradmin [**-A** *attr_name* [**-l** *local_attr*]]
attradmin -A *attr_name* **-a -r** *remote_attr* **-l** *local_attr*
attradmin -A *attr_name* **-d** [**-r** *remote_attr*] **-l** *local_attr*
attradmin -A *attr_name* **-I** *attr_descr*
attradmin -A *attr_name* [**-Dcf**]

DESCRIPTION

The **attradmin** command allows an administrator to display and update attribute mapping database entries. Attribute mapping databases are used by **attrmap**(3I) to map remote attributes into local ones.

The options to **attradmin** have the following meanings:

-A *attr_name* Specify the name of the attribute.

-l *local_attr* Specify the local value of the attribute into which the remote attribute value maps.

-a Add an entry to a map. The attribute name and the local and remote attribute values must be specified.

-r *remote_attr* Specify the value of the attribute on the remote machine.

-d Delete entries from a map. The attribute map filename and the local attribute value must be specified. Use of the remote attribute value is optional. If only the local attribute value is specified, all entries mapping to that local attribute value are deleted. If the remote attribute value is also specified, only a particular map entry is deleted.

-I *attr_descr* Install a new attribute map. A remote attribute value format descriptor *attr_descr* must be specified for the new attribute. The format descriptor is a string that describes the format of *remote_attr*; it includes field numbers, the letter M to indicate the field is mandatory, and field separators.

-D Delete an attribute map file. The attribute map filename must be specified.

-c Check consistency of a map file. The attribute map filename must be specified.

-f Fix an inconsistent attribute map file. The attribute map filename must be specified.

When no options are specified, **attradmin** lists the names of all installed attribute map files on the system. If an attribute map filename is specified, **attradmin** lists all entries in the map file. If an attribute map filename and a local attribute value are specified, **attradmin** lists all file entries that map to the specified local attribute value.

Transparent mapping may be achieved by using a regular expression including the metacharacters *****, **[**, **]** in *remote_attr* and a field specifier in *local_attr*. A field specifier **%** followed by a field number can be entered for *local_attr* to indicate that the value of *local_attr* is the same as the value in the specified field of *remote_attr*. If **%i** is entered for *local_attr*, attempts by **attrmap** to map the *remote_attr* will fail.

When **attrmap** searches for a *remote_attr*, it sequentially scans the attribute map file. Therefore, the ordering of remote attributes in this file is critical.

Remote attributes are sorted on the highest numbered field first. Entries with explicit values in this field appear first in the file. Entries which include regular expressions in this field are sorted from the most specific to the least specific based on the position of the metacharacters in the pattern. The more to the left the metacharacter is in the pattern, the less specific the pattern is. For example, **s*** is less specific than **sf***. Regular expressions containing brackets, **[ ]**, are considered more specific than expressions with asterisks and therefore come first in the file.

If two or more entries have patterns which are equally specific, the specificity of the next lower numbered field is examined. Fields are examined from highest to lowest until the remote attributes can be differentiated.

EXAMPLES

The following command line installs a new attribute map that maps GIDs:

```
attradmin -A gid -I M2:M1
```

In any format descriptor, the field numbers indicate the order of significance of the fields, where higher numbered fields contain entities of greater significance on the network. In the format descriptor **M2:M1**, the first field contains the remote machine name. **M1** contains the value of the remote attribute. When a machine name is specified, it precedes the attribute value, and the fields are separated by a colon.

The following command line adds an entry to the GID database that maps any user on the remote machine **macha** into the local system with the same GID. **%1** indicates that the value of *local_attr* is the same as the value in the *remote_attr* field that has 1 as its field number:

```
attradmin -A gid -a -r "macha:*" -l %1
```

The following command line adds an entry to the GID database that maps all GIDs from **100** to **119** on **macha** to GID **1** on the local system:

```
attradmin -A gid -a -r "macha:1[01][0-9]" -l 1
```

The **attradmin** command will insure that the second entry is found first in the map file, no matter which of the above two entries was actually added first.

FILES

/etc/idmap/attrmap/*attr_name***.map**	map file for attribute *attr_name*
/var/adm/log/idmap.log	log file

SEE ALSO

attrmap(3I), **idadmin**(1M), **namemap**(3I), **uidadmin**(1)

NOTES

All update operations are logged (whether successful or not) in the file `/var/adm/log/idmap.log`.

NAME

`atrm` – remove jobs spooled by at or batch

SYNOPSIS

`atrm` [`-a f i`] *arg* . . .

DESCRIPTION

`atrm` removes delayed-execution jobs that were created with the **`at`**(1) command, but not yet executed. The list of these jobs and associated job numbers can be displayed by using **`atq`**(1).

arg a user name or job-number. **`atrm`** removes each job-number you specify, and/or all jobs belonging to the user you specify, provided that you own the indicated jobs.

Jobs belonging to other users can only be removed by a privileged user.

The **`atrm`** command can be used with the following options:

`-a` All. Remove all unexecuted jobs that were created by the current user. If invoked by a privileged user, the entire queue will be flushed.

`-f` Force. All information regarding the removal of the specified jobs is suppressed.

`-i` Interactive. **`atrm`** asks if a job should be removed. If you respond with a **`y`**, the job will be removed.

FILES

`/var/spool/cron`
spool area

`/usr/lib/locale/`*locale***`/LC_MESSAGES/uxcore`**
language-specific message file [See **`LANG`** on **`environ`**(5).]

SEE ALSO

`at`(1), **`atq`**(1), **`cron`**(1M)

auditcnv (1M)

NAME

auditcnv – create default audit mask file

SYNOPSIS

auditcnv

DESCRIPTION

The **auditcnv** shell level command creates an audit mask file for the user login interface. **auditcnv** is invoked when the audit package is installed.

Information from the **/etc/passwd** and **/etc/default/useradd** files is used to assign an initial default audit mask for every user on the system. If either the **/etc/passwd** or **/etc/default/useradd file** does not exist or cannot be accessed, an error message is displayed (see DIAGNOSTICS).

If the audit mask file, **/etc/security/ia/audit** cannot be created or already exists, an error message is displayed (see DIAGNOSTICS).

When the **auditcnv** command is invoked and completes successfully, the following message is displayed:

```
/etc/security/ia/audit created
```

If the **/etc/security/ia/audit** file is corrupted or accidently removed, **auditcnv** needs to be invoked before the next reboot.

DIAGNOSTICS

Upon successful completion, the **auditcnv** command exits with a value of zero (0). If there are errors, it exits with one of the following values and prints the corresponding error message:

1 **usage: auditcnv**
  Invalid command syntax.

5 **file** *file* **does not exist**

5 **cannot access file** *file*

5 **cannot create audit mask file**

5 **audit mask file already exists**
  The audit mask file already exists when **auditcnv** is invoked.

5 **unable to stat()** *file*, **errno="***errno***"**

The following warning message may be displayed.

```
a default audit mask of none was set for all users
```

FILES

/etc/passwd
/etc/default/useradd
/etc/security/ia/audit

SEE ALSO

auditon(1M), **creatiadb**(1M), **defadm**(1M), **useradd**(1M), **usermod**(1M)

NAME

auditfltr – convert audit log file for inter-machine portability

SYNOPSIS

auditfltr [[**-iN**] [**-oX**]] | [**-iX -oN**]

DESCRIPTION

The **auditfltr** command is used to convert audit log files from native machine format into XDR (External Data Representation) format and vice versa. These conversions allow you to transport audit log files from one machine to another for processing with **auditrpt**.

The following options are available:

-i*type* Specifies the type of the input file. The input file is always standard in.

-o*type* Specifies the type of the output file. The output file is always standard out. The output file should be redirected, for example to a file or pipe, due to its data format.

The values for *type* may be **N**, for native machine format, or **X**, for XDR format. If an invalid conversion *type* or combination of conversion *types* is requested an error message is displayed (see DIAGNOSTICS). If no options are specified it is assumed the input file is in native machine format and the output file is in XDR format. If the format of the input file does not match the *type* specified by the **-i** option or the assumed format an error message is displayed (see DIAGNOSTICS).

The procedure for transferring an audit log file from one machine to another has basically three steps. First, the audit log is converted from native machine format to the portable XDR format, using a command like the following:

```
cat /var/audit/1125103 | auditfltr -iN -oX > /var/audit/1125103.xfer
```

Second, the file is transferred to another machine. This can be done by transferring the file to magnetic media on one with **cpio** or **tcpio** and then restoring it with the same command on the other. Third, the file is converted back to machine format with a command like the following:

```
cat /var/audit/1125103.xfer | auditfltr -iX -oN > /var/audit/1125103
```

NOTES

The **auditfltr** command accepts only audit log files as input.

DIAGNOSTICS

Upon successful completion, the **auditfltr** command exits with a value of zero (0). If there are errors, it exits with one of the following values and prints the corresponding error message:

1 **usage: auditfltr [[-iN] [-oX]] | [-iX -oN]**
Invalid command syntax.

1 **conversion type** *type* **is not supported**
usage: auditfltr [[-iN] [-oX]] | [-iX -oN]
The valid conversion types are X, for External Data Representation or N, for native machine format.

1 `invalid combination of conversion types`
`usage: auditfltr [[-iN] [-oX]] | [-iX -oN]`

5 `error manipulating file`
File manipulation error occurred during a write or read operation.

13 `bad log record type`
Invalid record type encountered in the audit log file.

24 `unable to allocate space`

32 `input file is in invalid format`
The format of the audit log used as input does not match the format specified by the **-i** option of the command.

39 `XDR encryption of an audit record field failed`

39 `XDR decryption of an audit record field failed`

FILES

`/var/audit/`*MMDD###*

SEE ALSO

`auditmap`(1M), `auditrpt`(1M)

NAME

auditlog – display or set audit log file attributes

SYNOPSIS

auditlog [**-P** *path*][**-p** *node*] [**-v** *high_water*] [**-x** *max_size*]
[**-s** | **-d** | [[**-A** *next_path]* [**-a** *next_node*] [**-n** *pgm*]]]

DESCRIPTION

The **auditlog** shell level command allows the administrator with the appropriate privileges to display and change audit log file attributes. The privleges required are **P_AUDIT** and **P_SETPLEVEL**.

The log file attributes that may be displayed and modified are the path to the event log file, a node name for the event log file, the value for the high water mark of the audit buffer(s), the maximum size of the event log file, the action taken when event log file is full, the next event log to be used, a node name for the next event log file and the program to be run when a log switch occurs. Additionally, the current status of auditing and the action to be taken after an audit error occurs are displayed. While auditing is enabled, execution of this command will result in an audit record being written to the event log file via the **auditdmp** system call. Without any options or arguments, **auditlog** will display the following information (Note: the default values are displayed first):

Current Status of Auditing:	**OFF**| **ON**
Current Event Log:	**/var/audit/***MMDD###*| [*path*]*MMDD###*[*node*]
Current Audit Buffer High Water Mark:	**ADT_BSIZE bytes**| *high_water* **bytes**
Current Maximum File Size Setting:	**none**| *max_size* **blocks**
Action To Be Taken Upon Full Event Log:	**auditing disabled|system shutdown|log switch**
Action To Be Taken Upon Error:	**auditing disabled|system shutdown**
Next Event Log To Be Used:	**none**| [*next_path*]*MMDD###*[*next_node*]
Program to Run When Event Log Is Full:	**none**| *pgm*

The **auditlog** command has the following options:

-P *path*
: The **-P** option specifies the absolute pathname to the primary event log. If the *path* argument is not a full pathname to a directory or a character special file, an error message is printed (see DIAGNOSTICS). The *path* to either a directory or character special file must exist. If the pathname does not exist, **auditlog** prints an error message (see DIAGNOSTICS). The **-P** option cannot be specified while auditing is enabled.

If the argument to **-P** is a valid directory, the next invocation of **auditon** will create a regular file in the directory *path*, with a name that includes the current month and day, followed by a three digit sequence number (for example, 1225001).

The valid range of sequence numbers is 001 to 999, and the default event log file to be used is the regular file **/var/audit/***MMDD###*.

-p *node*
: The **-p** option allows you to append an additional seven characters to the system generated event log file name. The **-p** option cannot be specified while auditing is enabled. For example, the command

```
auditlog -p abcdefg
```

creates the audit log file **/var/audit/***MMDD###***abcdefg**. If the *node* is larger than seven characters or if it contains a slash, an error message is displayed (see DIAGNOSTICS).

-v *high_water* The **-v** option specifies the *high_water* mark of the audit buffer(s). The default setting is equal to the audit buffer size (**ADT_BSIZE**). The *high_water* mark must be either zero (0) or a positive integer less than or equal to the size of the audit buffer (**ADT_BSIZE**). If the value is not valid, an error message is displayed (see DIAGNOSTICS). The *high_water* mark can be set while auditing is disabled or can be set dynamically while auditing is enabled to vary the frequency at which records are written to the audit log file. A setting of zero forces all audit records to be written directly to the audit log file. When used with the **-w** of **auditrpt**, this allows the administrator to monitor events as they occur.

-x *max_size* The **-x** option specifies the maximum file size, in 512 byte blocks, for all event logs that are regular files. If this option is used with event logs that are not regular files, **auditlog** prints a warning message (see DIAGNOSTICS) and ignores the option.

max_size must be greater than or equal to the size of the audit buffer tunable parameter **ADT_BSIZE**. If the value of *max_size* is zero, the size of the event log file is bounded by the amount of available free space on the file system. The default value of *none* implies a *max_size* setting of zero.

-s The **-s** option specifies that the system will be shut down when the event log is full. An event log file is considered full when either a regular file log reaches *max_size*, if specified, or the file system that the log resides in runs out of space, or a special character file log (for example, tape) cannot hold any more data. If this action is chosen and the event log file becomes full, the system will be brought down immediately.

-d The **-d** option specifies that auditing will be disabled when the event log becomes full. An event log file is considered full when either a regular file log reaches *max_size*, if specified, or the file system that the log resides in runs out of space, or a special character file log (for example, tape) cannot hold any more data.

-A *next_path* The **-A** option indicates that a log switch is to occur when the event log file becomes full and specifies the absolute pathname to the alternate event log. An event log file is considered full when either a regular file log reaches *max_size*, if specified, or the file system that the log resides in runs out of space, or a special character file log (for example, tape) cannot hold any more data. If the *next_path* argument is not a full pathname to a directory or a character special device, an error message is printed (see DIAGNOSTICS). The *next_path* to either a directory or special character device must exist. If the pathname does not exist an error message is printed (see DIAGNOSTICS).

When the log full condition is met, and *next_path* is a valid directory, the alternate log file is created relative to *next_path*. The filename format is the current month and day, followed by a three digit sequence number (for example, 1231002).

-a *next_node* The **-a** option allows you to append an additional seven characters to the system generated alternate event log file name. For example, the command

```
auditlog -a abcdefg
```

will create the file **/var/audit/***MMDD###***abcdefg** when a log switch occurs.

If the *next_node* is larger than seven characters or if it contains a slash, an error message is displayed (see DIAGNOSTICS).

-n *pgm* The **-n** option specifies either a shell file or binary executable (*pgm*) that will be run when a log switch occurs. The **-n** option may be used only if an alternate log is specified. The program will be invoked by **init**.

DIAGNOSTICS

If successful, the **auditlog** command exits with a value of zero. If there are errors, it exits with one of the following values and prints the corresponding error message:

1 **usage: auditlog [-P** *path*][-p *node*] [-v *high_water*] [-x *max_size*]
[-s |-d |[[-A *next_path]* [-a *next_node*] [-n *pgm*]]]
Invalid command syntax.

1 **invalid max_size value specified**
Audit Log File Size Must be >=# (512 byte)blocks

1 **invalid high water mark specified**
Audit Buffer High Water Mark Must Be >= 0 or <=*current buffer size in bytes* bytes

1 **cannot open/access path or device** *path/device name*

An invalid argument has been supplied to either the *-P, -A or -n* option.

1 **pathname component too long**

1 **event log node must be < 8 characters**

1 **event log node may not contain a slash**

1 **full pathname not specified**

1 **"***program***" is not a regular file**

1 *"program"* is not an executable file

3 **system service not installed**

The audit package is not installed.

4 **Permission denied**

Failure because of insufficient privilege.

6 **auditbuf() failed ABUFGET, errno=** *error*

A failure occurred while retrieving the audit buffer attributes.

7 **auditbuf() failed ABUFSET, errno=** *error*

A failure occurred while setting the audit buffer attributes.

8 **auditlog() failed ALOGGET, errno=** *error*

A failure occurred while retrieving the audit log attributes.

9 **auditlog() failed ALOGSET, errno=** *error*

A failure occurred while setting the audit log attributes.

12 **auditctl() failed ASTATUS, errno=** *error*

A failure occurred while retrieving the auditing status.

24 **unable to allocate space**

24 **argvtostr() failed**

27 *function name* **failed, errno =** *error*

Failure occurred while accessing level information.

34 *"-option"* **option not allowed while auditing is enabled**

The following warning or informational messages may be printed:

max_size value applies only to regular files
This warning message is printed if you attempt to use the **-x** option and the log file is a character special file.

cannot access /etc/default/audit
The system is unable to open the file that contains information about the default behavior of the auditing subsystem.

check the value of the *default parameter* **in the /etc/default/audit file**
The value of the default parameter in the **/etc/default/audit** file did not pass validation tests.

FILES

/etc/default/audit
/etc/conf/mtune.d/audit
/var/audit/*MMDD###*

SEE ALSO

auditoff(1M), **auditon**(1M), **auditrpt**(1M), **crash**(1M), **defadm**(1M)

NAME

auditmap – create and write audit map files

SYNOPSIS

auditmap [**-m** *dirname*]

DESCRIPTION

The **auditmap** shell level command allows an administrator with the appropriate privileges to create and write the audit map files. The privileges required are **P_AUDIT**, **P_DACREAD**, **P_MACWRITE** and **P_SETPLEVEL**. The **auditmap** command is invoked from the auditon command and may also be directly invoked by the auditing administrator.

The default directory for the audit map file(s) is **/var/audit/auditmap/**. The **-m** option allows the user to choose a directory where the audit map file(s) will be stored. If the directory, *dirname*, does not exist or is not writable, an error message is displayed (see DIAGNOSTICS).

In a base system, the **auditmap** command creates the auditmap file. The auditmap file contains file identification information and six maps.

* file-identification: audit software version, timezone information, privilege mechanism information, system name, machine node name, operating system release and version, and machine type
* all login names and their corresponding uids
* all group names and their gids including multiple groups
* all event type names and their corresponding event type numbers
* all event classes and their corresponding event types
* all privilege names and their corresponding numbers
* all system call names and their corresponding numbers

File locking mechanisms are in place to prevent file corruption during concurrent invocations of **auditmap**.

DIAGNOSTICS

On successful completion, the **auditmap** command exits with a value of zero (0). If there are errors, it exits with one of the following values and prints the corresponding error message:

1 **usage auditmap [-m dirname]**

Invalid command syntax.

3 **system service not installed**

The audit package is not installed.

4 **Permission denied**

Failure because of insufficient privilege.

5 **Invalid full path or pathname** *dirname* **specified**

The directory specified as an argument to the **-m** option does not exist.

5 *filename* **is not writable**

5 *filename* **is not readable**

Unable to open a master LTDB file.

5 **fcntl() failed**

12 **auditctl() failed ASTATUS**

Failure occurred while retrieving auditing status.

24 **malloc() failed**

24 **argvtostr() failed**

27 *function name* **failed, errno** = *error*

Failure occurred while accessing level information.

The following warning messages may be printed:

"resource name" **not written to audit map file** *"file"*

A localized copy of the master LTDB file was not created (for example, *resource name*: **/etc/security/mac/lid.internal** *filename*: **/var/audit/auditmap/lid.internal**) or the user, group or class map was not created (for example, *resource name*: UID *filename*: **/var/audit/auditmap/auditmap**)

Unable to create the auditmap file

filename **file busy**

Unable to place lock on said file.

unable to rename file *audit map file* to *audit map file*

Unable to rename the local audit map file.

stat() failed

FILES

/var/audit/auditmap/auditmap
/etc/security/audit/classes

SEE ALSO

auditon(1M), auditrpt(1M)

NAME

`auditoff` – disable auditing

SYNOPSIS

`auditoff`

DESCRIPTION

The **auditoff** shell level command allows the administrator with the appropriate privileges to disable auditing. The privileges required are **P_AUDIT** and **P_SETPLEVEL**.

The execution of **auditoff** while auditing is enabled will result in a flush of the audit buffer(s) to the audit log file. Additionally, a record indicating auditing has been disabled will be written to the audit log file via the **auditdmp** system call. When auditing is disabled the auditable events currently in progress will not have a record written to the audit log file since they did not complete while auditing was enabled.

When the **auditoff** command is invoked and returns success, the following message will be displayed:

`Auditing disabled`

DIAGNOSTICS

On successful completion, the **auditoff** command exits with a value of zero (0). If there are errors, it exits with one of the following values and prints the corresponding error message:

1 **usage: auditoff**

Invalid command syntax.

3 **system service not installed**

The audit package is not installed.

4 **Permission denied**

Failure because of insufficient privilege.

12 **auditctl() failed ASTATUS, errno =** *error*

Failure occurred while retrieving the status of auditing.

17 **auditctl() failed AUDITOFF, errno =** *error*

Failure occurred while attempting to disable auditing.

24 **argvtostr() failed**

27 *function name* **failed, errno =** *error*

Failure occurred while accessing level information.

The following warning messages may be printed:

`Auditing already disabled`

SEE ALSO

auditlog(1M), **auditon**(1M), **auditrpt**(1M), **auditset**(1M), **crash**(1M)

auditon (1M)

NAME

auditon – enable auditing

SYNOPSIS

auditon

DESCRIPTION

The **auditon** shell level command allows the administrator with the appropriate privileges to enable auditing. The privileges required are **P_AUDIT**, **P_DACREAD**, **P_MACWRITE** and **P_SETPLEVEL**.

When **auditon** is invoked, it retrieves the default values for the **AUDIT_LOGERR**, **AUDIT_LOGFULL**, and **AUDIT_DEFPATH** parameters from the **/etc/default/audit** file. If access to the file is denied or if any of the key words is missing or invalid, an error message is printed (see DIAGNOSTICS). The default value for the **AUDIT_LOGERR** and **AUDIT_LOGFULL** parameters in the distributed system is **DISABLE**. If the Enhanced Security package is installed the value is changed to **SHUTDOWN**. The default value for the **AUDIT_DEFPATH** parameter is **/var/audit**.

If the event log file is a regular file, the **AUDIT_NODE** parameter is evaluated. If the value of **AUDIT_NODE** is longer than 7 characters or contains a slash, it is not used and no node name is appended to the log file name. If the value of **AUDIT_NODE** is valid, it is appended to the log file name.

If the value of **AUDIT_LOGFULL** is **SWITCH**, the **AUDIT_PGM** parameter is evaluated. If the value of **AUDIT_PGM** is valid, it is used as the absolute pathname of a program to execute when a log switch occurs. The **AUDIT_DEFPATH** and **AUDIT_NODE** parameters are also evaluated, and their values used for the alternate log file name and alternate node name.

The **auditlog** command may be used to override all but the **AUDIT_LOGERR** parameter.

When **auditon** is invoked, it initializes the audit event log file. If the event log file cannot be accessed an error message is displayed (see DIAGNOSTICS). When the **auditon** command completes successfully, the following message is displayed:

```
Auditing enabled /var/audit/1215001
```

The **auditon** command invokes the **auditmap** command to create the audit map files.

Auditing remains enabled until the **auditoff** command is executed, or the log full condition of **DISABLE** or **SHUTDOWN** occurs, or an audit error is encountered.

DIAGNOSTICS

On successful completion, the **auditon** command exits with a value of zero (0). If there is an error, it exits one of the following values and prints the corresponding error message:

1 **usage: auditon**

Invalid command syntax.

3 **system service not installed**
The audit package is not installed.

4 **Permission denied**
Failure because of insufficient privilege.

8 **auditlog() failed ALOGGET, errno** = *errno*
Failure occurred while getting audit log file attributes.

9 **auditlog() failed ALOGSET, errno =** *errno*
Failure occurred while setting audit log file attributes.

12 **auditctl() failed ASTATUS, errno =** *errno*
Failure occurred while retrieving the status of auditing.

17 **cannot access event log** *current log file*
Failure occurred while attempting to enable auditing.

17 **Internal error, errno** = *errno*
Failure occurred while attempting to enable auditing.

17 **the maximum (999) number of audit event log files for a given day exist**

The maximum number of audit event log files exist, auditing is not enabled.

17 **auditing abnormally terminated** *log file*
Before command completion auditing was terminated by another process.

24 **unable to malloc space**

24 **argvtostr() failed**

27 *function name* **failed, errno =** *error*

Failure occurred while accessing level information.

33 **exec of** *program name* **failed**

36 **fork() failed**

The following warning messages may be printed:

Auditing already enabled

none or invalid AUDIT_LOGERR=value found in /etc/default/audit

cannot access /etc/default/audit
The **/etc/default/audit** file cannot be accessed. Default values described in the DESCRIPTION section are used. Auditing is enabled.

none or invalid AUDIT_LOGFULL=value found in /etc/default/audit

none or invalid AUDIT_DEFPATH=value found in /etc/default/audit

auditlog() failed ALOGGET, errno = *errno*
Auditing is enabled, however failure occurred when retrieving audit log attributes before changing owner/group of audit log file.

FILES

/etc/default/audit
/var/audit/*MMDD###*
/etc/init.d/audit

SEE ALSO

auditdmp(2), **auditlog**(1M), **auditmap**(1M), **auditoff**(1M), **auditrpt**(1M), **auditset**(1M), **defadm**(1M)

NAME

auditrpt – display recorded information from audit trail

SYNOPSIS

auditrpt [**-o**] [**-i**] [**-b** | **-w**] [**-e**[!]*event*[,. . .]] [**-u** *user*[,. . .]] [**-f** *object_id*[,. . .]]
[**-t** *object_type*[,. . .]] [**-l** *level* | **-r***levelmin-levelmax*]
[**-s** *time*] [**-h** *time*] [**-a** *outcome*] [**-m** *map*]
[**-p all** | *priv*[,. . .]] [**-v** *subtype*] [*log* . . .]]

DESCRIPTION

The **auditrpt** shell level command allows the administrator with the appropriate privileges to selectively display the contents of audit log files. The privileges required are **P_AUDIT** and **P_SETPLEVEL**. The following options are available:

-o Display the events that correspond to the union of the specified auditing criteria.

-i Take input audit records from standard input.

-b Display the events in reverse chronological order (backwards). This option cannot be used with the **-w** option.

-w Display the events as they are being written to the event log file. This option cannot be used with the **-b** option.

-e[!] *event*[,. . .] Display the selected event types or event classes. If **!** is specified, all the events except those listed are displayed. Event classes, which are aliases for groups of events, are defined in the **/etc/security/audit/classes** file.

-u *user*[,. . .] Display all the recorded events for the specified real and effective uids and/or login names.

-f *object_id*[,. . .]
Display all the recorded events for the specified *object_ids*. The *object_id* must be a full pathname of a regular file, special file, directory, or a named pipe, or the ID of an IPC object or loadable module.

-t *object_type*[,. . .]
Display all the recorded events for the specified *object_types*. Valid arguments are **f** (regular file), **c** (character special file), **l** (links), **d** (directories), **p** (named pipes or unnamed pipes), **s** (semaphores), **h** (shared memory), and **m** (messages).

-l *level* Display all the recorded events involving objects at the specified level. Only one level may be specified. Level information is recorded only if the Mandatory Access Control (MAC) feature was installed on the system that generated the audit log. This option cannot be used with the **-r** option.

-r *levelmin–levelmax*
Display all recorded events involving objects whose security level falls within the range defined by *levelmin* and *levelmax*. Only one level range may be specified, and the level specified by *levelmax* must dominate *levelmin*. Level information is recorded only if the

MAC feature was installed on the system that generated the audit log. This option cannot be used with the **-l** option.

-s *time* — Display all the events occurring at or after the specified *time*. The *time* should be specified in the format used by the **date** command. The following are valid values for times: for hours, 00 to 23; for minutes, 00 to 59; for days, 01 to 31; for months, 01 to 12; and for years, 00 to 99.

When both **-s** and **-h** are specified without the **-o** option, the start time (**-s**) must be earlier than the end time (**-h**).

-h *time* — Display all the events existing at or before the specified *time*. Format and valid values for *time* are as same as the **-s** option.

-a *outcome* — Display all the recorded events for the specified *outcome*: **s** (success) or **f** (failure).

-m *map* — Specify the path (absolute or relative) of the auditmap directory.

-p *all* | *priv*[,. . .]

Display the recorded events that use the specified privilege(s). If the word **all** follows the **-p** option, display all recorded events that use any privilege.

-v *subtype* — Display all miscellaneous records with the specified subtype. Only the first 20 characters of the specified subtype are considered for record matching. The command will parse the first field of the miscellaneous record, up to 20 characters or the colon separator, whichever comes first.

log[. . .] — Name (absolute or relative pathname) of the audit log(s) to use.

OUTPUT

The first part of the output of **auditrpt** consists of the command line entered by the administrator. For each log file, the output consists of two parts. First, **auditrpt** displays audit log file and system identification information to verify that the correct log file was specified. This includes the internal identification of the audit log file, the version of the audit software that produced the log file, and the identification of the machine that produced the log file. Second, all records that meet the selection criteria, are displayed one record per line. Records are displayed in the following format:

*time,event,pid,outcome,user,group(s),session,subj_lvl, *
(obj_id:obj_type:obj_lvl:device:maj:min:inode:fsid)(. . .)[,pgm_prm]

The meanings of the fields are explained below.

time — The time is printed as hour:minute:second:day:month:year. For example, **10:30:00:15:04:91** is 10:30am of April 15, 1991.

event — The event type.

process_id — The process ID number of the process that triggered the event, preceded by the letter **P**.

outcome The outcome of the event is either **s** for success or **f**(*exit value*) for failure.

user Real and effective user names are displayed. User names are separated by a colon (that is, *real_user_name*:*effective_user_name*).

group(s) Real and effective groups are displayed, followed by a list of supplementary groups, if any. Groups are separated by a colon (that is, *real_grp*:*effective_grp*:*suppl_grp1*:*suppl_grp2*: . . .).

session_id The session ID number, preceded by the letter **S**.

subj_lvl The security level of the process that triggered the event. The level name may contain colons and/or commas. For readability, the entire field will be enclosed in double quotes (for example, **"system:private,audit"**).

(obj_id:obj_type:obj_lvl:device:maj:min:inode:fsid)
This field contains file identification information, enclosed in parentheses. If multiple objects are accessed in a single event, the field is repeated. This field contains the following subfields:

- *obj_id* The the name of a regular file, special file, directory, named pipe, or the id of an IPC object. If the full pathname of a file system object cannot be determined, the partial pathname will be printed with an asterisk (*) as a prefix.
- *obj_type* The object type, using the codes described in the description of the **-t** option.
- *obj_lvl* The level of the object that was accessed during the event. The level name may contain colons and/or commas. For readability, the entire field will be enclosed in double quotes (for example, **"system:private,audit"**).
- *device* The object's device number.
- *maj* The major number component of the object's device.
- *min* The minor number component of the object's device.
- *inode* The object's **inode** number.
- *fsid* The object's file system ID number.

pgm_prm This field is specific to each audit event and may be composed of several subfields. The subfields described for each event will be displayed in the order shown below and will be separated by commas, unless otherwise specified.

The *pgm_prm* field can be one of the following:

- For the **audit_ctl/audit_evt/audit_log/audit_map** events when generated by the audit user level commands **auditon,auditoff,auditset,auditlog,auditmap**, respectively: the entire command line.

- For the **add_grp/add_usr/add_usr_grp/mod_grp/mod_usr** events: the entire command line.
- For the **tfadmin** event: the entire command line.
- For the **assign_lid/assign_nm/deactivate_lid/del_nm** events: the entire command line.
- For the **chg_times/date** events: the new date.
- For the **fork** event: the child process ID.
- For the **init** event: if generated by the user level command **init(1M)**, the entire command line. If generated by the **init** process (''process 1''), the init state that the machine was in (preceded by current_state:) and the new init state (preceded by new_state:).
- For the **set_uid** event: new user.
- For the **set_gid** event: the new group.
- For the **set_pgrps** event: the name of the system call that generated the event (**setpgrp** or **setpgid**). In addition, if generated by the **setpgid** system call, the process ID and process group ID passed to the system call.
- For the **set_grps** event: the supplementary group access list.
- For the **link** event: the pathname of the target file.
- For the **pipe** event: the two file descriptors returned by the **pipe** system call.
- For the **dac_own_grp** event: if the owner was changed, the new user ID (preceded by user:) or if the group was changed, the new group ID (preceded by group:). In addition, for the **fchown** system call, the file descriptor.
- For the **dac_mode** event: the new mode. In addition, for the **fchmod** system call, the file descriptor.
- For the **msg_ctl/msg_get/msg_op/sem_ctl/sem_get/sem_op/shm_ctl/shm_get/shm_op** events: the operation code, flag and command value. If a subfield does not pertain to an event type, a zero will be displayed.
- For the **login/bad_auth/bad_lvl/def_lvl** events: the terminal identification (tty), user, group and level (enclosed in double quotes) of user attempting to log on (if valid). In addition, for the **def_lvl** event: the old default level (enclosed in double quotes) and requested new default level (enclosed in double quotes) In addition, for the **bad_auth** event: the error message (**LOGIN**, **PASWD** or **AUDIT**)
- For the **passwd** event: the user whose password is being changed (if valid).
- For the **pm_denied** event: the requested privilege, system call name, and maximum set of privileges.

- For the **cron** event: user's effective uid, user's effective gid, user's level (enclosed in double quotes), and cron job name. User refers to the user that cron is running on behalf of.
- For the **open_rd/open_wr** events: the file descriptor.
- For the **cov_chan_1/cov_chan_2** events: covert channel event name and bits per second
- For the **file_lvl/set_lvl_rng/proc_lvl** events: new security level (enclosed in double quotes). In addition, for the **flvlfile** system call, the file descriptor.
- For the **disp_attr/set_attr** events: the release flag (**persistent**, **last-close**, or **system**), device mode (**static** or **dynamic**), low_level (enclosed in double quotes), high_level (enclosed in double quotes) and device state (**private** or **public**. In addition, for the **disp_attr** event: the inuse flag (**inuse** or **unused**). For the **fdevstat** system call, the file descriptor.
- For the **file_acl** event: all ACL entries.
- For the **ipc_acl** event: the ipc type, the ipc id and all ACL entries.
- For the **ulimit** event: the new limit.
- For the **setrlimit** event: the resource (**RLIMIT_CORE,RLIMIT_CPU, RLIMIT_DATA,RLIMIT_FSIZE,RLIMIT_NOFILE,RLIMIT_STACK RLIMIT_VMEM**), soft limit and hard limit.
- For the **sched_lk** event: the action (**PROCLOCK,TXTLOCK,DATLOCK**) if generated by the **plock** system call. The page mapping attributes (**PRIVATE**, or **SHARED**) and page protection attributes (one or more of the following: **PROT_READ**, **PROT_WRITE**, **PROT_EXEC**) if generated by the **memctl** system call.
- For the **sched_rt/sched_ts** events: If generated by the **priocntl** system call with the **PC_ADMIN** command, the function name (**RT_SETDPTBL** or **TS_SETDPTBL**), global priority and time quantum. In addition, if **TS_SETDPTBL** the time-sharing dispatcher parameters: tqexp, slpret, maxwait and lwait. If generated by the **priocntl** system call with the **PC_SETPARMS** command, the function name (**RT_NEW**, **TS_NEW**, **RT_PARMSET**, **TS_PARMSET**), process id and user priority. In addition, if the **sched_ts** event, user priority limit. If **sched_rt** event, the seconds in time quantum and additional nanoseconds in quantum.
- For the **modadm** event: the module type (**character device**, **block device**, **streams**, **filesystem**, **misc**, **none**), the command (**register**), and the module name. Also, module type specific data as follows: if module type is **character device** or **block device**, the major number; if module type is **filesystem**, the filesystem name; if module type is **misc** or **none**, no specific data is displayed.
- For the **modload** event: the load type (**demand** or **auto**) and the loadable module id.

- For the **moduload** event: the load type (**demand** or **auto**).
- For the **modpath** event: the absolute pathname added to the loadable module search path or <NULL> if the default search path is set.
- For the **iocntl** event: the file descriptor passed to the system call, the command argument id passed to the system call, the flags found in the file table entry, if any (separated by colons), (**FOPEN**, **FREAD**, **FWRITE**, **FNDELAY**, **FAPPEND**, **FSYNC**, **FNONBLOC**, **FMASK**, **FCREAT**, **FTRUNC**, **FEXCL**, **FNOCTTY**, **FASYNC**, **FNMFS**).
- For the **fcntl** event: the file descriptor passed to the system call and the command argument passed to the system call. If command is **F_DUPFD**, the new file descriptor. If command is **F_SETFD**, close-on-exec flag (0 or 1). If command is **F_SETFL**, status flags (separated by colons) (**O_APPEND**, **O_NDELAY**, **O_NONBLOCK**, **O_SYNC**). If a **struct flock** was passed to the system call: the file descriptor passed to the system call, the command argument passed to the system call, (**F_ALLCOSP**, **F_FREESP**, **F_SETLCK**, **F_SETLKW**, **F_RSETLCK**, **F_RSERLKW**) and the following structure members: l_type,l_whence,l_start,l_len.
- For the **mount** event: the flags passed to the system call and one or more of the following: **RDONLY** (read-only), **FSS** (old (4-argument) mount), **DATA** (6-argument mount), **NOSUID** (setuid disallowed), **REMOUNT** (remount), **NOTRUNC** (return **ENAMETOOLONG** for long filenames).
- For the **file_priv** event: all information in the **priv_t** masks passed to the system call, in the following format:

  priv_type1:priv_name[:priv_name],priv_type2:. . .

  priv_type will be the name of the privilege type, if it is recognized by the privilege mechanism of the audited system. If it is not recognized, it will be the character representation of the first byte of the **priv_t** mask (for example, **i** for inheritable). For a list of privileges, see **intro**(2).
- For the **recvfd** event: the sender's process ID, the sender's file descriptor, the receiver's process ID, and the receiver's file descriptor.
- For the **misc** event: the free form string provided by the application.
- For the **audit_buf** event: the high water mark value.
- For the **audit_ctl** event when generated by the **auditctl** system call: the action taken (**AUDITON or AUDITOFF**).
- For the **audit_log** event when generated by the **auditlog** system call: all information passed in the **alog** structure to the system call. This will include: log file attributes (**PPATH:PNODE:APATH:ANODE:PSIZE :ASPECIAL:PSPECIAL**), the action taken when the log is full (**ASHUT,ADISA,AALOG, AALOG:APROG**), the action taken when there is an audit error (**ASHUT** or **ADISA**), the maximum log size, the primary node name, the alternate node name, the primary log pathname, the alternate log pathname and the program to be run during a log switch.

- For the **audit_dmp** event when generated by the **auditdmp** system call: the event type and the status (if success: **SUCCESS**, if failure: **FAILURE**(status)).
- For the **audit_evt** event when generated by the **auditevt** system call: all information passed in the **aevt** structure to the system call. This will include: command argument (**ASETME,ASETSYS,ASETUSR, ASETLVL,ANAUDIT,AYAUDIT**). If the command is **ASETME**, the new user event mask for the invoking process. If the command is **ASETSYS**, the new system event mask. If the command is **ASETUSR**, the user whose mask has been modified, the new user event mask. If the command is **ASETLVL**, the list of security levels (each level enclosed in double quotes) or the level range (displayed as "level_min"-"level_max") , or the object level mask.
- For all events generated from file descriptor based system calls: the file descriptor.

All the commas in the output line, except possibly the last one (if *pgm_prm* is empty), will be displayed as place holders. For all the output fields, null will be displayed if the field is not appropriate for the event type being displayed. For example, the *date* event has no objects related to it, so the *obj_id:obj_type:obj_lvl:device:maj:min:inode:fsid* fields will be null (only the comma separator will be displayed for these fields). Also, in a base system the MAC level fields will be null.

The **auditrpt** command will use the audit map to translate users, groups,security levels, privileges, events and system calls from IDs(numbers) to names. If the information for translating a number to a name is not found in the map, raw data (ASCII representation of the numeric value) will be displayed for the corresponding field.

All numeric values are displayed in decimal representation unless preceded by **0x**, which indicates hexadecimal representation.

If a field is appropriate for an event but its value is "invalid," a **?** will be displayed. For example, if a *login* event fails because the logname used is unknown to the system (cannot be translated into a UID in the log record), the *user* will be flagged as "invalid" and a **?** will be displayed.

MISCELLANEOUS RECORDS

Application programs can generate audit records with the **auditdmp** system call. The **auditrpt** command processes these records as events of the type **misc**. The **misc** record will have a string in the final field of its output; this string will contain all the information written by the application program that created the **misc** audit record.

DIAGNOSTICS

If successful, **auditrpt** exits with a value of zero (0). If there are errors, it exits with one of the following values and prints the corresponding error message:

1

usage:
auditrpt [-o] [-i] [-b | -w] [-e [!]*event*[,. . .]] [**-u** *user*[,. . .]]
[**-f** *object_id*[,. . .]] [**-t** *object_type*[,. . .]] [**-s** *time*]
[**-h** *time*] [**-l** *level* **|** **-r** *levelmin-levelmax*] [**-a** *outcome*]
[**-m** *map*] [**-p** *all* | *priv*[,. . .]] [**-v** *subtype*] [*log* [. . .]]

Invalid command syntax.

1 **maximum security level does not dominate minimum security level**

The level range specified by the **-r** option is not valid.

1 **invalid minimum security level specified**

1 **invalid maximum security level specified**

1 **too many levels specified**
usage:
auditrpt [-o] [-i] [-b | -w] [-e [!]*event*[,. . .]] [**-u** *user*[,. . .]]
[**-f** *object_id*[,. . .]] [**-t** *object_type*[,. . .]] [**-s** *time*]
[**-h** *time*] [**-l** *level* | **-r** *levelmin-levelmax*] [**-a** *outcome*]
[**-m** *map*] [**-p** *all* | *priv*[,. . .]] [**-v** *subtype*] [*log* [. . .]]

More than one level was specified as an argument to the **-l** option, or more than one level range was specified as an argument to the **-r** option.

1 **security level specified does not exist in map**

1 **argument list for option** *option* **too long**

The argument list exceeds the current implementation limits.

1 **Option requires an argument** -- *e*

1 **start time must be earlier than the end time**

When the **-s** and **-h** options are used without **-o**, the time specified by **-s** must be earlier than that specified by **-h**.

1 **invalid argument given to option** *option*
user specified with the -u option contains at least one non-alphanumeric character.

1 **event type or class** *event* **does not exist**

The argument to the **-e** option was an invalid event type or class (that is, an event not found in the audit map information).

1 **full pathname must be specified for** *object_id*

1 **invalid object type specified:** *object_type*

The object type was not a **f**, **c**, **d**, **p**, **l**, **s**, **h**, or **m**.

1 **invalid outcome specified**

The outcome specified by **-a** must be either **s** or **f**.

1 **invalid option combination** *option1, option2,. . .*
usage:
auditrpt [-o] [-i] [-b | -w] [-e [!]*event*[,. . .]] [**-u** *user*[,. . .]]
[**-f** *object_id*[,. . .]] [**-t** *object_type*[,. . .]] [**-s** *time*]
[**-h** *time*] [**-l** *level* | **-r** *levelmin-levelmax*] [**-a** *outcome*]
[**-m** *map*] [**-p** *all* | *priv*[,. . .]] [**-v** *subtype*] [*log* [. . .]]

1 **auditing currently disabled, logfile must be specified**

1 **auditing disabled**

The **-w** option was specified while auditing was disabled.

1 **cannot open auditmap directory** *dirname*

1 **invalid time format**

The argument to the **-h** or **-s** option is not correct.

1 **invalid privilege "***priv***" supplied**

3 **system service not installed**

if the -w option is used or no log file is specified, then auditing must be installed on the machine in which auditing is executing.

4 **Permission denied**

Failure because of insufficient privilege.

5 **chmod(2) failed for temporary file, errno =** *number*

5 **error manipulating file**

6 **could not get buffer attributes**

The call to the **auditbuf** system call to get the audit buffer attributes failed.

8 **could not get current log attributes**

The call to the **auditlog** system call to get the current log file attributes failed.

12 **could not determine status of auditing**

The call to the **auditctl** system call to get the current status of auditing failed.

13 **bad log record type** *record number*

An invalid record type was encountered in the audit event log file.

15 **all event log files specified are inaccessible**

24 **unable to allocate space**

26 **additional options required**
usage:
auditrpt [-o] [-i] [-b | -w] [-e [!]*event*[,. . .]] [**-u** *user*[,. . .]]
[**-f** *object_id*[,. . .]] [**-t** *object_type*[,. . .]] [**-s** *time*]
[**-h** *time*] [**-l** *level* | **-r** *levelmin-levelmax*] [**-a** *outcome*]
[**-m** *map*] [**-p** *all* | *priv*[,. . .]] [**-v** *subtype*] [*log* [. . .]]

The **-o** option was specified without additional criteria selection options.

27 *function name* **failed, errno =** *error*

Failure occurred while accessing level information.

28 **bad map record type** *record number*

An invalid element was encountered in an audit map file.

32 **log file's format or byte ordering (***format id***)**
is not readable in current architecture

The event log file is in External Data Representation (XDR).

The following warning messages may be displayed:

event log file(s) are not in sequence or missing
The log files specified on the command line may not be in order, or a file may be missing.

missing pathname for process P*pid*
auditrpt did not find the expected number of filename records for the given process.

process information for P*pid* **is incomplete**
Process and/or group records for the given process were not found previously in the audit log file(s).

event log file *log* **does not exist**
A log file specified on the command line does not exist.

no match found in event log file(s)
The log file or files do not contain a record that matches the selection criteria.

machines in log file "*filename*" (*mach_info*) **and map file** (*mach_info*) **do not match**
The event log file and the audit map files were generated on different machines.

data in audit buffer will not be immediately displayed
The **-w** option is specified, but the audit log high water mark is not zero.

log file *"filename"* **ignored**
The **-i** option or the **-w** option was used along with a log file argument.

the ltdb files are missing or incomplete in the auditmap directory
auditrpt could not access some or all the audit map files containing security level information.

cannot open audit map file *map_file*
auditrpt could not open the **auditmap** directory for reading.

misformed miscellaneous record
The miscellaneous record did not have a subtype name followed by a colon (:) in the first 20 characters of the ASCII string.

cannot read and write character special device simultaneously
The specified (or default) log file is a character special device and is also the current active log file.

`user id` *user* does not exist in audit map

`keyword "all" should not be used in conjunction with individual privileges`
The privilege list specified with the **`-p`** option can not contain both the keyword *all* and individual privileges

FILES

`/var/tmp/`
`/var/audit/`*MMDD###*
`/var/audit/auditmap/auditmap`

SEE ALSO

`auditfltr`(1M), `auditlog`(1M), `auditmap`(1M), `auditoff`(1M), `auditon`(1M), `auditset`(1M)

auditset (1M)

NAME

auditset – select or display audit criteria

SYNOPSIS

auditset [-d [-u *user*[,. . .]|-a] [-m]]

auditset [-s [*operator*]*event*[,. . .]] [[-u *user*[,. . .]|-a] -e[*operator*]*event*[,. . .]] [-o [*operator*]*event*[,. . .]] [-r [-]*levelmin-levelmax*] [-l [+|-]*level*]

DESCRIPTION

The **auditset** shell level command allows the administrator with the appropriate privileges to set or display the system, user and object level audit criteria. The privileges required are **P_AUDIT**, **P_DACREAD**, **P_MACREAD** and **P_SETPLEVEL**.

To set or display user auditing criteria auditing must be enabled and the specified user(s) must be active. The -o, -l, -r, and -m options are only valid if the Mandatory Access Control feature (MAC) is installed. If no options are supplied on the command line, then the System and User level audit criteria are displayed.

The *event* input list must be separated by commas, and can be the name of an event class or event type. Event classes are defined in the **/etc/security/audit/classes** system file. Additionally, **all** and **none** may be used as *event* keywords. For the system and user audit criteria the keyword **none** is defined to be the set of fixed event types and the keyword **all** is defined to be the set of all fixed and pre-selectable event types. For the object audit criteria the keyword **none** is defined as no event types and the keyword **all** is defined to be the set of all pre-selectable object event types. Keyword(s) will be ignored if intermixed with event classes or event types.

The *user* input list must be separated by commas, and can be specified by either login name or uid. (Note: auditing is based on real uid).

Only one *operator* may be specified per option on the command line. *Operators* will be ignored when used with the keywords **all** and **none**. The following are the valid *operator* values:

[*no operator*]
: Replace the current auditable event(s), level, or level range with the specified input.

+
: Add the specified auditable event(s) or level to the current audit criteria.

-
: Delete the specified auditable event(s), level or level range from the current audit criteria.

!
: All auditable events except those specified replace the current auditable events.

The following are the valid command line options.

-d
: Display the current system audit criteria in the format:

System Audit Criteria:
system: *all* | *none* | *events*[,. . .]

-u *user*[,. . .] | **-a**

The **-u and -a** options are modifiers to the **-d** option and the **-e** option. The **-u** option is used to request a specific active user or a list of active users. The **-a** option is used to request all currently active users. The **-u and -a** options can not be used on the same command line. When used with the **-e** option user audit criteria is set (see explanation of **-e** option). When used with the **-d** option and auditing is enabled the user audit criteria is displayed. The format is:

User Audit Criteria:
user1 (uid1): all | *none* | *events*[,. . .]
user2 (uid2): all | *none* | *events*[,. . .]

(Note: *user* will be the login name and *uid*, the user ID).

When used with the *-d* option and auditing is *not* enabled the following is displayed:

User Audit Criteria: Auditing not enabled

-s [*operator*]*event*[,. . .]

Set the system wide auditing criteria. Any valid event type or event class will be recorded regardless of the current user or object level criteria.

-e [*operator*]*event*[,. . .] -u *user*[,. . .] | -a

Set the auditing criteria for the specified active user(s) or all users. All processes belonging to the specified user(s) will have their auditing information updated.

NOTES

The **auditset** command sets audit criteria for users dynamically. When you set audit criteria for a user with the **-e,-u,-a** options, the criteria are in effect only for that login session. If the user logs out or logs in from another terminal, the criteria are no longer in effect. If you want to set audit criteria for all a user's login sessions, use either the **useradd** or **usermod** commands.

DIAGNOSTICS

When invoked successfully, the **auditset** command exits with a value of zero (0). If there are errors, it exits with one of the following values and prints the corresponding error message:

1 **usage: auditset [-d [-u** *user*[,. . .] | **-a**]]
auditset [**-s** [*operator*]*event*[,. . .]] [[**-u** *user*[,. . .] | **-a**]
-e[*operator*]*event*[,. . .]]

Invalid command syntax.

1 **usage: auditset [-d [-u** *user*[,. . .] | **-a**] [**-m**]]
auditset [**-s** [*operator*]*event*[,. . .]] [[**-u** *user*[,. . .] | **-a**]
-e[*operator*]*event*[,. . .]] [**-o** [*operator*]*event*[,. . .]]
[**-l** [*operator*]*level*] [**-r** [*operator*]*levelmin-levelmax*]

Invalid command syntax.

1 **auditing is not enabled**

User audit criteria can not be set if auditing is disabled.

1 **invalid security level "*level*" specified**

An invalid level was specified as an argument to the **-l** or **-r** options.

1 **maximum security level does not dominate minimum security level "*level–level*"**

An invalid security level range was used as the argument to the **-r** option.

3 **invalid option -o, -l, -r**
system service not installed
usage: auditset [-d [-u *user*[,. . .] | **-a]]**
auditset [**-s** [*operator*]*event*[,. . .]] [[**-u** *user*[,. . .] | **-a**] **-e**[*operator*]*event*[,. . .]]

The MAC feature must be installed to use the **-o**, **-l**, and **-r** options.

3 **system service not installed**

The audit package is not installed.

4 **Permission denied**

Failure because of insufficient privilege.

5 **opendir() failed for directory /proc**

Unable to obtain a list of the active users on the system.

10 **auditevt() failed AGETSYS, errno** = *errno*

A failure occurred while retrieving the system audit mask.

10 **auditevt() failed ACNTLVL, errno** = *errno*

A failure occurred while retrieving the object level audit mask.

10 **auditevt() failed AGETLVL, errno** = *errno*

A failure occurred while retrieving the object level audit mask.

10 **auditevt() failed AGETUSR, errno** = *errno*

A failure occurred while retrieving a user's audit mask.

11 **auditevt() failed ASETSYS, errno** = *errno*

A failure occurred while setting the system audit mask.

11 **auditevt() failed ASETUSR, errno** = *errno*

A failure occurred while setting a user's audit mask.

11 **auditevt() failed ASETLVL, errno** = *errno*

A failure occurred while setting the object level audit mask.

12 **auditctl() failed ASTATUS, errno** = *errno*

A failure occurred while retrieving the status of auditing.

24 **unable to allocate space**

24 **argvtostr() failed**

27 *function name* **failed, errno** = *error*

Failure occurred while accessing level information.

31 **lvlout() error, errno** = *error*

A failure occurred while accessing level information.

37 **lvlin() error, errno** = *error*

A failure occurred while accessing level information.

37 **LTDB is inaccessible**

Cannot open the Level Translation Database (LTDB).

The following warning messages may be displayed:

invalid or inactive user *"user"* **specified**
The argument to the **-u** option contained an invalid or inactive user.

no current object levels in effect

no object level event type(s) or class(es) in effect

system defined level limit exceeded, level "*level***" not set**
The total number of levels that can be audited is defined by the tunable parameter **ADT_NLVLS** in **/etc/conf/mtune.d/audit**. If the level to be set would exceed this parameter, the system prints this warning message and continues processing the remaining options, if any.

level *level* **not currently in effect**
An attempt was made to delete a level that was not set for auditing.

FILES

/etc/security/audit/classes

SEE ALSO

auditoff(1M), **auditon**(1M), **auditrpt**(1M), **useradd**(1M), **usermod**(1M)

automount (1M)

NAME

automount – automatically mount NFS file systems

SYNOPSIS

/usr/lib/nfs/automount [-mnTv] [-D *name=value*] **[-M** *mount-directory*] **[-f** *master-file*]
  [-t *sub-options*] [*directory map* [*–mount-options*]] . . .

DESCRIPTION

automount is a daemon that automatically and transparently mounts an NFS file system as needed. It monitors attempts to access directories that are associated with an **automount** map, along with any directories or files that reside under them. When a file is to be accessed, the daemon mounts the appropriate NFS file system. You can assign a map to a directory using an entry in a direct **automount** map, by specifying a master-map on the command line, or by specifying an indirect map.

automount uses a map to locate an appropriate NFS file server, exported file system, and mount options, for an automatically mounted resource. It then mounts the file system in a temporary location (**/tmp_mnt**), and replaces the file system entry for the directory or subdirectory with a symbolic link to the temporary location. If the file system is not accessed within an appropriate interval (five minutes by default), the daemon unmounts the file system and removes the symbolic link. If the indicated directory (**/tmp_mnt**) has not already been created, the daemon creates it, and then removes it upon exiting.

Since the name-to-location binding is dynamic, updates to an **automount** map are transparent to the user. This obviates the need to pre-mount shared file systems for applications that have hard coded references to files.

If you specify the dummy directory /–**,** **automount** treats the *map* argument that follows as the name of a direct map. In a direct map, each entry associates the full pathname of a mount point with a remote file system to mount.

If the **directory** argument is a pathname, the *map* argument points to a file called an indirect map. An indirect map contains a list of the subdirectories contained within the indicated **directory**. With an indirect map, it is these subdirectories that are mounted automatically. The *map* argument must be a full pathname.

The *–mount-options* argument, when supplied, is a comma-separated list of **mount**(1M) options, preceded by a hyphen (–). If mount options are specified in the indicated map, however, those in the map take precedence.

Only a privileged user can execute this command.

The following options are available:

–m Disable the search of the Network Interface Services map file. This option can only be used in conjunction with the **–f** option.

–n Disable dynamic mounts. With this option, references through the **automount** daemon only succeed when the target file system has been previously mounted. This can be used to prevent NFS servers from cross-mounting each other.

-T Trace. Expand each NFS call and display it on the standard output.

-v Verbose. Log status messages to the console.

-D *name=value*
Assign *value* to the indicated **automount** (environment) variable.

-f *master-file*
Specify all arguments in *master-file* and instruct the daemon to look in it for instructions.

-M *mount-directory*
Mount temporary file systems in the named directory, instead of **/tmp_mnt**.

-t *sub-options*
Specify *sub-options* as a comma-separated list that contains any combination of the following:

l *duration*
Specify a *duration*, in seconds, that a file system is to remain mounted when not in use. The default is 5 minutes.

m *interval*
Specify an *interval*, in seconds, between attempts to mount a file system. The default is 30 seconds.

w *interval*
Specify an *interval*, in seconds, between attempts to unmount file systems that have exceeded their cached times. The default is 1 minute.

ENVIRONMENT

Environment variables can be used within an **automount** map. For instance, if **$HOME** appeared within a map, **automount** would expand it to its current value for the **HOME** variable.

If a reference needs to be protected from affixed characters, enclose the variable name within braces.

USAGE

Direct/Indirect Map Entry Format

A simple map entry (mapping) takes the form:

directory [-*mount-options*] *location* ...

where **directory** is the full pathname of the directory to mount when used in a direct map, or the basename of a subdirectory in an indirect map. *mount-options* is a comma-separated list of **mount** options, and *location* specifies a remote file system from which the directory may be mounted. In the simple case, *location* takes the form:

host:*pathname*

Multiple *location* fields can be specified, in which case **automount** sends multiple **mount** requests; **automount** mounts the file system from the first host that replies to the **mount** request. This request is first made to the local net or subnet. If there is no response, any connected server may respond.

If *location* is specified in the form:

host:*path*:*subdir*

host is the name of the host from which to mount the file system, *path* is the pathname of the directory to mount, and *subdir*, when supplied, is the name of a subdirectory to which the symbolic link is made. This can be used to prevent duplicate mounts when multiple directories in the same remote file system may be accessed. With a map for **/home** such as:

```
able  homebody:/home/homebody:able
baker homebody:/home/homebody:baker
```

and a user attempting to access a file in **/home/able**, **automount** mounts **homebody:/home/homebody**, but creates a symbolic link called **/home/able** to the **able** subdirectory in the temporarily mounted file system. If a user immediately tries to access a file in **/home/baker**, **automount** needs only to create a symbolic link that points to the **baker** subdirectory; **/home/homebody** is already mounted. With the following map:

```
able  homebody:/home/homebody/able
baker homebody:/home/homebody/baker
```

automount would have to mount the file system twice.

A mapping can be continued across input lines by escaping the NEWLINE with a backslash. Comments begin with a # and end at the subsequent NEWLINE.

Directory Pattern Matching

The & character is expanded to the value of the **directory** field for the entry in which it occurs. In this case:

```
able  homebody:/home/homebody:&
```

the **&** expands to **able**.

The * character, when supplied as the **directory** field, is recognized as the catch-all entry. Such an entry resolves to any entry not previously matched. For instance, if the following entry appeared in the indirect map for **/home**:

```
*       &:/home/&
```

this would allow automatic mounts in **/home** of any remote file system whose location could be specified as:

hostname:**/home/***hostname*

Hierarchical Mappings

A hierarchical mapping takes the form:

directory [/ [*subdirectory*]] [*–mount-options*] *location*. . .
[/ [*subdirectory*] [*–mount-options*] *location*. . .] . . .

The initial /[*subdirectory*] is optional for the first location list and mandatory for all subsequent lists. The optional *subdirectory* is taken as a filename relative to the **directory**. If *subdirectory* is omitted in the first occurrence, the / refers to the directory itself.

Given the direct map entry:

```
/arch/src    \
/          -ro,intr  arch:/arch/src           alt:/arch/src     \
/1.0       -ro,intr  alt:/arch/src/1.0        arch:/arch/src/1.0   \
/1.0/man   -ro,intr  arch:/arch/src/1.0/man   alt:/arch/src/1.0/man
```

automount would automatically mount **/arch/src**, **/arch/src/1.0** and **/arch/src/1.0/man**, as needed, from either **arch** or **alt**, whichever host responded first.

Direct Maps

A direct map contains mappings for any number of directories. Each directory listed in the map is automatically mounted as needed. The direct map as a whole is not associated with any single directory.

Indirect Maps

An indirect map allows you to specify mappings for the subdirectories you wish to mount under the **directory** indicated on the command line. It also obscures local subdirectories for which no mapping is specified. In an indirect map, each **directory** field consists of the basename of a subdirectory to be mounted as needed.

Included Maps

The contents of another map can be included within a map with an entry of the form

+*mapname*

where *mapname* is a filename.

Special Maps

The **-null** map is the only special map currently available. The **-null** map, when indicated on the command line, cancels a previous map for the directory indicated.

FILES

/tmp_mnt parent directory for dynamically mounted file systems

SEE ALSO

df(1M), **mount**(1M), **passwd**(4)

NOTES

Mount points used by **automount** are not recorded in **/etc/mnttab**. **mount**(1M) on such mount points will fail, saying mount point busy, although the mount point is not in **/etc/mnttab**.

Shell filename expansion does not apply to objects not currently mounted.

Since **automount** is single-threaded, any request that is delayed by a slow or non-responding NFS server will delay all subsequent automatic mount requests until it completes.

NAME

autopush – configure lists of automatically pushed STREAMS modules

SYNOPSIS

autopush -f *file*
autopush -r -M *major* **-m** *minor*
autopush -g -M *major* **-m** *minor*

DESCRIPTION

This command allows one to configure the list of modules to be automatically pushed onto the stream when a device is opened. It can also be used to remove a previous setting or get information on a setting.

The following options apply to **autopush**:

-f This option sets up the **autopush** configuration for each driver according to the information stored in the specified file. An **autopush** file consists of lines of at least four fields each where the fields are separated by a space as shown below:

```
maj_  min_  last_min_  mod1 mod2 ... modn
```

The first three fields are integers that specify the major device number, minor device number, and last minor device number. The fields following represent the names of modules. If *min_* is -1, then all minor devices of a major driver specified by *maj_* are configured and the value for *last_min_* is ignored. If *last_min_* is 0, then only a single minor device is configured. To configure a range of minor devices for a particular major, *min_* must be less than *last_min_*.

The last fields of a line in the **autopush** file represent the list of module names where each is separated by a space. The maximum number of modules that can be automatically pushed on a stream is defined to be eight. The modules are pushed in the order they are specified. Comment lines start with a # sign.

-r This option removes the previous configuration setting of the particular *major* and *minor* device number specified with the **-M** and **-m** options respectively. If the values of *major* and *minor* correspond to a setting of a range of minor devices, where *minor* matches the first minor device number in the range, the configuration would be removed for the entire range.

-g This option gets the current configuration setting of a particular *major* and *minor* device number specified with the **-M** and **-m** options respectively. It will also return the starting minor device number if the request corresponds to a setting of a range (as described with the **-f** option).

SEE ALSO

streamio(7)

NAME

awk – pattern scanning and processing language

SYNOPSIS

awk [**-F***c*] [**-f** *file* | *'cmds'*] [*parameters*] [*files*]

DESCRIPTION

awk scans each input *file* for lines that match any of a set of patterns specified in *cmds*. Patterns are arbitrary Boolean combinations of regular expressions and relational expressions. With each pattern in *cmds* there can be an associated action that will be performed when a line of a *file* matches the pattern. The set of patterns may appear literally as *cmds*, or in a file specified as **-f** *file*. The *cmds* string should be enclosed in single quotes (') to protect it from the shell.

awk processes supplementary code set characters in pattern-action statements and comments, and recognizes supplementary code set characters as field separators (see below) according to the locale specified in the **LC_CTYPE** environment variable [see **LANG** on **environ**(5)]. In regular expressions, pattern searches are performed on characters, not bytes, as described on **ed**(1).

Parameters, in the form x=... y=... and so on, may be passed to **awk**.

Files are read in order; if there are no files, the standard input is read. The file name - means the standard input. Each line is matched against the pattern portion of every pattern-action statement; the associated action is performed for each matched pattern.

An input line is made up of fields separated by white space. (This default can be changed by using **FS**, described below). The fields are denoted **$1**, **$2**, ... ; **$0** refers to the entire line.

A pattern-action statement has the form:

pattern { *action* }

A missing action means print the line; a missing pattern always matches. An action is a sequence of statements. A statement can be one of the following:

if (*conditional* **)** *statement* [*else statement*]
while (*conditional* **)** *statement*
for (*expression* **;** *conditional* **;** *expression* **)** *statement*
break
continue
{ [*statement*] . . . **}**
variable = *expression*
print [*expression-list*] [>*expression*]
printf *format* [, *expression-list*] [>*expression*]
next # skip remaining patterns on this input line
exit # skip the rest of the input

Statements are terminated by semicolons, new-lines, or right braces. An empty expression-list stands for the whole line. Expressions take on string or numeric values as appropriate, and are built using the operators **+**, **-**, *****, **/**, **%**, and concatenation (indicated by a blank). The C operators **++**, **--**, **+=**, **-=**, ***=**, **/=**, and **%=** are also available in expressions. Variables may be scalars, array elements (denoted **x[i]**), or fields. Variables are initialized to the null string. Array subscripts may be any string, not necessarily numeric; this allows for a form of associative memory. String constants are quoted (**"**).

The **print** statement prints its arguments on the standard output (or on a file if **>***expr* is present), separated by the current output field separator, and terminated by the output record separator. The **printf** statement formats its expression list according to the format [see **printf**(3S)].

The built-in function **length** returns the length in bytes of its argument taken as a string, or of the whole line if no argument. There are also built-in functions **exp**, **log**, **sqrt**, and **int**. The last truncates its argument to an integer. **substr (***s***,** *m***,** *n***)** returns the *n*-byte substring of *s* that begins at position *m*. The function **sprintf(***fmt***,** *expr***,** *expr***,** . . .**)** formats the expressions according to the **printf**(3S) format given by *fmt* and returns the resulting string.

As noted, patterns are arbitrary Boolean combinations (**!**, **||**, **&&**, and parentheses) of regular expressions and relational expressions. Regular expressions must be surrounded by slashes and are as in **egrep**(1). Isolated regular expressions in a pattern apply to the entire line. Regular expressions may also occur in relational expressions. A pattern may consist of two patterns separated by a comma; in this case, the action is performed for all lines between an occurrence of the first pattern and the next occurrence of the second.

A relational expression is one of the following:

> *expression matchop regular-expression*
> *expression relop expression*

where a *relop* is any of the six relational operators in C, and a *matchop* is either **~** (for *contains*) or **!~** (for *does not contain*). A conditional is an arithmetic expression, a relational expression, or a Boolean combination of these.

The special patterns **BEGIN** and **END** may be used to capture control before the first input line is read and after the last. **BEGIN** must be the first pattern, **END** the last.

A single character *c* may be used to separate the fields by starting the program with:

> **BEGIN { FS =** *c* **}**

or by using the **-F***c* option.

Other variable names with special meanings include **NF**, the number of fields in the current record; **NR**, the ordinal number of the current record; **FILENAME**, the name of the current input file; **OFS**, the output field separator (default blank); **ORS**, the output record separator (default new-line); and **OFMT**, the output format for numbers (default **%.6g**). The field separators specified with the **-F** option or with the variables **OFS**, **ORS**, and **FS** may be supplementary code set characters.

EXAMPLES

Print lines longer than 72 characters:

```
length > 72
```

Print first two fields in opposite order:

```
{ print $2, $1 }
```

Add up first column, print sum and average:

```
     { s += $1 }
END  { print "sum is", s, " average is", s/NR }
```

Print fields in reverse order:

```
{ for (i = NF; i > 0; --i) print $i }
```

Print all lines between *start/stop* pairs:

```
/start/, /stop/
```

Print all lines whose first field is different from previous one:

```
$1 != prev { print; prev = $1 }
```

Print file, filling in page numbers starting at 5:

```
/Page/ { $2 = n++; }
       { print }
```

command line: **awk -f** *program* **n=5** *input*

FILES

/usr/lib/locale/*locale***/LC_MESSAGES/uxawk**
language-specific message file [See **LANG** on **environ**(5).]

SEE ALSO

egrep(1), **grep**(1), **lex**(1), **nawk**(1), **printf**(3S), **sed**(1)

NOTES

Input white space is not preserved on output if fields are involved.

There are no explicit conversions between numbers and strings. To force an expression to be treated as a number, add 0 to it; to force it to be treated as a string, concatenate the null string (**""**) to it.

awk is obsolescent. **nawk**, which is a new version of **awk** that provides capabilities unavailable in previous versions, will become the default **awk** in the next release.

The implementation of **awk** for internationalization is based on **nawk** in System V, Release 4.

backup (1M)

NAME

backup – initiate or control a system backup session

SYNOPSIS

backup [**-t** *table*] [**-o** *oname*[**:***odevice*]] [**-m** *user*] [**-en**] [**-c** *week***:***day* | **demand**]
backup [**-i**] [**-t** *table*] [**-o** *oname*[**:***odevice*]] [**-m** *user*] [**-en**] [**-s** | **-v**]] [**-c** *week***:***day* | **demand**]
backup **-S** | **-R** | **-C** [**-u** *user* | **-A** | **-j** *jobid*]
backup [**-T**] [**-p** | **-w** | **-f** *files* | **-u** "*user1*[*user2*]"] **-d** *device*
backup -h

DESCRIPTION

Two backup facilities are delivered with UNIX System V Release 4.2: the basic version and the extended version. A basic **backup** command (providing seven options) is delivered in the Foundation Set. It provides a facility that is adequate for most small machines and machines with a minimal amount of software installed. If you install the Extended Backup and Restore Package, however, you'll have access to the extended backup command. This section describes the options available with both facilities.

Although many options cannot be run unless a user has privileges to do so, some options to the basic **backup** command can be executed by any user without special privileges.

The Extended Backup Facility

Without options, the **backup** command performs all backup operations specified for the current day and week of the backup rotation in the backup register. This set of backup operations is considered a single job and is assigned a **backup** job ID which can be used to control the progress of the session. As backup operations are processed, the status of each is tracked. [See **bkstatus**(1M).] As backup operations are completed, they are recorded in the backup history log.

A backup job can be controlled in three ways: it can be canceled, suspended or resumed (after being suspended).

The extended **backup** command may be executed only by a privileged user.

Modes of Operator Intervention in Extended Backup/Restore

Backup operations may require operator intervention to perform such tasks as inserting volumes into devices or confirming proper volume labels. **backup** provides three modes of operator interaction.

backup with no options assumes that an operator is present, but not at the terminal where the **backup** command was issued. This mode sends a **mail** message to the operator. The mail identifies the device requiring service and the volume required. The operator reads the mail message, invokes the **bkoper** command, responds to the prompts, and the backup operation continues.

backup -i establishes interactive mode, which assumes that an operator is present at the terminal where the **backup** command was issued. In this mode, **bkoper** is automatically invoked at the terminal where the **backup** command was entered. The operator responds to the prompts as they arrive.

Register Validations for Extended Backups

A number of backup service databases must be consistent before the backups listed in a backup register can be performed [see **bkreg**(1M)]. These consistencies can only be validated at the time **backup** is initiated. If any of them fail, **backup** will terminate. Invoking **backup -ne** performs the validation checks in addition to displaying the set of backup operations to be performed. The validations are:

1. The backup method must be a default method or be an executable file in `/bkup/method`.
2. The dependencies for an entry are all defined in the register. Circular dependencies (such as entry **abc** depends on entry **def;** entry **def** depends on entry **abc**) are allowed.
3. The device group for a destination must be defined in the device group table, `/etc/dgroup.tab`.

Options Available with the Foundation Set

`-d` *device* Used to specify the device to be used. If you don't use this option, **backup** checks to see how many floppy diskette drives you have. If you have only one, it's used. If you have more than one, **backup** prompts you to specify which you want used.

`-f` *files* Back up files specified by the *files* argument. Filenames may contain special characters (such as * and .), which will be expanded later by the shell. The argument (*files*) must be in quotes.

`-h` Produces a history of backups. Tells the user when the last complete and incremental/partial backups were done.

`-p` Performs a partial (also know as incremental) backup. All files modified since the most recent complete or partial backup are backed up. At least one complete backup must be done before a partial backup can be done.

`-T` Used when the device is a tape. This option must be used with the `-d` option when the tape device is specified.

`-u` Back up a user's home directory. All files in the user's home directory will be backed up. At least one user must be specified but it can be more. The argument must be in quotes if more than one user is specified. If the user name is **all**, then all users' home directories will be backed up.

`-w` A complete backup. All files changed since the system was installed are backed up.

Options Available with Extended Backup/Restore

`-c` *week:day* | **demand**
Selects from the backup register only those backup operations for the specified week and day of the backup rotation, instead of the current day and week of the rotation. If **demand** is specified, selects only those backup operations scheduled to be performed on demand.

-e This option displays an estimate of the number of volumes required to perform each backup operation.

-i Selects interactive operation

-j *jobid* Controls only the backup job identified by *jobid*. *jobid* is a **backup** job ID.

-m *user* Sends mail to the named *user* when all backup operations for the backup job are complete.

-n Displays the set of backup operations that would be performed but does not actually perform the backup operations. The display is ordered according to the dependencies and priorities specified in the backup register.

-o *name* Initiates backup operations only on the named originating object. *name* is an item in the following form [see **bkreg**(1M)]:
oname:*odevice*[:*omname*]

-p Performs a partial (also know as incremental) backup. All files modified since the most recent complete or partial backup are backed up. At least one complete backup must be done before a partial backup can be done.

-s Displays a "." for each 100 (512-byte) blocks transferred to the destination device. The dots are displayed while each backup operation is progressing.

-t *table* Initiates backup operations described in the specified backup register instead of the default register (**/etc/bkup/bkreg.tab**). *table* is a backup register.

-u *user* Controls backup jobs started by the named *user* instead of those started by the user invoking the command. *user* is a valid login ID.

-v While each backup operation is progressing, display the name of each file or directory as soon as it has been transferred to the destination device.

-A Controls backup jobs for all users instead of those started by the user invoking the command.

-C Cancels backup jobs.

-R Resumes suspended backup jobs.

-S Suspends backup jobs.

DIAGNOSTICS

The exit codes for the extended **backup** command are as follows:

0 = successful completion of the task
1 = one or more parameters to **backup** are invalid.
2 = an error has occurred which caused **backup** to fail to complete *all* portions of its task.

EXAMPLES

The following examples show several uses of the extended **backup** command.

Example 1:

```
backup -i -v -c 2:1 -m admin3
```

initiates those backups scheduled for Monday of the second week in the rotation period instead of backups for the current day and week. Performs the backup in interactive mode and displays on standard output the name of each file, directory, file system partition, or data partition as soon as it is transferred to the destination device. When all backups are completed, sends mail notification to the user with login ID **admin3**.

Example 2:

```
backup -o /home
```

Initiates backups from only the *usr* file system that is mounted on the home directory and is labeled **usr**.

Another way to do this is by specifying the originating device on which the *usr* file system is mounted (and labeled **usr**):

```
backup -o /dev/rdsk/c1d0s2
```

Example 3:

```
backup -S
```

Suspends the backup jobs requested by the invoking user.

Example 4:

```
backup -R -j back-359
```

resumes the backup operations included in backup job ID **back-359**.

FILES

The following files are used by the basic **backup** command.

/etc/Backup
/etc/Ignore

The following files are used by the extended **backup** command.
/etc/bkup/method/*
/etc/bkup/bkreg.tab
/etc/device.tab
/etc/dgroup.tab

SEE ALSO

bkhistory(1M), **bkoper**(1M), **bkreg**(1M), **bkstatus**(1M)

NAME

backup – (XENIX) perform backup functions

SYNOPSIS

backup [-t] [-p | -c | -f *files* | -u "*user1* [*user2*]"] -d *device*
backup -h

DESCRIPTION

- **-h** produces a history of backups. Tells the user when the last complete and incremental/partial backups were done.
- **-c** complete backup. All files changed since the system was installed are backed up.
- **-p** partial backup. If an incremental/partial backup was done, all files modified since that time are backed up. Otherwise all files modified since the last complete backup are backed up. A complete backup must be done before a partial backup.
- **-f** backup files specified by the *files* argument. file names may contain characters to be expanded (that is, *, .) by the shell. The argument must be in quotes.
- **-u** backup a user's home directory. All files in the user's home directory will be backed up. At least one user must be specified but it can be more. The argument must be in quotes if more than one user is specified. If the user name is "all", then all the user's home directories will be backed up.
- **-d** used to specify the device to be used. It defaults to a machine-specific value.
- **-t** used when the device is a tape. This option must be used with the **-d** option when the tape device is specified.

A complete backup must be done before a partial backup can be done. Raw devices rather than block devices should always be used. The program can handle multi-volume backups. The program will prompt the user when it is ready for the next medium. The program will give you an estimated number of floppies/tapes that will be needed to do the backup. Floppies must be formatted before the backup is done. Tapes do not need to be formatted. If backup is done to tape, the tape must be rewound.

NAME

`banner` – make posters

SYNOPSIS

`banner` *strings*

DESCRIPTION

`banner` prints its arguments (each up to 10 characters long) in large letters on the standard output.

FILES

`/usr/lib/locale/`*locale*`/LC_MESSAGES/uxue`
: language-specific message file [See `LANG` on `environ`(5).]

SEE ALSO

`echo`(1)

NOTES

Non-ASCII characters specified in *strings* will not be displayed correctly.

basename (1)

NAME

basename, **dirname** – deliver portions of path names

SYNOPSIS

basename *string* [*suffix*]
dirname *string*

DESCRIPTION

basename deletes any prefix ending in **/** and the *suffix* (if present in *string*) from *string*, and prints the result on the standard output. It is normally used inside substitution marks (\` \`) within shell procedures. The *suffix* is a pattern as defined on the **ed**(1) manual page.

dirname delivers all but the last level of the path name in *string*.

EXAMPLES

The following example, invoked with the argument **/home/sms/personal/mail** sets the environment variable **NAME** to the file named **mail** and the environment variable **MYMAILPATH** to the string **/home/sms/personal**.

```
NAME=`basename $HOME/personal/mail`
MYMAILPATH=`dirname $HOME/personal/mail`
```

This shell procedure, invoked with the argument **/usr/src/bin/cat.c**, compiles the named file and moves the output to **cat** in the current directory:

```
cc $1
mv a.out `basename $1 .c`
```

FILES

/usr/lib/locale/*locale***/LC_MESSAGES/uxcore**
language-specific message file [See **LANG** on **environ**(5).]

SEE ALSO

ed(1), **sh**(1)

NAME

basename – (BSD) display portions of pathnames

SYNOPSIS

/usr/ucb/basename *string* [*suffix*]

DESCRIPTION

basename deletes any prefix ending in '/' and the *suffix*, if present in *string*. It directs the result to the standard output, and is normally used inside substitution marks (` `) within shell procedures. The *suffix* is a pattern as defined on the **ed**(1) manual page.

EXAMPLE

This shell procedure invoked with the argument **/usr/src/bin/cat.c** compiles the named file and moves the output to **cat** in the current directory:

```
cc $1
mv a.out `basename $1 .c`
```

SEE ALSO

ed(1), **sh**(1)

NAME

bc – arbitrary-precision arithmetic language

SYNOPSIS

bc [**-c**] [**-l**] [*file* . . .]

DESCRIPTION

bc is an interactive processor for a language that resembles C but provides unlimited precision arithmetic. It takes input from any files given, then reads the standard input. **bc** is actually a preprocessor for the desk calculator program **dc**, which it invokes automatically unless the **-c** option is present. In this case the **dc** input is sent to the standard output instead. The options are as follows:

-c Compile only. The output is sent to the standard output.

-l Argument stands for the name of an arbitrary precision math library.

The syntax for **bc** programs is as follows: *L* means letter **a–z**, *E* means expression, *S* means statement.

Comments

are enclosed in /* and */.

Names

simple variables: *L*
array elements: *L* [*E*]
the words **ibase**, **obase**,**and scale**

Other operands

arbitrarily long numbers with optional sign and decimal point
(*E*)
sqrt (*E*)
length (*E*) number of significant decimal digits
scale (*E*) number of digits right of decimal point
L (*E* , . . . , *E*)

Operators

\+ - * / % ^
(% is remainder; ^ is power)
++ -- (prefix and postfix; apply to names)
== <= >= != < >
= =+ =- =* =/ =% =^

Statements

E
{ *S* ; . . . ; *S* }
if (*E*) *S*
while (*E*) *S*
for (*E* ; *E* ; *E*) *S*
null statement
break
quit

Function definitions

```
define L ( L , . . . , L ) {
      auto L , . . . , L
"     S" ; . . . S
      return ( E )
}
```

Functions in **-l** math library

s(*x*)	sine
c(*x*)	cosine
e(*x*)	exponential
l(*x*)	log
a(*x*)	arctangent
j(*n*,*x*)	Bessel function

All function arguments are passed by value.

The value of a statement that is an expression is printed unless the main operator is an assignment. Either semicolons or new-lines may separate statements. Assignment to **scale** influences the number of digits to be retained on arithmetic operations in the manner of **dc**. Assignments to **ibase** or **obase** set the input and output number radix respectively.

The same letter may be used as an array, a function, and a simple variable simultaneously. All variables are global to the program. **auto** variables are pushed down during function calls. When using arrays as function arguments or defining them as automatic variables, empty square brackets must follow the array name.

EXAMPLES

```
scale = 20
define e(x){
      auto a, b, c, i, s
      a = 1
      b = 1
      s = 1
      for(i=1; 1==1; i++){
            a = a*x
            b = b*i
            c = a/b
            if(c == 0) return(s)
            s = s+c
      }
}
```

defines a function to compute an approximate value of the exponential function and

```
for(i=1; i<=10; i++) e(i)
```

prints approximate values of the exponential function of the first ten integers.

FILES

/usr/lib/lib.b	mathematical library
/usr/bin/dc	desk calculator proper

SEE ALSO

dc(1)

NOTES

The **bc** command does not recognize the logical operators **&&** and **||**.

The **for** statement must have all three expressions (*E*'s).

The **quit** statement is interpreted when read, not when executed.

For certain operations, the value of **scale** might be calculated to be larger than the current specified scale value. When you set **scale** to a large value, take this into account when performing operations that could overflow the specified scale value.

NAME

bdftosnf – BDF to SNF font compiler for X11

SYNOPSIS

bdftosnf [**-s**] [**-p***num*] [**-u***num*] [**-m**] [**-l**] [**-M**] [**-L**] [**-w**] [**-W**] [**-t**] [**-i**] [*bdf-file*]

DESCRIPTION

The **bdftosnf** command reads a Bitmap Distribution Format (BDF) font from the specified file (or from standard input if no file is specified) and writes an X11 Server Normal Font (SNF) to standard output.

Options

-s force byte swapping.

-p*num* force the glyph padding to a specific number. The valid values are 1, 2, 4, and 8.

-u*num* force the scanline unit padding to a specific number. The valid values are 1, 2, and 4.

-m force the bit order to most significant bit first

-l force the bit order to least significant bit first

-M force the byte order to most significant byte first

-L force the byte order to least significant byte first

-w print warnings if the character bitmaps have bits set to one outside of their defined widths

-W print warnings for characters with an encoding of -1; the default is to silently ignore such characters

-t expand glyphs in "terminal-emulator" fonts to fill the bounding box

-i don't compute correct ink metrics for "terminal-emulator" fonts

Examples

```
bdftosnf -L -l -t 10x20.bdf > 10x20.snf
```

SEE ALSO

X(1)

NOTES

Portions of the page are derived from material which is copyright Massachusetts Institute of Technology.

bdiff(1)

NAME

`bdiff` – big `diff`

SYNOPSIS

`bdiff` *file1 file2* [*n*] [-s]

DESCRIPTION

bdiff is used in a manner analogous to **diff** to find which lines in *file1* and *file2* must be changed to bring the files into agreement. Its purpose is to allow processing of files too large for **diff**. If *file1 (file2)* is –, the standard input is read.

Valid options to **bdiff** are:

n The number of line segments. The value of *n* is 3500 by default. If the optional third argument is given and it is numeric, it is used as the value for *n*. This is useful in those cases in which 3500-line segments are too large for **diff**, causing it to fail.

-s Specifies that no diagnostics are to be printed by **bdiff** (silent option). Note, however, that this does not suppress possible diagnostic messages from **diff**, which **bdiff** calls.

bdiff ignores lines common to the beginning of both files, splits the remainder of each file into *n*-line segments, and invokes **diff** on corresponding segments. If both optional arguments are specified, they must appear in the order indicated above.

The output of **bdiff** is exactly that of **diff**, with line numbers adjusted to account for the segmenting of the files (that is, to make it look as if the files had been processed whole). Note that because of the segmenting of the files, **bdiff** does not necessarily find a smallest sufficient set of file differences.

FILES

`/tmp/bd`*?????*

SEE ALSO

`diff`(1)

NAME

bfs – big file scanner

SYNOPSIS

bfs [-] *file*

DESCRIPTION

The **bfs** command is similar to **ed** except that it is read-only and processes much larger files. Files can be up to 1024K bytes and 32K lines, with up to 512 bytes, including new-line, per line (255 for 16-bit machines). **bfs** is usually more efficient than **ed** for scanning a file, since the file is not copied to a buffer. It is most useful for identifying sections of a large file where the **csplit** command can be used to divide it into more manageable pieces for editing.

bfs processes supplementary code set characters in *file*, and recognizes supplementary code set characters in the *label*s given to the **:**, **xb**, **xbn**, and **xbz** commands (see below) according to the locale specified in the **LC_CTYPE** environment variable [see **LANG** on **environ**(5)]. In regular expressions, pattern searches are performed on characters, not bytes [see **ed**(1)].

Normally, the size in bytes of the file being scanned is printed, as is the size of any file written with the **w** command. The optional **-** suppresses printing of sizes. Input is prompted with * if **P** and a RETURN are typed, as in **ed**. Prompting can be turned off again by inputting another **P** and RETURN. Messages are given in response to errors if prompting is turned on.

All address expressions described under **ed** are supported. In addition, regular expressions may be surrounded with two symbols besides **/** and **?**: **>** indicates downward search without wrap-around, and **<** indicates upward search without wrap-around.

The **e**, **g**, **v**, **k**, **p**, **q**, **w**, **=**, **!** and null commands operate as described under **ed**. Commands such as **---**, **+++-**, **+++=**, **-12**, and **+4p** are accepted. Note that **1,10p** and **1,10** both print the first ten lines. The **f** command only prints the name of the file being scanned; there is no remembered file name. The **w** command is independent of output diversion, truncation, or crunching (see the **xo**, **xt**, and **xc** commands, below). The following additional commands are available:

xf *file* Further commands are taken from the named *file*. When an end-of-file is reached, an interrupt signal is received or an error occurs, reading resumes with the file containing the **xf**. The **xf** commands may be nested to a depth of 10.

xn List the marks currently in use (marks are set by the **k** command).

xo [*file*] Further output from the **p** and null commands is diverted to the named *file*, which, if necessary, is created with mode 666 (readable and writable by everyone), unless your **umask** setting dictates otherwise; see **umask**(1). If *file* is missing, output is diverted to the standard output. Note that each diversion causes truncation or creation of the file.

: *label* This positions a *label* in a command file. The *label* is terminated by new-line, and blanks between the **:** and the *label* are ignored. This command may also be used to insert comments into a command file, since labels need not be referenced. *label* may contain supplementary code set characters.

(**. , .**)**xb**/*regular expression*/*label*

A jump (either upward or downward) is made to *label* if the command succeeds. It fails under any of the following conditions:

1. Either address is not between `1` and `$`.
2. The second address is less than the first.
3. The regular expression does not match at least one line in the specified range, including the first and last lines.

On success, **.** is set to the line matched and a jump is made to *label*. This command is the only one that does not issue an error message on bad addresses, so it may be used to test whether addresses are bad before other commands are executed. Note that the command

```
xb/^/ label
```

is an unconditional jump.

The **xb** command is allowed only if it is read from someplace other than a terminal. If it is read from a pipe only a downward jump is possible. *label* may contain supplementary code set characters.

xt *number* Output from the **p** and null commands is truncated to at most *number* displayed columns. The initial number is 255.

xv[*digit*] [*spaces*] [*value*]

The variable name is the specified *digit* following the **xv**. The commands **xv5100** or **xv5 100** both assign the value `100` to the variable `5`. The command **xv61,100p** assigns the value `1,100p` to the variable `6`. To reference a variable, put a `%` in front of the variable name. For example, using the above assignments for variables `5` and `6`:

```
1,%5p
1,%5
%6
```

all print the first 100 lines.

```
g/%5/p
```

globally searches for the characters `100` and prints each line containing a match. To escape the special meaning of `%`, a `\` must precede it.

```
g/".*\%[cds]/p
```

could be used to match and list lines containing a **printf** of characters, decimal integers, or strings.

Another feature of the **xv** command is that the first line of output from a UNIX system command can be stored into a variable. The only requirement is that the first character of *value* be an `!`. For example:

```
.w junk
xv5!cat junk
!rm junk
!echo "%5"
xv6!expr %6 + 1
```

puts the current line into variable **5**, prints it, and increments the variable **6** by one. To escape the special meaning of **!** as the first character of *value*, precede it with a ****.

```
xv7\!date
```

stores the value **!date** into variable **7**.

xbz *label*
xbn *label* These two commands test the last saved *return code* from the execution of a UNIX system command (**!***command*) for zero or nonzero value, respectively, and jump to the specified label. *label* may contain supplementary code set characters. The two examples below both search for the next five lines containing the string **size**.

```
xv55
: l
/size/
xv5!expr %5 - 1
!test 0 = %5
xbn l

xv45
: l
/size/
xv4!expr %4 - 1
!test 0 != %4
xbz l
```

xc [*switch*] If *switch* is **1**, output from the **p** and null commands is crunched; if *switch* is **0** it is not. Without an argument, **xc** reverses *switch*. Initially *switch* is set for no crunching. Crunched output has strings of tabs and blanks reduced to one blank and blank lines suppressed.

SEE ALSO

csplit(1), **ed**(1), **regexp**(5), **umask**(1)

DIAGNOSTICS

? for errors in commands, if prompting is turned off. Self-explanatory error messages when prompting is on.

NAME

biff – (BSD) give notice of incoming mail messages

SYNOPSIS

/usr/ucb/biff [**y** | n]

DESCRIPTION

biff turns mail notification on or off for the terminal session. With no arguments, **biff** displays the current notification status for the terminal.

The **y** option allows mail notification for the terminal. The **n** option disables notification for the terminal.

biff operates asynchronously. For synchronized notices, use the **MAIL** variable of **sh**(1) or the **mail** variable of **csh**(1).

A '**biff y**' command can be included in your **~/.login** or **~/.profile** file for execution when you log in.

FILES

~/.login
~/.profile

SEE ALSO

csh(1), **mail**(1), **sh**(1)

NAME

biod – NFS daemon

SYNOPSIS

/usr/lib/nfs/biod [*nservers*]

DESCRIPTION

biod starts *nservers* asynchronous block I/O daemons. This command is used on an NFS client to buffer read-ahead and write-behind. Four is the usual number for *nservers*.

The **biod** daemons are automatically invoked in run level 3.

Only a privileged user can execute this command.

SEE ALSO

mountd(1M), **nfsd**(1M), **nfsping**(1M), **sharetab**(4)

NAME

`bkexcept` – change or display an exception list for incremental backups

SYNOPSIS

`bkexcept` [`-t` *file*] [`-d` *patterns*]
`bkexcept` [`-t` *file*] `-a` | `-r` *patterns*
`bkexcept -C` [*files*]

DESCRIPTION

The **bkexcept** command displays a list of patterns describing files that are to be excluded when backup operations occur using **incfile**. The list is known as the "exception list."

bkexcept may be executed only by a privileged user.

bkexcept -a adds patterns to the list.

bkexcept -d displays patterns from the list.

bkexcept -r removes patterns from the list.

Patterns

Patterns describe individual pathnames or sets of pathnames. Patterns must conform to pathname naming conventions specified under DEFINITIONS on the **intro**(2) page. A pattern is taken as a filename and is interpreted in the manner of **cpio**. A pattern can include the shell special characters *, **?**, and **[]**. Asterisk (*) and question mark (**?**) will match period (**.**) and slash(**/**). Because these are shell special characters, they must be escaped on the command line.

There are three general methods of specifying entries to the exception list:

- To specify all files under a particular directory, specify the directory name (and any desired subdirectories) followed by an asterisk:

  */directory/subdirectories/**

- To specify all instances of a filename regardless of its location, specify the filename preceded by an asterisk:

  **/filename*

- To specify one instance of a particular file, specify the entire pathname to the file:

  /directory/subdirectories/filename

If *pattern* is a dash (-), standard input is read for a list of patterns (one per line until EOF) to be added or deleted.

Compatibility

Prior versions of the backup service created exception lists using **ed** syntax. **bkexcept -C** provides a translation facility for exception lists created by **ed**. The translation is not perfect; not all **ed** patterns have equivalents in **cpio**. For those patterns that have no automatic translation, an attempt at translation is made, and the translated version is flagged with the word **QUESTIONABLE.** The exception list translation is directed to standard output. Redirect the standard output to a translation file, review the contents of the translation file (correcting entries that were not translated properly and deleting the **QUESTIONABLE** flags), and then use the resulting file as input to a subsequent **bkexcept -a**. For example, if the translated file was named **checkfile** the **-a** option would appear as follows:

```
bkexcept -a - < checkfile
```

Options

-t *file* The filename used in place of the default file.

-a *pattern. . .* Adds *pattern* to the exception list where *pattern* is one or more patterns (comma-separated or blank-separated and enclosed in quotes) describing sets of paths.

-d *pattern. . .* Displays entries in the exception list. If *pattern* begins with a slash (/), **-d** displays all entries whose names begin with *pattern*. If *pattern* does not begin with a slash, **-d** displays all entries that include *pattern* anywhere in the entry. If *pattern* is a dash (**-**), input is taken from standard input. *pattern* is not a pattern -- it matches patterns. *pattern* **a*b** matches **/a*b** but does not match **/adb**. For files containing a carriage return, a null exception list is returned. For files of zero length (no characters), an error is returned (search of table failed).

The entries are displayed in ASCII collating sequence order (special characters, numbers, then alphabetical order).

-r *pattern. . .* Removes *pattern* from the exception list. *pattern* is one or a list of patterns (comma-separated or blank-separated and enclosed in quotes) describing sets of paths. *pattern* must be an exact match of an entry in the exception list for *pattern* to be removed. Patterns that are removed are echoed to standard output, **stdout**.

-C [*files*] Displays on standard output the translation of each *file* (a prior version's exception list) to the new syntax. Each *file* contains **ed** patterns, one per line.

If *file* is omitted, the default UNIX exception list, **/etc/save.d/except**, is translated. If *file* is a dash (–), input is taken from standard input, one per line.

DIAGNOSTICS

The exit codes for the **bkexcept** command are the following:

0 = the task completed successfully
1 = one or more parameters to **bkexcept** are invalid
2 = an error has occurred, causing **bkexcept** to fail to complete *all* portions of its task

EXAMPLES

Example 1:

```
bkexcept -a /tmp/*,/var/tmp/*,/usr/rje/*,*/trash,
```

adds the four sets of files to the exception list, (all files under **/tmp**, all files under **/var/tmp**, all files under **/usr/rje**, and any file on the system named **trash**).

Example 2:

```
bkexcept -d /tmp
```

displays the following patterns from those added to the exception list in Example 1.

```
/tmp/*
bkexcept -d tmp
```

displays the following patterns from those added to the exception list in Example 1.

```
/tmp/*, /var/tmp/*
```

displays one per line, with a heading.

Example 3:

```
bkexcept -r /var/tmp/*,/usr/rje/*
```

removes the two patterns from the exception list.

Example 4:

```
bkexcept -C /save.d/old.except > trans.except
```

translates the file **/save.d/old.except** from its **ed** format to **cpio** format and sends the translations to the file **trans.except**. The translations of **/save.d/old.except** may be added to the current exception list by using **bkexcept -a** as follows:

```
bkexcept -a - < trans.except
```

FILES

/etc/bkup/bkexcept.tab	the default exception list for UNIX System V Release 4.0.
/etc/save.d/except	the default exception list for pre-UNIX System V Release 4.0.

SEE ALSO

backup(1M), **cpio**(1), **ed**(1), **intro**(2), **sh**(1)

NAME

bkhistory – report on completed backup operations

SYNOPSIS

bkhistory [**-hl**] [**-f** *field_separator*] [**-d** *dates*] [**-o** *names*] [**-t** *tags*]
bkhistory -p *period*

DESCRIPTION

bkhistory without options reports a summary of the contents of the backup history log, **bkhist.tab**. Backup operations are sorted alphabetically by tag. For each tag, operations are listed from most to least recent. **backup**(1M) updates this log after each successful backup operation.

bkhistory may be executed only by a privileged user.

bkhistory -p assigns a rotation *period* (in weeks) for the history log; all entries older than the specified number of weeks are deleted from the log. The default rotation period is one (1) week.

Options

-d *dates* — Restricts the report to backup operations performed on the specified dates. *dates* are in the **date** format. *day, hour, minute,* and *year,* are optional and will be ignored. The list of *dates* is either comma-separated or blank-separated and surrounded by quotes.

-f *field_separator* — Suppresses field wrap on the display and specifies an output field separator to be used. The value of *c* is the character that will appear as the field separator on the display output. For clarity of output, do not use a separator character that is likely to occur in a field. For example, do not use the colon as a field separator character if the display will contain dates that use a colon to separate hours from minutes. To use the default field separator (tab), specify the null character ("") for *c*.

-h — Suppresses header for the reports.

-l — Displays a long form of the report. This produces an **ls -l** listing of the files included in the backup archive (if backup tables of contents are available on-line).

-o *names* — Restricts the report to the specified originating objects (file systems or data partitions). *names* is a list of *onames* and/or *odevices*. [See **bkreg**(1M).]

The list of names is either comma-separated or blank-separated and surrounded by quotes.

-p *period* — Sets the number of weeks of information that will be saved in the backup history table. The minimum value of *period* is 1, which is also the default value. the size of int. By default, *period* is 1.

-t *tags* — Restricts the report to backups with the specified *tags*. *tags* is a list of tag values as specified in the backup register. The list of *tags* is either comma-separated or blank-separated and surrounded by quotes.

DIAGNOSTICS

The exit codes for the **bkhistory** command are the following:

0 =	the task completed successfully
1 =	one or more parameters to **bkhistory** are invalid
2 =	an error has occurred, causing **bkhistory** to fail to complete all portions of its task

EXAMPLES

Example 1:

```
bkhistory -p 3
```

sets the rotation period for the history log to three weeks. Entries older than three weeks are deleted from the log.

Example 2:

```
bkhistory -t SpoolDai,UsrDaily,TPubsWed
```

displays a report of completed backup operations for the three tags listed.

Example 3:

```
bkhistory -l -o /usr
```

Displays an **ls -l** listing of the files that were backed up from **/usr** (the originating object) if there is a table of contents.

FILES

/etc/bkup/bkhist.tab	the backup history log that contains information about successfully completed backup operations
/etc/bkup/bkreg.tab	description of the backup policy established by the administrator
/var/sadm/bkup/toc	list of directories with on-line tables of contents

SEE ALSO

backup(1M), **bkreg**(1M), **date**(1), **ls**(1)

NAME

bkoper – interact with backup operations to service media insertion prompts

SYNOPSIS

bkoper [**-u** *users*]

DESCRIPTION

Backup operations may require an operator to insert media and to confirm proper volume labels. The **bkoper** command provides a **mailx**-like interface for these operator interactions. It begins by printing a list of headers. Each header describes a backup operation requiring interaction, the device requiring attention including the media type and label of the volume to be inserted (see EXAMPLE). The system displays prompts and the operator issues commands to resolve the backup operation. Typing a carriage return invokes the current header. If no headers have been serviced, the current header is the first header on the list. If a header has been selected and serviced, the current header is the next one following.

bkoper may be executed only by a privileged user. By default, the operator may interact only with backup operations that were started by the same user ID .

If the **-u** *users* option is given, the operator interacts only with backup operations started by the specified *user*(s).

Commands

!*shell-command*	Escapes to the shell. The remainder of the line after the ! is sent to the UNIX system shell (**sh**) to be interpreted as a command.
=	Prints the current backup operation number.
?	Prints this summary of commands.
[**p**|**t**] [*n*]	Both the **p** and **t** options operate in the same way. Either option will interact with the backup operation described by the *n*'th header. *n* defaults to the current header number.
h	Prints the list of backup operations.
q	Quits from **bkoper**.

DIAGNOSTICS

The exit codes for **bkoper** are the following:

0 = successful completion of the task
1 = one or more parameters to **bkoper** are invalid.
2 = an error has occurred which caused **bkoper** to fail to complete *all* portions of its task.

EXAMPLE

A sample header is shown below. Items appearing in the header are listed in the following order: header number, job-ID, tag, originating device, destination group, destination device, destination volume labels. [See **bkreg**(1M) for descriptions of items.] Not every header contains values for all these fields; if a destination group is not specified in **/etc/bkup/bkreg.tab**, then no value for "destination group" appears in the header.

```
1 back-111 usrsun /dev/dsk/c1d0s1  disk /dev/dsk/c2d1s9 usrsave
2 back-112 fs2daily /dev/dsk/c1d0s8 ctape /dev/ctape/c4d0s2 -
```

Backup headers are numbered on the basis of arrival; the oldest header has the lowest number. If the destination device does not have a volume label, a dash is displayed in the header.

SEE ALSO

bkreg(1M), **bkstatus**(1M), **getvol**(1M), **mailx**(1)

NAME

bkreg – change or display the contents of a backup register

SYNOPSIS

bkreg -p *period* [**-w** *cweek*] [**-t** *table*]

bkreg -a *tag* **-o** *orig* **-c** *weeks:days* | **demand -d** *ddev* –m *method* | **migration** [**-b** *moptions*] [**-t** *table*] [**-D** *depend*] [**-P** *prio*]

bkreg -e *tag* [**-o** *orig*] [**-c** *weeks:days* | **demand**] [**-m** *method* | **migration**] [**-d** *ddev*] [**-t** *table*] [**-b** *moptions*] [**-D** *depend*] [**-P** *prio*]

bkreg -r *tag* [**-t** *table*]

bkreg [**-A** | **-O** | **-R**] [**-hsv**] [**-t** *table*] [**-c** *weeks*[:*days*] | **demand**]

bkreg -C *fields* [**-hv**] [**-t** *table*] [**-c** *weeks*[:*days*] | **demand**] [**-f** *c*]

DESCRIPTION

A backup register is a file containing descriptions of backup operations to be performed on a UNIX system. The default backup register is located in **/etc/bkup/bkreg.tab**. Other backup registers may be created.

The **bkreg** command may be executed only by a privileged user.

Each entry in a backup register describes backup operations to be performed on a given disk object (called the originating object) for some set of days and weeks during a rotation period. There may be several register entries for an object, but only one entry may specify backup operations for an object on a specific day and week of the rotation period. The entry describes the object, the backup method to be used to archive the object, and the destination volumes to be used to store the archive. Each entry has a unique *tag* that identifies it. *Tag*s must conform to file naming conventions.

Rotation Period

Backups are performed in a rotation period specified in weeks. When the end of a rotation period is reached, a new period begins. Rotation periods begin on Sundays. The default rotation period is one week.

Originating Objects

An originating object is either a raw data partition or a filesystem. An originating object is described by its originating object name, its device name, and optional volume labels.

Several backup operations for different originating objects may be active concurrently by specifying priorities and dependencies. During a backup session, higher priority backup operations are attempted before lower priority backup operations. All backup operations of a given priority may proceed concurrently unless dependencies are specified. If one backup is declared to be dependent on others, it will not be started until all its antecedents have completed successfully.

Destination Devices

Each backup archive is written to a set of storage volumes inserted into a destination device. A destination device can have destination device group, a destination device name, media characteristics, and volume labels. Default characteristics for a medium (as specified in the device table) may be overridden.

Backup Methods

An originating object is backed up to a destination device archive using a method. The method determines the amount of information backed up and the representation of that information. Different methods may be used for a given originating object on different days of the rotation. Each method accepts a set of options that are specific to the method.

Several default methods are provided with the Backup service. Other methods may be added by a UNIX system site. [See **fdisk**(1M) for details.]

A backup archive may be migrated to a different destination by specifying **migration** as the backup method. The device name of the originating object for a migration must have been the destination device for a previously successful backup operation. This form of backup does not re-archive the originating object. It copies an archive from one destination to another, updating the backup service's databases so that restores can still be done automatically.

Register Validations

There are items in a single backup register entry and items across register entries that must be consistent for the backup service to conduct a backup session correctly. Some of these consistencies are checked at the time the backup register is created or changed. Others can be checked only at the time the backup register is used by **backup**(1M). See **backup**(1M) for a complete list of validations.

Modes

The **bkreg** command has two modes: changing the contents of a backup register and displaying the contents of a backup register.

Changing Contents

bkreg -p changes the rotation period for a backup register. The default rotation period is one week.

bkreg -a adds an entry to a backup register. This option requires other options to be specified. These are listed below under **Options**.

bkreg -e edits an existing entry in a backup register.

bkreg -r removes an existing entry from a backup register.

Displaying Contents

bkreg -C produces a customized display of the contents of a backup register.

bkreg [**-A** | **-R** | **-O**]
produces a summary display of the contents of a backup register.

Options

-a Adds a new entry to the default backup register. Options required with **-a** are: *tag, originating device, weeks:days, destination device*, and *method*. If other options are not specified, the following defaults are used: the default backup register is used, no method options are specified, the priority is 0, and no dependencies exist between entries.

-b *moptions*
Each backup method supports a specific set of options that modify its behavior. *moptions* is specified as a list of options that are blank-separated and enclosed in quotes. The argument string provided here is passed to the

method exactly as entered, without modification. For lists of valid options, see **fdisk**(1M).

-c *weeks:days*| **demand**

Sets the week(s) and day(s) of the rotation period during which a backup entry should be performed or for which a display should be generated. *weeks* is a set of numbers including 1 and 52. The value of *weeks* cannot be greater than the value of **-p***period. weeks* is specified as a combination of lists or ranges (either comma-separated or blank-separated and enclosed in quotes). An example set of weeks is

```
''1 3-10,13''
```

indicating the first week, each of the third through tenth weeks, and the thirteenth week of the rotation period.

days is a set of numbers between 0 (Sunday) and 6 (Saturday). In addition, *days* are specified as a combination of lists or ranges (either comma-separated or blank-separated and enclosed in quotes).

demand indicates that an entry is used only when explicitly requested by

```
backup -c demand
```

-d *ddev*

Specifies *ddev* as the destination device for the backup operation. *ddev* is of the form:

[*dgroup***] [: [***ddevice***] [:***dchar***] [:***dmname***]]**

where either *dgroup* or *ddevice* must be specified and *dchar* and *dmname* are optional. (Both *dgroup* and *ddev* may be specified together.) Colons delineate field boundaries and must be included as indicated above.

dgroup is the device group for the destination device. If omitted, *ddevice* must be specified.

ddevice is the device name of a specific destination device. If omitted, *dgroup* must be specified and any available device in *dgroup* may be used.

dchar describes media characteristics. If specified, they override the default characteristics for the device and group. *dchar* is of the form:

keyword=*value*

where **keyword** is a valid device characteristic keyword (as it appears in the device table.) *dchar* entries may be separated by commas or blanks. If separated by blanks, the entire string of arguments to *ddev* must be enclosed in quotes.

dlabels is a list of volume names of the destination volumes. The list of *dlabels* must be either comma-separated or blank-separated. If blank-separated, the entire *ddev* argument must be surrounded by quotes. Each *dlabel* corresponds to a *volumename* specified on the **labelit** command. If *dlabels* is omitted, **backup** and **restore** do not validate the volume labels on this entry.

-e Edits an existing entry. If any of the options **-b**, **-c**, **-d**, **-m**, **-o**, **-D**, or **-P** are present, they replace the current settings for the specified entry in the register.

-f *c* Overrides the default output field separator. *c* is the character that will appear as the field separator on the display output. The default output field separator is colon (**:**).

-h Suppresses headers when generating displays.

-m *method* **|** **migration**

Performs the backup using the specified *method.* Default methods are: **incfile**, **ffile**, **fdisk**, **fimage**, and **fdp**. If the method to be used is not a default method, it must appear as the executable file in the standard method directory **/etc/bkup/method**. **migration** indicates that the value of *orig* (following the **-o** option) matches the value of *ddev* during a prior backup operation. The originating object is not rearchived; it is simply copied to the location specified by *ddev* (following the **-d** option). The backup history (if any) and tables of contents (if any) are updated to reflect the changed destination for the original archive.

-o *orig*

Specifies *orig* as the originating object for the backup operation. *orig* is specified in the following format:

*oname***:***odevice***[:***omname***]**

where *oname* is the name of an originating object. For file system partitions, it is the nodename on which the file system is usually mounted, **mount**. For data partitions, it is any valid path name. This value is provided to the backup method and validated by **backup**. The default data partition backup methods, **fdp** and **fdisk**, do not validate this name.

odevice is the device name for the originating object. In all cases, it is a raw disk partition device name. For Intel 386/486 computers, this name is specified in the following format: **/dev/rdsk/c?t?d?s?**.

olabel is the volume label for the originating object. For file system partitions, it corresponds to the *volumename* displayed by the **labelit** command. A data partition may have an associated volume name that appears nowhere except on the outside of the volume (where it is taped); **getvol** may be used to have an operator validate the name.

On Intel 386/486 computers, the special data partition **/dev/rdsk/c?t?d?s0** names an entire disk and is used when disk formatting or repartitioning is done to reference the disk's volume table of contents (VTOC). [See **prtvtoc**(1M).] **backup** validates this special full disk partition with the disk volume name specified when the disk was partitioned. If the disk volume name is omitted, **backup** does not validate the volume labels for this originating object.

-p *period*

Sets the rotation period (in weeks) for the backup register to *period*. The minimum value is 1; the maximum value is 52. By default the current week of the rotation is set to 1.

-r Removes the specified entries from the register.

-s Suppresses wrap-around behavior when generating displays. Normal behavior is to wrap long values within each field.

-t *table*
Uses *table* instead of the default register, **bkreg.tab**.

-v Generates displays using (vertical) columns instead of (horizontal) rows. This allows more information to be displayed without encountering problems displaying long lines.

-w *cweek*
Overrides the default behavior by setting the current week of the rotation period to *cweek*. *cweek* is an integer between 1 and the value of *period*. The default is 1.

-A Displays a report describing all fields in the register. The display produced by this option is best suited as input to a filter, since in horizontal mode it produces extremely long lines.

-C *fields*
Generates a display of the contents of a backup register, limiting the display to the specified fields. The output is a set of lines, one per register entry. Each line consists of the desired fields, separated by a field separator character. *fields* is a list of field names (either comma-separated or blank-separated and enclosed in quotes) for the fields desired. The valid field names are **period, cweek, tag, oname, odevice, olabel, weeks, days, method, moptions, prio, depend, dgroup, ddevice, dchar,** and **dlabel**.

-D *depend*
Specifies a set of backup operations that must be completed successfully before this operation may begin. *depend* is a list of *tag*(s) (either comma-separated or blank-separated and enclosed in quotes) naming the antecedent backup operations.

-f *c* Overrides the default output field separator. *c* is the character that will appear as the field separator on the display output. The default output field separator is colon (":").

-O Displays a summary of all originating objects with entries in the register.

-P *prio*
Sets a priority of *prio* for this backup operation. The default priority is 0; the highest priority is 100. All backup operations with the same priority may run simultaneously, unless the priority is 0. All backups with priority 0 run sequentially in an unspecified order.

-R Displays a summary of all destination devices with entries in the register.

DIAGNOSTICS

The exit codes for **bkreg** are the following:

0 = the task completed successfully
1 = one or more parameters to **bkreg** are invalid
2 = an error has occurred, causing **bkreg** to fail to complete *all* portions of its task

Errors are reported on standard error if any of the following occurs:

1. The **tag** specified in **bkreg** –e or **bkreg** –r does not exist in the backup register.
2. The tag specified in **bkreg -a** already exists in the register.

EXAMPLES

Example 1:

```
bkreg -p 15 -w 3
```

establishes a 15-week rotation period in the default backup register and sets the current week to the 3rd week of the rotation period.

Example 2:

```
bkreg -a acct5 -t wklybu.tab \
-o /usr:/dev/rdsk/c1d0s2:usr -c "2 4-6 8 10:0,2,5" \
-m incfile -b -txE \
-d diskette:capacity=1404:acctwkly1,acctwkly2,acctwkly3 \
```

adds an entry named *acct5* to the backup register named **wklybu.tab**. If **wklybu.tab** does not already exist, it will be created. The originating object to be backed up is the **/usr** file system on the **/dev/rdsk/c1d0s2** device which is known as **usr**. The backup will be performed each Sunday, Tuesday, and Friday of the second, fourth through sixth, eighth, and tenth weeks of the rotation period using the **incfile** (incremental file) method. The method options specify that a table of contents will be created on additional media instead of in the backup history log, the exception list is to be ignored, and an estimate of the number of volumes for the archive is to be provided before performing the backup. The backup will be done to the next available diskette device using the three diskette volumes **acctwkly1, acctwkly2,** and **acctwkly3**. These volumes have a capacity of 1404 blocks each.

Example 3:

```
bkreg -e services2 -t wklybu.tab \
-o /back:/dev/rdsk/c1d0s8:back -m migration \
-c demand -d ctape:/dev/rdsk/c4d0s3 \
```

changes the specifications for the backup operation named **services2** on the backup table **wklybu.tab** so that whenever the command **backup -c demand** is executed, the backup that was performed to the destination device **back:dev/rdsk/c1d0s2:back** will be migrated from that device (now serving as the originating device) to a cartridge tape.

Example 4:

```
bkreg -e pubsfri -P 10 -D develfri,marketfri,acctfri
```

changes the priority level for the backup operation named **pubsfri** to 10 and makes this backup operation dependent on the three backup operations **develfri, marketfri,** and **acctfri**. The **pubsfri** operation will be done only after all backup operations with priorities greater than 10 have begun and after the **develfri**, **marketfri**, and **acctfri** operations have been completed successfully.

Example 5:

```
bkreg -c 1-8:0-6
```

provides the default display of the contents of the default backup register, for all weekdays for the first through eighth weeks of the rotation period. The information in the register will be displayed in the following format:

```
Rotation Period = 10    Current Week = 4



Originating Device: / /dev/root
Tag        Weeks   Days   Method   Options   Pri   Dgroup
- - - - - - - - - - - - - - - - - - - - - - - - - - - - - - - - - - - -
rootdai    1-8     1-6    incfile                  diskette
rootsp     1-8     0      ffile    -bxt      20    ctape

Originating Device:  /usr /dev/dsk/c1d0s2

Tag        Weeks   Days   Method   Options   Pri   Dgroup
- - - - - - - - - - - - - - - - - - - - - - - - - - - - - - - - - - - -
usrdai     1-8     1-5    incfile                  diskette
usrsp      1-8     0      ffile    -bxt      15    ctape
```

FILES

/etc/bkup/method/*	
/etc/bkup/bkreg.tab	describes the backup policy established by the administrator
/etc/dgroup.tab	lists logical groupings of devices as determined by the administrator
/etc/device.tab	describes specific devices and their attributes

SEE ALSO

backup(1M), **fdisk**(1M), **getvol**(1M), **labelit**(1M), **mkfs**(1M), **mount**(1M), **prtvtoc**(1M), **restore**(1M)

bkstatus (1M)

NAME

bkstatus – display the status of backup operations

SYNOPSIS

bkstatus [-h] [**-f** *field_separator*] [**-j** *jobids*] [**-s** *states* | **-a**] [**-u** *users*]

bkstatus -p *period*

DESCRIPTION

Without options, the **bkstatus** command displays the status of backup operations that are in progress: either **active**, **pending**, **waiting** or **suspended**. When used with the **-a** option, the **backup** command includes **failed** and **completed** backup operations in the display.

bkstatus -p defines the amount of status information that is saved for display.

bkstatus may only be executed by a privileged user.

Each backup operation goes through a number of states as described below. The keyletters listed in parentheses after each state are used with the **-s** option and also appear on the display.

pending(p)
: **backup** has been invoked and the operations in the backup register for the specified day are scheduled to occur.

active(a)
: The backup operation has been assigned a destination device and archiving is currently underway; or a suspended backup has been resumed.

waiting(w)
: The backup operation is waiting for operator interaction, such as inserting the correct volume.

suspended(s)
: The backup operation has been suspended by an invocation of **backup -S**.

failed(f)
: The backup operation failed or has been canceled.

completed(c)
: The backup operation has completed successfully.

The **-a** and **-s** options are mutually exclusive.

Options

-a
: Include **failed** and **completed** backup operations in the display. All backup operations that have occurred within the rotation period are displayed.

-f *field_separator*
: Suppresses field wrap on the display and specifies an output field separator to be used. The value of *c* is the character that will appear as the field separator on the display output. For clarity of output, do not use a separator character that is likely to occur in a field. For example, do not use the colon as a field separator character if the display will

contain dates that use a colon to separate hours from minutes. To use the default field separator (tab), specify the null character (`""`) for *c*.

-h Suppress header on the display.

-j *jobids* Restrict the display to the specified list of **backup** job ids (either comma-separated or blank-separated and enclosed in quotes). [See **backup**(1M)].

-p *period* Define the amount of backup status information that is saved and made available for display as *period*. *period* is the number of weeks that information is saved in **/bkup/bkstatus.tab**. Status information that is older than the number of weeks specified in *period* is deleted from the status table. The minimum valid entry is 1. The maximum valid entry is 52. The default is 1 week.

-s *states* Restrict the report to backup operations with the specified *states*. *states* is a list of state key-letters (concatenated, comma-separated or blank-separated and surrounded by quotes). For example,

```
apf
a,p,f
"a p f"
```

all specify that the report should only include backup operations that are **active**, **pending** or **failed**.

-u *users* Restrict the display to backup operations started by the specified list of *users* (either comma-separated or blank-separated and enclosed in quotes). *users* must be in the **passwd** file.

DIAGNOSTICS

The exit codes for the **bkstatus** command are the following:

0 = successful completion of the task
1 = one or more parameters to **bkstatus** are invalid.
2 = an error has occurred which caused **bkstatus** to fail to complete *all* portions of its task.

EXAMPLES

Example 1:

```
bkstatus -p 4
```

specifies that backup status information is to be saved for four weeks. Any status information older than four weeks is deleted from the system.

Example 2:

```
bkstatus -a -j back-459,back-395
```

produces a display that shows status for the two backup jobs specified, even if they have **completed** or **failed**.

Example 3:

```
bkstatus -s a,c -u "oper3 oper4"
```

produces a display that shows only those backup jobs issued by users **oper3** and **oper4** that have a status of either **active** or **completed**.

FILES

/etc/bkup/bkstatus.tab	lists the current status of backups that have occurred or are still in progress
/etc/bkup/bkreg.tab	describes the backup policy decided on by the System Administrator

SEE ALSO

backup(1M), **bkreg**(1M)

NAME

boot – UNIX system boot program

DESCRIPTION

The **boot** program loads and executes stand-alone UNIX programs. While **boot** is used primarily for loading and executing the UNIX system kernel, it can load and execute any other programs that are linked for stand-alone execution. During installation of the UNIX system, the **boot** program is placed on the hard disk starting at logical block 0 of the active partition.

The system invokes the **boot** program each time the computer is started. It tries to locate the **boot** program on the floppy disk drive first; if the floppy disk drive is empty, the system invokes the hard-disk boot procedure. The boot procedure depends on whether you are booting from a floppy disk or hard disk, as described below.

The floppy-disk boot procedure has two stages:

1. The boot block in sector 0 of the file system loads **boot**.
2. **boot** loads and executes the UNIX kernel.

The hard-disk boot procedure has three stages:

1. The ROMs load in the **masterboot** block from absolute sector 0 on the hard disk.
2. The **masterboot** boot block then loads the partition boot block from logical sector 0 of the active partition [see **fdisk**(1M)].
3. The remainder of **boot** is loaded from the next 29 sectors of the hard disk.

When first invoked, **boot** displays the following status message:

```
Booting the UNIX System...
```

To load a program that is not the default program (**unix**), press any key to interrupt **boot**. The **boot** program pauses and prompts you with the following message for the name of the program you want to load:

```
Enter the name of a kernel to boot:
```

The system waits at this point for you to type the name of the program you want to load and press RETURN. If you have not typed something after 30 seconds, **boot** times out and resumes loading the default program.

If you provide a name like **unix.old** or **unix.good**, the boot code will load that kernel from the boot filesystem. If you give an absolute pathname (e.g. **/etc/conf/cf.d/unix**) and your root file system type is s5, the boot code will load that kernel.

If you specify an absolute pathname and you do not have an s5 root file system, or you specify a file that does not exist or cannot be loaded for some reason, you will warned and prompted again.

Note: if you specify **/stand/unix**, the boot code will try to load **unix** from the directory **/stand** in the root file system, not from the boot file system that is n-ormally mounted on **/stand**.

FILES

/etc/boot
/etc/fboot
/etc/initprog/sip
/etc/initprog/mip

SEE ALSO

boot(4), **disksetup**(1M), **fd**(7), **fdisk**(1M), **sd01**(7)

DIAGNOSTICS

The **masterboot** and **boot** programs have different error messages. The **masterboot** program displays an error message and locks the system. The following is a list of the most common **masterboot** messages and their meanings:

IO ERR — An error occurred when trying to read in the partition boot of the active operating system.

BAD TBL — The bootable partition indicator of at least one of the operating systems in the **fdisk** table contains an unrecognizable code.

NO OS — There was an unrecoverable error after trying to execute the active operating system's partition boot.

The **boot** program displays an error message, then returns to its prompt. When one of these messages occurs, you will need to correct the problem described in the message and reboot the system:

Error reading bootstrap
: The **boot** program could not locate the bootstrap, or the bootstrap is not readable. Make sure that the bootstrap is properly located on the specified boot device and is compatible with the kernel you are booting. Then reboot the system.

No active partition on hard disk
: There is currently no active partition from which to run the **boot** program. Activate an appropriate partition and reboot the system.

No file system to boot
: The **boot** program could not locate a **/stand** or an s5 root file system on the specified boot device. Make sure the boot device has a **/stand** or an s5 root file system and reboot the system.

command **argument missing or incorrect**
: The **boot** program received a command with no argument or with an invalid argument. Make sure that *command* in **/stand/boot** has the correct number of arguments and that all the arguments are valid, then restart **boot**.

Cannot load *file*; **file not opened**
: The **boot** program cannot locate *file* on the specified device, or *file* is not set up properly for execution. Check that *file* exists on the specified device and restart **boot**.

Cannot load *file*; **cannot read COFF header**
: The specified Common Object File Format (COFF) file contains no file header, or the file header is not readable. Make sure that *file* contains a readable file header, then restart **boot**.

`Cannot load` *file*`; not an 80386 ELF or COFF binary`
The specified file is not an 80386 ELF or COFF binary. Check that the file you want to load is a valid COFF binary that is compatible with 80386 systems and restart **boot**.

`Cannot load` *file*`; cannot read segment/sections`
The specified file does not contain a section header, or the section header is not readable. Check that *file* contains a readable section header and restart **boot**.

`Cannot load` *file*`; cannot read BKI section`
The specified file does not include the bootstrap-kernel interface (BKI) section, or the BKI section is not readable. Make sure the BKI section of *file* is accurate for your version of the kernel and bootstrap, then restart **boot**.

`Cannot load` *file*`; BKI too old`
The BKI of the current bootstrap is not compatible with the BKI of the program (*file*) you are loading. Make sure that the BKI of the bootstrap and *file* are compatible and restart **boot**.

`Cannot load` *file*`; BKI too new`
The BKI of the current bootstrap is not compatible with the BKI of the program (*file*) you are loading. Make sure that the BKI of the bootstrap and *file* are compatible and restart **boot**.

`Cannot load` *file*`; missing text or data segment`
The specified file does not contain a necessary text or data segment. Check that *file* contains the proper text and data segments, then restart **boot**.

`Cannot load` *file*`; missing BKI segment`
The specified file does not contain the BKI segment. Make sure that the BKI segment in *file* exists and is compatible with the BKI of the bootstrap.

`Cannot load` *file*
not present The amount of memory available for the kernel is not present or is inadequate. Make sure you have allocated enough memory for the kernel you want to load, then restart **boot**.

`Too many lines in defaults file; extra lines ignored`
The file **/stand/boot** contains too many lines. All extra lines will be ignored.

NOTES

The computer always tries to boot from any diskette in the floppy diskette drive first. If the diskette does not contain a valid bootstrap program, errors occur.

The **boot** program cannot be used to load programs that have not been linked for standalone execution. To create stand-alone programs, use the option of the UNIX system linker [`ld` (1)] and special stand-alone libraries.

Although stand-alone programs can operate in real or protected mode, they must not be large or huge model programs. Programs in real mode can use the input/output routines of the computer's startup ROM.

bootparamd (1M)

NAME

`bootparamd` – boot parameter server

SYNOPSIS

`/usr/lib/nfs/bootparamd` [`-d`]

DESCRIPTION

`bootparamd` is a server process that provides information necessary for booting to diskless clients. It obtains its information from the `/etc/bootparams` file.

The `bootparamd` daemon is automatically invoked in run level 3.

The `-d` option displays the debugging information.

Only a privileged user can execute this command.

FILES

`/etc/bootparams`

SEE ALSO

`bootparams`(4), `inetd`(1M), `nfsping`(1M)

NAME

brc, **bcheckrc** – system initialization procedures

SYNOPSIS

/sbin/brc

/sbin/bcheckrc

DESCRIPTION

The **bcheckrc** procedure first checks the status of the root file system. If the root file system is found to be bad, **bcheckrc** repairs it. Then, it mounts the **/stand**, **/proc**, and **/var** (if it exists) file systems (**/var** may exist as a directory in the root file system, or as a separate file system). **bcheckrc** is executed by an entry in **/etc/inittab** by **init** whenever the system is booted.

The **brc** script performs administrative tasks related to file sharing. The functionality of **brc** has been incorporated into other startup routines, and is no longer executed by **/etc/inittab**. It is kept for compatibility reasons.

After **bcheckrc** has executed, **init** checks for the **initdefault** value in **/etc/inittab**. This tells **init** in which run level to place the system. If, for example, **initdefault** is set to **2**, the system will be placed in the multi-user state via the **rc2** procedure.

Note that **bcheckrc** should always be executed before **brc**. Also, these shell procedures may be used for several run-level states.

SEE ALSO

fsck(1M), **init**(1M), **inittab**(4), **mnttab**(4), **rc2**(1M), **shutdown**(1M)

cal (1)

NAME

`cal` – print calendar

SYNOPSIS

`cal` [[*month*] *year*]

DESCRIPTION

`cal` prints a calendar for the specified year. If a month is also specified, a calendar just for that month is printed. If neither is specified, a calendar for the present month is printed. The *month* is a number between 1 and 12. The *year* can be between 1 and 9999. The calendar produced is that for England and the United States.

NOTES

An unusual calendar is printed for September 1752. That is the month 11 days were skipped to make up for lack of leap year adjustments. To see this calendar, type: `cal 9 1752`

The command `cal 83` refers to the year 83, not 1983.

The year is always considered to start in January even though this is historically naive.

NAME

calendar – reminder service

SYNOPSIS

calendar [–]

DESCRIPTION

calendar consults the file **calendar** in the current directory and prints out lines that contain today's or tomorrow's date anywhere in the line. Most reasonable month-day dates such as **Aug. 24**, **august 24**, **8/24**, and so on, are recognized, but not **24 August** or **24/8**. On weekends "tomorrow" extends through Monday. **calendar** can be invoked regularly by using the **crontab**(1) or **at**(1) commands.

When an argument is present, **calendar** does its job for every user who has a file **calendar** in his or her login directory and sends them any positive results by **mail**(1). Normally this is done daily by facilities in the UNIX operating system (see **cron**(1M)).

If the environment variable **DATEMSK** is set, **calendar** will use its value as the full path name of a template file containing format strings. The strings consist of field descriptors and text characters and are used to provide a richer set of allowable date formats in different languages by appropriate settings of the environment variable **LANG** or **LC_TIME** (see **environ**(5)). (See **date**(1) for the allowable list of field descriptors.)

EXAMPLES

The following example shows the possible contents of a template:

```
%B %eth of the year %Y
```

%B represents the full month name, **%e** the day of month and **%Y** the year (4 digits).

If **DATEMSK** is set to this template, the following **calendar** file would be valid:

```
March 7th of the year 1989 < Reminder>
```

FILES

/usr/lib/calprog   program used to figure out today's and tomorrow's dates
/etc/passwd
/tmp/cal*

SEE ALSO

at(1), **cron**(1M), **crontab**(1), **date**(1), **environ**(5), **mail**(1)

NOTES

Appropriate lines beginning with white space will not be printed.
Your calendar must be public information for you to get reminder service.
calendar's extended idea of "tomorrow" does not account for holidays.

captoinfo (1M)

NAME

captoinfo — convert a *termcap* description into a *terminfo* description

SYNOPSIS

captoinfo [**-v** . . .] [**-V**] [**-1**] [**-w** *width*] *file* . . .

DESCRIPTION

captoinfo looks in *file* for **termcap** descriptions. For each one found, an equivalent **terminfo** description is written to standard output, along with any comments found. A description which is expressed as relative to another description (as specified in the **termcap tc = field**) will be reduced to the minimum superset before being output.

If no *file* is given, then the environment variable **TERMCAP** is used for the filename or entry. If **TERMCAP** is a full pathname to a file, only the terminal whose name is specified in the environment variable **TERM** is extracted from that file. If the environment variable **TERMCAP** is not set, then the file **/usr/share/lib/termcap** is read.

-v print out tracing information on standard error as the program runs. Specifying additional **-v** options will cause more detailed information to be printed.

-V print out the version of the program in use on standard error and exit.

-1 cause the fields to print out one to a line. Otherwise, the fields will be printed several to a line to a maximum width of 60 characters.

-w change the output to *width* characters.

FILES

/usr/share/lib/terminfo/?/* Compiled terminal description database.

NOTES

captoinfo should be used to convert **termcap** entries to **terminfo** entries because the **termcap** database (from earlier versions of UNIX System V) may not be supplied in future releases.

SEE ALSO

curses(3curses), **infocmp**(1M), **terminfo**(4)

NAME

cat – concatenate and print files

SYNOPSIS

cat [**-u**] [**-s**] [**-v** [[**-t**] [**-e**]] *file* . . .

DESCRIPTION

cat reads each *file* in sequence and writes it on the standard output. Thus

```
cat file
```

prints the contents of **file** on your terminal, and

```
cat file1 file2 >file3
```

concatenates **file1** and **file2**, and writes the results in **file3**. If no input file is given, or if the argument **-** is encountered, **cat** reads from the standard input. **cat** processes supplementary code set characters according to the locale specified in the **LC_CTYPE** environment variable [see **LANG** on **environ**(5)].

The following options apply to **cat**:

-u The output is not buffered. (The default is buffered output.)

-s **cat** is silent about non-existent files.

-v Causes non-printing characters (with the exception of tabs, new-lines, and form-feeds) to be printed visibly. ASCII control characters (octal 000 – 037) are printed as ^*n*, where *n* is the corresponding ASCII character in the range octal 100 – 137 (@, A, B, C, . . ., X, Y, Z, [, \,], ^, and _); the DEL character (octal 0177) is printed **^?**. Other non-printable characters are printed as **M-***x*, where *x* is the ASCII character specified by the low-order seven bits. All supplementary code set characters are considered to be printable.

The following options may be used with the **-v** option:

-t Causes tabs to be printed as **^I**'s and formfeeds to be printed as **^L**'s.

-e Causes a **$** character to be printed at the end of each line (prior to the new-line).

The **-t** and **-e** options are ignored if the **-v** option is not specified.

FILES

/usr/lib/locale/*locale***/LC_MESSAGES/uxcore.abi**
language-specific message file [See **LANG** on **environ**(5).]

SEE ALSO

cp(1), **pg**(1), **pr**(1)

NAME

`catman` – (BSD) create the cat files for the manual

SYNOPSIS

`/usr/ucb/catman` [`-nptw`] [`-M` *directory*] [`-T` *mac_file*] [*sections*]

DESCRIPTION

The **catman** command creates the preformatted versions of the on-line manual from the **nroff**(1) input files. Each manual page is examined and those whose preformatted versions are missing or out of date are recreated. If any changes are made, **catman** recreates the **whatis** database.

If there is one parameter not starting with a "-", it is taken to be a list of manual sections to look in. For example

```
catman 123
```

only updates manual sections 1, 2, and 3.

The following options are available:

- **-n** Do not (re)create the **whatis** database.
- **-p** Print what would be done instead of doing it.
- **-t** Create **troff**ed entries in the appropriate **fmt** subdirectories instead of **nroff**ing into the **cat** subdirectories.
- **-w** Only create the **whatis** database. No manual reformatting is done.
- **-M** Update manual pages located in the specified **directory** (**/usr/share/man** by default).
- **-T** Use **mac_file** in place of the standard manual page macros.

ENVIRONMENT

TROFF The name of the formatter to use when the **-t** flag is given. If not set, "**troff**" is used.

FILES

/usr/share/man	default manual directory location
/usr/share/man/man?/*.*	raw (nroff input) manual sections
/usr/share/man/cat?/*.*	preformatted **nroff**ed manual pages
/usr/share/man/fmt?/*.*	preformatted **troff**ed manual pages
/usr/share/man/whatis	**whatis** database location
/usr/ucblib/makewhatis	command script to make **whatis** database

SEE ALSO

man(1), **nroff**(1), **troff**(1), **whatis**(1)

DIAGNOSTICS

man?/xxx.? (.so'ed from man?/yyy.?): No such file or directory
The file outside the parentheses is missing, and is referred to by the file inside them.

target of .so in man?/xxx.? must be relative to /usr/man
catman only allows references to filenames that are relative to the directory **/usr/share/man**.

`opendir:man?: No such file or directory`
A harmless warning message indicating that one of the directories `catman` normally looks for is missing.

`*.*: No such file or directory`
A harmless warning message indicating `catman` came across an empty directory.

NAME

`cb` – C program beautifier

SYNOPSIS

`cb` [`-s`] [`-j`] [`-l` *leng*] [`-V`] [*file* . . .]

DESCRIPTION

The `cb` command reads syntactically correct C programs either from its arguments or from the standard input, and writes them on the standard output with spacing and indentation that display the structure of the C code. By default, it preserves all user new-lines. `cb` processes supplementary code set characters according to the locale specified in the `LC_CTYPE` environment variable [see `LANG` on `environ`(5)].

`cb` accepts the following options:

- `-s` Write the code in the style of Kernighan and Ritchie found in *The C Programming Language*.
- `-j` Put split lines back together.
- `-l` *leng* Split lines that are longer than *leng*.
- `-V` Print on standard error output the version of `cb` invoked.

SEE ALSO

`cc`(1)

Kernighan, B. W., and Ritchie, D. M., *The C Programming Language*, Second Edition, Prentice-Hall, 1988

NOTES

`cb` treats `asm` as a keyword.

The format of structure initializations is unchanged by `cb`.

Punctuation that is hidden in preprocessing directives causes indentation errors.

NAME

cc – C compiler

SYNOPSIS

cc [*options*] *file* . . .

DESCRIPTION

The cc command is the interface to the C compilation system. The compilation system consists of the following conceptual phases: preprocessing, compiling, optimizing, basic block profiling, assembling, and linking. The cc command examines its options and filename suffixes, and then executes the proper phases with appropriate options and arguments.

The cc command recognizes the following filename suffixes:

.c A file that contains unprocessed C source; all phases are applicable.

.i A file that contains preprocessed C source; all phases except for preprocessing are applicable.

.s A file that contains assembly language source; only the assembling and linking phases are applicable.

other A file that contains input applicable only to the linking phase. This category commonly includes object files (.o), archive libraries (.a), and shared object libraries (.so).

If no options are present, the cc command sends all files through those phases (as appropriate to their suffixes) as are necessary to combine them into a dynamically linked executable with the name **a.out** in the current directory. If an intermediate result is requested instead, it is similarly placed in the current directory, with a filename derived by replacing the incoming suffix with a suffix appropriate to the resultant file. If the assembling phase occurs, the cc command places the object file (.o) in the current directory, but this file will be removed if a single source file is being compiled through to an executable. All other intermediate files are placed in a temporary directory. (The choice of directory can be controlled with the environment variable **TMPDIR**.)

The following options are applicable to all phases.

-Q *str* Controls the inclusion of compilation tool identification information in the output. If *str* is y (the default), then the information will be present; if *str* is n, it will not.

-V Causes the cc command and each invoked tool to print its version information, one per line, on the standard error output.

-W *phase*, *list*

Hands the argument(s) specified by the comma-separated *list* (in order) to the single compilation phase named by *phase*. An argument in *list* can include a comma by escaping it by a preceding \. If more than one conceptual phase is implemented by a single tool, all the associated argument *list*s are passed to the tool. The phase names are the following:

`p` preprocessor
`0` compiler
`2` optimizer
`b` basic block profiler
`a` assembler
`l` linker

Relative to the regular options and arguments passed to the compilation phase, the location of the arguments specified by *list* is unspecified and may change.

-X *str* Controls the degree of conformance to the ANSI and ISO C standards. The option argument *str* can be one of the following:

`a` Specifies standards conformance except for some elided warnings and a license for an extended name space. All C constructions behave as specified in the standards. All implemented language and library extensions beyond the standards are also available.

`c` Specifies strict standards conformance. Because the name space of the language and headers is reduced from that of **-Xa**, certain extensions (such as the **asm** keyword) and some commonly expected header file declarations are not available. The latter may be helped by use of **-D_POSIX_SOURCE** or **-D_XOPEN_SOURCE**.

`t` Specifies standards conformance except where the semantics differ from "classic" C. (See Kernighan & Ritchie, First Edition.) In addition, warnings are issued about preprocessing phase semantic changes such as new escape sequences (like **\x**) and any trigraph replacements (like **??!**). Certain potential optimizations available in the other **-X** modes are also disabled.

In all **-X** modes, the compiling phase will warn about expressions in which the modified promotion rules for narrower unsigned values may cause an otherwise hidden behavior change.

The default mode is **-Xt**, but will be changed to be **-Xa** in a future release.

-Y *str***,***dir*

Changes to *dir* the directory in which to find the item(s) named by *str*. The option argument *str* is one or more of the following:

phase Causes the phase (spelled the same as for **-W**) to be found in the directory *dir*. If more than one conceptual phase is implemented by a single tool and differing directories are specified for the phases, it is unspecified which directory is used.

I Changes the directory searched last for preprocessing phase include files.

P Changes the basic linking phase default library search path to be the colon-separated list of one or more directories, *dir*. (More directories can be added to the front of the path due to other options.)

`s` Changes the directory in which to find the implementation's start-up object files.

In addition to the ability to specify the directory in which to find the various compilation phases, if the **cc** command is invoked as *prefix***cc**, then each tool executed will be similarly prefixed, as will the filenames for the start-up object files. For example, if the command **./abccc** is invoked with **-Ya,../xyz**, then the assembler would be expected to have the pathname **../xyz/abcas**.

The following options are applicable only to the preprocessing phase. During this phase, the macros __STDC__ and __USLC__ are always predefined. While __USLC__ always has a positive integer value (which signifies that a USL C compilation system is being used), __STDC__ has the value **1** only for **-Xc**, and the value **0** otherwise.

-A *name*[**(***tokens***)**]
Causes *name* to be asserted as a predicate associated with the optional parenthesized *tokens* as if by a **#assert** directive.

-A - Causes all predefined macros (other than those that begin with __) to be undefined and all preassertions to be unasserted.

The affected predefined macros and preassertions are the following:

```
#define i386 1        /* not present if -Xc */
#define unix 1        /* not present if -Xc */
#assert system(unix)
#assert cpu(i386)
#assert machine(i386)
```

-C Causes all comments other than on directive lines to be retained; otherwise, they are are removed.

-D *name*[=*tokens*]
Causes *name* to be defined as a macro to be replaced by *tokens*, or by **1** if =*tokens* is not present, as if by a **#define** directive.

-E Supresses all phases but preprocessing, and sends the result to the standard output. The result will contain directives intended for a subsequent compiling phase.

-H Causes the pathnames of all files included to be printed, one per line, on the standard error output.

-I *dir* Causes *dir* to be searched for included files whose names do not begin with / before searching the usual directories. The directories for multiple **-I** options are searched in the order specified.

-P Supresses all phases but preprocessing, and places the result in a **.i**-suffixed file. Unlike **-E**, the result will contain no directives.

-U *name*
Causes *name* to be undefined as a macro as if by a **#undef** directive, even if *name* is a predefined macro (including those that begin with __) or is also the subject of a **-D** option.

The following options are applicable to all phases other than the preprocessing. All options affecting only the linking phase are also handed to the **ld**(1) command.

-B *str* Controls the linking phase library name search mechanism for subsequent **-l** options. The option argument *str* can be either **dynamic** (the initial setting) or **static**. The order of the **-B**, **-L**, and **-l** options is significant; see the **-l** option.

-c Supresses the linking phase. No produced object files (**.o**) are removed.

-d *str* Determines the mode of the executable result of the linking phase. If *str* is **y** (the default), a dynamically linked executable is to be produced; if *str* is **n**, the result will be statically linked.

-G Causes the linking phase to produce a shared object instead of an executable.

-g Causes the generation of information that facilitates symbolic debugging. This option clashes with **-O** but has lower precedence: no debugging information is generated if both are specified.

-K *list* Enables certain variations in code generation, or optimization, or linking, or a combination thereof. For those items in the following list presented in groups of two or more, the first item is the default choice, and at most one of each such group will be effective. The option argument *list* is a comma-separated list of one or more of the following items:

PIC Changes code generation to be position-independent.

minabi Changes the linking phase default library search path (**-YP**) to check first in the directory that contains a C library with minimized dynamic linking.

i486
P5
i386 Causes code generation specifically tuned to the selected processor.

ieee
noieee Controls whether the generated floating point code strictly conforms to the IEEE floating point and C standards. The default specifies strict conformance.

no_frame
frame Specifies whether the generated code must use the **%ebp** register as the stack frame pointer. The default permits **%ebp** to be allocated as a general purpose register, which can cause debugging stack traces to be unreliable, but usually produces faster code.

Multiple **-K** options have the same effect as if the separate *list* arguments were merged into one option.

-L *dir* Adds *dir* to the linking phase list of directories to be searched for subsequent **-l** options. The order of the **-B**, **-L**, and **-l** options is significant; see the **-l** option.

-l *str* — Causes the linking phase to search the library **lib***str***.so** or **lib***str***.a**. The order of the **-B**, **-L**, and **-l** options is significant: A **-l** option causes the linker to check first in the directories specified by preceding **-L** options (in order) and then in the directories of the default library search path (**-YP**). If **-Bdynamic** is set at the point of the **-l** option, each directory is checked first for **lib***str***.so** and then **lib***str***.a**; otherwise, only **lib***str***.a** is checked for.

-O — Enables the optimization phase. This phase clashes with **-g** but has higher precedence: no debugging information is generated if both are specified. This phase also clashes with **-ql** but has lower precedence: the optimization phase is disabled if both are specified.

-o *pathname*
Causes the linking phase to place its result in *pathname* instead of **a.out**.

-p — Causes extra code to be generated that counts the number of calls to each routine. If the linking phase is enabled, the default library search path (**-YP**) is altered to check directories that are intended to contain similarly instrumented libraries before the usual directories. Moreover, different start-up object files are used that arrange to record (in the file **mon.out**) the time spent in each routine; see **prof**(1).

-q *str* — Causes extra code that instruments the program to be generated. If *str* is **p**, the behavior is the same as the **-p** option. If *str* is **l**, the basic block profiling phase is enabled which generates extra code that counts the number of times each source lines is executed; see **lprof**(1). The **-O** option clashes with **-ql** but has lower precedence: the optimization phase is not enabled if both are specified.

-S — Supresses the assembling and linking phases, and places the result in a **.s**-suffixed file.

-v — Causes the compiling phase to perform extra syntactic, semantic, and **lint**(1)-like checks.

-Z *str* — Controls the packing of structures in the compiling phase. The option argument *str* is one of the following:

- **p1** Selects at least one byte alignment for all structure members; or, in other words, include no padding. (This can also be specified as **-Zp**.)
- **p2** Selects at least two byte alignment for structure members of at least two bytes in size.
- **p4** Selects two byte alignment for two byte sized structure members and four byte alignment for larger structure members. This is the default choice.

The **cc** command recognizes **-e**, **-h**, **-u**, and **-z** as linking phase options with arguments. These, and all other unrecognized option-like arguments are handed to **ld**(1).

Finally, the `cc` command also recognizes the option `-#`. If one `-#` option is present, the `cc` command will print each tool with its options and argument just before it is invoked. With two `-#` options, the pathname of each tool is also printed; with three, the invocations are skipped.

FILES

`a.out`	default name of resulting executable
INCDIR	last directory to search for include files
LIBDIR`/*crt*.o`	startup code object files
LIBDIR`/acomp`	preprocessor and compiler
LIBDIR`/optim`	optimizer
LIBDIR`/basicblk`	basic block profiler
BINDIR`/as`	assembler
BINDIR`/ld`	linker
LIBDIR`/libc.so`	dynamic shared standard C library
LIBDIR`/libc.a`	archive standard C library
DIR`/libp`	subdirectory of each *LIBPATH* entry in which to check for profiled libraries

INCDIR	usually `/usr/include`
LIBDIR	usually `/usr/ccs/lib`
BINDIR	usually `/usr/ccs/bin`
LIBPATH	usually `/usr/ccs/lib:/usr/lib`
TMPDIR	usually `/var/tmp` but can be overridden by the environment variable `TMPDIR`.

SEE ALSO

`as`(1), `debug`(1), `ld`(1), `lint`(1), `lprof`(1), `monitor`(3C), `prof`(1), `tmpnam`(3S)

Kernighan, B. W., and Ritchie, D. M., *The C Programming Language*, Second Edition, Prentice-Hall, 1988

American National Standard for Information Systems – Programming Language C, X3.159-1989

International Standard ISO/IEC 9899:1990, Programming Languages – C

International Standard ISO/IEC 9945-1:1990, Information Technology – Portable Operating System Interface (POSIX) – Part 1: System Application Program Interface (API) [C Language]

NOTES

The `cc` command accepts a number of obsolescent options including `-YL` and `-YU` which are subsumed by `-YP`, and `-f` which at one time requested floating point support. Options with option arguments, such as `-K`, sometimes accept more values than listed above. If a mode choice option (such as `-Q` or `-X`) is specified more than once, generally the last is used.

New code should use `-Xa` and `-v`; older code is best handled with `-Xt`.

For a typical multiuser Intel486™ microprocessor-based system, the fastest code will probably be generated by using the `-Xa`, `-Knoieee`, and `-O` options, and by using the standard include files such as `<string.h>`. However, if the system has *lots* of memory, or if a single run of the program is critical, the `-dn` option should also be used.

NAME

cc – (BSD) C compiler

SYNOPSIS

/usr/ucb/cc [*options*] *file* . . .

DESCRIPTION

/usr/ucb/cc is the C compiler for the BSD Compatibility Package. **/usr/ucb/cc** is identical to **/usr/bin/cc** [see **cc**(1)] except that BSD header files are used. BSD libraries are linked before System V libraries.

/usr/ucb/cc accepts the same options as **/usr/bin/cc**, with the following exceptions:

-I *dir* Search *dir* for included files whose names do not begin with a '**/**', prior to the usual directories. The directories fro multiple **-I** options are searched in the order specified. The preprocessor first searches for **#include** files in the directory containing *sourcefile*, and then in directories named with **-I** options (if any), then **/usr/ucbinclude**, and finally, in **/usr/include**.

-L *dir* Add *dir* to the list of directories searched for libraries by **/usr/bin/cc**. This option is passed to **/usr/bin/ld**. Directories specified with this option are searched before **/usr/ucblib** and **/usr/lib**.

-Y LU, *dir* Change the default directory used for finding libraries.

FILES

/usr/ucblib
/usr/lib/ld
/usr/ucblib/libucb.a
/usr/lib/libucb.a

SEE ALSO

a.out(4), **ar**(1), **as**(1), **cc**(1), **ld**(1), **lorder**(1), **strip**(1), **tsort**(1)

NOTES

The **-Y LU,***dir* option may have unexpected results, and should not be used. This option is not in the UNIX System V base.

If the **-p** option to **/usr/ucb/cc** is being used with the **-dn** and **-lm** options, then this invocation of the **/usr/ucb/cc** command will fail. This occurs because **/usr/ucb/cc** executes as the following command:

```
(/usr/bin/cc  -YP,:/usr/ucblib:/usr/ccs/lib:/usr/lib  $@  -I
/usr/ucbinclude -l ucb -l socket -l nsl)
```

This command requests a search of the library **libnsl** (**-l nsl**) which is a shared object, rather than an archive library. To fix this problem, you must invoke **/usr/bin/cc** directly, using the same format as shown above for **/usr/ucb/cc**, but without the **-l nsl** option.

An example would be:

```
/usr/bin/cc -YP,:/usr/ucblib:/usr/ccs/lib:/usr/lib -p -dn -lm
prog.c -I /usr/ucbinclude -l ucb -l socket
```

cd(1)

NAME

cd – change working directory

SYNOPSIS

cd [*directory*]

DESCRIPTION

If *directory* is not specified, the value of shell parameter **$HOME** is used as the new working directory. If *directory* specifies a complete path starting with /, ., or .., *directory* becomes the new working directory. If neither case applies, **cd** tries to find the designated directory relative to one of the paths specified by the **$CDPATH** shell variable. **$CDPATH** has the same syntax as, and similar semantics to, the **$PATH** shell variable. **cd** must have execute (search) permission in *directory*.

Because a new process is created to execute each command, **cd** would be ineffective if it were written as a normal command; therefore, it is recognized by and is internal to the shell.

FILES

/usr/lib/locale/*locale***/LC_MESSAGES/uxcore.abi**
language-specific message file [See **LANG** on **environ** (5).]

SEE ALSO

pwd(1), **chdir**(2), **sh**(1)

NAME

cdc – change the delta comment of an SCCS delta

SYNOPSIS

cdc -r *SID* [**-m**[*mrlist*]] [**-y**[*comment*]] *file* . . .

DESCRIPTION

cdc changes the delta comment, for the SID (SCCS identification string) specified by the **-r** keyletter, of each named SCCS file.

The delta comment is the Modification Request (MR) and comment information normally specified via the **-m** and **-y** keyletters of the **delta** command.

If *file* is a directory, **cdc** behaves as though each file in the directory were specified as a named file, except that non-SCCS files (last component of the path name does not begin with **s.**) and unreadable files are silently ignored. If a name of – is given, the standard input is read (see the NOTES section) and each line of the standard input is taken to be the name of an SCCS file to be processed.

Arguments to **cdc**, which may appear in any order, consist of keyletter arguments and file names.

All the described keyletter arguments apply independently to each named file:

-r*SID* Used to specify the *SCCS IDentification* (SID) string of a delta for which the delta comment is to be changed.

-m*mrlist* If the SCCS file has the **v** flag set [see **admin**(1)] then a list of MR numbers to be added and/or deleted in the delta comment of the SID specified by the **-r** keyletter may be supplied. A null MR list has no effect.

mrlist entries are added to the list of MRs in the same manner as that of **delta**. In order to delete an MR, precede the MR number with the character **!** (see the EXAMPLES section). If the MR to be deleted is currently in the list of MRs, it is removed and changed into a comment line. A list of all deleted MRs is placed in the comment section of the delta comment and preceded by a comment line stating that they were deleted.

If **-m** is not used and the standard input is a terminal, the prompt **MRs?** is issued on the standard output before the standard input is read; if the standard input is not a terminal, no prompt is issued. The **MRs?** prompt always precedes the **comments?** prompt (see **-y** keyletter).

mrlist entries in a list are separated by blanks and/or tab characters. An unescaped new-line character terminates the MR list.

Note that if the **v** flag has a value [see **admin**(1)], it is taken to be the name of a program (or shell procedure) that validates the correctness of the MR numbers. If a non-zero exit status is returned from the MR number validation program, **cdc** terminates and the delta comment remains unchanged.

-y[*comment*] Arbitrary text used to replace the *comment*(s) already existing for the delta specified by the **-r** keyletter. The previous comments are kept and preceded by a comment line stating that they were changed. A null *comment* has no effect.

If **-y** is not specified and the standard input is a terminal, the prompt **comments?** is issued on the standard output before the standard input is read; if the standard input is not a terminal, no prompt is issued. An unescaped new-line character terminates the *comment* text.

If you made the delta and have the appropriate file permissions, you can change its delta comment. If you own the file and directory you can modify the delta comment.

EXAMPLES

```
cdc -r1.6 -m"bl88-12345 !bl87-54321 bl89-00001" -ytrouble s.file
```

adds bl88-12345 and bl89-00001 to the MR list, removes bl87-54321 from the MR list, and adds the comment **trouble** to delta 1.6 of **s.file**.

Entering:

```
cdc -r1.6 s.file
MRs? !bl87-54321 bl88-12345 bl89-00001
comments? trouble
```

produces the same result.

FILES

x.*file* [see **delta**(1)]
z.*file* [see **delta**(1)]

SEE ALSO

admin(1), **delta**(1), **get**(1), **help**(1), **prs**(1), **sccsfile**(4)

DIAGNOSTICS

Use **help** for explanations.

NOTES

If SCCS file names are supplied to the **cdc** command via the standard input (- on the command line), then the **-m** and **-y** keyletters must also be used.

NAME

cddevsuppl – Set or get major and minor numbers of a CD-ROM device file

SYNOPSIS

cddevsuppl [**-m** *mapfile* | **-u** *unmapfile*] [**-c**]

DESCRIPTION

cddevsuppl sets or gets the major and minor number of any or all of the device files so the appropriate device on the host system is accessed. The major and minor number of a device file on a CD-ROM are assigned by the CD-ROM publisher during manufacturing. These values may not match the major and minor numbers assigned to the physical devices on the host system. Only a privileged user can set the major/minor number assignments of a device file.

Mappings should be established before affected device files are used. Any device files that are in use and have their mappings changed by the **cddevsuppl** utility will continue to use the previous mappings until they are closed.

With no options **cddevsuppl** returns the current major/minor number assignments of all of the device files on the mounted CD-ROM.

Options

The following options are available:

-m *mapfile* Sets the major and minor number for the device files, as specified in *mapfile*. *mapfile* has one entry for each device file to be set. **CD_MAXDMAP** specifies the maximum number of device mappings that *mapfile* may contain. Each field in *mapfile* is separated by white space (tab, space), and each entry is separated by a new line. Anything beyond the third field on a line is considered to be a comment. The format for an entry in *mapfile* is:

device_file_path *new_major_number* *new_minor_number*

-u *unmapfile* Unsets the major and minor number assignment for the device files specified in *unmapfile*. (The default major/minor number assignments for the device file as recorded on the CD-ROM are then used.) The *unmapfile* file has one entry for each device file assignment. Each entry is separated by a new line. Anything beyond the first field on a line is considered to be a comment.

The format for an entry in *unmapfile* is:

device_file_path

-c Causes **cddevsuppl** to continue processing file entries even if an error occurs for an individual entry. The default action is to stop processing. The **-c** option is used with the **-m** *mapfile* or **-u** *unmapfile* options.

An error message for the specific device file is printed to standard error.

Exit Codes

If the **-m** option successfully completes, the new major/minor number settings are output to standard error.

If the **-u** option successfully completes, the major/minor numbers for the device files recorded on the CD-ROM are displayed.

cddevsuppl exits with one of the following values:

0	Successful completion
1	File is not found.
1	File is not a file or directory within a CD-ROM file hierarchy.
1	Access is denied.
2	Not a user with appropriate privileges. The user must have read/write permission for the device file to change the major/minor settings of the device file and must have read permission to see the settings.
3	Too many assignments
4	Parameter error.
4	Bad format in *mapfile* or *unmapfile*.
5	File is not a device file.
6	A device file listed in *unmapfile* (specified with the **-u** option) was not previously set.

USAGE

The **-m** *mapfile* and **-u** *unmapfile* options are mutually exclusive.

When the CD-ROM is unmounted, any new major and minor number assignments are voided.

If the major and minor number settings of a device file are reset, previous settings are overridden.

The maximum number of device files per CD-ROM that can be reset is defined in the header file **sys/cdrom.h**.

REFERENCES

cdsuf(1M), **cd_setdevmap**(3X), **cd_suf**(3X), **environ**(5), *Rock Ridge Interchange Protocol* from Rock Ridge Technical Working Group

NAME

cddrec – read CD-ROM Directory Record

SYNOPSIS

cddrec [-s *number*] **[-b]** *file*

DESCRIPTION

cddrec lists the contents of the directory record for a CD-ROM file or directory.

cddrec produces a table that lists the names of the fields in the Directory Record and their values. If the **-b** option is not used, the System Use field is not listed because it may contain non-printable characters.

Options

file File or directory within the CD-ROM file system.

-s *number*
File Section for which the Directory Record should be read. The numbering starts with one. If this option is omitted, the last File Section of that file is assumed.

-b Lists the contents of the Directory Record, including the System Use Field, in binary format.

Environment Variables

IF **LC_TIME** (which determines the format and contents of the date and time strings) is not set or is set to the empty string, then **cddrec** uses the value of **LANG**. If **LANG** is not set, or is set to the empty string, **cddrec** uses the value from the implementation-specific default locale. If both **LC_TIME** and **LANG** contain invalid settings, **cddrec** behaves as if all of the variables are undefined.

Exit Codes

0 Successful completion

1 *file* not found, *file* is not within the CD-ROM file hierarchy, or access permission is denied.

2 File Section indicated by **-s** does not exist.

REFERENCES

cd_drec(3X), **environ**(5)

cdmntsuppl (1M)

NAME

`cdmntsuppl` – set and get administrative CD-ROM features

SYNOPSIS

`cdmntsuppl [-D` *mode*`] [-F` *mode*`] [-g` *group*`] [-G` *gmfile*`]`
`[-u` *owner*`] [-U` *umfile*`] [-c | [-l] [-m]] [-s | -x]` *mountpoint*

DESCRIPTION

`cdmntsuppl` sets CD-ROM default features, such as ownership of files and directories, file permissions, user and group IDs, file name conversion, and execute permission for directories. You cannot use the `-c` option with either `-l` or `-m`. Nor can you use `-x` with `-s`.

Use `cdmntsuppl` without options to display the current settings.

You need read permission on the mount point to read the current settings. You must have appropriate permissions to change administrative CD-ROM features. Change the default features after the CD-ROM has been mounted, but before any CD-ROM access occurs or that change may not be consistently visible.

Options

`-c` Use file names as they are recorded on the CD-ROM. This option cannot be used with the `-m` or `-l` options.

`-D` *mode* Sets the default permissions for directories the same way as with the `-F` option.

`-F` *mode* Sets the default permission for files. Specify *mode* either as symbolic or absolute.

An absolute *mode* is a bit-wise inclusive OR of zero or more of the following octal values:

`0400`	Read by owner.
`0100`	Execute by owner.
`0040`	Read by group.
`0010`	Execute by group.
`0004`	Read by others.
`0001`	Execute by others.

A symbolic *mode* has the form:

`[`*who*`]` *op* `[`*permission*`]`

who is a combination of the letters; `u` (user), `g` (group), and `o` (other). `a` stands for `ugo`.

op is one of these symbols:

- `+` adds *permission* to the file's mode
- `-` removes *permission*
- `=` assigns *permission* absolutely (all other bits are reset).

permission is a combination of the letters **r** (read), and **x** (execute). Omitting *permission* is only useful when used with = to take away all permission.

-g *group* Sets the default group of files and directories, where *group* is a group ID or a valid group name.

-G *gmfile* Specifies a file that maps default group IDs on CD-ROM files and directories to group IDs or group names on the file system on which the CD-ROM is mounted. The files and directories on the CD-ROM must have an unrestricted final XAR. Entries in *gmfile* must have the following syntax:

value of group ID on CD-ROM, a colon **:**, value of group ID or group name.

Multiple entries must be separated by a newline character. The **sys/cdrom.h** header file defines the maximum number of mappings allowed in *gmfile* (**CD_MAXGMAP**).

-u *owner* Sets the default ownership of files and directories, where *owner* is a user ID or a valid login name.

-U *umfile* Specifies a file that maps default user IDs on CD-ROM files and directories to user IDs or user names on the file system on which the CD-ROM is mounted. The files and directories on the CD-ROM must have an unrestricted final XAR. Entries in *umfile* must have the following syntax:

value of user ID on CD-ROM, a colon **:**, value of user ID or user name.

Multiple entries must be separated by a newline character. The **sys/cdrom.h** header file defines the maximum number of mappings allowed in *umfile* (**CD_MAXUMAP**).

-l Convert upper case characters in File or Directory Identifiers to lower case. If the File Identifier does not contain a File Name Extension, do not display the period separator. **(.)** is not represented. This option can be used with the **-m** option.

-m Do not display the Version Number and semicolon separator (;) of File or Directory Identifiers on CD-ROM. This option can be used with the **-l** option.

-s Grants search permission for directories on which the searcher has read or execute permission.

-x Grants search permission for directories on which the searcher has execute permission.

Environment Variables

LC_CTYPE is not used in file name conversion.

Exit Codes

0 Successful completion.

1 *mountpoint* not found, access permission is denied, or *mountpoint* is not a mount point of a CD-ROM file system.

2 User does not have appropriate permission.

3 Too many mappings.

4 Bad format in a mapping file or parameter error.

REFERENCES

cd_defs, **cd_idmap**, **cd_mnconv**, **cdfs**-specific **mount**(1M)

NAME

`cdptrec` – read CD-ROM Path Table Record

SYNOPSIS

`cdptrec [-b]` *directory*

DESCRIPTION

`cdptrec` produces a table that lists the name of each field in the Path Table Record and its value, as recorded on the CD-ROM. A Path Table contains a variable length record for each directory in the file system.

directory Directory within the CD-ROM file system.

`-b` Produce table in binary format.

Exit Codes

On success, `cdptrec` returns `0`. On failure `cdptrec` returns `1`, which indicates that *directory* is not found or access permission is denied.

REFERENCES

`cd_pvd`(3X), `cd_ptrec`(3X)

cdsuf (1M)

NAME

cdsuf – read the System Use Fields from a System Use Area on CD-ROM

SYNOPSIS

cdsuf [**-s** *number*] [**-b**] *file*

DESCRIPTION

cdsuf lists the contents of the System Use Fields (which conform to the System Use Sharing Protocol) of the System Use Area associated with a File Section of a file or directory. Information in any continuation fields that are present is also displayed.

The output is in the form of a table containing an entry for each System Use Field in the System Use Area recorded on the CD-ROM. Each entry of the table has the fields *Signature, Length, Version,* and *Data,* as specified in the System Use Sharing Protocol.

Only a privileged user can execute the command successfully.

Options

The following options are available:

-s *number* Specifies the File Section number for which the System Use Area shall be read. The numbering starts with 1. If this option is omitted, the last File Section of that file is assumed.

-b Copies all of the System Use Fields of the System Use Area from the CD-ROM to standard output, in binary format.

file Names the file or directory within the CD-ROM file hierarchy.

Environment Variables

LC_TIME determines the format and contents of date and time strings. If **LC_TIME** is not set in the environment or is set to the empty string, the value of **LANG** is used as the default. If **LANG** is not set or is set to the empty string, the corresponding value from the implementation-specific default locale is used. If **LC_TIME** or **LANG** contain an invalid setting, the utility behaves as if none of the variables are defined.

Exit Codes

cdsuf exits with one of the following values:

0	Successful completion
1	File is not found.
1	File is not a file or directory within a CD-ROM file hierarchy.
1	Access is denied.
2	File section indicated by **-s** does not exist.
3	File section indicated by **-s** has no System Use Area.

REFERENCES

cddevsuppl(1M), **cd_getdevmap**(3X), **cd_setdevmap**(3X), **cd_suf**(3X), **environ**(5), *Rock Ridge Interchange Protocol* from the Rock Ridge Technical Working Group

NAME

cdvd – read the CD-ROM Primary Volume Descriptor

SYNOPSIS

cdvd [-b] *file*

DESCRIPTION

cdvd reads the Primary Volume Descriptor from the CD-ROM and produces a table that lists each field and its contents. If the **-b** option is not used, the Application Use field is not listed because it may contain non-printable characters.

file A file or directory in the CD-ROM file system, or a block special file that holds a CD-ROM file system.

-b Copies the entire Primary Volume Descriptor from CD-ROM to standard output in binary format, including the Application Use field.

Environment Variables

IF **LC_TIME** (which determines the format and contents of the date and time strings) is not set or is set to the empty string, then **cdvd** uses the value of **LANG**. If **LANG** is not set, or is set to the empty string, **cdvd** uses the value from the implementation-specific default locale. If both **LC_TIME** and **LANG** contain invalid settings, **cdvd** behaves as if all of the variables are undefined.

Exit Codes

0 Successful completion

1 *file* not found, *file* is not within the CD-ROM file hierarchy, *file* is not a block special file for a CD-ROM file system, or access permission is denied.

2 *file* is a block special file and a read error occurred, or the file system format is not recognized.

REFERENCES

cd_pvd(3X)

cdxar (1M)

NAME

`cdxar` – read CD-ROM Extended Attribute Record (XAR)

SYNOPSIS

`cdxar [-s` *number*`] [-b]` *file*

DESCRIPTION

`cdxar` displays the Extended Attribute Record (XAR) associated with a File Section of a file or directory. The output is a table that lists each field in the XAR and its contents. If the `-b` option is not used, the Application Use field and the Escape Sequences field are not listed because they may contain non-printable characters.

file — File or directory in the CD-ROM file system.

`-s` *number* — Specifies the File Section for which the XAR shall be read. The numbering starts with one. If this option is omitted, the last File Section of that file is assumed.

`-b` — Displays the XAR in binary format, including the Application Use Field and the Escape Sequences field.

Environment Variables

IF `LC_TIME` (which determines the format and contents of the date and time strings) is not set or is set to the empty string, then `cdxar` uses the value of `LANG`. If `LANG` is not set, or is set to the empty string, `cdxar` uses the value from the implementation-specific default locale. If both `LC_TIME` and `LANG` contain invalid settings, `cdxar` behaves as if all of the variables are undefined.

Exit Codes

0 Successful completion

1 *file* not found, *file* is not a file or directory in the CD-ROM file system, or access permission is denied.

2 File section specified by `-s` does not exist.

3 File Section specified by `-s` does not have a XAR.

REFERENCES

`cd_xar`(3X)

NAME

`cflow` – generate C flowgraph

SYNOPSIS

`cflow [-r] [-ix] [-i_] [-d`*num*`]` *files*

DESCRIPTION

The **cflow** command analyzes a collection of C, **yacc**, **lex**, assembler, and object files and builds a graph charting the external function references. Files suffixed with `.y`, `.l`, and `.c` are processed by **yacc**, **lex**, and the C compiler as appropriate. The results of the preprocessed files, and files suffixed with **.i**, are then run through the first pass of **lint**. Files suffixed with **.s** are assembled. Assembled files, and files suffixed with `.o`, have information extracted from their symbol tables. The results are collected and turned into a graph of external references that is written on the standard output. **cflow** processes supplementary code set characters in literals and constants according to the locale specified in the **LC_CTYPE** environment variable [see **LANG** on **environ**(5)].

Each line of output begins with a reference number, followed by a suitable number of tabs indicating the level, then the name of the global symbol followed by a colon and its definition. Normally only function names that do not begin with an underscore are listed (see the **-i** options below). For information extracted from C source, the definition consists of an abstract type declaration (for example, **char** *), and, delimited by angle brackets, the name of the source file and the line number where the definition was found. Definitions extracted from object files indicate the file name and location counter under which the symbol appeared (for example, *text*). If the compilation system adds a leading underscore to external names, it is removed. Once a definition of a name has been printed, subsequent references to that name contain only the reference number of the line where the definition may be found. For undefined references, only **< >** is printed.

As an example, suppose the following code is in **file.c**:

```
int  i;

main()
{
        f();
        g();
        f();
}

f()
{
        i = h();
}
```

The command

```
cflow -ix file.c
```

produces the output

```
1       main: int(), <file.c 4>
2               f: int(), <file.c 11>
3                       h: <>
4                       i: int, <file.c 1>
5               g: <>
```

When the nesting level becomes too deep, the output of **cflow** can be piped to the **pr** command, using the **-e** option, to compress the tab expansion to something less than every eight spaces.

In addition to the **-D**, **-I**, and **-U** options (which are interpreted just as they are by **cc**), the following options are interpreted by **cflow**:

-r Reverse the "caller:callee" relationship producing an inverted listing showing the callers of each function. The listing is also sorted in lexicographical order by callee.

-ix Include external and static data symbols. The default is to include only functions in the flowgraph.

-i_ Include names that begin with an underscore. The default is to exclude these functions (and data if **-ix** is used).

-d*num* The *num* decimal integer indicates the depth at which the flowgraph is cut off. By default this number is very large. Attempts to set the cutoff depth to a nonpositive integer will be ignored.

SEE ALSO

as(1), **cc**(1), **lex**(1), **lint**(1), **nm**(1), **yacc**(1)

DIAGNOSTICS

Complains about multiple definitions and only believes the first.

NOTES

Files produced by **lex** and **yacc** cause the reordering of line number declarations, which can confuse **cflow**. To get proper results, feed **cflow** the **yacc** or **lex** input.

NAME

charconv – NLS conversion tool

SYNOPSIS

charconv [**-7abcdlmpqsuvxz**] [*infile* [*outfile*]]

DESCRIPTION

The **/usr/bin/charconv** command is a general-purpose conversion tool that you can modify to do what you want using the options described below. Depending upon how you invoke it, **charconv** converts between the code set used by your UNIX operating system and the code page used by your personal computer and vice versa. **charconv** is a very powerful command and is most useful in mixed language (NLS) environments. For simple file conversion cases, use **dos2unix** and **unix2dos**. Unlike **dos2unix** or **unix2dos**, there are no default settings for **charconv**. You must specify the –i and –o options for **charconv** to work.

The first file specified (*infile*) is the source file. The second file specified (*outfile*) is the target file. The source file and the target file must not be the same. When neither file parameter is specified, **charconv** reads from standard input and writes to standard output. If you specify only one file parameter, that file is considered the source file, and the output is written to standard output.

All of the options below can be set on the command line or with the **CONVOPTS** (conversion options) environment variable. By specifying options with **CONVOPTS**, you can set the conversion options you always want to use without having to type them at the command line each time. **CONVOPTS** is explained at the end of this section.

-7 Notifies you if **charconv** encounters any 8-bit characters and translates them to 7-bit characters. You cannot use this option with **-b**.

-a Causes the **charconv** program to quit if it encounters a character it cannot translate accurately. This option supersedes the **-c**, **-m**, and **-s** options.

-b Preserves 8-bit (binary) character representations. This option is on by default.

-c *x* Specifies *x* as the character to use for untranslatable characters. The default character is an asterisk (*) if you do not specify the **-c** option. You cannot use this option with **-s**.

-d Converts a text file from DOS to UNIX operating system format.

-i *tbl* Identifies the code page or code set used for the input file. This option is required.

-o *tbl* Identifies the code page or code set used for the output file. This option is required.

For example, if you want to convert a DOS file from code page 437 to code page 850, use the **charconv** command as follows:

charconv -i pc437 -o pc850 *input_file output_file*

-l Converts text to lowercase.

`-m` Translates single, untranslatable characters into multibyte characters, if possible. For example, ¾ translates to 3/4.

`-p` Converts a text file from UNIX operating system to DOS format.

`-q` Prevents **charconv** from displaying warning messages and character conversion statistics on your screen. This option is on by default. This option overrides `-v`, unless you specify `-v` after specifying `-q`—that is, the last option specified is used.

`-s` Converts single, untranslatable characters into the best single character representation. For example, (the DOS graphic character for intersection), translates to +. If there is no best single translation, **charconv** uses the default asterisk (*) character. You cannot use this option with `-c`.

`-u` Converts text to uppercase.

`-v` Displays warning messages and character conversion statistics on your screen. This option overrides `-q`, unless you specify `-q` after specifying `-v`—that is, the last option specified is used.

`-x` Specifies that **charconv** should not translate from code page to code set or vice versa. Use this command with the `-d` or `-p` options when you want to translate between DOS and UNIX operating system text format without changing code pages. When you specify `-x`, **charconv** does not allow you to use the `-i` or `-o` options.

`-z` Causes **charconv** to stop processing when it encounters the DOS end-of-file (EOF) character, ^Z.

Use `-?` or `-h` to display the syntax for the **charconv** command on your screen.

Setting The CONVOPTS Environment Variable

The **CONVOPTS** environment variable allows you to set the **charconv** options once so you only need to type **charconv** *filename* to accomplish a task.

For example, suppose you want to convert a series of files from code page 437 to code page 850 and make all of the characters uppercase.

To do this, you would set the **CONVOPTS** environment variable on the UNIX operating system command line as follows, using the Bourne shell:

```
CONVOPTS= -u -ipc437 -opc850 export CONVOPTS
```

Now, you can just type:

charconv *filename*

for each file, and code page 437 is converted to code page 850 and all characters appear in uppercase.

The settings for **CONVOPTS** remain in effect until you reset them.

NOTES

The `-c` and `-s`, `-u` and `-l`, `-b` and `-7`, and `-d` and `-p` options are mutually exclusive.

If you use **charconv** with a file name that begins with a minus sign (–, you must precede the file name with two minus signs (– –), slashes, or any combination thereof. For example: `charconv -i pc437 -o pc850 --` *-file*

NAME

checknr – (BSD) check nroff and troff input files; report possible errors

SYNOPSIS

/usr/ucb/checknr [**-fs**] [**-a.***x1***.***y1***.***x2***.***y2*. . . **.***xn***.***yn*]
[**-c.***x1***.***x2***.***x3*. . . **.***xn*] [*file* . . .]

DESCRIPTION

The **checknr** command checks a list of **nroff** or **troff** input files for certain kinds of errors involving mismatched opening and closing delimiters and unknown commands. If no files are specified, **checknr** checks the standard input. Delimiters checked are:

Font changes using **\f***x* . . . **\fP**.

Size changes using **\s***x* . . . **\s0**.

Macros that come in open . . . close forms, for example, the **.TS** and **.TE** macros which must always come in pairs.

checknr knows about the **ms** and **me** macro packages.

checknr is intended to be used on documents that are prepared with **checknr** in mind. It expects a certain document writing style for **\f** and **\s** commands, in that each **\f***x* must be terminated with **\fP** and each **\s***x* must be terminated with **\s0**. While it will work to directly go into the next font or explicitly specify the original font or point size, and many existing documents actually do this, such a practice will produce complaints from **checknr**. Since it is probably better to use the **\fP** and **\s0** forms anyway, you should think of this as a contribution to your document preparation style.

The following options are available:

-f Ignore **\f** font changes.

-s Ignore **\s** size changes.

-a.*x1***.***y1* . . .
Add pairs of macros to the list. The pairs of macros are assumed to be those (such as **.DS** and **.DE**) that should be checked for balance. The **-a** option must be followed by groups of six characters, each group defining a pair of macros. The six characters are a period, the first macro name, another period, and the second macro name. For example, to define a pair **.BS** and **.BE**, use **-a.BS.BE**

-c.*x1* . . .
Define commands which **checknr** would otherwise complain about as undefined.

SEE ALSO

eqn(1), **me**(5), **ms**(5), **nroff**(1), **troff**(1)

NOTES

There is no way to define a one-character macro name using the **-a** option.

chgrp (1)

NAME

chgrp – change the group ownership of a file

SYNOPSIS

chgrp [-R] [-h] *group file* . . .

DESCRIPTION

chgrp changes the group ID of the *files* given as arguments to *group*. The group may be either a decimal group ID or a group name found in the group ID file, **/etc/group**.

You must be the owner of the file, or have appropriate privilege to use this command.

The operating system has a configuration option {**_POSIX_CHOWN_RESTRICTED**}, to restrict ownership changes. When this option is in effect, the owner of the file may change the group of the file only to a group to which the owner belongs. Only a privileged user can arbitrarily change owner **ID**s whether this option is in effect or not.

chgrp has two options:

-R Recursive. **chgrp** descends through the directory, and any subdirectories, setting the specified group ID as it proceeds. When symbolic links are encountered, they are traversed.

-h If the file is a symbolic link, change the group of the symbolic link. Without this option, the group of the file referenced by the symbolic link is changed.

FILES

/etc/group

/usr/lib/locale/*locale***/LC_MESSAGES/uxcore.abi**

language-specific message file [See **LANG** on **environ** (5).]

SEE ALSO

chmod(1), **chown**(1), **chown**(2), **group**(4), **id**(1M), **passwd**(4)

NAME

chkey – change user encryption key

SYNOPSIS

`chkey [-f]`

DESCRIPTION

The **chkey** command prompts for a password and uses it to encrypt a new user encryption key. The encrypted key is stored in the **publickey**(4) database.

Options

`-f` indicates to **chkey** that if the password given doesn't match the login password, it should be treated as a warning, and not a fatal error. This option can be used if the user believes that their password on the local NIS server may be out of date (due to a recently changed password, and the possibility that the new password hasn't been propagated through the system).

REFERENCES

keylogin(1), **keylogout**(1), **keyserv**(1M), **newkey**(1M), **publickey**(4)

chmod (1)

NAME

chmod – change file mode

SYNOPSIS

chmod [**-R**] *mode file* . . .
chmod [**ugoa**]{ + | - | = }[**rwxlstugo**] *file* . . .

DESCRIPTION

chmod changes or assigns the mode of a file. The mode of a file specifies its permissions and other attributes. The mode may be absolute or symbolic.

An absolute *mode* is specified using octal numbers:

chmod *nnnn file* . . .

where *n* is a number from 0 to 7. An absolute mode is constructed from the OR of any of the following modes:

4000	Set user ID on execution.
20#0	Set group ID on execution if # is **7**, **5**, **3**, or **1**. Enable mandatory locking if # is **6**, **4**, **2**, or **0**. This bit is ignored if the file is a directory; it may be set or cleared only using the symbolic mode.
1000	Turn on sticky bit [(see **chmod**(2)].
0400	Allow read by owner.
0200	Allow write by owner.
0100	Allow execute (search in directory) by owner.
0070	Allow read, write, and execute (search) by group.
0007	Allow read, write, and execute (search) by others.

Upon execution, the **setuid** and **setgid** modes affect interpreter scripts only if the first line of those scripts is

#! *pathname* [*arg*]

where *pathname* is the path of a command interpreter, such as **sh**. [See **exec**(2).]

A symbolic *mode* is specified in the following format:

chmod [*who*] *operator* [*permission(s)*] *file* . . .

who is zero or more of the characters **u**, **g**, **o**, and **a** specifying whose permissions are to be changed or assigned:

u	user's permissions
g	group's permissions
o	others' permissions
a	all permissions (user, group, and other)

If *who* is omitted, it defaults to **a**.

operator is one of +, –, or =, signifying how permissions are to be changed:

+	Add permissions.
–	Take away permissions.
=	Assign permissions absolutely.

Unlike other symbolic operations, = has an absolute effect in that it resets all other bits. Omitting *permission*(s) is useful only with = to take away all permissions.

permission(s) is any compatible combination of the following letters:

`r`	read permission
`w`	write permission
`x`	execute permission
`s`	user or group set-ID
`t`	sticky bit
`l`	mandatory locking
`u, g, o`	indicate that *permission* is to be taken from the current user, group or other mode respectively.

Permissions to a file may vary depending on your user identification number (UID) or group identification number (GID). Permissions are described in three sequences each having three characters:

User	Group	Other
`rwx`	`rwx`	`rwx`

This example (user, group, and others all have permission to read, write, and execute a given file) demonstrates two categories for granting permissions: the access class and the permissions themselves.

Multiple symbolic modes separated by commas may be given, though no spaces may intervene between these modes. Operations are performed in the order given. Multiple symbolic letters following a single operator cause the corresponding operations to be performed simultaneously.

The letter **s** is only meaningful with `u` or `g`, and `t` only works with `u`.

Mandatory file and record locking (`l`) refers to a file's ability to have its reading or writing permissions locked while a program is accessing that file. When locking is requested, the group ID of the user must be the same as the group ID of the file. It is not possible to permit group execution and enable a file to be locked on execution at the same time. In addition, it is not possible to turn on the set-group-ID bit and enable a file to be locked on execution at the same time. The following examples, therefore, are invalid and elicit error messages:

chmod g+x,+l *file*
chmod g+s,+l *file*

Only the owner of a file or directory (or a privileged user) may change that file's or directory's mode. Only a privileged user may set the sticky bit on a non-directory file. Otherwise, **chmod** will mask the sticky-bit but will not return an error. In order to turn on a file's set-group-ID bit, your own group ID must correspond to the file's and group execution must be set.

The **-R** option recursively descends through directory arguments, setting the mode for each file as described above. If a symbolic link is encountered whose target is a directory, the permission of the directory is changed. That directory's contents are *not* recursively traversed.

EXAMPLES

Deny execute permission to everyone:

```
chmod a-x file
```

Allow read permission to everyone:

```
chmod 444 file
```

Make a file readable and writable by the group and others:

```
chmod go+rw file
chmod 066 file
```

Cause a file to be locked during access:

```
chmod +l file
```

Allow everyone to read, write, and execute the file and turn on the set group-ID.

```
chmod =rwx,g+s file
chmod 2777 file
```

Absolute changes don't work for the set-group-ID bit of a directory. You must use **g+s** or **g-s**.

FILES

/usr/lib/locale/*locale***/LC_MESSAGES/uxcore.abi**
language-specific message file [See **LANG** on **environ** (5).]

SEE ALSO

chmod(2), **ls**(1)

NOTES

chmod permits you to produce useless modes so long as they are not illegal (e.g., making a text file executable). **chmod** does not check the file type to see if mandatory locking is available.

Normally, the effective user and group ID of a process is the user and group ID of the invoking process. If the set-user-ID (set-group-ID) on execution mode bit of an executable file is set, the effective user (group) ID of the process, when the file is invoked, is the owner (group) ID of the executable file. The real user ID and real group ID of the new process remain the same as those of the calling process.

Setting the "set-group-ID on execution" bit on a directory (via the **g+s** option) means that any files subsequently created in that directory will automatically be given the group ID of that directory.

Neither set-user-ID nor set-group-ID mode bits affect shell script privileges.

When symbolic links are created by **ln**, they are made with permissions set to read, write, and execute for owner, group, and world (**777**). A **chmod** applied to a symbolic link acts on the target of the link, not on the link itself.

NAME

chown – change file owner

SYNOPSIS

chown [-R] [-h] *owner file . . .*

DESCRIPTION

chown changes the owner of the *files* to *owner*. The value of *owner* may be either a decimal user ID or a login name found in the **/etc/passwd** file. Login names in **/etc/passwd** must begin with a non-numeric character; an alphabetic character or any special character except colon is acceptable.

If **chown** is invoked by someone other than a privileged user, the set-user-ID bit of the file mode, 04000, is cleared.

Only the owner of a file (or a privileged user) may change the owner of that file.

Valid options to **chown** are:

-R Recursive. **chown** descends through the directory, and any subdirectories, setting the ownership ID as it proceeds. When symbolic links are encountered, they are traversed.

-h If the file is a symbolic link, change the owner of the symbolic link. Without this option, the owner of the file referenced by the symbolic link is changed.

The operating system has a configuration option {**_POSIX_CHOWN_RESTRICTED**}, to restrict ownership changes. When this option is in effect the owner of the file is prevented from changing the owner ID of the file. Only a privileged user can arbitrarily change owner IDs whether this option is in effect or not.

FILES

/etc/passwd

/usr/lib/locale/*locale***/LC_MESSAGES/uxcore.abi**

language-specific message file [See **LANG** on **environ** (5).]

SEE ALSO

chgrp(1), **chmod**(1), **chown**(2), **passwd**(4)

NAME

chown – (BSD) change file owner

SYNOPSIS

/usr/ucb/chown [**-fhR**] *owner*[**.***group*] *file* . . .

DESCRIPTION

chown changes the owner of the *file*s to *owner*. The *owner* may be either a decimal user ID or a login name found in **/etc/passwd** file. The optional **.***group* suffix may be used to change the group at the same time.

If **chown** is invoked by other than the super-user, the set-user-ID bit of the file mode, 04000, is cleared.

Only the super-user may change the owner of a file.

Valid options to **chown** are:

- **-f** Suppress error reporting
- **-h** If the file is a symbolic link, change the owner of the symbolic link. Without this option, the owner of the file referenced by the symbolic link is changed.
- **-R** Descend recursively through directories setting the ownership ID of all files in each directory entered.

FILES

/etc/group
/etc/passwd

NOTES

In a Remote File Sharing environment, you may not have the permissions that the output of the **ls -l** command leads you to believe.

SEE ALSO

chgrp(1), **chmod**(1), **chown**(2), **passwd**(4)

NAME

chroot – change root directory for a command

SYNOPSIS

/usr/sbin/chroot *newroot command*

DESCRIPTION

chroot causes the given command to be executed relative to the new root. The meaning of any initial slashes (**/**) in the path names is changed for the command and any of its child processes to *newroot* . Furthermore, upon execution, the initial working directory is *newroot* .

Notice, however, that if you redirect the output of the command to a file:

chroot *newroot command* >**x**

will create the file **x** relative to the original root of the command, not the new one.

The new root path name is always relative to the current root: even if a **chroot** is currently in effect, the *newroot* argument is relative to the current root of the running process.

This command can be run only by a privileged user.

SEE ALSO

cd(1), **chroot**(2)

NOTES

One should exercise extreme caution when referencing device files in the new root file system.

When using **chroot**, do not exec a command that uses shared libraries. This will result in killing your process.

NAME

`chrtbl` – generate character classification and conversion tables

SYNOPSIS

`chrtbl` [*file*]

DESCRIPTION

The **chrtbl** command creates two tables containing information on character classification, upper/lowercase conversion, character-set width, and numeric formatting. One table is an array of (257∗2) + 7 bytes that is encoded so a table lookup can be used to determine the character classification of a character, convert a character [see **ctype**(3C)], and find the byte and screen width of a character in one of the supplementary code sets. The other table contains information about the format of non-monetary numeric quantities: the first byte specifies the decimal delimiter; the second byte specifies the thousands delimiter; and the remaining bytes comprise a null-terminated string indicating the grouping (each element of the string is taken as an integer that indicates the number of digits that comprise the current group in a formatted non-monetary numeric quantity).

chrtbl reads the user-defined character classification and conversion information from *file* and creates three output files in the current directory. To construct *file*, use the file supplied in **/usr/lib/locale/C/chrtbl_C** as a starting point. You may add entries, but do not change the original values supplied with the system. For example, for other locales you may wish to add eight-bit entries to the ASCII definitions provided in this file.

One output file, **ctype.c** (a C language source file), contains a (257*2)+7-byte array generated from processing the information from *file*. You should review the content of **ctype.c** to verify that the array is set up as you had planned. (In addition, an application program could use **ctype.c**.) The first 257 bytes of the array in **ctype.c** are used for character classification. The characters used for initializing these bytes of the array represent character classifications that are defined in **ctype.h**; for example, **_L** means a character is lowercase and **_S** | **_B** means the character is both a spacing character and a blank. The second 257 bytes of the array are used for character conversion. These bytes of the array are initialized so that characters for which you do not provide conversion information will be converted to themselves. When you do provide conversion information, the first value of the pair is stored where the second one would be stored normally, and vice versa; for example, if you provide **<0x41 0x61>**, then **0x61** is stored where **0x41** would be stored normally, and **0x61** is stored where **0x41** would be stored normally. The last 7 bytes are used for character width information for up to three supplementary code sets.

The second output file (a data file) contains the same information, but is structured for efficient use by the character classification and conversion routines [see **ctype**(3C)]. The name of this output file is the value you assign to the keyword **LC_CTYPE** read in from *file*. Before this file can be used by the character classification and conversion routines, it must be installed in the **/usr/lib/locale/***locale* directory with the name **LC_CTYPE** by someone who is super-user or a member of group **bin**. This file must be readable by user, group, and other; no other permissions should be set. To use the character classification and conversion tables in this file, set the **LC_CTYPE** environment variable appropriately [see **environ**(5) or **setlocale**(3C)].

The third output file (a data file) is created only if numeric formatting information is specified in the input file. The name of this output file is the value you assign to the keyword **LC_NUMERIC** read in from *file*. Before this file can be used, it must be installed in the **/usr/lib/locale/***locale* directory with the name **LC_NUMERIC** by someone who is super-user or a member of group **bin**. This file must be readable by user, group, and other; no other permissions should be set. To use the numeric formatting information in this file, set the **LC_NUMERIC** environment variable appropriately [see **environ**(5) or **setlocale**(3C)].

The name of the locale where you install the files **LC_CTYPE** and **LC_NUMERIC** should correspond to the conventions defined in *file*. For example, if French conventions were defined, and the name for the French locale on your system is **french**, then you should install the files in **/usr/lib/locale/french**.

If no input file is given, or if the argument "–" is encountered, **chrtbl** reads from standard input.

The syntax of *file* allows the user to define the names of the data files created by **chrtbl**, the assignment of characters to character classifications, the relationship between upper and lowercase letters, byte and screen widths for up to three supplementary code sets, and three items of numeric formatting information: the decimal delimiter, the thousands delimiter, and the grouping. The keywords recognized by **chrtbl** are:

LC_CTYPE	name of the data file created by **chrtbl** to contain character classification, conversion, and width information
isupper	character codes to be classified as uppercase letters
islower	character codes to be classified as lowercase letters
isdigit	character codes to be classified as numeric
isspace	character codes to be classified as spacing (delimiter) characters
ispunct	character codes to be classified as punctuation characters
iscntrl	character codes to be classified as control characters
isblank	character code for the blank (space) character
isxdigit	character codes to be classified as hexadecimal digits
ul	relationship between upper- and lowercase characters
cswidth	byte and screen width information (by default, each is one character wide)
LC_NUMERIC	name of the data file created by **chrtbl** to contain numeric formatting information
decimal_point	decimal delimiter
thousands_sep	thousands delimiter

grouping string in which each element is taken as an integer that indicates the number of digits that comprise the current group in a formatted non-monetary numeric quantity.

Any lines with the number sign (**#**) in the first column are treated as comments and are ignored. Blank lines are also ignored.

Characters for **isupper**, **islower**, **isdigit**, **isspace**, **ispunct**, **iscntrl**, **isblank**, **isxdigit**, and **ul** can be represented as a hexadecimal or octal constant (for example, the letter **a** can be represented as **0x61** in hexadecimal or **0141** in octal). Hexadecimal and octal constants may be separated by one or more space and/or tab characters.

The dash character (**-**) may be used to indicate a range of consecutive numbers. Zero or more space characters may be used for separating the dash character from the numbers.

The backslash character (\) is used for line continuation. Only a carriage return is permitted after the backslash character.

The relationship between upper- and lowercase letters (**ul**) is expressed as ordered pairs of octal or hexadecimal constants: *<uppercase_character lowercase_character>*. These two constants may be separated by one or more space characters. Zero or more space characters may be used for separating the angle brackets (< >) from the numbers.

The following is the format of an input specification for **cswidth**:

```
cswidth n1[[:s1][,n2[:s2][,n3[:s3]]]]
```

where,

n1 byte width for supplementary code set 1, required
s1 screen width for supplementary code set 1
n2 byte width for supplementary code set 2
s2 screen width for supplementary code set 2
n3 byte width for supplementary code set 3
s3 screen width for supplementary code set 3

decimal_point and **thousands_sep** are specified by a single character that gives the delimiter. **grouping** is specified by a quoted string in which each member may be in octal or hex representation. For example, **\3** or **\x3** could be used to set the value of a member of the string to 3.

In a C locale, or in a locale where the decimal point character is not defined, the decimal point character defaults to a period (.).

EXAMPLE

The following is an example of an input file used to create the USA-ENGLISH code set definition table in a file named **usa** and the non-monetary numeric formatting information in a file name **num-usa**.

```
LC_CTYPE   usa
isupper    0x41 - 0x5a
islower    0x61 - 0x7a
isdigit    0x30 - 0x39
isspace    0x20 0x9 - 0xd
```

```
ispunct    0x21 - 0x2f 0x3a - 0x40       \
           0x5b - 0x60 0x7b - 0x7e
iscntrl    0x0 - 0x1f  0x7f
isblank    0x20
isxdigit   0x30 - 0x39 0x61 - 0x66       \
           0x41 - 0x46
ul        <0x41 0x61> <0x42 0x62> <0x43 0x63>  \
          <0x44 0x64> <0x45 0x65> <0x46 0x66>  \
          <0x47 0x67> <0x48 0x68> <0x49 0x69>  \
          <0x4a 0x6a> <0x4b 0x6b> <0x4c 0x6c>  \
          <0x4d 0x6d> <0x4e 0x6e> <0x4f 0x6f>  \
          <0x50 0x70> <0x51 0x71> <0x52 0x72>  \
          <0x53 0x73> <0x54 0x74> <0x55 0x75>  \
          <0x56 0x76> <0x57 0x77> <0x58 0x78>  \
          <0x59 0x79> <0x5a 0x7a>
cswidth         1:1,0:0,0:0
LC_NUMERIC num_usa
decimal_point         .
thousands_sep         ,
grouping              "\3"
```

FILES

/usr/lib/locale/*locale*/LC_CTYPE
: data files containing character classification, conversion, and character-set width information created by **chrtbl**

/usr/lib/locale/*locale*/LC_NUMERIC
: data files containing numeric formatting information created by **chrtbl**

/usr/include/ctype.h
: header file containing information used by character classification and conversion routines

/usr/lib/locale/C/chrtbl_C
: input file used to construct **LC_CTYPE** and **LC_NUMERIC** in the default locale.

SEE ALSO

ctype(3C), **environ**(5), **setlocale**(3C)

DIAGNOSTICS

The error messages produced by **chrtbl** are intended to be self-explanatory. They indicate errors in the command line or syntactic errors encountered within the input file.

NOTES

Changing the files in **/usr/lib/locale/C** will cause the system to behave unpredictably.

ckbinarsys (1M)

NAME

ckbinarsys – determine whether remote system can accept binary messages

SYNOPSIS

ckbinarsys [**-S**] **-s** *remote_system_name* **-t** *msg_type*

DESCRIPTION

Because **rmail** can transport binary data, it may be important to determine whether a particular remote system (typically the next hop) can handle binary data via the chosen transport layer agent (uux, SMTP, and so on).

ckbinarsys consults the file **/etc/mail/binarsys** for information on a specific remote system. **ckbinarsys** returns its results via an appropriate exit code. An exit code of zero implies that it is OK to send a message with the indicated content type to the system specified. An exit code other than zero indicates either that the remote system cannot properly handle messages with binary content, or that there is no **binarsys** file.

Command-line arguments are:

-s *remote_system_name*	Name of remote system to look up in **/etc/mail/binarsys**
-t *content_type*	Content type of message to be sent. When invoked by **rmail**, this will be one of two strings: **text** or **binary**, as determined by **mail** independent of any **Content-Type:** header lines that may be present within the message header. All other arguments are treated as equivalent to **binary**.
-S	Normally, **ckbinarsys** will print a message (if the binary mail is rejected) which would be suitable for **rmail** to return in the negative acknowledgement mail. When **-S** is specified, no message will be printed.

In the absence of the **binarsys** file, the default is to not accept non-text mail messages.

FILES

/etc/mail/binarsys
/usr/lib/mail/surrcmd/ckbinarsys

SEE ALSO

binarsys(4), **mail**(1), **mailsurr**(4), **uux**(1C)

NAME

ckdate, **errdate**, **helpdate**, **valdate** – prompt for and validate a date

SYNOPSIS

ckdate [**-Q**] [**-W** *width*] [**-f** *format*] [**-d** *default*] [**-h** *help*] [**-e** *error*] [**-p** *prompt*]
[**-k** *pid* [**-s** *signal*]]

errdate [**-W** *width*] [**-e** *error*] [**-f** *format*]

helpdate [**-W** *width*] [**-h** *help*] [**-f** *format*]

valdate [**-f** *format*] *input*

DESCRIPTION

ckdate prompts a user and validates the response. It defines, among other things, a prompt message whose response should be a date, text for help and error messages, and a default value (which is returned if the user responds with a RETURN). The user response must match the defined format for a date.

All messages are limited in length to 70 characters and are formatted automatically. Any white space used in the definition (including newline) is stripped. The **-W** option cancels the automatic formatting. When a tilde is placed at the beginning or end of a message definition, the default text is inserted at that point, allowing both custom text and the default text to be displayed.

If the prompt, help or error message is not defined, the default message (as defined under NOTES) is displayed.

Three visual tool modules are linked to the **ckdate** command. They are **errdate** (which formats and displays an error message), **helpdate** (which formats and displays a help message), and **valdate** (which validates a response). These modules should be used in conjunction with FMLI objects. In this instance, the FMLI object defines the prompt. When *format* is defined in the **errdate** and **helpdate** modules, the messages describe the expected format.

The options and arguments for this command are:

-Q Do not allow quit as a valid response..

-W Use *width* as the line length for prompt, help, and error messages.

-f Verify input using *format*. Possible formats and their definitions are:
%b = abbreviated month name
%B = full month name
%d = day of month (01 – 31)
%D = date as *%m/%d/%y* (the default format)
%e = day of month (1 – 31; single digits are preceded by a blank)
%h = abbreviated month name (for example, **jan**, **feb**, **mar**)
%m = month number (01 – 12)
%y = year within century (for example, 91)
%Y = year as *CCYY* (for example, 1991)

-d The default value is *default*. The default is not validated and so does not have to meet any criteria.

`-h`	The help message is *help*.
`-e`	The error message is *error*.
`-p`	The prompt message is *prompt*.
`-k`	Send process ID *pid* a signal if the user chooses to abort.
`-s`	When quit is chosen, send *signal* to the process whose *pid* is specified by the **-k** option. If no signal is specified, use **SIGTERM**.
input	Input to be verified against format criteria.

EXIT CODES

0 = Successful execution
1 = EOF on input
1 = Usage error
3 = User termination (quit)
4 = Garbled format argument

NOTES

The default prompt for **ckdate** is:

```
Enter the date [?,q]
```

The default error message is:

```
ERROR - Please enter a date. Format is format.
```

The default help message is:

```
Please enter a date. Format is format.
```

When the quit option is chosen (and allowed), **q** is returned along with the return code 3. The **valdate** module does not produce any output. It returns zero for success and non-zero for failure.

NAME

ckgid, **errgid**, **helpgid**, **valgid** – prompt for and validate a group ID

SYNOPSIS

ckgid [**-Q**] [**-W** *width*] [**-m**] [**-d** *default*] [**-h** *help*] [**-e** *error*] [**-p** *prompt*] [**-k** *pid* [**-s** *signal*]]

errgid [**-W** *width*] [**-e** *error*]

helpgid [**-W** *width*] [**-m**] [**-h** *help*]

valgid *input*

DESCRIPTION

ckgid prompts a user and validates the response. It defines, among other things, a prompt message whose response should be an existing group ID, text for help and error messages, and a default value (which is returned if the user responds with a RETURN).

All messages are limited in length to 70 characters and are formatted automatically. Any white space used in the definition (including newline) is stripped. The **-W** option cancels the automatic formatting. When a tilde is placed at the beginning or end of a message definition, the default text is inserted at that point, allowing both custom text and the default text to be displayed.

If the prompt, help or error message is not defined, the default message (as defined under NOTES) is displayed.

Three visual tool modules are linked to the **ckgid** command. They are **errgid** (which formats and displays an error message), **helpgid** (which formats and displays a help message), and **valgid** (which validates a response). These modules should be used in conjunction with FML objects. In this instance, the FML object defines the prompt.

The options and arguments for this command are:

- **-Q** Do not allow quit as a valid response.
- **-W** Use *width* as the line length for prompt, help, and error messages.
- **-m** Display a list of all groups when help is requested or when the user makes an error.
- **-d** The default value is *default*. The default is not validated and so does not have to meet any criteria.
- **-h** The help message is *help*.
- **-e** The error message is *error*.
- **-p** The prompt message is *prompt*.
- **-k** Send process ID *pid* a signal if the user chooses to abort.
- **-s** When quit is chosen, send *signal* to the process whose *pid* is specified by the **-k** option. If no signal is specified, use **SIGTERM**.
- *input* Input to be verified against **/etc/group**

EXIT CODES

0 = Successful execution
1 = EOF on input
1 = Usage error
3 = User termination (quit)

NOTES

The default prompt for **ckgid** is:

```
Enter the name of an existing group [?,q]
```

The default error message is:

```
ERROR - Please enter the name of an existing group.
```
(if the **-m** *option of* **ckgid** *is used, a list of valid groups is displayed here)*

The default help message is:

```
Please enter an existing group name.
```
(if the **-m** *option of* **ckgid** *is used, a list of valid groups is displayed here)*

When the quit option is chosen (and allowed), **q** is returned along with the return code 3. The **valgid** module does not produce any output. It returns zero for success and non-zero for failure.

NAME

`ckint` – display a prompt; verify and return an integer value

SYNOPSIS

ckint [**-Q**] [**-W** *width*] [**-b** *base*] [**-d** *default*] [**-h** *help*] [**-e** *error*]
[**-p** *prompt*] [**-k** *pid* [**-s** *signal*]]

errint [**-W** *width*] [**-b** *base*] [**-e** *error*]

helpint [**-W** *width*] [**-b** *base*] [**-h** *help*]

valint [**-b** *base*] *input*

DESCRIPTION

ckint prompts a user, then validates the response. It defines, among other things, a prompt message whose response should be an integer, text for help and error messages, and a default value (which is returned if the user responds with a RETURN).

All messages are limited in length to 70 characters and are formatted automatically. Any white space used in the definition (including newline) is stripped. The **-W** option cancels the automatic formatting. When a tilde is placed at the beginning or end of a message definition, the default text is inserted at that point, allowing both custom text and the default text to be displayed.

If the prompt, help or error message is not defined, the default message (as defined under NOTES) is displayed.

Three visual tool modules are linked to the **ckint** command. They are **errint** (which formats and displays an error message), **helpint** (which formats and displays a help message), and **valint** (which validates a response). These modules should be used in conjunction with FML objects. In this instance, the FML object defines the prompt. When *base* is defined in the **errint** and **helpint** modules, the messages includes the expected base of the input.

The options and arguments for this command are:

-Q Do not allow quit as a valid response.

-W Use *width* as the line length for prompt, help, and error messages.

-b The base for input is *base*. Must be 2 to 36, default is 10.

-d The default value is *default*. The default is not validated and so does not have to meet any criteria.

-h The help message is *help*.

-e The error message is *error*.

-p The prompt message is *prompt*.

-k Send process ID *pid* a signal if the user chooses to abort.

-s When quit is chosen, send *signal* to the process whose *pid* is specified by the **-k** option. If no signal is specified, use **SIGTERM**.

input Input to be verified against *base* criterion.

EXIT CODES

`0` = Successful execution
`1` = EOF on input
`1` = Usage error
`3` = User termination (quit)

NOTES

The default base 10 prompt for **ckint** is:

```
Enter an integer [?,q]
```

The default base 10 error message is:

```
ERROR - Please enter an integer.
```

The default base 10 help message is:

```
Please enter an integer.
```

The messages are changed from "**integer**" to "**base** *base* **integer**" *if the base is set to a number other than 10.*

When the quit option is chosen (and allowed), **q** is returned along with the return code `3`. The **valint** module does not produce any output. It returns zero for success and non-zero for failure.

NAME

ckitem – build a menu; prompt for and return a menu item

SYNOPSIS

ckitem [**-Q**] [**-W** *width*] [**-uno**] [**-f** *file*] [**-l** *label*]
[[**-i** *invis*] [**-i** *invis*] . . .] [**-m** *max*] [**-d** *default*] [**-h** *help*] [**-e** *error*]
[**-p** *prompt*] [**-k** *pid* [**-s** *signal*]] [*choice1 choice2* . . .]

erritem [**-W** *width*] [**-e** *error*] [*choice1 choice2* . . .]

helpitem [**-W** *width*] [**-h** *help*] [*choice1 choice2* . . .]

DESCRIPTION

ckitem builds a menu and prompts the user to choose one item from a menu of items. It then verifies the response. Options for this command define, among other things, a prompt message whose response is a menu item, text for help and error messages, and a default value (which is returned if the user responds with a RETURN).

By default, the menu is formatted so that each item is prepended by a number and is printed in columns across the terminal. Column length is determined by the longest choice. Items are alphabetized.

All messages are limited in length to 70 characters and are formatted automatically. Any white space used in the definition (including newline) is stripped. The **-W** option cancels the automatic formatting. When a tilde is placed at the beginning or end of a message definition, the default text is inserted at that point, allowing both custom text and the default text to be displayed.

If the prompt, help or error message is not defined, the default message (as defined under NOTES) is displayed.

Two visual tool modules are linked to the **ckitem** command. They are **erritem** (which formats and displays an error message) and **helpitem** (which formats and displays a help message). These modules should be used in conjunction with FML objects. In this instance, the FML object defines the prompt. When *choice* is defined in these modules, the messages describe the available menu choice (or choices).

The options and arguments for this command are:

-Q Do not allow quit as a valid response.

-W Use *width* as the line length for prompt, help, and error messages.

-u Display menu items as an unnumbered list.

-n Do not display menu items in alphabetical order.

-o Return only one menu token.

-f *file* contains a list of menu items to be displayed. [The format of this file is: *token<tab>description*. Lines beginning with a pound sign ("#") are comments and are ignored.]

-l Print *label* above the menu.

- `-i` *invis* specifies invisible menu choices (choices not to be printed in the menu). For example, "**all**" used as an invisible choice would mean it is a valid option but does not appear in the menu. Any number of invisible choices may be defined. Invisible choices should be made known to a user either in the prompt or in a help message.
- `-m` The maximum number of menu choices allowed is *m*.
- `-d` The default value is *default*. The default is not validated and so does not have to meet any criteria.
- `-h` The help message is *help*.
- `-e` The error message is *error*.
- `-p` The prompt message is *prompt*.
- `-k` Send process ID *pid* a signal if the user chooses to abort.
- `-s` When quit is chosen, send *signal* to the process whose *pid* is specified by the **-k** option. If no signal is specified, use **SIGTERM**.
- *choice* Defines menu items. Items should be separated by white space or newline.

EXIT CODES

0 = Successful execution
1 = EOF on input
1 = Usage error
3 = User termination (quit)
4 = No choices from which to choose

NOTES

The user may input the number of the menu item if choices are numbered or as much of the string required for a unique identification of the item. Long menus are paged with 10 items per page.

When menu entries are defined both in a file (by using the **-f** option) and also on the command line, they are usually combined alphabetically. However, if the **-n** option is used to suppress alphabetical ordering, then the entries defined in the file are shown first, followed by the options defined on the command line.

The default prompt for **ckitem** is:

```
Enter selection [?,??,q]:
```

One question mark gives a help message and then redisplays the prompt. Two question marks gives a help message and then redisplays the menu label, the menu and the prompt.

The default error message is:

```
ERROR - Does not match an available menu selection.
Enter one of the following:
- the number of the menu item you wish to select
- the token associated withe the menu item,
- partial string which uniquely identifies the token
   for the menu item
- ?? to reprint the menu
```

The default help message is:

```
Enter one of the following:
– the number of the menu item you wish to select
– the token associated with the menu item,
– partial string which uniquely identifies the token
   for the menu item
– ?? to reprint the menu
```

When the quit option is chosen (and allowed), `q` is returned along with the return code `3`.

ckkeywd (1)

NAME

ckkeywd – prompt for and validate a keyword

SYNOPSIS

ckkeywd [**-Q**] [**-W** *width*] [**-d** *default*] [**-h** *help*] [**-e** *error*] [**-p** *prompt*]
[**-k** *pid* [**-s** *signal*]] [*keyword* . . .]

DESCRIPTION

ckkeywd prompts a user and validates the response. It defines, among other things, a prompt message whose response should be one of a list of keywords, text for help and error messages, and a default value (which is returned if the user responds with a RETURN). The answer returned from this command must match one of the defined list of keywords.

All messages are limited in length to 70 characters and are formatted automatically. Any white space used in the definition (including newline) is stripped. The **-W** option cancels the automatic formatting. When a tilde is placed at the beginning or end of a message definition, the default text is inserted at that point, allowing both custom text and the default text to be displayed.

If the prompt, help or error message is not defined, the default message (as defined under NOTES) is displayed.

-Q Do not allow quit as a valid response.

-W Use *width* as the line length for prompt, help, and error messages.

-d The default value is *default*. The default is not validated and so does not have to meet any criteria.

-h The help message is *help*.

-e The error message is *error*.

-p The prompt message is *prompt*.

-k Send process ID *pid* a signal if the user chooses to abort.

-s When quit is chosen, send *signal* to the process whose *pid* is specified by the **-k** option. If no signal is specified, use **SIGTERM**.

keyword The keyword, or list of keywords, against which the answer is to be verified is *keyword*.

EXIT CODES

0 = Successful execution
1 = EOF on input
1 = Usage error
3 = User termination (quit)
4 = No keywords from which to choose

NOTES

The default prompt for **ckkeywd** is:

Enter appropriate value [*keyword*[, . . .],?,q]

The default error message is:

```
ERROR - Please enter one of the following keywords:
```
keyword`[, . . . ]`

The default help message is:

```
Please enter one of the following keywords:
```
keyword`[, . . . ]`

When the quit option is chosen (and allowed), `q` is returned along with the return code `3`.

ckpath (1)

NAME

ckpath – display a prompt; verify and return a pathname

SYNOPSIS

ckpath [**-Q**] [**-W** *width*] [**-a**| **l**] [*file_options*] [**-rtwx**] [**-d** *default*]
[**-h** *help*] [**-e** *error*] [**-p** *prompt*] [**-k** *pid* [**-s** *signal*]]

errpath [**-W** *width*] [**-a**| **l**] [*file_options*] [**-rtwx**] [**-e** *error*]

helppath [**-W** *width*] [**-a**| **l**] [*file_options*] [**-rtwx**] [**-h** *help*]

valpath [**-a**| **l**] [*file_options*] [**-rtwx**] *input*

DESCRIPTION

ckpath prompts a user and validates the response. It defines, among other things, a prompt message whose response should be a pathname, text for help and error messages, and a default value (which is returned if the user responds with a RETURN).

The pathname must obey the criteria specified by the first group of options. If no criteria are defined, the pathname must be for a normal file that does not yet exist. If neither **-a** (absolute) or **-l** (relative) is given, then either is assumed to be valid.

All messages are limited in length to 70 characters and are formatted automatically. Any white space used in the definition (including newline) is stripped. The **-W** option cancels the automatic formatting. When a tilde is placed at the beginning or end of a message definition, the default text is inserted at that point, allowing both custom text and the default text to be displayed.

If the prompt, help or error message is not defined, the default message (as defined under NOTES) is displayed.

Three visual tool modules are linked to the **ckpath** command. They are **errpath** (which formats and displays an error message), **helppath** (which formats and displays a help message), and **valpath** (which validates a response). These modules should be used in conjunction with FACE objects. In this instance, the FACE object defines the prompt.

The options and arguments for this command are:

-Q Do not allow quit as a valid response.

-W Use *width* as the line length for prompt, help, and error messages.

-a Pathname must be an absolute path.

-l Pathname must be a relative path.

-r Pathname must be readable.

-t Pathname must be creatable (touchable). Pathname is created if it does not already exist.

-w Pathname must be writable.

-x Pathname must be executable.

-d The default value is *default*. The default is not validated and so does not have to meet any criteria.

`-h` The help message is *help*.

`-e` The error message is *error*.

`-p` The prompt message is *prompt*.

`-k` Send process ID *pid* a signal if the user chooses to abort.

`-s` When quit is chosen, send *signal* to the process whose *pid* is specified by the **-k** option. If no signal is specified, use **SIGTERM**.

input Input to be verified against validation options.

file_options are:

`-b` Pathname must be a block special file.

`-c` Pathname must be a character special file.

`-f` Pathname must be a regular file.

`-y` Pathname must be a directory.

`-n` Pathname must not exist (must be new).

`-o` Pathname must exist (must be old).

`-z` Pathname must be a file with the size greater than 0 bytes.

The following *file_options* are mutually exclusive: **-bcfy**, **-no**, **-nz**, **-bz**, **-cz**.

EXIT CODES

0 = Successful execution
1 = EOF on input
1 = Usage error
3 = User termination (quit)
4 = Mutually exclusive options

NOTES

The text of the default messages for **ckpath** depends upon the criteria options that have been used. An example default prompt for **ckpath** (using the **-a** option) is:

```
Enter an absolute pathname [?,q]
```

An example default error message (using the **-a** option) is:

```
ERROR - Pathname must begin with a slash (/).
```

An example default help message is:

```
A pathname is a filename, optionally preceded by parent
directories. The pathname you enter:
– must contain 1 to NAME_MAX characters
– must not contain a spaces or special characters
```

NAME_MAX is a system variable is defined in **limits.h**.

When the quit option is chosen (and allowed), **q** is returned along with the return code 3. The **valpath** module does not produce any output. It returns zero for success and non-zero for failure.

NAME

ckrange – prompt for and validate an integer

SYNOPSIS

ckrange [**-Q**] [**-W** *width*] [**-l** *lower*] [**-u** *upper*] [**-b** *base*] [**-d** *default*] [**-h** *help*] [**-e** *error*] [**-p** *prompt*] [**-k** *pid* [**-s** *signal*]]

errange [**-W** *width*] [**-l** *lower*] [**-u** *upper*] [**-e** *error*] [**-b** *base*]

helprange [**-W** *width*] [**-l** *lower*] [**-u** *upper*] [**-h** *help*] [**-b** *base*]

valrange [**-l** *lower*] [**-u** *upper*] [**-b** *base*] *input*

DESCRIPTION

ckrange prompts a user and validates the response. It defines, among other things, a prompt message whose response should be an integer in the range specified, text for help and error messages, and a default value (which is returned if the user responds with a RETURN).

This command also defines a range for valid input. If either the lower or upper limit is left undefined, then the range is bounded on only one end.

All messages are limited in length to 70 characters and are formatted automatically. Any white space used in the definition (including newline) is stripped. The **-W** option cancels the automatic formatting. When a tilde is placed at the beginning or end of a message definition, the default text is inserted at that point, allowing both custom text and the default text to be displayed.

If the prompt, help or error message is not defined, the default message (as defined under NOTES) is displayed.

Three visual tool modules are linked to the **ckrange** command. They are **errange** (which formats and displays an error message), **helprange** (which formats and displays a help message), and **valrange** (which validates a response). These modules should be used in conjunction with FACE objects. In this instance, the FACE object defines the prompt.

The options and arguments for this command are:

-Q Do not allow quit as a valid response.

-W Use *width* as the line length for prompt, help, and error messages.

-l The lower limit of the range is *lower*. Default is the machine's largest negative integer or long.

-u The upper limit of the range is *upper*. Default is the machine's largest positive integer or long.

-b The base for input is *base*. Must be 2 to 36, default is 10.

-d The default value is *default*. The default is not validated and so does not have to meet any criteria. If *default* is non-numeric, **ckrange** returns 0 and not the alphabetic string.

-h The help message is *help*.

`-e` The error message is *error*.

`-p` The prompt message is *prompt*.

`-k` Send process ID *pid* a signal if the user chooses to abort.

`-s` When quit is chosen, send *signal* to the process whose *pid* is specified by the `-k` option. If no signal is specified, use `SIGTERM`.

input Input to be verified against upper and lower limits and base.

EXIT CODES

`0` = Successful execution
`1` = EOF on input
`1` = Usage error
`3` = User termination (quit)

NOTES

The default base 10 prompt for **`ckrange`** is:

`Enter an integer between` *lower* **`and`** *upper* `[`*lower–upper*`,q,?]`

The default base 10 error message is:

`ERROR - Please enter an integer between` *lower* **`and`** *upper*`.`

The default base 10 help message is:

`Please enter an integer between` *lower* **`and`** *upper*`.`

The messages are changed from "**`integer`**" to "**`base`** *base* **`integer`**" *if the base is set to a number other than 10.*

When the quit option is chosen (and allowed), **`q`** is returned along with the return code `3`. The **`valrange`** module does not produce any output. It returns zero for success and non-zero for failure.

NAME

ckroot(vxfs) – set mount options for root file system

SYNOPSIS

/etc/fs/vxfs/ckroot

DESCRIPTION

ckroot reads the mount options for the root file system from /etc/vfstab and uses the VX_SETROOTFSOPT ioctl to set the mount options for the root file system.

ckroot is invoked by the /sbin/ckroot script before the root file system is mounted for read/write access. If the root is dirty, fsck is run by /sbin/ckroot before ckroot is invoked.

SEE ALSO

vxfs-specific fsck(1M), init(1M), vxfsio(7)

NAME

`ckstr` – display a prompt; verify and return a string answer

SYNOPSIS

ckstr [-Q] [-W *width*] [[-r *regexp*] [-r *regexp*] . . .] [-l *length*]
[-d *default*] [-h *help*] [-e *error*] [-p *prompt*] [-k *pid* [-s *signal*]]

errstr [-W *width*] [-e *error*] [[-r *regexp*] [-r *regexp*] . . .] [-l *length*]

helpstr [-W *width*] [-h *help*] [[-r *regexp*] [-r *regexp*] . . .] [-l *length*]

valstr *input* [[-r *regexp*] [-r *regexp*] . . .] [-l *length*]

DESCRIPTION

`ckstr` prompts a user and validates the response. It defines, among other things, a prompt message whose response should be a string, text for help and error messages, and a default value (which is returned if the user responds with a RETURN).

The answer returned from this command must match the defined regular expression and be no longer than the length specified. If no regular expression is given, valid input must be a string with a length less than or equal to the length defined with no internal white space. Leading and/or trailing white spaces are ignored. If no length is defined, the length is not checked. Either a regular expression or a length must be given with the command.

All messages are limited in length to 70 characters and are formatted automatically. Any white space used in the definition (including newline) is stripped. The `-W` option cancels the automatic formatting. When a tilde is placed at the beginning or end of a message definition, the default text is inserted at that point, allowing both custom text and the default text to be displayed.

If the prompt, help or error message is not defined, the default message (as defined under NOTES) is displayed.

Three visual tool modules are linked to the `ckstr` command. They are **errstr** (which formats and displays an error message), **helpstr** (which formats and displays a help message), and **valstr** (which validates a response). These modules should be used in conjunction with FACE objects. In this instance, the FACE object defines the prompt.

The options and arguments for this command are:

`-Q` Do not allow quit as a valid response.

`-W` Use *width* as the line length for prompt, help, and error messages.

`-r` Validate the input against regular expression *regexp*. May include white space. If multiple expressions are defined, the answer need match only one of them.

`-l` The maximum length of the input is *length*.

`-d` The default value is *default*. The default is not validated and so does not have to meet any criteria.

`-h` The help message is *help*.

-e	The error message is *error*.
-p	The prompt message is *prompt*.
-k	Send process ID *pid* a signal if the user chooses to abort.
-s	When quit is chosen, send *signal* to the process whose *pid* is specified by the **-k** option. If no signal is specified, use **SIGTERM**.
input	Input to be verified against format length and/or regular expression criteria.

EXIT CODES

0 = Successful execution
1 = EOF on input
1 = Usage error
3 = User termination (quit)

NOTES

The default prompt for **ckstr** is:

```
Enter an appropriate value [?,q]
```

The default error message is dependent upon the type of validation involved. The user is told either that the length or the pattern matching failed.

The default help message is also dependent upon the type of validation involved. If a regular expression has been defined, the message is:

Please enter a string which matches the following pattern:
regexp

Other messages define the length requirement and the definition of a string.

When the quit option is chosen (and allowed), **q** is returned along with the return code 3. The **valstr** module does not produce any output. It returns zero for success and non-zero for failure.

Unless a "**q**" for "quit" is disabled by the **-Q** option, a single "**q**" to the following

```
ckstr -rq
```

is treated as a "quit" and not as a pattern match.

NAME

cktime – display a prompt; verify and return a time of day

SYNOPSIS

cktime [**-Q**] [**-W** *width*] [**-f** *format*] [**-d** *default*] [**-h** *help*] [**-e** *error*] [**-p** *prompt*]
[**-k** *pid* [**-s** *signal*]]

errtime [**-W** *width*] [**-e** *error*] [**-f** *format*]

helptime [**-W** *width*] [**-h** *help*] [**-f** *format*]

valtime [**-f** *format*] *input*

DESCRIPTION

cktime prompts a user and validates the response. It defines, among other things, a prompt message whose response should be a time, text for help and error messages, and a default value (which is returned if the user responds with a RETURN). The user response must match the defined format for the time of day.

All messages are limited in length to 70 characters and are formatted automatically. Any white space used in the definition (including newline) is stripped. The **-W** option cancels the automatic formatting. When a tilde is placed at the beginning or end of a message definition, the default text is inserted at that point, allowing both custom text and the default text to be displayed.

If the prompt, help or error message is not defined, the default message (as defined under NOTES) is displayed.

Three visual tool modules are linked to the **cktime** command. They are **errtime** (which formats and displays an error message), **helptime** (which formats and displays a help message), and **valtime** (which validates a response). These modules should be used in conjunction with FMLI objects. In this instance, the FMLI object defines the prompt. When *format* is defined in the **errtime** and **helptime** modules, the messages describe the expected format.

The options and arguments for this command are:

-Q Do not allow quit as a valid response.

-W Use *width* as the line length for prompt, help, and error messages.

-f Verify the input against *format*. Possible formats and their definitions are:

%H = hour (00 – 23)
%I = hour (00 – 12)
%M = minute (00 – 59)
%p = ante meridian or post meridian
%r = time as **%I:%M:%S %p**
%R = time as **%H:%M** (the default format)
%S = seconds (00 – 59)
%T = time as **%H:%M:%S**

-d The default value is *default*. The default is not validated and so does not have to meet any criteria.

-h The help message is *help*.

-e The error message is *error*.

-p The prompt message is *prompt*.

-k *pid* Send process ID *pid* a signal if the user chooses to abort.

-s *signal*
When quit is chosen, send *signal* to the process whose *pid* is specified by the **-k** option. If no signal is specified, use **SIGTERM**.

input Input to be verified against format criteria.

EXIT CODES

0 = Successful execution
1 = EOF on input
1 = Usage error
3 = User termination (quit)
4 = Garbled format argument

NOTES

The default prompt for **cktime** is:

Enter a time of day [?,q]

The default error message is:

ERROR - Please enter the time of day. Format is *format*.

The default help message is:

Please enter the time of day. Format is *format*.

When the quit option is chosen (and allowed), **q** is returned along with the return code 3. The **valtime** module does not produce any output. It returns zero for success and non-zero for failure.

NAME

ckuid – prompt for and validate a user ID

SYNOPSIS

ckuid [**-Q**] [**-W** *width*] [**-m**] [**-d** *default*] [**-h** *help*] [**-e** *error*] [**-p** *prompt*]
[**-k** *pid* [**-s** *signal*]]

erruid [**-W** *width*] [**-e** *error*]

helpuid [**-W** *width*] [**-m**] [**-h** *help*]

valuid *input*

DESCRIPTION

ckuid prompts a user and validates the response. It defines, among other things, a prompt message whose response should be an existing user ID, text for help and error messages, and a default value (which is returned if the user responds with a RETURN).

All messages are limited in length to 70 characters and are formatted automatically. Any white space used in the definition (including newline) is stripped. The **-W** option cancels the automatic formatting. When a tilde is placed at the beginning or end of a message definition, the default text is inserted at that point, allowing both custom text and the default text to be displayed.

If the prompt, help or error message is not defined, the default message (as defined under NOTES) is displayed.

Three visual tool modules are linked to the **ckuid** command. They are **erruid** (which formats and displays an error message), **helpuid** (which formats and displays a help message), and **valuid** (which validates a response). These modules should be used in conjunction with FML objects. In this instance, the FML object defines the prompt.

The options and arguments for this command are:

-Q Do not allow quit as a valid response.

-W Use *width* as the line length for prompt, help, and error messages.

-m Display a list of all logins when help is requested or when the user makes an error.

-d The default value is *default*. The default is not validated and so does not have to meet any criteria.

-h The help message is *help*.

-e The error message is *error*.

-p The prompt message is *prompt*.

-k Send process ID *pid* a signal if the user chooses to abort.

-s When quit is chosen, send *signal* to the process whose *pid* is specified by the **-k** option. If no signal is specified, use **SIGTERM**.

input Input to be verified against **/etc/passwd**.

EXIT CODES

`0` = Successful execution
`1` = EOF on input
`1` = Usage error
`3` = User termination (quit)

NOTES

The default prompt for **ckuid** is:

Enter the login name of an existing user [?,q]

The default error message is:

ERROR - Please enter the login name of an existing user.
(If the **-m** *option of* **ckuid** *is used, a list of valid users is also displayed.)*

The default help message is:

Please enter the login name of an existing user.
(If the **-m** *option of* **ckuid** *is used, a list of valid users is also displayed.)*

When the quit option is chosen (and allowed), **q** is returned along with the return code `3`. The **valuid** module does not produce any output. It returns zero for success and non-zero for failure.

NAME

ckyorn – prompt for and validate yes/no

SYNOPSIS

ckyorn [**-Q**] [**-W** *width*] [**-d** *default*] [**-h** *help*] [**-e** *error*] [**-p** *prompt*]
[**-k** *pid* [**-s** *signal*]]

erryorn [**-W** *width*] [**-e** *error*]

helpyorn [**-W** *width*] [**-h** *help*]

valyorn *input*

DESCRIPTION

ckyorn prompts a user and validates the response. It defines, among other things, a prompt message for a yes or no answer, text for help and error messages, and a default value (which is returned if the user responds with a RETURN).

All messages are limited in length to 70 characters and are formatted automatically. Any white space used in the definition (including newline) is stripped. The **-W** option cancels the automatic formatting. For the **-h** and **-e** options, placing a tilde at the beginning or end of a message definition causes the default text to be inserted at that point. This allows both custom text and the default text to be displayed.

If the prompt, help or error message is not defined, the default message (as defined under NOTES) is displayed.

Three visual tool modules are linked to the **ckyorn** command. They are **erryorn** (which formats and displays an error message), **helpyorn** (which formats and displays a help message), and **valyorn** (which validates a response). These modules should be used in conjunction with FACE objects. In this instance, the FACE object defines the prompt.

The options and arguments for this command are:

-Q Do not allow quit as a valid response.

-W Use *width* as the line length for prompt, help, and error messages.

-d The default value is *default*. The default is not validated and so does not have to meet any criteria.

-h The help message is *help*.

-e The error message is *error*.

-p The prompt message is *prompt*.

-k Send process ID *pid* a signal if the user chooses to abort.

-s When quit is chosen, send *signal* to the process whose *pid* is specified by the **-k** option. If no signal is specified, use **SIGTERM**.

input Input to be verified as **y**, **yes**, **Y**, **Yes**, **YES** or **n**, **no**, **N**, **No**, **NO**.

EXIT CODES

0 = Successful execution
1 = EOF on input
1 = Usage error
3 = User termination (quit)

NOTES

The default prompt for **ckyorn** is:

```
Yes or No [y,n,?,q]
```

The default error message is:

```
ERROR - Please enter yes or no.
```

The default help message is:

```
Enter y or yes if your answer is yes;
or no if your answer is no.
```

When the quit option is chosen (and allowed), **q** is returned along with the return code 3. The **valyorn** module does not produce any output. It returns zero for success and non-zero for failure.

NAME

`clear` – clear the terminal screen

SYNOPSIS

`clear`

DESCRIPTION

`clear` clears your screen if this is possible. It looks in the environment for the terminal type and then in the `terminfo` database to figure out how to clear the screen.

SEE ALSO

`terminfo`(4), `tput`(1)

cmp(1)

NAME

cmp – compare two files

SYNOPSIS

cmp [**-l**] [**-s**] *file1 file2* [*skip1* [*skip2*]]

DESCRIPTION

The two files are compared. (If *file1* is **-**, the standard input is used.) Under default options, **cmp** makes no comment if the files are the same; if they differ, it announces the byte and line number at which the difference occurred. If one file is an initial subsequence of the other, that fact is noted. *skip1* and *skip2* are initial byte offsets into *file1* and *file2* respectively, and may be either octal or decimal; a leading **0** denotes octal.

Options:

-l Print the byte number (decimal) and the differing bytes (octal) for each difference.

-s Print nothing for differing files; return codes only.

FILES

/usr/lib/locale/*locale***/LC_MESSAGES/uxcore.abi**
language-specific message file [See **LANG** on **environ**(5).]

SEE ALSO

comm(1), **diff**(1)

DIAGNOSTICS

Exit code **0** is returned for identical files, **1** for different files, and **2** for an inaccessible or missing argument.

NAME

`cof2elf` – COFF to ELF object file translation

SYNOPSIS

`cof2elf [-iqV] [-Q{yn}] [-s` *directory*`]` *files*

DESCRIPTION

`cof2elf` converts one or more COFF object *files* to ELF. This translation occurs in place, meaning the original file contents are modified. If an input file is an archive, each member will be translated as necessary, and the archive will be rebuilt with its members in the original order. `cof2elf` does not change input files that are not COFF.

Options have the following meanings.

`-i` Normally, the files are modified only when full translation occurs. Unrecognized data, such as unknown relocation types, are treated as errors and prevent translation. Giving the `-i` flag ignores these partial translation conditions and modifies the file anyway.

`-q` Normally, `cof2elf` prints a message for each file it examines, telling whether the file was translated, ignored, and so forth. The `-q` flag (for quiet) suppresses these messages.

`-Q`*arg* If *arg* is `y`, identification information about `cof2elf` will be added to the output files. This can be useful for software administration. Giving `n` for *arg* explicitly asks for no such information, which is the default behavior.

`-s`*directory* As mentioned above, `cof2elf` modifies the input files. This option saves a copy of the original files in the specified *directory*, which must exist. `cof2elf` does not save files it does not modify.

`-V` This flag tells `cof2elf` to print a version message on standard error.

SEE ALSO

`a.out`(4), `ar`(4), `elf`(3E), `ld`(1)

NOTES

Some debugging information is discarded. Although this does not affect the behavior of a running program, it may affect the information available for symbolic debugging.

`cof2elf` translates only COFF relocatable files. It does not translate executable or static shared library files for two main reasons. First, the operating system supports executable files and static shared libraries, making translation unnecessary. Second, those files have specific address and alignment constraints determined by the file format. Matching the constraints with a different object file format is problematic.

When possible, programmers should recompile their source code to build new object files. `cof2elf` is provided for those times when source code is unavailable.

col(1)

NAME

`col` – filter reverse line-feeds

SYNOPSIS

`col` [`-b`] [`-f`] [`-x`] [`-p`]

DESCRIPTION

`col` reads from the standard input and writes onto the standard output. It performs the line overlays implied by reverse line feeds (ASCII code ESC-`7`), and by forward and reverse half-line-feeds (ESC-`9` and ESC-`8`). `col` is particularly useful for filtering multicolumn output made with the `.rt` command of `nroff` and output resulting from use of the `tbl`(1) preprocessor.

If the `-b` option is given, `col` assumes that the output device in use is not capable of backspacing. In this case, if two or more characters are to appear in the same place, only the last one read will be output.

Although `col` accepts half-line motions in its input, it normally does not emit them on output. Instead, text that would appear between lines is moved to the next lower full-line boundary. This treatment can be suppressed by the `-f` (fine) option; in this case, the output from `col` may contain forward half-line-feeds (ESC-`9`), but will still never contain either kind of reverse line motion.

Unless the `-x` option is given, `col` will convert white space to tabs on output wherever possible to shorten printing time.

The ASCII control characters SO (\017) and SI (\016) are assumed by `col` to start and end text in an alternate character set. The character set to which each input character belongs is remembered, and on output SI and SO characters are generated as appropriate to ensure that each character is printed in the correct character set.

On input, the only control characters accepted are space, backspace, tab, return, new-line, SI, SO, VT (\013), and ESC followed by `7`, `8`, or `9`. The VT character is an alternate form of full reverse line-feed, included for compatibility with some earlier programs of this type. All other non-printing characters are ignored.

Normally, `col` will ignore any escape sequences unknown to it that are found in its input; the `-p` option may be used to cause `col` to output these sequences as regular characters, subject to overprinting from reverse line motions. The use of this option is highly discouraged unless the user is fully aware of the textual position of the escape sequences.

FILES

`/usr/lib/locale/`*locale*`/LC_MESSAGES/uxdfm`
language-specific message file [See `LANG` on `environ`(5).]

NOTES

The input format accepted by `col` matches the output produced by `nroff` with either the `-T37` or `-Tlp` options. Use `-T37` (and the `-f` option of `col`) if the ultimate disposition of the output of `col` will be a device that can interpret half-line motions, and `-Tlp` otherwise.

`col` cannot back up more than 128 lines or handle more than 800 characters per line.

Local vertical motions that would result in backing up over the first line of the document are ignored. As a result, the first line must not have any superscripts.

SEE ALSO

ascii(5), **nroff**(1), **tbl**(1)

NAME

colltbl – create collation database

SYNOPSIS

colltbl [*file* | -]

DESCRIPTION

The **colltbl** command takes as input a specification file, *file*, that describes the collating sequence for a particular language and creates a database that can be read by **strxfrm**(3C) and **strcoll**(3C). **strxfrm**(3C) transforms its first argument and places the result in its second argument. The transformed string is such that it can be correctly ordered with other transformed strings by using **strncmp**(3C). **strcoll**(3C) transforms its arguments and does a comparison.

If no input file is supplied, *stdin* is read.

The output file produced contains the database with collating sequence information in a form usable by system commands and routines. The name of this output file is the value you assign to the keyword **codeset** read in from *file*. Before this file can be used, it must be installed in the **/usr/lib/locale/***locale* directory with the name **LC_COLLATE** by someone who is super-user or a member of group **bin**. *locale* corresponds to the language area whose collation sequence is described in *file*. This file must be readable by user, group, and other; no other permissions should be set. To use the collating sequence information in this file, set the **LC_COLLATE** environment variable appropriately [see **environ**(5) or **setlocale**(3C)].

The **colltbl** command can support languages whose collating sequence can be completely described by the following cases:

Ordering of single characters within the code set. For example, in Swedish, **V** is sorted after **U**, before **X**, and with **W** (**V** and **W** are considered identical as far as sorting is concerned).

Ordering of "double characters" in the collation sequence. For example, in Spanish, **ch** and **ll** are collated after **c** and **l**, respectively.

Ordering of a single character as if it consists of two characters. For example, in German, the "sharp s," β, is sorted as **ss**. This is a special instance of the next case below.

Substitution of one character string with another character string. In the example above, the string β is replaced with **ss** during sorting.

Ignoring certain characters in the code set during collation. For example, if **-** were ignored during collation, then the strings **re-locate** and **relocate** would compare as equal.

Secondary ordering between characters. In the case where two characters are sorted together in the collation sequence, (that is, they have the same "primary" ordering), there is sometimes a secondary ordering that is used if two strings are identical except for characters that have the same primary ordering. For example, in French, the letters **e** and **è** have the same primary ordering but **e** comes before **è** in the secondary ordering. Thus the word **lever** would be ordered before **lèver**, but **lèver** would be sorted before **levitate**. (Note that if **e** came before **è** in the primary ordering, then **lèver** would be sorted after **levitate**.)

The specification file consists of three types of statements:

1. **codeset** *filename*

   filename is the name of the output file to be created by **colltbl**.

2. **order is** *order_list*

   order_list is a list of symbols, separated by semicolons, that defines the collating sequence. The special symbol, . . . , specifies symbols that are lexically sequential in a short-hand form. For example,

   ```
   order is a;b;c;d;...;x;y;z
   ```

   would specify the list of lowercase letters. Of course, this could be further compressed to just **a;...;z**.

   A symbol can be up to two bytes in length and can be represented in any one of the following ways:

   the symbol itself (for example, **a** for the lowercase letter **a**),

   in octal representation (for example, **\141** or **0141** for the letter **a**), or

   in hexadecimal representation (for example, **\x61** or **0x61** for the letter **a**).

   Any combination of these may be used as well.

   The backslash character, \ , is used for continuation. No characters are permitted after the backslash character.

   Symbols enclosed in parentheses are assigned the same primary ordering but different secondary ordering. Symbols enclosed in curly brackets are assigned only the same primary ordering. For example,

   ```
   order is a;b;c;ch;d;(e;è);f;...;z;\
            {1;...;9};A;...;Z
   ```

   In the above example, **e** and **è** are assigned the same primary ordering and different secondary ordering, digits 1 through 9 are assigned the same primary ordering and no secondary ordering. Only primary ordering is assigned to the remaining symbols. Notice how double letters can be specified in the collating sequence (letter **ch** comes between **c** and **d**).

   If a character is not included in the **order is** statement, it is excluded from the ordering and will be ignored during sorting.

3. **substitute** *string* **with** *repl*

   The **substitute** statement substitutes the string *string* with the string *repl*. This can be used, for example, to provide rules to sort the abbreviated month names numerically:

   ```
   substitute "Jan" with "01"
   substitute "Feb" with "02"
         .
         .
         .
   substitute "Dec" with "12"
   ```

A simpler use of the **substitute** statement would be to substitute a single character with two characters, as with the substitution of β with **ss** in German.

The **substitute** statement is optional. The **order is** and **codeset** statements must appear in the specification file.

Any lines in the specification file with a **#** in the first column are treated as comments and are ignored. Empty lines are also ignored.

EXAMPLE

The following example shows the collation specification required to support a hypothetical telephone book sorting sequence.

The sorting sequence is defined by the following rules:

a. Upper- and lowercase letters must be sorted together, but uppercase letters have precedence over lowercase letters.

b. All special characters and punctuation should be ignored.

c. Digits must be sorted as their alphabetic counterparts (for example, **0** as **zero**, **1** as **one**).

d. The **Ch**, **ch**, **CH** combinations must be collated between **C** and **D**.

e. **V** and **W**, **v** and **w** must be collated together.

The input specification file to **colltbl** will contain:

```
codeset     telephone

order is    A;a;B;b;C;c;CH;Ch;ch;D;d;E;e;F;f;\
            G;g;H;h:I;i;J;j;K;k;L;l;M;m;N;n;O;o;P;p;\
            Q;q;R;r;S;s;T;t;U;u;{V;W};{v;w};X;x;Y;y;Z;z

substitute "0" with "zero"
substitute "1" with "one"
substitute "2" with "two"
substitute "3" with "three"
substitute "4" with "four"
substitute "5" with "five"
substitute "6" with "six"
substitute "7" with "seven"
substitute "8" with "eight"
substitute "9" with "nine"
```

FILES

/lib/locale/*locale***/LC_COLLATE**
  LC_COLLATE database for *locale*

/usr/lib/locale/C/colltbl_C
  input file used to construct **LC_COLLATE** in the default locale.

SEE ALSO

environ(5), **memory**(3C), **setlocale**(3C), **strcoll**(3C), **string**(3C), **strxfrm**(3C)

NAME

comb – combine SCCS deltas

SYNOPSIS

comb [**-o**] [**-s**] [**-p***SID*] [**-c***list*] *file* . . .

DESCRIPTION

comb generates a shell procedure [see **sh**(1)] that, when run, reconstructs the given SCCS files. The reconstructed files are typically smaller than the original files. The arguments may be specified in any order, but all keyletter arguments apply to all named SCCS files. If a directory is named, **comb** behaves as though each file in the directory were specified as a named file, except that non-SCCS files (last component of the path name does not begin with **s.**) and unreadable files are silently ignored. If a name of **-** is given, the standard input is read; each line of the input is taken to be the name of an SCCS file to be processed; non-SCCS files and unreadable files are silently ignored. The generated shell procedure is written on the standard output.

The keyletter arguments are as follows. Each argument is explained as if only one named file is to be processed, but the effects of any keyletter argument apply independently to each named file.

-o For each **get -e**, this argument causes the reconstructed file to be accessed at the release of the delta to be created, otherwise the reconstructed file would be accessed at the most recent ancestor. Use of the **-o** keyletter may decrease the size of the reconstructed SCCS file. It may also alter the shape of the delta tree of the original file.

-s This argument causes **comb** to generate a shell procedure that, when run, produces a report that gives for each file: the file name, size (in blocks) after combining, original size (also in blocks), and percentage change computed by:

$$100 * (original - combined) / original$$

It is recommended that before any SCCS files are actually combined, one should use this option to determine exactly how much space is saved by the combining process.

-p*SID* The SCCS identification string (SID) of the oldest delta to be preserved. All older deltas are discarded in the reconstructed file.

-c*list* A *list* of deltas to be preserved. All other deltas are discarded. See **get**(1) for the syntax of a *list*.

If no keyletter arguments are specified, **comb** preserves only leaf deltas and the minimal number of ancestors needed to preserve the tree.

FILES

s.COMB	the reconstructed SCCS file
comb?????	temporary file

SEE ALSO

admin(1), **delta**(1), **get**(1), **help**(1), **prs**(1), **sccsfile**(4), **sh**(1)

DIAGNOSTICS

Use **help**(1) for explanations.

NOTES

comb may rearrange the shape of the tree of deltas.

comb may not save any space; in fact, it is possible for the reconstructed file to be larger than the original.

NAME

comm – select or reject lines common to two sorted files

SYNOPSIS

comm [– [123]] *file1 file2*

DESCRIPTION

comm reads *file1* and *file2*, which should be ordered in ASCII collating sequence [see sort(1)], and produces a three-column output: lines only in *file1*; lines only in *file2*; and lines in both files. The file name – means the standard input.

Flags 1, 2, or 3 suppress printing of the corresponding column. Thus comm -12 prints only the lines common to the two files; comm -23 prints only lines in the first file but not in the second; comm -123 prints nothing.

FILES

/usr/lib/locale/*locale*/LC_MESSAGES/uxdfm
language-specific message file [See LANG on environ(5).]

SEE ALSO

cmp(1), diff(1), sort(1), uniq(1)

compress (1)

NAME

compress, **uncompress**, **zcat** – compress data for storage, uncompress and display compressed files

SYNOPSIS

compress [**-cfv**] [**-b** *bits*] *file*

uncompress [**-cfv**] *file*

zcat [**-cfv**] *file*

DESCRIPTION

compress takes a file and compresses it to the smallest possible size, creates a compressed output file, and removes the original file unless the **-c** option is present. Compression is achieved by encoding common strings within the file. **uncompress** restores a previously compressed file to its uncompressed state and removes the compressed version. **zcat** uncompresses and displays a file on the standard output.

If no file is specified on the command line, input is taken from the standard input and the output is directed to the standard output. Output defaults to a file with the same filename as the input file with the suffix **.Z** or it can be directed through the standard output. The output files have the same permissions and ownership as the corresponding input files or the user's standard permissions if output is directed through the standard output.

If no space is saved by compression, the output file is not written unless the **-F** flag is present on the command line.

OPTIONS

The following options are available from the command line:

-b *bits* Specifies the maximum number of bits to use in encoding.

-c Writes output on the standard output and does not remove original file.

-f Forces output file to be written, even if one already exists, and even if no space is saved by compressing.

-v Prints the name of the file being compressed and the percentage of compression achieved. With **uncompress**, the name of the uncompressed file is printed.

SEE ALSO

ar(1), **cat**(1), **pack**(1), **tar**(1)

NAME

comsat, in.comsat – biff server

SYNOPSIS

in.comsat

DESCRIPTION

comsat is the server process which listens for reports of incoming mail and notifies users who have requested to be told when mail arrives. It is invoked as needed by **inetd**(1M), and times out if inactive for a few minutes.

comsat listens on a datagram port associated with the **biff** service specification [see **services**(4)] for one line messages of the form

user@*mailbox*-*offset*

If the *user* specified is logged in to the system and the associated terminal has the owner execute bit turned on (by a **biff y**), the *offset* is used as a seek offset into the appropriate mailbox file and the first 7 lines or 560 characters of the message are printed on the user's terminal. Lines which appear to be part of the message header other than the **From**, **To**, **Date**, or **Subject** lines are not printed when displaying the message.

FILES

/var/utmp	who's logged on and on what terminals

SEE ALSO

inetd(1M), **services**(4)

NOTES

The message header filtering is prone to error.

NAME

configure – Internet-specific network boot parameters configuration

SYNOPSIS

/etc/confnet.d/inet/configure -i -d *device* **[-d** *device***]**
/etc/confnet.d/inet/configure -d *device*
    [-H *ip_host* **-A** *ip_addr* **-I** *ifconfig_opt* **-S** *slink_opt***]**
/etc/confnet.d/inet/configure -r
/etc/confnet.d/inet/configure -r -d *device* **[-d** *device***]**

DESCRIPTION

The **/etc/confnet.d/inet/configure** is called by **/etc/confnet.d/configure** [see configure(1M)]. **/etc/confnet.d/inet/configure** is used to manipulate the TCP/IP **slink** [see **slink**(1M)] and **ifconfig** [see **ifconfig**(1M)] boot configuration information stored in **/etc/confnet.d/inet/interface** [see **interface**(4)]. The manipulation of a device that already has an entry in the **interface** file results in replacing the existing entry. Generic configure operations intended to remove devices will remove the appropriate entries from the interface file.

If there is only one network device installed in the **/etc/confnet.d/netdrivers** [see **netdrivers**(4)] file at the time the Internetworking package is installed, and that device is not mapped, the post-installation script will automatically use the generic **configure** script to map that device in **netdrivers** and use the **/etc/confnet.d/inet/configure** script to create an entry in the **interface** file with default configuration parameters for this device.

The default for *ifconfig_opt* is **-trailers**. The default for *slinkopts* is **add_interface**.

If you have installed more than one board and/or more than one protocol, then the postinstallation script can not automatically generate any device to protocol mappings, and the **interface** entries for each device will not be automatically configured. In these cases, the system owner and administrator are sent mail to run the generic **configure** script (**/etc/confnet.d/configure -i**) to assign device and protocol mappings.

Before you run **configure -i**, check that all of the installed network devices are correctly listed in **/etc/confnet.d/netdrivers**. For the format of an entry in the **netdrivers** file, see **netdrivers**(4). A reason for checking the **netdrivers** file is if you had to manually edit this file. For example, if you are using an unsupported networking board, you may have to manually create an entry in the **netdrivers** file. The entry must be properly formatted, otherwise **configure** will not know how to process it, and the board will not be configured. The proper format of an entry is a line containing only the device. Once the protocol-specific **configure** script has completed, a second field indicates the protocol that has been mapped to the device.

Options

/etc/confnet.d/inet/configure can be used with the following option templates:

NAME

coproc: **cocreate**, **cosend**, **cocheck**, **coreceive**, **codestroy** – communicate with a process

SYNOPSIS

cocreate [**-r** *rpath*] [**-w** *wpath*] [**-i** *id*] [**-R** *refname*] [**-s** *send_string*]
[**-e** *expect_string*] *command*

cosend [**-n**] *proc_id string*

cocheck *proc_id*

coreceive *proc_id*

codestroy [**-R** *refname*] *proc_id* [*string*]

DESCRIPTION

These co-processing functions provide a flexible means of interaction between FMLI and an independent process; especially, they enable FMLI to be responsive to asynchronous activity.

The **cocreate** function starts *command* as a co-process and initializes communications by setting up pipes between FMLI and the standard input and standard output of *command*. The argument *command* must be an executable and its arguments (if any). This means that *command* expects strings on its input (supplied by **cosend**) and sends information on its output that can be handled in various ways by FMLI. The following options can be used with **cocreate**.

-r *rpath* If **-r** is specified, *rpath* is the pathname from which FMLI reads information. This option is usually used to set up communication with processes that naturally write to a certain path. If **-r** is not specified, **cocreate** will choose a unique path in **/var/tmp**.

-w *wpath* If **-w** is specified, *wpath* is the pathname to which **cosend** writes information. This option is usually used so that one process can talk to many different FMLI processes through the same pipe. If **-w** is not specified, **cocreate** will choose a unique path in **/var/tmp**.

-i *id* If **-i** is specified, *id* is an alternative name for the co-process initialized by this **cocreate**. If **-i** is not specified, *id* defaults to *command*. The argument *id* can later be used with the other co-processing functions rather than *command*. This option is typically used, since it facilitates the creation of two or more co-processes generated from the same *command*. (For example, **cocreate -i ID1 program args** and **cocreate -i ID2 program different_args**.)

-R *refname* If **-R** is specified, *refname* is a local name for the co-process. Since the **cocreate** function can be issued more than once, a *refname* is useful when the same co-process is referenced a second or subsequent time. With the **-R** option, if the co-process already exists a new one will not be created: the same pipes will be shared. Then, *refname* can be used as an argument to the **-R** option to **codestroy** when you want to end a particular connection to a co-process and leave other connections undisturbed. (The co-process is only killed after **codestroy -R** has been called as many times as **cocreate -R** was called.)

-s *send_string* The **-s** option specifies *send_string* as a string that will be appended to all output sent to the co-process using **cosend**. This option allows a co-process to know when input from FMLI has completed. The default *send_string* is a newline if **-s** is not specified.

-e *expect_string* The **-e** option specifies *expect_string* as a string that identifies the end of all output returned by the co-process. (Note: *expect_string* need only be the initial part of a line, and there must be a newline at the end of the co-process output). This option allows FMLI to know when output from the co-process has completed. The default *expect_string* is a newline if **-e** is not specified.

The **cosend** function sends *string* to the co-process identified by *proc_id* via the pipe set up by **cocreate** (optionally *wpath*), where *proc_id* can be either the *command* or *id* specified in **cocreate**. By default, **cosend** blocks, waiting for a response from the co-process. Also by default, FMLI does not send a *send_string* and does not expect an *expect_string* (except a newline). That is, it reads only one line of output from the co-process. If **-e** *expect_string* was not defined when the pipe was created, then the output of the co-process is any single string followed by a newline: any other lines of output remain on the pipe. If the **-e** option was specified when the pipe was created, **cosend** reads lines from the pipe until it reads a line starting with *expect_string*. All lines except the line starting with *expect_string* become the output of **cosend**. The following option can be used with **cosend**:

-n If the **-n** option is specified, **cosend** will not wait for a response from the co-process. It simply returns, providing no output. If the **-n** option is not used, a co-process that does not answer will cause FMLI to permanently hang, waiting for input from the co-process.

The **cocheck** function determines if input is available from the process identified by *proc_id*, where *proc_id* can be either the *command* or *id* specified in **cocreate**. It returns a Boolean value, which makes **cocheck** useful in **if** statements and in other backquoted expressions in Boolean descriptors. **cocheck** receives no input from the co-process; it simply indicates if input is available from the co-process. You must use **coreceive** to actually accept the input. The **cocheck** function can be called from a **reread** descriptor to force a frame to update when new data is available. This is useful when the default value of a field in a form includes **coreceive**.

The **coreceive** function is used to read input from the co-process identified by *proc_id*, where *proc_id* can be either the *command* or *id* specified in **cocreate**. It should only be used when it has been determined, using **cocheck**, that input is actually available. If the **-e** option was used when the co-process was created, **coreceive** will continue to return lines of input until *expect_string* is read. At this point, **coreceive** will terminate. The output of **coreceive** is all the lines that were read excluding the line starting with *expect_string*. If the **-e** option was not used in the **cocreate**, each invocation of **coreceive** will return exactly one line from the co-process. If no input is available when **coreceive** is invoked, it will simply terminate without producing output.

The **codestroy** function terminates the read/write pipes to *proc-id*, where *proc_id* can be either the *command* or *id* specified in **cocreate**. It generates a **SIGPIPE** signal to the (child) co-process. This kills the co-process, unless the co-process ignores the **SIGPIPE** signal. If the co-process ignores the **SIGPIPE**, it will not die, even after the FMLI process terminates (the parent process id of the co-process will be 1).

The optional argument *string* is sent to the co-process before the co-process dies. If *string* is not supplied, a NULL string is passed, followed by the normal *send_string* (newline by default). That is, **codestroy** will call **cosend** *proc_id string*: this implies that **codestroy** will write any output generated by the co-process to **stdout**. For example, if an interactive co-process is written to expect a "**quit**" string when the communication is over, the **close** descriptor could be defined;

```
close=`codestroy ID 'quit' | message`
```

and any output generated by the co-process when the string **quit** is sent to it via **codestroy** (using **cosend**) would be redirected to the message line.

The **codestroy** function should usually be given the **-R** option, since you may have more than one process with the same name, and you do not want to kill the wrong one. **codestroy** keeps track of the number of *refnames* you have assigned to a process with **cocreate**, and when the last instance is killed, it kills the process (*id*) for you. **codestroy** is typically called as part of a **close** descriptor because **close** is evaluated when a frame is closed. This is important because the co-process will continue to run if **codestroy** is not issued.

When writing programs to use as co-processes, the following tips may be useful. If the co-process program is written in C language, be sure to flush output after writing to the pipe. [Currently, **awk**(1) and **sed**(1) cannot be used in a co-process program because they do not flush after lines of output.] Shell scripts are well-mannered, but slow. C language is recommended. If possible, use the default *send_string*, *rpath* and *wpath*. In most cases, *expect_string* will have to be specified. This, of course, depends on the co-process.

In the case where asynchronous communication from a co-process is desired, a co-process program should use **vsig** to force strings into the pipe and then signal FMLI that output from the co-process is available. This causes the **reread** descriptor of all frames to be evaluated immediately.

EXAMPLE

```
  .
  .
  .
init=`cocreate -i BIGPROCESS initialize`
close=`codestroy BIGPROCESS`
  .
  .
  .
reread=`cocheck BIGPROCESS`

name=`cosend -n BIGPROCESS field1`
  .
  .
```

```
name="Receive field"
inactive=TRUE
value=`coreceive BIGPROCESS`
```

NOTES

Co-processes for trusted FMLI applications should use named pipes created by the application with the appropriate permissions; the default pipes created by FMLI are readable and writable by everyone. Handshaking can also be used to enhance security.

If **cosend** is used without the **-n** option, a co-process that does not answer will cause FMLI to permanently hang.

The use of non-alphabetic characters in input and output strings to a co-process should be avoided because they may not get transferred correctly.

NAME

copy – (XENIX) copy groups of files

SYNOPSIS

copy [*option*] . . . *source* . . . *dest*

DESCRIPTION

The **copy** command copies the contents of directories to another directory. It is possible to copy whole file systems since directories are made when needed.

If files, directories, or special files do not exist at the destination, then they are created with the same modes and flags as the source. In addition, the super-user may set the user and group ID. The owner and mode are not changed if the destination file exists. Note that there may be more than one source directory. If so, the effect is the same as if the **copy** command had been issued for each source directory with the same destination directory for each copy.

All of the options must be given as separate arguments, and they may appear in any order even after the other arguments. The arguments are:

-a Asks the user before attempting a copy. If the response does not begin with a **y**, then a copy is not done. This option also sets the **ad** option.

-l Uses links instead whenever they can be used. Otherwise a copy is done. Note that links are never done for special files or directories.

-n Requires the destination file to be new. If not, then the **copy** command does not change the destination file. The **-n** flag is meaningless for directories. For special files an **-n** flag is assumed (that is, the destination of a special file must not exist).

-o If set then every file copied has its owner and group set to those of source. If not set, then the file's owner is the user who invoked the program.

-m If set, then every file copied has its modification time and access time set to that of the source. If not set, then the modification time is set to the time of the copy.

-r If set, then every directory is recursively examined as it is encountered. If not set, then any directories that are found are ignored.

-ad Asks the user whether an **-r** flag applies when a directory is discovered. If the answer does not begin with a **y**, then the directory is ignored.

-v If the verbose option is set, messages are printed that reveal what the program is doing.

source This may be a file, directory or special file. It must exist. If it is not a directory, then the results of the command are the same as for the **cp** command.

dest The destination must be either a file or directory that is different from the source. If *source* and *destination* are anything but directories, then **copy** acts just like a **cp** command. If both are directories, then **copy** copies each file into the destination directory according to the flags that have been set.

NOTES

Special device files can be copied. When they are copied, any data associated with the specified device is not copied.

NAME

cp – copy files

SYNOPSIS

cp [**-i**] [**-r**] [**-e** *extent_opt*] *file1* [*file2* . . .] *target*

DESCRIPTION

The **cp** command copies *filen* to *target*. *filen* and *target* may not have the same name. [Care must be taken when using **sh**(1) metacharacters.] If *target* is not a directory, only one file may be specified before it; if it is a directory, more than one file may be specified. If *target* does not exist, **cp** creates a file named *target*. If *target* exists and is not a directory, its contents are overwritten. If *target* is a directory, the file(s) are copied to that directory.

The following options are recognized:

-i Prompt for confirmation whenever the copy would overwrite an existing *target*. A **y** answer means the copy should proceed. Any other answer prevents **cp** from overwriting *target*. The **-i** option remains in effect even if the standard input is not a terminal.

-r (if *filen* is a directory) Copy the directory and all its files, including any sub-directories and their files. (*target* must be a directory.)

-e *extent_opt*
Specify how to handle a **vxfs** file that has extent attribute information. Extent attributes include reserved space, a fixed extent size, and extent alignment. It may not be possible to preserve the information if the destination file system does not support extent attributes, has a different block size than the source file system, or lacks free extents appropriate to satisfy the extent attribute requirements. Valid values for *extent_opt* are:

warn Issue a warning message if extent attribute information cannot be kept (default).

force Fail the copy if extent attribute information cannot be kept.

ignore Ignore extent attribute information entirely.

If *filen* is a file and *target* is a link to another file with links, the other links remain and *target* becomes a new file.

FILES

/usr/lib/locale/*locale***/LC_MESSAGES/uxcore.abi**
language-specific message file [See **LANG** on **environ** (5).]

SEE ALSO

chmod(1), **cpio**(1), **ln**(1), **mv**(1), **rm**(1)

NOTES

A **--** permits the user to mark the end of any command line options explicitly, thus allowing **cp** to recognize filename arguments that begin with a **-**. If a **--** and a **-** both appear on the same command line, the second will be interpreted as a filename.

cp will hang if *file* is a pipe.

cpio (1)

NAME

cpio – copy file archives in and out

SYNOPSIS

cpio -i [**bBcdfkmrsSTtuvV6**] [**-C** *bufsize*] [**-E** *file*] [**-G** *file*] [**-H** *hdr*] [**-e** *extent_opt*] [**-I** *file* [**-M** *message*]] [**-R** *ID*]] [*pattern . . .*]

cpio -o [**aABcLvV**] [**-C** *bufsize*] [**-G** *file*] [**-H** *hdr*] [**-K** *mediasize*] [**-e** *extent_opt*] [**-O** *file* [**-M** *message*]]

cpio -p [**adlLmuvV**] [**-R** *ID*] [**-e** *extent_opt*] *directory*

DESCRIPTION

The **-i**, **-o**, and **-p** options select the action to be performed. The following list describes each of the actions (which are mutually exclusive).

cpio -i (copy in) extracts files from the standard input, which is assumed to be the product of a previous **cpio -o**. Only files with names that match *patterns* are selected. *patterns* are regular expressions given in the filename-generating notation of **sh**(1). In *patterns*, meta-characters **?**, *, and **[. . .]** match the slash (**/**) character, and backslash (\) is an escape character. A **!** meta-character means *not*. (For example, the **!abc*** pattern would exclude all files that begin with **abc**.) Multiple *patterns* may be specified and if no *patterns* are specified, the default for *patterns* is * (that is, select all files). Each pattern must be enclosed in double quotes; otherwise, the name of a file in the current directory might be used. Extracted files are conditionally created and copied into the current directory tree based on the options described below.

The permissions of the files will be those of the previous **cpio -o**. Owner and group permissions will be the same as the current user unless the current user is super-user. If this is true, owner and group permissions will be the same as those resulting from the previous **cpio -o**.

NOTE: If **cpio -i** tries to create a file that already exists and the existing file is the same age or younger (newer), **cpio** will output a warning message and not replace the file. (The **-u** option can be used to overwrite, unconditionally, the existing file.) If file names are given as absolute pathnames to **cpio -o**, then when the files are restored via **cpio -i**, they will be written to their original directories regardless of the current directory. This behavior can be circumvented by using the **-r** option. When **cpio** is invoked from the shell, each *pattern* should be quoted; otherwise the pattern may be expanded. Extracted files are conditionally created based upon the options described below. The permissions of the files will be those of the previous **cpio -o**. The owner and group of the files will be that of the current user unless the user is super-user, which causes **cpio** to retain the owner and group of the files of the previous **cpio -o**.

cpio -o (copy out) reads the standard input to obtain a list of pathnames and copies those files onto the standard output together with pathname and status information.

In normal circumstances, **cpio** sets the **Hdr_type** variable (which defines the header type) to **NONE** before checking the actual header type. It does this even if you have specified a different header type on the command line. When you use the **-k** option, however, **cpio** does not set **Hdr_type** to **NONE** if you've specified a header type on the command line (with the **-c** or **-H** option). In this case, **cpio** sets

Hdr_type to the header type you've specified. Thus you have a way of making sure the correct header file type is specified, which improves your chances of recovering files correctly. For this reason, we recommend you specify the header type for the file (with **-c** or **-H**) whenever you use the **-k** option.

cpio -p (pass) reads the standard input to obtain a list of pathnames of files that are conditionally created and copied into the destination *directory* tree based on the options described below.

cpio processes supplementary code set characters, and recognizes supplementary code set characters in the *message* given to the **-M** option (see below) according to the locale specified in the **LC_CTYPE** environment variable [see **LANG** on **environ**(5)]. In regular expressions, pattern searches are performed on characters, not bytes, as described on **sh**(1). Under the **-vt** option (see below), the date is displayed according to the locale specified in the **LC_TIME** environment variable.

The meanings of the available options are

-a Reset access times of input files after they have been copied. Access times are not reset for linked files when **cpio -pla** is specified.

-A Append files to an archive. The **-A** option requires the **-O** option. Valid only with archives that are files, or that are on floppy diskettes or hard disk partitions.

-b Reverse the order of the bytes within each word. (Use only with the **-i** option.)

-B Input/output is to be blocked 5120 bytes to the record. The default buffer size is device dependent when neither this nor the **-C** option is used.

-c Read or write header information in ASCII character form for portability. Always use this option (or the **-H** option) when the origin and the destination machines are different types (mutually exclusive with **-H** and **-6**). (The **-c** option implies expanded device numbers.)

-C *bufsize*
Input/output is to be blocked *bufsize* bytes to the record, where *bufsize* is replaced by a positive integer. The default buffer size is device dependent when neither this nor the **-B** option is used. If used with **-K**, *bufsize* must be a multiple of 1K.

-d Directories are to be created as needed.

-E *file* Specify an input file (*file*) that contains a list of filenames to be extracted from the archive (one filename per line).

-e *extent_opt*
Specify how to handle a **vxfs** file that has extent attribute information. Extent attributes include reserved space, a fixed extent size, and extent alignment. It may not be possible to preserve the information if the destination file system does not support extent attributes, has a different block size than the source file system, or lacks free extents appropriate to satisfy the extent attribute requirements. Valid values for *extent_opt* are:

- `warn` — Issue a warning message if extent attribute information cannot be kept (default).
- `force` — Fail the file save or restore or copy if extent attribute information cannot be kept.
- `ignore` — Ignore extent attribute information entirely.

-f Copy in all files except those in *patterns*. (See the paragraph about **cpio -i** for a description of *patterns*.)

-G *file* NOTE: This option is intended for use by front-end or application programs that invoke **cpio**. If you're running **cpio** at the shell level, you probably won't need this option.

The **-G** option allows a program to specify *file* as the interface through which **cpio** communicates with a user. Specifically, this interface is used for end-of-medium processing; it is used both for writing the prompts to the user and for reading the user's input. By default, **/dev/tty** is the interface. However, in some situations (such as graphics application environments), **/dev/tty** is not available. Therefore an alternative interface, such as a pseudo-**tty**, may be needed.

-H *hdr* Read or write header information in *hdr* format. Always use this option or the **-c** option when the origin and the destination machines are different types (mutually exclusive with **-c** and **-6**). Valid values for *hdr* are:

- **crc** or **CRC** — ASCII header with expanded device numbers and an additional per-file checksum
- **ustar** or **USTAR** — IEEE/P1003 Data Interchange Standard header and format
- **tar** or **TAR** — **tar** header and format
- **odc** — ASCII header with small device numbers

-I *file* Read the contents of *file* as an input archive. If *file* is a character special device, and the current medium has been completely read, replace the medium and press RETURN to continue to the next medium. This option is used only with the **-i** option.

-k Attempt to skip corrupted file headers and I/O errors that may be encountered. If you want to copy files from a medium that is corrupted or out of sequence, this option lets you read only those files with good headers. (For **cpio** archives that contain other **cpio** archives, if an error is encountered, **cpio** may terminate prematurely. **cpio** will find the next good header, which may be one for a smaller archive, and terminate when the smaller archive's trailer is encountered.) Used only with the **-i** option.

-K *mediasize*
Specify the media size as a multiple of 1K. If used with **-C** *bufsize*, then *bufsize* must be a multiple of 1K. Use only with the **-o** option.

-l Whenever possible (only with the **-p** option), link files rather than copying them. (Even if a file cannot be linked, it will be copied.)

`-L` Follow symbolic links. The default is not to follow symbolic links.

`-m` Retain previous file modification time. The modification time and access time of a restored file is set to the modification time of the file when it was backed up. Modification time of directories is not retained.

`-M` *message*
Define a *message* to use when switching media. When you use the `-O` or `-I` options and specify a character special device, you can use this option to define the message that is printed when you reach the end of the medium. One `%d` can be placed in *message* to print the sequence number of the next medium needed to continue. *message* may contain supplementary code set characters.

`-O` *file* Direct the output of **cpio** to *file*. If *file* is a character special device and the current medium is full, replace the medium and type a carriage return to continue to the next medium. Use only with the `-o` option.

`-r` Interactively rename files. If the user types a carriage return alone, the file is skipped. If the user types a "." the original pathname will be retained. (Should be used only with `cpio -i`.)

`-R` *ID* Reassign ownership and group information for each file to *user ID* (*ID* must be a valid login ID from **/etc/passwd**). This option is valid only for a privileged user.

`-s` Swap bytes within each half word.

`-S` Swap halfwords within each word.

`-t` Print a table of contents of the input. No files are created (mutually exclusive with `-V`).

`-T` Truncate long file names to 14 characters. Use only with the `-i` option.

`-u` Copy unconditionally (normally, an older file will not replace a newer file with the same name).

`-v` Verbose: causes a list of file names to be printed. When used with the `-t` option, the table of contents looks like the output of an `ls -l` command [see `ls`(1)]; dates are displayed according to the locale specified in the **LC_TIME** environment variable [see **LANG** on **environ**(5)].

`-V` Special Verbose: print a dot for each file read or written. Useful to assure the user that **cpio** is working without printing out all file names.

`-6` Process a UNIX System Sixth Edition archive format file. Use only with the `-i` option (mutually exclusive with `-c` and `-H`).

NOTE: **cpio** assumes four-byte words.

If, when writing to a character device (`-o`) or reading from a character device (`-i`), **cpio** reaches the end of a medium (such as the end of a diskette), and the `-O` and `-I` options aren't used, **cpio** will print the following message:

```
If you want to go on, type device/file name when ready.
```

To continue, you must replace the medium and type the character special device name (**/dev/rdsk/f0** for example) and press RETURN. You may want to continue by directing **cpio** to use a different device. For example, if you have two floppy drives you may want to switch between them so **cpio** can proceed while you are changing the floppies.

EXAMPLES

Output (–o)

When standard input is directed through a pipe to **cpio -o**, files are grouped so they can be directed (>) to a single file (**../newfile**). The **-c** option insures that the file will be portable to other machines (as would the **-H** option). Instead of **ls**(1), you could use **find**(1), **echo**(1), **cat**(1), and so on, to pipe a list of names to **cpio**. You could direct the output to a device instead of a file.

```
ls | cpio -oc > ../newfile
```

Input (–i)

cpio -i uses the output file of **cpio -o** (directed through a pipe with **cat** in the example below), extracts those files that match the patterns (**memo/a1**, **memo/b***), creates directories below the current directory as needed (**-d** option), and places the files in the appropriate directories. The **-c** option is used if the input file was created with a portable header. If no patterns were given, all files from **newfile** would be placed in the directory.

```
cat newfile | cpio -icd "memo/a1" "memo/b*"
```

Pass (–p)

cpio -p takes the file names piped to it and copies or links (**-l** option) those files to another directory (**newdir** in the example below). The **-d** option allows you to create directories as needed. The **-m** option lets you retain the modification time and security level. [It is important to use the **-depth** option of **find**(1) to generate pathnames for **cpio**. Use of this option eliminates problems **cpio** could have in trying to create files under read-only directories.] The destination directory, **newdir**, must exist.

```
find . -depth -print | cpio -pdlmv newdir
```

Note that when you use **cpio** in conjunction with **find**, if you use the **-L** option with **cpio** then you must use the **-follow** option with **find** and vice versa. Otherwise there will be undesirable results.

EXIT CODES

1 usage error

2 file error (but **cpio** completes, displaying error number)

3 fatal error (**cpio** dies immediately)

FILES

/usr/lib/locale/*locale***/LC_MESSAGES/uxcore.abi**
language-specific message file [See **LANG** on **environ** (5).]

SEE ALSO

ar(1), **archives**(4), **cat**(1), **echo**(1), **find**(1), **ls**(1), **tar**(1)

NOTES

An archive created with the `-c` option on a System V Release 4 system cannot be read on System V Release 3.2 systems, or earlier. Use the `-H odc` option, which is equivalent to the header created by the `-c` option in earlier System V Releases, if the `cpio` image will be read by a pre-System V Release 4 version of `cpio`.

In releases of UNIX System V prior to Release 4, symbolic links are not understood. The result of copying in a symbolic link on an older release will be a regular file that contains the pathname of the referenced file.

Pathnames are restricted to 256 characters for the binary (the default) and `-H odc` header formats. Otherwise, pathnames are restricted to 1024 characters.

Only a privileged user can copy block or character special files.

Blocks are reported in 512-byte quantities.

The `st01` tape driver does not always require block sizes that are in multiples of 512 bytes, but block size is device dependent. Use `tapecntl` to set the tape driver to use the block size supported by the tape device. Failure to set the block size correctly will result in an error when the driver attempts to write a block of the unsupported size.

If a file has `000` permissions and contains more than 0 characters of data, and the user does not have the appropriate privilege, the file will not be saved or restored.

When attempting to redirect standard input or standard output from or to a block or character special device (such as `/dev/rmt/0m`), you may get an error message such as `Cannot read from device` or `Cannot write to device`. The appearance of such a message does not necessarily mean a true I/O error has occurred. It is more likely to mean the user does not have access to that device; the user should ask the system administrator to allocate the device for him or her.

Prior to Release 4, the default buffer size was 512 bytes. Beginning with Release 4, the default buffer size is optimized for the device and using the `-C` option to specify a different block size may cause `cpio` to fail. Therefore, care must be taken when choosing the block size. To avoid wasting space on streaming tape drives, use the `-C` option and specify an appropriate block size.

If your attempt to direct `cpio` output to a floppy diskette fails, regardless of the method used (output redirection or use of the `-O` option), the reason for the failure may be that the diskette is write-protected.

cr1 (1M)

NAME

cr1 – bilateral IAF authentication scheme

SYNOPSIS

cr1 [**-r**] [**-u** *local_user*] [**-s** *local_service*] [**-U** *remote_user*]
[**-M** *remote_machine*] [**-S** *remote_service*]

DESCRIPTION

The **cr1** scheme executable implements the cr1 identification and authentication protocol. The cr1 scheme is a bilateral scheme that operates within the framework of the Identification and Authentication Facility (IAF).

cr1 identifies and authenticates users on both the server and the client machines at the time a connection is established. Both parties in the communication are authenticated through the use of a key [see **cryptkey**(1)]. The effective UID of the process running **cr1** determines the key that is used in the authentication.

To instruct a port monitor to use **cr1** to protect a service, a **cr1** command line must be registered in the *scheme* field of the service's entry in the port monitor's **_pmtab** file. When a remote user attempts to access a service on the local system, the port monitor passes the command to the **invoke** function, which executes the program.

The options to **cr1** have the following meanings:

-r Indicates that the scheme will operate in the role of responder. If this option is not specified, the scheme operates in the role of imposer.

-u *local_user* Indicates the local logname *local_user*.

-s *local_service* Indicates the local service name *local_service*.

-U *remote_user* Indicates the remote logname *remote_user*.

-M *remote_machine* Indicates the remote system *remote_machine*.

-S *remote_service* Indicates the remote service name *remote_service*.

If the **-u** option is used in the responder role, the cr1 scheme attempts to use the key shared by the local and remote machines. If this key is not available to the application (or if no **-u** option is used), the cr1 scheme will attempt to use the key shared by the local effective user and the principal indicated by the **-M** and **-U** options.

The imposer will use the corresponding key shared by the responder and the local effective user.

The options **-u** and **-s** indicate that the local user name and the name of the local service, respectively, are to be passed to the remote machine in the authentication exchange. The **-U** and **-M** options instruct **cr1** to use the remote machine name and the remote user name, respectively, to look up keys in its database.

The **cr1** executable program implements the **cr1** protocol, assuming that file descriptors 0, 1, and 2 have been set to the connection to be authenticated. The file descriptors are set by the **invoke** library function [see **invoke**(3I)].

Upon successful completion of an authentication exchange, the **cr1** program exits with a value of 0 and associates appropriate values with the authenticated connection, using the **putava** and **setava** functions. The associated values may then be used by applications using the authenticated connection, using the **getava** and **retava** functions.

FILES

/etc/iaf/cr1/keys	cr1 key database
/var/iaf/cr1/log	cr1 log file

SEE ALSO

cryptkey(1), **getava**(3I), **getkey**(3N), **invoke**(3I), **keymaster**(1M)

DIAGNOSTICS

If authentication fails, **cr1** exits with a non-zero return value and logs a reason or reasons in its log file.

NOTES

By default, **cr1** uses DES encryption. For this to work, both machines using authentication must have the Encryption Utilities package installed. If this package is not available, the machines can use authentication using ENIGMA encryption, by invoking **cr1** as **cr1.enigma**.

NAME

crash – examine system images

SYNOPSIS

/usr/sbin/crash [**-d** *dumpfile*] [**-n** *namelist*] [**-m** *moduledir*] [**-w** *outputfile*]

DESCRIPTION

The **crash** command is used to examine the system memory image of a running or a crashed system by formatting and printing control structures, tables, and other information.

Options

crash takes the following options:

-d *dumpfile*
: Use *dumpfile* for the file containing the system memory image. The default *dumpfile* is **/dev/mem**. If you enter a value other than **/dev/mem**, it is assumed that the system is crashed.

-n *namelist*
: Use the text file *namelist*, containing the symbol table information needed for symbolic access to the system memory image to be examined. The default *namelist* is **/stand/unix**. If a system image from another machine is to be examined, the corresponding text file must be copied from that machine. For active systems, **crash** uses system calls to the running kernel to get symbol table information. For that reason, only global symbols are available.

-m *moduledir*
: Use the specified directory, *moduledir* to look for modules. When working on a dump, **crash** looks for the modules that were loaded at the time of the dump, and adds those symbols to its symbol table information. By default, **crash** tries to find the modules in the directories from which there were loaded. The **-m** option specifies a directory where **crash** should look for the modules instead. If you use the **-m** option, **crash** only looks in the specified directory. You can only use a single instance of the **-m** option on the command line, and if you attempt to use the **-m** option more than once, only the last one is valid; the others are ignored.

-w *outputfile*
: The output from a **crash** session is directed to *outputfile*. The default *outputfile* is the standard output.

Input

When you execute the **crash** command, a session is initiated. If you enter the "?" character at the command prompt, **crash** provides a help menu of the available commands.

Input during a **crash** session is of the form:

function [*argument* . . .]

where *function* is one of the **crash** functions described below under "FUNCTIONS" and *arguments* are qualifying data that indicate which items of the system image are to be printed.

The default for process-related items is the current process for a running system or the process that was running at the time of the crash for a crashed system. If the contents of a table are being dumped, the default is all active table entries.

The following function options are available to **crash** functions wherever they are semantically valid.

-e Display every entry in a table.

-f Display the full structure.

-n Display privilege names symbolically. Default is to display in hexadecimal.

-p Interpret all address arguments in the command line as physical addresses. If they are not physical addresses, results are inconsistent.

-s *process*
Specify a process slot other than the default.

-w *file* Redirect the output of a function to *file*.

The functions **mode**, **defproc**, and **redirect** correspond to the function options **-p**, **-s**, and **-w**. The **mode** function may be used to set the address translation mode to physical or virtual for all subsequently entered functions; **defproc** sets the value of the process slot argument for subsequent functions; and **redirect** redirects all subsequent output.

Output

Output from **crash** functions may be piped to another program as follows:

function [*argument* . . .] **!** *shell_command*

For example,

```
mount ! grep rw
```

writes all mount table entries with an **rw** flag to the standard output. The redirection option (**-w**) cannot be used with this feature.

An argument can be either a symbol or a numeric argument. Numeric arguments are assumed to be decimal unless preceded by **0x** or **0b** prefixes for hexadecimal or binary numbers. Any argument not either a symbol or a number will be reported as a error. Each function, when executed, determines whether the argument specified a valid slot or address.

Default bases on all arguments may be overridden. The C conventions for designating the bases of numbers are recognized.

Aliases for functions may be any uniquely identifiable initial substring of the function name. Traditional aliases of one letter, such as **p** for **proc**, remain valid.

Many functions accept different forms of entry for the same argument. Requests for table information will accept a table entry number or a range. A range of slot numbers may be specified in the form *a–b* where *a* and *b* are decimal numbers. An expression consists of two operands and an operator. An operand may be an address, a symbol, or a number; the operator may be +, –, *, /, &, or | . An operand that is a number should be preceded by a radix prefix if it is not a decimal number (**0** for octal, **0x** for hexadecimal, **0b** for binary). The expression must be enclosed in parentheses. Other functions accept any of these argument forms that are meaningful.

Two abbreviated arguments to **crash** functions are] used throughout. Both accept data entered in several forms. They may be expanded into the following:

tabel_entry = *address* | *slot* | *range*

start_addr = *address* | *symbol* | *expression*

USAGE

Following are the available functions in **crash**:

? [**-w** *file*]
: List available functions.

! *command*
: Escape to the shell and execute *command*.

abuf [**-w** *file*] [**-***mode*]
: Print audit buffer data in *mode* format. *mode* is one of long (**-l**), short (**-t**), or byte (**-b**). The default mode for character and ASCII formats is byte; the default mode for decimal, hexadecimal, and octal formats is long. When mode is omitted, the previous value is used. At the start of a **crash** session, the mode is long.

as [**-e**] [**-f**] [**-w** *file*] [*proc* . . .]
: Print address space information on process segments.

base [**-w** *file*] *number* . . .
: Print *number* in binary, octal, decimal, and hexadecimal. A number in a radix other than decimal should be preceded by a prefix that indicates its radix as follows: **0x**, hexadecimal; **0**, octal; and **0b**, binary.

buffer [**-w** *file*] [*-format*] [**-p**] *addr*
: Alias: **b**.
: Print the contents of a buffer in the designated format. The following format designations are recognized: **-b**, byte: **-c**, character; **-d**, decimal; **-x**, hexadecimal; **-o**, octal; and, **-i**, inode. If no format is given, the previous format is used. The default format at the beginning of a **crash** session is hexadecimal.

bufhdr [**-f**] [**-w** *file*] [[**-p**] *addr* . . .]
: Alias: **buf**.
: Print system buffer headers. The **-f** option produces different output depending on whether the buffer is local or remote (contains RFS data).

callout [**-w** *file*]
: Alias: **c**.
: Print the callout table.

class [**-w** *file*] [*table_entry* . . .]
: Print information about process scheduler classes.

defproc [**-w** *file*] [**-c**]

defproc [**-w** *file*] [*slot*]
Set the value of the default process slot argument. The default process slot argument may be set to the current slot number (**-c**) or the slot number may be specified. If no argument is entered, the value of the previously set slot number is printed. At the start of a **crash** session, the process slot is set to the current process.

dis [**-w** *file*] [**-a**] *start_addr* [*count*]
dis [**-w** *file*] [**-a**] **-c** [*count*]
Disassemble *count* instructions starting at *start_addr*. The default count is 1. The absolute option (**-a**) specifies a non-symbolic disassembly. The **-c** option can be used in place of *start_addr* to continue disassembly at the address at which a previous disassembly ended.

dispq [**-w** *file*] [*table_entry* . . .]
Print the dispatcher (scheduler) queues.

ds [**-w** *file*] *virtual_address* . . .
Print the data symbol whose address is closest to, but not greater than, the address entered.

evactive [**-w** *file*] [**-f**] [*event_name*]
Print the active event queue. The **-f** option provides a verbose display.

evmm [**-w** *file*]
Print the events memory management information.

file [**-e**] [**-w** *file*] [[**-p**] *table_entry* . . .]
Alias: **f**.
Print the file table.

filepriv [**-e**] [**-n**] [**-w** *file*] [[**-p**] *table_entry* . . .]
Print the kernel privilege table.

findaddr [**-w** *file*] *table slot*
Print the address of *slot* in *table*. Only tables available to the **size** function are available to **findaddr**.

findslot [**-w** *file*] *virtual_address* . . .
Print the table, entry slot number, and offset for the address entered. Only tables available to the **size** function are available to **findslot**.

fs [**-w** *file*] [[**-p**] *table_entry* . . .]
Print the file system information table.

gdp [**-e**] [**-f**] [**-w** *file*] [[**-p**] *table_entry* . . .]
Print the gift descriptor protocol table.

gdt [**-e**] [**-w** *file*] [**slot** [**count**]]
table_entry . . .] Print the global descriptor table.

help [**-w** *file*] *function* . . .
Print a description of the named function, including syntax and aliases.

idt [**-e**] [**-w** *file*] [**slot** [**count**]]
Print the interrupt descriptor table.

hrt [**-w** *file*]
Print the high resolution timer information.

inode [**-e**] [**-f**] [**-w** *file*] [[**-p**] *table_entry . . .*]
Alias: **i**.
Print the inode table, including file system switch information.

kfp [**-w** *file*] [*value . . .*]
Print the kernel frame pointer (kfp) for the start of a kernel stack trace. If the value argument is supplied, the **p** is set to that value. If no argument is entered, the current value of the kfp is printed.

kmastat [**-w** *file*]
Print kernel memory allocator statistics.

lck [**-e**] [**-w** *file*] [[**-p**] *table_entry . . .*]
Alias: **l**.
Print record locking information. If the **-e** option is used or table address arguments are given, the record lock list is printed. If no argument is entered, information on locks relative to inodes is printed.

ldt [**-e**] [**-w** *file*] [**process** [**slot** [**count**]]]
Print the local descriptor table for the given process, for the current process if none is given.

lidcache [**-w** *file*] [ ]
Print out the level identifier (LID) translation cache. The LID cachhe is supported only if the Enhanced Security Utilities are installed and running.

linkblk [**-e**] [**-w** *file*] [[**-p**] *table_entry . . .*]
Print the linkblk table.

map [**-w** *file*] *mapname . . .*
Print the map structure of the given mapname.

mode [**-w** *file*] [*mode*]
Set address translation of arguments to virtual (**v**) or physical (**p**) mode. If no mode argument is given, the current mode is printed. At the start of a **crash** session, the mode is virtual.

mount [**-e**] [**-w** *file*] [[**-p**] *table_entry . . .*]
Alias: **m**, **vfs**.
Print information about mounted file systems.

nm [**-w** *file*] *symbol . . .*
Print value and type for the given symbol.

od [**-p**] [**-w** *file*] [*-format*] [*-mode*] [**-s** *process*] *start_addr* [*count*]
Alias: **rd**.
Print *count* values starting at *start_addr* in one of the following formats: character (**-c**), decimal (**-d**), hexadecimal (**-x**), octal (**-o**), ASCII (**-a**), or hexadecimal/character (**-h**), and one of the following modes: long (**-l**), short (**-t**), or byte (**-b**). The default mode for character and ASCII formats is byte; the default mode for decimal, hexadecimal, and octal formats is long. The format **-h** prints both hexadecimal and character representations of the addresses dumped; no mode needs to be specified. When format or

mode is omitted, the previous value is used. At the start of a **crash** session, the format is hexadecimal and the mode is long. If no count is entered, 1 is assumed.

panic Print the latest system notices, warnings, and panic messages from the limited circular buffer kept in memory.

page [**-e**] [**-w***file*] [[**-p**] *table_entry* . . .]
Print information about pages.

pcb [**-w** *file*] [*process*]
Print the process control block (TSS). If no arguments are given, the active TSS for the current process is printed.

prnode [**-e**] [**-w** *file*] [[**-p**] *table_entry* . . .]
Print information about the private data of processes being traced.

proc [**-e**] [**-f** [**-n**]] [**-w** *file*] [[**-p**] *table_entry* . . . **#***procid* . . .]
proc [**-f** [**-n**]] [**-w** *file*] [**-r**]
Alias: **p**.
Print the process table. Process table information may be specified in two ways. First, any mixture of table entries and process IDs may be entered. Each process ID must be preceded by a **#**. Alternatively, process table information for runnable processes may be specified with the runnable option (**-r**). The full option (**-f**) details most of the information in the process table as well as the region for that process.

ptbl [**-e**] [**-w** *file*] [**-s***process*] [[**-p**] *addr* [*count*]]
Print information on page descriptor tables.

pty [**-f**] [**-e**] [**-w** *file*] [**-s**] [**-h**] [**-l**]
Print the pseudo ttys presently configured. The **-l**, **-h** and **-h** options give information about the STREAMS modules **ldterm**, **ptem** and **pckt**, respectively.

qrun [**-w** *file*]
Print the list of scheduled streams queues.

queue [**-e**] [**-w** *file*] [[**-p**] *table_entry* . . .]
Print streams queues.

quit Alias: **q**.
Terminate the **crash** session.

rcvd [**-e**] [**-f**] [**-w** *file*] [[**-p**] *table_entry* . . .]
Print the receive descriptor table.

rduser [**-e**] [**-f**] [**-w** *file*] [[**-p**] *table_entry* . . .]
Print the receive descriptor user table.

redirect [**-w** *file*] [**-c**]
redirect [**-w** *file*] [*newfile*]
Used with a file name, redirects output of a **crash** session to *newfile*. If no argument is given, the file name to which output is being redirected is printed. Alternatively, the close option (**-c**) closes the previously set file and redirects output to the standard output.

resource [**-e**] [**-w** *file*] [[**-p**] *table_entry* . . .]
Print the advertise table.

rtdptbl [**-w** *file*] [*table_entry* . . .]
Print the real-time scheduler parameter table. See **rt_dptbl**(4).

rtproc [**-w** *file*]
Print information about processes in the real-time scheduler class.

search [**-p**] [**-w** *file*] [**-m** *mask*] [**-s** *process*] *pattern start_addr length*
Print the long words in memory that match *pattern*, beginning at the *start_addr* for *length* long words. The mask is ANDed (&) with each memory word and the result compared against the pattern. The mask defaults to **0xffffffff**.

sinode [**-e**] [**-f**] [**-w** *file*] [[**-p**] *table_entry* . . .]
Alias: **si**.
Print the inode table for **ufs** or **sfs** file systems. Since the **ufs/sfs** incore inode contains the **icommon** inode and the alternate inode, this function displays, in addition to the **icommon** inode information, all security data stored in the alternate inode. This includes the level identifier, the Access Control List (ACL) count, the extended ACL disk block pointer, and any inode resident ACL entries.

size [**-w** *file*] [**-x**] [*structure_name* . . .]
Print the size of the designated structure. The (**-x**) option prints the size in hexadecimal. If no argument is given, a list of the structure names for which sizes are available is printed.

sndd [**-e**] [**-f**] [**-w** *file*] [[**-p**] *table_entry* . . .]
Print the send descriptor table.

snode [**-e**] [**-f**] [**-w** *file*] [[**-p**] *table_entry* . . .]
Print information about open special files. Along with other information, it prints the security attributes of a device: mode, stat, high level range, low level range, release flag, and other security flags; these attributes are supported only if the Enhanced Security Utilities are installed and running.

srmount [**-e**] [**-w** *file*] [[**-p**] *table_entry* . . .]
Print the server mount table.

stack [**-w** *file*] [*process*]
Alias: **s**.
Dump the stack. If no arguments are entered, the kernel stack for the current process is printed. The interrupt stack and the stack for the current process are not available on a running system.

stat [**-w** *file*]
Print system statistics.

stream [**-e**] [**-f**] [**-w** *file*] [[**-p**] *table_entry* . . .]
Print the streams table.

strstat [**-w** *file*]
Print streams statistics.

trace [**-w** *file*] [**-r**] [*process*]
Alias: **t**.
Print stack trace. The kfp value is used with the **-r** option; the **kfp** function prints or sets the kfp (kernel frame pointer) value.

ts [**-w** *file*] *virtual_address . . .*
Print text symbol closest to the designated address.

tsdptbl [**-w** *file*] [*table_entry . . .*]
Print the time-sharing scheduler parameter table. See **ts_dptbl**(4).

tsproc [**-w** *file*]
Print information about processes in the time-sharing scheduler class.

tty [**-e**] [**-f**] [**-l**] [**-w** *file*] [**-t** *type* [[**-p**] *table_entry . . .*] | [**-p**] *start addr*]
Valid types: **console, sr, sx, sc**.
Print the tty table. If no arguments are given, the tty table for both tty types is printed. If the **-t** option is used, the table for the single tty type specified is printed. If no argument follows the type option, all entries in the table are printed. A single tty entry may be specified using *start_addr*. The **-l** option prints the line discipline information.

user [**-f**] [**-w** *file*] [*process*]
Alias: **u**.
Print the ublock for the designated process.

var [**-w** *file*]
Alias: **v**.
Print the tunable system parameters.

vfs [**-e**] [**-w** *file*] [[**-p**] *table_entry . . .*]
Alias: **mount**, **m**.
Print information about mounted file systems.

vfssw [**-w** *file*] [[**-p**] *table_entry . . .*]
Print information about configured file system types.

vnode [**-w** *file*] [[**-p**] *vnode_addr . . .*]
Print information about vnodes.

vtop [**-w** *file*] [**-s** *process*] *start_addr . . .*
Print the physical address translation of the virtual address *start_addr*.

vxinode [**-e**] [**-f**] [**-w** *file*] [[**-p**] *table_entry . . .*]
Alias: **vxi**.
Print the VxFS file system (**vxfs**) inode table; valid only for **vxfs** type file systems.

creatiadb (1M)

NAME

creatiadb – create **/etc/security/ia/index** and **/etc/security/ia/master** files

SYNOPSIS

creatiadb

DESCRIPTION

The **creatiadb** command creates the **/etc/security/ia/index** and **/etc/security/ia/master** files. It is invoked by **init** through an entry in the **inittab**(4) file at system initialization time. The files are created after each system boot.

If there are errors, a message is written to the console and to the file **/var/adm/creatialog**.

FILES

/etc/group
/etc/shadow
/etc/passwd
/etc/security/ia/audit
/etc/security/ia/level/*login-name*
/var/adm/creatialog

SEE ALSO

group(4), **init**(1M), **login**(1), **passwd**(4), **shadow**(4), **useradd**(1M), **userdel**(1M), **usermod**(1M)

DIAGNOSTICS

The **creatiadb** command exits with one of the following values:

0 SUCCESS.

1 Failure. Master and index files unchanged.

2 Failure. I&A data file(s) missing.

NAME

`cron` – clock daemon

SYNOPSIS

`/usr/sbin/cron` [*nofork*]

DESCRIPTION

The **cron** command starts a process that executes commands at specified dates and times. Regularly scheduled commands can be specified according to instructions found in **crontab** files in the directory **/var/spool/cron/crontabs**. Users can submit their own **crontab** file via the **crontab** command. Commands to be executed only once may be submitted via the **at** command.

cron normally forks itself and places itself into the background. When the *nofork* option is specified, this initial fork is not performed. This would allow **cron** to be started via **inittab** rather than during system boot time.

The commands are not executed if, at the time of execution, the requesting user ID or level ID has been deleted, or if the level is no longer a valid login level for the requesting user.

cron only examines **crontab** files and **at** command files during process initialization and when a file changes via the **crontab** or **at** commands. This reduces the overhead of checking for new or changed files at regularly scheduled intervals.

Because **cron** never exits, it should be executed only once, normally through **/etc/rc2.d/S75cron** at system boot time. The file **/etc/cron.d/LCK_CRON** is used as a lock file to prevent the execution of more than one **cron**.

Use the following files, described in **cron**(4), to control **cron**:

> To specify whether **cron** is to log all actions, set **CRONLOG** to **YES** or to **NO** in **/etc/default/cron**. **cron** usually creates huge log files.
>
> Specify the number of concurrent jobs per user, their priority, and a retry interval in the file **/etc/cron.d/queuedefs**.

NOTE

Changing the time of day clock on the system affects the execution of jobs specified in **crontab** files. If the clock is moved ahead, the jobs scheduled for the skipped time interval will not be run. If the clock is moved back, the jobs already executed in the time interval to be revisited will be run a second time. Adjusting the system time because of standard or alternate time zone changes, including daylight time changes, causes this problem.

FILES

`/etc/cron.d`	main cron directory
`/etc/cron.d/queuedefs`	concurrency, priority, retry options file
`/etc/cron.d/LCK_CRON`	lock file
`/etc/default/cron`	log options file
`/var/cron/log`	accounting information
`/var/spool/cron`	spool area
`/usr/lib/locale/`*locale*`/LC_MESSAGES/uxcore`	language-specific message file [See **LANG** on **environ**(5).]

SEE ALSO

`at`(1), `cron`(4), `crontab`(1)

DIAGNOSTICS

A history of all actions taken by **`cron`** is recorded in **`/var/cron/log`** if logging is turned on.

NAME

`crontab` – user `crontab` file

SYNOPSIS

`crontab` [*file*]
`crontab -e` [`-u` *username*]
`crontab -r` [`-u` *username*]
`crontab -l` [`-u` *username*]

DESCRIPTION

`crontab` copies the specified file, or standard input if no file is specified, into a directory that holds all users' `crontab`s.

The –e option edits a copy of the current user's `crontab` file, or creates an empty file to edit if `crontab` does not exist. When editing is complete, the file is installed as the user's `crontab` file. If `-u` *username* is given, the specified user's `crontab` file is edited, rather than the current user's `crontab` file; this may only be done by a privileged user. The `-e` option invokes the editor specified by the `VISUAL` environment variable, and if that is null, it looks at the `EDITOR` environment variable, and if that is null, it invokes `ed`(1).

The `-r` option removes a user's `crontab` from the `crontab` directory.

The –l options lists the `crontab` file for the invoking user.

Only a privileged user can use `-u` *username* following the `-e`, `-l`, or `-r` options, to edit, list, or remove the `crontab` file of the specified user.

Users are permitted to use `crontab` if their names appear in the file `/etc/cron.d/cron.allow.` If that file does not exist, the file `/etc/cron.d/cron.deny` is checked to determine if the user should be denied access to `crontab`. If neither file exists, only root is allowed to submit a job. If `cron.allow` does not exist and `cron.deny` exists but is empty, global usage is permitted. The allow/deny files consist of one user name per line.

A crontab file consists of lines of six fields each. The fields are separated by spaces or tabs. The first five are integer patterns that specify the following:

minute (0–59)
hour (0–23)
day of the month (1–31)
month of the year (1–12)
day of the week (0–6 with 0=Sunday)

Each of these patterns may be either an asterisk (meaning all valid values) or a list of elements separated by commas. An element is either a number or two numbers separated by a minus sign (meaning an inclusive range). Note that the specification of days may be made by two fields (day of the month and day of the week). If both are specified as a list of elements, both are adhered to. For example, `0 0 1,15 * 1` runs a command on the first and fifteenth of each month, as well as on every Monday. To specify days by only one field, the other field should be set to * (for example, `0 0 * * 1` runs a command only on Mondays).

The sixth field of a line in a crontab file is a string to be executed by the shell at the specified times. A percent character in this field (unless escaped by \) is translated to a newline character. Only the first line (up to a % or end of line) of the command field is executed by the shell. The other lines are made available to the command as standard input.

Any line beginning with a # is a comment and is ignored.

The shell is invoked from your **HOME** directory with an **arg0** of **sh**. Users who want to have their **.profile** executed must explicitly do so in the **crontab** file. **cron** supplies a default environment for every shell, defining **HOME**, **LOGNAME**, **SHELL(=/bin/sh)**, and **PATH(=:/bin:/usr/bin:/usr/lbin)**.

If you do not redirect the standard output and standard error of your commands, any generated output or errors will be mailed to you.

FILES

/usr/sbin/cron.d	main cron directory
/var/spool/cron/crontabs	spool area
/var/cron/log	accounting information
/etc/cron.d/cron.allow	list of allowed users
/etc/cron.d/cron.deny	list of denied users
/usr/lib/locale/*locale***/LC_MESSAGES/uxcore**	
	language-specific message file [See **LANG** on **environ**(5).]

NOTES

If you inadvertently enter the **crontab** command with no arguments, do not exit with a CTRL-**d**. If you do, all entries in your **crontab** file are removed. Instead, exit with a DEL.

If a privileged user modifies another user's **crontab** file, resulting behavior may be unpredictable. Instead, the privileged user should first **su**(1M) to the other user's login before making any changes to the **crontab** file.

The **-u** before the *username* needs to be specified only on systems based on Intel processors. Others can specify *username* without the **-u**.

SEE ALSO

at(1), **cron**(1M), **sh**(1), **su**(1M)

NAME

crypt – encode/decode

SYNOPSIS

crypt [*password*]
crypt [-k]

DESCRIPTION

crypt reads from the standard input and writes on the standard output. The *password* is a key that selects a particular transformation. If no argument is given, **crypt** demands a key from the terminal and turns off printing while the key is being typed in. If the **-k** option is used, **crypt** will use the key assigned to the environment variable **CRYPTKEY**. **crypt** encrypts and decrypts with the same key:

```
crypt key <clear >cypher
crypt key <cypher | pr
```

Files encrypted by **crypt** are compatible with those treated by the editors **ed**(1), **edit**(1), **ex**(1), and **vi**(1) in encryption mode.

The security of encrypted files depends on three factors: the fundamental method must be hard to solve; direct search of the key space must be infeasible; "sneak paths" by which keys or clear text can become visible must be minimized.

crypt implements a one-rotor machine designed along the lines of the German Enigma, but with a 256-element rotor. Methods of attack on such machines are known, but not widely; moreover the amount of work required is likely to be large.

The transformation of a key into the internal settings of the machine is deliberately designed to be expensive, that is, to take a substantial fraction of a second to compute. However, if keys are restricted to (say) three lower-case letters, then encrypted files can be read by expending only a substantial fraction of five minutes of machine time.

If the key is an argument to the **crypt** command, it is potentially visible to users executing **ps**(1) or a derivative. The choice of keys and key security are the most vulnerable aspect of **crypt**.

FILES

/dev/tty for typed key

SEE ALSO

ed(1), **edit**(1), **ex**(1), **makekey**(1), **nroff**(1), **pg**(1), **ps**(1), **stty**(1), **vi**(1)

NOTES

This command is provided with the Encryption Utilities, which is only available in the United States. If two or more files encrypted with the same key are concatenated and an attempt is made to decrypt the result, only the contents of the first of the original files will be decrypted correctly.

If output is piped to **nroff** and the encryption key is not given on the command line then do not pipe **crypt** through **pg**(1) or any other program that changes the **tty** settings. Doing so may cause **crypt** to leave terminal modes in a strange state [see **stty**(1)].

NAME

cryptkey – add, delete, or modify a key in the cr1 key database

SYNOPSIS

cryptkey [-a | -c | -d] [-s *scheme*] [*local_principal*] *remote_principal*

DESCRIPTION

cryptkey adds, deletes, or modifies the key shared by two principals in an authentication exchange.

Typically, a shared key is used in a cr1 exchange [see **cr1**(1M)]. A shared key is a bit string, known only to the parties in an exchange, that is used to authenticate a connection.

The **cryptkey** command is used to enter the shared key and the identities of the principals (the local and remote hosts or users) that are required to use the key to complete authentication. The **cryptkey** command can be used by both privileged and non-privileged users. The privileged user is the owner of the **keys** file. A non-privileged user must be the local principal for whom the key is being added, deleted, or modified.

Once the shared key has been entered using the **cryptkey** command, it is stored in the **keys** file by a daemon process. If a master key exists, the shared keys in the file are encrypted, using that master key.

The options to **cryptkey** have the following meanings:

-a Indicates that an entry for the specified principals is to be added to the **keys** file. The user will be prompted for the new key. To confirm the entry, the system prompts the user to enter the key a second time.

-c Indicates that the entry in the **keys** file for the specified principals is to be changed. The system prompts a non-privileged user to enter the old key. The system then prompts the user for a new key. To confirm the new key, the system prompts the user to enter it a second time. A privileged user is not required to enter the old key.

-d Indicates that the entry for the specified principals is to be deleted from the **keys** file. The system prompts a non-privileged user to enter the old key. A privileged user is not required to enter the old key.

-s *scheme* Specifies the name of the scheme to be used. The default for *scheme* is **cr1**, which uses DES encryption, and requires that the Encryption Utilities package be installed. If this package is not available, ENIGMA encryption can be used by specifying **cr1.enigma** as the *scheme*.

local_principal The name of the local principal sharing the key. The name has one of the following forms, where *local_user* is any logname in **/etc/passwd**:

[*local_user*][**@***local_system*]
[*local_system***!**][*local_user*]

If *local_principal* is omitted, the principal name of the effective user is assumed.

remote_principal The name of the remote principal sharing the key. The name has one of the following forms, where *remote_user* is the logname of a remote user:

[*remote_user*@]*remote_system*
remote_system[!*remote_user*]

If **cryptkey** is entered without options, the **-c** option is assumed and an existing key for the specified principals will be modified.

The system confirms a request to enter a new key by prompting the user to enter the key a second time. If the second entry does not match the first, the operation is not executed.

DIAGNOSTICS

If the daemon has been installed and is running, **cryptkey** determines success or failure based on the response of the daemon and indicates the result to the user. If the request is processed successfully, **cryptkey** exits with a value of 0; otherwise, it prints an error message and exits with a non-zero value.

FILES

/etc/iaf/cr1/keys cr1 key database

SEE ALSO

cr1(1M), **getkey**(3N), **keymaster**(1M)

NOTES

For the *local-principal*, **cryptkey** does not validate the existence of system names when they are entered, although it requires that they be printable characters. When entered by a privileged user, **cryptkey** does not validate lognames.

For the *remote-principal*, **cryptkey** does not validate system names or log names at any time.

cs(1M)

NAME

cs – Connection Server, a daemon that establishes connections for TLI/serial network services

SYNOPSIS

/usr/sbin/cs [-d | -x]

DESCRIPTION

The Connection Server (**cs**) is used to establish connections for all network services that communicate over TLI connection-oriented and serial connections. The Connection Server is automatically started when the system goes to multi-user mode. It receives connection requests for network services from client machine applications (via **cs_connect**(3N) and **dial**(3N) function calls), maps machine and service names into transport–dependent addresses, establishes connections to the services, authenticates the connections if necessary, and passes the connections back to the applications. **cs** is used by the **cu** and **uucp** commands to establish network connections. See "The Connection Server" in *Network Administration*.

cs information/status is written to **/var/adm/log/cs.log**.

Options

The following options are available to the **cs** command:

-d Invokes the Connection Server in debug mode. If the Connection Server is already running, you must **kill** the **cs** process and then restart the Connection Server with the **-d** option. The debug information is written to **/var/adm/log/cs.debug**.

-x Forces the Connection Server to reread the authentication file (**/etc/cs/auth**). The authentication file is normally only read when **cs** is started. This option must be used if the **/etc/cs/auth** file is updated while **cs** is running.

Files

/etc/cs/auth	optional file that lists authentication scheme and role associated with a particular host, service, or network tuple
/etc/iaf/serve.alias	optional file that contains a list of server names, network service names, and their aliases
/etc/iaf/serve.allow	list of network services that client applications expect to use and the authentication scheme(s) for each service
/var/adm/log/cs.debug	Connection Server debug file
/var/adm/log/cs.log	Connection Server log file

USAGE

Examples

To force the Connection Server to reread the authentication file, use:

```
cs -x
```

To put the Connection Server into debug mode, you must **kill** the current **cs** process and enter **/usr/sbin/cs -d** to start the Connection Server in debug mode.

To turn off the debug mode, you must **kill** the current Connection Server that is running in debug mode, and restart it with no options.

REFERENCES

cs_connect(3N), **dial**(3N), **reportscheme**(1M)

cscope (1)

NAME

cscope – interactively examine a C program

SYNOPSIS

cscope [*options*] [*file* . . .]

DESCRIPTION

cscope is an interactive, screen-oriented tool that allows the user to browse through C source files for specified elements of code.

By default, **cscope** examines the C (**.c** and **.h**), **lex** (**.l**), and **yacc** (**.y**) source files in the current directory. **cscope** may also be invoked for source files named on the command line. In either case, **cscope** searches the standard directories for **#include** files that it does not find in the current directory. **cscope** uses a symbol cross-reference, **cscope.out** by default, to locate functions, function calls, macros, variables, and preprocessor symbols in the files.

cscope builds the symbol cross-reference the first time it is used on the source files for the program being browsed. On a subsequent invocation, **cscope** rebuilds the cross-reference only if a source file has changed or the list of source files is different. When the cross-reference is rebuilt, the data for the unchanged files are copied from the old cross-reference, which makes rebuilding faster than the initial build.

The following options can appear in any combination:

-b Build the cross-reference only.

-C Ignore letter case when searching.

-c Use only ASCII characters in the cross-reference file, that is, do not compress the data.

-d Do not update the cross-reference.

-e Suppress the **CTRL-e** command prompt between files.

-F *symfile* Read symbol reference lines from *symfile*. (A symbol reference file is created by **>** and **>>**, and can also be read using the **<** command, described under "Issuing Subsequent Requests," below.)

-f *reffile* Use *reffile* as the cross-reference file name instead of the default **cscope.out**.

-I *incdir* Look in *incdir* (before looking in *INCDIR*, the standard place for header files, normally **/usr/include**) for any **#include** files whose names do not begin with **/** and that are not specified on the command line or in *namefile* below. (The **#include** files may be specified with either double quotes or angle brackets.) The *incdir* directory is searched in addition to the current directory (which is searched first) and the standard list (which is searched last). If more than one occurrence of **-I** appears, the directories are searched in the order they appear on the command line.

-i *namefile* Browse through all source files whose names are listed in *namefile* (file names separated by spaces, tabs, or new-lines) instead of the default (**cscope.files**). If this option is specified, **cscope** ignores any files appearing on the command line.

-L Do a single search with line-oriented output when used with the *-num pattern* option.

-l Line-oriented interface (see "Line-Oriented Interface" below).

-num pattern Go to input field *num* (counting from 0) and find *pattern*.

-P *path* Prepend *path* to relative file names in a pre-built cross-reference file so you do not have to change to the directory where the cross-reference file was built. This option is only valid with the **-d** option.

-p *n* Display the last *n* file path components instead of the default (1). Use 0 to not display the file name at all.

-q Build an inverted index for quick symbol searching. If you use this option with the **-f** option, you must use **-f** on every call to **cscope**, including when you build the cross-reference file, because it changes the names of the inverted index files.

-s *dir* Look in *dir* for additional source files. This option is ignored if source files are given on the command line.

-T Use only the first eight characters to match against C symbols. A regular expression containing special characters other than a period (.) will not match any symbol if its minimum length is greater than eight characters.

-U Do not check file time stamps (assume that no files have changed).

-u Unconditionally build the cross-reference file (assume that all files have changed).

-V Print on the first line of screen the version number of **cscope**.

The **-I**, **-p**, **-q**, and **-T** options can also be in the **cscope.files** file.

Requesting the Initial Search

After the cross-reference is ready, **cscope** will display this menu:

```
Find this C symbol:
Find this function definition:
Find functions called by this function:
Find functions calling this function:
Find this text string:
Change this text string:
Find this egrep pattern:
Find this file:
Find files #including this file:
```

Press the TAB key repeatedly to move to the desired input field, type the text to search for, and then press the RETURN key.

Issuing Subsequent Requests

If the search is successful, any of these single-character commands can be used:

`1-9`	Edit the file referenced by the given line number.
SPACE	Display next set of matching lines.
`+`	Display next set of matching lines.
–	Display previous set of matching lines.
`^e`	Edit displayed files in order.
`>`	Write the displayed list of lines to a file.
`>>`	Append the displayed list of lines to a file.
`<`	Read lines from a file that is in symbol reference format (created by `>` or `>>`), just like the `-F` option.
`^`	Filter all lines through a shell command and display the resulting lines, replacing the lines that were already there.
`|`	Pipe all lines to a shell command and display them without changing them.

At any time these single-character commands can also be used:

TAB	Move to next input field.
RETURN	Move to next input field.
`^n`	Move to next input field.
`^p`	Move to previous input field.
`^y`	Search with the last text typed.
`^b`	Move to previous input field and search pattern.
`^f`	Move to next input field and search pattern.
`^c`	Toggle ignore/use letter case when searching. (When ignoring letter case, search for **FILE** will match **File** and **file**.)
`^r`	Rebuild the cross-reference.
`!`	Start an interactive shell (type `^d` to return to **cscope**).
`^l`	Redraw the screen.
`?`	Give help information about **cscope** commands.
`^d`	Exit **cscope**.

Note: If the first character of the text to be searched for matches one of the above commands, escape it by typing a \ (backslash) first.

Substituting New Text for Old Text

After the text to be changed has been typed, **cscope** will prompt for the new text, and then it will display the lines containing the old text. Select the lines to be changed with these single-character commands:

`1-9`	Mark or unmark the line to be changed.
*	Mark or unmark all displayed lines to be changed.
SPACE	Display next set of lines.
`+`	Display next set of lines.
–	Display previous set of lines.
`a`	Mark or unmark all lines to be changed.
`^d`	Change the marked lines and exit.
ESCAPE	Exit without changing the marked lines.
`!`	Start an interactive shell (type `^d` to return to **cscope**).
`^l`	Redraw the screen.

? Give help information about **cscope** commands.

Special Keys

If your terminal has arrow keys that work in **vi**(1), you can use them to move around the input fields. The up-arrow key is useful to move to the previous input field instead of using the TAB key repeatedly. If you have CLEAR, NEXT, or PREV keys they will act as the `^l`, `+`, and `-` commands, respectively.

Line-Oriented Interface

The `-l` option lets you use **cscope** where a screen-oriented interface would not be useful, for example, from another screen-oriented program.

cscope will prompt with `>>` when it is ready for an input line starting with the field number (counting from 0) immediately followed by the search pattern, for example, `1main` finds the definition of the `main` function.

If you just want a single search, instead of the `-l` option use the `-L` and *-num pattern* options, and you won't get the `>>` prompt.

For `-l`, **cscope** outputs the number of reference lines

```
cscope: 2 lines
```

For each reference found, **cscope** outputs a line consisting of the file name, function name, line number, and line text, separated by spaces, for example,

```
main.c main 161 main(argc, argv)
```

Note that the editor is not called to display a single reference, unlike the screen-oriented interface.

You can use the `c` command to toggle ignore/use letter case when searching. (When ignoring letter case, search for `FILE` will match `File` and `file`.)

You can use the `r` command to rebuild the database.

cscope will quit when it detects end-of-file, or when the first character of an input line is `^d` or `q`.

ENVIRONMENT VARIABLES

EDITOR	Preferred editor, which defaults to **vi**(1).
HOME	Home directory, which is automatically set at login.
INCLUDEDIRS	Colon-separated list of directories to search for `#include` files.
SHELL	Preferred shell, which defaults to **sh**(1).
SOURCEDIRS	Colon-separated list of directories to search for additional source files.
TERM	Terminal type, which must be a screen terminal.
TERMINFO	Terminal information directory full path name. If your terminal is not in the standard **terminfo** directory, see **curses**(3curses) and **terminfo**(4) for how to make your own terminal description.
TMPDIR	Temporary file directory, which defaults to `/var/tmp`.
VIEWER	Preferred file display program [such as **pg**(1)], which overrides **EDITOR** (see above).

VPATH A colon-separated list of directories, each of which has the same directory structure below it. If **VPATH** is set, **cscope** searches for source files in the directories specified; if it is not set, **cscope** searches only in the current directory.

FILES

cscope.files Default files containing **-I**, **-p**, **-q**, and **-T** options and the list of source files (overridden by the **-i** option).

cscope.out Symbol cross-reference file (overridden by the **-f** option), which is put in the home directory if it cannot be created in the current directory.

cscope.in.out
cscope.po.out Default files containing the inverted index used for quick symbol searching (**-q** option). If you use the **-f** option to rename the cross-reference file (so it's not **cscope.out**), the names for these inverted index files will be created by adding **.in** and **.po** to the name you supply with **-f**. For example, if you indicated **-f xyz**, then these files would be named **xyz.in** and **xyz.po**.

INCDIR Standard directory for **#include** files (usually **/usr/include**).

NOTES

cscope recognizes function definitions of the form:

fname blank **(** *args* **)** *white arg_decs white* **{**

where:

fname	is the function name
blank	is zero or more spaces or tabs, not including newlines
args	is any string that does not contain a **"** or a newline
white	is zero or more spaces, tabs, or newlines
arg_decs	are zero or more argument declarations (*arg_decs* may include comments and white space)

It is not necessary for a function declaration to start at the beginning of a line. The return type may precede the function name; **cscope** will still recognize the declaration. Function definitions that deviate from this form will not be recognized by **cscope**.

The **Function** column of the search output for the menu option **Find functions called by this function:** input field will only display the first function called in the line, that is, for this function

```
e()
{
        return (f() + g());
}
```

the display would be

```
Functions called by this function: e

File Function Line
a.c  f     3 return(f() + g());
```

Occasionally, a function definition or call may not be recognized because of braces inside `#if` statements. Similarly, the use of a variable may be incorrectly recognized as a definition.

A `typedef` name preceding a preprocessor statement will be incorrectly recognized as a global definition, for example,

```
LDFILE *
#if AR16WR
```

Preprocessor statements can also prevent the recognition of a global definition, for example,

```
char flag
#ifdef ALLOCATE_STORAGE
     = -1
#endif
;
```

A function declaration inside a function is incorrectly recognized as a function call, for example,

```
f()
{
     void g();
}
```

is incorrectly recognized as a call to `g()`.

`cscope` recognizes C++ classes by looking for the class keyword, but doesn't recognize that a `struct` is also a class, so it doesn't recognize inline member function definitions in a structure. It also doesn't expect the class keyword in a `typedef`, so it incorrectly recognizes `X` as a definition in

```
typedef class X * Y;
```

It also doesn't recognize operator function definitions

```
Bool Feature::operator==(const Feature & other)
{
     ...
}
```

Nor does it recognize function definitions with a function pointer argument

```
ParseTable::Recognize(int startState, char *pattern,
        int finishState, void (*FinalAction)(char *))
{
        ...
}
```

csh(1)

NAME

csh – shell command interpreter with a C-like syntax

SYNOPSIS

csh [**-bcefinstvVxX**] [*argument* . . .]

DESCRIPTION

csh, the C shell, is a command interpreter with a syntax reminiscent of the C language. It provides a number of convenient features for interactive use that are not available with the standard (Bourne) shell, including filename completion, command aliasing, history substitution, job control, and a number of built-in commands. As with the standard shell, the C shell provides variable, command and filename substitution.

Initialization and Termination

When first started, the C shell normally performs commands from the **.cshrc** file in your home directory, provided that it is readable and you either own it or your real group ID matches its group ID. If the shell is invoked with a name that starts with '–', as when started by **login**(1), the shell runs as a **login** shell. In this case, after executing commands from the **.cshrc** file, the shell executes commands from the **.login** file in your home directory; the same permission checks as those for **.cshrc** are applied to this file. Typically, the **.login** file contains commands to specify the terminal type and environment.

As a login shell terminates, it performs commands from the **.logout** file in your home directory; the same permission checks as those for **.cshrc** are applied to this file.

Interactive Operation

After startup processing is complete, an interactive C shell begins reading commands from the terminal, prompting with *hostname*% (or *hostname*# for the privileged user). The shell then repeatedly performs the following actions: a line of command input is read and broken into *words*. This sequence of words is placed on the history list and then parsed, as described under USAGE, below. Finally, the shell executes each command in the current line.

Noninteractive Operation

When running noninteractively, the shell does not prompt for input from the terminal. A noninteractive C shell can execute a command supplied as an *argument* on its command line, or interpret commands from a script.

The following options are available:

-b Force a break from option processing. Subsequent command-line arguments are not interpreted as C shell options. This allows the passing of options to a script without confusion. The shell does not run a set-user-ID script unless this option is present.

-c Read commands from the first filename *argument* (which must be present). Remaining arguments are placed in **argv**, the argument-list variable.

-e Exit if a command terminates abnormally or yields a nonzero exit status.

-f Fast start. Read neither the **.cshrc** file, nor the **.login** file (if a login shell) upon startup.

-i Forced interactive. Prompt for command-line input, even if the standard input does not appear to be a terminal (character-special device).

-n Parse (interpret), but do not execute commands. This option can be used to check C shell scripts for syntax errors.

-s Take commands from the standard input.

-t Read and execute a single command line. A '\' (backslash) can be used to escape each newline for continuation of the command line onto subsequent input lines.

-v Verbose. Set the **verbose** predefined variable; command input is echoed after history substitution (but before other substitutions) and before execution.

-V Set **verbose** before reading **.cshrc**.

-x Echo. Set the **echo** variable; echo commands after all substitutions and just before execution.

-X Set **echo** before reading **.cshrc**.

Except with the options **-c**, **-i**, **-s** or **-t**, the first nonoption *argument* is taken to be the name of a command or script. It is passed as argument zero, and subsequent arguments are added to the argument list for that command or script.

USAGE

Filename Completion

When enabled by setting the variable **filec**, an interactive C shell can complete a partially typed filename or user name. When an unambiguous partial filename is followed by an ESC character on the terminal input line, the shell fills in the remaining characters of a matching filename from the working directory.

If a partial filename is followed by the EOF character (usually typed as CTRL-d), the shell lists all filenames that match. It then prompts once again, supplying the incomplete command line typed in so far.

When the last (partial) word begins with a tilde (~), the shell attempts completion with a user name, rather than a file in the working directory.

The terminal bell signals errors or multiple matches; this can be inhibited by setting the variable **nobeep**. You can exclude files with certain suffixes by listing those suffixes in the variable **fignore**. If, however, the only possible completion includes a suffix in the list, it is not ignored. **fignore** does not affect the listing of filenames by the EOF character.

Lexical Structure

The shell splits input lines into words at space and tab characters, except as noted below. The characters **&**, **|**, **;**, **<**, **>**, **(**, and **)** form separate words; if paired, the pairs form single words. These shell metacharacters can be made part of other words, and their special meaning can be suppressed by preceding them with a '\' (backslash). A newline preceded by a \ is equivalent to a space character.

In addition, a string enclosed in matched pairs of single-quotes (´), double-quotes ("), or backquotes (` ), forms a partial word; metacharacters in such a string, including any space or tab characters, do not form separate words. Within pairs of backquote ( `) or double-quote (") characters, a newline preceded by a '\' (backslash) gives a true newline character. Additional functions of each type of quote are described, below, under **Variable Substitution**, **Command Substitution**, and **Filename Substitution**.

When the shell's input is not a terminal, the character # introduces a comment that continues to the end of the input line. Its special meaning is suppressed when preceded by a \ or enclosed in matching quotes.

Command Line Parsing

A *simple command* is composed of a sequence of words. The first word (that is not part of an I/O redirection) specifies the command to be executed. A simple command, or a set of simple commands separated by | or |& characters, forms a *pipeline*. With |, the standard output of the preceding command is redirected to the standard input of the command that follows. With |&, both the standard error and the standard output are redirected through the pipeline.

Pipelines can be separated by semicolons (;), in which case they are executed sequentially. Pipelines that are separated by && or || form conditional sequences in which the execution of pipelines on the right depends upon the success or failure, respectively, of the pipeline on the left.

A pipeline or sequence can be enclosed within parentheses '( )' to form a simple command that can be a component in a pipeline or sequence.

A sequence of pipelines can be executed asynchronously, or in the background by appending an '&'; rather than waiting for the sequence to finish before issuing a prompt, the shell displays the job number (see **Job Control**, below) and associated process IDs, and prompts immediately.

History Substitution

History substitution allows you to use words from previous command lines in the command line you are typing. This simplifies spelling corrections and the repetition of complicated commands or arguments. Command lines are saved in the history list, the size of which is controlled by the **history** variable. The most recent command is retained in any case. A history substitution begins with a **!** (although you can change this with the **histchars** variable) and may occur anywhere on the command line; history substitutions do not nest. The **!** can be escaped with \ to suppress its special meaning.

Input lines containing history substitutions are echoed on the terminal after being expanded, but before any other substitutions take place or the command gets executed.

Event Designators

An event designator is a reference to a command-line entry in the history list.

! Start a history substitution, except when followed by a space character, tab, newline, = or (.

`!!`	Refer to the previous command. By itself, this substitution repeats the previous command.
`!`*n*	Refer to command-line *n* .
`!-`*n*	Refer to the current command-line minus *n*.
`!str`	Refer to the most recent command starting with **`str`**.
`!?`*str*`[?]`	Refer to the most recent command containing **`str`**.
`!{...}`	Insulate a history reference from adjacent characters (if necessary).

Word Designators

A '`:`' (colon) separates the event specification from the word designator. It can be omitted if the word designator begins with a `^`, `$`, `*`, `-` or `%`. If the word is to be selected from the previous command, the second `!` character can be omitted from the event specification. For instance, `!!:1` and `!:1` both refer to the first word of the previous command, while `!!$` and `!$` both refer to the last word in the previous command. Word designators include:

`#`	The entire command line typed so far.
`0`	The first input word (command).
n	The *n*'th argument.
`^`	The first argument, that is, `1`.
`$`	The last argument.
`%`	The word matched by (the most recent) `?`*s* search.
x`-`*y*	A range of words; `-`*y* abbreviates `0-`*y*.
`*`	All the arguments, or a null value if there is just one word in the event.
x`*`	Abbreviates *x*`-$`.
x`-`	Like *x** but omitting word `$`.

Modifiers

After the optional word designator, you can add a sequence of one or more of the following modifiers, each preceded by a `:`.

`h`	Remove a trailing pathname component, leaving the head.
`r`	Remove a trailing suffix of the form '`.`*xxx*', leaving the basename.
`e`	Remove all but the suffix.
`s/`*l*`/`*r*`[/]`	Substitute *r* for *l*.
`t`	Remove all leading pathname components, leaving the tail.
`&`	Repeat the previous substitution.
`g`	Apply the change to the first occurrence of a match in each word, by prefixing the above (for example, `g&`).
`p`	Print the new command but do not execute it.
`q`	Quote the substituted words, escaping further substitutions.
`x`	Like `q`, but break into words at each space character, tab or newline.

Unless preceded by a `g`, the modification is applied only to the first string that matches *l*; an error results if no string matches.

The left-hand side of substitutions are not regular expressions, but character strings. Any character can be used as the delimiter in place of `/`. A backslash quotes the delimiter character. The character `&`, in the right hand side, is replaced by the text from the left-hand-side. The `&` can be quoted with a backslash. A null *l* uses the previous string either from a *l* or from a contextual scan string *s* from **!?***s*. You can omit the rightmost delimiter if a newline immediately follows *r*; the rightmost **?** in a context scan can similarly be omitted.

Without an event specification, a history reference refers either to the previous command, or to a previous history reference on the command line (if any).

Quick Substitution

^*l*^*r*[^] This is equivalent to the history substitution: **!:s**^*l*^*r*[^].

Aliases

The C shell maintains a list of aliases that you can create, display, and modify using the **alias** and **unalias** commands. The shell checks the first word in each command to see if it matches the name of an existing alias. If it does, the command is reprocessed with the alias definition replacing its name; the history substitution mechanism is made available as though that command were the previous input line. This allows history substitutions, escaped with a backslash in the definition, to be replaced with actual command-line arguments when the alias is used. If no history substitution is called for, the arguments remain unchanged.

Aliases can be nested. That is, an alias definition can contain the name of another alias. Nested aliases are expanded before any history substitutions is applied. This is useful in pipelines such as

```
alias lm ´ls -l \!* | more´
```

which when called, pipes the output of **ls**(1) through **more**(1).

Except for the first word, the name of the alias may not appear in its definition, nor in any alias referred to by its definition. Such loops are detected, and cause an error message.

I/O Redirection

The following metacharacters indicate that the subsequent word is the name of a file to which the command's standard input, standard output, or standard error is redirected; this word is variable, command, and filename expanded separately from the rest of the command.

< Redirect the standard input.

< < *word* Read the standard input, up to a line that is identical with *word*, and place the resulting lines in a temporary file. Unless *word* is escaped or quoted, variable and command substitutions are performed on these lines. Then, invoke the pipeline with the temporary file as its standard input. *word* is not subjected to variable, filename, or command substitution, and each line is compared to it before any substitutions are performed by the shell.

> >! >& >&! Redirect the standard output to a file. If the file does not exist, it is created. If it does exist, it is overwritten; its previous contents are lost.

When set, the variable **noclobber** prevents destruction of existing files. It also prevents redirection to terminals and **/dev/null**, unless one of the **!** forms is used. The **&** forms redirect both standard output and the the standard error (diagnostic output) to the file.

>> >>& >>! >>&!
Append the standard output. Like **>**, but places output at the end of the file rather than overwriting it. If **noclobber** is set, it is an error for the file not to exist, unless one of the **!** forms is used. The **&** forms append both the standard error and standard output to the file.

Variable Substitution

The C shell maintains a set of *variables*, each of which is composed of a *name* and a *value*. A variable name consists of up to 20 letters and digits, and starts with a letter (the underscore is considered a letter). A variable's value is a space-separated list of zero or more words.

To refer to a variable's value, precede its name with a '**$**'. Certain references (described below) can be used to select specific words from the value, or to display other information about the variable. Braces can be used to insulate the reference from other characters in an input-line word.

Variable substitution takes place after the input line is analyzed, aliases are resolved, and I/O redirections are applied. Exceptions to this are variable references in I/O redirections (substituted at the time the redirection is made), and backquoted strings (see Command Substitution).

Variable substitution can be suppressed by preceding the **$** with a \, except within double-quotes where it always occurs. Variable substitution is suppressed inside of single-quotes. A **$** is escaped if followed by a space character, tab or newline.

Variables can be created, displayed, or destroyed using the **set** and **unset** commands. Some variables are maintained or used by the shell. For instance, the **argv** variable contains an image of the shell's argument list. Of the variables used by the shell, a number are toggles; the shell does not care what their value is, only whether they are set or not.

Numerical values can be operated on as numbers (as with the **@** built-in). With numeric operations, an empty value is considered to be zero; the second and subsequent words of multiword values are ignored. For instance, when the **verbose** variable is set to any value (including an empty value), command input is echoed on the terminal.

Command and filename substitution is subsequently applied to the words that result from the variable substitution, except when suppressed by double-quotes, when **noglob** is set (suppressing filename substitution), or when the reference is quoted with the **:q** modifier. Within double-quotes, a reference is expanded to form (a portion of) a quoted string; multiword values are expanded to a string with embedded space characters. When the **:q** modifier is applied to the reference, it is expanded to a list of space-separated words, each of which is quoted to prevent subsequent command or filename substitutions.

Except as noted below, it is an error to refer to a variable that is not set.

`$`*var*
`${`*var*`}` These are replaced by words from the value of *var*, each separated by a space character. If *var* is an environment variable, its value is returned (but '`:`' modifiers and the other forms given below are not available).

`$`*var*`[`*index*`]`
`${`*var*`[`*index*`]}` These select only the indicated words from the value of *var*. Variable substitution is applied to *index*, which may consist of (or result in) a either single number, two numbers separated by a '–', or an asterisk. Words are indexed starting from 1; a '`*`' selects all words. If the first number of a range is omitted (as with **`$argv[-2]`**), it defaults to 1. If the last number of a range is omitted (as with **`$argv[1-]`**), it defaults to **`$#`***var* (the word count). It is not an error for a range to be empty if the second argument is omitted (or within range).

`$#`*name*
`${#`*name*`}` These give the number of words in the variable.

`$0` This substitutes the name of the file from which command input is being read. An error occurs if the name is not known.

`$`*n*
`${`*n*`}` Equivalent to **`$argv`**`[`*n*`]`.

`$*` Equivalent to **`$argv`**`[*]`.

The modifiers **`:e`**, **`:h`**, **`:q`**, **`:r`**, **`:t`** and **`:x`** can be applied (see **`History Substitution`**), as can **`:gh`**, **`:gt`** and **`:gr`**. If **`{ }`** (braces) are used, then the modifiers must appear within the braces. The current implementation allows only one such modifier per expansion.

The following references may not be modified with **`:`** modifiers.

`$?`*var*
`${?`*var*`}` Substitutes the string 1 if *var* is set or 0 if it is not set.

`$?0` Substitutes 1 if the current input filename is known, or 0 if it is not.

`$$` Substitute the process number of the (parent) shell.

`$<` Substitutes a line from the standard input, with no further interpretation thereafter. It can be used to read from the keyboard in a C shell script.

Command and Filename Substitutions

Command and filename substitutions are applied selectively to the arguments of built-in commands. Portions of expressions that are not evaluated are not expanded. For non-built-in commands, filename expansion of the command name is done separately from that of the argument list; expansion occurs in a subshell, after I/O redirection is performed.

Command Substitution

A command enclosed by backquotes (` ... `) is performed by a subshell. Its standard output is broken into separate words at each space character, tab and newline; null words are discarded. This text replaces the backquoted string on the current command line. Within double-quotes, only newline characters force new words; space and tab characters are preserved. However, a final newline is ignored. It is therefore possible for a command substitution to yield a partial word.

Filename Substitution

Unquoted words containing any of the characters `*`, `?`, `[` or `{`, or that begin with `~`, are expanded (also known as *globbing*) to an alphabetically sorted list of filenames, as follows:

`*` Match any (zero or more) characters.

`?` Match any single character.

`[...]` Match any single character in the enclosed list(s) or range(s). A list is a string of characters. A range is two characters separated by a minus-sign (-), and includes all the characters in between in the ASCII collating sequence [see **ascii**(5)].

`{` *str*, *str*, ... `}` Expand to each string (or filename-matching pattern) in the comma-separated list. Unlike the pattern-matching expressions above, the expansion of this construct is not sorted. For instance, `{b,a}` expands to '`b`' '`a`', (not '`a`' '`b`'). As special cases, the characters `{` and `}`, along with the string `{}`, are passed undisturbed.

~[*user*] Your home directory, as indicated by the value of the variable **home**, or that of *user*, as indicated by the password entry for *user*.

Only the patterns `*`, `?` and `[...]` imply pattern matching; an error results if no filename matches a pattern that contains them. The '`.`' (dot character), when it is the first character in a filename or pathname component, must be matched explicitly. The `/` (slash) must also be matched explicitly.

Expressions and Operators

A number of C shell built-in commands accept expressions, in which the operators are similar to those of C and have the same precedence. These expressions typically appear in the **@**, **exit**, **if**, **set** and **while** commands, and are often used to regulate the flow of control for executing commands. Components of an expression are separated by white space.

Null or missing values are considered 0. The result of all expressions are strings, which may represent decimal numbers.

The following C shell operators are grouped in order of precedence:

`( ... )`	grouping
`~`	one's complement
`!`	logical negation
`*  /  %`	multiplication, division, remainder (These are right associative, which can lead to unexpected results. Group combinations explicitly with parentheses.)
`+  -`	addition, subtraction (also right associative)
`<<  >>`	bitwise shift left, bitwise shift right
`<  >  <=  >=`	less than, greater than, less than or equal to, greater than or equal to
`==  !=  =~  !~`	equal to, not equal to, filename-substitution pattern match (described below), filename-substitution pattern mismatch
`&`	bitwise AND
`^`	bitwise XOR (exclusive or)
`|`	bitwise inclusive OR
`&&`	logical AND
`||`	logical OR

The operators: `==`, `!=`, `=~`, and `!~` compare their arguments as strings; other operators use numbers. The operators `=~` and `!~` each check whether or not a string to the left matches a filename substitution pattern on the right. This reduces the need for **`switch`** statements when pattern-matching between strings is all that is required.

Also available are file inquiries:

-r *filename* Return true, or 1 if the user has read access. Otherwise it returns false, or 0.

-w *filename* True if the user has write access.

-x *filename* True if the user has execute permission (or search permission on a directory).

-e *filename* True if *file* exists.

-o *filename* True if the user owns *file*.

-z *filename* True if *file* is of zero length (empty).

-f *filename* True if *file* is a plain file.

-d *filename* True if *file* is a directory.

If *file* does not exist or is inaccessible, then all inquiries return false.

An inquiry as to the success of a command is also available:

`{` *command* `}` If *command* runs successfully, the expression evaluates to true, 1. Otherwise it evaluates to false 0. (Note that, conversely, *command* itself typically returns 0 when it runs successfully, or some other value if it encounters a problem. If you want to get at the status directly, use the value of the **`status`** variable rather than this expression).

Control Flow

The shell contains a number of commands to regulate the flow of control in scripts, and within limits, from the terminal. These commands operate by forcing the shell either to reread input (to *loop*), or to skip input under certain conditions (to *branch*).

Each occurrence of a **foreach**, **switch**, **while**, **if**...**then** and **else** built-in must appear as the first word on its own input line.

If the shell's input is not seekable and a loop is being read, that input is buffered. The shell performs seeks within the internal buffer to accomplish the rereading implied by the loop. (To the extent that this allows, backward **goto** commands will succeed on nonseekable inputs.)

Command Execution

If the command is a C shell built-in, the shell executes it directly. Otherwise, the shell searches for a file by that name with execute access. If the command-name contains a /, the shell takes it as a pathname, and searches for it. If the command-name does not contain a /, the shell attempts to resolve it to a pathname, searching each directory in the **path** variable for the command. To speed the search, the shell uses its hash table (see the **rehash** built-in) to eliminate directories that have no applicable files. This hashing can be disabled with the **-c** or **-t**, options, or the **unhash** built-in.

As a special case, if there is no / in the name of the script and there is an alias for the word **shell**, the expansion of the **shell** alias is prepended (without modification), to the command line. The system attempts to execute the first word of this special (late-occurring) alias, which should be a full pathname. Remaining words of the alias's definition, along with the text of the input line, are treated as arguments.

When a pathname is found that has proper execute permissions, the shell forks a new process and passes it, along with its arguments to the kernel (using the **execve** system call). The kernel then attempts to overlay the new process with the desired program. If the file is an executable binary (in **a.out**(4) format) the kernel succeeds, and begins executing the new process. If the file is a text file, and the first line begins with **#!**, the next word is taken to be the pathname of a shell (or command) to interpret that script. Subsequent words on the first line are taken as options for that shell. The kernel invokes (overlays) the indicated shell, using the name of the script as an argument.

If neither of the above conditions holds, the kernel cannot overlay the file (the **execve** call fails); the C shell then attempts to execute the file by spawning a new shell, as follows:

- If the first character of the file is a **#**, a C shell is invoked.
- Otherwise, a standard (Bourne) shell is invoked.

Signal Handling

The shell normally ignores QUIT signals. Background jobs are immune to signals generated from the keyboard, including hangups (HUP). Other signals have the values that the C shell inherited from its environment. The shell's handling of interrupt and terminate signals within scripts can be controlled by the **onintr** built-in. Login shells catch the TERM signal; otherwise this signal is passed on to child processes. In no case are interrupts allowed when a login shell is reading the `.logout` file.

Job Control

The shell associates a numbered *job* with each command sequence, to keep track of those commands that are running in the background or have been stopped with TSTP signals (typically CTRL-z). When a command, or command sequence (semi-colon separated list), is started in the background using the **&** metacharacter, the shell displays a line with the job number in brackets, and a list of associated process numbers:

```
[1] 1234
```

To see the current list of jobs, use the **jobs** built-in command. The job most recently stopped (or put into the background if none are stopped) is referred to as the *current* job, and is indicated with a '+'. The previous job is indicated with a '–'; when the current job is terminated or moved to the foreground, this job takes its place (becomes the new current job).

To manipulate jobs, refer to the **bg**, **fg**, **kill**, **stop** and **%** built-ins.

A reference to a job begins with a '%'. By itself, the percent-sign refers to the current job.

`% %+ %%`	The current job.
`%–`	The previous job.
`%`*j*	Refer to job *j* as in: '**kill -9 %***j*'. *j* can be a job number, or a string that uniquely specifies the command-line by which it was started; '**fg %vi**' might bring a stopped **vi** job to the foreground, for instance.
`%?`*string*	Specify the job for which the command-line uniquely contains *string*.

A job running in the background stops when it attempts to read from the terminal. Background jobs can normally produce output, but this can be suppressed using the '**stty tostop**' command.

Status Reporting

While running interactively, the shell tracks the status of each job and reports whenever a finishes or becomes blocked. It normally displays a message to this effect as it issues a prompt, so as to avoid disturbing the appearance of your input. When set, the **notify** variable indicates that the shell is to report status changes immediately. By default, the **notify** command marks the current process; after starting a background job, type **notify** to mark it.

Built-In Commands

Built-in commands are executed within the C shell. If a built-in command occurs as any component of a pipeline except the last, it is executed in a subshell.

: Null command. This command is interpreted, but performs no action.

alias [*name* [*def*]]
Assign *def* to the alias *name*. *def* is a list of words that may contain escaped history-substitution metasyntax. *name* is not allowed to be **alias** or **unalias**. If *def* is omitted, the alias *name* is displayed along with its current definition. If both *name* and *def* are omitted, all aliases are displayed.

bg [%*job*] . . .
Run the current or specified jobs in the background.

break Resume execution after the **end** of the nearest enclosing **foreach** or **while** loop. The remaining commands on the current line are executed. This allows multilevel breaks to be written as a list of **break** commands, all on one line.

breaksw Break from a **switch**, resuming after the **endsw**.

case *label*:
A label in a **switch** statement.

cd [*dir*]
chdir [*dir*]
Change the shell's working directory to directory *dir*. If no argument is given, change to the home directory of the user. If *dir* is a relative pathname not found in the current directory, check for it in those directories listed in the **cdpath** variable. If *dir* is the name of a shell variable whose value starts with a /, change to the directory named by that value.

continue Continue execution of the nearest enclosing **while** or **foreach**.

default: Labels the default case in a **switch** statement. The default should come after all **case** labels. Any remaining commands on the command line are first executed.

dirs [**-l**]
Print the directory stack, most recent to the left; the first directory shown is the current directory. With the **-l** argument, produce an unabbreviated printout; use of the ~ notation is suppressed.

echo [**-n**] *list*
The words in *list* are written to the shell's standard output, separated by space characters. The output is terminated with a newline unless the **-n** option is used.

eval *argument* ...
Reads the arguments as input to the shell, and executes the resulting command(s). This is usually used to execute commands generated as the result of command or variable substitution, since parsing occurs before these substitutions. See **tset**(1) for an example of how to use **eval**.

exec *command*
Execute *command* in place of the current shell, which terminates.

exit [(*expr*)]
The shell exits, either with the value of the STATUS variable, or with the value of the specified by the expression **expr**.

fg % [*job*]
Bring the current or specified *job* into the foreground.

foreach *var* (*wordlist*)
...
end The variable *var* is successively set to each member of *wordlist*. The sequence of commands between this command and the matching **end** is executed for each new value of *var*. (Both **foreach** and **end** must appear alone on separate lines.)

The built-in command **continue** may be used to continue the loop prematurely and the built-in command **break** to terminate it prematurely. When this command is read from the terminal, the loop is read up once prompting with **?** before any statements in the loop are executed.

glob *wordlist*
Perform filename expansion on *wordlist*. Like **echo**, but no \ escapes are recognized. Words are delimited by **NULL** characters in the output.

goto *label* The specified *label* is filename and command expanded to yield a label. The shell rewinds its input as much as possible and searches for a line of the form *label*: possibly preceded by space or tab characters. Execution continues after the indicated line. It is an error to jump to a label that occurs between a **while** or **for** built-in, and its corresponding **end**.

hashstat Print a statistics line indicating how effective the internal hash table has been at locating commands (and avoiding **exec**s). An **exec** is attempted for each component of the *path* where the hash function indicates a possible hit, and in each component that does not begin with a '/'.

history [**-hr**] [*n*]
Display the history list; if *n* is given, display only the *n* most recent events.

-r Reverse the order of printout to be most recent first rather than oldest first.

-h Display the history list without leading numbers. This is used to produce files suitable for sourcing using the **-h** option to *source*.

if (*expr*) *command*
If the specified expression evaluates to true, the single *command* with arguments is executed. Variable substitution on *command* happens early, at the same time it does for the rest of the *if* command. *command* must be a simple command, not a pipeline, a command list, or a parenthesized command list. Note: I/O redirection occurs even if **expr** is false, when *command* is *not* executed (this is a bug).

`if` (*expr*) `then`
...
`else if` (*expr2*) `then`
...
`else`
...
`endif` If **expr**"" is true, commands up to the first **else** are executed. Otherwise, if *expr2* is true, the commands between the **else if** and the second **else** are executed. Otherwise, commands between the **else** and the **endif** are executed. Any number of **else if** pairs are allowed, but only one **else**. Only one **endif** is needed, but it is required. The words **else** and **endif** must be the first nonwhite characters on a line. The **if** must appear alone on its input line or after an **else**.)

`jobs`[`-l`]
List the active jobs under job control.

`-l` List process IDs, in addition to the normal information.

`kill` [-*sig*] [*pid*] [%*job*] ...
`kill -l` Send the TERM (terminate) signal, by default, or the signal specified, to the specified process ID, the *job* indicated, or the current *job*. Signals are either given by number or by name. There is no default. Typing **kill** does not send a signal to the current job. If the signal being sent is TERM (terminate) or HUP (hangup), then the job or process is sent a CONT (continue) signal as well.

`-l` List the signal names that can be sent.

`limit` [`-h`] [*resource* [*max-use*]]
Limit the consumption by the current process or any process it spawns, each not to exceed *max-use* on the specified *resource*. If *max-use* is omitted, print the current limit; if *resource* is omitted, display all limits.

`-h` Use hard limits instead of the current limits. Hard limits impose a ceiling on the values of the current limits. Only the privileged user may raise the hard limits.

resource is one of:

cputime	Maximum CPU seconds per process.
filesize	Largest single file allowed.
datasize	Maximum data size (including stack) for the process.
stacksize	Maximum stack size for the process.
coredumpsize	Maximum size of a core dump (file).
descriptors	Maximum number of file descriptors per process.
memoryuse	Maximum size of mapped virtual memory for the process.

max-use is a number, with an optional scaling factor, as follows:

*n***h**	Hours (for **cputime**).
*n***k**	*n* kilobytes. This is the default for all but **cputime**.
*n***m**	*n* megabytes or minutes (for **cputime**).
*mm***:***ss*	Minutes and seconds (for **cputime**).

login [*username* | **-p**]
Terminate a login shell and invoke **login**(1). The **.logout** file is not processed. If *username* is omitted, **login** prompts for the name of a user.

-p Preserve the current environment (variables).

logout Terminate a login shell.

nice [+*n* | -*n*] [*command*]
Increment the process priority value for the shell or for *command* by *n*. The higher the priority value, the lower the priority of a process, and the slower it runs. When given, *command* is always run in a subshell, and the restrictions placed on commands in simple **if** commands apply. If *command* is omitted, **nice** increments the value for the current shell. If no increment is specified, **nice** sets the process priority value to 4. The range of process priority values is from –20 to 20. Values of *n* outside this range set the value to the lower, or to the higher boundary, respectively.

+*n* Increment the process priority value by *n*.
-*n* Decrement by *n*. This argument can be used only by the privileged user.

nohup [*command*]
Run *command* with HUPs ignored. With no arguments, ignore HUPs throughout the remainder of a script. When given, *command* is always run in a subshell, and the restrictions placed on commands in simple **if** commands apply. All processes detached with **&** are effectively **nohup**'d.

notify [%*job*] . . .
Notify the user asynchronously when the status of the current, or of specified jobs, changes.

onintr [- | *label*]
Control the action of the shell on interrupts. With no arguments, **onintr** restores the default action of the shell on interrupts. (The shell terminates shell scripts and returns to the terminal command input level). With the **-** argument, the shell ignores all interrupts. With a *label* argument, the shell executes a **goto** *label* when an interrupt is received or a child process terminates because it was interrupted.

popd [+*n*] Pop the directory stack, and **cd** to the new top directory. The elements of the directory stack are numbered from 0 starting at the top.

+*n* Discard the *n*'th entry in the stack.

pushd [+*n* | *dir*]
Push a directory onto the directory stack. With no arguments, exchange the top two elements.

+*n* Rotate the *n*'th entry to the top of the stack and **cd** to it.

dir Push the current working directory onto the stack and change to *dir*.

rehash Recompute the internal hash table of the contents of directories listed in the *path* variable to account for new commands added.

repeat *count command*

Repeat *command count* times. *command* is subject to the same restrictions as with the one-line **if** statement.

set [*var* [= *value*]]
set *var*[*n*] = *word*

With no arguments, **set** displays the values of all shell variables. Multiword values are displayed as a parenthesized list. With the *var* argument alone, **set** assigns an empty (null) value to the variable *var*. With arguments of the form *var* = *value* **set** assigns *value* to *var*, where *value* is one of:

word	A single word (or quoted string).
(*wordlist*)	A space-separated list of words enclosed in parentheses.

Values are command and filename expanded before being assigned. The form **set** *var*[*n*] = *word* replaces the *n*'th word in a multiword value with *word*.

setenv [*VAR* [*word*]]

With no arguments, **setenv** displays all environment variables. With the *VAR* argument sets the environment variable *VAR* to have an empty (null) value. (By convention, environment variables are normally given upper-case names.) With both *VAR* and *word* arguments **setenv** sets the environment variable **NAME** to the value *word*, which must be either a single word or a quoted string. The most commonly used environment variables, **USER**, **TERM**, and **PATH**, are automatically imported to and exported from the **csh** variables **user**, **term**, and **path**; there is no need to use **setenv** for these. In addition, the shell sets the **PWD** environment variable from the **csh** variable **cwd** whenever the latter changes.

shift [*variable*]

The components of **argv**, or *variable*, if supplied, are shifted to the left, discarding the first component. It is an error for the variable not to be set, or to have a null value.

source [**-h**] *name*

Reads commands from *name*. **source** commands may be nested, but if they are nested too deeply the shell may run out of file descriptors. An error in a sourced file at any level terminates all nested **source** commands.

-h Place commands from the the file *name* on the history list without executing them.

stop [%*job*] ...

Stop the current or specified background job.

suspend Stop the shell in its tracks, much as if it had been sent a stop signal with **^Z**. This is most often used to stop shells started by **su**.

switch (*string*)
case *label*:
...
breaksw
...
default:
...
breaksw
endsw Each *label* is successively matched, against the specified *string*, which is first command and filename expanded. The file metacharacters *****, **?** and **[...]** may be used in the case labels, which are variable expanded. If none of the labels match before a default label is found, execution begins after the default label. Each **case** statement and the **default** statement must appear at the beginning of a line. The command **breaksw** continues execution after the **endsw**. Otherwise control falls through subsequent **case** and **default** statements as with C. If no label matches and there is no default, execution continues after the **endsw**.

time [*command*]

With no argument, print a summary of time used by this C shell and its children. With an optional *command*, execute *command* and print a summary of the time it uses.

umask [*value*]

Display the file creation mask. With *value* set the file creation mask. *value* is given in octal, and is XORed with the permissions of 666 for files and 777 for directories to arrive at the permissions for new files. Common values include 002, giving complete access to the group, and read (and directory search) access to others, or 022, giving read (and directory search) but not write permission to the group and others.

unalias *pattern*

Discard aliases that match (filename substitution) *pattern*. All aliases are removed by **unalias ***.

unhash Disable the internal hash table.

unlimit [**-h**] [*resource*]
Remove a limitation on *resource*. If no *resource* is specified, then all *resource* limitations are removed. See the description of the **limit** command for the list of *resource* names.

-h Remove corresponding hard limits. Only the privileged user may do this.

unset *pattern*
Remove variables whose names match (filename substitution) *pattern*. All variables are removed by '**unset ***'; this has noticeably distasteful side-effects.

unsetenv *variable*
Remove *variable* from the environment. Pattern matching, as with **unset** is not performed.

wait Wait for background jobs to finish (or for an interrupt) before prompting.

while (*expr*)
...
end While **expr** is true (evaluates to non-zero), repeat commands between the **while** and the matching **end** statement. **break** and **continue** may be used to terminate or continue the loop prematurely. The **while** and **end** must appear alone on their input lines. If the shell's input is a terminal, it prompts for commands with a question-mark until the **end** command is entered and then performs the commands in the loop.

% [*job*] [**&**]
Bring the current or indicated *job* to the foreground. With the ampersand, continue running *job* in the background.

@ [*var* **=expr**]
@ [*var* **[***n***]** **=expr**]
With no arguments, display the values for all shell variables. With arguments, the variable *var*, or the *n*'th word in the value of *var* , to the value that **expr** evaluates to. (If **[***n***]** is supplied, both *var* and its *n*'th component must already exist.)

If the expression contains the characters **>**, **<**, **&** or **|**, then at least this part of **expr** must be placed within parentheses.

The operators ***=**, **+=**, etc., are available as in C. The space separating the name from the assignment operator is optional. Spaces are, however, mandatory in separating components of **expr** that would otherwise be single words.

Special postfix operators, **++** and **--** increment or decrement *name*, respectively.

Environment Variables and Predefined Shell Variables

Unlike the standard shell, the C shell maintains a distinction between environment variables, which are automatically exported to processes it invokes, and shell variables, which are not. Both types of variables are treated similarly under variable substitution. The shell sets the variables **argv**, **cwd**, **home**, **path**, **prompt**, **shell**, and **status** upon initialization. The shell copies the environment variable **USER** into the shell variable **user**, **TERM** into **term**, and **HOME** into **home**, and copies each back into the respective environment variable whenever the shell variables are reset. **PATH** and **path** are similarly handled. You need only set **path** once in the **.cshrc** or **.login** file. The environment variable **PWD** is set from **cwd** whenever the latter changes. The following shell variables have predefined meanings:

argv Argument list. Contains the list of command line arguments supplied to the current invocation of the shell. This variable determines the value of the positional parameters **$1**, **$2**, and so on.

cdpath Contains a list of directories to be searched by the **cd**, **chdir**, and **popd** commands, if the directory argument each accepts is not a subdirectory of the current directory.

cwd The full pathname of the current directory.

echo Echo commands (after substitutions), just before execution.

fignore A list of filename suffixes to ignore when attempting filename completion. Typically the single word '**.o**'.

filec Enable filename completion, in which case the CTRL-d character and the ESC character have special significance when typed in at the end of a terminal input line:

- EOT Print a list of all filenames that start with the preceding string.
- ESC Replace the preceding string with the longest unambiguous extension.

hardpaths If set, pathnames in the directory stack are resolved to contain no symbolic-link components.

histchars A two-character string. The first character replaces **!** as the history-substitution character. The second replaces the carat (^) for quick substitutions.

history The number of lines saved in the history list. A very large number may use up all of the C shell's memory. If not set, the C shell saves only the most recent command.

home The user's home directory. The filename expansion of ~ refers to the value of this variable.

ignoreeof If set, the shell ignores EOF from terminals. This protects against accidentally killing a C shell by typing a CTRL-d.

mail A list of files where the C shell checks for mail. If the first word of the value is a number, it specifies a mail checking interval in seconds (default 5 minutes).

nobeep Suppress the bell during command completion when asking the C shell to extend an ambiguous filename.

`noclobber` Restrict output redirection so that existing files are not destroyed by accident. `>` redirections can only be made to new files. `>>` redirections can only be made to existing files.

`noglob` Inhibit filename substitution. This is most useful in shell scripts once filenames (if any) are obtained and no further expansion is desired.

`nonomatch` Returns the filename substitution pattern, rather than an error, if the pattern is not matched. Malformed patterns still result in errors.

`notify` If set, the shell notifies you immediately as jobs are completed, rather than waiting until just before issuing a prompt.

`path` The list of directories in which to search for commands. **`path`** is initialized from the environment variable **`PATH`**, which the C shell updates whenever **`path`** changes. A null word specifies the current directory. The default is typically: `(. /usr/ucb /usr/bin)`. If **`path`** becomes unset only full pathnames will execute. An interactive C shell will normally hash the contents of the directories listed after reading **`.cshrc`**, and whenever **`path`** is reset. If new commands are added, use the **`rehash`** command to update the table.

`prompt` The string an interactive C shell prompts with. Noninteractive shells leave the **`prompt`** variable unset. Aliases and other commands in the **`.cshrc`** file that are only useful interactively, can be placed after the following test: '**`if ($?prompt == 0) exit`**', to reduce startup time for noninteractive shells. A `!` in the **`prompt`** string is replaced by the current event number. The default prompt is *hostname*`%` for mere mortals, or *hostname*`#` for the privileged user.

`savehist` The number of lines from the history list that are saved in **`~/.history`** when the user logs out. Large values for **`savehist`** slow down the C shell during startup.

`shell` The file in which the C shell resides. This is used in forking shells to interpret files that have execute bits set, but that are not executable by the system.

`status` The status returned by the most recent command. If that command terminated abnormally, 0200 is added to the status. Built-in commands that fail return exit status 1, all other built-in commands set status to 0.

`time` Control automatic timing of commands. Can be supplied with one or two values. The first is the reporting threshold in CPU seconds. The second is a string of tags and text indicating which resources to report on. A tag is a percent sign (`%`) followed by a single *upper-case* letter (unrecognized tags print as text):

- `%D` Average amount of unshared data space used in Kilobytes.
- `%E` Elapsed (wall clock) time for the command.

%F	Page faults.
%I	Number of block input operations.
%K	Average amount of unshared stack space used in Kilobytes.
%M	Maximum real memory used during execution of the process.
%O	Number of block output operations.
%P	Total CPU time — U (user) plus S (system) — as a percentage of E (elapsed) time.
%S	Number of seconds of CPU time consumed by the kernel on behalf of the user's process.
%U	Number of seconds of CPU time devoted to the user's process.
%W	Number of swaps.
%X	Average amount of shared memory used in Kilobytes.

The default summary display outputs from the **%U**, **%S**, **%E**, **%P**, **%X**, **%D**, **%I**, **%O**, **%F** and **%W** tags, in that order.

`verbose` Display each command after history substitution takes place.

FILES

`~/.cshrc`	Read at beginning of execution by each shell.
`~/.login`	Read by login shells after **.cshrc** at login.
`~/.logout`	Read by login shells at logout.
`~/.history`	Saved history for use at next login.
`/usr/bin/sh`	Standard shell, for shell scripts not starting with a '**#**'.
`/tmp/sh*`	Temporary file for '**<<**'.
`/etc/passwd`	Source of home directories for '~*name*'.

SEE ALSO

a.out(4), **access**(2), **ascii**(5), **environ**(4), **exec**(2), **fork**(2), **login**(1), **pipe**(2), **sh**(1), **termio**(7)

DIAGNOSTICS

You have stopped jobs.

You attempted to exit the C shell with stopped jobs under job control. An immediate second attempt to exit will succeed, terminating the stopped jobs.

NOTES

Words can be no longer than 1024 characters. The system limits argument lists to 1,048,576 characters. However, the maximum number of arguments to a command for which filename expansion applies is 1706. Command substitutions may expand to no more characters than are allowed in the argument list. To detect looping, the shell restricts the number of **alias** substitutions on a single line to 20.

When a command is restarted from a stop, the shell prints the directory it started in if this is different from the current directory; this can be misleading (that is, wrong) as the job may have changed directories internally.

Shell built-in functions are not stoppable/restartable. Command sequences of the form *a* **;** *b* **;** *c* are also not handled gracefully when stopping is attempted. If you suspend *b*, the shell never executes *c*. This is especially noticeable if the expansion results from an alias. It can be avoided by placing the sequence in parentheses to force it into a subshell.

Control over terminal output after processes are started is primitive; use the Sun Window system if you need better output control.

Multiline shell procedures should be provided, as they are with the standard (Bourne) shell.

Commands within loops, prompted for by **?**, are not placed in the *history* list.

Control structures should be parsed rather than being recognized as built-in commands. This would allow control commands to be placed anywhere, to be combined with **|**, and to be used with **&** and **;** metasyntax.

It should be possible to use the **:** modifiers on the output of command substitutions. There are two problems with **:** modifier usage on variable substitutions: not all of the modifiers are available, and only one modifier per substitution is allowed.

The **g** (global) flag in history substitutions applies only to the first match in each word, rather than all matches in all words. The the standard text editors consistently do the latter when given the **g** flag in a substitution command.

Quoting conventions are confusing. Overriding the escape character to force variable substitutions within double quotes is counterintuitive and inconsistent with the Bourne shell.

Symbolic links can fool the shell. Setting the **hardpaths** variable alleviates this.

'**set path**' should remove duplicate pathnames from the pathname list. These often occur because a shell script or a **.cshrc** file does something like '**set path=(/usr/local /usr/hosts $path)**' to ensure that the named directories are in the pathname list.

The only way to direct the standard output and standard error separately is by invoking a subshell, as follows:

> **example%** (*command* > *outfile*) >& *errorfile*

Although robust enough for general use, adventures into the esoteric periphery of the C shell may reveal unexpected quirks.

csplit (1)

NAME

csplit – context split

SYNOPSIS

csplit [**-s**] [**-k**] [**-f** *prefix*] *file arg1* [. . . *argn*]

DESCRIPTION

csplit reads *file* and separates it into *n*+1 sections, defined by the arguments *arg1* . . . *argn*. By default the sections are placed in **xx00** . . . **xx***n* (*n* may not be greater than 99). These sections get the following pieces of *file*:

00: From the start of *file* up to (but not including) the line referenced by *arg1*.

01: From the line referenced by *arg1* up to the line referenced by *arg2*.

⋮

n: From the line referenced by *argn* to the end of *file*.

If the *file* argument is a **-**, then standard input is used.

csplit processes supplementary code set characters, and recognizes supplementary code set characters in the *prefix* given to the **-f** option (see below) according to the locale specified in the **LC_CTYPE** environment variable [see **LANG** on **environ**(5)]. In regular expressions, pattern searches are performed on characters, not bytes, as described on **ed**(1).

The options to **csplit** are:

-s — **csplit** normally prints the number of bytes in each file created. If the **-s** option is present, **csplit** suppresses the printing of all byte counts.

-k — **csplit** normally removes created files if an error occurs. If the **-k** option is present, **csplit** leaves previously created files intact.

-f *prefix* — If the **-f** option is used, the created files are named *prefix***00** . . . *prefixn*. The default is **xx00** . . . **xx***n*. Supplementary code set characters may be used in *prefix*.

The arguments (*arg1* . . . *argn*) to **csplit** can be a combination of the following:

/rexp/ — A file is to be created for the section from the current line up to (but not including) the line containing the regular expression *rexp*. The line containing *rexp* becomes the current line. This argument may be followed by an optional **+** or **-** some number of lines (for example, **/Page/-5**). See **ed**(1) for a description of how to specify a regular expression.

%rexp% — This argument is the same as */rexp/*, except that no file is created for the section.

lnno — A file is to be created from the current line up to (but not including) *lnno*. *lnno* becomes the current line.

{*num*} — Repeat argument. This argument may follow any of the above arguments. If it follows a *rexp* type argument, that argument is applied *num* more times. If it follows *lnno*, the file will be split every *lnno* lines (*num* times) from that point.

Enclose all *rexp* type arguments that contain blanks or other characters meaningful to the shell in the appropriate quotes. Regular expressions may not contain embedded new-lines. **csplit** does not affect the original file; it is the user's responsibility to remove it if it is no longer wanted.

EXAMPLES

```
csplit -f cobol file '/procedure division/' /par5./ /par16./
```

This example creates four files, **cobol00** . . . **cobol03**. After editing the "split" files, they can be recombined as follows:

```
cat cobol0[0-3] > file
```

Note that this example overwrites the original file.

```
csplit -k file 100 {99}
```

This example splits the file at every 100 lines, up to 10,000 lines. The **-k** option causes the created files to be retained if there are less than 10,000 lines; however, an error message would still be printed.

```
csplit -k prog.c '%main(%' '/^}/+1' {20}
```

If **prog.c** follows the normal C coding convention (the last line of a routine consists only of a **}** in the first character position), this example creates a file for each separate C routine (up to 21) in **prog.c**.

FILES

/usr/lib/locale/*locale***/LC_MESSAGES/uxdfm**
language-specific message file [See **LANG** on **environ**(5).]

SEE ALSO

ed(1), **regexp**(5), **sh**(1)

DIAGNOSTICS

Self-explanatory except for:

arg – out of range

which means that the given argument did not reference a line between the current position and the end of the file.

ct(1C)

NAME

ct – spawn login to a remote terminal

SYNOPSIS

ct [*options*] *telno . . .*

DESCRIPTION

ct dials the telephone number of a modem that is attached to a terminal and spawns a **login** process to that terminal. *Telno* is a telephone number, with equal signs for secondary dial tones and minus signs for delays at appropriate places. (The set of legal characters for *telno* is **0** through **9**, **–**, **=**, ***,** and **#**. The maximum length of *telno* is 31 characters). If more than one telephone number is specified, **ct** tries each in succession until one answers; this is useful for specifying alternate dialing paths.

ct tries each line listed in the file **/etc/uucp/Devices** until it finds an available line with appropriate attributes, or runs out of entries. **ct** uses the following options:

-h Normally, **ct** hangs up the current line so it can be used to answer the incoming call. The **-h** option prevents this action. The **-h** option also waits for the termination of the specified **ct** process before returning control to the user's terminal.

-s *speed* The data rate may be set with the **-s** option. *speed* is expressed in baud rates. The default baud rate is 1200.

-v If the **-v** (verbose) option is used, **ct** sends a running narrative to the standard error output stream.

-w *n* If there are no free lines **ct** asks if it should wait for one, and if so, for how many minutes it should wait before it gives up. **ct** continues to try to open the dialers at one-minute intervals until the specified limit is exceeded. This dialogue may be overridden by specifying the **-w** *n* option where *n* is the maximum number of minutes that **ct** is to wait for a line.

-x*n* This option is used for debugging; it produces a detailed output of the program execution on standard error. *n* is a single number between **0** and **9**. As *n* increases to **9**, more detailed debugging information is given.

After the user on the destination terminal logs out, there are two things that could occur, depending on what type of port monitor is monitoring the port. In the case of no port monitor, **ct** prompts: **Reconnect?** If the response begins with the letter **n**, the line is dropped; otherwise, **ttymon** is started again and the **login:** prompt is printed. In the second case, where a port monitor is monitoring the port, the port monitor reissues the **login:** prompt.

The user should log out properly before disconnecting.

FILES

/etc/uucp/Devices

SEE ALSO

cu(1C), login(1), uucp(1C) ttymon(1M)

NOTES

The ct program will not work with a DATAKIT Multiplex interface.

For a shared port, one used for both dial-in and dial-out, the ttymon program running on the line must have the -r and -b options specified [see ttymon(1M)].

ctags (1)

NAME

ctags – create a tags file for use with **vi**

SYNOPSIS

ctags [**-aBFtuvwx**] [**-f** *tagsfile*] *file* . . .

DESCRIPTION

ctags makes a tags file for **ex**(1) from the specified C, Pascal, FORTRAN, YACC, and LEX sources. A tags file gives the locations of specified objects (in this case functions and typedefs) in a group of files. Each line of the tags file contains the object name, the file in which it is defined, and an address specification for the object definition. Functions are searched with a pattern, typedefs with a line number. Specifiers are given in separate fields on the line, separated by SPACE or TAB characters. Using the tags file, **ex** can quickly find these objects definitions.

Normally **ctags** places the tag descriptions in a file called **tags**; this may be overridden with the **-f** option.

Files with names ending in **.c** or **.h** are assumed to be C source files and are searched for C routine and macro definitions. Files with names ending in **.y** are assumed to be YACC source files. Files with names ending in **.l** are assumed to be LEX files. Others are first examined to see if they contain any Pascal or FORTRAN routine definitions; if not, they are processed again looking for C definitions.

The tag **main** is treated specially in C programs. The tag formed is created by prepending **M** to *file*, with a trailing **.c** removed, if any, and leading pathname components also removed. This makes use of **ctags** practical in directories with more than one program.

The following options are available:

-a Append output to an existing **tags** file.

-B Use backward searching patterns (**?** . . . **?**).

-F Use forward searching patterns (**/** . . . **/**) (default).

-t Create tags for typedefs.

-u Update the specified files in tags, that is, all references to them are deleted, and the new values are appended to the file. Beware: this option is implemented in a way which is rather slow; it is usually faster to simply rebuild the **tags** file.

-v Produce on the standard output an index listing the function name, file name, and page number (assuming 64 line pages). Since the output will be sorted into lexicographic order, it may be desired to run the output through **sort -f**.

-w Suppress warning diagnostics.

-x Produce a list of object names, the line number and file name on which each is defined, as well as the text of that line and prints this on the standard output. This is a simple index which can be printed out as an off-line readable function index.

FILES

`tags`　　output tags file

USAGE

The **-v** option is mainly used with **vgrind** which may be part of the optional BSD Compatibility Package.

SEE ALSO

ex(1), **vi**(1)

NOTES

Recognition of **functions**, **subroutines** and **procedures** for FORTRAN and Pascal is done in a very simple-minded way. No attempt is made to deal with block structure; if you have two Pascal procedures in different blocks with the same name you lose.

The method of deciding whether to look for C or Pascal and FORTRAN functions is a hack.

ctags does not know about **#ifdefs**.

ctags should know about Pascal types. Relies on the input being well formed to detect typedefs. Use of **-tx** shows only the last line of typedefs.

NAME

`ctrace` – C program debugger

SYNOPSIS

`ctrace` [*options*] [*file*]

DESCRIPTION

The `ctrace` command allows the user to monitor the sequential execution of a C program as each program statement executes. The effect is similar to executing a shell procedure with the `-x` option. `ctrace` reads the C program in *file* (or from standard input if the user does not specify *file*), inserts statements to print the text of each executable statement and the values of all variables referenced or modified, and writes the modified program to the standard output. The output of `ctrace` must be placed into a temporary file because the `cc`(1) command does not allow the use of a pipe. This file can then be compiled and executed.

As each statement in the program executes, it will be listed at the terminal, followed by the name and value of any variables referenced or modified in the statement; these variable names and values will be followed by any output from the statement. Loops in the trace output are detected and tracing is stopped until the loop is exited or a different sequence of statements within the loop is executed. A warning message is printed after each 1000 loop cycles to help the user detect infinite loops. The trace output goes to the standard output so the user can put it into a file for examination with an editor or the `bfs`(1) or `tail`(1) commands.

The options commonly used are:

`-f` *functions* Trace only these *functions.*
`-v` *functions* Trace all but these *functions.*

The user may want to add to the default formats for printing variables. Long and pointer variables are always printed as signed integers. Pointers to character arrays are also printed as strings if appropriate. `char`, `short`, and `int` variables are also printed as signed integers and, if appropriate, as characters. `float`, `double`, and `long double` variables are printed as floating point numbers in scientific notation. The user can request that variables be printed in additional formats, if appropriate, with these options:

`-o` Octal
`-x` Hexadecimal
`-u` Unsigned
`-e` Floating point

These options are used only in special circumstances:

`-l` *n* Check *n* consecutively executed statements for looping trace output, instead of the default of 20. Use 0 to get all the trace output from loops.

`-s` Suppress redundant trace output from simple assignment statements and string copy function calls. This option can hide a bug caused by use of the = operator in place of the == operator.

`-t` *n* Trace *n* variables per statement instead of the default of 10 (the maximum number is 20). The diagnostics section explains when to use this option.

-P Preprocess the input before tracing it. The user can also use the **-D**, **-I**, and **-U** cc(1) options.

-p *string*
Change the trace print function from the default of **printf**. For example, **fprintf(stderr,** would send the trace to the standard error output.

-r *f* Use file *f* in place of the **runtime.c** trace function package. This replacement lets the user change the entire print function, instead of just the name and leading arguments (see the **-p** option).

-V Prints version information on the standard error.

-Q*arg* If *arg* is **y**, identification information about **ctrace** will be added to the output files. This can be useful for software administration. Giving **n** for *arg* explicitly asks for no such information, which is the default behavior.

EXAMPLES

If the file **lc.c** contains this C program:

```
#include <stdio.h>
main()  /* count lines in input */
{
    int c, nl;

    nl = 0;
    while ((c = getchar()) != EOF)
          if (c = '\n')
                ++nl;
    printf("%d\n", nl);
}
```

these commands and test data are entered:

```
cc lc.c
a.out
1
(CTRL-d)
```

the program will be compiled and executed. The output of the program will be the number **2**, which is incorrect because there is only one line in the test data. The error in this program is common, but subtle. If the user invokes **ctrace** with these commands:

```
ctrace lc.c >temp.c
cc temp.c
a.out
```

the output will be:

```
 2 main()
 6    nl = 0;
      /* nl == 0 */
 7    while ((c = getchar()) != EOF)
```

The program is now waiting for input. If the user enters the same test data as before, the output will be:

```
        /* c == 49 or '1' */
8                 if (c = '0)
                  /* c  == 10 or '0 */
9                         ++nl;
                          /* nl == 1 */
7          while ((c = getchar()) != EOF)
           /* c  == 10 or '0 */
8                 if (c = '0)
                  /* c  == 10 or '0 */
9                         ++nl;
                          /* nl == 2 */
       /* repeating */
```

Once the end-of-file character (CTRL-d) is entered, the final output will be:

```
        /* repeated < 1 time */
 7          while ((c = getchar()) != EOF)
            /* c  == -1 */
10          printf("%d0, nl);
            /* nl == 2 */2

        /* return */
```

Note the information printed out at the end of the trace line for the **nl** variable following line 10. Also note the **return** comment added by **ctrace** at the end of the trace output. This shows the implicit return at the terminating brace in the function.

The trace output shows that variable **c** is assigned the value '**1**' in line 7, but in line 8 it has the value '**\n**'. Once user attention is drawn to this **if** statement, he or she will probably realize that the assignment operator (=) was used in place of the equality operator (==). This error can easily be missed during code reading.

Execution-time Trace Control

The default operation for **ctrace** is to trace the entire program file, unless the **-f** or **-v** options are used to trace specific functions. The default operation does not give the user statement-by-statement control of the tracing, nor does it let the user turn the tracing off and on when executing the traced program.

The user can do both of these by adding **ctroff**() and **ctron**() function calls to the program to turn the tracing off and on, respectively, at execution time. Thus, complex criteria can be arbitrarily coded for trace control with **if** statements, and this code can even be conditionally included because **ctrace** defines the **CTRACE** preprocessor variable. For example:

```
#ifdef CTRACE
        if (c == '!' && i > 1000)
                ctron();
#endif
```

These functions can also be called from **debug**(1) if they are compiled with the **-g** option. For example, to trace all but lines 7 to 10 in the main function, enter:

```
debug a.out
debug> stop lc.c @7  {set ctroff();} EVENT [1] assigned
debug> stop lc.c @11  {set ctron();} EVENT [2] assigned
debug> run
```

The trace can be turned off and on by setting static variable `tr_ct_` to `0` and `1`, respectively. This on/off option is useful if a user is using a debugger that can not call these functions directly.

FILES

`/usr/ccs/lib/ctrace/runtime.c` run-time trace package

SEE ALSO

cc(1), **ctype**(3C), **debug**(1), **fclose**(3S), **printf**(3S)

DIAGNOSTICS

This section contains diagnostic messages from both **ctrace** and **cc**(1), since the traced code often gets some **cc** warning messages. The user can get **cc** error messages in some rare cases, all of which can be avoided.

ctrace Diagnostics

warning: some variables are not traced in this statement
: Only 10 variables are traced in a statement to prevent the C compiler "out of tree space; simplify expression" error. Use the **-t** option to increase this number.

warning: statement too long to trace
: This statement is over 400 characters long. Make sure that tabs are used to indent the code, not spaces.

`cannot handle preprocessor code, use -P option`
: This is usually caused by **#ifdef**/**#endif** preprocessor statements in the middle of a C statement, or by a semicolon at the end of a **#define** preprocessor statement.

`'if . . . else if' sequence too long`
: Split the sequence by removing an **else** from the middle.

`possible syntax error, try -P option`
: Use the **-P** option to preprocess the **ctrace** input, along with any appropriate **-D**, **-I**, and **-U** preprocessor options.

NOTES

Defining a function with the same name as a system function may cause a syntax error if the number of arguments is changed. Just use a different name.

ctrace assumes that **BADMAG** is a preprocessor macro, and that **EOF** and **NULL** are #defined constants. Declaring any of these to be variables, for example, "**int EOF**;", will cause a syntax error.

Pointer values are always treated as pointers to character strings.

`ctrace` does not know about the components of aggregates like structures, unions, and arrays. It cannot choose a format to print all the components of an aggregate when an assignment is made to the entire aggregate. `ctrace` may choose to print the address of an aggregate or use the wrong format (for example, `3.149050e-311` for a structure with two integer members) when printing the value of an aggregate.

The loop trace output elimination is done separately for each file of a multi-file program. Separate output elimination can result in functions called from a loop still being traced, or the elimination of trace output from one function in a file until another in the same file is called.

NAME

cu – call another UNIX system

SYNOPSIS

cu [*options*] [*destination*]

DESCRIPTION

cu calls up another UNIX system, a terminal, or possibly a non-UNIX system. It manages an interactive conversation with possible transfers of files. It is convenient to think of **cu** as operating in two phases. The first phase is the connection phase in which the connection is established. **cu** then enters the conversation phase. The **-d** option is the only one that applies to both phases.

-d Causes diagnostic traces to be printed.

If you need to use the **-d** option of **cu**, you must first make sure that the Connection Server (**cs**) is in debug mode. To see if **cs** is in debug mode, enter:

```
ps -eaf | grep cs
```

If you don't see output similar to the following:

```
root    236     1  0    Jun 08 ?         0:01 /usr/sbin/cs -d
```

you must kill the current **cs** process, and restart **cs** with the **-d** option by entering:

```
/usr/sbin/cs -d
```

To turn off **cs** debugging, you must kill the **cs** process that is running the debug mode, and restart **cs** normally.

The **cu** command sets the input and output conversion mode to on or off, as appropriate, to avoid a character conversion on the local system when accessing the remote system.

On the remote system, the input and output conversion should be set manually, as **cu** cannot know whether input conversion is required or not. In most cases, remote systems can be used with input conversion on; however, when transferring files, this should be set to off before invoking the file transfer command in order to avoid unexpected conversion of the file contents.

Connection Phase

cu uses the same mechanism that **uucp** does to establish a connection. This means that it will use the **uucp** control files **/etc/uucp/Devices** and **/etc/uucp/Systems**. This gives **cu** the ability to choose from several different media to establish the connection. The possible media include telephone lines, direct connections, and local area networks (LANs). The **Devices** file contains a list of media that are available on your system. The **Systems** file contains information for connecting to remote systems, but it is not generally readable.

The *destination* parameter from the command line is used to tell **cu** what system you wish to connect to. The *destination* can be blank, a telephone number, a system name, or a LAN-specific address. A telephone number is a string consisting of the tone dial characters (the digits 0 through 9, *, and #) plus the special characters = and –. The equal sign designates a secondary dial tone and the minus sign creates a 4 second delay. A system name is the name of any computer that **uucp** can call; the

uuname [see **uucp**(1C)] command prints a list of these names. The documentation for your LAN will show the form of the LAN-specific address.

If **cu**'s default behavior is invoked (not using the **-c** or **-l** options), **cu** will use *destination* to determine which medium to use. If *destination* is a telephone number, **cu** will assume that you wish to use a telephone line and it will select an automatic call unit (ACU). If the *destination* is not a telephone number, then **cu** will assume that it is a system name. **cu** will follow the **uucp** calling mechanism and use the **Systems** and **Devices** files to obtain the best available connection. Since **cu** will choose a speed that is appropriate for the medium that it selects, you may not use the **-s** option when *destination* is a system name.

The **-c** and **-l** options modify this default behavior. **-c** is most often used to select a LAN by specifying a Type field from the **Devices** file. Here, *destination* is assumed to be a system name. If the connection attempt to *system name* fails, a connection will be attempted using *destination* as a LAN-specific address. The **-l** option is used to specify a device associated with a direct connection. If the connection is truly a direct connection to the remote machine, then there is no need to specify a *destination*. This is the only case where a blank *destination* is allowed. On the other hand, there may be cases in which the specified device connects to a dialer, so it is valid to specify a telephone number as a *destination*. The **-c** and **-l** options should not be specified on the same command line.

cu accepts many options. The **-c**, **-l**, and **-s** options play a part in selecting the medium; the remaining options are used in configuring the line.

-s*speed* Specifies the transmission speed (300, 1200, 2400, 4800, 9600). The default value is "Any" speed which will depend on the order of the lines in the **/etc/uucp/Devices** file. Most modems are either 300, 1200, or 2400 baud. Directly connected lines may be set to a speed higher than 2400 baud.

-c*type* The first field in the **Devices** file is the "Type" field. The **-c** option forces **cu** to only use entries in the "Type" field that match the user specified *type*. The specified *type* is usually the name of a local area network.

-l*line* Specifies a device name to use as the communication line. This can be used to override the search that would otherwise take place for the first available line having the right speed. When the **-l** option is used without the **-s** option, the speed of a line is taken from the **Devices** file record in which *line* matches the second field (the Line field). When the **-l** and **-s** options are both used together, **cu** will search the **Devices** file to check if the requested speed for the requested line is available. If so, the connection will be made at the requested speed, otherwise, an error message will be printed and the call will not be made. In the general case where a specified device is a directly connected asynchronous line (e.g., **/dev/term/***ab*), a telephone number (*telno*) is not required. The specified device need not be in the **/dev** directory. If the specified device is associated with an auto dialer, a telephone number must be provided. If *destination* is used with this option, it must be a telephone number.

`-b`*n*	Forces *n* to be the number of bits processed on the line. *n* is either 7 or 8. This allows connection between systems with different character sizes. By default, the character size of the line is set to the same as the current local terminal.
`-e`	Set an EVEN data parity. This option designates that EVEN parity is to be generated for data sent to the remote system.
`-h`	Set communication mode to half-duplex. This option emulates the local **echo**(1) command in order to support calls to other computer systems that expect terminals to be set to half-duplex mode.
`-n`	Request user prompt for telephone number. For added security, this option will prompt the user to provide the telephone number to be dialed, rather than taking it from the command line.
`-o`	Set an ODD data parity. This option designates that ODD parity is to be generated for data sent to the remote system.
`-t`	Used to dial a terminal which has been set to auto answer. Appropriate mapping of carriage-return to carriage-return-line-feed pairs is set.

Conversation Phase

After making the connection, **cu** runs as two processes: the *transmit* process reads data from the standard input and, except for lines beginning with ~, passes it to the remote system; the *receive* process accepts data from the remote system and, except for lines beginning with ~, passes it to the standard output. Normally, an automatic DC3/DC1 protocol is used to control input from the remote so the buffer is not overrun. Lines beginning with ~ have special meanings.

The *transmit* process interprets the following user-initiated commands:

`~.`	terminate the conversation.
`~!`	escape to an interactive shell on the local system.
`~!`*cmd* ...	run *cmd* on the local system (via `sh -c`).
`~$`*cmd* ...	run *cmd* locally and send its output to the remote system.
`~+`*cmd* ...	run *cmd* locally and connect its input and output to the remote system.
`~%cd`	change the directory on the local system. Note: `~!cd` will cause the command to be run by a sub-shell, probably not what was intended.
`~%take` *from* [*to*]	copy file *from* (on the remote system) to file *to* on the local system. If *to* is omitted, the *from* argument is used in both places.
`~%put` *from* [*to*]	copy file *from* (on local system) to file *to* on remote system. If *to* is omitted, the *from* argument is used in both places.
`~~` *line*	send the line ~ *line* to the remote system.

~%break transmit a BREAK to the remote system (which can also be specified as **~%b**).

~%debug toggles the **-d** debugging option on or off (which can also be specified as **~%d**).

~t prints the values of the termio structure variables for the user's terminal (useful for debugging).

~l prints the values of the termio structure variables for the remote communication line (useful for debugging).

~%ifc toggles between DC3/DC1 input control protocol and no input control. This is useful when the remote system does not respond properly to the DC3 and DC1 characters. (can also be specified as ~**%nostop**).

~%ofc toggles the output flow control setting. When enabled, outgoing data flow may be controlled by the remote host (can also be specified as ~**%noostop**).

~%divert allow/disallow unsolicited diversions. That is, diversions not specified by **~%take**.

~%old allow/disallow old style syntax for received diversions.

The *receive* process normally copies data from the remote system to the standard output of the local system. It may also direct the output to local files.

The use of **~%put** requires **stty**(1) and **cat**(1) on the remote side. It also requires that the current control characters on the remote system be identical to the current control characters on the local system. Backslashes are inserted at appropriate places for these control characters.

The use of **~%take** requires the existence of **echo**(1) and **cat**(1) on the remote system. Also, **tabs** mode [see **stty**(1)] should be set on the remote system if tabs are to be copied without expansion to spaces.

When **cu** is used on system X to connect to system Y and subsequently used on system Y to connect to system Z, commands on system Y can be executed by using ~~. Executing a tilde command reminds the user of the local system **uname**. For example, **uname** can be executed on Z, X, and Y as follows:

```
uname
Z
~[X]!uname
X
~~[Y]!uname
Y
```

In general, ~ causes the command to be executed on the original machine. ~~ causes the command to be executed on the next machine in the chain.

EXAMPLES

To dial a system whose telephone number is 9 1 201 555 1234 using 1200 baud (where dialtone is expected after the 9):

```
cu  -s1200  9=12015551234
```

If the speed is not specified, "Any" is the default value.

To log on a system that is on a Datakit VCS local area network, but which has not been defined by your administrator [i.e., is not entered in the **/etc/uucp/Systems** file(s)]:

```
cu -c DK address
```

DK is the name of the Datakit local area network, and *address* is the Datakit address which is of the form, /area/exchange/machine.

To log on a system connected by a direct line:

```
cu  -l  /dev/term/XX
```

or

```
cu -l term/XX
```

To dial a system with a specific line and speed:

```
cu  -s1200  -l  term/XX
```

To dial a system using a specific line associated with an auto dialer:

```
cu  -l  culXX  9=12015551234
```

To use a system name:

```
cu systemname
```

FILES

/etc/uucp/Sysfiles
/etc/uucp/Systems
/etc/uucp/Devices
/var/spool/locks/*

SEE ALSO

cat(1), **ct**(1C), **echo**(1), **stty**(1), **uname**(1), **uucp**(1C)

DIAGNOSTICS

Exit code is zero for normal exit, otherwise, one.

NOTES

The **cu** command does not do any integrity checking on data it transfers. Data fields with special **cu** characters may not be transmitted properly. Depending on the interconnection hardware, it may be necessary to use a ~. to terminate the conversion, even if **stty 0** has been used. Non-printing characters are not dependably transmitted using either the **~%put** or **~%take** commands. **cu**, between an IMBR1 and a PENRIL modem, will not return a login prompt immediately upon connection. A carriage return will return the prompt.

~%put and **~%take** cannot be used over multiple links. Files must be moved one link at a time.

There is an artificial slowing of transmission by **cu** during the **~%put** operation so that loss of data is unlikely. Files transferred using **~%take** or **~%put** must contain a trailing newline, otherwise, the operation will hang. Entering a CTRL-d command usually clears the hang condition.

NAME

custom – (XENIX) install specific portions of SCO UNIX or XENIX packages

SYNOPSIS

/sbin/custom

/sbin/custom -a [*package* . . .] [**-m /dev/install** | **/dev/install1**]

/sbin/custom -s *existing_product* [**-ilr** [*package* . . .]] [**-f** [*file*]]
[**-m /dev/install** | **/dev/install1**]

DESCRIPTION

custom allows a privileged user to create a custom installation by selectively installing or deleting portions of SCO UNIX or XENIX packages. If you don't provide information **custom** needs, it will prompt you (see "Non-interactive Mode" and "Interactive Mode," below).

Use **pkgadd** to install UNIX System V packages which were created using the packaging format provided beginning with UNIX System V Release 4 [see **pkgadd**(1M) and **pkginfo**(4)]. For pre-Release 4 packages, use **installpkg**.

Products are made up of one or more packages. In turn, packages are made up of one or more files. You can use **custom** to install or remove one or more packages for a product or list all the packages in a product. In addition, you can list the files in a package or install a single file from a package. By default, **custom** expects to install packages from floppy drive 0 (**/dev/install**).

Non-interactive Mode

-a If you haven't installed a product before, you can provide the names of the *packages* to install from that product. If you want to install all the packages from the product, use **ALL**, instead of naming *packages*. If you don't provide a *package* argument, **custom** will prompt you for the names of the packages you wish to install.

-s If you want to install an additional package from a product that you previously installed, follow the **-s** option with the *existing_product* name and follow the **-i** option with the *package* name(s). *existing_product* can be a product id or a product name. If you don't provide these arguments, **custom** will prompt you for them.

-i Install the specified *package*(s)

-r Remove the specified *package*(s)

-l List the files in the specified *package*(s)

-f Install the specified *file*

-m Install from device **/dev/install** for floppy drive 0 (the default) or **/dev/install1** for floppy drive 1

Interactive Mode

If you invoke **custom** with no arguments, **custom** provides a menu of the *existing_products*, beginning with the choice of adding a new product. Select this first choice, "Add a Supported Product," if you want to install packages from a new product whose distribution medium is in floppy drive drive 0. If you want to install, remove, or list packages from an *existing_product*, select the number corresponding to that *existing_product*. If you choose to install packages from *existing_product*, its distribution medium must be in floppy drive drive 0.

Once you have made your selection from this first menu, you will be offered the following menu:

1. Install one or more packages
2. Remove one or more packages
3. List the available packages
4. List the files in a package
5. Install a single file
6. Select a new product to customize
7. Display current disk usage
8. Help

When you enter a menu option, you are prompted for further information. Options 1, 2, and 3 list available packages in the selected product. Each line describes the package name; whether the package is fully installed, not installed or partially installed; the size of the package (in 512-byte blocks); and a one line description of the package contents.

The following describes what actions are necessary for each menu option:

1. Install Package
After listing the packages available in a product, this option prompts for one or more package names. To specify multiple packages, separate the names by spaces. It calculates which installation volumes (distribution media) are needed and then prompts for the correct volume numbers.

2. Remove Package
After listing the packages available in a product, this option prompts for one or more package names to remove. To specify multiple packages, separate the names by spaces. It deletes the correct files in the specified package(s).

3. List Available Packages
This option lists all the packages in a product.

4. List Files in a Package
After listing the packages available in a product, this option prompts for one or more package names. To specify multiple packages, separate the names by spaces. It lists all files in the specified package(s).

5. Install File
This option prompts for the name of a file from the product and retrieves that file from the distribution medium. The filename should be a full pathname relative to the root directory "/".

6. Select New Product
This option allows the user to work from a different product.

7. Display Current Disk Usage
This option reports current disk usage.

8. Help
This option prints a page of instructions to help you use **custom**.

NOTES

When installing some XENIX applications, error messages such as "**bad gid**" or "**bad uid**" may be printed. These messages occur because XENIX and UNIX systems assign UID and GID numbers differently. If necessary, the file and/or directory permissions can be altered with **chmod**(1) after installation.

Some packages require that **SCOMPAT=3.2** be set before **custom** is run [see the NOTES section of **scompat**(1)]; however, some package installation procedures may not allow this to occur.

FILES

/etc/perms/* information about *existing_products*

SEE ALSO

chmod(1), **df**(1M), **du**(1M), **fixperm**(1M), **fixshlib**(1M), **pkgadd**(1M), **pkginfo**(4), **scompat**(1), **xinstall**(1M)

NAME

`cut` – cut out selected fields of each line of a file

SYNOPSIS

`cut` [*–s*] [`-d`*char*] [`-c`*list* | `-f`*list*] *file* . . .

DESCRIPTION

Use **cut** to cut out columns from a table or fields from each line of a file; in data base parlance, it implements the projection of a relation. The fields as specified by *list* can be fixed length, that is, character positions as on a punched card (`-c` option) or the length can vary from line to line and be marked with a field delimiter character like *tab* (`-f` option). **cut** can be used as a filter; if no files are given, the standard input is used. A file name of "–" explicitly refers to standard input.

`cut` processes supplementary code set characters, and recognizes supplementary code set characters in the *char* given to the **-d** option (see below) according to the locale specified in the **LC_CTYPE** environment variable [see **LANG** on **environ**(5)]. For special treatment of multibyte characters, see the `-c`*list* option below.

The meanings of the options are:

list A comma-separated list of integer field numbers (in increasing order), with optional `-` to indicate ranges [for example, `1,4,7`; `1-3,8`; `-5,10` (short for `1-5,10`); or `3-` (short for third through last field)].

`-c`*list* The *list* following `-c` (no space) specifies column positions (for example, `-c1-72` would pass the first 72 single-byte characters of each line). When multibyte characters are split at a specified position, the remaining column positions are filled with an appropriate number of ASCII spaces instead of characters.

`-f`*list* The *list* following `-f` is a list of fields assumed to be separated in the file by a delimiter character (see `-d`); for example, `-f1,7` copies the first and seventh field only. Lines with no field delimiters will be passed through intact (useful for table subheadings), unless `-s` is specified.

`-d`*char* The character following `-d` is the field delimiter (`-f` option only). Default is *tab*. Space or other characters with special meaning to the shell must be quoted. *char* may be a supplementary code set character.

`-s` Suppresses lines with no delimiter characters in case of `-f` option. Unless specified, lines with no delimiters will be passed through untouched.

Either the `-c` or `-f` option must be specified.

Use **grep**(1) to make horizontal "cuts" (by context) through a file, or **paste**(1) to put files together column-wise (that is, horizontally). To reorder columns in a table, use `cut` and `paste`.

EXAMPLES

`cut -d: -f1,5 /etc/passwd`	mapping of user IDs to names
``name=`who am i	cut -f1 -d" "` ``	to set **name** to current login name.

FILES

/usr/lib/locale/*locale***/LC_MESSAGES/uxcore**
language-specific message file [See **LANG** on **environ**(5).]

SEE ALSO

grep(1), **paste**(1)

DIAGNOSTICS

UX:cut:ERROR:line too long
A line can have no more than 1023 bytes or fields, or there is no new-line character.

UX:cut:ERROR:bad list for c / f option
Missing **-c** or **-f** option or incorrectly specified *list*. No error occurs if a line has fewer fields than the *list* calls for.

UX:cut:ERROR:no fields
The *list* is empty.

UX:cut:ERROR:no delimiter
Missing *char* on **-d** option.

UX:cut:ERROR:cannot handle multiple adjacent backspaces
Adjacent backspaces cannot be processed correctly.

UX:cut:WARNING:cannot open <*filename***>**
Either *filename* cannot be read or does not exist. If multiple filenames are present, processing continues.

NAME

cvtomflib - convert OMF (XENIX) libraries to ELF

SYNOPSIS

cvtomflib [-v] [-o *outfile*] *library* [*library*. . .]

DESCRIPTION

cvtomflib converts libraries of OMF objects to libraries of ELF objects. It is intended for use with application packages that provide only OMF libraries that could not otherwise be used in an ELF-based environment.

The options have the following meanings.

-v Verbose output is produced for each converted object. Without this option, **cvtomflib** does its work silently.

-o This option allows the user to specify a new name, *outfile*, for the converted library without changing the original. This option is only available when a single library is being converted.

SEE ALSO

elf(3E)

NOTES

The original order of objects within the library is retained.

Each library is converted in the directory in which it's located. Without the -o option, the converted library will overwrite the original; therefore, you may want to copy the original library before conversion.

cxref (1)

NAME

`cxref` – generate C program cross-reference

SYNOPSIS

`cxref` `[`*options*`]` *files*

DESCRIPTION

The **`cxref`** command analyzes a collection of C files and builds a cross-reference table. **`cxref`** uses a special version of **`cc`** to include **`#define`**'d information in its symbol table. It generates a list of all symbols (auto, static, and global) in each individual file, or, with the **`-c`** option, in combination. The table includes four fields: NAME, FILE, FUNCTION, and LINE. The line numbers appearing in the LINE field also show reference marks as appropriate. The reference marks include:

assignment	=
declaration	–
definition	*

If no reference marks appear, you can assume a general reference.

`cxref` processes supplementary code set characters according to the locale specified in the **`LC_CTYPE`** environment variable [see **`LANG`** on **`environ`**(5)].

The `-D`, `-I`, and `-U` options are interpreted as by **`cc`**. In addition, **`cxref`** interprets the following options:

`-c` Combine the source files into a single report. Without the **`-c`** option, **`cxref`** generates a separate report for each file on the command line.

`-d` Disables printing declarations, making the report easier to read.

`-l` Does not print local variables; prints only global and file scope statistics.

`-o`*file* Direct output to *file*.

`-s` Operates silently; does not print input file names.

`-t` Format listing for 80-column width.

`-w`*num* Width option that formats output no wider than *num* (decimal) columns. This option will default to 80 if *num* is not specified or is less than 51.

`-C` Runs only the first pass of **`cxref`**, creating a **`.cx`** file that can later be passed to **`cxref`**. This is similar to the **`-c`** option of **`cc`** or **`lint`**.

`-F` Prints the full path of the referenced file names.

`-L`*cols* Modifies the number of table columns in the LINE field. If you do not specify a number, **`cxref`** defaults to five columns.

`-V` Prints version information on the standard error.

`-W`*name, file, function, line*
Changes the default width of at least one field. The default widths are:

Field	Columns
NAME	15
FILE	13
FUNCTION	15
LINE	20 (4 per table column)

FILES

TMPDIR/**tcx.***	temporary files
TMPDIR/**cx.***	temporary files
LIBDIR/**xref**	accessed by **cxref**
LIBDIR	usually **/usr/ccs/lib**
TMPDIR	usually **/var/tmp** but can be redefined by setting the environment variable **TMPDIR** [see **tempnam** in **tmpnam**(3S)].

EXAMPLES

```
a.c
1     main()
2     {
3           int i;
4           extern char c;
5
6           i=65;
7           c=(char)i;
8     }
```

Resulting cross-reference table:

```
NAME  FILE        FUNCTION  LINE
c     a.c         ---       4-     7=
i     a.c         main      3*     6=    7
main  a.c         ---       2*
u3b2  predefined  ---       0*
unix  predefined  ---       0*
```

SEE ALSO

cc(1), lint(1)

DIAGNOSTICS

Error messages usually mean you cannot compile the files.

NAME

`date` – print and set the date

SYNOPSIS

date [**-u**] [+*format]*

date [**-a** [-] *sss*.*fff*] [**-u**] [[*mmdd*] | *HHMM* | *mmddHHMM* [**cc**] **yy**]

DESCRIPTION

If no argument is given, or if the argument begins with **+**, the current date and time are printed. Otherwise, the current date is set if the user is a privilege user.

Supplementary code set characters in +*format* (see below) are recognized and displayed according to the locale specified in the **LC_CTYPE** environment variable [see **LANG** on **environ**(5)]. Month and weekday names are recognized according to the locale specified in the **LC_TIME** environment variable, as described below.

-a [-] *sss*.*fff* Slowly adjust the time by *sss*.*fff* seconds (*fff* represents fractions of a second). This adjustment can be positive or negative. The system's clock will be sped up or slowed down until it has drifted by the number of seconds specified.

-u Display (or set) the date in Greenwich Mean Time (GMT—universal time), bypassing the normal conversion to (or from) local time.

mm is the month number

dd is the day number in the month

HH is the hour number (24 hour system)

MM is the minute number

cc is the century minus one

yy is the last 2 digits of the year number

The month, day, year, and century may be omitted; the current values are supplied as defaults. For example:

```
date 10080045
```

sets the date to Oct 8, 12:45 AM. The current year is the default because no year is supplied. The system operates in GMT. **date** takes care of the conversion to and from local standard and daylight time. Only a privileged user may change the date. After successfully setting the date and time, **date** displays the new date according to the default format. The **date** command uses **TZ** to determine the correct time zone information [see **environ**(5)].

+*format* If the argument begins with **+**, the output of **date** is under the control of the user. Each Field Descriptor, described below, is preceded by **%** and is replaced in the output by its corresponding value. A single **%** is encoded by **%%**. All other characters are copied to the output without change. The string is always terminated with a new-line character. If the argument contains embedded blanks it must be quoted (see the EXAMPLE section). Supplementary code set characters may be used in *format*.

As noted, month and weekday names are recognized according to the locale specified in the `LC_TIME` environment variable [see `LANG` on `environ`(5)]. The names are taken from a file whose format is specified in `strftime`(4). This file also defines country-specific date and time formats such as `%c`, which specifies the default date format. The following form is the default for `%c`:

`%a %b %e %T %Z %Y`
for example, Fri Dec 23 10:10:42 EST 1988

Field Descriptors (must be preceded by a `%`):

- `a` abbreviated weekday name
- `A` full weekday name
- `b` abbreviated month name
- `B` full month name
- `c` country-specific date and time format
- `d` day of month – 01 to 31
- `D` date as `%m/%d/%y`
- `e` day of month – 1 to 31 (single digits are preceded by a blank)
- `h` abbreviated month name (alias for `%b`)
- `H` hour – 00 to 23
- `I` hour – 01 to 12
- `j` day of year – 001 to 366
- `m` month of year – 01 to 12
- `M` minute – 00 to 59
- `n` insert a new-line character
- `p` string containing ante-meridian or post-meridian indicator (by default, AM or PM)
- `r` time as `%I:%M:%S %p`
- `R` time as `%H:%M`
- `S` second – 00 to 61, allows for leap seconds
- `t` insert a tab character
- `T` time as `%H:%M:%S`
- `U` week number of year (Sunday as the first day of the week) – 00 to 53
- `w` day of week – Sunday = 0
- `W` week number of year (Monday as the first day of the week) – 00 to 53
- `x` country-specific date format
- `X` country-specific time format
- `y` year within century – 00 to 99
- `Y` year as *ccyy* (4 digits)
- `Z` timezone name

EXAMPLE

The command

```
date '+DATE: %m/%d/%y%nTIME: %H:%M:%S'
```

generates as output:

```
DATE: 08/01/76
TIME: 14:45:05
```

FILES

/usr/lib/locale/*locale*/LC_MESSAGES/uxcore.abi
language-specific message file [See **LANG** on **environ** (5).]

SEE ALSO

environ(5), **strftime**(4), **sysadm**(1M)

DIAGNOSTICS

UX:date:ERROR:No permission
You are not a privileged user and you try to change the date.

UX:date:ERROR:bad conversion
The date set is syntactically incorrect.

NOTES

Should you need to change the date while the system is running multi-user, use the **datetime** command of **sysadm**(1M).

If you attempt to set the current date to one of the dates on which the standard and alternate time zones change (for example, the date that daylight time is starting or ending), and you attempt to set the time to a time in the interval between the end of standard time and the beginning of the alternate time (or the end of the alternate time and the beginning of standard time), the results are unpredictable.

NAME

dc – desk calculator

SYNOPSIS

dc [*file*]

DESCRIPTION

dc is an arbitrary precision arithmetic package. Ordinarily it operates on decimal integers, but one may specify an input base, output base, and a number of fractional digits to be maintained. [bc is a preprocessor for dc that provides infix notation and a C-like syntax that implements functions. bc also provides reasonable control structures for programs. See bc(1).] The overall structure of dc is a stacking (reverse Polish) calculator. If an argument is given, input is taken from that file until its end, then from the standard input. The following constructions are recognized:

number
: The value of the number is pushed on the stack. A number is an unbroken string of the digits 0–9. It may be preceded by an underscore (_) to input a negative number. Numbers may contain decimal points.

+ - / * % ^
: The top two values on the stack are added (+), subtracted (-), multiplied (*), divided (/), remaindered (%), or exponentiated (^). The two entries are popped off the stack; the result is pushed on the stack in their place. Any fractional part of an exponent is ignored.

s*x*
: The top of the stack is popped and stored into a register named *x*, where *x* may be any character. If the s is capitalized, *x* is treated as a stack and the value is pushed on it.

l*x*
: The value in register *x* is pushed on the stack. The register *x* is not altered. All registers start with zero value. If the l is capitalized, register *x* is treated as a stack and its top value is popped onto the main stack.

d
: The top value on the stack is duplicated.

p
: The top value on the stack is printed. The top value remains unchanged.

P
: Interprets the top of the stack as an ASCII string, removes it, and prints it.

f
: All values on the stack are printed.

q
: Exits the program. If executing a string, the recursion level is popped by two.

Q
: Exits the program. The top value on the stack is popped and the string execution level is popped by that value.

x
: Treats the top element of the stack as a character string and executes it as a string of dc commands.

X
: Replaces the number on the top of the stack with its scale factor.

[...]
: Puts the bracketed ASCII string onto the top of the stack.

`<x  >x  =x`
: The top two elements of the stack are popped and compared. Register *x* is evaluated if they obey the stated relation.

`v`
: Replaces the top element on the stack by its square root. Any existing fractional part of the argument is taken into account, but otherwise the scale factor is ignored.

`!`
: Interprets the rest of the line as a UNIX system command.

`c`
: All values on the stack are popped.

`i`
: The top value on the stack is popped and used as the number radix for further input.

`I`
: Pushes the input base on the top of the stack.

`o`
: The top value on the stack is popped and used as the number radix for further output.

`O`
: Pushes the output base on the top of the stack.

`k`
: The top of the stack is popped, and that value is used as a non-negative scale factor: the appropriate number of places are printed on output, and maintained during multiplication, division, and exponentiation. The interaction of scale factor, input base, and output base will be reasonable if all are changed together.

`z`
: The stack level is pushed onto the stack.

`Z`
: Replaces the number on the top of the stack with its length.

`?`
: A line of input is taken from the input source (usually the terminal) and executed.

`; :`
: are used by **bc**(1) for array operations.

EXAMPLES

This example prints the first ten values of n!:

```
[la1+dsa*pla10>y]sy
0sa1
lyx
```

SEE ALSO

bc(1)

DIAGNOSTICS

x is unimplemented: *x* is an octal number.

stack empty: not enough elements on the stack to do what was asked.

Out of space: the free list is exhausted (too many digits).

Out of headers: too many numbers being kept around.

Out of pushdown: too many items on the stack.

Nesting Depth: too many levels of nested execution.

NAME

dcopy (generic) – copy file systems for optimal access time

SYNOPSIS

dcopy [**-F** *FSType*] [**-V**] [*current_options*] [**-o** *specific_options*] *inputfs outputfs*

DESCRIPTION

dcopy copies file system *inputfs* to *outputfs*. *inputfs* is the device file for the existing file system; *outputfs* is the device file to hold the reorganized result. For the most effective optimization *inputfs* should be the raw device and *outputfs* should be the block device. Both *inputfs* and *outputfs* should be unmounted file systems.

current_options are options supported by the **s5**-specific module of **dcopy**. Other FSTypes do not necessarily support these options. *specific_options* indicate suboptions specified in a comma-separated list of suboptions and/or keyword-attribute pairs for interpretation by the *FSType*-specific module of the command.

The options are:

-F Specify the *FSType* on which to operate. The *FSType* should either be specified here or be determinable from **/etc/vfstab** by matching the *inputfs* (device) with an entry in the table.

-V Echo the complete command line, but do not execute the command. The command line is generated by using the options and arguments provided by the user and adding to them information derived from **/etc/vfstab**. This option should be used to verify and validate the command line.

-o Specify FSType-specific options.

NOTE

This command may not be supported for all FSTypes.

FILES

/etc/vfstab list of default parameters for each file system

SEE ALSO

s5-specific **dcopy**(1M), **vfstab**(4)

NAME

dcopy (s5) – copy **s5** file systems for optimal access time

SYNOPSIS

dcopy [**-F s5**] [*generic_options*] [**-s***X*] [**-a***n*] [**-d**] [**-v**] [**-f***fsize*[*:isize*]] *inputfs outputfs*

DESCRIPTION

generic_options are options supported by the generic **dcopy** command.

With no options, **dcopy** copies files from *inputfs* compressing directories by removing vacant entries, and spacing consecutive blocks in a file by the optimal rotational gap.

The options are:

-F s5 Specifies the **s5**-FSType. Need not be supplied if the information may be obtained from **/etc/vfstab** by matching the *inputfs* device with an entry in the file.

-s*X* Supply device information for creating an optimal organization of blocks in a file. *X* must be of the form *cylinder size:gap size*.

-a*n* Place the files not accessed in *n* days after the free blocks of the destination file system If no *n* is specified then no movement occurs.

-d Leave order of directory entries as is. The default is to sort the directory based on how recently each entry has been accessed. Entries accessed within the last 24 hours will be placed at the beginning of the directory. All subdirectories will be treated as if they were accessed within the last 24 hours.

-v Reports how many files were processed and how big the source and destination freelists are.

-f *fsize*[*:isize*] Specify the *outputfs* file system (*fsize*) and inode list (*isize*) sizes in logical blocks. If the suboption (or *:isize*) is not given, the values from *inputfs* are used.

dcopy catches interrupts and quits and reports on its progress. To terminate **dcopy**, send a quit signal followed by an interrupt or quit.

NOTES

fsck should be run on the new file system created by **dcopy** before it is mounted.

FILES

/etc/mnttab list of file systems currently mounted

SEE ALSO

generic **dcopy**(1M), **fsck**(1M), **mkfs**(1M)

NAME

dd – convert and copy a file

SYNOPSIS

dd [option=value] . . .

DESCRIPTION

dd copies the specified input file to the specified output with possible conversions. The standard input and output are used by default. The input and output block sizes may be specified to take advantage of raw physical I/O. **dd** processes supplementary code set characters according to the locale specified in the **LC_CTYPE** environment variable [see **LANG** on **environ**(5)], except as noted below.

option	*values*
if=*file*	input file name; standard input is default.
of=*file*	output file name; standard output is default.
ibs=*n*	input block size *n* bytes (default 512).
obs=*n*	output block size *n* bytes (default 512).
bs=*n*	set both input and output block size, superseding *ibs* and *obs*; also, if no conversion is specified, preserve the input block size instead of packing short blocks into the output buffer (this is particularly efficient since no in-core copy need be done).
cbs=*n*	conversion buffer size (logical record length).
files=*n*	copy and concatenate *n* input files before terminating (makes sense only where input is a magnetic tape or similar device).
skip=*n*	skip *n* input blocks before starting copy (appropriate for magnetic tape, where *iseek* is undefined).
iseek=*n*	seek *n* blocks from beginning of input file before copying (appropriate for disk files, where *skip* can be slow).
oseek=*n*	seek *n* blocks from beginning of output file before copying.
seek=*n*	identical to *oseek*, retained for backward compatibility.
count=*n*	copy only *n* input blocks.
conv=ascii	convert EBCDIC to ASCII. Conversion results cannot be assured when supplementary code set characters are also subject to conversion.
ebcdic	convert ASCII to EBCDIC. Conversion results cannot be assured when supplementary code set characters are also subject to conversion.
ibm	slightly different map of ASCII to EBCDIC. Conversion results cannot be assured when supplementary code set characters are also subject to conversion.

`conv=block`	convert new-line terminated ASCII records to fixed length.
`unblock`	convert fixed length ASCII records to new-line terminated records.
`lcase`	map alphabetics to lower case. Multibyte characters are not converted.
`ucase`	map alphabetics to upper case. Multibyte characters are not converted.
`swab`	swap every pair of bytes.
`noerror`	do not stop processing on an error (limit of 5 consecutive errors).
`sync`	pad every input block to *ibs*.
`... , ...`	several comma-separated conversions.

Where sizes are specified, a number of bytes is expected. A number may end with **k**, **b**, or **w** to specify multiplication by 1024, 512, or 2, respectively; a pair of numbers may be separated by **x** to indicate multiplication.

cbs is used only if **ascii**, **unblock**, **ebcdic ibm**, or **lock** conversion is specified. In the first two cases, *cbs* characters are copied into the conversion buffer, any specified character mapping is done, trailing blanks are trimmed, and a new-line is added before sending the line to the output. In the latter three cases, characters are read into the conversion buffer and blanks are added to make up an output record of size *cbs*. If **cbs** is unspecified or zero, the **ascii**, **ebcdic**, and **ibm** options convert the character set without changing the block structure of the input file; the **unblock** and **block** options become a simple file copy.

After completion, **dd** reports the number of whole and partial input and output blocks.

EXAMPLE

This command will read an EBCDIC tape blocked ten 80-byte EBCDIC card images per tape block into the ASCII file *x*:

```
dd  if=/dev/rmt*  of=x  ibs=800  obs=8k  cbs=80  conv=ascii,lcase
```

Note the use of raw magnetic tape. **dd** is especially suited to I/O on the raw physical devices because it allows reading and writing in arbitrary block sizes. Note also that **/rmt*** represents the raw magnetic tape device name.

FILES

/usr/lib/locale/*locale***/LC_MESSAGES/uxcore.abi**
language-specific message file [See **LANG** on **environ** (5).]

SEE ALSO

cp(1)

DIAGNOSTICS

f+p **records in(out)** numbers of full and partial blocks read(written)

NOTES

Do not use dd to copy files between file systems having different block sizes.

dd does not always require block sizes that are in multiples of 512 bytes. Block size is device dependent.

Using a blocked device to copy a file will result in extra nulls being added to the file to pad the final block to the block boundary.

Using dd with a cartridge tape is not recommended.

ddbconv (1M)

NAME

ddbconv – converts device table to Device Database format

SYNOPSIS

ddbconv [-v]

DESCRIPTION

ddbconv converts the device table located in the **/etc/device.tab** file to Device Database (DDB) format, a format which recognized by the device management commands. Pathnames of device special files defined for the **cdevice**, **bdevice**, **cdevlist**, and **bdevlist** attributes are moved into a new file, **/etc/security/ddb/ddb_dsfmap**. This file contains mappings between device special files and device names (**aliases**). The device management software requires that these mappings be unique.

Options

ddbconv takes the following options:

-v Verbose format. Displays the names of all device aliases whose attributes were modified.

USAGE

ddbconv should be executed only once, when upgrading to DDB format. If it is executed when the system is already in DDB format, the command returns normally, taking no action and producing no error messages.

DIAGNOSTICS

If successful, **ddbconv** exits with a value of zero (0). If there are errors, **ddbconv** returns one of the following exit codes and prints the corresponding error message.

1 **syntax incorrect, invalid options**
USAGE:ddbconv [-v]

4 **Device Database could not be accessed or created**

FILES

/etc/device.tab

REFERENCES

getdev(1M), putdev(1M)

NAME

debug — source-level, interactive, object file debugger

SYNOPSIS

debug [*opts*] [[**-f none|procs|all**] [**-r**] *cmd_line*]
debug [*opts*] [**-f none|procs|all**] [**-l** *object_file*] *live_object* . . .
debug [*opts*] **-c** *core_file object_file*
opts: [**-V**] [**-i c|x**] [**-X** *opt*] [**-d** *defaults*] [**-s** *path*] [**-Y***item,dir*]

DESCRIPTION

debug is a tool that facilitates the finding of errors in user programs by allowing the user to control the execution of a program and examine its state. The user can create a new process from an executable program, take over control of an existing process, or examine the state of a process that terminated abnormally with a **core** dump (see **core**(4)). Live programs can be executed one source statement or machine instruction at a time, or can be instructed to run until some event occurs. Program variables and the processor registers may be examined or modified, and the user can request a trace back of active functions, disassembly of a portion of the program's executable code or a raw dump of any area of the program's memory.

To take full advantage of the symbolic capabilities of **debug**, the programs examined and controlled by **debug** should be compiled with the **-g** option to the compiler (see **cc**(1)). If the controlled program has not been compiled with **-g**, the capabilities of **debug** will be limited, but the program can still be controlled and examined.

debug provides both a command line interface and an X Windows based graphical user interface. Only the command line interface is described here.

debug can be invoked in one of three ways. In the first, the user may specify a *cmd_line*. *cmd_line* consists of one or more executable files, and their associated arguments. The individual commands can be linked by shell-style pipes, and the input and output of the *cmd_line* can be redirected (characters special to the shell must be quoted). **debug** creates a new controlled process for each command specified in *cmd_line* , taking care of any necessary redirections of input and output. The processes are set-up to stop at the starting address specified by the object file. **debug** then **exec**'s each command, passing each the specified arguments.

If no *cmd_line* is specified, **debug** simply enters interactive mode.

In the second form of invocation, the user specifies one or more existing processes by giving a list of *live_object*s (either pathnames, entries in the **/proc** directory, or process ids). In either case, the debugger attempts to control the specified objects as live processes and, if successful, suspends their execution.

Finally, the user may specify an executable program in one of the object file formats understood by **debug**, along with a *core_file*. **debug** interprets the *core_file* as a record of the process state at the time of the death of the process associated with the *object_file* and lets the user examine the contents of the process stack, registers and data segments.

debug associates the name of each object (program name) with all processes derived from the current invocation of that object. This name may be used in any command that accepts a process list. If the object name matches the name of an already existing debugger-controlled program, the debugger will create a new name for the program. The default program name may be reset using the **rename** command (see below).

The following options are recognized:

- **-c** Associate the **core** image *core_file* with the specified *object_file*.
- **-d** Specify a *defaults* file containing debugger commands. If no *defaults* is given, **debug** will search for a file called **.debugrc** in the user's home directory. If a default command file exists, **debug** executes the commands it contains before it processes any other command line options or user requests.
- **-f** Specify whether **debug** will follow all child processes created by any of the *live_objects* or by any of the programs given in the *cmd_line*, (**procs**, or **all**) or none of the child processes (**none**). See *Process Control*.
- **-i** The interface mode for the debugger. **-i c** instructs **debug** to use the command line interface. **-i x** instructs **debug** to use the X Window based interface. If no **-i** option is given, **debug** uses the X Window interface, if the necessary hardware and software is present, otherwise the command line interface.
- **-l** Specify an alternate *object_file* from which to load symbolic information when debugging a *live_object*. If **-l** is used, only one *live_object* may be specified. See **grab** under *Commands*.
- **-r** Redirect input and output of the created objects to a pseudo-terminal (this does not affect subsequent redirection by the shell or the processes themselves). See *Redirection of Process I/O*.
- **-s** Specify initial value for the global search path, **%global_path**. The *path* is a colon separated list of directory pathnames. See *Directory Search Paths*.
- **-V** Print out version information about **debug**.
- **-X** Specify option to be passed to the X Windows initialization routine. This option may be specified multiple times.
- **-Y** Specify a new directory *dir* for the location of *item*. *item* can consist of any of the following:
  - **a** file containing definitions of built-in aliases for **debug**.
  - **f** follower process used by **debug** to control other processes.
  - **g** graphical user interface for **debug**.

Command Language

debug provides a simple, user-extensible command language, with a syntax similar to **sh**(1) in style, using keywords and dash options. Command options may appear in any order. Multiple options may be specified together, as in **symbols -lf** or separately, as in **symbols -l -f**, but multiple occurrences of the same option letter are invalid.

Several commands separated by semi-colons (**;**) may be given on a single line. A backslash (\) at the end of a line indicates that the command is continued on the following line. The output of a command may be redirected to a file or shell pipeline using the **sh** syntax of **>**, **>>** and **|**. (For example, **symbols -g | pg**). As in the shell, **>** and **>>** may appear anywhere within a command, but **|** must appear at the end of a debugger command, since the rest of the line is treated as a shell command that will receive the output of the debugger command. A sequence of debugger commands may be enclosed in curly braces (**{}**), forming a command *block*. The output of such a block may be redirected as a whole. A debugger comment is introduced by a pound sign (**#**). Any characters following a pound sign on a line will be ignored.

Many debugger commands have built-in aliases. These are one or two character names that may be used wherever the full command is used. The user can redefine any of the built-in aliases, or may define his or her own aliases. An alias can consist of any valid debugger command sequence and may take parameters. See **alias** under *Commands* for more details.

On-line help is available for all debugger commands and on many other topics, as well. See **help** for details.

Built-In Variables

debug maintains a set of special variables that describe the current debugger state and allow the user to customize certain debugger features. These variables all begin with a percent sign (%). The processor registers are also considered to be built-in variables and use the same naming convention. The current value of a debugger variable may be seen with the **print** or **symbols** commands. Some built-in variables are read-only. Those that can be modified may be changed using the **set** command.

User-Defined Variables

The user may also define variables in the debugger. The names of these variables consist of a dollar sign followed by a C-style identifier (*$username*). A user-defined variable is defined by assigning it an initial value using the **set** command, and may subsequently be modified. All of the user's environment variables are imported to debugger variables of the same name when **debug** is invoked.

User-defined variables are polymorphic, having either string or numeric values, according to the type of the last value assigned to them. Any variable, string or numeric, may be used where a string value is required, and any string-valued variable which is convertible to an integer via the **strtol**(3C) function may be used where a numeric value is required.

Command Editing and History

debug supports a subset of the **ksh**(1) command-line editing facility (see **ksh**(1)). Both **vi** and **emacs** modes are available. The initial mode is determined by examining the values of the **VISUAL** and **EDITOR** environment variables, as in **ksh**. The current mode is available in the debugger built-in variable **%mode**, and may be changed using the **set** command. The debugger command history is written to the file specified by the environment variable **DEBUG_HISTORY**, if this variable exists and is non-null. Otherwise, the command history is written to the file **.debug_hist** in the user's home directory. The debugger command history file is preserved across invocations of **debug** and is subject to the **ksh** history file size monitoring constraints.

debug also supports the **ksh fc** command, which allows command history searching, editing, listing and rerunning.

Process Control

An application designed to run in the UNIX System V environment can consist of one or more processes coordinated through some interprocess communication mechanism. These processes may have been created from a common ancestor via **fork**(2), or may have no particular ancestral relationship. A process is derived from an object file and zero or more static or dynamic shared libraries via **exec**(2), and is modified by attaching or detaching dynamic shared libraries during its execution.

debug provides control over both single and multiprocess applications. It maintains knowledge of an arbitrary number of object files and shared library files together with an arbitrary number of processes derived from those files.

For each active process under its control, **debug** detects when the object program and shared library association changes and maintains current knowledge of the associations. In particular, processes may attach or detach shared objects into/from their address spaces using the **libdl** interfaces (**dlopen**(3X), **dlclose**(3X), **dlsym**(3X)).

By default, **debug** detects when a new process is created by one of its controlled processes and includes the new process in its set of controlled objects. The user can release such newly created objects from debugger control by using the **release** command (see below). The default behavior may be overridden by individual **create** or **grab** commands, or may be changed by setting the value of the built-in variable **%follow**. Legal values are:

none Do not control child processes.

procs Follow all child processes.

all Follow all child processes (same as **procs**).

debug assigns a unique identifier to each process under its control. Process identifiers are in the form **p***id* (**p1**, **p2**, **p3**, ...). **debug** maintains a record of the current process in the built-in variable **%proc**. For all debugger commands that accept an optional list of processes, the default action, if no such list is given, is to apply the command to the current process, unless otherwise specified under individual commands.

When **debug** begins execution, the current process is set to the first process specified on the command line, whether a live process or one the debugger creates. The user may change the debugger's notion of the current process by changing the contents of **%proc** with the **set** command.

Foreground and Background Execution

Most users of traditional single-process debuggers are accustomed to a synchronous interface with the debugger: the user enters a command that sets a process in motion, and the debugger suspends its own execution until the process stops, only then returning control to the user. In a multiprocess application, if a debugger synchronously watches one process for too long, or takes too long to address a breakpoint or other event in some component, the timing of process interactions is affected. While it is impossible to avoid the problem of affecting the subject application entirely, the debugger can minimize this effect by reacting very quickly to all processes at the same time. This implies asynchronous process interaction, which in turn implies an asynchronous user interface.

When the user enters a command that sets a controlled object in motion, **debug**, by default, waits for that process to stop before returning control to the user. If the debugger built-in variable **%wait** is set to **0** or **no**, or **background**, the debugger does not wait for the affected object to stop. The default behavior may be re-asserted by setting **%wait** to **1** or **yes**, or **foreground**. This global behavior may be overridden by each command that sets a process in motion.

Redirection of Process I/O

When debugging a multiprocess application, a user can quickly get confused by output coming to the terminal from several different processes at once, especially if several processes are running in asynchronous mode. There is also a potential for confusion if more than one process is waiting for input from the user.

When the user creates a debugger-controlled object, **debug** does not, by default, attempt to intercept the input or output for the generated processes. Subject process output is unlabeled, and the subject competes with the debugger for the terminal input. If the debugger variable **%redir** is set to **1** or **yes**, the process I/O is redirected to a pseudo-terminal. All output from that process is labeled with an indication of which pseudo-terminal has been written. Subsequent input to the process must be made through the **input** command (see below). The default behavior may be re-asserted by setting **%redir** to **0** or **no**. This global behavior may be overridden by an individual **create** command.

debug does not attempt to redirect the I/O of grabbed processes, or of the child processes of some created subject, since it cannot tell what those processes may have already done to redirect their own I/O. Note, too, that all of the processes that result from a single **create** command read and write from/to the same pseudo-terminal.

Process Lists

A *process list* is a way to specify one or more processes as the target of a command. Many debugger commands take an argument (**-p** *proc_list*) that lists the names of those processes which should be affected by the command. A *program* is the set of all processes created as the result of invoking a single binary executable. It does not include processes created from different executables when a process within a program **exec**s.

The command language represents process lists as comma-separated lists of process names. A *process name* is defined as either:

the keyword **all**, denoting all controlled processes,

a user or debugger-generated *program name*, denoting all processes created from the current invocation of the same executable,

a debugger-generated *process id*, of the form **p***integer*, denoting a specific controlled object,

the debugger built-in variable **%program**, denoting all active processes derived from the current program,

the debugger built-in variable **%proc**, the current process, a decimal integer, denoting the process which has the given integer as its system *pid*,

any user-defined variable that has an integer value, interpreted as a system *pid*,

any user-defined variable that has a string value, which can be interpreted as one of the above forms, or as a list of the above forms.

Context Variables

The context for the execution of most debugger commands that describe the state of controlled objects is determined by a subset of the debugger built-in variables. **%program** and **%proc** determine the object(s) to which a command applies. Setting one affects the other. In addition, there is a set of context variables specific to each process. For each controlled process, the following debugger built-in variables are available:

%db_lang	The source language of the current context.
%frame	The current frame (an integer representing the frame number).
%func	The current function.
%file	The current source file.
%line	The current source line number.
%list_file	The next file to be displayed by the **list** command.
%list_line	The next line to be displayed by the **list** command.
%loc	The current program address.

These variables are reset whenever the process that owns them stops for any reason. **%frame** may be explicitly set by the user to any active frame and changes the value of the other context variables accordingly. **%func** may be explicitly set to any function with a currently active frame and results in setting **%frame** to the most recent instance of that function. **%db_lang**, **%file**, **%line**, and **%loc** are read-only. If no debugging or symbolic information is available for the current function, **%db_lang**, **%func**, **%file**, and **%line** may be null.

Verbosity Levels

When a user process under the debugger's control stops for any reason, single step, breakpoint, signal, *etc.*, the debugger generates output to the terminal. This output can sometimes be more voluminous than the user would desire. For that reason the amount of user-visible output can be adjusted on a global basis by setting the **%verbose** variable. The legal values are:

quiet	No output is generated for debugger events.
source	The debugger displays the next source line.
events	If the process stops for an event (system call, signal or stop event) the debugger announces the type of event and the current location. For all stops, it displays the next source line.

reason (default)	This is the same as **events**, except that the debugger announces each single step in addition to all of the events.
all	The highest verbosity level. Currently, this is the same as **reason**.

Certain commands allow the user to specify the **quiet** verbosity level, with a **-q** option, overriding the global **%verbose** setting.

Directory Search Paths

To associate program addresses with source listings, **debug** must know where to look for the source of the programs being debugged. The built-in variable **%global_path** contains a colon-separated list of directory pathnames. **debug** combines this information with the names of source files it derives from the debugging information in the object file, to search for source code. In addition to the global path, each *program* may have a program-specific path. This path is stored in the built-in variable **%path**. Each program has its own version of this variable. When attempting to find the source for a given program, **debug** searches first the list of directories in that program's **%path** variable, and then the list specified by **%global_path**.

Events

Events in the debugger are triggers in the execution sequence of a process that cause control to pass from the process to the debugger. These triggers are activated at the user's request and consist of changes in the process address space, signals and entry to or exit from system calls. Events may also consist of user-specified actions taken by the debugger when a controlled entity stops for any reason.

Event triggers may apply to a single process or to a set of processes. The event fires if any of the specified objects encounter the trigger. Commands that create events apply, by default, to the current program, rather than the current process.

With each event, the user may specify an optional debugger command block. This block is executed whenever the event triggers. Events and their associated commands can be deleted, or temporarily deactivated and then reactivated.

For each user-specified event, **debug** assigns a unique identifier in a common name space. This identifier may be used in the commands that delete, enable, disable and list events. The last event identifier assigned is maintained in the special variable **%lastevent**, which is updated automatically by the debugger. When an event triggers, **debug** executes the commands associated with the event, after setting the special variables **%program**, **%proc**, **%file**, **%line**, **%func**, **%frame**, **%loc**, **%db_lang** to indicate the process and location at which the event occurred, and **%thisevent** to the event number of the triggered event.

These variables are set only for the execution of the commands associated with the triggering event. They revert to their previous values (or are updated to reflect the new debugger state) when those commands complete.

The default action for each event is to announce the occurrence of the event and display the current source line (or current instruction, if no line number information or source is available).

When a controlled process dies, **debug** remembers the events created for that process. If a new process is created for the same program, all events that applied to the entire program (the default) are re-instantiated for the new process. Events that were created to apply only to a single process within a multiprocess program are not recreated. Similarly, when a process creates a new child process via **fork**(2), all events that apply to the entire program from which the parent process is derived are copied in the child process. Events that apply to the parent process only are not copied.

Expressions

Many debugger commands accept programming language *expressions*. Each expression is evaluated using the syntax and semantics of the current language, subject to possible limitations of the debugger on that language. The current language, **%db_lang,** is determined dynamically from the source language of the current file. The debugging information in an object file supplies a language attribute describing the programming language of the source file. If the debugger cannot determine the program's source language, **%db_lang** defaults to C. The user may override the information in the object file by setting the variable **%lang.** If the user sets **%lang** to the null string (**""**), the debugger reverts to using **%db_lang.** Expressions referencing variables defined in files compiled from different languages do not change the current language.

debug accepts expressions containing any combination of program variables or functions, qualified names, built-in debugger variables, and user-defined debugger variables. A qualified name specifies a program identifier that may not be visible in the current context. The syntax is:

> [[*process id*]@] [[*file*]@] [[*function*]@] [*line number*]@]*identifier*
> [[*process id*]@] [[*frame number*]@]*identifier*

The qualified name is evaluated left to right, and may be disambiguated by supplying **@**'s as needed.

When **%db_lang** is set to **C**, **debug** supports evaluation of all legal ANSI C expressions, except those involving macro expansion, or structure, union, or enumeration type declarations. An example of a type declaration in an expression is

```
((struct { int i; char c; } *)p)->c = 'a';
```

debug evaluates C expressions using ANSI C semantics rather than the pre-ANSI C (or *transition mode*) semantics. The main effect is on type promotions involving unsigned types, where ANSI C semantics are value preserving rather than unsigned preserving. The debugger's behavior may differ from the behavior of programs compiled with **cc -Xt** (for transition mode).

When **%db_lang** is set to **C++**, The debugger accepts a subset of C++ expressions, including:

> all expressions accepted when **%db_lang** is **C**,
> expressions using overloaded function names,
> expressions using the scoping operator (**::**), and
> expressions referencing non-virtual member functions.

Within this subset, **debug** conforms to the C++ Reference Manual. **debug** accepts and print names as they appear in the C++ source, not as they appear in the object file.

Expressions beginning with a dash (-) or containing character sequences with special meanings to **debug** must be enclosed in parens, square brackets or curly braces. The special character sequences are: >, >>, |, ||, &&, #, ',', ;, **newline**.

Definitions

The syntax and semantics for each command are described below. The following terms are used in the synopses and descriptions:

address	A constant, user-defined variable, built-in variable or register name that evaluates to an address (an integer or pointer value).
block	A list of commands, enclosed in braces, separated by newlines or semicolons.
call	A system call name or number. Case is not significant.
cmd	A simple command or a *block*.
cmd_line	A shell-style command line (possibly including shell scripts, environment variables, pipes, and I/O redirection) which will be interpreted by the shell, but the resulting processes will be controlled by the debugger.
core_file	The relative or complete pathname of a file which was created by the kernel upon abnormal termination of some process. It may be an ELF file or an "old-style" core file.
count	An unsigned decimal integer.
event_command	Any of **onstop**, **stop**, **signal** or **syscall**.
event_num	A small integer, assigned by the debugger when any event is created, that identifies the resulting set of actions.
expr	An expression in the current language. See *Expressions*, above.
func_name	The name of a function in the current process.
location	A designation of an address in a subject process. It includes line numbers, program symbols, processor registers, and limited expressions involving these components. The syntax is: *address* [±*constant*] # includes debugger and user variables [*process_id*@] [*filename*@]*func_name* [±*constant*] [*process_id*@] [*filename*@] *line_number*
object_file	The relative or complete pathname of an executable object file (an "*a.out*") in COFF or ELF format.
pattern	Simple regular expressions used to restrict a list of names. **sh**(1) syntax is used.
process_id	A system process identifier.

proc_list	See *Process Lists*.
reg_exp	A simple internationalized regular expression using the syntax accepted by **ed**(1).
signal	A signal name or number. A signal name may be specified with or without the **SIG** prefix, and case is not significant.
stop_expr	An expression denoting conditions under which specified processes should be stopped. See **stop**.
...	Denotes optional repetition of the preceding element.
xxx | *yyy*	Denotes that either *xxx* or *yyy*, but not both, may appear.

Commands

`!` *shell-command*

This command passes the entire command line, less the exclamation mark, to the shell (**$SHELL**, if set, or else **/usr/bin/sh**) for execution. Note that any redirection will be interpreted by the shell, not the debugger.

If the shell escape operator is given twice, with no arguments, that is, **!!**, **debug** re-executes the last shell escape specified.

alias [-r] [*name* **[***tokens***]]**

The **alias** command, with no arguments, lists the current aliases and their definitions. If the **-r** option is present, it removes the alias with the given *name* from the list of aliases. If no **-r** option is present, but a *name* is given, the **alias** command displays the definition, if any, for the alias with the given *name* . If any characters, other than spaces, tabs, or comments, follow the *name* argument, the command establishes a new alias for the *name* , consisting of all the characters up to, but not including, the comment or newline.

Alias definitions may contain the special identifiers **$1**, **$2**, ... Each such special identifier **$***n* in an alias definition is replaced by the *n*th argument in an alias invocation, where the arguments are numbered beginning at 1. Each argument must be preceded by whitespace and is terminated by whitespace, a newline, the comment character (**#**) or the beginning of a block (**{**). The special identifiers **$1**, **$2**, ... will not be replaced within a quoted string.

If an alias definition contains the special identifier **$#**, it will be replaced during invocation of the alias with the number of arguments actually used during the current alias invocation. If an alias definition contains the special identifier **$***, it will be replaced during invocation of the alias with a list of all arguments passed during the current alias invocation, each separated from the next by a single space.

Aliases may be defined in terms of other aliases, but not recursively. At least 20 levels of nested alias definitions are supported.

If the *name* given is the same as any existing built-in command, a warning will be generated. Aliases take precedence over built-in commands.

break The **break** command causes the debugger to exit from the innermost enclosing **while** loop (see **while**).

cancel [-p *proc_list*] [*signal*...]
cancel takes a list of signals, that are specified as in the **kill** command. If **debug** has intercepted any of the listed signals for any of the specified objects, it will ensure that those objects do not see the specified signals when they continue execution. If no signals are specified, **debug** cancels all pending signals for the specified objects.

cd [*pathname*]
The **cd** command changes the debugger's current working directory to *pathname*. If no *pathname* is given, **cd** uses the directory specified by the environment variable **HOME**.

change *event_num* **[-p** *proc_list*] **[-eqvx] [-c** *count*] [*stop_expr*|*call*...| *signal*...] [*block*]
The **change** command allows the user to modify various attributes associated with a previously assigned event. *event_num* must come before the optional stop expression, signal or system call specifications and must be the number of an event that is currently defined (although it may be disabled).

The list of processes to which the event is applied may be changed with the **-p** option.

The **-q** option specifies that **debug** will not announce the occurrence of the event. **-v** specifies that the event occurrence will be announced.

The **-e** and **-x** options work as in the **syscall** command, and specify whether the system call will be trapped on entry, exit or both entry and exit.

The **-c** option specifies the number of times the event must occur before it triggers. The **-c** option is valid only for **stop** and **syscall** events.

Alternate expressions, signals or system calls and/or an alternate command block, may be specified.

The resulting event will have the same event number as *event_num* . Note that the **change** command does not allow the type of event: **onstop**, **stop**, **signal** or **syscall**, to be changed. Further note that the command list must be in the form of a *block* (*i.e.* with enclosing braces) to distinguish it from a stop expression, system call or signal name.

continue
The **continue** command causes the debugger to begin execution of the next iteration of the innermost enclosing **while** loop. The debugger continues by re-evaluating the **expr** part of the **while** command (see **while**).

create [-f none|procs|all] [-dr] [*cmd_line*]
cmd_line consists of one or more executable files, in any of the object file formats understood by the debugger, and their associated arguments. The individual commands can be linked by shell-style pipes, and the input and output of the *cmd_line* can be redirected. Shell meta-characters need not be quoted. The length of *cmd_line* is limited only by the length of the argument list accepted by **exec** (**ARG_MAX**).

debug creates a new controlled process for each command specified in *cmd_line* , taking care of any necessary redirections of input and output. The processes are set-up to stop at the starting address specified by the object file. **debug** then **exec**'s each command, passing each the specified arguments.

If no *cmd_line* is specified to **create**, **debug** re-executes the last **create** command issued, (first killing all processes created as a result of the last **create** command, if they still exist) in effect, re-running the last process (or processes) created with the same set of arguments.

If the **-r** option is specified, **debug** redirects the I/O of the resulting subjects to a pseudo-terminal, as described above. If the **-d** option is given (the default), no redirection is attempted.

debug resets its notion of the current program to the first executable specified on the *cmd_line* . The current process is reset to the process generated from that executable.

The **-f** option may be used to override the default behavior of the debugger with respect to whether it takes control of child processes. The arguments to the **-f** option have the same meanings as do the legal values for the **%follow** built-in variable (see *Process Control*).

debug associates the name of each object (program name) with all processes derived from the current invocation of that object. This name may be used in any command that accepts a process list. If the command name matches the name of an already existing debugger-controlled program, **debug** creates a new name for the program. The default program name may be reset with the **rename** command (see below).

delete *event_num ...*
delete -a [-p *proc_list***] [***event_command***]**

delete can be invoked in one of two ways. In the first, the user specifies a list of previously assigned event identifiers. **debug** deletes any associated events, removing the planted breakpoint or canceling the signal or system call trigger.

In the second form, all debugger events for the current process (or all events associated with the optional *proc_list)* are deleted. If an *event_command* (**onstop**, **stop**, **signal** or **syscall**) is given, only events of the type specified are deleted.

dis [-p *proc_list***] [-c** *instr_count***] [***location***]**

The **dis** command with no arguments displays the result of disassembling **%num_lines** instructions. **%num_lines** starts out at 10 and may be reset by the user. If an *instr_count* is given, **dis** displays *instr_count* instructions, instead.

If a *location* is given, **dis** begins disassembling at that address. If no location has been specified, and the context for the specified process has not changed since the last **dis** invocation on that process, **dis** begins with the address following the last instruction displayed for that process. Otherwise, **dis** begins its display with the current location, as specified by the debugger variable **%loc**, which is reset whenever the context for the specified process changes.

If more than one process is specified by the *proc_list* argument, the disassembly request is performed for each process in turn.

disable *event_num ...*
disable -a [-p *proc_list*] [*event_command*]

disable can be invoked in one of two ways. In the first, the user specifies a list of previously assigned event identifiers. The debugger marks any associated events as inactive, but does not delete them. The event identifiers are still valid, but the actions specified by the events are not performed.

In the second form, all debugger events for the current process (or all events associated with the optional *proc_list)* are disabled. If an *event_command* is given, only events of the type specified are disabled.

dump [-p *proc_list*] [**-c** *byte_count*] *location*

The **dump** command displays **%num_bytes** bytes of memory, 16 bytes per line, starting at the address specified by the *location* truncated to a multiple of 16, in hexadecimal and ASCII. If a *byte_count* is given, that many bytes of memory are dumped instead. **%num_bytes** starts out at 256 and may be set by the user.

If more than one process is specified by the *proc_list* argument, the dump request is performed for each process in turn.

enable *event_num ...*
enable -a [-p *proc_list*] [*event_command*]

enable can be invoked in one of two ways. In the first, the user specifies a list of previously assigned event identifiers. For each, if the associated event is currently disabled, the debugger reactivates it.

In the second form, all disabled debugger events for the current process (or all events associated with the optional *proc_list)* are enabled. If an *event_command* is given, only events of the type specified are enabled.

events [-p *proc_list*] [*event_num ...*]

The **events** command without any arguments prints the entire list of user-specified events for the current process. For each, the event identifier and status (active or disabled), event type, list of associated processes, the event trigger (stop expression, system call or signal) and the beginning of the associated command list is printed.

If a *proc_list* is specified, those events associated with the list of processes are printed. If a list of event numbers is given, a more detailed record of the specified events is printed, including the full set of associated commands.

export $*username*

The **export** command makes a user-defined variable and its value available in the debugger's environment. The variable is thereafter passed to all processes created by **debug**. If the value of **$***username* is changed using the **set** command, after it has been exported, it must be explicitly re-exported for the new value to be visible in the environment. **$***username* is exported without the leading **$** sign.

fc [-e *ename*] **[-nlr]** [*first* [*last*]]
fc -e - [*old=new*] [*command*]

In the first form, a range of commands from *first* to *last* is selected from the last **HISTSIZE** commands (environment variable, default 128) that were entered. The arguments *first* and *last* may be specified as numbers or as strings. A string is used to locate the most recent command starting with the given string. A negative number is used as an offset to the current command number. If the **-l** option is given, the commands are listed on standard output. Otherwise, the editor program *ename* is invoked on a temporary file containing the commands. If *ename* is not supplied, the value of the environment variable **FCEDIT** (default **/usr/bin/ed**) is used as the editor. When editing is completed, the edited commands are executed.

If *first* is not specified, the default is the previous command for editing and the previous 16 commands for listing. The **-r** option reverses the order of the commands; the **-n** option suppresses command numbers when listing.

In the second form, the *command* is re-executed after the substitution *old=new* is performed. If *command* is not supplied, the default is the previous command.

grab [-f none|procs|all] [-l *object_file*] *live_object ...*
grab -c *core_file object_file*

The **grab** command can take one of two forms. In the first, the user specifies one or more existing processes by giving a list of *live_object*s (either pathnames, entries in the **/proc** directory, or process ids). In either case, **debug** attempts to control the specified objects as live processes and, if successful, suspends their execution. **debug** resets its notion of the current program to the executable from which the first process specified was derived. The current process is reset to the first process specified.

debug, by default, loads symbolic information for the process from the object file from which the process was created. The **-l** option specifies an alternate *object_file* from which to load symbolic information. If **-l** is used, only one *live_object* may be specified. This option is useful when debugging long running applications that have no symbol information.

The **-f** option may be used to override the default behavior of the debugger with respect to whether it takes control of child processes. The arguments to the **-f** option have the same meanings as do the legal values for the **%follow** built-in variable (see *Process Control*)

In the second form of **grab**, the user specifies an executable program in one of the object file formats understood by the debugger. **debug** interprets the *core_file* as a kernel-created record of the process state at the time of the death of the process associated with the *object_file* and lets the user examine the contents of the process stack, registers and data segments.

debug associates the name of each object with all processes derived from the current invocation of that object. This name may be used in any command that accepts a process list. If the command name matches the name of an already existing debugger-controlled program, **debug** creates a new name for the program. The default program name may be reset using the **rename**

command (see below).

halt [-p *proc_list***]**

debug instructs the specified processes to stop execution and waits for them to stop.

help [*topic***]**

The **help** command, with no arguments, lists all of the available commands and help topics. If a command name is given, it gives a detailed syntax and usage message for that command. If a ''help topic'' name is given, it lists the help available on that topic. Each debugger command has a help message which describes its syntax, options, and usage, and gives examples of its use. In addition, there are help topics which are not also command names, to explain the syntax for process lists, expressions, command output redirection and ''locations,'' and to list the available languages for expression evaluation.

if (*expr***)** *cmd* **[else** *cmd***]**

This is the traditional conditional branch statement, similar to that present in C, with the exception that semicolons are not necessary, except to separate multiple commands on a single line.

expr can be any valid expression in the current language (see *Expressions*). The expression is evaluated, and if it evaluates to ''true'' in the semantics of the current language, the *cmd* associated with the **if** clause is executed. Otherwise, if there is an *else* clause, the **cmd** associated with it is executed.

The **if** construct is more likely to be used in commands associated with events, or in scripts, than to be typed interactively as a top-level command.

input [-p *proc_name* **| -r** *pseudo_tty***] [-n]** *string*

The **input** command is used to send user input to a process whose I/O has been redirected by the debugger to a pseudo-terminal (see *Redirection of Process I/O*). The first argument may be either the name of a single program or process (as specified in a process list), or the name of a pseudo-terminal, as used by **debug** to label process output. If a *proc_name* is specified, **debug** finds the pseudo-terminal (if any) associated with that program. If neither a program nor a pseudo-terminal is specified, **debug** attempts to find a pseudo-terminal associated with the current program.

debug sends the input *string* to the specified pseudo-terminal, after appending a new-line. If the **-n** option is given, no new-line is appended.

It is an error if the specified **proc_name** has no associated pseudo-terminal.

jump [-p *proc_list***]** *location*

location may be any debugger expression that resolves to an address in one of the specified processes. For each process specified, if the given process is currently stopped, and if the specified *location* is valid for that process, **debug** adjusts the program counter for that object to that *location*. Subsequent **run** or **step** commands for that object continue execution from the specified *location* . **debug** does not attempt to adjust the process stack if the specified *location* is in a different function.

kill [**-p** *proc_list*] [*signal*]

kill sends a single, user-specified signal to a list of processes. If no *signal* is specified, the default is **SIGKILL**. *signal* may be either a valid signal number (as defined in **<sys/signal.h>**) or a symbolic name, formed from the manifest constant name listed in **<sys/signal.h>**, with or without the **SIG** prefix. Case is ignored.

list [**-c** *count*] [*line*|*func_name*|*reg_exp*]

The **list** command with no arguments displays **%num_lines** source lines. **%num_lines** starts out at 10 and may be reset by the user. If a *count* is given, **list** displays *count* lines, instead.

The starting place for the listing may be specified in several ways. If a regular expression is given, the current file is searched for the next occurrence of a line which matches the given *reg_exp* , beginning from the line immediately following the current line (preceding, if the *reg_exp* is surrounded by question marks). If a match is found, and no *count* is given, only the line containing the match is listed. If a *count* is given, the line containing the match begins the display. **ed**(1) syntax is used for regular expressions.

A function name as an argument causes the **list** command to begin its display at the first line of the named function. The function may be specified as in the location syntax: a name, the debugger built-in variable **%func**, or *filename*@*func_name*.

A line number may be specified as in the location syntax: a single decimal constant, the debugger built-in variables **%line** or **%list_line**, or *filename*@*line*.

If no starting location is specified, the **list** command begins the display with **%list_file@%list_line**. **%list_file** is set to the current file (**%file**) and **%list_line** is set to the current line (**%line**) whenever the current context changes. In addition, **%list_line** is set to the last line displayed each time **list** is invoked. Thus, if the current context has not changed and no starting location is specified, **list** begins with the last line displayed in the previous **list** invocation.

logoff

The **logoff** command stops session logging.

logon [*filename*]

The **logon** command starts debugger session logging. All debugger input and output are sent to *filename* in addition to being echoed at the terminal. Output lines are printed as comments.

If no *filename* is given, the last *filename* used in a **logon** command is assumed, and new debugger commands and output are appended to that file.

map [**-p** *proc_list*]

The **map** command prints out a list of all mapped segments for the current process, or for each process specified in *proc_list* . The listing includes the virtual address range and access permissions for all segments, and the pathname, for all segments associated with the **a.out** and associated shared libraries.

onstop [-p *proc_list*] [*cmd*]

The **onstop** command, by default, applies to all processes derived from the current program. The **onstop** command with no arguments prints out the list of **onstop** events with their associated commands.

cmd is a debugger command block. The commands are executed whenever the specified list of processes stops for any reason.

print [-p *proc_list*] [-f *fmt*] *expr* [, *expr*] ...

The **print** command displays the results of evaluating the (comma-separated) list of expressions. The expressions are evaluated in the context of the current process, unless other processes are specified in the *proc_list* argument. If more than one process is specified, the expressions are evaluated and printed in the context of each specified process, with the **%proc** debugger variable set to the process identifier of the process in which the expressions are being evaluated. All events which would be triggered as a side effect of evaluating an expression (breakpoints in a function, a call to which appears in the expression, for example) are ignored, as if they had been disabled.

The **-f** option allows specification of a list of format expressions to be used when printing values. The *fmt* is a string enclosed in quotation marks ("") and may contain a subset of the format expressions accepted by **printf**(3C). A format expression may have the following form:

%[*flags*][*width*][.[*precision*]][*conversion*]*specifier*

The *flags*, *width*, *precision*, and *conversion* fields have the same meanings as in the **printf** routine, with the exception that positional parameters are not accepted. The *specifier* may be one of the following characters:

c	unsigned char
d,i	signed decimal integer
e,E	floating point in style [-]*d.ddde±dd*
f	floating point in style [-]*ddd.dddd*
g,G	floating point in either of above 2 styles
o	unsigned octal integer
p	**void *** (generic data pointer; hexadecimal address)
s	string
u	unsigned decimal integer
x,X	unsigned hexadecimal integer
z	debugger default style for the expression
%	%

Any character in the *fmt* that is not part of a format expression is printed as given. The default format for a particular expression is determined by the expression evaluator for the current language. The expression evaluators will attempt to present information formatted in a way that is meaningful for the given language. For example, for C, a pointer to a character would be printed as a character string, a reference to an array variable would print all members of that array and dereferencing a pointer to a structure would print each member of that structure. Each *expr* may be any valid expression in the current language (see *Expressions*).

Each expression in the list is converted to its printable representation, a newline is added, and the result displayed. This process is repeated for each process named in the *proc_list* . If a *fmt* is given, no terminating newline is printed unless specified in the *fmt* .

ps [**-p** *proc_list*]
: The **ps** command prints the debugger-generated identifiers, kernel-generated identifiers, current state, location, if the process is stopped, and object name for all controlled processes, or for only those objects specified by the **-p** option, if present.

pwd
: The **pwd** command prints the debugger's current working directory. The current working directory may be changed using the **cd** command.

quit
: The **quit** command causes the debugger to exit, releasing and running any grabbed processes and killing any processes created by the debugger.

If a user wishes to leave a grabbed process suspended, perhaps to be grabbed at a later time from a different invocation of the debugger, he or she should use the **release** command with the **-s** option before quitting.

regs [**-p** *proc_list*]
: The **regs** command displays in hexadecimal the contents of the processor registers for the current process. If more than one process is specified by the *proc_list* argument, the register display is performed for each process in turn.

release [**-s**] [**-p** *proc_list*]
: **debug** removes all planted breakpoints from all processes specified in *proc_list* and relinquishes its control of them. If the **-s** option is specified, the processes are released, but halted. Otherwise, the released processes are allowed to continue execution. If the current process is released, **debug** chooses a new process to become current.

Processes released in the halted state may be grabbed by the debugger in a different **debug** session.

release can be used on core images as well as live processes. The debugger deletes the core image and associated object file from the list of objects that can be examined.

rename *prog_name name*
: The **rename** command changes the name by which a related group of processes are known. All processes derived from a single invocation of the executable from which *prog_name* was derived, can be referred to by the new *name*. *name* can be used in any command that accepts a *proc_list* and will appear in any debugger output that would have used *prog_name*.

run [-p *proc_list*] [-bfr] [-u *location*]

debug starts the specified processes. Execution continues from the program address at which it was suspended when the given process last stopped, or at the address specified in a preceding **jump** command.

The **-f** and **-b** options allow the global behavior set by the **%wait** debugger variable to be overridden. **-f** specifies foreground execution for the processes. **-b** specifies background execution.

The **-r** option causes **debug** to continue execution of the given processes until each returns from its current stack frame, that is, until the return address of the current function is reached (or until some other event causes execution to halt).

The **-u** option allows the specification of an address to run to. **debug** continues execution of the specified objects until that address is reached (or until some other event causes execution to halt).

script [-q] *fname*

The **script** command reads and executes debugger commands from the named file. Commands are echoed before execution, unless the **-q** option is given.

Scripts may nest; the debugger implementation does not place a limit on the number of nested scripts (although external limits, such as the number of open files supported by **stdio**, may apply).

set [-p *proc_list*] *expr*
set [-p *proc_list*] *debug_or_user_var* [=] *expr* [, *expr*] ...

The **set** command has two forms. In the first, *expr* may be any valid expression in the current language (see *Expressions*). While any valid language expression may be given, the typical use of the **set** command is to evaluate assignment expressions.

In the second form of the command, **set** is used to change the value of a debugger built-in variable name or user-defined variable name. Debugger built-in variables may have special semantics associated with them, such as **%path**, which requires a string value having a particular structure, or **%frame**, which denotes a frame number and must be within the range of currently active frame numbers. Setting a built-in variable such as **%frame**, may cause the values of other built-in variables to change as well (*e.g.* **%line** or **%func**). There is also an implied string concatenation operator. Any pair of string-valued expressions which appear separated by commas will be concatenated into a single string-valued expression before the assignment is performed.

The *debug_or_user_var* and *expr* are both evaluated in the context of the current process, unless one or more other processes have been specified in the *proc_list* argument. If more than one process is specified, the **set** command is evaluated in the context of each of the specified processes, in turn.

signal [-p *proc_list*] [[-iq] *signal* ... [*cmd*]]

The **signal** command, by default, applies to all processes derived from the current program. Signals are different from other debugger events in that the debugger catches all signals by default. When a signal is posted to a process, the debugger stops the process and announces that the signal has been posted. The user can then request that the signal be canceled before the process actually receives it (see **cancel**).

debug can be instructed to ignore a given signal for a particular process (or set of processes) with the **-i** option to the **signal** command. So **signal -i sigusr1** instructs the debugger to let **SIGUSR1** go directly to the current process, while **signal sigusr1** re-establishes the default action for **SIGUSR1** for the current process.

The **signal** command can also be used to create events triggered by the receipt of a signal. If a user associates a command block with a signal or set of signals, the debugger creates an event number for that signal in the same name space as the other event commands. These events may be manipulated using **events**, **delete**, **disable** or **enable**. Multiple events may be assigned for the same signal in any given process. The creation of an event for a signal takes precedence over any instruction to ignore that signal (using **signal -i**).

The **-q** option specifies that **debug** will not announce the occurrence of the signal and applies only to signal events.

The **signal** command with no *signal* arguments prints the current signal disposition for each signal and the current list of user-specified signal events, including the event identifier and current status (active or disabled), list of associated processes, signal name and the beginning of any associated command block.

stack [-p *proc_list***] [-c** *count***] [-f** *frame***]**

The **stack** command with no arguments prints the entire call stack for the current process. Frames are numbered from 0 for the bottom of the stack (initial stack frame). Displays begin with the top of the stack, unless the **-f** option is given, in which case they begin with *frame.* The *count* argument restricts the display to at most *count* frames from each stack. If more than one process is specified by the *proc_list* argument, the stack request is performed for each process in turn.

step [-p *proc_list***] [-bfioq] [-c** *count***]**

The **step** command continues execution of the specified processes. The **-i** option specifies stepping at the machine instruction level. The specified objects are instructed to execute a single machine instruction, or *count* instructions, if a *count* is specified.

The default is stepping at the source statement level. **debug** continues execution until the object reaches the next source statement as defined by the compiler-generated debugging information. If a *count* is specified, the debugger repeats the **step** command *count* times, or until execution is interrupted by some other event. An explicit *count* of zero is interpreted to mean "step forever."

The **-o** option specifies stepping over function calls. When the debugger encounters a subroutine call while stepping with the **-o** option, it will set a temporary breakpoint at the return point of the call and run at "full speed" until the temporary breakpoint is reached. Stepping over function calls is available with both the instruction and source level stepping.

The `-f` and `-b` options allow the global behavior set by the `%wait` debugger variable to be overridden. `-f` specifies foreground execution for the processes. `-b` specifies background execution.

The `-q` option specifies quiet stepping: the debugger does not announce the step action nor the new source line.

stop [-p *proc_list*] [[-q] [-c *count*] *stop_expr* [*cmd*]]

The **stop** command specifies conditions in the address space of one or more controlled objects that should cause a list of processes to stop. By default, the **stop** command applies to all processes derived from the current program.

A *stop_expr* consists of one or more *stop events* , joined by the special debugger conjunction (`&&`) or disjunction (`||`) operators. These operators are left-associative, and **debug** does not guarantee the order in which their operands are evaluated. A *stop event* can take one of three forms:

location
**lvalue*
(*expr*)

Each type of *stop event* has some action that will cause the event to be noticed by the debugger. When such an action occurs, the entire *stop_expr* is evaluated for "truth". If true, the event triggers in the normal way (**debug** informs the user of the event and executes any associated commands).

A *location* is an address in the process's text where **debug** can set a breakpoint. When the process reaches the specified location **debug** notices the event. For location stop events that refer to function names, the expression is true as long as that function is active. For location stop events that apply to a particular address or line number, the expression is true only when the process is at that address or line.

lvalue may be any expression in the current language that would be valid on the left-hand side of an assignment statement in that language. The debugger notices this event when the contents of the location change. The change itself makes this kind of stop event true.

expr can be any valid expression in the current language. The debugger notices the stop event when any of the identifiers involved in the expression changes value. The entire expression is then evaluated in the context of the current language.

stop events are evaluated continuously while the process is executing. The debugger is free to choose whatever means it has available to achieve this effect. This may include hardware support or may involve continuous single stepping of the process.

The optional *count* specifies the number of times the *stop_expr* must evaluate to true before the event triggers. After *count* times, the event triggers each time the *stop_expr* evaluates to true.

The **-q** option specifies that **debug** will not announce the occurrence of the event.

The **stop** command with no *stop_expr* arguments prints the list of user-specified stop expressions including the event identifier and current status (active or disabled).

symbols [-p *proc_list***] [-o** *object***] [-n** *filename***] [-dfgltuv] [***pattern***]**

The **symbols** command with no arguments displays "local" symbols; that is, names of variables which are defined within the current function (**%frame**) and are visible from the current location. This is also the behavior of the **-l** option.

The **-g** option displays only the names of global variables which are visible from the current location. This includes only those symbols defined within the current object (executable program or shared library). The **-o** option, in conjunction with **-g**, displays the names of global variables in the named *object*.

The **-f** option displays only the names of variables which are local to the current file (**%file**) and are visible from the current location (**%loc**). If the **-n** option is used, the symbols local to *filename* are displayed instead.

The **-d** option displays the debugger built-in variables. The **-u** option displays the debugger-maintained, user-defined variables.

If a *pattern* is given, the display is further restricted to symbols which match the *pattern*. **sh**(1) syntax is used.

If the **-v** option is specified, the value of each symbol is displayed, along with its name. The **-t** option displays the type of the variable.

If more than one process is specified by the *proc_list* argument, the **symbols** request is performed in the context of each process in turn.

syscall [-p *proc_list***] [[-eqx] [-c** *count***]** *call* . . . [*cmd*]]

The **syscall** command, by default, applies to all processes derived from the current program. The **syscall** command with no *call* arguments prints the current list of user-specified system call actions, including the event identifier and current status (active or disabled), list of associated processes, system call name and the beginning of any associated command block.

Each *call* may be given as either a system call entry number, or as the name used in the C language interface to the call. The **-e** option specifies system call entry, and is the default. The **-x** option specifies system call exit. Both may be given on a single invocation of the **syscall** command. For each *call* listed, the debugger arranges for the specified processes to stop on entry to or exit from that *call*, or on both entry and exit. The resulting set of actions is then assigned a unique event identifier.

The optional *count* specifies the number of times the *call* must occur before the event triggers. After *count* times, the event triggers each time the *call* occurs.

The `-q` option specifies that **debug** will not announce the occurrence of the system call.

`while` `(`*expr*`)` *cmd*
This is the traditional conditional loop statement, similar to that present in C, with the exception that semicolons are not necessary, except to separate multiple commands on a single line.

expr can be any valid expression in the current language (see *Expressions*). The expression is evaluated, and if it evaluates to "true" in the semantics of the current language, the *cmd* is executed. The expression is then re-evaluated.

Unlike `if`, the `while` construct is often useful as a top-level command.

Built-In Command Aliases

`b`	→	`stop`
`exit`	→	`quit`
`h`	→	`help`
`history`→	`fc -l`	
`l`	→	`list`
`n`	→	`step -o`
`next`	→	`step -o`
`ni`	→	`step -io`
`p`	→	`print`
`q`	→	`quit`
`r`	→	`run`
`rr`	→	`fc -e -`
`s`	→	`step`
`si`	→	`step -i`
`sig`	→	`signal`
`syms`	→	`symbols`
`sys`	→	`syscall`
`t`	→	`stack`

Summary of Built-In Variables

`%db_lang` The current language as determined from the object file (read-only, process specific).

`%file` The current file (read-only, process specific).

`%follow` Should **debug** follow child processes? Valid values are **all**, **none**, **procs** (global).

`%frame` The current active stack frame. Affects `%db_lang`, `%func`, `%file`, `%line`, `%list_file`, `%list_line`, `%loc` (process specific).

`%func` The current function. Affects `%frame` (process specific).

`%global_path` The list of directory pathnames used to search for source files for all processes. Searched after the program specific list `%path` (global).

`%lang`	The current language. Setting **`%lang`** overrides the language as determined from the object file and maintained in **`%db_lang`** (global) .
`%lastevent`	The id of the last event created (read-only, global).
`%line`	The current line (read-only, process specific).
`%list_file`	The name of the file to be displayed by the **`list`** command. Reset when the current context changes (process specific).
`%list_line`	The number of the next source line to be displayed by the **`list`** command. Reset when the current context changes. Set to the last line displayed by any invocation of **`list`** (process specific).
`%loc`	The current location (read-only, process specific).
`%mode`	Mode for command line editing (global). Valid values are **`vi`** and **`emacs`**. Setting **`%mode`** to **`NULL`** turns off command line editing.
`%num_bytes`	The default number of bytes printed by the **`dump`** command (global).
`%num_lines`	The default number of lines printed by the **`dis`** and **`list`** commands (global).
`%path`	The list of directory pathnames used to search for source files for a given program. Searched before the global list **`%global_path`** (program specific).
`%proc`	The current process (global).
`%program`	The current program (global).
`%prompt`	The string used by **`debug`** to prompt the user for input; default is **`debug>`** (global).
`%redir`	Should process I/O be redirected to a pseudo-terminal for processes created by **`debug`**? Valid values are `0`, `1`, **`no`**, **`yes`** (global).
`%result`	The result status of any debugger command. `0` indicates success, non-zero failure.
`%thisevent`	The id of the event whose associated command list is currently being executed (read-only, global).
`%verbose`	Level of verbosity for event notification (global). Valid values are **`quiet`**, **`source`**, **`events`**, **`reason`**, **`all`**.
`%wait`	Should processes run in the foreground or background? Valid values are `0`, `1`, **`background`**, **`foreground`**, **`no`**, **`yes`** (global).
%*register*	The processor registers.

DIAGNOSTICS

If **debug** is invoked with invalid arguments, it prints a diagnostic message and exits with a non-zero exit status. If the command-line processing fails for any other reason, **debug** continues execution, allowing the user to enter requests interactively. **debug** prints diagnostics for any failure in processing user requests. The result status of each command is recorded in the debugger variable **%result**. A value of 0 indicates successful execution; a non-zero value indicates failure.

If **debug** cannot create or execute processes for any of the commands specified in *cmd_line*, it acts as if the entire *cmd_line* request had failed. In particular, any processes that had been created as part of the same *cmd_line* request are killed.

On the other hand, if **debug** cannot gain control of one or more of the *live_object*s specified in the second form of invocation, it continues to attempt to control the other objects specified.

If **debug** is invoked with the **-i x** option and cannot start the X Window based interface, it prints a diagnostic message and exits with a non-zero exit status.

FILES

$HOME/.debug_hist	command history log
$HOME/.debugrc	defaults file
LIBDIR/**debug_alias**	built-in alias definitions
LIBDIR/**follow**	follower process
LIBDIR/**debug.ol.ui**	graphical interface
LIBDIR	usually **/usr/ccs/lib**

SEE ALSO

cc(1), **core**(4), **dlclose**(3X), **dlopen**(3X), **dlsym**(3X), **ed**(1), **exec**(2), **fork**(2), **ksh**(1), **printf**(3C), **sh**(1), **strtol**(3C)

defadm (1M)

NAME

defadm – display/modify default values

SYNOPSIS

defadm

defadm [*filename* [*name*[=*value*]] [*name*[=*value*]] [. . .]]

defadm [**-d** *filename name* [*name*] [. . .]]

DESCRIPTION

The **defadm** command prints, modifies, adds, or deletes system and command default values contained in the file given by *filename*; where *filename* is a file in the **/etc/default** directory.

If **defadm** is executed with no arguments, it lists the files in the **/etc/default** directory.

If **defadm** is given a *filename*, it prints all the defaults contained in *filename*. If one or more *names* are specified together with a *filename*, then **defadm** prints the specified *names* together with their *values*.

If **defadm** is given a *filename* and one or more *names* and *values*, then the default file is modified so that the *name* is set to the respective *value*. If the *value* is an empty string, the *name* has a null value. If *name* is not found, a warning message is printed and processing continues.

If **defadm** is given the **-d** option, a *filename*, and one or more *names*, it removes the specified *names* from the *filename*.

FILES

/etc/default/* directory of files containing system or command default values

SEE ALSO

cron(1M), **login**(1), **passwd**(1), **su**(1M), **useradd**(1M), **userdel**(1M)

DIAGNOSTICS

The **defadm** command exits with one of the following values:

0	SUCCESS.
1	UX:defadm: ERROR: invalid option.
2	UX:defadm: ERROR: directory **directory** does not exist.
3	UX:defadm: ERROR: cannot access directory **directory**.
4	UX:defadm: ERROR: file **filename** does not exist.
5	UX:defadm: ERROR: cannot access file **filename**.
6	UX:defadm: WARN: name **name** does not exist.
7	UX:defadm: ERROR: file **filename** is locked, try again later.
8	UX:defadm: ERROR: unexpected error.

NAME

delsysadm – **sysadm** interface menu or task removal tool

SYNOPSIS

delsysadm *task* | [**-r**] *menu*

DESCRIPTION

The **delsysadm** command deletes a *task* or *menu* from the **sysadm** interface and modifies the interface directory structure on the target machine.

task | *menu* The logical name and location of the menu or task within the interface menu hierarchy. Begin with the top menu **main** and include the name of all other menus that must be traversed (in the order they are traversed) to reach the menu or task, separating each name with colons. See EXAMPLES.

If the **-r** option is used, this command will recursively remove all sub-menus and tasks for this menu. If the **-r** option is not used, the menu must be empty.

delsysadm should only be used to remove items added as "on-line" changes with the **edsysadm** command. Such an addition will have a package instance tag of ONLINE. If the task or menu (and its sub-menus and tasks) have any package instance tags other than ONLINE, you are asked whether to continue with the removal or to exit. Under these circumstances, you probably do not want to continue and you should rely on the package involved to take the necessary actions to delete this type of entry.

The command exits successfully or provides the error code within an error message.

EXAMPLES

To remove the **nformat** task, execute:

```
delsysadm main:applications:ndevices:nformat.
```

DIAGNOSTICS

0 Successful execution
2 Invalid syntax
3 Menu or task does not exist
4 Menu not empty
5 Unable to update interface menu structure

NOTES

Any menu that was originally a placeholder menu (one that only appears if sub-menus exist under it) will be returned to placeholder status when a deletion leaves it empty.

When the **-r** option is used, **delsysadm** checks for dependencies before removing any subentries. (A dependency exists if the menu being removed contains an entry placed there by an application package). If a dependency is found, the user is shown a list of packages that depend on the menu being deleted and asked whether to continue. If the answer is yes, the menu and all its menus and tasks are removed (even those shown to have dependencies). If the answer is no, the menu is not deleted.

delsysadm should only be used to remove menu or task entries that have been added to the interface with **edsysadm**.

SEE ALSO

edsysadm(1M), **sysadm**(1M)

NAME

delta – make a delta (change) to an SCCS file

SYNOPSIS

delta [**-r***SID*] [**-s**] [**-n**] [**-g***list*] [**-m**[*mrlist*]] [**-y**[*comment*]] [**-p**] *file* . . .

DESCRIPTION

delta is used to introduce changes into the named SCCS *file*; *file* must have been retrieved previously by using **get -e** (called the **g.***file* or generated file). The file name specified must be in the form **s.***file* or be the name of a directory. If a directory is named, **delta** behaves as though each file in the directory were specified as a named file, except that non-SCCS files (last component of the path name does not begin with **s.**) and unreadable files are silently ignored. If a name of **-** is given, the standard input is read (see the NOTES section); each line of the standard input is taken to be the name of an SCCS file to be processed.

delta may issue prompts on the standard output depending on certain keyletters specified and flags [see **admin**(1)] that may be present in the SCCS file (see **-m** and **-y** keyletters below).

Keyletter arguments apply independently to each named file.

-r*SID* Uniquely identifies which delta is to be made to the SCCS file. The use of this keyletter is necessary only if two or more outstanding **get**s for editing (**get -e**) on the same SCCS file were done by the same person (login name). The SID value specified with the **-r** keyletter can be either the SID specified on the **get** command line or the SID to be made as reported by the **get** command [see **get**(1)]. A diagnostic results if the specified SID is ambiguous, or, if necessary and omitted on the command line.

-s Suppresses the issue, on the standard output, of the created delta's SID, as well as the number of lines inserted, deleted and unchanged in the SCCS file.

-n Specifies retention of the edited **g.***file* (normally removed at completion of delta processing).

-g*list* Specify a *list* [see **get**(1) for the definition of *list*] of deltas that are to be ignored when the file is accessed at the change level (SID) created by this delta.

-m[*mrlist*] If the SCCS file has the **v** flag set [see **admin**(1)] then a Modification Request (MR) number must be supplied as the reason for creating the new delta. If **-m** is not used and the standard input is a terminal, the prompt **MRs?** is issued on the standard output before the standard input is read; if the standard input is not a terminal, no prompt is issued. The **MRs?** prompt always precedes the **comments?** prompt (see **-y** keyletter). MRs in a list are separated by blanks and/or tab characters. An unescaped new-line character terminates the MR list. Note that if the **v** flag has a value [see **admin**(1)], it is taken to be the name of a program (or shell procedure) that will validate the correctness of the MR numbers. If a non-zero exit status is returned from the MR number validation program, **delta** terminates. (It is assumed that the MR numbers were not all valid.)

-y[*comment*] Arbitrary text used to describe the reason for making the delta. A null string is considered a valid *comment*. If **-y** is not specified and the standard input is a terminal, the prompt **comments?** is issued on the standard output before the standard input is read; if the standard input is not a terminal, no prompt is issued. An unescaped new-line character terminates the comment text. Supplementary code set characters may be used in *comment*.

-p Causes **delta** to print (on the standard output) the SCCS file differences before and after the delta is applied in a **diff**(1) format.

FILES

g.*file* Existed before the execution of **delta**; removed after completion of **delta**.
p.*file* Existed before the execution of **delta**; may exist after completion of **delta**.
q.*file* Created during the execution of **delta**; removed after completion of **delta**.
x.*file* Created during the execution of **delta**; renamed to SCCS file after completion of **delta**.
z.*file* Created during the execution of **delta**; removed during the execution of **delta**.
d.*file* Created during the execution of **delta**; removed after completion of **delta**.
bdiff Program to compute differences between the "gotten" file and the **g.***file*.

SEE ALSO

admin(1), **bdiff**(1) **cdc**(1), **get**(1), **help**(1), **prs**(1), **rmdel**(1), **sccsfile**(4)

DIAGNOSTICS

Use **help**(1) for explanations.

NOTES

A **get** of many SCCS files, followed by a **delta** of those files, should be avoided when the **get** generates a large amount of data. Instead, multiple **get/delta** sequences should be used.

If the standard input (**-**) is specified on the **delta** command line, the **-m** (if necessary) and **-y** keyletters must also be present. Omission of these keyletters causes an error.

Comments are limited to text strings of at most 1024 bytes. Line lengths greater than 1000 bytes cause undefined results.

NAME

deluser – remove a login from the system

SYNOPSIS

deluser *login_name* **Yes** | **No** *logdir*

DESCRIPTION

deluser is used to remove a user ID from the system. Once the ID has been removed, its owner will no longer have access to the system.

login_name
This is the login name for the user account that's being removed from the system.

Yes | **No** This argument determines whether or not the user's files should be saved when his or her login name is removed.

If **Yes** is specified, all files in the user's home directory are copied to **/lost+found/***login_name* before the home directory is removed.

If **No** is specified, the files in **$HOME** are not removed.

logdir This is the user's home directory.

SEE ALSO

adduser(1M)

deroff(1)

NAME

deroff – remove **nroff/troff**, **tbl**, and **eqn** constructs

SYNOPSIS

deroff [-w] [-m(msl)] [-i] [*file*] . . .

DESCRIPTION

deroff reads each of the *files* in sequence and removes all **troff**(1) requests, macro calls, backslash constructs, **eqn**(1) constructs (between **.EQ** and **.EN** lines, and between delimiters), and **tbl**(1) descriptions, perhaps replacing them with white space (blanks and blank lines), and writes the remainder of the file on the standard output. **deroff** follows chains of included files (**.so** and **.nx troff** commands); if a file has already been included, a **.so** naming that file is ignored and a **.nx** naming that file terminates execution. If no input file is given, **deroff** reads the standard input.

Options

-w The output is a word list, one "word" per line, with all other characters deleted. Otherwise, the output follows the original, with the deletions mentioned above. In text, a "word" is any string that contains at least two letters and is composed of letters, digits, ampersands (&), and apostrophes ('). In a macro call, however, a "word" is a string that begins with at least two letters and contains a total of at least three letters. Delimiters are any characters other than letters, digits, apostrophes, and ampersands. Trailing apostrophes and ampersands are removed from "words."

The **-m** option may be followed by an **m**, **s**, or **l**.

-mm or **-ms**
: cause the macros to be interpreted so that only running text (that is, no text from macro lines) is output.

-ml forces the **-mm** option and also causes deletion of lists associated with the **mm** macros.

-i causes deroff to ignore .so and .nx commands

SEE ALSO

eqn(1), **nroff**(1), **tbl**(1), **troff**(1)

NOTES

deroff is not a complete **troff** interpreter, so it can be confused by subtle constructs. Most such errors result in too much rather than too little output.

The **-ml** option does not handle nested lists correctly.

NAME

deroff – (BSD) remove **nroff**, **troff**, **tbl** and **eqn** constructs

SYNOPSIS

/usr/ucb/deroff [**-w**] *file* . . .

DESCRIPTION

The **deroff** command reads each file in sequence and removes all **nroff** and **troff** command lines, backslash constructions, macro definitions, **eqn** constructs (between **.EQ** and **.EN** lines or between delimiters), and table descriptions and writes the remainder on the standard output. **deroff** follows chains of included files (**.so** and **.nx** commands); if a file has already been included, a **.so** is ignored and a **.nx** terminates execution. If no input file is given, **deroff** reads from the standard input file.

OPTIONS

-w Generate a word list, one word per line. A "word" is a string of letters, digits, and apostrophes, beginning with a letter; apostrophes are removed. All other characters are ignored.

SEE ALSO

eqn(1), **nroff**(1), **tbl**(1), **troff**(1)

NOTES

deroff is not a complete **troff** interpreter, so it can be confused by subtle constructs. Most errors result in too much rather than too little output.

deroff does not work well with files that use **.so** to source in the standard macro package files.

desktop (1)

NAME

desktop - initialize the UNIX desktop

SYNOPSIS

desktop [[*client*] *options*] [-- [*server*] [*display*] *options*]

DESCRIPTION

The **desktop** command initializes the UNIX desktop. It is similar to the X Window System **xinit** command.

The **desktop** command is used to start the X Window System server (**X**), a primary client program (**dtm**), and (optionally through an **.olinitrc** file) secondary clients (for example, **dsdm** and **olwm**). When the primary client exits, **desktop** will kill the X server and then terminate. If the X server exits, **desktop** will kill the primary client and the secondary clients and then terminate.

Unless otherwise specified on the command line, **desktop** assumes that there are programs called **X** and **dtm** in the current search path. It starts the server on display 0 and then runs **dtm**.

An alternate primary client and/or server may be specified on the command line. The desired client program and its arguments should be given as the first command line arguments to **desktop**. To specify a particular server command line, append a double dash (--) to the **desktop** command line (after any client and arguments) followed by the desired server command.

A relative or full pathname must be provided for the primary client program and the server program. Otherwise, they are treated as arguments to be appended to their respective startup lines. This makes it possible to add arguments (for example, foreground and background colors) without having to retype the whole command line.

If an explicit server name is not given and the first argument following the double dash (--) is a digit, the **desktop** program uses that number as the display number instead of zero. All remaining arguments are appended to the server command line.

desktop also creates files called **.oliniterr** and **.olinitout** and places them in the user's home directory. All errors and warnings are put in the **.oliniterr** file. Output to **stdout** is written out to the **.olinitout** file.

Files

$HOME/.olinitrc
$HOME/.oliniterr
$HOME/.olinitout

USAGE

An **.olinitrc** file can be used to start secondary clients if **dtm** is the primary client. Since it is the responsibility of **dtm** to execute the **.olinitrc** file, the contents of **.olinitrc** will be ignored if an application other than **dtm** is the primary client for **desktop**. **dtm** looks for this file in the user's home directory. The format of this file is typically:

```
client_a &
client_b &
. . .
```

All applications in the **/usr/X/bin** directory or set up using the desktop icon set up mechanism are assumed to be X applications. Other applications are assumed to be character based and the system will create an **xterm** for each one invoked. Note that character based applications which use shell scripts that place processes in the background (for example, **my_app &**) will behave as follows:

an **xterm** will be created and the shell script will be executed from the **xterm**

the shell script invokes the process in the background and then exits

xterm exits because the shell script has exited

the background process exits

Shell scripts should either not place processes in the background, or use the **wait** command to wait for child processes to complete.

Before making a change to the localization property window, all applications should be terminated. This is necessary for applications to change to the new locale. There is no dynamic adjustment by clients to a change in locale.

NOTE

desktop can only be used for starting the server and clients on the same machine. Using **desktop** with remote servers is not supported.

SEE ALSO

sh(1), **wait**(1)

devattr (1M)

NAME

`devattr` – lists device attributes

SYNOPSIS

`devattr` [`-v`] *device* [*attribute* [. . .]]

DESCRIPTION

`devattr` displays the values for a device's attributes. The display can be presented in two formats. When run without the **`-v`** option, **`devattr`** shows only the attribute values. When run with **`-v`**, **`devattr`** shows the attributes in the format *attribute=value*[*,value* . . .]. When no attributes are given on the command line, all attributes for the specified device are displayed in alphabetical order by attribute name. If attributes are given on the command line, only those are shown and they are displayed in command line order.

Options and Arguments

`devattr` takes the following options and arguments:

`-v` Specifies verbose format, where attribute values are displayed in an *attribute=value* format.

device Defines the device for which attributes should be displayed. This value can be the absolute pathname of the device or the device alias. If the provided value is an absolute pathname, **`devattr`** gets the device alias name to which the pathname maps, and displays all the attributes defined for that alias. If the alias is a secure device alias, then security attributes are also displayed.

attribute
Defines which attributes should be shown. The default is to show all attributes for a device. See **`putdev`**(1M) for a complete list of device attributes.

Return Values

If successful, the command exits with a value of zero (0). If there is an error, the `devattr` exits with one of the following values and prints the corresponding error message:

1 `syntax incorrect, invalid options`
`USAGE: devattr [-v] device [attribute [ . . . ]]`

1 `Insufficient memory`

2 `Device Database could not be opened for reading`

2 `Device Database in inconsistent state - notify administrator`

3 `Requested device not found in Device Database`

Files

`/etc/device.tab`
`/etc/security/ddb/ddb_dsfmap`

REFERENCES

`getdev`(1M), `putdev`(1M)

NAME

devfree – release devices from exclusive use

SYNOPSIS

devfree *key* [*device* [. . .]]

DESCRIPTION

devfree releases devices from exclusive use. Exclusive use is requested with the command **devreserv**.

When **devfree** is invoked with only the *key* argument, it releases all devices that have been reserved for that *key*. When called with *key* and *device* arguments, **devfree** releases the specified devices that have been reserved with that *key*.

Arguments

devfree takes the following arguments:

key Designates the unique key on which the device was reserved.

device Defines device that this command will release from exclusive use. Can be the pathname of the device or the device alias.

Return Values

devfree exits with one of the following values:

0 Successful completion of the task

1 Command syntax incorrect, invalid option used, or internal error occurred.

2 Device table or device reservation table could not be opened for reading.

3 Reservation release could not be completely fulfilled because one or more of the devices was not reserved or was not reserved on the specified key.

Files

/etc/device.tab
/etc/devlkfile

USAGE

The commands **devreserv** and **devfree** are used to manage the availability of devices on a system. These commands do not place any constraints on the access to the device. They serve only as a centralized bookkeeping point for those who wish to use them. Processes that do not use **devreserv** may concurrently use a device with a process that has reserved that device.

REFERENCES

devreserv(1M)

devnm (1M)

NAME

devnm – device name

SYNOPSIS

/usr/sbin/devnm [*name* . . .]

DESCRIPTION

The **devnm** command identifies the special file associated with the mounted file system where the argument *name* resides. One or more *names* can be specified.

Files

/dev/dsk/*

/etc/mnttab

/usr/lib/locale/*locale***/LC_MESSAGES/uxcore.abi**
language-specific message file [See **LANG** on **environ**(5)]

USAGE

The **devnm** command is most commonly used by the **brc** command to construct a mount table entry for the **root** device.

Examples

The command:

```
/usr/sbin/devnm /usr
```

produces:

```
/dev/dsk/c0t0d0s3 /usr
```

if **/usr** is mounted on **/dev/dsk/c0t0d0s3**.

REFERENCES

brc(1M), **mnttab**(4)

NAME

devreserv – reserve devices for exclusive use

SYNOPSIS

devreserv [*key* [*devicelist* . . .]]

DESCRIPTION

devreserv reserves devices for exclusive use. When the device is no longer required, use **devfree** to release it.

devreserv reserves at most one device per *devicelist*. Each list is searched in linear order until the first available device is found. If a device cannot be reserved from each list, the entire reservation fails.

If you execute **devreserv** without arguments, devices that are currently reserved are listed, and the keys to which they are reserved. When **devreserv** is executed with only the *key* argument, it lists the devices currently reserved to that key.

Arguments

devreserv takes the following arguments:

key Designates a unique key on which the device will be reserved. The key must be a positive integer.

devicelist
Defines a list of devices that **devreserv** will search to find an available device. (The list must be formatted as a single argument to the shell.)

Return Values

devreserv exits with one of the following values:

0 Successful completion of the task

1 Command syntax incorrect, invalid option used, or internal error occurred

2 Device table or device reservation table could not be opened for reading

3 Device reservation request could not be fulfilled

Files

/etc/device.tab
/etc/devlkfile

NOTES

The commands **devreserv** and **devfree** are used to manage the availability of devices on a system. Their use is on a participatory basis and they do not place any constraints on actual access to the device. They provide a centralized bookkeeping point for those who want to use them. To summarize, devices that have been reserved cannot be used by processes that utilize the device reservation functions until the reservation has been canceled. However, processes that do not use device reservation may use a device that has been reserved since such a process would not have checked for its reservation status.

devreserv (1M)

USAGE

Example

To reserve a floppy disk and a cartridge tape:

```
$ key=$$
$ echo "The current Process ID is equal to: $key"
The Current Process ID is equal to: 10658
$ devreserv $key diskette1,ctape1
```

To list all devices currently reserved:

```
$ devreserv
disk1          2423
diskette1      10658
ctape1         10658
```

To list all devices currently reserved to a particular key:

```
$ devreserv $key
diskette1
ctape1
```

REFERENCES

devfree(1M)

NAME

`df` (generic), `dfspace` – report number of free disk blocks and files/free disk space

SYNOPSIS

`df` [`-F` *FSType*] [`-begiklntV`] [*current_options*] [`-o` *specific_options*]
  [*directory* | *special* | *resource*. . .]

`dfspace` [`-F` *FSType*]

DESCRIPTION

The `df` command prints the allocation portions of the generic superblock for mounted or unmounted file systems, directories or mounted resources. *directory* represents a valid directory name. If *directory* is specified, `df` reports on the device that contains the *directory*. *special* represents a special device (for example, `/dev/dsk/*f1`, where `*` is implementation dependent). *resource* is an RFS/NFS resource name. If arguments to `df` are pathnames, `df` produces a report on the file system containing the named file.

The `df` command reports sizes in 512 byte blocks. It will report 2 blocks less free space, rather than 1 block, since the file uses one system block of 1-24 bytes.

The directory `/etc/fscmd.d/TYPE` contains programs for each filesystem type; `df` invokes the appropriate binary. `/etc/fscmd.d` is linked to `/etc/fs`.

current_options are options supported by the `s5`-specific module of `df`. Other FSTypes do not necessarily support these options. *specific_options* indicate suboptions specified in a comma-separated list of suboptions and/or keyword-attribute pairs for interpretation by the *FSType*-specific module of the command.

The generic options are:

`-F` Specify the *FSType* on which to operate. This is only needed if the file system is unmounted. The *FSType* should be specified here or are determined from `/etc/vfstab` by matching the *mount_point*, *special*, or *resource* with an entry in the table.

`-b` Print only the number of kilobytes free.

`-e` Print only the number of files free.

`-g` Print the entire `statvfs` structure. Used only for mounted file systems. Cannot be used with *current_options* or with the `-o` option. This option overrides the `-b`, `-e`, `-k`, `-n`, and `-t` options. The numbers for `available`, `total`, and `free` blocks are reported in 512 byte blocks.

`-i` Display the total number of inodes, the number of free inodes, the number of used inodes, and the percentage of inodes in use.

`-k` Print allocation in kilobytes. This option should be invoked by itself because its output format is different from that of the other options.

`-l` Report on local file systems only. Used only for mounted file systems. Can not be used with *current_options* or with the `-o` option.

`-n` Print only the *FSType* name. Invoked with no arguments this option prints a list of mounted file system types. Used only for mounted file systems. Can not be used with *current_options* or with the `-o` option.

`-t` Causes total allocated block figures to be reported as well as number of free blocks.

`-V` Echo the complete command line, but do not execute the command. The command line is generated by using the options and arguments provided by the user and adding to them information derived from **/etc/mnttab** or **/etc/vfstab**. This option should be used to verify and validate the command line.

`-o` Specify FSType-specific options.

`-v` Reports percent of blocks used as well as the number of blocks used and free. The **-v** option cannot be used with other options.

If no arguments or options are specified, the free space on all local and remotely mounted file systems is printed.

dfspace is a shell script that uses the **df** command. **dfspace** reports the available disk space for all mounted file systems with the exception of pseudo file systems such as **/proc**. **dfspace** reports the free disk space in mega bytes and also as a percentage of total disk space.

Without arguments, **dfspace** reports the free disk space on all file systems.

The option for **dfspace** is:

-F *FSType* find free disk space on *FSType* file system.

NOTES

The **-F** option is intended for use with unmounted file systems, except for the **bfs** *FSType*. **df -F bfs** is not supported when **/stand** is not mounted.

This command may not be supported for all FSTypes.

If options **-g** or **-n** are used when there are remotely mounted resources, **df** will try to determine the remote resource's file system type. If it can be determined, **df** will print the file system type; otherwise, it will print **unknown**.

FILES

/dev/dsk/*
/etc/mnttab list of filesystems currently mounted
/etc/vfstab list of default parameters for each file system

SEE ALSO

FSType-specific **df**(1M), **mnttab**(4), **mount**(1M), **statvfs**(2), **vfstab**(4)

NAME

`df` – (BSD) report free disk space on file systems

SYNOPSIS

`/usr/ucb/df` [`-i`] [`-a`] [`-t` *type* | *file* . . .]

DESCRIPTION

df displays the amount of disk space occupied by currently mounted file systems, the amount of used and available space, and how much of the file system's total capacity has been used. Used without arguments, **df** reports on all mounted file systems, producing something like:

```
Filesystem  kbytes  used  avail  capacity  Mounted on
/dev/root    7445   4714  1986     70%     /
/dev/0s10    5148   3279  1868     64%     /stand
```

Note that **used**+**avail** is less than the amount of space in the file system (kbytes); this is because the system reserves a fraction of the space in the file system to allow its file system allocation routines to work well. The amount reserved is typically about 10%; this may be adjusted using **tunefs**(1M). When all the space on a file system except for this reserve is in use, only the super-user can allocate new files and data blocks to existing files. When a file system is overallocated in this way, **df** may report that the file system is more than 100% utilized.

If arguments to **df** are disk partitions (for example, **/dev/root** or *pathnames*, **df** produces a report on the file system containing the named file. Thus **df .** shows the amount of space on the file system containing the current directory.

Options

The options for **df** are as follows:

`-a` Reports on all filesystems including the uninteresting ones which have zero total blocks. (For example, *automounter*)

`-i` Report the number of used and free inodes.

`-t` *type* Report on filesystems of a given *type* (for example, **nfs**).

FILES

`/etc/mnttab` List of filesystems currently mounted.

SEE ALSO

du(1M), **quot**(1M), **tunefs**(1M)

NAME

`df` (s5) – report number of free disk blocks and i-nodes for **s5** file systems

SYNOPSIS

`df [-F s5]` [*generic_options*] `[-f]` [*directory* . . . | *special* . . .]

DESCRIPTION

generic_options are options supported by the generic **df** command.

The **df** command prints out the number of free blocks and free i-nodes in **s5** file systems or directories by examining the counts kept in the super-blocks. The *special* device name (for example, **/dev/dsk/***, where the value of * is machine-dependent) or mount point *directory* name (for example, **/usr**) must be specified. If *directory* is specified, the report presents information for the device that contains the directory.

The options are:

`-F s5` Specifies the **s5**-FSType.

`-f` An actual count of the blocks in the free list is made, rather than taking the figure from the super-block.

NOTE

The `-f` option can be used with the `-t`, `-b`, and `-e` options. The `-k` option overrides the `-f` option.

FILES

`/dev/dsk/*`

SEE ALSO

generic **df**(1M)

NAME

df (sfs) – report free disk space on **sfs** file systems

SYNOPSIS

df [**-F sfs**] [*generic_options*] [**-o i**] [*directory* | *special*]

DESCRIPTION

generic_options are options supported by the generic **df** command.

df displays the amount of disk space occupied by **sfs** file systems, the amount of used and available space, and how much of the file system's total capacity has been used.

The options are:

-F sfs
: Specifies the **sfs**-FSType.

-o
: Specify **sfs** file system specific options. The available option is:

  i Report the number of used and free inodes. May not be used with *generic_options*.

NOTES

Unlike **ufs**, **sfs** does not support the **minfree** tunable.

The **-b** and **-e** options override the **-t** option [see generic **df**(1M)].

FILES

/etc/mnttab list of file systems currently mounted

SEE ALSO

generic **df**(1M), **du**(1M), **mnttab**(4)

NAME

`df` (ufs) – report free disk space on **ufs** file systems

SYNOPSIS

df [**-F ufs**] [*generic_options*] [**-o i**] [*directory* | *special*]

DESCRIPTION

generic_options are options supported by the generic **df** command.

df displays the amount of disk space occupied by **ufs** file systems, the amount of used and available space, and how much of the file system's total capacity has been used.

Note that the amount of space reported as used and available is less than the amount of space in the file system; this is because the system reserves a fraction of the space in the file system to allow its file system allocation routines to work well. The amount reserved is typically about 10%; this may be adjusted using **tunefs**(1M). When all the space on the file system except for this reserve is in use, only a privileged user can allocate new files and data blocks to existing files. When the file system is overallocated in this way, **df** may report that the file system is more than 100% utilized.

The options are:

-F ufs Specifies the **ufs**-FSType.

-o Specify **ufs** file system specific options. The available option is:

- **i** Report the number of used and free inodes. May not be used with *generic_options*.

NOTES

df calculates its results differently for mounted and unmounted file systems. For mounted systems the 10% reserved space mentioned above is included in the number of blocks used. For unmounted systems the 10% reservation is not included in the number of blocks used. The generic **-k option displays the free space as a percentage.**

The **-b** and **-e** options override the **-t** option.

FILES

`/etc/mnttab` list of file systems currently mounted

SEE ALSO

generic **df**(1M), **du**(1M), **mnttab**(4), **mount**(1M), **quot**(1M), **tunefs**(1M)

NAME

`df` (vxfs) – report number of free disk blocks and inodes for **vxfs** file systems

SYNOPSIS

df [**-F vxfs**] [*generic_options*] [**-o s**] *directory* | *special* . . .

DESCRIPTION

generic_options are options supported by the generic **df** command.

The **df** command prints out the number of free blocks and free inodes in **vxfs** file systems or directories by examining the counts kept in the super-blocks. The *special* device name (for example, **/dev/dsk/c0t1d0s5**) or mount point *directory* name (for example, **/usr**) must be specified. If *directory* is a directory name, the report presents information for the device that contains the directory.

The options are:

-F vxfs Specify the **vxfs** FSType.

-o Specify **vxfs** file system specific options. The following option is available:

- **s** Print the number of free extents of each size. Free extents are always an integral power of 2 in length, ranging from a minimum of 1 block to a maximum of the size of an allocation unit.

FILES

`/dev/dsk/*`

SEE ALSO

generic **df**(1M), **vxfs**-specific **fs**(4)

NAME

dfmounts – display mounted resource information

SYNOPSIS

dfmounts [-F *fstype*] **[-h] [-o** *specific_options*] [*restriction* **...]**

DESCRIPTION

dfmounts shows the local resources currently mounted by clients through a distributed file system *fstype* along with a list of clients that have the resource mounted. the local system. *specific_options* as well as the availability and semantics of *restriction* are specific to particular distributed file system types. *specific_options* and *restriction* should be used in conjunction with the **-F** option.

If **dfmounts** is entered without the **-F** option, the **dfmounts** command is executed for each configured distributed file system type.

The output of **dfmounts** consists of an optional header line (suppressed with the **-h** flag) followed by a list of lines containing whitespace-separated fields. For each resource, the fields are:

resource server path clients
resource server pathname clients

where

resource The meaning of *resource* is dependent upon the distributed file system type that is being used.

server Specifies the system from which the resource was mounted.

path Specifies the pathname that was given to the **share**(1M) command.

pathname Identical to *path*.

clients The format of *clients* is dependent upon the distributed file system type that is being used.

A field may be null. Each null field is indicated by a hyphen (–) unless the remainder of the fields on the line are also null. In this case, it is blank.

Only a privileged user can execute this command.

FILES

/etc/dfs/fstypes

SEE ALSO

nfs-specific **dfmounts**, **rfs**-specific **dfmounts**, **dfshares**(1M), **mount**(1M), **share**(1M), **unshare**(1M)

NAME

`dfmounts` – display mounted NFS resource information

SYNOPSIS

`dfmounts [-F nfs] [-h] [`*server*` . . .]`

DESCRIPTION

`dfmounts` shows the local resources currently mounted by clients through Network File System (NFS), along with a list of clients that have mounted the resource.

`dfmounts` may not indicate the correct state if you mount a single resource on more than one directory.

Only a privileged user can execute this command.

Options

The following options are available to the `dfmounts` command:

`-F` Specifies the File System Type (*fstype*). This option may be omitted if NFS is the only file system type listed in the file `/etc/dfs/fstypes`.

`-h` Suppress the header line in the output of `dfmounts`.

server Any system on the network that has made resources available to your machine. If *server* is specified, it shows the resources available from that machine, along with the current clients using each resource.

If no *server* is specified, then *server* is assumed to be the local system. The resources on the local system that are currently mounted by other clients, along with a list of those clients, are displayed.

`dfmounts` without options displays any remote systems that have mounted resources that you have made available.

Files

`/etc/dfs/fstypes`

Output

The output from `dfmounts` prints the header, followed by a list of lines containing whitespace-separated fields. For each resource, the fields are:

resource server pathname clients . . .

where

resource This field has no meaning for NFS, and is filled with a hyphen (–).

server Specifies the machine from which the resource was mounted.

pathname Specifies the pathname of the shared resource.

clients A comma-separated list of systems that currently have the resource mounted.

Exit Codes

0 Successful exit

33 Usage error

34 RPC error

36 System call **gethostname** (**uname**) failed

REFERENCES

mount(1M), **share**(1M), **unshare**(1M)

NAME

dfmounts – display mounted RFS resource information

SYNOPSIS

dfmounts -F rfs [-h] [*resource_name* **...]**

DESCRIPTION

dfmounts shows the local resources available to clients, along with a list of clients (if any) that have the resource(s) currently mounted.

Only a privileged user can execute this command.

Options

-h Suppress the header line in the output of **dfmounts**.

resource_name
Print information about the specified RFS resource(s).

Output

The output of *dfmounts* consists of an optional header line (suppressed with the **-h** flag) followed by a list of lines containing whitespace-separated fields. For each resource, the fields are:

resource server path clients ...

where

resource Specifies the resource name that was given to the **share(1M)** command.

server The name of the system that made the resource available.

path Specifies the full pathname that was given to the **share(1M)** command.

clients A comma-separated list of systems (if any) that currently have the resource mounted. This field may be blank.

REFERENCES

dfmounts(1M), **fumount**(1M), **mount**(1M), **share**(1M), **unshare**(1M)

dfshares (1M)

NAME

dfshares – list available resources from remote or local systems

SYNOPSIS

dfshares [-F *fstype*] **[-h] [-o** *specific_options*] [*server* ...]

DESCRIPTION

dfshares provides information about resources available to the host through a distributed file system of type *fstype*.

Options

The following options are available to the **dfshares** command:

-F Specifies the File System Type (fstype). If this option is not specified, the first file system type listed in the **/etc/dfs/fstypes** file is used.

-h Suppress the header line in the output of **dfshares**.

specific_options
Depends upon the distributed file system (*fstype*) being used. For a list of *specific_options*, refer to the documentation on the regarding the *fstype* that is being used.

If **dfshares** is entered without arguments, all resources currently shared on the local system, along with resources that are available for mounting, are displayed, regardless of file system type.

Files

/etc/dfs/fstypes

Output

dfshares prints a header line, followed by a list of lines containing whitespace-separated fields. For each resource, the fields are:

resource server access transport description

where

resource Specifies the resource name that must be given to the **mount**(1M) command.

server Specifies the name of the system that is making the resource available.

access Specifies the access permissions granted to the client systems, either **ro** (for read-only) or **rw** (for read/write). If **dfshares** cannot determine access permissions, a hyphen (-) is displayed.

transport Specifies the transport provider over which the *resource* is shared.

description Describes the resource. This field is not printed for all file system types.

A field may be null. Each null field is indicated by a hyphen (–) unless the remainder of the fields on the line are also null. In this case, it may be omitted.

REFERENCES

dfmounts(1M), **nfs**-specific **dfshares**(1M), **rfs**-specific **dfshares**(1M), **mount**(1M), **share**(1M), **unshare**(1M)

NAME

dfshares – list available NFS resources from remote systems

SYNOPSIS

dfshares [-F nfs] [-o] [-h] [*server* . . .]

DESCRIPTION

dfshares provides information about resources available to the host through Network File System.

Options

The following options are available to the **dfshares** command:

- **-F** Specifies the File System Type (FSType). This option may be omitted if NFS is the only file system type listed in the **/etc/dfs/fstypes** file.
- **-h** Suppress the header line in the output of **dfshares**.
- **-o** Use only **udp** to gather **dfshares** information. This option will decrease the time it takes the command to return if a host is down. The default is to try to get the **dfshares** information over **tcp** first. If that fails, then **udp** is tried.
- *server* Any system on the network that has made resources available to your machine. If no *server* is specified, then *server* is assumed to be the local system. More than one *server* can be specified with **dfshares**

dfshares without arguments displays all of the NFS resources shared on the local system.

Files

/etc/dfs/fstypes

Output

dfshares prints a header line, followed by a list of lines containing whitespace-separated fields. For each resource, the fields are:

resource server access transport

where

- *resource* Specifies the resource name (*server*:*path*) that must be given to the **mount**(1M) command.
- *server* Specifies the system that is making the resource available.
- *access* Specifies the access permissions granted to the client systems; however, **dfshares** cannot determine this information for an NFS resource and populates the field with a hyphen (-).
- *transport* Specifies the transport provider over which the *resource* is shared; however, **dfshares** cannot determine this information for an NFS resource and populates the field with a hyphen (-).

Exit Codes

0	Successful exit
33	Usage error
34	RPC error
35	No exports list
36	System call **gethostname** (**uname**) failed

REFERENCES

mount(1M), **share**(1M), **unshare**(1M)

NAME

dfshares – list available RFS resources from remote systems

SYNOPSIS

dfshares [**-F rfs**] [**-h**] [*server* . . .]

DESCRIPTION

This command is obsolete and will not be supported after this release. **dfshares** provides information about resources available to the host through Remote File Sharing. The **-F** flag may be omitted if **rfs** is the first file system type listed in the file **/etc/dfs/fstypes**.

The query may be restricted to the output of resources available from one or more servers. If no *server* is specified, all resources in the host's domain are displayed. A *server* may be given in the following form:

system	Specifies a system in the host's domain.
domain.	Specifies all systems in *domain*.
domain.system	Specifies *system* in *domain*.

The output of **dfshares** consists of an optional header line (suppressed with the **-h** flag) followed by a list of lines containing whitespace-separated fields. For each resource, the fields are:

resource server access transport description

where

resource	Specifies the resource name that must be given to the **mount**(1M) command.
server	Specifies the system that is making the resource available.
access	Specifies the access permissions granted to the client systems, either **ro** (for read-only) or **rw** (for read and write).
transport	Specifies the transport provider over which the *resource* is shared.
description	Describes the resource.

A field may be null. Each null field is indicated by a hyphen (–) unless the remainder of the fields on the line are also null. In this case, it may be omitted.

ERRORS

If your host machine cannot contact the domain name server, or the argument specified is syntactically incorrect, an error message is sent to standard error.

FILES

/etc/dfs/fstypes

SEE ALSO

mount(1M), **share**(1M), **unshare**(1M)

NAME

`diff` – differential file comparator

SYNOPSIS

diff [**-bitw**] [**-c** | **-e** | **-f** | **-h** | **-n**] *filename1 filename2*
diff [**-bitw**] [**-C** *number*] *filename1 filename2*
diff [**-bitw**] [**-D** *string*] *filename1 filename2*
diff [**-bitw**] [**-c** | **-e** | **-f** | **-h** | **-n**] [**-l**] [**-r**] [**-s**] [**-S** *name*]
directory1 directory2

DESCRIPTION

diff tells what lines must be changed in two files to bring them into agreement. If *filename1* (*filename2*) is **-**, the standard input is used. If *filename1* (*filename2*) is a directory, then a file in that directory with the name *filename2* (*filename1*) is used. The normal output contains lines of these forms:

n1 **a** *n3,n4*
n1,n2 **d** *n3*
n1,n2 **c** *n3,n4*

These lines resemble **ed** commands to convert *filename1* into *filename2*. The numbers after the letters pertain to *filename2*. In fact, by exchanging **a** for **d** and reading backward one may ascertain equally how to convert *filename2* into *filename1*. As in **ed**, identical pairs, where *n1* = *n2* or *n3* = *n4*, are abbreviated as a single number.

Following each of these lines come all the lines that are affected in the first file flagged by **<**, then all the lines that are affected in the second file flagged by **>**.

-b Ignores trailing blanks (spaces and tabs) and treats other strings of blanks as equivalent.

-i Ignores the case of letters; for example, '**A**' will compare equal to '**a**'.

-t Expands TAB characters in output lines. Normal or **-c** output adds character(s) to the front of each line that may adversely affect the indentation of the original source lines and make the output lines difficult to interpret. This option will preserve the original source's indentation.

-w Ignores all blanks (SPACE and TAB characters) and treats all other strings of blanks as equivalent; for example, '**if (a == b)**' will compare equal to '**if(a==b)**'.

The following options are mutually exclusive:

-c Produces a listing of differences with three lines of context. With this option output format is modified slightly: output begins with identification of the files involved and their creation dates, then each change is separated by a line with a dozen *****'s. The lines removed from *filename1* are marked with '—'; those added to *filename2* are marked '+'. Lines that are changed from one file to the other are marked in both files with '!'.

-C *number*
Produces a listing of differences identical to that produced by **-c** with *number* lines of context.

`-e` Produces a script of *a, c*, and *d* commands for the editor **ed**, which will recreate *filename2* from *filename1*. In connection with **-e**, the following shell program may help maintain multiple versions of a file. Only an ancestral file ($1) and a chain of version-to-version **ed** scripts ($2,$3, . . .) made by **diff** need be on hand. A "latest version" appears on the standard output.

```
(shift; cat $*; echo '1,$p') | ed - $1
```

Except in rare circumstances, **diff** finds a smallest sufficient set of file differences.

`-f` Produces a similar script, not useful with **ed**, in the opposite order.

`-h` Does a fast, half-hearted job. It works only when changed stretches are short and well separated, but does work on files of unlimited length. Options **-e** and **-f** are unavailable with **-h**.

`-n` Produces a script similar to **-e**, but in the opposite order and with a count of changed lines on each insert or delete command.

`-D` *string*
Creates a merged version of *filename1* and *filename2* with C preprocessor controls included so that a compilation of the result without defining *string* is equivalent to compiling *filename1*, while defining *string* will yield *filename2*.

The following options are used for comparing directories:

`-l` Produce output in long format. Before the **diff**, each text file is piped through **pr**(1) to paginate it. Other differences are remembered and summarized after all text file differences are reported.

`-r` Applies **diff** recursively to common subdirectories encountered.

`-s` Reports files that are identical; these would not otherwise be mentioned.

`-S` *name*
Starts a directory **diff** in the middle, beginning with the file *name*.

FILES

/tmp/d?????

/usr/lib/diffh
for **-h**

/usr/bin/pr

/usr/lib/locale/*locale***/LC_MESSAGES/uxcore.abi**
language-specific message file [See **LANG** on **environ** (5).]

SEE ALSO

bdiff(1), **cmp**(1), **comm**(1), **ed**(1), **pr**(1)

DIAGNOSTICS

Exit status is 0 for no differences, 1 for some differences, 2 for trouble.

UX:diff:WARNING:Missing newline at end of file X

indicates that the last line of file X did not have a new-line. If the lines are different, they will be flagged and output; although the output will seem to indicate they are the same.

NOTES

Editing scripts produced under the `-e` or `-f` option are naive about creating lines consisting of a single period (`.`).

NAME

`diff3` – 3-way differential file comparison

SYNOPSIS

`diff3` [`-exEX3`] *file1 file2 file3*

DESCRIPTION

`diff3` compares three versions of a file, and publishes disagreeing ranges of text flagged with these codes:

`====`	all three files differ
`====1`	*file1* is different
`====2`	*file2* is different
`====3`	*file3* is different

The type of change suffered in converting a given range of a given file to some other is indicated in one of these ways:

f **:** *n1* **a**	Text is to be appended after line number *n1* in file *f*, where *f* = 1, 2, or 3.
f **:** *n1* **,** *n2* **c**	Text is to be changed in the range line *n1* to line *n2*. If *n1* = *n2*, the range may be abbreviated to *n1*.

The original contents of the range follows immediately after a **c** indication. When the contents of two files are identical, the contents of the lower-numbered file is suppressed.

-e Produce a script for the editor **ed**(1) that will incorporate into *file1* all changes between *file2* and *file3*, that is, the changes that normally would be flagged `====` and `====3`.

-x Produce a script to incorporate only changes flagged `====`.

-3 Produce a script to incorporate only changes flagged `====3`.

-E Produce a script that will incorporate all changes between *file2* and *file3*, but treat overlapping changes (that is, changes that would be flagged with `====` in the normal listing) differently. The overlapping lines from both files will be inserted by the edit script, bracketed by `<<<<<<` and `>>>>>>` lines.

-X Produce a script that will incorporate only changes flagged `====`, but treat these changes in the manner of the **-E** option.

The following command will apply the resulting script to *file1*.

```
(cat script; echo '1,$p') | ed - file1
```

FILES

`/tmp/d3*`
`/usr/lib/diff3prog`

SEE ALSO

`diff`(1)

NOTES

Text lines that consist of a single `.` will defeat `-e`. Files longer than 64K bytes will not work.

NAME

diffmk – (BSD) mark differences between versions of a **troff** input file

SYNOPSIS

/usr/ucb/diffmk *oldfile newfile markedfile*

DESCRIPTION

The **diffmk** command compares two versions of a file and creates a third version that includes "change mark" (**.mc**) commands for **nroff** and **troff**. *oldfile* and *newfile* are the old and new versions of the file. **diffmk** generates *markedfile*, which, contains the text from *newfile* with **troff**(1) "change mark" requests (**.mc**) inserted where *newfile* differs from *oldfile*. When *markedfile* is formatted, changed or inserted text is shown by a | at the right margin of each line. The position of deleted text is shown by a single *.

diffmk can also be used in conjunction with the proper **troff** requests to produce program listings with marked changes. In the following command line:

```
diffmk old.c new.c marked.c ; nroff reqs marked.c | pr
```

the file **reqs** contains the following **troff** requests:

```
.pl 1
.ll 77
.nf
.eo
.nh
```

which eliminate page breaks, adjust the line length, set no-fill mode, ignore escape characters, and turn off hyphenation, respectively.

If the characters | and * are inappropriate, you might run *markedfile* through **sed** to globally change them.

SEE ALSO

diff(1), **nroff**(1), **sed**(1), **troff**(1)

NOTES

Aesthetic considerations may dictate manual adjustment of some output. File differences involving only formatting requests may produce undesirable output, that is, replacing **.sp** by **.sp 2** will produce a "change mark" on the preceding or following line of output.

NAME

dinit – run commands performed for multi-user environment after login processes

SYNOPSIS

/sbin/dinit

DESCRIPTION

This file is executed via an entry in **/etc/inittab**. **dinit** is responsible for completing portions of initializations (traditionally performed by **rc2**), for multi-user states 2 and 3 that can be delayed until after the login processes have been created. The purpose of this command is to improve the performance of system startup to multi-user states.

The actions performed by **dinit** are found in files in the directory **/etc/dinit.d**. Files in **/etc/dinit.d** must begin with an **S** or a **K** followed by a number and the rest of the filename. Files beginning with **S** are executed with the **start** option; files beginning with **K**, are executed with the **stop** option. Files beginning with other characters are ignored. These files are executed by **/usr/bin/sh** in ASCII sort-sequence order.

When functions are added that need to be initialized when the system goes multi-user, but that do not need to complete before the user logs into the system, an appropriate file should be added in **/etc/dinit.d**.

Examples of functions done by the **dinit** command and its associated **/etc/dinit.d** files include:

> Starting the connection server
>
> Starting printer services
>
> Starting the **cron** daemon by executing **/usr/sbin/cron**.

Other functions can be added, as required, to support the addition of hardware and software features.

SEE ALSO

inittab(4), **rc2**(1M), **shutdown**(1M)

dircmp(1)

NAME

dircmp – directory comparison

SYNOPSIS

dircmp [**-d**] [**-s**] [**-w***n*] *dir1 dir2*

DESCRIPTION

dircmp examines *dir1* and *dir2* and generates various tabulated information about the contents of the directories. Listings of files that are unique to each directory are generated for all the options. If no option is entered, a list is output indicating whether the file names common to both directories have the same contents. **dircmp** processes supplementary code set characters in directory and file names according to the locale specified in the **LC_CTYPE** environment variable [see **LANG** on **environ**(5)].

-d Compare the contents of files with the same name in both directories and output a list telling what must be changed in the two files to bring them into agreement. The list format is described in **diff**(1).

-s Suppress messages about identical files.

-w*n* Change the width of the output line to *n* columns. The default width is 72.

SEE ALSO

cmp(1), **diff**(1), **pr**(1)

NAME

dis – object code disassembler

SYNOPSIS

dis [**-o**] [**-V**] [**-L**] [**-s**] [**-d** *sec*] [**-D** *sec*] [**-F** *function*] [**-t** *sec*] [**-l** *string*] *file* . . .

DESCRIPTION

The **dis** command produces an assembly language listing of *file*, which may be an object file or an archive of object files. The listing includes assembly statements and an octal or hexadecimal representation of the binary that produced those statements.

The following *options* are interpreted by the disassembler and may be specified in any order.

-d *sec* — Disassemble the named section as data, printing the offset of the data from the beginning of the section.

-D *sec* — Disassemble the named section as data, printing the actual address of the data.

-F *function* — Disassemble only the named function in each object file specified on the command line. The **-F** option may be specified multiple times on the command line.

-L — Lookup source labels for subsequent printing. This option works only if the file was compiled with additional debugging information (for example, the **-g** option of **cc**).

-l *string* — Disassemble the archive file specified by *string*. For example, one would issue the command **dis -l x -l z** to disassemble **libx.a** and **libz.a**, which are assumed to be in *LIBDIR*.

-o — Print numbers in octal. The default is hexadecimal.

-s — Perform symbolic disassembly where possible. Symbolic disassembly output will appear on the line following the instruction. Symbol names will be printed using C syntax.

-t *sec* — Disassemble the named section as text.

-V — Print, on standard error, the version number of the disassembler being executed.

If the **-d**, **-D** or **-t** options are specified, only those named sections from each user-supplied file name will be disassembled. Otherwise, all sections containing text will be disassembled.

On output, a number enclosed in brackets at the beginning of a line, such as **[5]**, indicates that the break-pointable line number starts with the following instruction. These line numbers will be printed only if the file was compiled with additional debugging information [for example, the **-g** option of **cc**]. An expression such as **<40>** in the operand field or in the symbolic disassembly, following a relative displacement for control transfer instructions, is the computed address within the section to which control will be transferred. A function name will appear in the first column, followed by **( )** if the object file contains a symbol table.

FILES

LIBDIR usually **/usr/ccs/lib**

SEE ALSO

a.out(4), **as**(1), **cc**(1), **ld**(1)

DIAGNOSTICS

The self-explanatory diagnostics indicate errors in the command line or problems encountered with the specified files.

NOTES

Since the **-da** option did not adhere to the command syntax rules, it has been replaced by **-D**.

At this time, symbolic disassembly does not take advantage of additional information available if the file is compiled with the **-g** option.

NAME

disable_glogin – disable UNIX Desktop graphical login

SYNOPSIS

disable_glogin

DESCRIPTION

This command disables the UNIX Desktop graphical login by removing the file /etc/rc2.d/S69xdm from the /etc/rc2.d directory if the file exists [see rc2(1M)].

SEE ALSO

enable_glogin(1M), rc2(1M)

diskadd (1M)

NAME

diskadd – disk set up utility

SYNOPSIS

diskadd [*disk_number*]
diskrm [*disk_number*]

DESCRIPTION

The initial system disk is set up during system installation. Additional disks must be set up using **diskadd**; the **diskrm** command is used to remove disk drives from the system.

diskadd is an interactive command which prompts you for information about the setup of the disk.

Arguments

The optional argument *disk_number* is used to represent the SCSI or non-SCSI disk device to be added to the system. If you specify 1 as the *disk_number*, **diskadd** defaults to the non-SCSI nomenclature (for example, **/dev/rdsk/1s?**, and so on). For SCSI disks, the format of the *disk_number* argument is:

c*x*t*y*d*z*

x = controller number, (0, 1, 2)
y = Target controller SCSI ID, (0, 1, 2, 3, 4, 5, 6)
z = Logical Unit ID number, (0, 1, 2, 3).

Files

/dev/dsk/1s?
/dev/dsk/c?t?d?s?
/dev/rdsk/1s*
/dev/rdsk/c?t?d?s0
/etc/vfstab

USAGE

To setup a hard disk, first the **fdisk**(1M) command is invoked to partition the disk. This step breaks up the disk into logical portions for the UNIX Operating system and for the DOS Operating system.

Next, the **disksetup**(1M) command is executed for surface analysis, creating/writing the **pdinfo**, VTOC and alternates info (for non-SCSI drives) to the disk, issuing the needed **mkfs** calls, and mounting filesystems.

The surface analysis is performed to catch any detectable defects and remap them. On SCSI disks, the formatting of the disk remaps any detectable defects, so the surface analysis is optional, but recommended. The creation of the VTOC divides the UNIX system partition into slices. Slices are created to contain a filesystem or act as a raw device (for example, the **swap** or **dump** device). Executing the **mkfs**(1M) command for the needed filesystems handles the creation of a specific type of filesystem on a slice. If you requested automatic mounting, directories are created in the root filesystem to hold the new filesystems, they are mounted, and **/etc/vfstab** is updated to remount them on subsequent bootups of the system.

The device files will be present prior to running **diskadd**. The device files for a second integral disk, **/dev/rdsk/1s*** and **/dev/dsk/1s***, are always present.

If you add swap/paging space on the new drive, you must make it available for system use with the **swap**(1M) command.

As mentioned previously, the **diskrm** command can be used to remove disk drives from the system and update the **/etc/vfstab** file. The drive to be removed is designated in the same way as for the **diskadd** command.

REFERENCES

fdisk(1M), **mkdir**(1), **mkfs**(1M), **swap**(1M)

diskcfg (1M)

NAME

diskcfg – generate System files for PDI drivers

SYNOPSIS

/etc/scsi/diskcfg [**-R** *ROOT*] [*filename*]

DESCRIPTION

diskcfg generates System files for the Portable Device Interface (PDI) drivers from information provided. It reads input from the provided file, or from **stdin** if a file is not provided, and generates a new PDI configuration based on the information. The input provided describes the PDI drivers to be turned on and off, and must exactly match the required format or **diskcfg** will fail. **diskcfg** is intended for use with the **pdiconfig**(1M) command or any command producing similar output.

Options

diskcfg takes the following options:

-R *ROOT* Uses this value instead of **/** for the root of a kernel source tree.

filename Read input from *filename* instead of from standard input.

Input

The format of the input for **diskcfg** is:

> *driver name long driver name driver type configure flag unit number dma channel 1 dma channel 2 ipl level interrupt vector interrupt sharing flag starting I/O address ending I/O address starting memory address ending memory address*

Each field must have a value present, and the input must be tab separated. Each input line represents one PDI device.

Note that **diskcfg** does not use the shell variable *ROOT* from the user environment as its starting path. You can specify a value for *ROOT* by using the **-R** option. The **-R** option should not be used except for the special case of kernel development in a non-root source tree.

Return Values

diskcfg exits with a return code of zero on success and non-zero on failure.

NOTES

diskcfg is an administrative command and must be run in single user mode. See **init**(1M) for information on switching the machine to single user mode.

Any loadable target drivers, such as **st01**(7), **sc01**(7), or **sw01**(7), that deal with PDI devices, must be demand loaded before executing **diskcfg**. See **modadmin**(1M) for information on loading loadable drivers.

SEE ALSO

disk.cfg(4), **init**(1M), **modadmin**(1M), **pdiadd**(1M), **pdiconfig**(1M), **pdirm**(1M)

NAME

disksetup – disk set up utility

SYNOPSIS

/etc/disksetup -I -B [**-d** *defaults-file*] **-b***boot-file raw-device* (Install primary disk) [**-s**]
/etc/disksetup -I [**-d** *defaults-file*] *raw-device* (Install additional disk) [**-s**]
/etc/disksetup -b *boot-file raw-device* (write boot code to the disk) [**-s**]

DESCRIPTION

disksetup performs the low level activities required to install the primary drive or additional drives. The tasks required for disk setup include surface analysis, assisting you to create the layout of slices (either through a set of defaults or by asking you for details), writing the pdinfo, VTOC and alternates tables out to the drive, issuing needed **mkfs** *calls, creating mount points, mounting filesystems, and updating the* **/etc/vfstab** *file.*

Options

-I Directs the *raw-device* to be installed, performing the surface analysis, creation/writing the pdinfo, VTOC, and alternates tables (for non-SCSI drives).

-B Denotes that the raw-device will be the system boot device.

-d *defaults-file*
Passes in a default layout for the raw-device. The arguments are in the form *x*[R], where *x* describes the minimum size of the file in megabytes, and *R* is an optional parameter to determine whether the partition entry is required. The information from the defaults file is used to generate the default slices for the UNIX System partition. The layout of the file is described later in this manual page.

-s Denotes that the **disksetup** command should operate without returning any queries, information, or error messages (silent mode). This option can be useful for automatic installation.

-b *boot-file*
Write the boot code found in the boot file into the boot slice of the UNIX System partition. The boot code can be in either **ELF** or **COFF** format. Only the required sections/segments will be loaded. The boot file provided with the system is **/etc/boot**.

Arguments

raw-device
The required raw-device argument is the character special device for the accessed disk drive. It should use the slice 0 device to represent the entire device (for example, **/dev/rdsk/0s0** or **/dev/rdsk/c0t0d0s0**).

Files

/dev/dsk/1s?
/dev/dsk/c?t?d?s?
/dev/rdsk/1s*
/dev/rdsk/c?t?d?s0
/etc/vfstab

USAGE

If you do not specify a defaults-file, you are asked first which slices you wish to create, and then what size you wish them to be. (you must ultimately confirm these choices, and you can repeat the above steps if you are unsatisfied with your selections.) If you provide a defaults-file, a default layout of slices will be created, based on the defaults-file. If you select the default layout, a VTOC representing the default layout is written to the drive. If you do not select the default layout, you are then given the opportunity to specify the sizes for slices defined in the defaults-file.

The layout for the defaults-file is as follows:

slice #	slicename	FStype	FSblksz	slicesize	minsz
1	/	s5	1024	35M	12
2	/dev/swap	-	-	2m	8
3	/usr	ufs	4096	60W	26
5	/home	ufs	4096	40W	3
10	/stand	bfs	512	5M	5

The slice number is the entry in VTOC where the slice will be located. Note that the primary DOS partition should be assigned to slice number 5. Up to two additional DOS partitions can be assigned to slice numbers 14 and 15, although the UNIX System takes precedence if assigned to either or both of these slices.

Slice name is the mount point if the slice is a filesystem or descriptive name if no file system is to be created. *FStype* is the file system type for the slice, where s5, **ufs**, and **bfs** denote that particular type of **mkfs** command is to be issued; a dash in the *FStype* field instructs **disksetup** to issue no **mkfs** command for this slice. *FSblksz* is the primary block size for the specified file system.

Slice size is an integer value greater than zero, followed by size specifier character. The *minsz* denotes the minimum slice size, which can be followed by the character "R" to denote a required slice.

The *M* size specifier character denotes a size in megabytes (MB), so for example, 35M specifies a 35 MB slice size. The *m* size specifier defines a file system size in terms of the amount of memory in the system, with *m* defining a multiple of memory. For example, given a system with 4 MB of memory, 2m specifies an 8 MB slice size.

The *W* size specifier character requests a weighted proportion. To calculate a weighted proportion of *xW*, *x* is divided by the sum of the *W* requests, and then that value is multiplied with the remaining disk space (after all M and m type requests are handled) to define the slice size. For example, assuming a system with a 100 MB disk and 4 MB of memory, the example defaults file provided here would yield:

```
slice 1 35M = 35 MB size
slice 2 2m = (2 * 4MB) = 8 MB size
slice 3 60W = (60/100 * 52 MB) = 31 MB size
slice 5 40W = (40/100 * 52 MB) = 21 MB size
slice 10 5M = 5 MB size
```

NOTES

If you use **disksetup** to add a drive, and request a surface analysis, normally the surface analysis is performed a track at a time. However, on some SCSI drives, including IBM models, the SCSI Mode Sense command fails, preventing **disksetup** from obtaining the track size parameters. If this happens, **disksetup** will provide you the options of performing the disk surface analysis, but do so one sector at a time, or to skip the surface analysis entirely.

Warnings

If you install a hard disk using incorrect disk hardware description parameters (for example, in system CMOS), in many cases, system diagnostics will not inform you that you have made a mistake. In addition, UNIX System installation will not be affected, and the system will appear to function normally. However, several commands will be affected; specifically, any command that deals with the physical space values on the disk will report incorrect values.

To correct this situation, you must not only correct the CMOS or firmware setting, but you should also perform a low level format of the affected partition, and then reinstall UNIX. If you cannot perform the low level format, you should move the UNIX partition up a cylinder and then reinstall UNIX.

REFERENCES

fdisk(1M), **mkdir**(1) **mkfs**(1M), **mount**(1M), **sd01**(7), **swap**(1M)

diskusg (1M)

NAME

diskusg, **bfsdiskusg**, **sfsdiskusg**, **ufsdiskusg**, **vxdiskusg** – generate disk accounting data by user ID

SYNOPSIS

/usr/lib/acct/diskusg [*options*] [*files*]
/usr/lib/acct/bfsdiskusg [*options*] [*files*]
/usr/lib/acct/sfsdiskusg [*options*] [*files*]
/usr/lib/acct/ufsdiskusg [*options*] [*files*]
/usr/lib/acct/vxdiskusg [*options*] [*files*]

DESCRIPTION

diskusg, **bfsdiskusg**, **sfsdiskusg**, **ufsdiskusg**, and **vxdiskusg** generate intermediate disk accounting information from data in *files*, or the standard input if omitted. **diskusg**, **bfsdiskusg**, **sfsdiskusg**, **ufsdiskusg** and **vxdiskusg** output lines on the standard output (one per user) in the following format:

uid login #blocks

where

uid	is the numerical user ID of the user,
login	is the login name of the user, and
#blocks	is the total number of disk blocks allocated to this user.

diskusg is normally used to read the inodes of s5 file systems for disk accounting. In this case, *files* are the special filenames of these devices. **bfsdiskusg**, **sfsdiskusg**, **ufsdiskusg**, and **vxdiskusg** are used to read the inodes of bfs, sfs, ufs, and vxfs file systems, respectively, for disk accounting.

Options

diskusg, **bfsdiskusg**, **sfsdiskusg**, **ufsdiskusg**, and **vxdiskusg** recognize the following options:

-s Combine all lines for a single user into a single line. (The input data is already in **diskusg** output format.)

-v Print (on standard error) a list of all files charged to no one.

-p *file* Use *file* as the name of the password file to generate login names. **/etc/passwd** is used by default.

-u *file* Write (to *file*) records of files that are charged to no one. Records consist of the special filename, the inode number, and the user ID.

The **diskusg**, **sfsdiskusg**, **ufsdiskusg**, and **vxdiskusg** commands recognize the following option:

-i *fnmlist*
Ignore the data on those file systems for which a name is recorded in *fnmlist*. (*fnmlist* is a list of file system names separated by commas or enclosed within quotes.) **diskusg** compares each name in this list with the file system name stored in the volume ID. [See **labelit**(1M).]

Files

/etc/passwd, used for conversions of user IDs to login names

USAGE

The output of the **diskusg**, **bfsdiskusg**, **sfsdiskusg**, **ufsdiskusg**, and **vxdiskusg** commands is normally the input to **acctdisk** [see **acct**(1M)], which generates total accounting records that can be merged with other accounting records. **diskusg**, **bfsdiskusg**, **sfsdiskusg**, **ufsdiskusg**, and **vxdiskusg** are normally run in **dodisk**. [See **acctsh**(1M).]

Examples

Generate daily disk accounting information for the root file system on `/dev/dsk/c1d0s0` (where root is an s5 file system):

```
diskusg /dev/dsk/c1d0s0 | acctdisk > disktacct
```

NOTES

acctdusg [see **acct(1M)**] can be used on all file system types but is slower than **diskusg**.

REFERENCES

acct(1M), **acct**(4), **acctsh**(1M)

NAME

dispadmin – process scheduler administration

SYNOPSIS

dispadmin -l
dispadmin -c *class* **-g [-r** *res***]**
dispadmin -c *class* **-s** *file*

DESCRIPTION

The **dispadmin** command displays or changes process scheduler parameters while the system is running.

The **-l** option lists the scheduler classes currently configured in the system.

The **-c** option specifies the class whose parameters are to be displayed or changed. Valid *class* values are **RT** for the real-time class and **TS** for the time-sharing class.

The **-g** option gets the parameters for the specified class and writes them to the standard output. Parameters for the real-time class are described on **rt_dptbl**(4). Parameters for the time-sharing class are described on **ts_dptbl**(4).

When using the **-g** option you may also use the **-r** option to specify a resolution to be used for outputting the time quantum values. If no resolution is specified, time quantum values are in milliseconds. If *res* is specified it must be a positive integer between 1 and 1000000000 inclusive, and the resolution used is the reciprocal of *res* in seconds. For example, a *res* value of 10 yields time quantum values expressed in tenths of a second; a *res* value of 1000000 yields time quantum values expressed in microseconds. If the time quantum cannot be expressed as an integer in the specified resolution, it is rounded up to the next integral multiple of the specified resolution.

The **-s** option sets scheduler parameters for the specified class using the values in *file*. These values overwrite the current values in memory—they become the parameters that control scheduling of processes in the specified class. The values in *file* must be in the format output by the **-g** option. Moreover, the values must describe a table that is the same size (has same number of priority levels) as the table being overwritten. Super-user privileges are required in order to use the **-s** option.

The **-g** and **-s** options are mutually exclusive: you may not retrieve the table at the same time you are overwriting it.

dispadmin does some limited sanity checking on the values supplied in *file* to verify that they are within their required bounds. The sanity checking, however, does not attempt to analyze the effect that the new values have on the performance of the system. Inappropriate values can have a dramatic negative effect on system performance.

EXAMPLES

The following command retrieves the current scheduler parameters for the real-time class from kernel memory and writes them to the standard output. Time quantum values are in microseconds.

```
dispadmin -c RT -g -r 1000000
```

The following command overwrites the current scheduler parameters for the real-time class with the values specified in **rt.config**.

```
dispadmin -c RT -s rt.config
```

The following command retrieves the current scheduler parameters for the time-sharing class from kernel memory and writes them to the standard output. Time quantum values are in nanoseconds.

```
dispadmin -c TS -g -r 1000000000
```

The following command overwrites the current scheduler parameters for the time-sharing class with the values specified in **ts.config**.

```
dispadmin -c TS -s ts.config
```

DIAGNOSTICS

dispadmin prints an appropriate diagnostic message if it fails to overwrite the current scheduler parameters due to lack of required permissions or a problem with the specified input file.

SEE ALSO

priocntl(1), **priocntl**(2), **rt_dptbl**(4), **ts_dptbl**(4)

dispgid(1)

NAME

`dispgid` – displays a list of all valid group names

SYNOPSIS

`dispgid`

DESCRIPTION

`dispgid` displays a list of all group names on the system (one group per line).

EXIT CODES

0 = Successful execution
1 = Cannot read the group file

NAME

`dispuid` – displays a list of all valid user names

SYNOPSIS

`dispuid`

DESCRIPTION

`dispuid` displays a list of all user names on the system (one line per name).

EXIT CODES

0 = Successful execution
1 = Cannot read the password file

NAME

dname – print/set Remote File Sharing domain and network names

SYNOPSIS

dname [-D *domain*] [-N *netspec*] [-**dna**]

DESCRIPTION

This command is obsolete and will not be supported after this release. **dname** defines or prints a host's Remote File Sharing (RFS) domain name or the network(s) used by RFS as transport provider(s).

Options

The following options are available to the **dname** command:

-d Print the host's RFS domain name.

-n Print the host's RFS transport provider.

-a Prints the host's RFS domain name and RFS transport provider.

The following **dname** commands can only be executed by a privileged user and when RFS is not running.

-D *domain*
: Set the host's RFS domain name. The *domain* entry must consist of no more than 14 characters and can be any combination of letters (upper and lower case), digits, hyphens (–), and underscores (_). When the -D option is used to change a domain name, the host's password is removed. The administrator will be prompted for a new password the next time RFS is started [see **rfstart**(1M)].

-N *netspec*
: Set the host's RFS transport provider(s). *netspec* is a comma-separated list of transport providers (*tp1*, *tp2*, . . .). The value of each transport provider is the network device name, relative to the **/dev** directory.

If **dname** is used with no options, it defaults to **dname -d**.

USAGE

Examples

To print the RFS domain name, use:

```
dname
```

or

```
dname -d
```

To print the RFS transport provider, use:

```
dname -n
```

To print both the RFS domain name and the RFS transport provider, use:

```
dname -a
```

The following examples are for use by a privileged user and can only be used when RFS is not running.

To set the domain name to **krusty**, use:

```
dname -D krusty
```

If RFS is running, you will see the following error message:

```
dname: cannot change domain name while RFS is running
```

To set the RFS transport provider for TCP/IP, use:

```
dname -N tcp
```

If RFS is running, you will see the following error message:

```
dname: cannot change network specification while RFS is running
```

To stop RFS, you must unshare and unmount your RFS resources. To unshare your RFS resources you can use:

fumount -w *sec resource*

where *sec* is the number of seconds before the RFS resource will be made unavailable, and *resource* is the name of the RFS resource that will be made unavailable. This will unshare your RFS resource and unmount it on any client machines. See **fumount**(1M) for more information on the usage of **fumount**.

To unmount all of the RFS resources you have mounted, use:

```
umountall -F rfs
```

This will unmount all of the RFS resources you have mounted. See **mountall**(1M) for more information on **umountall**. You should send a message to the users on your machine using **wall**, [see **wall**(1M)] to inform them that RFS resource(s) will be made unavailable.

To stop RFS, use:

```
rfstop
```

This will stop RFS once all resources have been unmounted and unshared. You can then use the **dname -D** and **dname -N** commands. For more information on **rfstop**, see **rfstop**(1M).

To restart RFS, use:

```
rfstart
```

For more information on **rfstart**, see **rfstart**(1M).

REFERENCES

fumount(1M), **mountall**(1M), **rfstart**(1M), **rfstop**(1M), **shareall**(1M)

domainname (1M)

NAME

domainname – get/set name of current secure RPC domain

SYNOPSIS

domainname [*newname*]

DESCRIPTION

The **domainname** command is used on secure RPC machines. With no argument, the name of the machine's secure RPC domain is written to standard output.

The **domainname** command with an argument sets the name of the secure RPC domain to *newname*. *newname* may be up to 255 characters long.

domainname is normally run by the RPC administrator on all machines to set the name of the secure RPC domain. To use secure RPC, machines must have secure RPC domain names.

NOTES

Secure RPC domain names are not related to and should not be confused with RFS domains.

The RPC package expects the *newname* argument to be a valid filename for the underlying file system in use on the networked machines using secure RPC. For example, machines based on the s5 file system should not have domain names longer than 14 characters in length or problems may occur when using secure RPC.

The secure RPC domain name set by **domainname** will not be remembered across reboots. To give a machine a "permanent" name, set the **SRPC_DOMAIN** tunable in **/etc/master.d/name** to the secure RPC domain name.

NAME

dos: doscat, doscp, dosdir, dosformat, dosmkdir, dosls, dosrm, dosrmdir – access and manipulate DOS files

SYNOPSIS

doscat [**-r** | **-m**] *file* . . .

doscp [**-r** | **-m**] *file1 file2*

doscp [**-r** | **-m**] *file* . . . *directory*

dosdir *directory*

dosformat [**-fqv**] *drive*

dosls *directory* . . .

dosmkdir *directory* . . .

dosrm *file* . . .

dosrmdir *directory* . . .

DESCRIPTION

The **dos** commands allow access to files and directories on a DOS hard disk partition or diskette. The DOS partition must be bootable, although not active.

Below is a description of the **dos** commands:

doscat Copies one or more DOS files to the standard output. If **-r** is given, the files are copied without newline conversions. If **-m** is given, the files are copied with newline conversions.

doscp Copies files from/to a DOS diskette or a DOS hard disk partition to/from a UNIX file system. **doscp** will rename a file while it is copying. For example, the command:

```
doscp a:file1 file2
```

copies the file named **file1** from the DOS disk to the UNIX file system and renames it file2.

If *directory* is given, one or more *files* are copied to that directory. If **-r** is given, the files are copied without new line conversions. If **-m** is given, the files are copied with newline conversions.

doscp cannot be used to copy files between two floppy drives.

dosdir Lists DOS files in the standard DOS style directory format. (See the DOS **DIR** command.)

dosformat Creates a DOS 2.0 formatted diskette. It cannot be used to format a hard disk partition. The drive must be specified using the UNIX special file names. For example, if your system has two floppy drives, the first a 3.5" and the second a 5.25", then the following special file names would be used to format low and high density floppies:

DOS Format	UNIX special file name
1.4 MB	/dev/rdsk/f03ht
720 KB	/dev/rdsk/f03dt
1.2 MB	/dev/rdsk/f15ht
360 KB	/dev/rdsk/f15d9t

In the above special file names, **f0** refers to the first floppy drive, and **f1** refers to the second floppy drive.

The **-f** option suppresses the interactive feature. The **-q** (quiet) option is used to suppress information normally displayed during **dosformat**, but it does not suppress the interactive feature. The **-v** option prompts the user for a volume label after the diskette has been formatted. The maximum size of the volume label is 11 characters.

dosls Lists DOS directories and files in a UNIX system style format [see **ls**(1)].

dosrm Removes DOS files.

dosmkdir Creates DOS directories.

dosrmdir Deletes DOS directories.

The *file* and *directory* arguments for DOS files and directories have the form:

device:*name*

where *device* is a UNIX system path name for the special device file containing the DOS disk, and *name* is a path name to a file or directory on the DOS disk. The two components are separated by a colon (:). For example, the argument:

/dev/rdsk/f0t:/src/file.c

specifies the DOS file **file.asm** in the directory **/src** on diskette **/dev/rdsk/fd0t**. Note that slashes (and not backslashes) are used as file name separators for DOS path names. Arguments without a *device*: are assumed to be UNIX files.

For convenience, the user-configurable default file **/etc/default/msdos** can define DOS drive names to be used in place of the special device file path names. It may contain the following lines:

```
A=/dev/rdsk/f0t
C=/dev/rdsk/0s5
D=/dev/rdsk/1s5
```

The drive letter **A** may be used in place of special device file path name **/dev/rdsk/f0t** when referencing DOS files (see "Examples" below). The drive letter **C** or **D** refer to the DOS partition on the first or second hard disk.

The commands operate on the following types of disks:

DOS partitions on a hard disk
5-1/4 inch DOS
3-1/2 inch DOS
8, 9, 15, or 18 sectors per track
40 tracks per side
1 or 2 sides
DOS versions 1.0, 2.0, or 3.0

In the case of **doscp**, certain name conversions can be performed when copying a UNIX system file. File names with a base name longer than eight characters are truncated. Filename extensions (the part of the name following the separating period) longer than three characters are truncated. For example, the file 123456789.12345 becomes 12345678.123. A message informs the user that the name has been changed and the altered name is displayed. File names containing illegal DOS characters are stripped when writing to the DOS format. A message informs the user that characters have been removed and displays the name as written.

All DOS text files use a carriage-return/linefeed combination, CR-LF, to indicate a newline. UNIX system text files use a single newline LF character. When the **doscat** and **doscp** commands transfer DOS text files to UNIX system text files, they automatically strip the CR. When text files are transferred to DOS, the commands insert a CR before each LF character.

Under some circumstances, the automatic newline conversions do not occur. The `-m` option may be used to ensure the newline conversion. The **-r** option can be used to override the automatic conversion and force the command to perform a true byte copy regardless of file type.

EXAMPLES

```
doscat /dev/rdsk/f0t:tmp/output.1
doscat A:prog/output.1

dosdir /dev/rdsk/f0t:/prog
dosdir /D:/prog

doscp /mine/file.out /dev/rdsk/f0t:/mine/file.2
doscp /tmp/f1 /tmp/f2 D:

dosformat /dev/rdsk/f0d8dt

dosls /dev/rdsk/f0t:/src
dosls B:

dosmkdir /dev/fd0:/usr/docs

dosrm /dev/rdsk/f0t:/docs/memo.txt
dosrm /A:/docs/memo1.txt

dosrmdir /dev/rdsk/f0t:/usr/docs
```

FILES

`/etc/default/msdos`	Default information
`/dev/rdsk/f0t`	Floppy disk devices
`/dev/rdsk/0s5`	Hard disk devices

SEE ALSO

`directory`(3C)

See your MS-DOS Documentation.

NOTES

It is not possible to refer to DOS files or directories with wild card specifications.

The programs mentioned above cooperate among themselves so no two programs will access the same DOS disk simultaneously. If a process attempts to access a device already in use, it displays the error message **`Device Busy`**, and exits with and exit code of 1.

The device argument to dosformat must be specific. For example, use **`/dev/rdsk/f03ht`** not **`/dev/rdsk/f0t`** or **`a:`**.

The DOS partition hard disk device names correspond as follows:

/dev/dsk/0s5	is equivalent to /dev/hd0d
/dev/rdsk/0s5	is equivalent to /dev/rhd0d
/dev/dsk/1s5	is equivalent to /dev/hd1d
/dev/rdsk/1s5	is equivalent to /dev/rhd1d

All of the DOS utilities leave temporary files in **`/tmp`**. These files are automatically removed when the system is rebooted. They can also be manually removed.

You must have DOS 3.3 or earlier. Extended DOS partitions are not supported.

NAME

dos2unix – converts DOS text files to UNIX operating system format

SYNOPSIS

dos2 [-z] [*infile* [*outfile*]]
dos2 [-? h]

DESCRIPTION

The **dos2unix** command makes DOS text files viewable under the UNIX operating system. It accomplishes this by removing all end-of-file marks, ^Z (octal 032), and converting lines ending in a carriage-return line-feed sequence to lines ending in a new-line (ASCII line-feed). Additionally, it translates from the UNIX operating system code set to the DOS code page used by your personal computer.

The first file (*infile*) specified is the source file. The second file specified (*outfile*) is the target file. The source file and the target file must not have the same name. When neither file parameter is specified, **dos2unix** reads from standard input and writes to standard output. When only one file parameter is specified, that file is considered the source file, and the output is written to standard output.

If the source file is already in UNIX operating system format, **dos2unix** does not alter the format of the file, but it does translate between code page and code set by default.

Use the **-z** option if you want **dos2unix** to stop processing when it encounters the DOS end-of-file (EOF) character, ^Z.

If **dos2unix** doesn't convert characters as you expect, use **-?** or **-h** to display the options available. Refer to **charconv** in this appendix for more information.

You can use **dos2unix** in combination with DOS and UNIX operating system pipes and redirection. For example, the command:

> **sort** < *text* | **dos2unix** > *newtext*

sorts the DOS file TEXT, converts the sorted text, and writes it to a UNIX operating system file called **newtext**. Note that you cannot redirect a converted file to itself.

dosslice (1)

NAME

dosslice – set up UNIX nodes for accessing DOS partitions

SYNOPSIS

dosslice [*0* | *1*]

DESCRIPTION

The **dosslice** command sets up the UNIX device nodes to allow access to the MS-DOS partitions from the UNIX system. The argument to **dosslice** is the hard disk drive that is being used, **0** or **1**. If you omit the argument, the command prompts for the drive number.

The node created for the DOS partition may be readable/writable by all. You make this choice when prompted whether to make the DOS partition public. If the node is not made public, then you must enter the user login name at the next prompt, and the node is made private to that user.

If multiple DOS partitions are found, each one is given a unique node name. The node name is printed for each DOS partition that is found.

The **dosslice** command is needed only when DOS is installed after UNIX has been installed.

SEE ALSO

dos(1), **dos2unix**(1), **pcidossvr(1), unix2dos(1)**

NAME

`download` – host resident PostScript Type 1 font downloader

SYNOPSIS

`download` [*options*] [*files*]

DESCRIPTION

`download` prepends host resident Type 1 fonts to *files* and writes the results on the standard output. If no *files* are specified, or if - is one of the input *files*, the standard input is read. `download` assumes the input *files* make up a single PostScript job and that requested fonts can be included at the start of each input *file*. The following *options* are understood:

`-f` Force a complete scan of each input *file*. In the absence of an explicit comment pointing `download` to the end of the file, the default scan stops immediately after the PostScript header comments.

`-p` *printer* Before downloading, check the list of printer-resident Type 1 fonts in `/etc/lp/printers/`*printer*`/residentfonts`. This file may have to be updated manually with the names of the ROM-resident Type 1 fonts when the PostScript printer named *printer* is installed. Otherwise, this option will point to an empty or non-existent file and ROM-resident fonts will be downloaded from the host when not needed. See the section below "Defining ROM-resident PostScript Fonts."

`-m` *name* Use *name* as the font map table. A *name* that begins with `/` is the full pathname of the map table and is used as is; otherwise *name* defaults to `map` and is appended to the pathname of the host font directory.

`-H` *dir* Use *dir* as the host font directory. The default is the directory `/usr/share/lib/hostfontdir`.

Requested fonts are named in a comment (marked with `%%DocumentFonts:`) in the input *files*. Available Type 1 fonts are the ones listed in the map table selected using the `-m` option.

The map table consists of font name–filename pairs. The font name is the name of the PostScript Type 1 font, exactly as it would appear in a `%%DocumentFonts:` comment and exactly as it appears in the literal `/FontName` in the Type 1 font program itself. The filename is the pathname of the host resident Type 1 font. A filename that begins with a `/` is used as is; otherwise the pathname is relative to the host font directory. Comments in the map table are introduced by `%` (as in PostScript) and extend to the end of the line.

The only candidates for downloading are fonts listed in the map table that point `download` to readable files. A Type 1 font is downloaded once, at most, for a single document, even if it occurs multiple times in the `%%DocumentFonts:` comment or PostScript file. The downloading of fonts occurs only for the duration of the PostScript job; however, permanent downloading of fonts to the printer's RAM can be done with special PostScript programming techniques using the `exitserver` operator.

Requests for unlisted fonts or inaccessible files are ignored; all requests are ignored if the map table can't be read.

Retail Type 1 Fonts Installed Using the UNIX Desktop

The UNIX Desktop provides a capability for installing retail Type 1 fonts from diskette for use with XWin and **lp**. This capability installs the fonts in the XWIN directory **/usr/X/lib/fonts/type1** and updates the **map** file in the directory **/usr/share/lib/hostfontdir** to make their location available to **download**. The updating of the **map** file is done with the **mkfontscale** utility. If Adobe Font Metric files with the file suffix **.afm** exist on the DOS diskette, these are copied as well, to the directory **/usr/X/lib/fonts/type1/afm**, for use by application developers.

On installation, the desktop converts Type 1 fonts files in the compressed (binary) format (files with a suffix of **.pfb**) to the uncompressed (ASCII) format (with a suffix of **.pfa**). Both formats contain most of their data in an encrypted form. Since, generally, only ASCII files should be downloaded to PostScript printers, this conversion by the desktop means that the **download** filter does not do any conversion on the files.

Defining ROM-resident PostScript Fonts

The **-p** option to **download** tells it to check a file named **/etc/lp/printers/***printer-name***/residentfonts** to see what Type 1 fonts are ROM-resident and disk-resident (some PostScript printers have directly attached fonts disks) in the printer so that it does not download such fonts. But this file is not automatically created when a PostScript printer is first set up on your system using **lpadmin**; you may need to create this file yourself.

A list of the Type 1 fonts in ROM or on disk of an attached PostScript printer can be obtained from the printer manufacturer's documentation and entered into the file **/etc/lp/printers/***printer-name***/residentfonts**. For PostScript printers attached via a serial line to an SVR4.2 system, a list of these fonts can also be generated using the **postio** command and a PostScript program available in SVR4.2 (this does not work for PostScript printers attached on a parallel port).

To obtain the list of ROM fonts in a PostScript printer attached on a serial line, first, obtain the device that the PostScript printer is connected on:

```
lpstat -s
```

Given a system on which the PostScript printer **prlocal** is attached on a serial line, this would return output like:

```
scheduler is running
no system default destination
device for prlocal: /dev/tty01
character set ^D
```

This shows that the printer is attached on device **/dev/tty01**. Then, as **root**, run the commands

```
cd /usr/lib/lp/postscript
postio -L /tmp/postio.o -l /dev/tty01 -t romfonts
```

The **romfonts** program is a PostScript program that queries the PostScript printer for a list of resident fonts. For our sample **prlocal** printer, this will produce output in the file **/tmp/postio.o** that looks like:

```
printer startup
%%[ status: waiting; source: serial 25 ]%%
%%[ status: endofjob ]%%
%%[ status: idle ]%%
sending file romfonts
waiting for end of job
%%[ status: busy; source: serial 25 ]%%
/AGaramond-Bold
/AGaramond-BoldItalic
/AGaramond-Italic
/AGaramond-Regular
/AvantGarde-Book
/AvantGarde-BookOblique
/AvantGarde-Demi
/AvantGarde-DemiOblique
  . . . more PostScript font names . . .
/ZapfChancery-MediumItalic
/ZapfDingbats
%%[ status: endofjob ]%%
job complete
```

This file can be edited to contain only the font names in the printers memory (from **AGaramond-Bold** through **ZapfDingbats** in the output shown above for the printer **prlocal**) and placed into the file **/etc/lp/printers/prlocal/residentfonts** to prevent downloading of these fonts from the host computer.

Obtaining the PostScript Font Name for PostScript Application Output

For an application to generate PostScript output that contains the required **%%DocumentFonts:** comment naming the Type 1 PostScript fonts needed by the PostScript job, the application must be able to obtain the PostScript font name. Since the PostScript Type 1 font name is named in the **/FontName** literal in a Type 1 program, but is not part of the XLFD font name, it is made available as the atom **_ADOBE_POSTSCRIPT_FONTNAME** in the X font structure for an outline font that is open as an X font. Application writers must use this mechanism to allow their PostScript fonts to be downloaded and used correctly.

This name can be obtained by an application from the X font structure; this code sample shows the mechanism:

```
#include <stdio.h>
#include <Xlib.h>

#define false 0

main(int argc, char *argv[])
{
    Display *display;
    Atom adobePostScriptFontNameAtom, psfontNameAtom;
    char *XLFDString;
    XFontStruct *newFont;
    char *psfontName;
```

```
if (argc > 1)
 XLFDString = argv[1];
else {
 fprintf(stderr, "usage: %s XLFDname0, argv[0]);
 exit(1);
}

display = XOpenDisplay(NULL);

adobePostScriptFontNameAtom = XInternAtom(display,
                              "_ADOBE_POSTSCRIPT_FONTNAME",
                              false);

/* Do some gratuitous error checking... */
if (adobePostScriptFontNameAtom == None) {
 adobePostScriptFontNameAtom = 0L;
 /* Some sort of error report - if ATM is in the server, this
    atom should have been registered at X startup time -
    unless, of course, ATM is done as a dynamic extension.
    But then, an atom should have been created anyway. */
}

/* This is the part that actually gets the font name from out
   of the font.  newFont is an (XFontStruct *) as returned by
   XLoadQueryFont. */
if ((newFont = XLoadQueryFont(display, XLFDString)) == NULL) {
 fprintf(stderr, "Can't load font %s0, XLFDString);
 exit(1);
}
if (adobePostScriptFontNameAtom) {
 /* psfontNameAtom is an unsigned long (Atom). */
 if (XGetFontProperty(newFont, adobePostScriptFontNameAtom,
                &psfontNameAtom)) {

     /* psfontName is a (char *).  According to the X
        documentation, XGetAtomName is doing the allocating
        here, and the application is expected to XFree the
        psfontName when it is done. */

     psfontName = XGetAtomName(display, psfontNameAtom);
     if (psfontName)
      printf("psfontName=%s0, psfontName);
     else        { /* ...Error, do something... */ }

     /* Do whatever is wanted with the psfontName - store it
        away, use it in outputting to a file, etc. */
     if (psfontName)
      (void)XFree(psfontName);
 }
```

```
        else /* XGetFontProperty */ {
              /* This font didn't come through a path which put the
                 PostScript Type 1 font name into the properties list.
                 Do some sort of backup thing, or error handling... */
          }
         }
    }
```

EXAMPLES

The following map table could be used to control the downloading of the Bookman font family:

```
%
% The first string is the full PostScript font name.
% The second string is the file name - relative to the
% host font directory unless it begins with a /.
%
  Bookman-Light              bookman/light
  Bookman-LightItalic        bookman/lightitalic
  Bookman-Demi               bookman/demi
  Bookman-DemiItalic         bookman/demiitalic
```

The following entry would be created in the **map** file if the Copperplate Gothic font from the Adobe TypeSet™ 2 retail fonts package were installed using the UNIX Desktop:

```
Copperplate-ThirtyOneAB /usr/X/lib/fonts/type1/CP31A___.pfa
```

Using the file **myprinter/map** (in the default host font directory) as the map table, you could download fonts by issuing the following command:

download -m myprinter/map *file*

DIAGNOSTICS

An exit status of 0 is returned if *files* were successfully processed.

NOTES

The **download** program should be part of a more general program.

The **download** utility does not look for **%%PageFonts:** comments and there is no way to force multiple downloads of a particular font.

SEE ALSO

dpost(1), **lp**(1), **mkfontscale**(1), **pfb2pfa**(1), **postdaisy**(1), **postdmd**(1), **postio**(1), **postmd**(1), **postprint**(1), **posttek**(1)

dpost(1)

NAME

dpost – **troff** postprocessor for PostScript printers

SYNOPSIS

/usr/lib/lp/postscript/dpost [*options*] [*files*]

DESCRIPTION

dpost translates *files* created by **troff**(1) into PostScript and writes the results on the standard output. If no *files* are specified, or if – is one of the input *files*, the standard input is read. The following *options* are understood:

-c *num* — Print *num* copies of each page. By default only one copy is printed.

-e *num* — Sets the text encoding level to *num*. The recognized choices are 0, 1, and 2. The size of the output file and print time should decrease as *num* increases. Level 2 encoding will typically be about 20 percent faster than level 0, which is the default and produces output essentially identical to previous versions of **dpost**.

-m *num* — Magnify each logical page by the factor *num*. Pages are scaled uniformly about the origin, which is located near the upper left corner of each page. The default magnification is 1.0.

-n *num* — Print *num* logical pages on each piece of paper, where *num* can be any positive integer. By default, *num* is set to 1.

-o *list* — Print those pages for which numbers are given in the comma-separated *list*. The list contains single numbers *N* and ranges *N1*–*N2*. A missing *N1* means the lowest numbered page, a missing *N2* means the highest.

-p *mode* — Print *files* in either portrait or landscape *mode*. Only the first character of *mode* is significant. The default *mode* is portrait.

-w *num* — Set the line width used to implement *troff* graphics commands to *num* points, where a point is approximately 1/72 of an inch. By default, *num* is set to 0.3 points.

-x *num* — Translate the origin *num* inches along the positive x axis. The default coordinate system has the origin fixed near the upper left corner of the page, with positive x to the right and positive y down the page. Positive *num* moves everything right. The default offset is 0 inches.

-y *num* — Translate the origin *num* inches along the positive y axis. Positive *num* moves text up the page. The default offset is 0.

-F d*ir* — Use *dir* as the font directory. The default *dir* is **/usr/lib/font**, and *dpost* reads binary font files from directory **/usr/lib/font/devpost**.

-H *dir* — Use *dir* as the host resident font directory. Files in this directory should be complete PostScript font descriptions, and must be assigned a name that corresponds to the appropriate two-character **troff** font name. Each font file is copied to the output file only when needed and at most once during each job. There is no default directory.

-L *file* — Use *file* as the PostScript prologue which, by default, is **/usr/lib/postscript/dpost.ps**.

-O — Disables PostScript picture inclusion. A recommended option when **dpost** is run by a spooler in a networked environment.

-T *name* — Use font files for device *name* as the best description of available PostScript fonts. By default, *name* is set to **post** and **dpost** reads binary files from **/usr/lib/font/devpost**.

The *files* should be prepared by **troff**. The default font files in **/usr/lib/font/devpost** produce the best and most efficient output. They assume a resolution of 720 dpi, and can be used to format files by adding the **-Tpost** option to the **troff** call. Older versions of the **eqn** and **pic** preprocessors need to know the resolution that **troff** will be using to format the *files*. If those are the versions installed on your system, use the **-r720** option with **eqn** and **-T720** with **pic**.

dpost makes no assumptions about resolutions. The first **x res** command sets the resolution used to translate the input *files*, the **DESC.out** file, usually **/usr/lib/font/devpost/DESC.out**, defines the resolution used in the binary font files, and the PostScript prologue is responsible for setting up an appropriate user coordinate system.

EXAMPLES

If the old versions of **eqn** and **pic** are installed on your system, you can obtain the best possible looking output by issuing a command line such as the following:

```
pic -T720 file | tbl | eqn -r720 | troff -mm -Tpost | dpost
```

Otherwise,

```
pic file | tbl | eqn | troff -mm -Tpost | dpost
```

should give the best results.

NOTES

Output files often do not conform to Adobe's file structuring conventions. Piping the output of **dpost** through **postreverse** should produce a minimally conforming PostScript file.

Although **dpost** can handle files formatted for any device, emulation is expensive and can easily double the print time and the size of the output file. No attempt has been made to implement the character sets or fonts available on all devices supported by **troff**. Missing characters will be replaced by white space, and unrecognized fonts will usually default to one of the Times fonts (that is, **R**, **I**, **B**, or **BI**).

An **x res** command must precede the first **x init** command, and all the input *files* should have been prepared for the same output device.

Use of the **-T** option is not encouraged. Its only purpose is to enable the use of other PostScript font and device description files, that perhaps use different resolutions, character sets, or fonts.

Although level 0 encoding is the only scheme that has been thoroughly tested, level 2 is fast and may be worth a try.

DIAGNOSTICS

An exit status of 0 is returned if *files* have been translated successfully, while 2 often indicates a syntax error in the input *files*.

FILES

```
/usr/lib/font/devpost/*.out
/usr/lib/font/devpost/charlib/*
/usr/lib/lp/postscript/dpost.ps
/usr/lib/lp/postscript/color.ps
/usr/lib/lp/postscript/draw.ps
/usr/lib/lp/postscript/forms.ps
/usr/lib/lp/postscript/ps.requests
/usr/lib/macros/pictures
/usr/lib/macros/color
```

SEE ALSO

`download`(1), `postdaisy`(1), `postdmd`(1), `postio`(1), `postmd`(1), `postprint`(1), `postreverse`(1), `posttek`(1), `troff`(1)

NAME

`dsdm` – Drop Site Database Manager

SYNOPSIS

`dsdm &`

DESCRIPTION

The **`dsdm`** command (Drop Site Database Manager) maintains the information from all drag-and-drop participants. This information is used to provide the drag-and-drop user feedback.

The line

```
dsdm
```

should be in the **`$HOME/.olinitrc`** file (created when executing **`dtadduser`**).

SEE ALSO

`dtadduser`(1M)
section 3DnD (Drag and Drop) functions

dtadduser (1M)

NAME

dtadduser - add a UNIX Desktop user

SYNOPSIS

dtadduser [-m] [-r *remote*] [*user*]

DESCRIPTION

The **dtadduser** command adds a new UNIX Desktop user. It is normally invoked thru the UNIX Desktop User Setup window.

-m use the MOTIF Graphical User Interface look and feel, the default is the OPEN LOOK Graphical User Interface look and feel

-r specify the X-terminal or system name the user frequently logs in from

user specify the user to add

dtadduser creates the files **.olinitrc**, **.olsetup**, and **.xsession** in the user's home directory and adding the line

```
. $HOME/.olsetup<TAB>#!@ Do not edit this line !@
```

to the end of the user's **.profile**. The user is specified by login name using either the optional argument *user* or by the **$LOGNAME** environment variable.

dtadduser also creates the file **.Xdefaults**, and places the **numMouseBtns** default in it if the file **/etc/default/mouse** exists, and the file **.olinitrc**, with the following lines:

```
olwm
dsdm
```

If the user already exists, these files (excluding **.Xdefaults**) will be overwritten. If write permissions are not granted on any of these files, **dtadduser** will write an error message on standard error stating so, and exit.

The **.olsetup** procedure automatically sets and exports the **XWINFONTPATH** environment variable which ensures that the MOTIF and OPEN LOOK GUI fonts are found by the XWIN server. If the **dtadduser** command is not executed when the desktop is installed, and the user has not explicitly set the **XWINFONTPATH** environment variable, the system-wide default will be used.

dtadduser also sets up

default directories in **$HOME** containing files that link to tools such as **xterm** and **shutdown**,

a mailbox directory in **$HOME**,

UUCP_InBox directory under the **$HOME/utilities** directory with a link to **/var/spool/uucppublic/receive/***user*,

a **.wastebasket** directory,

puts *user* in **cron.allow**,

grants default desktop permissions, and

adds *user* to the TFM database.

Files

`$HOME/.profile`
`$HOME/.olinitrc`
`$HOME/.olsetup`
`$HOME/.Xdefaults`
`$HOME/.xsession`
`/etc/security/tfm/users/`*user*
`/usr/lib/cron/cron.allow`
`/usr/X/adm/dtuser.msgs` read only
`/usr/X/desktop/LoginMgr/PrivTable` read only
`/usr/X/desktop/LoginMgr/Users/`*user*
`/usr/X/desktop/`*directory templates*

Exit Codes

The **dtadduser** command exists with one of the following values:

0 success, user added

1 user not in **/etc/passwd**

2 user **$HOME** missing

3 user **$HOME** access denied

4 user **.profile** access denied

5 copy of **.olinitrc**, **.olsetup**, or **.xsession** failed

6 **adminuser** failed

USAGE

dtadduser resides in **/usr/X/adm**. Since the **PATH** environment variable does not normally include that path, either specify the full pathname or add **/usr/X/adm** to the **PATH** variable.

If **dtadduser** is invoked from the UNIX shell or via a user-supplied shell script, and if *user* was already a UNIX Desktop user, the UNIX Desktop User Setup window will show that the user has no administrative permissions. Use **dtdeluser** to remove *user* as a UNIX Desktop user, and then invoke **dtadduser**.

SEE ALSO

adminuser(1M), **cron**(1M), **crontab**(1), **dtdeluser**(1M), **dtmodem**(1M), **dtprinter**(1M), **dtprivilege**(1M), **dtstatus**(1M), **make-owner**(1M), **tfadmin**(1M), **uucp**(1c)

dtdeluser (1M)

NAME

dtdeluser - delete a UNIX Desktop user

SYNOPSIS

dtdeluser [*user*]

DESCRIPTION

The **dtdeluser** command deletes a UNIX Desktop user. If *user* is not specified, and the **$LOGNAME** environment variable is not set, it defaults to the login executing the command.

dtdeluser removes the files **.olinitrc**, **.olsetup**, **.Xdefaults**, and **.xsession** in the user's home directory and deletes the line

```
. $HOME/.olsetup<TAB>#!@ Do not edit this line !@
```

from the user's **.profile**.

If write permissions are not granted on any of these files, **dtdeluser** will write an error message on standard error stating so.

dtdeluser also removes:

default directories in **$HOME** with links to tools such as **xterm** and **shutdown**

a mailbox directory in **$HOME**, if it is empty

UUCP_InBox with a link to **/var/spool/uucppublic/receive/***user*

a **.wastebasket**, if it is empty

files such as **.lastsession**, **.dtprops**, and **.dtinfo** from **$HOME**

moves **$HOME/.dtfclass** to **$HOME/.dtfclass_old**

removes those entries in the TFM database added by the UNIX Desktop for *user*

Files

$HOME/.profile	
$HOME/.olinitrc	
$HOME/.olsetup	
$HOME/.Xdefaults	
$HOME/.xsession	
/etc/security/tfm/users/*user*	
/usr/X/adm/dtuser.msgs	read only
/usr/X/desktop/LoginMgr/PrivTable	read only
/usr/X/desktop/LoginMgr/Users/*user*	
/usr/X/desktop/*directory templates*	

Exit Codes

The **dtdeluser** command exits with one of the following values:

0 success, user deleted

1 user not in **/etc/passwd**

2 user **$HOME** missing

3 user **$HOME** access denied

USAGE

dtdeluser resides in **/usr/X/adm**. Since the **PATH** environment variable does not normally include that path, either specify the full pathname or add **/usr/X/adm** to the **PATH** variable.

SEE ALSO

adminuser(1M), **cron**(1M), **crontab**(1), **dtadduser**(1M), **make-owner**(1M), **tfadmin**(1M)

dtfilter (1M)

NAME

dtfilter - add an entry to the printer filter table

SYNOPSIS

dtfilter -a [-o] *file* . . .

dtfilter -d *entry* . . .

DESCRIPTION

The **dtfilter** command adds or deletes an entry to the printer filter table. The printer filter table is used by the desktop printer setup application to prompt users for printer filter options.

-a add entries in *file*, to the printer filter table

-o overwrite existing entries of the same name

-d remove *entry* from the filter table

A filter table *entry* has the format:

EntryName<TAB>*LabelString*[^*CatalogFile*:*Index*]<TAB>*OptionString*

EntryName
tag used to reference the entry

LabelString[^*CatalogFile*:*Index*]
checkbox label, for example, **Landscape mode:** or **Reverse order printing:** Note that [*CatalogFile*:*Index*:] translates *LabelString*. *CatalogFile* is the file of locale specific translations. *index* is the line number of the translation.

OptionString
option syntax, this can be a simple string (no % may be included in the entry) or complex string (a % must be in the entry). A %% may be used to embed a percent character in either simple or complex strings.

A simple string will be presented as a simple checkbox. It is passed to **lp** via the **-y** option and should match one of the "mode strings" already defined for the print filter [see **lp**(1) and **lpfilter**(1M)].

A complex string will require textual user input. The entry uses a **printf**-like format.

%d integer field

%s string field

%c character field

%u unsigned integer field

%f floating point field

Environment

The **dtfilter** command uses the **XWINHOME** environment variable to locate printer filter tables. The default value of **XWINHOME** is **/usr/X**, so **/usr/X/desktop/PrintMgr/Filters** will be searched.

Files

`$XWINHOME/desktop/PrintMgr/Filters/*`
`/usr/X/desktop/PrintMgr/Filters/*`

Exit Codes

The **dtfilter** command returns

0 success

1 usage error

2 format error

3 item exists and **-o** not specified

4 cannot read/write file

USAGE

dtfilter resides in **/usr/X/adm**. Since the **PATH** environment variable does not normally include that path, either specify the full pathname or add **/usr/X/adm** to the **PATH** variable.

Examples

The examples show filter strings and their corresponding user interfaces:

Entry Name	User Interface	Passed to **lp**
landscape	Landscape Mode: [x]	landscape
pages	Maximum Pages:_______	maxpages=%u
pages	Range of Pages:_____	range=%u-%u

If, in the above example, the user inputs 44, 22, and 23, in that order, the arguments passed to **lp** will be

```
-ylandscape
-ymaxpages=44
-yrange=22-23
```

SEE ALSO

dtprinter(1M), **dttypes**(1M), **lp**(1), **lpfilter**(1M)

dtm(1)

NAME

`dtm` - Desktop Manager

SYNOPSIS

`dtm` [-*display*]

DESCRIPTION

`dtm`, the Desktop Manager, provides file and workspace management for the UNIX Desktop.

`dtm` takes one optional command line argument: **`motif`** or **`openlook`**. If no argument is specified, the default is **`motif`**. **`dtm`** relies on the existence of the file class database, **`$HOME/.dtfclass`**. The file class database is accessed via the Icon Setup program in the System Setup Folder of the UNIX Desktop. This file is copied to a users directory by **`dtadduser`**.

`dtm` looks in the **`$HOME/.Xdefaults`** file for user-specifiable parameters and puts files that are deleted (through the UNIX desktop) in the directory **`$HOME/.wastebasket`**. If **`.Xdefaults`** or **`.wastebasket`** do not exist, **`dtm`** creates them.

Files

`$HOME/.dtfclass`
`$HOME/.wastebasket`
`$HOME/.Xdefaults`

USAGE

Before making a change to the localization property window, all applications should be terminated. This is necessary for applications to change to the new locale. There is no dynamic adjustment by clients to a change in locale.

SEE ALSO

`desktop`(1), **`dtadduser`**(1M), **`olwm`**(1)

dtmodem(1M)

NAME

dtmodem - add an entry to the modem table

SYNOPSIS

dtmodem -a [**-o**] *file* . . .

dtmodem -d *entry* . . .

DESCRIPTION

The **dtmodem** command adds or deletes an entry to the modem table. The modem table is used by the UNIX Desktop Dialup Setup application to prompt users on the modems available.

-a add entries in *file*, to the modem table

-o overwrite existing entries of the same name

-d remove *entry* from the modem table

A modem table *entry* has the format:

EntryName<TAB>*ModemType*[^*CatalogFile*:*Index*]<TAB>*DialersName*

EntryName
: tag used to reference the entry

ModemType[^*CatalogFile*:*Index*]
: string presented to the user. Note that [*CatalogFile*:*Index*:] translates *ModemType*. *CatalogFile* is the file of locale specific translations. *index* is the line number of the translation.

DialersName
: device name as it appears in the Dialers file (**/usr/lib/uucp/Dialers**)

Files

/usr/X/desktop/DialupMgr/Modems

Exit Codes

The **dtmodem** command returns

0 success

1 usage error

2 format error

3 item exists and **-o** not specified

4 cannot read/write file

5 no memory

USAGE

dtmodem resides in **/usr/X/adm**. Since the **PATH** environment variable does not normally include that path, either specify the full pathname or add **/usr/X/adm** to the **PATH** variable.

SEE ALSO

uucp(1C)

dtprinter (1M)

NAME

`dtprinter` - add an entry to the printer table

SYNOPSIS

`dtprinter -a` [`-o`] *file* . . .

`dtprinter -d` *entry* . . .

DESCRIPTION

The **`dtprinter`** command adds or deletes an entry to the printer table. The printer table is used by the desktop Printer setup application to prompt users on the printer they want to use.

`-a` add entries in *file*, to the printer table

`-o` overwrite existing entries of the same name

`-d` remove *entry* from the printer table

A printer table entry contains the following lines, of which only **`entry`** and **`name`** are required:

`entry:`*EntryName*
`name:`*PrinterName*[^*CatalogFile*`:`*Index*]
`terminfo:`*Terminfo Name*
`interface:`*Interface Program Name*
`contents:`*list of content types*
`stty:`*stty argument list*
`modules:`*streams module names*

`entry` tag used to reference the entry

`name` name of printer presented to user. Note that [*CatalogFile*`:`*Index*`:`] translates *PrinterName*. *CatalogFile* is the file of locale specific translations. *index* is the line number of the translation.

`terminfo`
`terminfo` name of printer. This may be a comma seperated list. The default is **`unknown`**.

`interface`
program to use with the printer. This may be an absolute path or a path that is relative to the LP model directory, that is **`/usr/lib/lp/model`**. The standard interface supplied with LP is the default.

`contents`
comma separated list of types of files the printer can support. For example, **`simple`** for simple ASCII text (the default) and **`PS`** for postscript input.

`stty` any **`stty`** options needed when initializing the printer. The default is "".

`modules`
comma separated list of all streams modules to be pushed when the printer is initialized. The default is the users default modules.

Environment

The **`dtprinter`** command uses the **`XWINHOME`** environment variable to locate printer tables. The default value of **`XWINHOME`** is **`/usr/X`**, so **`/usr/X/desktop/PrintMgr/Printers`** will be searched.

Files

`$XWINHOME/desktop/PrintMgr/Printers`
`/usr/X/desktop/PrintMgr/Printers`

Exit Codes

The **dtprinter** command returns

- 0 success
- 1 usage error
- 2 format error
- 3 item exists and **-o** not specified
- 4 cannot read/write file
- 5 no memory

USAGE

dtprinter resides in **/usr/X/adm**. Since the **PATH** environment variable does not normally include that path, either specify the full pathname or add **/usr/X/adm** to the **PATH** variable.

All streams modules listed under **modules** are assumed to already have been built into the kernel. This is most likely to occur during installation of the printer package.

Examples

The example shows an entry for an HP Laser Jet:

```
entry:HPlaser
name:HP Laser Jet
terminfo:hplaserjet
contents:simple
```

SEE ALSO

dtfilter(1M), **dttypes**(1M), **lp**(1), **lpfilter**(1)

dtprivilege (1M)

NAME

dtprivilege - add an entry to the privilege table

SYNOPSIS

dtprivilege -a [*entry*]

dtprivilege -d *entry . . .*

DESCRIPTION

The **dtprivilege** command adds or deletes an entry to a privilege table.

-a add *entry* or entries to the privilege table

-d delete *entry* from the privilege table

The Trusted Facilities Management facility (TFM) maintains a database of logins and associated privileges. This allows UNIX Desktop users permission to execute commands that require special privileges. The privilege table is a list of privileged commands to be registered with TFM when a user is granted permission via the User Setup window.

PrivTable File

PrivTable is a list of permissions that can be granted users through the desktop User_Setup client. Each entry includes a list of commands a user is able to execute, if granted permissions via User Setup.

A privilege table *entry* has the format:

[*CatalogFile*:*Index*:]*CheckboxString*<TAB>*EntryList*<TAB>*HelpFile*

[*CatalogFile*:*Index*:]
: translate *CheckboxString*. *CatalogFile* is the file of locale specific translations. *index* is the line number of the translation.

CheckboxString
: label to use for the checkbox in User_Setup Account Permissions window. If the checkbox is checked, *EntryList* will be registered with TFM

EntryList
: comma separated list of entries. This takes the form

entryname1:*fullpath*:*priv1*:*priv2*:. . .,*entryname2* . . .

HelpFile
: help file to use with this privilege checkbox. This may be a full path name or a locale-specific file in

/usr/X/lib/locale/*locale***/help/LoginMgr**

Files

/etc/security/tfm/users/*user*
/usr/X/desktop/LoginMgr/PrivTable
/usr/X/lib/locale/*locale***/help/LoginMgr**

USAGE

dtprivilege resides in **/usr/X/adm**. Since the **PATH** environment variable does not normally include that path, either specify the full pathname or add **/usr/X/adm** to the **PATH** variable.

Examples

Ordinarily, users can only use date to see the time and date. This example creates an "Update System Clock" checkbox that adds the command **date** to the list of commands the user can invoke with privilege so the user can change the date.

```
Update System Clock  date:/usr/bin/date:sysops:macwrite:dacwrite
```

SEE ALSO

adminuser(1M), **dtadduser**(1M), **gettxt**(1), **make-owner**(1M), **PrivTable**(4), **tfadmin**(1M)

dtstatus (1M)

NAME

`dtstatus` – update desktop system status parameters

SYNOPSIS

dtstatus -a *filename*

dtstatus -d *entry . . .*

dtstatus -f *flag entry . . .*

DESCRIPTION

The **dtstatus** command modifies the template file used to control the display of the System_Status desktop administration client. Each line of this file is either a comment (a blank line, or one beginning with **#**), or defines a component of the status display. The syntax of these entries is:

entry flag command

with the fields separated by TAB characters. *entry* is the string displayed in the System Status window. The *command* field is either a UNIX command producing one output line or the word **builtin** specifying one of the components present in the factory defaults.

The *flag* field indicates whether the component is (temporarily) suppressed (initial **-**) or displayed (**+** or neither sign present), and whether the component is on the right (**r**) or left (**l** or no marker) side of the display. For the clock and disk gauge components, there may be a following number indicating the interval in seconds between updates of the status information (with **0** meaning that the initial display is not updated).

Options

The options available are

-a *filename* append the contents of *filenamed* to the system **StatusFile**

-d *entry* delete *entry* from the system **StatusFile**, *entry* being the name of the component, the first field of the entry in the **StatusFile**

-f *nflag entry* modify each *entry*'s *flag* to be *nflag*. This can be used to "turn off" the display of components or to "move" them from side to side in the display.

Examples

To eliminate the display of the system memory component in the factory settings, either eliminate it altogether, using

```
dtstatus -d memory
```

or leave it in the file, but not displaying, by changing the flag

```
dtstatus -f -r memory
```

To add a new component, for example a date command that is updated every 10 seconds, presumably as a replacement for the factory clock and calendar (which can be turned off by the **-d** or **-f** flags), one could have a file datestat containing the line

```
date +10  date
```

and attach this to the System_Status display via

```
dtstatus -a datestat
```

This example shows the standard line for display of hard disk space usage:

```
disk +60r builtin
```

indicating that the display, with its gauge of the space usage on mounted hard disk file systems, is updated and displayed every 60 seconds, on the right side of the System_Status screen.

Files

`/usr/X/desktop/dashboard/StatusFile`

USAGE

Minimal checking of the syntax is done for added files.

dttypes (1M)

NAME

dttypes - add an entry to the document types table

SYNOPSIS

dttypes -a [**-o**] *file* . . .

dttypes -d *entry* . . .

DESCRIPTION

The **dttypes** command adds or deletes an entry to the document types table. The document types table is used by the desktop Printer Setup application to add or change the type of document to be printed. The list of document types is presented when the user selects the "File to be printed is" button when the file is submitted to the printer.

-a add entries in *file*, to the document types table

-o overwrite existing entries of the same name

-d remove *entry* from the document types table

A document types table **entry** has the format:

EntryName<TAB>*TypeString*[^*CatalogFile*:*Index*]<TAB>*InputType*

EntryName
: tag used to reference the entry

TypeString[^*CatalogFile*:*Index*]
: string presented to the user. Note that [*CatalogFile*:*Index*:] translates *TypeString*. *CatalogFile* is the file of locale specific translations. *index* is the line number of the translation.

InputType
: input type, as predefined by the Line Printer utilities

Files

/usr/X/desktop/PrintMgr/Types

Exit Codes

The **dtfilter** command returns

0 success

1 usage error

2 format error

3 item exists and **-o** not specified

4 cannot read/write file

5 no memory

USAGE

dttypes resides in **/usr/X/adm**. Since the **PATH** environment variable does not normally include that path, either specify the full pathname or add **/usr/X/adm** to the **PATH** variable.

SEE ALSO

lp(1), lpfilter(1M)

du(1M)

NAME

du – summarize disk usage

SYNOPSIS

du [**-sar**] [*name* . . .]

DESCRIPTION

The **du** command reports the number of blocks contained in all files and (recursively) directories within each directory and file specified. The block count includes the indirect blocks of the file. If no *names* are given, the current directory is used.

A user with the appropriate privileges is able to display information about all files and directories.

The optional arguments are as follows:

-s causes only the grand total (for each of the specified *names*) to be given.

-a causes an output line to be generated for each file.

If neither **-s** or **-a** is specified, an output line is generated for each directory only.

-r will cause **du** to generate messages about directories that cannot be be read, files that cannot be opened, etc., rather than being silent (the default).

A file with two or more links is only counted once.

NOTES

If the **-a** option is not used, non-directories given as arguments are not listed.

If there are links between files in different directories where the directories are on separate branches of the file system hierarchy, **du** will count the excess files more than once.

NAME

du – (BSD) display the number of disk blocks used per directory or file

SYNOPSIS

/usr/ucb/du [**-a**] [**-s**] [*filename* **. . .**]

DESCRIPTION

du gives the number of kilobytes contained in all files and, recursively, directories within each specified directory or file *filename*. If *filename* is missing, '**.**' (the current directory) is used.

A file which has multiple links to it is only counted once.

OPTIONS

-a Generate an entry for each file.

-s Only display the grand total for each of the specified *filename*s.

Entries are generated only for each directory in the absence of options.

EXAMPLE

Here is an example of using **du** in a directory. We used the **pwd**(1) command to identify the directory, then used **du** to show the usage of all the subdirectories in that directory. The grand total for the directory is the last entry in the display:

```
% pwd
/usr/ralph/misc
% du
5     ./jokes
33    ./squash
44    ./tech.papers/lpr.document
217   ./tech.papers/new.manager
401   ./tech.papers
144   ./memos
80    ./letters
388   ./window
93    ./messages
15    ./useful.news
1211  .
%
```

SEE ALSO

df(1M), **pwd**(1), **quot**(1M)

NOTES

Filename arguments that are not directory names are ignored, unless you use **-a**.

If there are too many distinct linked files, **du** will count the excess files more than once.

dump(1)

NAME

`dump` – dump selected parts of an object file

SYNOPSIS

`dump` *options file* . . .

DESCRIPTION

The **dump** command dumps selected parts of each of its object *file* arguments. You must provide at least one option.

This command will accept both object files and archives of object files. It processes each file argument according to one or more of the following options:

`-a` Dump the archive header of each member of an archive.

`-C` Dump decoded C++ symbol table names.

`-c` Dump the string table(s).

`-D` Dump debugging information.

`-f` Dump each file header.

`-g` Dump the global symbols in the symbol table of an archive.

`-h` Dump the section headers.

`-L` Dump dynamic linking information and static shared library information, if available.

`-l` Dump line number information.

`-o` Dump each program execution header.

`-r` Dump relocation information.

`-s` Dump section contents in hexadecimal.

`-T` *index* or `-T` *index1*`,`*index2*
Dump only the indexed symbol table entry defined by *index* or a range of entries defined by *index1*`,`*index2*.

`-t` Dump symbol table entries.

`-u` When reading a COFF object file, **dump** translates the file to ELF internally (this translation does not affect the file contents). This option controls how much translation occurs from COFF values to ELF. Normally (without **`-u`**), the COFF values are preserved as much as possible, showing the actual bytes in the file. If **`-u`** is used, **dump** updates the values and completes the internal translation, giving a consistent ELF view of the contents. Although the bytes displayed under this option might not match the file itself, they show how the file would look if it were converted to ELF. (See **`cof2elf`**(1) for more information.)

`-V` Print version information.

The following modifiers are used in conjunction with the options listed above to modify their capabilities.

`-d` *number* or `-d` *number1*`,`*number2*
Dump the section number indicated by *number* or the range of sections starting at *number1* and ending at *number2*. This modifier can be used with `-h`, `-s`, and `-r`. When `-d` is used with `-h` or `-s`, the argument is treated as the number of a section or range of sections. When `-d` is used with `-r`, the argument is treated as the number of the section or range of sections to which the relocation applies. For example, to print out all relocation entries associated with the `.text` section, specify the number of the section as the argument to `-d`. If `.text` is section number 2 in the file, `dump -r -d 2` will print all associated entries. To print out a specific relocation section use `dump -s -n` *name* for raw data output, or `dump -sv -n` *name* for interpreted output.

`-n` *name*
Dump information pertaining only to the named entity. This modifier can be used with `-h`, `-s`, `-r`, and `-t`. When `-n` is used with `-h` or `-s`, the argument will be treated as the name of a section. When `-n` is used with `-t` or `-r`, the argument will be treated as the name of a symbol. For example, `dump -t -n .text` will dump the symbol table entry associated with the symbol whose name is `.text`, where `dump -h -n .text` will dump the section header information for the `.text` section.

`-p`
Suppress printing of the headings.

`-v`
Dump information in symbolic representation rather than numeric. This modifier can be used with `-a` (date, user id, group id), `-f` (class, data, type, machine, version, flags), `-h` (type, flags), `-o` (type, flags), `-r` (name, type), `-s` (interpret section contents wherever possible), `-t` (type, bind), and `-L` (value). When `-v` is used with `-s`, all sections that can be interpreted, such as the string table or symbol table, will be interpreted. For example, `dump -sv -n .symtab` *file* will produce the same formatted output as `dump -tv` *file*, but `dump -s -n .symtab` *file* will print raw data in hexadecimal. Without additional modifiers, `dump -sv` *file* will dump all sections in *file* interpreting all those that it can and dumping the rest (such as `.text` or `.data`) as raw data.

The `dump` command attempts to format the information it dumps in a meaningful way, printing certain information in character, hexadecimal, octal or decimal representation as appropriate.

SEE ALSO

`a.out`(4), `ar`(4), `cof2elf`(1)

echo(1)

NAME

echo – echo arguments

SYNOPSIS

echo [*arg*] . . .
echo [**-n**] [*arg*]

DESCRIPTION

echo writes its arguments separated by blanks and terminated by a new-line on the standard output. It processes supplementary code set characters according to the locale specified in the **LC_CTYPE** environment variable [see **LANG** on **environ**(5)].

The **/usr/bin/sh** version understands the following C-like escape conventions; beware of conflicts with the shell's use of \ :

\b	backspace
\c	print line without new-line
\f	form-feed
\n	new-line
\r	carriage return
\t	tab
\v	vertical tab
\\	backslash
\0*n*	where *n* is the 1-, 2-, or 3-digit octal encoding of an 8-bit character. Each byte of multibyte characters should be preceded by backslash (\).

The following option is available to **/usr/bin/sh** users only if **/usr/ucb** precedes **/usr/bin** in the user's PATH. It is available to **/usr/csh** users, regardless of PATH:

-n Do not add the newline to the output.

echo is useful for producing diagnostics in command files, for sending known data into a pipe, and for displaying the contents of environment variables.

SEE ALSO

sh(1)

NOTES

The **-n** option is a transition aid for BSD applications, and may not be supported in future releases.

When representing an 8-bit character by using the escape convention \0*n*, the *n* must **always** be preceded by the digit zero (0).

For example, typing: **echo 'WARNING:\07'** will print the phrase **WARNING:** and sound the "bell" on your terminal. The use of single (or double) quotes (or two backslashes) is required to protect the " \" that precedes the "07".

Following the \0, up to three digits are used in constructing the octal output character. If, following the \0*n*, you want to echo additional digits that are not part of the octal representation, you must use the full 3-digit *n*. For example, if you want to echo "ESC 7" you must use the three digits "033" rather than just the two digits "33" after the \0.

2 digits	Incorrect:	`echo "\0337"  | od -xc`	
	produces:	`df0a`	(hex)
		`337`	(ascii)
3 digits	Correct:	`echo "\00337" | od -xc`	
	produces:	`1b37 0a00`	(hex)
		`033 7`	(ascii)

echo (1F)

NAME

echo – put string on virtual output

SYNOPSIS

echo [*string* . . .]

DESCRIPTION

The **echo** function directs each string it is passed to *stdout*. It is often used in conditional execution or for passing a string to another command.

EXAMPLES

Set the **done** descriptor to **help** if a test fails:

```
done=`if [ -s $F1 ];
      then echo close;
      else echo help;
      fi`
```

SEE ALSO

echo(1)

NAME

echo – (BSD) echo arguments

SYNOPSIS

/usr/ucb/echo [arg] . . .
/usr/ucb/echo [**-n**] [arg]

DESCRIPTION

echo writes its arguments separated by blanks and terminated by a new-line on the standard output.

The **/usr/bin/sh** version understands the following C-like escape conventions; beware of conflicts with the shell's use of \:

\b	backspace
\c	print line without new-line
\f	form-feed
\n	new-line
\r	carriage return
\t	tab
\v	vertical tab
****	backslash
\0*n*	where *n* is the 8-bit character whose ASCII code is the 1-, 2- or 3-digit octal number representing that character.

The following option is available to **/usr/bin/sh** users only if **/usr/ucb** precedes **/usr/bin** in the user's PATH. It is available to **/usr/csh** users, regardless of PATH:

-n Do not add the newline to the output.

echo is useful for producing diagnostics in command files and for sending known data into a pipe.

SEE ALSO

sh(1)

NOTES

The **-n** option is a transition aid for BSD applications, and may not be supported in future releases.

The When representing an 8-bit character by using the escape convention **\0***n*, the *n* must **always** be preceded by the digit zero (0).

For example, typing: **echo ´WARNING:\07´** will print the phrase **WARNING:** and sound the "bell" on your terminal. The use of single (or double) quotes (or two backslashes) is required to protect the "\" that precedes the "07".

For the octal equivalents of each character, see ascii(5).

NAME

ed, **red** – text editor

SYNOPSIS

ed [**-s**] [**-p** *string*] [**-x**] [**-C**] [*file*]

red [**-s**] [**-p** *string*] [**-x**] [**-C**] [*file*]

DESCRIPTION

ed is the standard text editor. If the *file* argument is given, **ed** simulates an **e** command (see below) on the named file; that is to say, the file is read into **ed**'s buffer so that it can be edited. Both **ed** and **red** process supplementary code set characters in *file*, and recognize supplementary code set characters in the prompt string given to the **-p** option (see below) according to the locale specified in the **LC_CTYPE** environment variable [see **LANG** on **environ**(5)]. In regular expressions, pattern searches are performed on characters, not bytes, as described below.

-s Suppresses the printing of byte counts by **e**, **r**, and **w** commands, of diagnostics from **e** and **q** commands, and of the **!** prompt after a **!***shell command*.

-p Allows the user to specify a prompt string. The string may contain supplementary code set characters.

-x Encryption option; when used, **ed** simulates an **X** command and prompts the user for a key. This key is used to encrypt and decrypt text using the algorithm of **crypt**(1). The **X** command makes an educated guess to determine whether text read in is encrypted or not. The temporary buffer file is encrypted also, using a transformed version of the key typed in for the **-x** option. See **crypt**(1). Also, see the NOTES section at the end of this manual page.

-C Encryption option; the same as the **-x** option, except that **ed** simulates a **C** command. The **C** command is like the **X** command, except that all text read in is assumed to have been encrypted.

ed operates on a copy of the file it is editing; changes made to the copy have no effect on the file until a **w** (write) command is given. The copy of the text being edited resides in a temporary file called the *buffer*. There is only one buffer.

red is a restricted version of **ed**. It will only allow editing of files in the current directory. It prohibits executing shell commands via **!***shell command*. Attempts to bypass these restrictions result in an error message (restricted shell).

Both **ed** and **red** support the **fspec**(4) formatting capability. After including a format specification as the first line of *file* and invoking **ed** with your terminal in **stty -tabs** or **stty tab3** mode [see **stty**(1)], the specified tab stops will automatically be used when scanning *file*. For example, if the first line of a file contained:

```
<:t5,10,15 s72:>
```

tab stops would be set at columns 5, 10, and 15, and a maximum line length of 72 would be imposed. NOTE: when you are entering text into the file, this format is not in effect; instead, because of being in **stty -tabs** or **stty tab3** mode, tabs are expanded to every eighth column.

Commands to **ed** have a simple and regular structure: zero, one, or two *addresses* followed by a single-character *command*, possibly followed by parameters to that command. These addresses specify one or more lines in the buffer. Every command that requires addresses has default addresses, so that the addresses can very often be omitted.

In general, only one command may appear on a line. Certain commands allow the input of text. This text is placed in the appropriate place in the buffer. While **ed** is accepting text, it is said to be in *input mode*. In this mode, no commands are recognized; all input is merely collected. Leave input mode by typing a period (**.**) at the beginning of a line, followed immediately by pressing RETURN.

ed supports a limited form of *regular expression* notation; regular expressions are used in addresses to specify lines and in some commands (for example, **s**) to specify portions of a line that are to be substituted. A regular expression specifies a set of character strings. A member of this set of strings is said to be matched by the regular expression. The regular expressions allowed by **ed** are constructed as follows:

The following one-character regular expressions match a single character:

1.1 An ordinary character (not one of those discussed in 1.2 below) is a one-character regular expression that matches itself.

1.2 A backslash (\) followed by any special character is a one-character regular expression that matches the special character itself. The special characters are:

a. **.**, *, **[**, and \ (period, asterisk, left square bracket, and backslash, respectively), which are always special, except when they appear within square brackets (**[ ]**; see 1.4 below).

b. ^ (caret or circumflex), which is special at the beginning of a regular expression (see 4.1 and 4.3 below), or when it immediately follows the left of a pair of square brackets (**[ ]**) (see 1.4 below).

c. **$** (dollar sign), which is special at the **end** of a regular expression (see 4.2 below).

d. The character that is special for that specific regular expression, that is used to bound (or delimit) a regular expression. (For example, see how slash (**/**) is used in the **g** command, below.)

1.3 A period (**.**) is a one-character regular expression that matches any character, including supplementary code set characters, except new-line.

1.4 A non-empty string of characters enclosed in square brackets (**[ ]**) is a one-character regular expression that matches one character, including supplementary code set characters, in that string. If, however, the first character of the string is a circumflex (^), the one-character regular expression matches any character, including supplementary code set characters, except new-line and the remaining characters in the string. The ^ has this special meaning only if it occurs first in the string. The minus (–) may be used to indicate a range of consecutive characters, including supplementary code set characters; for example, **[0-9]** is equivalent to **[0123456789]**. Characters specifying the range must be from the same code set; when the characters are from different code sets, one of the characters specifying the range is matched. The – loses this special meaning if it occurs first (after an initial ^, if any) or last in the string. The right square bracket (]) does not terminate such a string when it is the first character within it (after an initial ^, if any); for example, **[]a-f]** matches either a right square bracket (]) or one of the ASCII letters **a** through **f** inclusive. The four characters listed in 1.2.a above stand for themselves within such a string of characters.

The following rules may be used to construct regular expressions from one-character regular expressions:

2.1 A one-character regular expression is an regular expression that matches whatever the one-character regular expression matches.

2.2 A one-character regular expression followed by an asterisk (*) is a regular expression that matches zero or more occurrences of the one-character regular expression, which may be a supplementary code set character. If there is any choice, the longest leftmost string that permits a match is chosen.

2.3 A one-character regular expression followed by \{m\}, \{m,\}, or \{m,n\} is a regular expression that matches a range of occurrences of the one-character regular expression. The values of m and n must be non-negative integers less than 256; \{m\} matches exactly m occurrences; \{m,\} matches at least m occurrences; \{m,n\} matches any number of occurrences between m and n inclusive. Whenever a choice exists, the regular expression matches as many occurrences as possible.

2.4 The concatenation of regular expressions is an regular expression that matches the concatenation of the strings matched by each component of the regular expression.

2.5 A regular expression enclosed between the character sequences \(and \) is an regular expression that matches whatever the unadorned regular expression matches.

2.6 The expression \$n$ matches the same string of characters as was matched by an expression enclosed between \(and \) earlier in the same regular expression. Here n is a digit; the sub-expression specified is that beginning with the n-th occurrence of \(counting from the left. For example, the expression **^\(.*\)\1$** matches a line consisting of two repeated appearances of the same string.

A regular expression may be constrained to match words.

3.1 **\<** constrains a regular expression to match the beginning of a string or to follow a character that is not a digit, underscore, or letter. The first character matching the regular expression must be a digit, underscore, or letter.

3.2 **\>** constrains a regular expression to match the end of a string or to precede a character that is not a digit, underscore, or letter.

A regular expression may be constrained to match only an initial segment or final segment of a line (or both).

4.1 A circumflex (^) at the beginning of a regular expression constrains that regular expression to match an initial segment of a line.

4.2 A dollar sign (**$**) at the end of an entire regular expression constrains that regular expression to match a final segment of a line.

4.3 The construction ^*regular expression* **$** constrains the regular expression to match the entire line.

The null regular expression (for example, //) is equivalent to the last regular expression encountered. See also the last paragraph of the DESCRIPTION section below.

To understand addressing in **ed** it is necessary to know that at any time there is a *current line*. Generally speaking, the current line is the last line affected by a command; the exact effect on the current line is discussed under the description of each command. *Addresses* are constructed as follows:

1. The character **.** addresses the current line.
2. The character **$** addresses the last line of the buffer.
3. A decimal number *n* addresses the *n*-th line of the buffer.
4. '*x* addresses the line marked with the mark name character *x*, which must be a lower-case letter (**a**–**z**). Lines are marked with the **k** command described below.
5. A regular expression enclosed by slashes (/) addresses the first line found by searching forward from the line following the current line toward the end of the buffer and stopping at the first line containing a string matching the regular expression. If necessary, the search wraps around to the beginning of the buffer and continues up to and including the current line, so that the entire buffer is searched. See also the last paragraph of the DESCRIPTION section below.
6. A regular expression enclosed in question marks (?) addresses the first line found by searching backward from the line preceding the current line toward the beginning of the buffer and stopping at the first line containing a string matching the regular expression. If necessary, the search wraps around to the end of the buffer and continues up to and including the current line. See also the last paragraph of the DESCRIPTION section below.
7. An address followed by a plus sign (+) or a minus sign (–) followed by a decimal number specifies that address plus (respectively minus) the indicated number of lines. A shorthand for .+5 is .5.
8. If an address begins with + or -, the addition or subtraction is taken with respect to the current line; for example, -5 is understood to mean .-5.
9. If an address ends with + or -, then 1 is added to or subtracted from the address, respectively. As a consequence of this rule and of Rule 8, immediately above, the address - refers to the line preceding the current line. (To maintain compatibility with earlier versions of the editor, the character ^ in addresses is entirely equivalent to –.) Moreover, trailing + and - characters have a cumulative effect, so -- refers to the current line less 2.

10. For convenience, a comma (,) stands for the address pair 1,$, while a semicolon (;) stands for the pair .,$.

Commands may require zero, one, or two addresses. Commands that require no addresses regard the presence of an address as an error. Commands that accept one or two addresses assume default addresses when an insufficient number of addresses is given; if more addresses are given than such a command requires, the last one(s) are used.

Typically, addresses are separated from each other by a comma (,). They may also be separated by a semicolon (;). In the latter case, the first address is calculated, the current line (.) is set to that value, and then the second address is calculated. This feature can be used to determine the starting line for forward and backward searches (see Rules 5 and 6, above). The second address of any two-address sequence must correspond to a line in the buffer that follows the line corresponding to the first address.

In the following list of **ed** commands, the parentheses shown prior to the command are not part of the address; rather they show the default address(es) for the command.

It is generally illegal for more than one command to appear on a line. However, any command (except **e**, **f**, **r**, or **w**) may be suffixed by **l**, **n**, or **p** in which case the current line is either listed, numbered or printed, respectively, as discussed below under the **l**, **n**, and **p** commands.

(.)a
<text>
. The **a**ppend command accepts zero or more lines of text and appends it after the addressed line in the buffer. The current line (.) is left at the last inserted line, or, if there were none, at the addressed line. Address 0 is legal for this command: it causes the "appended" text to be placed at the beginning of the buffer. The maximum number of bytes that may be entered from a terminal is 256 per line.

(.)c
<text>
. The **c**hange command deletes the addressed lines from the buffer, then accepts zero or more lines of text that replaces these lines in the buffer. The current line (.) is left at the last line input, or, if there were none, at the first line that was not deleted.

C Same as the **X** command, described later, except that **ed** assumes all text read in for the **e** and **r** commands is encrypted unless a null key is typed in.

(.,.)d
The **d**elete command deletes the addressed lines from the buffer. The line after the last line deleted becomes the current line; if the lines deleted were originally at the end of the buffer, the new last line becomes the current line.

e *file* The **e**dit command deletes the entire contents of the buffer and then reads the contents of *file* into the buffer. The current line (.) is set to the last line of the buffer. If *file* is not given, the currently remembered file name, if any, is used (see the **f** command). The number of characters read in is printed; *file* is remembered for possible use as a default file name in subsequent **e**, **r**, and

w commands. If *file* is replaced by **!**, the rest of the line is taken to be a shell [**sh**(1)] command whose output is to be read in. Such a shell command is not remembered as the current file name. See also DIAGNOSTICS below.

E *file* The **E**dit command is like **e**, except that the editor does not check to see if any changes have been made to the buffer since the last **w** command.

f *file* If *file* is given, the **f**ile-name command changes the currently remembered file name to *file*; otherwise, it prints the currently remembered file name.

(1,$)g/*regular expression***/***command list*
In the **g**lobal command, the first step is to mark every line that matches the given regular expression. Then, for every such line, the given *command list* is executed with the current line (**.**) initially set to that line. A single command or the first of a list of commands appears on the same line as the global command. All lines of a multi-line list except the last line must be ended with a \; **a**, **i**, and **c** commands and associated input are permitted. The **.** terminating input mode may be omitted if it would be the last line of the *command list*. An empty *command list* is equivalent to the **p** command. The **g**, **G**, **v**, and **V** commands are not permitted in the *command list*. See also the NOTES section and the last paragraph of the DESCRIPTION section below.

(1,$)G/*regular expression***/**
In the interactive **G**lobal command, the first step is to mark every line that matches the given regular expression. Then, for every such line, that line is printed, the current line (**.**) is changed to that line, and any one command (other than one of the **a**, **c**, **i**, **g**, **G**, **v**, and **V** commands) may be input and is executed. After the execution of that command, the next marked line is printed, and so on; a new-line acts as a null command; an **&** causes the re-execution of the most recent command executed within the current invocation of **G**. Note that the commands input as part of the execution of the **G** command may address and affect any lines in the buffer. The **G** command can be terminated by an interrupt signal (ASCII DEL or BREAK).

h The **h**elp command gives a short error message that explains the reason for the most recent **?** diagnostic.

H The **H**elp command causes **ed** to enter a mode in which error messages are printed for all subsequent **?** diagnostics. It will also explain the previous **?** if there was one. The **H** command alternately turns this mode on and off; it is initially off.

(.)i
<text>
. The **i**nsert command accepts zero or more lines of text and inserts it before the addressed line in the buffer. The current line (**.**) is left at the last inserted line, or, if there were none, at the addressed line. This command differs from the **a** command only in the placement of the input text. Address 0 is not legal for this command. The maximum number of characters that may be entered from a terminal is 256 per line.

`(.,.+1)j`
: The `join` command joins contiguous lines by removing the appropriate new-line characters. If exactly one address is given, this command does nothing.

`(.)k`*x*
: The **mark** command marks the addressed line with name *x*, which must be a lower-case letter (**a**–**z**). The address '*x* then addresses this line; the current line (**.**) is unchanged.

`(.,.)l`
: The `list` command prints the addressed lines in an unambiguous way: a few non-printing characters (for example, tab, backspace) are represented by visually mnemonic overstrikes. All other non-printing characters are printed in octal, and long lines are folded. An `l` command may be appended to any command other than **e**, **f**, **r**, or **w**.

`(.,.)m`*a*
: The **move** command repositions the addressed line(s) after the line addressed by *a*. Address **0** is legal for *a* and causes the addressed line(s) to be moved to the beginning of the file. It is an error if address *a* falls within the range of moved lines; the current line (**.**) is left at the last line moved.

`(.,.)n`
: The **number** command prints the addressed lines, preceding each line by its line number and a tab character; the current line (**.**) is left at the last line printed. The **n** command may be appended to any command other than **e**, **f**, **r**, or **w**.

`(.,.)p`
: The **print** command prints the addressed lines; the current line (**.**) is left at the last line printed. The **p** command may be appended to any command other than **e**, **f**, **r**, or **w**. For example, **dp** deletes the current line and prints the new current line.

`P`
: The editor will prompt with a * for all subsequent commands. The **P** command alternately turns this mode on and off; it is initially off.

`q`
: The **quit** command causes **ed** to exit. No automatic write of a file is done; however, see DIAGNOSTICS below.

`Q`
: The editor exits without checking if changes have been made in the buffer since the last **w** command.

`($)r` *file*
: The **read** command reads the contents of *file* into the buffer. If *file* is not given, the currently remembered file name, if any, is used (see the **e** and **f** commands). The currently remembered file name is not changed unless *file* is the very first file name mentioned since **ed** was invoked. Address 0 is legal for **r** and causes the file to be read in at the beginning of the buffer. If the read is successful, the number of characters read in is printed; the current line (**.**) is set to the last line read in. If *file* is replaced by **!**, the rest of the line is taken to be a shell [see **sh**(1)] command whose output is to be read in.

For example, `$r !ls` appends current directory to the end of the file being edited. Such a shell command is not remembered as the current file name.

`(.,.)s/`*regular expression*`/`*replacement*`/` or
`(.,.)s/`*regular expression*`/`*replacement*`/g` or
`(.,.)s/`*regular expression*`/`*replacement*`/`*n* n = 1-512

The **s**ubstitute command searches each addressed line for an occurrence of the specified regular expression. In each line in which a match is found, all (non-overlapped) matched strings are replaced by the *replacement* if the global replacement indicator `g` appears after the command. If the global indicator does not appear, only the first occurrence of the matched string is replaced. If a number *n*, appears after the command, only the *n*-th occurrence of the matched string on each addressed line is replaced. It is an error if the substitution fails on all addressed lines. Any character other than space or new-line may be used instead of `/` to delimit the regular expression and the *replacement*; the current line (`.`) is left at the last line on which a substitution occurred. See also the last paragraph of the DESCRIPTION section below.

An ampersand (`&`) appearing in the *replacement* is replaced by the string matching the regular expression on the current line. The special meaning of `&` in this context may be suppressed by preceding it by `\`. As a more general feature, the characters `\`*n*, where *n* is a digit, are replaced by the text matched by the *n*-th regular subexpression of the specified regular expression enclosed between `\(` and `\)`. When nested parenthesized subexpressions are present, *n* is determined by counting occurrences of `\(` starting from the left. When the character `%` is the only character in the *replacement*, the *replacement* used in the most recent substitute command is used as the *replacement* in the current substitute command. The `%` loses its special meaning when it is in a replacement string of more than one character or is preceded by a `\`.

A line may be split by substituting a new-line character into it. The new-line in the *replacement* must be escaped by preceding it by `\`. Such substitution cannot be done as part of a `g` or `v` command list.

`(.,.)t`*a*

This command acts just like the `m` command, except that a copy of the addressed lines is placed after address `a` (which may be 0); the current line (`.`) is left at the last line copied.

`u` The **u**ndo command nullifies the effect of the most recent command that modified anything in the buffer, namely the most recent `a`, `c`, `d`, `g`, `i`, `j`, `m`, `r`, `s`, `t`, `v`, `G`, or `V` command.

`(1,$)v/`*regular expression*`/`*command list*

This command is the same as the global command `g`, except that the lines marked during the first step are those that do not match the regular expression.

`(1,$)V/`*regular expression*`/`

This command is the same as the interactive global command `G`, except that the lines that are marked during the first step are those that do not match the regular expression.

(1,$)w*file*
The write command writes the addressed lines into *file*. If *file* does not exist, it is created with mode **666** (readable and writable by everyone), unless your file creation mask dictates otherwise; see the description of the **umask** special command on **sh**(1). The currently remembered file name is not changed unless *file* is the very first file name mentioned since **ed** was invoked. If no file name is given, the currently remembered file name, if any, is used (see the **e** and **f** commands); the current line (.) is unchanged. If the command is successful, the number of characters written is printed. If *file* is replaced by **!**, the rest of the line is taken to be a shell [see **sh**(1)] command whose standard input is the addressed lines. Such a shell command is not remembered as the current file name.

(1,$)W*file*
This command is the same as the write command above, except that it appends the addressed lines to the end of *file* if it exists. If *file* does not exist, it is created as described above for the **w** command.

X
A key is prompted for, and it is used in subsequent **e**, **r**, and **w** commands to decrypt and encrypt text using the **crypt**(1) algorithm. An educated guess is made to determine whether text read in for the **e** and **r** commands is encrypted. A null key turns off encryption. Subsequent **e**, **r**, and **w** commands will use this key to encrypt or decrypt the text [see **crypt**(1)]. An explicitly empty key turns off encryption. Also, see the **-x** option of **ed**.

($)=
The line number of the addressed line is typed; the current line (.) is unchanged by this command.

!*shell command*
The remainder of the line after the **!** is sent to the UNIX system shell [see **sh**(1)] to be interpreted as a command. Within the text of that command, the unescaped character **%** is replaced with the remembered file name; if a **!** appears as the first character of the shell command, it is replaced with the text of the previous shell command. Thus, **!!** will repeat the last shell command. If any expansion is performed, the expanded line is echoed; the current line (.) is unchanged.

(.+1)<new-line>
An address alone on a line causes the addressed line to be printed. A new-line alone is equivalent to **.+1p**; it is useful for stepping forward through the buffer.

If an interrupt signal (ASCII DEL or BREAK) is sent, **ed** prints a **?** and returns to its command level.

Some size limitations: 512 bytes in a line, 256 bytes in a global command list and in the pathname of a file (counting slashes). The limit on the number of lines depends on the amount of user memory: each line takes 1 word.

When reading a file, **ed** discards ASCII NUL characters.

If a file is not terminated by a new-line character, **ed** adds one and puts out a message explaining what it did.

If the closing delimiter of a regular expression or of a replacement string (for example, /) would be the last character before a new-line, that delimiter may be omitted, in which case the addressed line is printed. The following pairs of commands are equivalent:

```
s/s1/s2        s/s1/s2/p
g/s1           g/s1/p
?s1            ?s1?
```

FILES

$TMPDIR if this environmental variable is not null, its value is used in place of **/var/tmp** as the directory name for the temporary work file.

/var/tmp if **/var/tmp** exists, it is used as the directory name for the temporary work file.

/tmp if the environmental variable **TMPDIR** does not exist or is null, and if **/var/tmp** does not exist, then **/tmp** is used as the directory name for the temporary work file.

ed.hup work is saved here if the terminal is hung up.

/usr/lib/locale/*locale*/LC_MESSAGES/uxcore.abi
language-specific message file [See **LANG** on **environ** (5).]

SEE ALSO

edit(1), **ex**(1), **fspec**(4), **grep**(1), **regexp**(5), **sed**(1), **sh**(1), **stty**(1), **umask**(1), **vi**(1)

DIAGNOSTICS

? for command errors.

?*file* for an inaccessible file.
(use the **help** and **Help** commands for detailed explanations).

If changes have been made in the buffer since the last **w** command that wrote the entire buffer, **ed** warns the user if an attempt is made to destroy **ed**'s buffer via the **e** or **q** commands. It prints **?** and allows one to continue editing. A second **e** or **q** command at this point will take effect. The **-s** command-line option inhibits this feature.

NOTES

The **-** option, although it continues to be supported, has been replaced in the documentation by the **-s** option that follows the Command Syntax Standard [see **intro**(1)].

The encryption options and commands are provided with the Encryption Utilities package, which is available only in the United States.

A **!** command cannot be subject to a **g** or a **v** command.

The **!** command and the **!** escape from the **e**, **r**, and **w** commands cannot be used if the editor is invoked from a restricted shell [see **sh**(1)].

The sequence **\n** in a regular expression does not match a new-line character.

If the editor input is coming from a command file (for example, **ed** *file* < *ed_cmd_file*), the editor exits at the first failure.

NAME

edit – text editor (variant of ex for casual users)

SYNOPSIS

edit [**-r**] [**-x**] [**-C**] *name* . . .

DESCRIPTION

edit is a variant of the text editor **ex** recommended for new or casual users who want to use a command-oriented editor. It operates precisely as **ex** with the following options automatically set:

novice	**ON**
report	**1**
showmode	**ON**
magic	**OFF**

These options can be turned on or off via the **set** command in **ex**(1).

-r Recover file after an editor or system crash.

-x Encryption option; when used the file will be encrypted as it is being written and will require an encryption key to be read. **edit** makes an educated guess to determine if a file is encrypted or not. See **crypt**(1). Also, see the NOTES section at the end of this manual page.

-C Encryption option; the same as **-x** except that **edit** assumes files are encrypted.

edit processes supplementary code set characters according to the locale specified in the **LC_CTYPE** environment variable [see **LANG** on **environ**(5)].

The following brief introduction should help you get started with **edit**. If you are using a CRT terminal you may want to learn about the display editor **vi**.

To edit the contents of an existing file you begin with the command: **edit** *name* to the shell. **edit** makes a copy of the file that you can then edit, and tells you how many lines and bytes are in the file. To create a new file, you also begin with the command **edit** with a filename: **edit** *name;* the editor will tell you it is a **[New File]**.

The **edit** command prompt is the colon (**:**), which you should see after starting the editor. If you are editing an existing file, then you will have some lines in **edit**'s buffer (its name for the copy of the file you are editing). When you start editing, **edit** makes the last line of the file the current line. Most commands to **edit** use the current line if you do not tell them which line to use. Thus if you say **print** (which can be abbreviated **p**) and press RETURN (as you should after all **edit** commands), the current line will be printed. If you **delete** (**d**) the current line, **edit** will print the new current line, which is usually the next line in the file. If you **delete** the last line, then the new last line becomes the current one.

If you start with an empty file or want to add some new lines, then the **append** (**a**) command can be used. After you enter **append** or **a**, press RETURN. **edit** will read lines from your terminal until you type a line consisting of just a dot (**.**) and it will place these lines after the current line. The last line you type then becomes the current line. The **insert** (**i**) command is like **append**, but places the lines you type before, rather than after, the current line.

edit numbers the lines in the buffer, with the first line having number 1. If you execute the command **1**, then **edit** will type the first line of the buffer. If you then execute the command **d**, **edit** will delete the first line, line 2 will become line 1, and **edit** will print the current line (the new line 1) so you can see where you are. In general, the current line will always be the last line affected by a command.

You can make a change to some text within the current line by using the **substitute** (**s**) command: **s**/*old*/*new*/ where *old* is the string of characters you want to replace and *new* is the string of characters you want to replace *old* with.

The **file** (**f**) command will tell you how many lines there are in the buffer you are editing and will say **[Modified]** if you have changed the buffer. After modifying a file, you can save the contents of the file by executing a **write** (**w**) command. You can leave the editor by issuing a **quit** (**q**) command. If you run **edit** on a file, but do not change it, it is not necessary (but does no harm) to **write** the file back. If you try to **quit** from **edit** after modifying the buffer without writing it out, you will receive the message **No write since last change (:quit! overrides)**, and **edit** will wait for another command. If you do not want to write the buffer out, issue the **quit** command followed by an exclamation point (**q!**). The buffer is then irretrievably discarded and you return to the shell.

By using the **d** and **a** commands and giving line numbers to see lines in the file, you can make any changes you want. You should learn at least a few more things, however, if you will use **edit** more than a few times.

The **change** (**c**) command changes the current line to a sequence of lines you supply (as in **append**, you type lines up to a line consisting of only a dot (**.**). You can tell **change** to change more than one line by giving the line numbers of the lines you want to change, that is, **3,5c**. You can print lines this way too: **1,23p** prints the first 23 lines of the file.

The **undo** (**u**) command reverses the effect of the last command you executed that changed the buffer. Thus if you execute a **substitute** command that does not do what you want, type **u** and the old contents of the line will be restored. You can also **undo** an **undo** command. **edit** will give you a warning message when a command affects more than one line of the buffer. Note that commands such as **write** and **quit** cannot be undone.

To look at the next line in the buffer, press RETURN. To look at a number of lines, type **^D** (while holding down the control key, press **d**) rather than RETURN. This will show you a half-screen of lines on a CRT or 12 lines on a hardcopy terminal. You can look at nearby text by executing the **z** command. The current line will appear in the middle of the text displayed, and the last line displayed will become the current line; you can get back to the line where you were before you executed the **z** command by typing ´´. The **z** command has other options: **z-** prints a screen of text (or 24 lines) ending where you are; **z+** prints the next screenful. If you want less than a screenful of lines, type **z.11** to display five lines before and five lines after the current line. (Typing **z.***n*, when *n* is an odd number, displays a total of *n* lines, centered about the current line; when *n* is an even number, it displays *n*–1 lines, so that the lines displayed are centered around the current line.) You can give counts after other commands; for example, you can delete 5 lines starting with the current line with the command **d5 .**

To find things in the file, you can use line numbers if you happen to know them; since the line numbers change when you insert and delete lines this is somewhat unreliable. You can search backwards and forwards in the file for strings by giving commands of the form /*text*/ to search forward for *text* or ?*text*? to search backward for *text* . If a search reaches the end of the file without finding *text*, it wraps around and continues to search back to the line where you are. A useful feature here is a search of the form /^*text*/ which searches for *text* at the beginning of a line. Similarly /*text*$/ searches for *text* at the end of a line. You can leave off the trailing / or **?** in these commands.

The current line has the symbolic name dot (**.**); this is most useful in a range of lines as in **.,$p** which prints the current line plus the rest of the lines in the file. To move to the last line in the file, you can refer to it by its symbolic name $. Thus the command **$d** deletes the last line in the file, no matter what the current line is. Arithmetic with line references is also possible. Thus the line **$-5** is the fifth before the last and **.+20** is 20 lines after the current line.

You can find out the current line by typing **.=**. This is useful if you want to move or copy a section of text within a file or between files. Find the first and last line numbers you want to copy or move. To move lines 10 through 20, type **10,20d a** to delete these lines from the file and place them in a buffer named **a**. **edit** has 26 such buffers named **a** through **z**. To put the contents of buffer **a** after the current line, type **put a**. If you want to move or copy these lines to another file, execute an **edit** (**e**) command after copying the lines; following the **e** command with the name of the other file you want to edit, that is, **edit chapter2**. To copy lines without deleting them, use **yank** (**y**) in place of **d**. If the text you want to move or copy is all within one file, it is not necessary to use named buffers. For example, to move lines 10 through 20 to the end of the file, type **10,20m $**.

FILES

/usr/lib/locale/*locale***/LC_MESSAGES/uxed.abi**
language-specific message file [See **LANG** on **environ**(5).]

SEE ALSO

ed(1), **ex**(1), **vi**(1)

NOTES

The encryption options are provided with the Encryption Utilities package, which is available only in the United States.

NAME

edquota – edit user quotas for **ufs** file system

SYNOPSIS

edquota [**-p** *proto_user*] *username* . . .

edquota -t

DESCRIPTION

edquota is a quota editor. One or more users may be specified on the command line. For each user a temporary file is created with an ASCII representation of the current disk quotas for that user for each mounted ufs file system that has a **quotas** file, and an editor is then invoked on the file. The quotas may then be modified, new quotas added, and so on. Upon leaving the editor, **edquota** reads the temporary file and modifies the binary quota files to reflect the changes made.

The editor invoked is **vi**(1) unless the **EDITOR** environment variable specifies otherwise.

Only a privileged user may edit quotas.

In order for quotas to be established on a file system, the root directory of the file system must contain a file, owned by root, called **quotas**. See **quotaon**(1M) for details.

proto_user and **username** can be numeric, corresponding to the uid of a user. Unassigned uids may be specified; unassigned names may not. In this way, default quotas can be established for users who are later assigned a uid.

The options are:

-p Duplicate the quotas of the *proto_user* specified for each *username* specified. This is the normal mechanism used to initialize quotas for groups of users.

-t Edit the soft time limits for each file system. If the time limits are zero, the default time limits in **/usr/include/sys/fs/ufs_quota.h** are used. Time units of sec(onds), min(utes), hour(s), day(s), week(s), and month(s) are understood. Time limits are printed in the greatest possible time unit such that the value is greater than or equal to one.

FILES

quotas	quota file at the file system root
/etc/mnttab	table of mounted file systems

SEE ALSO

quota(1M), **quotacheck**(1M), **quotaon**(1M), **repquota**(1M), **vi**(1)

edsysadm (1M)

NAME

edsysadm – **sysadm** interface editing tool

SYNOPSIS

edsysadm

DESCRIPTION

edsysadm is an interactive tool that adds or changes either menu or task definitions in the **sysadm** interface. It can be used to make changes directly on-line on a specific machine or to create changes that will become part of a software package. The command creates the administration files necessary to achieve the requested changes in the interface and either places them in the appropriate place for on-line changes or saves them to be included in a software package.

edsysadm presents several screens, prompting first for which type of menu item you want to change (a **menu** or a **task**) and then for what type of action to take (**add** or **change**). When you select **add**, a blank menu or task definition (as described below) is provided for you to fill in. When you select **change**, a series of screens is presented to help identify the definition you want to change. The final screen presented is the menu or task definition filled in with its current values, which you can then edit.

The menu definition prompts are the following:

Menu Name — The name of the new menu (as it should appear in the left-hand column of the screen). This field has a maximum length of 16 alphanumeric characters.

Menu Description — A description of the new menu (as it should appear in the right-hand column of the screen). This field has a maximum length of 58 characters and can consist of any alphanumeric character except at sign (@), carat (^), tilde (~), back grave (‘), grave (’), and double quotes (").

Menu Location — The location of the menu in the menu hierarchy, expressed as a menu pathname. The pathname should begin with the main menu followed by all other menus that must be traversed (in the order they are traversed) to access this menu. Each menu name must be separated by colons. For example, the menu location for a menu entry being added to the Applications menu is **main:applmgmt**. Do not include the menu name in this location definition. The complete pathname to this menu entry will be the menu location plus the menu name defined at the first prompt.

This is a scrollable field, showing a maximum of 50 alphanumeric characters at a time.

Menu Help File Name Pathname to the item help file for this menu entry. If it resides in the directory from which you invoked **edsysadm**, you do not need to give a full pathname. If you name an item help file that does not exist, you are placed in an editor (as defined by **EDITOR**) so you can create one. The new file is created in the current directory and is named **Help**.

The task definition prompts are the following: **Task Name** The name of the new task (as it should appear in the left-hand column of the screen). This field has a maximum length of 16 alphanumeric characters.

Task Description A description of the new task (as it should appear in the right-hand column of the screen). This field has a maximum length of 58 characters and can consist of any alphanumeric character except at sign (@), carat (^), tilde (~), back grave (‘), grave (’), and double quotes (").

Task Location The location of the task in the menu hierarchy, expressed as a pathname. The pathname should begin with the main menu followed by all other menus that must be traversed (in the order they are traversed) to access this task. Each menu name must be separated by colons. For example, the task location for a task entry being added to the applications menu is **main:applmgmt**. Do not include the task name in this location definition. The complete pathname to this task entry will be the task location as well as the task name defined at the first prompt.

This is a scrollable field, showing a maximum of 50 alphanumeric characters at a time.

Task Help File Name Pathname to the item help file for this task entry. If it resides in the directory from which you invoked **edsysadm**, you do not need to give a full pathname. If you name an item help file that does not exist, you are placed in an editor (as defined by **EDITOR**) to create one. The new file is created in the current directory and named **Help**.

Task Action The FACE form name or executable that will be run when this task is selected. This is a scrollable field, showing a maximum of 58 alphanumeric characters at a time. This pathname can be relative to the current directory as well as absolute.

Task Files Any FACE objects or other executables that support the task action listed above and might be called from within that action. Do not include the help file name or the task action in this list. Pathnames can be relative to the current directory as well as absolute. A dot (.) implies "all files in the current directory" and includes files in subdirectories.

This is a scrollable field, showing a maximum of 50 alphanumeric characters at a time.

Once the menu or task has been defined, screens for installing the menu or task or saving them for packaging are presented. The package creation or on-line installation is verified and you are informed on completion.

NOTES

If the test option is selected, **edsysadm** places a copy of the menu or task structure into the directory defined by the **TESTBASE** environment variable in **edsysadm.sh** (default is **/var/tmp**). When it begins processing, **edsysadm** determines if there is enough disk space (at least 500 blocks) available in the directory. If there is not enough disk space, you can override the default by substituting a directory of your choice for the **TESTBASE** environment variable.

For package creation or modification, this command automatically creates a menu information file and a **prototype** file in the current directory (the directory from which the command is executed). The menu information file is used during package installation to modify menus in the menu structure. A **prototype** file is an installation file [in the format described on **prototype**(4)] that gives a listing of package contents. The **prototype** file created by **edsysadm** lists the files defined under task action and gives them the special installation class of **admin**. The contents of this **prototype** file must be incorporated in the package **prototype** file.

For on-line installation, **edsysadm** automatically creates a menu information file and adds or modifies the interface menu directly. When you request installation of your new menu (or changes to an existing one), **edsysadm** will respond in one of three ways: (a) it will install the menu (or changes) and display a message verifying this; (b) it will not install the menu (or changes) and display a message explaining why installation failed; or (c) it will display a message explaining that there's a conflict between the name you've chosen for this menu and an existing menu.

In the latter case, you'll be prompted to choose from four possible actions: (a) **install** (the menu or changes will be installed despite the collision between the names); (b) **rename** (the menu form will be displayed so you can change the name of the entry); (c) **relocate** (the menu form will be displayed so you can change the location of the entry); and (d) **do not install** (the default action, which you can select by pressing SAVE).

The item help file must follow the format shown in the *Advanced Administration* appendix about customizing the **sysadm** interface.

SEE ALSO

delsysadm(1M), **pkgmk**(1), **prototype**(4), **sysadm**(1M)

NAME

`edvtoc` – VTOC (Volume Table of Contents) editing utility

SYNOPSIS

`edvtoc -f` *vtoc-file raw-device*

DESCRIPTION

The **edvtoc** command allows you to edit the contents of the VTOC (Volume Table Of Contents).

Options and Arguments

`-f` *vtoc-file*

Specifies the path location of the updated (condensed format) VTOC file to be written to disk. The format of the file is slice number, slice tag value, slice flag value, slice start sector, slice size (in sectors). A copy of this file can be obtained for modification by using the **-f** option of the **prtvtoc** command.

raw-device

raw-device is the character special device for the disk drive to be accessed. It must be the slice 0 device to represent the entire device (for example, **/dev/rdsk/c0t0d0s0**).

Files

/dev/rdsk/c?t?d?s0

USAGE

The required procedure for editing the VTOC includes four steps. First, run **prtvtoc**(1M) using the **-f** option. Second, edit the file created by **prtvtoc** to reflect the needed changes to the VTOC. Third, run **edvtoc** using the edited file. Lastly, reboot the system, so the disk driver can read the new VTOC; the changes to the VTOC will not take place until you perform the reboot.

`edvtoc` provides four functions; reading/interpreting the *vtoc-file*, limited validity checking of the new VTOC, displaying the new VTOC, and writing the VTOC to the disk if the user requests it.

When editing the VTOC, the following entries are the valid slice tags and slice permission flags.

Slice Tags

```
#define V_BOOT     0x01    /* Boot slice */
#define V_ROOT     0x02    /* Root filesystem */
#define V_SWAP     0x03    /* Swap filesystem */
#define V_USR      0x04    /* Usr filesystem */
#define V_BACKUP   0x05    /* full disk */
#define V_ALTS     0x06    /* alternate sector space */
#define V_OTHER    0x07    /* non-unix space */
#define V_ALTTRK   0x08    /* alternate track space */
#define V_STAND    0x09    /* Stand slice */
#define V_VAR      0x0a    /* Var slice */
#define V_HOME     0x0b    /* Home slice */
#define V_DUMP     0x0c    /* dump slice */
```

Slice Permission Flags

```
#define V_UNMNT     0x01     /* Unmountable partition */
#define V_RONLY     0x10     /* Read only */
#define V_VALID     0x200    /* Partition is valid to use */
```

The start and size value are in absolute sector numbers where the first sector on the drive is 0 (which is reserved for the partition table). Slices should start and end on a cylinder boundary if possible. The head, cylinder and sectors/track information provided by **prtvtoc -p** assists in the calculations. Slices should not overlap (slice 0 is the exception, it describes the entire UNIX partition).

REFERENCES

prtvtoc(1M), **sd01**(7)

NAME

egrep – search a file for a pattern using full regular expressions

SYNOPSIS

egrep [*options*] *full_regular_expression* [*strings*] [*file* . . .]

DESCRIPTION

egrep (expression **grep**) searches files for a pattern of characters and prints all lines that contain that pattern. **egrep** uses full regular expressions (expressions that have string values that use the full set of alphanumeric and special characters) to match the patterns. It uses a fast deterministic algorithm that sometimes needs exponential space.

egrep processes supplementary code set characters according to the locale specified in the **LC_CTYPE** environment variable [see **LANG** on **environ**(5)], except as noted under the **-i** option below. In regular expressions, pattern searches are performed on characters, not bytes, as described on **ed**(1).

egrep accepts the same full regular expressions accepted by **ed**, with six exceptions:

```
\(   \<   \{m
\)   \>   n\}
```

(The regular expressions `\(` and `\)` should not be confused with parentheses used for grouping.) In addition, **egrep** accepts the following expressions:

1. A full regular expression followed by **+** that matches one or more occurrences of the full regular expression.
2. A full regular expression followed by **?** that matches 0 or 1 occurrences of the full regular expression.
3. Full regular expressions separated by | or by a newline that match strings that are matched by any of the expressions.
4. A full regular expression that may be enclosed in parentheses `()` for grouping.

Be careful using the characters **$**, *, **[**, ^, |, (,), and \ in *full_regular_expression*, because they are also meaningful to the shell. It is safest to enclose the entire *full_regular_expression* in single quotes ′ . . . ′.

The order of precedence of operators is **[ ]**, then * **? +**, then concatenation, then | and newline.

If no files are specified, **egrep** assumes standard input. Normally, each line found is copied to the standard output. The file name is printed before each line found if there is more than one input file.

Command line options are:

-b Precede each line by the block number on which it was found. This can be useful in locating block numbers by context (first block is 0).

-c Print only a count of the lines that contain the pattern.

-i Ignore uppercase/lowercase distinction during comparisons; valid for single-byte characters only.

-h Suppress printing of filenames when searching multiple files.

-l Print the names of files with matching lines once, separated by newlines. Does not repeat the names of files when the pattern is found more than once.

-n Precede each line by its line number in the file (first line is 1).

-v Print all lines except those that contain the pattern.

-e *special_expression*
Search for a *special_expression* (*full_regular_expression* that begins with a **-**).

-f *file*
Take the list of *full_regular_expressions* from *file*.

FILES

/usr/lib/locale/*locale***/LC_MESSAGES/uxcore**
language-specific message file [See **LANG** on **environ**(5).]

SEE ALSO

ed(1), **fgrep**(1), **grep**(1), **sed**(1), **sh**(1)

DIAGNOSTICS

Exit status is 0 if any matches are found, 1 if none, 2 for syntax errors or inaccessible files (even if matches were found).

NOTES

Ideally there should be only one **grep** command, but there is not a single algorithm that spans a wide enough range of space-time tradeoffs. Lines are limited to **BUFSIZ** bytes; longer lines are truncated. **BUFSIZ** is defined in **/usr/include/stdio.h.**

NAME

enable, **disable** – enable/disable LP printers

SYNOPSIS

enable *printers*
disable [*options*] *printers*

DESCRIPTION

The **enable** command activates the named *printers*, enabling them to print requests submitted by the **lp** command. If the printer is remote, the command will only enable the transfer of requests to the remote system; the **enable** command must be run again, on the remote system, to activate the printer. (Run **lpstat -p** to get the status of printers.)

When changes are made to the attributes of a print device, they are recognized by **enable**. Therefore to change the definition or allocation for a device, you must disable the printer on that device, change the device, and then run **enable**. The new device attributes will become effective when **enable** is executed.

The **disable** command deactivates the named *printers*, disabling them from printing requests submitted by **lp**. By default, any requests that are currently printing on the designated printers will be reprinted in their entirety either on the same printer or on another member of the same class of printers. If the printer is remote, this command will only stop the transmission of jobs to the remote system. The **disable** command must be run on the remote system to disable the printer. (Run **lpstat -p** to get the status of printers.) **disable** recognizes supplementary code set characters in the *reason* given to the **-r** option (see below) according to the locale specified in the **LC_CTYPE** environment variable [see **LANG** on **environ**(5)].

-c Cancel any requests that are currently printing on any of the designated printers. This option cannot be used with the **-W** option. If the printer is remote, the **-c** option will be silently ignored.

-r *reason* Assign a *reason* for the disabling of the printers. This *reason* applies to all *printers* specified. This *reason* is reported by **lpstat -p**. *reason* may contain supplementary code set characters, and must be enclosed in quotes if it contains blanks. The default reason is **unknown reason** for existing printers, and **new printer** for printers just added to the system but not yet enabled.

-W Wait until the request currently being printed is finished before disabling the specified printer. This option cannot be used with the **-c** option. If the printer is remote, the **-W** option will be silently ignored.

FILES

/var/spool/lp/*
/usr/lib/locale/*locale***/LC_MESSAGES/uxlp**
language-specific message file [See **LANG** on **environ**(5).]

SEE ALSO

lp(1), **lpstat**(1)

NOTES

Printer names are *system-defined words* and as such should be restricted to uppercase and lowercase ASCII characters.

NAME

enable_glogin – enable the UNIX Desktop graphical login

SYNOPSIS

enable_glogin

DESCRIPTION

This command enables the UNIX Desktop graphical login by adding the file /etc/rc2.d/S69xdm to the /etc/rc2.d directory if the file does not exist. The file is then used by rc2 when bringing the system to a ready-to-use state, traditionally state 2, called the "multi-user" state [see rc2(1M)].

The file S69xdm checks for the existence of the X server and the xdm command and executes xdm if both are found.

SEE ALSO

disable_glogin(1M), rc2(1M), xdm(1M)

env(1)

NAME

env, **printenv** – set environment for command execution

SYNOPSIS

env [–] [*name=value*] . . . [*command args*]

DESCRIPTION

env obtains the current *environment*, modifies it according to its arguments, then executes the *command* with the modified environment. Arguments of the form *name*=*value* are merged into the inherited environment before the command is executed. The **-** flag causes the inherited environment to be ignored completely, so that the command is executed with exactly the environment specified by the arguments. If no command is specified, the resulting environment is printed, one name-value pair per line. **env** recognizes supplementary code set characters in *value, command,* and *args* according to the locale specified in the **LC_CTYPE** environment variable [see **LANG** on **environ**(5)].

If the Application Compatibility Package is installed, then **printenv** replaces **env**.

SEE ALSO

environ(5), **exec**(2), **profile**(4), **sh**(1)

NAME

eqn, **neqn**, **checkeq** – (BSD) typeset mathematics

SYNOPSIS

/usr/ucb/eqn [**-d***xy*] [**-f***n*] [**-p***n*] [**-s***n*] [*file*] . . .

/usr/ucb/neqn [*file*] . . .

/usr/ucb/checkeq [*file*] . . .

DESCRIPTION

The **eqn** and **neqn** commands are language processors to assist in describing equations. **eqn** is a preprocessor for **troff**(1) and is intended for devices that can print **troff**'s output. **neqn** is a preprocessor for **nroff**(1) and is intended for use with terminals.

checkeq reports missing or unbalanced delimiters and **.EQ/.EN** pairs.

If no *file*s are specified, **eqn** and **neqn** read from the standard input. A line beginning with **.EQ** marks the start of an equation; the end of an equation is marked by a line beginning with **.EN**. Neither of these lines is altered, so they may be defined in macro packages to get centering, numbering, and so on. It is also possible to set two characters as "delimiters"; subsequent text between delimiters is also treated as **eqn** input.

The following options are available for **eqn** and **neqn**:

-d*xy* Set equation delimiters set to characters *x* and *y* with the command-line argument. The more common way to do this is with **delim** *xy* between **.EQ** and **.EN**. The left and right delimiters may be identical. Delimiters are turned off by **delim off** appearing in the text. All text that is neither between delimiters nor between **.EQ** and **.EN** is passed through untouched.

-f*n* Change font to *n* globally in the document. The font can also be changed globally in the body of the document by using the **gfont** directive.

-p*n* Reduce subscripts and superscripts by *n* point sizes from the prevailing size. In the absence of the **-p** option, subscripts and superscripts are reduced by 3 point sizes from the prevailing size.

-s*n* Set equations in point size *n* globally in the document. The point size can also be changed globally in the body of the document by using the **gsize** directive.

-T*dev* Prepare output for device *dev*. If no **-T** option is present, **eqn** looks at the environment variable **TYPESETTER** to see what the intended output device is. If no such variable is found in the environment, a system-dependent default device is assumed. Not available using **neqn**.

USAGE

eqn Language

Tokens within **eqn** are separated by braces, double quotes, tildes, circumflexes, SPACE, TAB, or NEWLINE characters. Braces **{ }** are used for grouping; generally speaking, anywhere a single character like *x* could appear, a complicated construction enclosed in braces may be used instead. Tilde (~) represents a full SPACE in the output, circumflex (^) half as much.

Subscripts and superscripts are produced with the keywords **sub** and **sup**. Thus '**x sub i**' makes x_i, '**a sub i sup 2**' produces a_i^2, and '**e sup {x sup 2 + y sup 2}**' gives $e^{x^2+y^2}$.

Fractions are made with **over**: '**a over b**' yields $\frac{a}{b}$.

sqrt makes square roots: '**1 over down 10 sqrt {ax sup 2 +bx+c}**' results in

$$\frac{1}{\sqrt{ax^2+bx+c}}.$$

Although **eqn** tries to get most things at the right place on the paper, occasionally you will need to tune the output to make it just right. Local motions such as, **up** *n*, **down** *n*, **fwd** *n* and **back** *n* allow you to change the default spacing. In the previous example, a local motion, **down 10**, was used to get more space between the square root and the line above it.

The keywords **from** and **to** introduce lower and upper limits on arbitrary things: $\lim_{n \to \infty} \sum_0^n x_i$ is made with '**lim from {n-> inf} sum from 0 to n x sub i**'.

Left and right brackets, braces, and so on, of the right height are made using **left** and **right**: '**left [x sup 2 + y sup 2 over alpha right] ~=~1**' produces

$$\left[x^2 + \frac{y^2}{\alpha} \right] = 1.$$

The **right** clause is optional. Legal characters after **left** and **right** are braces, brackets, bars, **c** and **f** for ceiling and floor, and **""** for nothing at all (useful for a right-side-only bracket).

Vertical piles of things are made with **pile**, **lpile**, **cpile**, and **rpile**: '**pile {a above b above c}**' produces $\begin{matrix} a \\ b \\ c \end{matrix}$. There can be an arbitrary number of elements in a pile. **lpile** left-justifies, **pile** and **cpile** center, with different vertical spacing, and **rpile** right justifies.

Matrices are made with **matrix**: '**matrix { lcol { x sub i above y sub 2 } ccol { 1 above 2 } }**' produces $\begin{matrix} x_i & 1 \\ y_2 & 2 \end{matrix}$. In addition, there is **rcol** for a right-justified column.

Diacritical marks are made with **dot**, **dotdot**, **hat**, **tilde**, **bar**, **vec**, **dyad**, and **under**: '**x dot = f(t) bar**' is $\dot{x} = \overline{f(t)}$, '**y dotdot bar ~=~ n under**' is $\bar{\ddot{y}} = \underline{n}$, and '**x vec ~=~ y dyad**' is $\vec{x} = \overleftrightarrow{y}$.

Size and font can be changed with **size** *n* or **size** ±*n*, **roman**, **italic**, **bold**, and **font** *n*. Size and font can be changed globally in a document by **gsize** *n* and **gfont** *n*, or by the command-line arguments **-s***n* and **-f***n*.

Successive display arguments can be lined up. Place **mark** before the desired lineup point in the first equation; place **lineup** at the place that is to line up vertically in subsequent equations.

Shorthands may be defined or existing keywords redefined with **define**:

`define` *thing* `%` *replacement* `%`

defines a new token called *thing* which will be replaced by *replacement* whenever it appears thereafter. The `%` may be any character that does not occur in *replacement*.

Keywords like **sum** ($\sum$), **int** ($\int$), **inf** (∞), and shorthands like `>=` ($\geq$), `->` ($\rightarrow$), and `!=` ($\neq$) are recognized. Greek letters are spelled out in the desired case, as in **alpha** or **GAMMA**. Mathematical words like sin, cos, and log are made Roman automatically. **troff**(1) four-character escapes like \(bu (•) can be used anywhere. Strings enclosed in double quotes `"..."` are passed through untouched; this permits keywords to be entered as text, and can be used to communicate with **troff** when all else fails.

EXAMPLE

`eqn` *file . . .* | **troff**

`neqn` *file . . .* | **nroff**

SEE ALSO

eqnchar(5), **ms**(5), **tbl**(1), **troff**(1)

NOTES

To embolden digits, parens, and so on, it is necessary to quote them, as in **bold** `"12.3"`.

NAME

`evgainit` – Extended VGA keyboard/display driver initialization

SYNOPSIS

`evgainit` *card-type*

DESCRIPTION

`evgainit` is used to initialize the keyboard/display driver [see **keyboard**(7)] if extended VGA graphics modes are being used on certain video cards.

The keyboard/display driver provides the interface to the video card. `evgainit` informs the keyboard/display driver which video card is installed and should be rerun each time the system is booted.

In many cases the keyboard/display driver can determine which card is being used and therefore this command need not be run. For example, you don't need to run `evgainit` for the following cards:

Any card that doesn't have extended VGA capability (that is, 800x600 pixels).

Any card that is only VGA (640x480 pixels) or EGA (640x350 pixels).

Any extended VGA cards (listed below) that will not be set to graphics modes with resolutions greater than 640x480 pixels.

`evgainit` must be run, however, for the following cards before attempting to use resolutions greater than 640x480 pixels. The following list shows the *card-type* argument value that should be used for each video card:

card-type	Video Card(s)
`vega`	Video 7 800x600, Video 7 VEGA VGA Adaptor
`stbga`	STB VGA Extra/EM, Extra/EM-16
`sigma/h`	SIGMA VGA/H
`pvga1a`	Paradise PVGA1A
`dell`	Dell VGA
`vram`	Video 7 VRAM VGA
`orvga`	Orchid Designer VGA, Designer 800 VGA, ProDesigner VGA
`orvgani`	Orchid Designer, ProDesigner VGA (non-interlaced)
`tvga`	Tseng Labs
`tvgani`	Tseng Labs (non-interlaced)
`gvga`	Genoa Super VGA
`pega`	Paradise PEGA2
`gega`	Genoa EGA
`fastwrite`	Video 7 FastWrite VGA
`won`	ATI VGA Wonder
`pvga1024`	Paradise 1024

The command can only be run with appropriate privilege.

EXAMPLES

For an STB Extra/EM-16 video card, **evgainit** should be invoked as:

```
evgainit stbga
```

This command can be run automatically from the **inittab** file [see **inittab**(4)] or can be run by a user with appropriate privilege after each system reboot.

SEE ALSO

console(7), **inittab**(4), **keyboard**(7)

ex(1)

NAME

ex – text editor

SYNOPSIS

ex [**-s**] [**-v**] [**-t** *tag*] [**-r** *file*] [**-L**] [**-R**] [**-x**] [**-C**] [**-c** *command*] *file* . . .

DESCRIPTION

ex is the root of a family of editors: **ex** and **vi**. **ex** is a superset of **ed**, with the most notable extension being a display editing facility. If you have a CRT terminal, you may wish to use a display based editor; in this case see **vi**(1). **ex** processes supplementary code set characters according to the locale specified in the **LC_CTYPE** environment variable [see **LANG** on **environ**(5)]. In regular expressions, pattern searches are performed on characters, not bytes, as described on **ed**(1).

For ed Users

If you have used **ed** you will find that, in addition to having all of the **ed** commands available, **ex** has a number of additional features useful on CRT terminals. Intelligent terminals and high speed terminals are very pleasant to use with **vi**. Generally, the **ex** editor uses far more of the capabilities of terminals than **ed** does, and uses the terminal capability data base [see **terminfo**(4)] and the type of the terminal you are using from the environmental variable **TERM** to determine how to drive your terminal efficiently. The editor makes use of features such as insert and delete character and line in its **visual** command (which can be abbreviated **vi**) and which is the central mode of editing when using the **vi** command.

ex contains a number of features for easily viewing the text of the file. The **z** command gives easy access to windows of text. Typing **^D** (control-d) causes the editor to scroll a half-window of text and is more useful for quickly stepping through a file than just typing return. Of course, the screen-oriented **visual** mode gives constant access to editing context.

ex gives you help when you make mistakes. The **undo** (**u**) command allows you to reverse any single change which goes astray. **ex** gives you a lot of feedback, normally printing changed lines, and indicates when more than a few lines are affected by a command so that it is easy to detect when a command has affected more lines than it should have.

The editor also normally prevents overwriting existing files, unless you edited them, so that you do not accidentally overwrite a file other than the one you are editing. If the system (or editor) crashes, or you accidentally hang up the line, you can use the editor **recover** command (or **-r** *file* option) to retrieve your work. This will get you back to within a few lines of where you left off.

ex has several features for dealing with more than one file at a time. You can give it a list of files on the command line and use the **next** (**n**) command to deal with each in turn. The **next** command can also be given a list of file names, or a pattern as used by the shell to specify a new set of files to be dealt with. In general, file names in the editor may be formed with full shell metasyntax. The metacharacter '%' is also available in forming file names and is replaced by the name of the current file.

The editor has a group of buffers whose names are the ASCII lower-case letters (**a**-**z**). You can place text in these named buffers where it is available to be inserted elsewhere in the file. The contents of these buffers remain available when you begin editing a new file using the **edit** (**e**) command.

There is a command **&** in **ex** which repeats the last **substitute** command. In addition, there is a confirmed substitute command. You give a range of substitutions to be done and the editor interactively asks whether each substitution is desired.

It is possible to ignore the case of letters in searches and substitutions. **ex** also allows regular expressions which match words to be constructed. This is convenient, for example, in searching for the word "edit" if your document also contains the word "editor."

ex has a set of options which you can set to tailor it to your liking. One option which is very useful is the **autoindent** option that allows the editor to supply leading white space to align text automatically. You can then use `^D` as a backtab and space or tab to move forward to align new code easily.

Miscellaneous useful features include an intelligent **join** (`j`) command that supplies white space between joined lines automatically, commands **<** and **>** which shift groups of lines, and the ability to filter portions of the buffer through commands such as **sort**.

Invocation Options

The following invocation options are interpreted by **ex** (previously documented options are discussed in the NOTES section at the end of this manual page):

- **-s** Suppress all interactive-user feedback. This is useful in processing editor scripts.
- **-v** Invoke `vi`.
- **-t** *tag* Edit the file containing the *tag* and position the editor at its definition. Note: tags in the *tag* file must be in ascending order.
- **-r** *file* Edit *file* after an editor or system crash. (Recovers the version of *file* that was in the buffer when the crash occurred.)
- **-L** List the names of all files saved as the result of an editor or system crash.
- **-R** **Readonly** mode; the **readonly** flag is set, preventing accidental overwriting of the file.
- **-x** Encryption option; when used, **ex** simulates an **X** command and prompts the user for a key. This key is used to encrypt and decrypt text using the algorithm of the **crypt** command. The **X** command makes an educated guess to determine whether text read in is encrypted or not. The temporary buffer file is encrypted also, using a transformed version of the key typed in for the **-x** option. See **crypt**(1). Also, see the NOTES section at the end of this manual page.
- **-C** Encryption option; the same as the **-x** option, except that **ex** simulates a **C** command. The **C** command is like the **X** command, except that all text read in is assumed to have been encrypted.
- **-c** *command* Begin editing by executing the specified editor *command* (usually a search or positioning command).

The *file* argument indicates one or more files to be edited.

ex States

Command	Normal and initial state. Input prompted for by **:**. Your line kill character cancels a partial command.
Insert	Entered by **a**, **i**, or **c**. Arbitrary text may be entered. Insert state normally is terminated by a line having only "**.**" on it, or, abnormally, with an interrupt.
Visual	Entered by typing **vi**; terminated by typing **Q** or ^\ (control-\).

ex Command Names and Abbreviations

abbrev	**ab**	map		set	**se**
append	**a**	mark	**ma**	shell	**sh**
args	**ar**	move	**m**	source	**so**
change	**c**	next	**n**	substitute	**s**
copy	**co**	number	**nu**	unabbrev	**unab**
delete	**d**	preserve	**pre**	undo	**u**
edit	**e**	print	**p**	unmap	**unm**
file	**f**	put	**pu**	version	**ve**
global	**g**	quit	**q**	visual	**vi**
insert	**i**	read	**r**	write	**w**
join	**j**	recover	**rec**	xit	**x**
list	**l**	rewind	**rew**	yank	**ya**

ex Commands

forced encryption	**C**	heuristic encryption	**X**
resubst	**&**	print next	CR
rshift	**>**	lshift	**<**
scroll	**^D**	window	**z**
shell escape	**!**		

ex Command Addresses

n	line *n*	**/***pat*	next with *pat*
.	current	**?***pat*	previous with *pat*
$	last	*x*-*n*	*n* before *x*
+	next	*x*,*y*	*x* through *y*
-	previous	´*x*	marked with *x*
+*n*	*n* forward	´´	previous context
%	1,$		

Initializing options

EXINIT	place **set**'s here in environment variable
$HOME/.exrc	editor initialization file
./.exrc	editor initialization file
set *x*	enable option *x*
set no*x*	disable option *x*
set *x*=**val**	give value *val* to option *x*
set	show changed options

set all	show all options
set *x*?	show value of option *x*

Most useful options and their abbreviations

Option	Abbreviation	Description
autoindent	**ai**	supply indent
autowrite	**aw**	write before changing files
directory		pathname of directory for temporary work files
exrc	**ex**	allow **vi/ex** to read the **.exrc** in the current directory. This option is set in the **EXINIT** shell variable or in the **.exrc** file in the **$HOME** directory.
ignorecase	**ic**	ignore case of letters in scanning
list		print **^I** for tab, $ at end
magic		treat **. [*** special in patterns
modelines		first five lines and last five lines executed as **vi/ex** commands if they are of the form **ex:***command***:** or **vi:***command***:**
number	**nu**	number lines
paragraphs	**para**	macro names that start paragraphs
redraw		simulate smart terminal
report		informs you if the number of lines modified by the last command is greater than the value of the **report** variable
scroll		command mode lines
sections	**sect**	macro names that start sections
shiftwidth	**sw**	for **< >**, and input **^D**
showmatch	**sm**	to **)** and **}** as typed
showmode	**smd**	show insert mode in **vi**
slowopen	**slow**	stop updates during insert
term		specifies to **vi** the type of terminal being used (the default is the value of the environmental variable **TERM**)
window		visual mode lines
wrapmargin	**wm**	automatic line splitting
wrapscan	**ws**	search around end (or beginning) of buffer

Scanning pattern formation

^	beginning of line
$	end of line
.	any character
\<	beginning of word
\>	end of word
[**str**]	any character in *str*
[^**str**]	any character not in *str*
[*x*–*y*]	any character between *x* and *y*
*	any number of preceding characters

AUTHOR

vi and **ex** are based on software developed by The University of California, Berkeley California, Computer Science Division, Department of Electrical Engineering and Computer Science.

FILES

/usr/lib/exstrings	error messages
/usr/lib/exrecover	recover command
/usr/lib/expreserve	preserve command
/usr/share/lib/terminfo/*	describes capabilities of terminals
$HOME/.exrc	editor startup file
./.exrc	editor startup file
/tmp/Ex*nnnnn*	editor temporary
/tmp/Rx*nnnnn*	named buffer temporary
/var/preserve/*login*	preservation directory
/usr/lib/locale/*locale***/LC_MESSAGES/uxed.abi**	language-specific message file [See **LANG** on **environ**(5).]

SEE ALSO

crypt(1), **ctags**(1), **curses**(3curses), **ed**(1), **edit**(1), **grep**(1), **sed**(1), **sort**(1), **term**(4), **terminfo**(4), **vi**(1)

NOTES

Several options, although they continue to be supported, have been replaced in the documentation by options that follow the Command Syntax Standard [see **intro**(1)]. The **-** option has been replaced by **-s**, a **-r** option that is not followed with an option-argument has been replaced by **-L**, and **+***command* has been replaced by **-c** *command*.

The encryption options and commands are provided with the Encryption Utilities package, which is available only in the United States.

The **z** command prints the number of logical rather than physical lines. More than a screen full of output may result if long lines are present.

File input/output errors do not print a name if the command line **-s** option is used.

There is no easy way to do a single scan ignoring case.

The editor does not warn if text is placed in named buffers and not used before exiting the editor.

Null characters are discarded in input files and cannot appear in resultant files.

NAME

exportfs – export and unexport directories to NFS clients

SYNOPSIS

/usr/sbin/exportfs [**-aiuv**] [**-o** *options*] [*pathname*]

DESCRIPTION

exportfs makes a local directory or filename available for mounting over the network by NFS clients. It uses information contained in the **/etc/dfs/dfstab** file to export *pathname* (which must be specified as a full pathname). The user with appropriate administrative privileges can run **exportfs** at any time to alter the list or characteristics of exported directories and filenames. Directories and files that are currently exported are listed in the file **/etc/dfs/sharetab.**

With no options or arguments, **exportfs** prints out the list of directories and filenames currently exported.

OPTIONS

-a All. Export all pathnames listed in **/etc/dfs/dfstab,** or if **-u** is also specified, unexport all of the currently exported pathnames.

-i Ignore the options in **/etc/dfs/dfstab**. Normally, **exportfs** will consult **/etc/dfs/dfstab** for the options associated with the exported pathname.

-u Unexport the indicated *pathname*. A *pathname* is required if **-u** is not used in conjunction with **-a**.

-v Verbose. Print each directory or filename as it is exported or unexported.

-o *options*
Specify a comma-separated list of optional characteristics for the pathname being exported. *options* can be selected from among:

ro Export the pathname read-only. If not specified, the pathname is exported read-write.

rw= *hostname*[: *hostname*] . . .
Export the pathname read-mostly. Read-mostly means exported read-only to most machines, but read-write to those specified. If not specified, the pathname is exported read-write to all.

anon= *uid*
If a request comes from an unknown user, use UID as the effective user. ID. Note: root users (UID 0) are always considered unknown by the NFS server, unless they are included in the **root** option below. The default value for this option is –2. Setting the value of anon to –1 disables anonymous access. Note: by default secure NFS accepts insecure requests as anonymous, and those wishing for extra security can disable this feature by setting anon to –1.

root= *hostname*[: *hostname*] . . .
Give root access only to the root users from a specified *hostname*. The default is for no hosts to be granted root access.

`access`= *client*[: *client*] . . .
Give mount access to each *client* listed.

`secure`
Require clients to use a more secure protocol when accessing the directory.

FILES

`/etc/dfs/dfstab` static export information
`/etc/dfs/sharetab` current state of exported pathnames

SEE ALSO

`showmount`(1M)

NOTES

You cannot export a directory that is either a parent- or a sub-directory of one that is currently exported and within the same filesystem. It would be illegal, for example, to export both **/usr** and **/usr/local** if both directories resided in the same disk partition.

NAME

expr – evaluate arguments as an expression

SYNOPSIS

expr *arguments*

DESCRIPTION

The *arguments* are taken as an expression. After evaluation, the result is written on the standard output. Terms of the expression must be separated by blanks. Characters special to the shell must be escaped. Note that **0** is returned to indicate a zero value, rather than the null string. Strings containing blanks or other special characters should be quoted. Integer-valued arguments may be preceded by a unary minus sign. Internally, integers are treated as 32-bit, 2s complement numbers. The length of the expression is limited to 512 characters. Expressions may be grouped using (escaped) parentheses.

The operators and keywords are listed below. Characters that need to be escaped in the shell [see **sh**(1)] are preceded by \. The list is in order of increasing precedence, with equal precedence operators grouped within **{ }** symbols.

expr **\|** *expr*
: Return the first *expr* if it is neither null nor **0**, otherwise return the second *expr*.

expr **\&** *expr*
: Return the first *expr* if neither *expr* is null or **0**, otherwise return **0**.

expr { **=, \>, \>=, \<, \<=, !=** } *expr*
: Return the result of an integer comparison if both arguments are integers, otherwise return the result of a lexical comparison.

expr { **+, -** } *expr*
: Add or subtract integer-valued arguments.

expr { ***, /, %** } *expr*
: Multiply, divide, or compute remainder of integer-valued arguments.

expr **:** *expr*
match *expr expr*
: Compare the first argument with the second argument, which must be a regular expression. Regular expression syntax is the same as that of **ed**(1), except that all patterns are "anchored" (that is, begin with ^) and, therefore, ^ is not a special character, in that context. Normally, the matching operator returns the number of characters matched (**0** on failure). Alternatively, the **\(. . . \)** pattern symbols can be used to return a portion of the first argument.

length *string*
: Return the length of *string*.

substr *string index count*
: Return the portion of *string* composed of at most *count* characters starting at the character position of *string* as expressed by *index* (where the first character of *string* is index 1, not 0).

index *string character_sequence*
Return the index of the first character in *string* that is also in *character_sequence* or 0 to indicate no match.

expr processes supplementary code set characters according to the locale specified in the **LC_CTYPE** environment variable [see **LANG** on **environ**(5)]. In regular expressions, pattern searches are performed on characters, not bytes, as described on **ed**(1).

DIAGNOSTICS

As a side effect of expression evaluation, **expr** returns the following exit values:

0 The expression is neither null nor 0.
1 The expression is null or 0.
2 An expression is invalid.

ERRORS

non-numeric argument arithmetic attempted on a non-numeric string

FILES

/usr/lib/locale/*locale***/LC_MESSAGES/uxcore.abi**
language-specific message file [See **LANG** on **environ** (5).]

EXAMPLES

Add 1 to the shell variable **a**:

```
a=`expr $a + 1`
```

The following example emulates **basename**(1)—it returns the last segment of the path name **$a**. For **$a** equal to either **/usr/abc/file** or just **file**, the example returns **file**. The **//** characters eliminate any ambiguity about the division operator.

```
expr //$a : '.*/\(.*\)'
```

SEE ALSO

ed(1), **sh**(1)

NOTES

After argument processing by the shell, **expr** cannot tell the difference between an operator and an operand except by the value. If **$a** is an =, the command:

```
expr $a = '='
```

looks like:

```
expr = = =
```

as the arguments are passed to **expr** (and they are all taken as the = operator). The following works:

```
expr X$a = X=
```

NAME

exstr – extract strings from source files

SYNOPSIS

exstr *file* . . .
exstr -e *file* . . .
exstr -r [**-d**] *file* . . .

DESCRIPTION

The **exstr** utility is used to extract strings from C language source files and replace them by calls to the message retrieval function [see **gettxt**(3C)]. This utility will extract all character strings surrounded by double quotes, not just strings used as arguments to the **printf** command or the **printf** routine. In the first form, **exstr** finds all strings in the source files and writes them on the standard output. Each string is preceded by the source file name and a colon. The meanings of the options are:

-e Extract a list of strings from the named C language source files, with positional information. This list is produced on standard output in the following format:

file:line:position:msgfile:msgnum:string

file	the name of a C language source file
line	line number in the file
position	character position in the line
msgfile	null
msgnum	null
string	the extracted text string

Normally you would redirect this output into a file. Then you would edit this file to add the values you want to use for *msgfile* and *msgnum*:

msgfile the file that contains the text strings that will replace *string*. A file with this name must be created and installed in the appropriate place by the **mkmsgs**(1) utility.

msgnum the sequence number of the string in *msgfile*.

The next step is to use **exstr -r** to replace *string*s in *file*.

-r Replace strings in a C language source file with function calls to the message retrieval function **gettxt**.

-d This option is used together with the **-r** option. If the message retrieval fails when **gettxt** is invoked at run time, then the extracted string is printed.

You would use the capability provided by **exstr** on an application program that needs to run in an international environment and have messages print in more than one language. **exstr** replaces text strings with function calls that point at strings in a message database. The database used depends on the runtime value of the **LC_MESSAGES** environment variable [see **environ**(5)].

The first step is to use **exstr -e** to extract a list of strings and save it in a file. Next, examine this list and determine which strings can be translated and subsequently retrieved by the message retrieval function. Then, modify this file by deleting lines that can't be translated and, for lines that can be translated, by adding the message file names and the message numbers as the fourth (*msgfile*) and fifth (*msgnum*) entries on a line. The message files named must have been created by **mkmsgs**(1) and exist in **/usr/lib/locale/***locale***/LC_MESSAGES**. The directory *locale* corresponds to the language in which the text strings are written [see **setlocale**(3C)]. The message numbers used must correspond to the sequence numbers of strings in the message files.

Now use this modified file as input to **exstr -r** to produce a new version of the original C language source file in which the strings have been replaced by calls to the message retrieval function **gettxt**. The *msgfile* and *msgnum* fields are used to construct the first argument to **gettxt**. The second argument to **gettxt** is printed if the message retrieval fails at run time. This argument is the null string, unless the **-d** option is used.

This utility cannot replace strings in all instances. For example, a static initialized character string cannot be replaced by a function call, or a string could be in the form of an escape sequence that cannot be translated. In order not to break existing code, the files created by invoking **exstr -e** must be examined and lines containing strings not replaceable by function calls must be deleted. In some cases the code may require modifications so that strings can be extracted and replaced by calls to the message retrieval function.

EXAMPLES

The following examples show uses of **exstr**.

Assume that the file **foo.c** contains two strings:

```
main()
{
        printf("This is an example\n");
        printf("Hello world!\n");
}
```

The **exstr** utility, invoked with the argument **foo.c**, extracts strings from the named file and prints them on the standard output.

exstr foo.c produces the following output:

```
foo.c:This is an example\n
foo.c:Hello world!\n
```

exstr -e foo.c > foo.stringsout produces the following output in the file **foo.stringsout**:

```
foo.c:3:8:::This is an example\n
foo.c:4:8:::Hello world!\n
```

You must edit **foo.stringsout** to add the values you want to use for the *msgfile* and *msgnum* fields before these strings can be replaced by calls to the retrieval function. If **UX** is the name of the message file, and the numbers **1** and **2** represent the sequence number of the strings in the file, here is what **foo.stringsout** looks like after you add this information:

```
foo.c:3:8:UX:1:This is an example\n
foo.c:4:8:UX:2:Hello world!\n
```

The **exstr** utility can now be invoked with the **-r** option to replace the strings in the source file by calls to the message retrieval function **gettxt**.

exstr -r foo.c <foo.stringsout >intlfoo.c produces the following output:

```
extern char *gettxt();
main()
{
     printf(gettxt("UX:1", ""));
     printf(gettxt("UX:2", ""));
}
```

exstr -rd foo.c <foo.stringsout >intlfoo.c uses the extracted strings as a second argument to **gettxt**.

```
extern char *gettxt();
main()
{
     printf(gettxt("UX:1", "This is an example\n"));
     printf(gettxt("UX:2", "Hello world!\n"));
}
```

FILES

/usr/lib/locale/*locale*/LC_MESSAGES/* files created by **mkmsgs**(1)

SEE ALSO

environ(5), **gettxt**(1), **gettxt**(3C), **mkmsgs**(1), **printf**(1), **printf**(3S), **setlocale**(3C), **srchtxt**(1)

DIAGNOSTICS

The error messages produced by **exstr** are intended to be self-explanatory. They indicate errors in the command line or format errors encountered within the input file.

face (1)

NAME

face – executable for the Framed Access Command Environment Interface

SYNOPSIS

face [**-i** *init_file*] [**-c** *command_file*] [**-a** *alias_file*] [*file* . . .]

DESCRIPTION

file is the full pathname of the file describing the object to be opened initially, and must follow the naming convention **Menu.***xxx* for a menu, **Form.***xxx* for a form, and **Text.***xxx* for a text file, where *xxx* is any string that conforms to the UNIX system file naming conventions. The FMLI descriptor **lifetime** will be ignored for all frames opened by argument to **face**. These frames have a lifetime of **immortal** by default. If *file* is not specified on the command line, the FACE Menu will be opened along with those objects specified by the **LOGINWIN** environment variables. These variables are found in the user's **.environ** file.

FILES

$HOME/pref/.environ

SEE ALSO

environ(4)

DIAGNOSTICS

The **face** command will exit with a non-zero exit code if the user is not properly set up as a FACE user.

NAME

`factor` – obtain the prime factors of a number

SYNOPSIS

`factor` [*integer*]

DESCRIPTION

When you use **`factor`** without an argument, it waits for you to give it an integer. After you give it a positive integer less than or equal to 10^{14}, it factors the integer, prints its prime factors the proper number of times, and then waits for another integer. **`factor`** exits if it encounters a zero or any non-numeric character.

If you invoke **`factor`** with an argument, it factors the integer as described above, and then it exits.

The maximum time to factor an integer is proportional to $\sqrt{n}$. **`factor`** will take this time when n is prime or the square of a prime.

DIAGNOSTICS

`factor` prints the error message, **`Ouch`**, for input out of range or for garbage input.

NAME

fastboot, **fasthalt** – (BSD) reboot/halt the system without checking the disks

SYNOPSIS

/usr/ucb/fastboot [*boot-options*]

/usr/ucb/fasthalt [*halt-options*]

DESCRIPTION

fastboot and **fasthalt** are shell scripts that invoke **reboot** and **halt** with the proper arguments.

These commands are provided for compatibility only.

FILES

/etc/rc*

SEE ALSO

fsck(1M), **halt**(1M), **init**(1M), **rc0**(1M), **rc2**(1M), **reboot**(1M)

NAME

`fdetach` – detach a name from a STREAMS-based file descriptor

SYNOPSIS

`fdetach` *path*

DESCRIPTION

The **`fdetach`** command detaches a STREAMS-based file descriptor from a name in the file system. *path* is the pathname of the object in the file system name space, which was previously attached [see **`fattach`**(3C)]. The user must be the owner of the file or a user with the appropriate privileges. All subsequent operations on *path* operate on the file system node and not on the STREAMS file. The permissions and status of the node are restored to the state they were in before the STREAMS file was attached to it.

SEE ALSO

`fattach`(3C), **`fdetach`**(3C), **`streamio`**(7)

NAME

`fdisk` – create or modify hard disk partition table

SYNOPSIS

`fdisk` [*argument*]

DESCRIPTION

This command is used to create and modify the partition table that is put in the first sector of the hard disk. This table is used by DOS and by the first-stage bootstrap to identify parts of the disk reserved for different operating systems, and to identify the partition containing the second-stage bootstrap (the active partition). The optional argument can be used to specify the raw device associated with the hard disk; the default value is **`/dev/rdsk/0s0`** for integral disks. For SCSI disks, there is no default value. However if the default on your system is set to **`0s0`**, then it is linked to **`/dev/rdsk/c0t0d0s0`**. If the default is set to **`1s0`**, then it is linked to **`/dev/rdsk/c0t1d0s0`**.

The program displays the partition table as it exists on the disk, and then presents a menu allowing you to modify the table. The menu, questions, warnings, and error messages are intended to be self-explanatory.

If there is no partition table on the disk, you are given the options to create a default partition or to specify the initial table values. The default partitioning allows 10% of the disk for MS-DOS and 90% for the UNIX System, and makes the UNIX System partition active. In either case, when the initial table is created, **`fdisk`** also writes out the first-stage bootstrap code [see **`sd01`**(7)] along with the partition table. After the initial table is created, only the table is changed; the bootstrap is not modified.

Menu Options

The following are the menu options given by the **`fdisk`** program:

`Create a partition`
: Allows you to create a new partition. The maximum number of partitions is 4. The program will ask for the type of the partition (MS-DOS, UNIX System, or other). It will then ask for the size of the partition as a percentage of the disk. For the UNIX desktop operating system, the minimum UNIX System disk partition size is 60 MB for disk 0 and 40 MB for disk 1. The user may also enter the letter **`c`** at this point, in which case the program will ask for the starting cylinder number and size of the partition in cylinders. If a **`c`** is not entered, the program will determine the starting cylinder number where the partition will fit. In either case, if the partition would overlap an existing partition, or will not fit, a message is displayed and the program returns to the original menu.

`Change Active (Boot from) partition`
: Allows you to specify the partition where the first-stage bootstrap will look for the second-stage bootstrap, otherwise known as the active partition.

`Delete a partition`
: Allows you to delete a previously created partition. Note that this will destroy all data in that partition. Use this option with extreme caution.

`Overwrite system master boot code`

Overwrites the in-core boot code portion of the boot sector with the UNIX System version of the master boot code. You will need to perform an update, using **fdisk**'s update menu option, to have the master boot code written to the disk. You should use the overwrite menu option if you have had OS/2 installed on the disk previously, because the OS/2 master boot will not boot UNIX. However, the overwrite option is not necessary for machines which have had MS-DOS and then OS/2 installed on them.

`Update`

Writes the new version of the table created during this session with **fdisk** out to the hard disk, and exits the program.

`Exit` Exits without modifying the partition table.

Errors

Most messages will be self-explanatory. The following may appear immediately after starting the program:

fdisk: cannot open <device>

This indicates that the device name argument is not valid.

fdisk: unable to get device parameters for device <device>

This indicates a problem with the configuration of the hard disk, or an error in the hard disk driver.

fdisk: error reading partition table

This indicates that some error occurred when trying initially to read the hard disk. This could be a problem with the hard disk controller or driver, or with the configuration of the hard disk.

This message may appear after selecting the **Exit** option from the menu.

fdisk: error writing boot record

This indicates that some error occurred when trying to write the new partition table out to the hard disk. This could be a problem with the hard disk controller, the disk itself, the driver, or the configuration of the hard disk.

Files

/dev/rdsk/0s0 for integral disks
/dev/rdsk/c?**t**?**d**?**s0** for SCSI disks

NOTES

Warnings

Use caution when using the **fdisk** command. If you select the option to delete a partition, the data on that partition is lost and cannot be retrieved. If you delete a partition accidentally, you will need a tape or disk backup to restore the lost data.

Compatibility

fdisk is compatible with MS-DOS Versions 3.2, 3.3, 4.0, and 5.0. Partitions set up using the MS-DOS 4.0 **fdisk** command that are greater than 32 MB will appear in the UNIX System display as "other". Partitions can be created at sizes greater than 32 MB for MS-DOS 5.0, and appear correctly as DOS partitions. Partitions created with MS-DOS at any release level that are less than 32 MB will appear correctly as DOS partitions.

The label of a created partition will be either **DOS** for MS-DOS 5.0 partitions or **pre-5.0DOS** for any version of MS-DOS lower than 5.0. Note, however, that the version of the partition can be **pre-5.0DOS** even when the operating system in use is MS-DOS 5.0. Therefore, do not depend on the partition label to determine which release of MS-DOS is running.

The DOS 4.01 **fdisk** program assumes it can store diagnostic information in cylinder 1020 on the hard disk. If a UNIX System partition is created that uses cylinder 1020, DOS 4.01 **fdisk** will be unable to create a DOS partition. Therefore, the user must either create the UNIX System partition at the front of the disk so that cylinder 1020 is not used, or create the DOS partition using the UNIX System **fdisk** (not DOS **fdisk**) and never delete it.

When setting up a DOS 4.01 partition on the hard disk to co-reside with a UNIX partition that has already been set up, do not allow **fdisk** to create the largest possible partition and make it active (as the **fdisk** prompt requests). Instead, the user should manually set it up to line up against the UNIX partition. Note that this applies to when the user boots DOS 4.01 from floppy disk (not from within UNIX) and runs **fdisk**.

Also note that there was a previous version of the **fdisk** command, intended for use with the UNIX System **bkrs** (backup/restore) utility. The current version of **fdisk** is used only for partitioning disks.

As noted in the section describing **fdisk**'s menu options, you need to use the overwrite option when installing UNIX on a disk that has had OS/2 installed on it. The **Overwrite system master boot code** option overwrites the in-core boot code portion of the boot sector with the UNIX System master boot code. This operation is necessary because the OS/2 boot code will not boot UNIX. The overwrite is not necessary, however, on systems which had MS-DOS and then OS/2 installed on them. To complete the overwrite, you need to use the update menu option in **fdisk**.

REFERENCES

sd01(7)

NAME

`ff` (generic) – list file names and statistics for a file system

SYNOPSIS

`ff` [`-F` *FSType*] [`-V`] [*current_options*] [`-o` *specific_options*] *special* . . .

DESCRIPTION

`ff` reads the files and directories of the *special* file. I-node data is saved for files which match the selection criteria which is either the *inode* number and/or *inode* age. Output consists of the path name and other file information. Output fields are positional. The output is produced in i-node order. The default line produced by `ff` is:

path-name i-number

current_options are options supported by the **s5**-specific module of `ff`. Other FSTypes do not necessarily support these options. *specific_options* indicate suboptions specified in a comma-separated list of suboptions and/or keyword-attribute pairs for interpretation by the *FSType*-specific module of the command.

The options are:

`-F` Specify the *FSType* on which to operate. The *FSType* should either be specified here or be determinable from **/etc/vfstab** by matching the *special* with an entry in the table.

`-V` Echo the complete command line, but do not execute the command. The command line is generated by using the options and arguments provided by the user and adding to them information derived from `/etc/vfstab`. This option should be used to verify and validate the command line.

`-o` Specify FSType-specific options.

NOTE

This command may not be supported for all FSTypes.

FILES

`/etc/vfstab` list of default parameters for each file system

SEE ALSO

`s5`-specific `ff`(1M), **ufs**-specific `ff`(1M), **vxfs**-specific `ff`(1M), **ncheck**(1M), **vfstab**(4), `find`(1)

NAME

`ff` (s5) – display i-list information

SYNOPSIS

ff [**-F s5**] [*generic_options*] [**-I**] [**-l**] [**-p***prefix*] [**-s**] [**-u**] [**-a***n*] [**-m***n*] [**-c***n*] [**-n***file*] [**-i***i-node-list*] *special* . . .

DESCRIPTION

generic_options are options supported by the generic **ff** command.

ff reads the i-list and directories of the *special* file, assuming it is an **s5** file system. I-node data is saved for files which match the selection criteria. Output consists of the pathname for each saved i-node, plus other file information requested using the print *options* below. Output fields are positional. The output is produced in i-node order; fields are separated by tab characters. The default line produced by **ff** is:

pathname i-number

The pathname is preceded by a **.** (dot) unless the **-p** option is specified.

The maximum information the command will provide is:

pathname i-number size uid

The argument *n* in the *option* descriptions that follow is used as a decimal integer (optionally signed), where **+** *n* means more than *n*, **-** *n* means less than *n*, and *n* means exactly *n*. A day is defined as a 24 hour period.

The options are:

-F s5 Specifies the **s5**-FSType.

-I Do not print the i-node number after each pathname.

-l Generate a supplementary list of all pathnames for multiply-linked files.

-p*prefix* The specified *prefix* will be added to each generated pathname. The default is **.** (dot).

-s Print the file size, in bytes, after each pathname.

-u Print the owner's login name after each pathname.

-a*n* Select if the i-node has been accessed in *n* days.

-m*n* Select if the i-node has been modified in *n* days.

-c*n* Select if the i-node has been changed in *n* days.

-n*file* Select if the i-node has been modified more recently than the argument *file*.

-i*i-node-list* Generate names for only those i-nodes specified in *i-node-list*. *i-node-list* is a list of numbers separated by commas and without spaces.

NOTE

If the `-l` option is not specified, only a single pathname out of all possible ones is generated for a multiply-linked i-node. If `-l` is specified, all possible names for every linked file on the file system are included in the output. If `-l` and `-i` are both specified, then only the names for linked files matching an i-node listed in the i-node list are displayed.

SEE ALSO

generic **ff**(1M), **find**(1), **ncheck**(1M)

NAME

ff (ufs) – list file names and statistics for a **ufs** file system

SYNOPSIS

ff [**-F ufs**] [*generic_options*] [**-I**] [**-l**] [**-p***prefix*] [**-s**] [**-u**] [**-a***n*] [**-m***n*] [**-c***n*] [**-n***file*] [**-i***i-node-list*] [**-o a,m,s**] *special*. . .

DESCRIPTION

generic_options are options supported by the generic **ff** command.

ff reads the i-list and directories of the *special* file, assuming it is a file system. Inode data is saved for files which match the selection criteria. Output consists of the pathname for each saved inode, plus other file information requested using the options below. Output fields are positional. The output is produced in inode order; fields are separated by TAB characters. The default line produced by **ff** is:

pathname i-number

Options

-F ufs Specifies the **ufs**-FSType.

-I Do not print the i-node number after each pathname.

-l Generate a supplementary list of all pathnames for multiply-linked files.

-p*prefix* The specified *prefix* will be added to each generated pathname. The default is **.** (dot).

-s Print the file size, in bytes, after each pathname.

-u Print the owner's login name after each pathname.

-a*n* Select if the i-node has been accessed in *n* days.

-m*n* Select if the i-node has been modified in *n* days.

-c*n* Select if the i-node has been changed in *n* days.

-n*file* Select if the i-node has been modified more recently than the argument *file*.

-i*i-node-list*
Generate names for only those i-nodes specified in *i-node-list*. *i-node-list* is a list of numbers separated by commas and without spaces.

-o Specify **ufs** file system specific options. The options available are:

- **a** Print the '**.**' and '**..**' directory entries.
- **m** Print mode information.
- **s** Print only special files and files with set-user-ID mode.

NOTE

If the **-l** option is not specified, only a single pathname out of all possible ones is generated for a multiply-linked inode. If **-l** is specified, all possible names for every linked file on the file system are included in the output. However, no selection criteria apply to the names generated.

SEE ALSO

find(1), generic **ff**(1M), **ncheck**(1M)

NAME

ff (vxfs) – list file names and inode information for a **vxfs** file system

SYNOPSIS

ff [**-F vxfs**] [*generic_options*] [**-I**] [**-l**] [**-p** *prefix*] [**-s**] [**-u**] [**-a** *n*] [**-m** *n*] [**-c** *n*] [**-n** *file*] [**-i** *inode_list*] [**-o s**] *special . . .*

DESCRIPTION

generic_options are options supported by the generic **ff** command.

ff reads the inode list and directories of the *special* file, assuming it is a **vxfs** file system. Inode data is saved for files that match all the selection criteria. Output consists of the pathname for each saved inode, plus other file information requested using the print options below. Output fields are positional. The output is produced in inode order; fields are separated by tabs. The default line produced by **ff** is:

pathname inumber

The pathname is preceded by a **.** (dot) unless the **-p** option is specified.

The maximum information the command will provide is:

pathname inumber size owner

The argument *n* in the following *option* descriptions is used as a decimal integer (optionally signed), where **+** *n* means more than *n*, **-** *n* means less than *n*, and *n* means exactly *n*. A day is defined as a 24-hour period.

The options are:

-F vxfs Specify the **vxfs** FSType.

-I Do not print the inode number after each pathname.

-l Generate a supplementary list of all pathnames for multiply-linked files.

-p*prefix* The specified *prefix* will be added to each generated pathname. The default is **.** (dot).

-s Print the file size, in bytes, after each pathname.

-u Print the owner's login name after each pathname.

-a *n* Select if the inode has been accessed in *n* days.

-m *n* Select if the inode has been modified in *n* days.

-c *n* Select if the inode has been changed in *n* days.

-n *file* Select if the inode has been modified more recently than the argument *file*.

-i *inode_list* Generate names for only those inodes specified in *inode_list*. *inode_list* is a list of numbers separated by commas and without spaces.

-o Specify **vxfs** file system specific options. The following option is available:

s Print only special files and files with set-user-ID mode.

NOTE

If the `-l` option is not specified, only a single pathname out of all possible pathnames is generated for a multiply-linked inode. If `-l` is specified, a supplementary list of all possible names for the selected file(s) is generated. This supplementary list is also sorted in inode order, separate from the initial output.

`ff` prints summary information to standard error output, in addition to the report sent to standard output.

SEE ALSO

generic **ff**(1M), **find**(1), **vxfs**-specific **fs**(4), generic **ncheck**(1M)

NAME

fgrep – search a file for a character string

SYNOPSIS

fgrep [*options*] *string* [*file* . . .]

DESCRIPTION

fgrep (fixed string **grep**) searches files for a character string and prints all lines that contain that string. **fgrep** is different from **grep** and **egrep** because it searches for a string instead of searching for a pattern that matches an expression. It uses a fast and compact algorithm.

fgrep processes supplementary code set characters according to the locale specified in the **LC_CTYPE** environment variable [see **LANG** on **environ**(5)], except as noted under the **-i** option below. Pattern searches are performed on characters, not bytes.

The characters **$**, *, [, ^, |, (,), and \ are interpreted literally by **fgrep**, that is, **fgrep** does not recognize full regular expressions as does **egrep**. Because these characters have special meaning to the shell, it is safest to enclose the entire *string* in single quotes ' . . . '.

If no files are specified, **fgrep** assumes standard input. Normally, each line found is copied to the standard output. The filename is printed before each line found if there is more than one input file.

Command line options are:

-b Precede each line by the block number on which it was found. This can be useful in locating block numbers by context (first block is 0).

-c Print only a count of the lines that contain the pattern.

-h Suppress printing of filenames when searching multiple files.

-i Ignore uppercase/lowercase distinction during comparisons; valid for single-byte characters only.

-l Print the names of files with matching lines once, separated by newlines. Does not repeat the names of files when the pattern is found more than once.

-n Precede each line by its line number in the file (first line is 1).

-v Print all lines except those that contain the pattern.

-x Print only lines matched entirely.

-e *special_string*
Search for a *special_string* (*string* begins with a -).

-f *file*
Take the list of *strings* from *file*.

FILES

/usr/lib/locale/*locale***/LC_MESSAGES/uxcore**
language-specific message file [See **LANG** on **environ**(5).]

SEE ALSO

ed(1), **egrep**(1), **grep**(1), **sed**(1), **sh**(1)

DIAGNOSTICS

Exit status is 0 if any matches are found, 1 if none, 2 for syntax errors or inaccessible files (even if matches were found).

NOTES

Ideally there should be only one **grep** command, but there is not a single algorithm that spans a wide enough range of space-time tradeoffs. Lines are limited to **BUFSIZ** bytes; longer lines are truncated. **BUFSIZ** is defined in **/usr/include/stdio.h**.

NAME

file – determine file type

SYNOPSIS

file [**-h**] [**-m** *mfile*] [**-f** *ffile*] *arg* . . .
file [**-h**] [**-m** *mfile*] **-f** *ffile*
file -c [**-m** *mfile*]

DESCRIPTION

file performs a series of tests on each file supplied by *arg* and, optionally, on each file supplied in *ffile* in an attempt to classify it. If *arg* appears to be a text file, **file** examines the first 512 bytes and tries to guess its programming language. If *arg* is an executable **a.out**, **file** prints the version stamp, provided it is greater than 0. If *arg* is a symbolic link, by default the link is followed and **file** tests the file that the symbolic link references.

-c Check the magic file for format errors. For reasons of efficiency, this validation is normally not carried out.

-f *ffile* *ffile* contains the names of the files to be examined.

-h Do not follow symbolic links.

-m *mfile* Use *mfile* as an alternate magic file, instead of **/etc/magic**.

file uses **/etc/magic** to identify files that have a magic number. A magic number is a numeric or string constant that indicates the file type. Commentary at the beginning of **/etc/magic** explains its format.

file classifies files containing supplementary code set characters according to the locale specified in the **LC_CTYPE** environment variable [see **LANG** on **environ**(5)]. **file** reads each argument and can distinguish data files, program text files, shell scripts, and executable files as follows:

Files	Classification
Data files containing supplementary characters	data
Shell scripts containing supplementary characters	command text
Language program text files containing literals or comments using supplementary characters	*xxx* text
Executable files	executable

FILES

/etc/magic
/usr/lib/locale/*locale***/LC_MESSAGES/uxcore**
language-specific message file [See **LANG** on **environ**(5).]

SEE ALSO

filehdr(4)

DIAGNOSTICS

If the **-h** option is specified and *arg* is a symbolic link, **file** prints the error message:

UX:file:ERROR:symbolic link to *arg*

NAME

filepriv – set, delete, or display privilege information associated with a file

SYNOPSIS

filepriv [**-f** *priv*[, . . .]] [**-i** *priv*[, . . .]] *file* . . .
filepriv -d *file* . . .

DESCRIPTION

filepriv is used to set, delete, or display the privilege information associated with a file.

The following options are available:

-d used to delete the privileges associated with the named file; also used to delete non-existent files from the Privilege Data File (PDF).

-f *priv,priv, . . .*
used to specify the fixed privileges associated with the named file.

-i *priv,priv, . . .*
used to specify the inheritable privileges associated with the named file.

Privilege information is stored in the Privilege Data File (PDF) located in **/etc/security/tcb/privs**.

filepriv must have the **P_SETSPRIV** and **P_SETUPRIV** privileges when setting or deleting file privileges, otherwise permission is denied.

The argument *priv* is defined as a process privilege name [see **intro**(2)]. The argument **allprivs** can be used to set or delete all the process privileges available. The *file* argument must be an absolute pathname of an executable file when setting or deleting file privileges. There must be at least one *file* argument specified; otherwise, **filepriv** exits with an error.

filepriv calls the **realpath** routine to resolve symbolic links. In this way, when new privileges are entered into the Privilege Data File for a symbolic link on a file that already exists in the the PDF, the privileges are associated correctly.

When setting file privileges, all fixed and inheritable privileges on the specified file are removed before those privileges specified by the **-f** and **-i** options are applied. Also, **filepriv** will set only privileges allowed by the maximum set of privileges on the process calling **filepriv**(2) as defined by the Privilege Data File.

The **filepriv** command exits with an error if the **-f** and **-i** options are specified and the same privilege exists in both.

When deleting privilege information from a file, the **-d** option is used. However, the **-d** option is also used to remove a non-existent file from the privilege database. If the file exists, then the **-d** option deletes privileges. If the file does not exist because it is a spurious file or has been removed from the system without the knowledge of the privilege administrator, then the **-d** option removes this file from the privilege database.

When no options are specified, **filepriv** displays the privileges associated with the named file(s).

Defaults

The file **/etc/default/privcmds** contains the following parameter:

GEN_CKSUM If the value of this parameter is **No**, then the **filepriv** command will not generate a check sum value for the Privilege Data File (PDF) located in **/etc/security/tcb/privs**; this results in faster performance compared to generating the check sum value each time the command is run. If the value of this parameter is anything other than **No** (including **NULL**, the default), then the **filepriv** command generates a check sum each time it is run.

EXAMPLE

The following is an example of the output when **filepriv** is executed with one file:

fixed *priv,priv, . . .*
inher *priv,priv, . . .*

If no fixed privileges exist on the file, the **fixed** privilege line is not displayed. If no inheritable privileges exist on the file, the **inher** privilege line is not displayed. The space between the privilege type and privileges is a single tab (\t) character.

If more than one file is specified, then the file name followed by a colon (**:**) and space character is printed before the privileges as follows:

file1: **fixed** *priv,priv, . . .*
file1: **inher** *priv,priv, . . .*
file2: **fixed** *priv,priv, . . .*
file2: **inher** *priv,priv, . . .*
file3: **fixed** *priv,priv, . . .*
file3: **inher** *priv,priv, . . .*

FILES

/etc/security/tcb/privs Privilege Data File
/etc/default/privcmds Default file.

SEE ALSO

initprivs(1M), **filepriv**(2),
intro(2) for a list of the available privileges and their meanings

DIAGNOSTICS

filepriv exits with a return code of 0 upon successful completion.

If **filepriv** detects errors, the following messages may be displayed:

undefined process privilege ''*priv*''

cannot use ''*priv*'' **as both fixed and inheritable privilege**

cannot access file ''*file*''

''*file*'' **is not an executable file**

permission denied

''*file*'' **is not an absolute pathname**

```
incompatible options specified
no such file or directory for file ''file''
''filepriv'' system call not in operation
Bad entry found in ''/etc/security/tcb/privs''
the file ''file'' was not found in the privilege data file
cannot create lock for ''/etc/security/tcb/privs''
```

NAME

find – find files

SYNOPSIS

find *path-list predicate-list*

DESCRIPTION

find recursively descends the directory hierarchy for each path name in the *path-list* (that is, one or more path names) seeking files that match a *predicate-list*, a boolean expression written in the primaries given below. It processes supplementary code set characters, and recognizes supplementary code set characters in *path-list* and as described below, according to the locale specified in the **LC_CTYPE** environment variable [see **LANG** on **environ**(5)]. Pattern searches are performed on characters, not bytes. In the descriptions, the argument *n* is used as a decimal integer where **+***n* means more than *n*, **-***n* means less than *n* and *n* means exactly *n*. Valid expressions are:

-name *pattern*
: True if *pattern* matches the current file name. Normal shell file name generation characters (see **sh**(1)) may be used. A backslash (\ ) is used as an escape character within the pattern. The pattern should be escaped or quoted when **find** is invoked from the shell. *pattern* may contain supplementary code set characters.

-perm [-]*onum*
: True if the file permission flags exactly match the octal number *onum* (see **chmod**(1)). If *onum* is prefixed by a minus sign (**-**), only the bits that are set in *onum* are compared with the file permission flags, and the expression evaluates true if they match.

-size *n*[**c**]
: True if the file is *n* blocks long (512 bytes per block). If *n* is followed by a **c**, the size is in bytes.

-atime *n*
: True if the file was accessed *n* days ago. The access time of directories in *path-list* is changed by **find** itself.

-mtime *n*
: True if the file's data was modified *n* days ago.

-ctime *n*
: True if the file's status was changed *n* days ago.

-exec *cmd*
: True if the executed *cmd* returns a zero value as exit status. A command argument **{}** is replaced by the current path name. The end of *cmd* must be punctuated by an escaped semicolon or a plus sign (+). When a plus sign is used, *cmd* aggregates a set of pathnames and executes on the set; when a semicolon is used, *cmd* executes on one pathname at a time. The net result is the same. *cmd* may contain supplementary code set characters.

-ok *cmd*
: Like **-exec** except that the generated command line is printed with a question mark first, and is executed only if the user responds by typing **y**. *cmd* may contain supplementary code set characters.

-print	Always true; causes the current path name to be printed.
-newer *file*	True if the current file has been modified more recently than the argument *file*.
-depth	Always true; causes descent of the directory hierarchy to be done so that all entries in a directory are acted on before the directory itself. This can be useful when **find** is used with **cpio**(1) to transfer files that are contained in directories without write permission.
-mount	Always true; restricts the search to the file system containing the directory specified.
-local	True if the file physically resides on the local system.
(*expression*)	True if the parenthesized expression is true (parentheses are special to the shell and must be escaped).
-type *c*	True if the type of the file is *c*, where *c* is **b**, **c**, **d**, **l**, **p**, or **f** for block special file, character special file, directory, symbolic link, fifo (named pipe), or plain file, respectively.
-follow	Causes symbolic links to be followed. When following symbolic links, **find** keeps track of the directories visited so that it can detect infinite loops; for example, such a loop would occur if a symbolic link pointed to an ancestor. This expression should not be used with the **-type l** expression.
-links *n*	True if the file has *n* links.
-user *uname*	True if the file belongs to the user *uname*. If *uname* is numeric and does not appear as a login name in the **/etc/passwd** file, it is taken as a user ID.
-nouser	True if the file belongs to a user not in the **/etc/passwd** file.
-group *gname*	True if the file belongs to the group *gname*. If *gname* is numeric and does not appear in the **/etc/group** file, it is taken as a group ID.
-nogroup	True if the file belongs to a group not in the **/etc/group** file.
-fstype *type*	True if the filesystem to which the file belongs is of type *type*.
-inum *n*	True if the file has inode number *n*.
-prune	Always yields true. Do not examine any directories or files in the directory structure below the *pattern* just matched. See the examples, below.

The primaries may be combined using the following operators (in order of decreasing precedence):

1. The negation of a primary (`!` is the unary *not* operator).
2. Concatenation of primaries (the *and* operation is implied by the juxtaposition of two primaries).
3. Alternation of primaries (`-o` is the *or* operator).

Note that when you use **find** in conjunction with **cpio**, if you use the **-L** option with **cpio** then you must use the **-follow** expression with **find** and vice versa. Otherwise there will be undesirable results.

EXAMPLES

Remove all files in your home directory named **a.out** or **.o* that have not been accessed for a week:

```
find $HOME \( -name a.out -o -name '*.o' \) -atime +7 -exec rm {} \;
```

Recursively print all file names in the current directory and below, but skipping SCCS directories:

```
find . -name SCCS -prune -o -print
```

Recursively print all file names in the current directory and below, skipping the contents of SCCS directories, but printing out the SCCS directory name:

```
find . -print -name S -prune
```

FILES

/etc/passwd
/etc/group
/usr/lib/locale/*locale***/LC_MESSAGES/uxcore.abi**
language-specific message file [See **LANG** on **environ** (5).]

SEE ALSO

chmod(1), **fs**(4), **sh**(1), **stat**(2), **test**(1), **umask**(2)

NOTE

When using **find** to determine files modified within a range of time, one must use the **?time** argument BEFORE the **-print** argument otherwise **find** will give all files.

The following option is obsolete and will not be supported in future releases.

-cpio *device* Always true; write the current file on *device* in **cpio**(1) format (5120-byte records).

finger (1)

NAME

finger – display information about local and remote users

SYNOPSIS

finger [**-bfhilmpqsw**] *username*. . .

finger [**-l**] *username@hostname*. . . (**TC/IP**)

DESCRIPTION

By default, the **finger** command displays information about each , logged-in user, including login name, full name, terminal name (prepended with a '*****' if write-permission is denied), idle time, login time, and location if known.

Idle time is minutes if it is a single integer, hours and minutes if a '**:**' is present, or days and hours if a **d** is present.

When one or more *username* arguments are given, more detailed information is given for each *username* specified, whether they are logged in or not. *username* must be that of a local user, and may be a first or last name, or an account name. When **finger** is used to find users on a remote device, the user and the name of the remote device are specified in the form *username@hostname.* Information is presented in a multi-line format, and includes, in addition to the information mentioned above:

> the user's home directory and login shell
>
> time the user logged in if currently logged in, or the time the user last logged in if not, as well as the terminal or host from which the user logged in and, if a terminal.
>
> last time the user received mail, and the last time the user read their mail
>
> any plan contained in the file **.plan** in the user's home directory
>
> and any project on which the user is working described in the file **.project** (also in the user's home directory)

The following options are available:

-b Suppress printing the user's home directory and shell in a long format printout.

-f Suppress printing the header that is normally printed in a non-long format printout.

-h Suppress printing of the **.project** file in a long format printout.

-i Force "idle" output format, which is similar to short format except that only the login name, terminal, login time, and idle time are printed.

-l Force long output format.

-m Match arguments only on user name (not first or last name).

-p Suppress printing of the **.plan** file in a long format printout.

-q Force quick output format, which is similar to short format except that only the login name, terminal, and login time are printed.

`-s` Force short output format.

`-w` Suppress printing the full name in a short format printout.

Within the **TCP/IP** network, the `-l` option can be used remotely.

FILES

`/var/adm/utmp`	who is logged in
`/etc/passwd`	for users' names
`/var/adm/lastlog`	last login times
`~/.plan`	plans
`~/.project`	projects

SEE ALSO

passwd(1), **who**(1), **whois**(1)

NOTES

Only the first line of the `~/.project` file is printed.

fingerd (1M)

NAME

fingerd, **in.fingerd** – remote user information server

SYNOPSIS

in.fingerd

DESCRIPTION

fingerd implements the server side of the Name/Finger protocol, specified in RFC 742. The Name/Finger protocol provides a remote interface to programs which display information on system status and individual users. The protocol imposes little structure on the format of the exchange between client and server. The client provides a single command line to the finger server which returns a printable reply.

fingerd waits for connections on TCP port 79. Once connected it reads a single command line terminated by a <RETURN-LINE-FEED> which is passed to **finger**(1). **fingerd** closes its connections as soon as the output is finished.

If the line is null (only a RETURN-LINEFEED is sent) then **finger** returns a default report that lists all users logged into the system at that moment.

If a user name is specified (for instance, **eric**<RETURN-LINE-FEED>) then the response lists more extended information for only that particular user, whether logged in or not. Allowable names in the command line include both login names and user names. If a name is ambiguous, all possible derivations are returned.

FILES

/var/utmp	who is logged in
/etc/passwd	for users' names
/var/adm/lastlog	last login times
$HOME/.plan	plans
$HOME/.project	projects

SEE ALSO

finger(1)

Harrenstien, Ken, *NAME/FINGER*, RFC 742, Network Information Center, SRI International, Menlo Park, Calif., December 1977

NOTES

Connecting directly to the server from a TIP or an equally narrow-minded TELNET-protocol user program can result in meaningless attempts at option negotiation being sent to the server, which will foul up the command line interpretation. **fingerd** should be taught to filter out IAC's and perhaps even respond negatively (IAC *will not)* to all option commands received.

NAME

fixperm – (XENIX) correct or initialize XENIX file permissions and ownership

SYNOPSIS

/usr/sbin/fixperm [**-aCcDfgiLlnOpSsUvwX** [**-d** *package*] [**-u** *package*]] *specfile*

DESCRIPTION

For each line in the specification file *specfile*, **fixperm** makes the listed pathname conform to a specification. **fixperm** is typically used by privileged users to configure a XENIX system upon installation. It has been provided for use with any existing XENIX packages that you want to install on the UNIX system. Non-privileged users can only use **fixperm** with the **-D** , **-f** , **-g** , **-i** , **-L** , **-l** , **-n**, **-O**, or **-X** options.

The following options are available:

Option	Description
-a	All files in the perm file must exist. This means that files marked as optional (type letter is in capital letters) must be present.
-C	Compress all C files.
-c	Creates empty files and missing directories.
-D	Lists directories only on standard output. Does not modify target files.
-d *package*	Processes input lines beginning with given package specifier string (see "Specification File Format," below). The default action is to process all lines.
-f	Lists files only on standard output. Does not modify target files.
-g	Lists all devices on the standard output. Target files are not modified (analogous to **-l**, **-f**, and **-D**).

-i	Checks to see if the selected packages are installed. Return values are
	`0:  package completely installed`
	`4:  package not installed`
	`5:  package partially installed`
	If the equivalent package was installed as a UNIX system package, **-i** will not detect it.

-L	List compressed C files.
-l	Lists files and directories on standard output. Does not modify target files.
-n	Reports errors only. Does not modify target files.
-O	Do not list link names. This option is ignored unless the **-f**, **-g**, **-l**, **-D**, or **-L** options are also specified.
-p	Check *specfile* for user id and group id before checking in **/etc/passwd** and **/etc/group**.

-S	Issues a complaint if files are not in x.out format.
-s	Modifies special device files in addition to the rest of the permlist.
-U	Uncompress all C files.
-u *package*	Causes similar action to **-d** option but processes items that are not part of the given package.
-v (*verbose*)	Issues a complaint if executable files are 1) word-swapped, 2) not fixed-stack, 3) not separate I and D, or 4) not stripped.
-w	Lists location (volume number) of the specified files or directories.
-X	Print only files and directories that are not installed. This option is ignored unless the **-f**, **-g**, **-l**, **-D**, or **-L** options are also specified.

Specification File Format

Each nonblank line in the specification file, **specfile**, consists of either a comment or an item specification. A comment is any text from a pound sign (**#**) up to the end of the line. There is one item specification per line. User and group id numbers must be specified at the top of the specification file for each user and group mentioned in the file.

An item specification consists of a package specifier, a permission specification, owner and group specifications, the number of links on the file, the filename, and an optional volume number.

The package specifier is an arbitrary string that is the name of a package within a distribution set. A package is a set of files.

A permission specification follows the package specifier. The permission specification consists of a file type, followed by a numeric permission specification. The item specification is one of the following characters:

Character	Description
x	executable
a	archive
e	empty file (create if **-c** option given)
b	block device
c	character device
d	directory
f	text file
p	named pipe

If the item specification is given as an uppercase letter, the file associated with it is optional, and **fixperm** will not return an error message if it does not exist.

The numeric permission conforms to the scheme described in **chmod** (1). The owner and group permissions are in the third column separated by a slash, such as **bin/bin**. The fourth column indicates the number of links. If there are links to the file, the next line contains the linked filename with no other information. The fifth column is a pathname. The pathname must be relative (not preceded by a slash (**/**).

The sixth column is only used for special files, major and minor device numbers, or volume numbers.

EXAMPLES

The following two lines make a distribution and invoke **tar**(1) to archive only the files in **my_package** on **/dev/sample** :

```
/usr/sbin/fixperm -f /etc/perm/my_package> list
tar cfF /dev/sample list
```

This command line reports package errors:

```
/usr/sbin/fixperm -nd my_package
```

NOTES

fixperm is usually only run by a shell script at installation.

fixperm should only be run from the directory to which the target files are relative.

SEE ALSO

chmod(1), **custom**(1M), **fixshlib**(1M), **tar**(1), **xinstall**(1M)

NAME

fixshlib – (XENIX) alters executables to call SCO UNIX System V/386 Release 3.2-compatible libnsl

SYNOPSIS

/usr/sbin/fixshlib *file*

DESCRIPTION

SCO applications installed with the **custom** command [see **custom**(1M)] will automatically have references to **libnsl** changed to reference a SCO UNIX System V/386 Release 3.2-compatible **libnsl** (**/shlib/libNSL_s**). However, you may need to run **fixshlib** on any SCO UNIX System V/386 Release 3.2 application that is not installed using the **custom** command. The **fixshlib** command will alter the executable to use the SCO UNIX System V/386 Release 3.2-compatible **libnsl**.

When executing the command, *file* is the pathname of the executable to be modified.

SEE ALSO

custom(1M), **fixperm**(1M), **xinstall**(1M)

DIAGNOSTICS

If *file* is not a COFF format **a.out** executable, you will see the following error message:

```
unknown file type - possibly bad magic: Error 0
```

NOTES

If **fixshlib** is run on a non-SCO UNIX executable, the executable will no longer execute properly and will be unusable. Therefore, as a precaution, we recommend that you make a copy of each executable before you run **fixshlib** on it. If your executable fails because **fixshlib** should not have been run on it, you can restore it from the copy you made. Otherwise, you will have to re-install the application that contained the executable.

NAME

`fmlcut` – cut out selected fields of each line of a file

SYNOPSIS

`fmlcut -c`*list* [*file* . . .]
`fmlcut -f`*list* [`-d`*char*] [`-s`] [*file* . . .]

DESCRIPTION

The `fmlcut` function cuts out columns from a table or fields from each line in *file*; in database parlance, it implements the projection of a relation. `fmlcut` can be used as a filter; if *file* is not specified or is `-`, the standard input is read. *list* specifies the fields to be selected. Fields can be fixed length (character positions) or variable length (separated by a field delimiter character), depending on whether `-c` or `-f` is specified.

Note that either the `-c` or the `-f` option must be specified.

The meanings of the options are:

list A comma-separated list of integer field numbers (in increasing order), with optional `-` to indicate ranges For example: `1,4,7`; `1-3,8`; `-5,10` (short for `1-5,10`); or `3-` (short for third through last field).

`-c`*list* If `-c` is specified, *list* specifies character positions (for example, `-c1-72` would pass the first 72 characters of each line). Note that no space intervenes between `-c` and *list*.

`-f`*list* If `-f` is specified, *list* is a list of fields assumed to be separated in the file by the default delimiter character, **TAB**, or by *char* if the `-d` option is specified. For example, `-f1,7` copies the first and seventh field only. Lines with no delimiter characters are passed through intact (useful for table subheadings), unless `-s` is specified. Note that no space intervenes between `-f` and *list*. The following options can be used if you have specified `-f`.

> `-d`*char* If `-d` is specified, *char* is the field delimiter. Space or other characters with special meaning to FMLI must be quoted. Note that no space intervenes between `-d` and *char*. The default field delimiter is **TAB**.
>
> `-s` Suppresses lines with no delimiter characters. If `-s` is not specified, lines with no delimiters will be passed through untouched.

EXAMPLES

`fmlcut -d: -f1,5 /etc/passwd`	gets login IDs and names
`` `who am i	fmlcut -f1 -d" "` ``	gets the current login name

DIAGNOSTICS

`fmlcut` returns the following exit values:

0 when the selected field is successfully cut out
2 on syntax errors

The following error messages may be displayed on the FMLI message line:

ERROR: `line too long`
A line has more than 1023 characters or fields, or there is no new-line character.

ERROR: `bad list for c / f option`
Missing `-c` or `-f` option or incorrectly specified *list*. No error occurs if a line has fewer fields than the *list* calls for.

ERROR: `no fields`
The *list* is empty.

ERROR: `no delimiter`
Missing *char* on `-d` option.

NOTES

`fmlcut` cannot correctly process lines longer than 1023 characters, or lines with no newline character.

SEE ALSO

`fmlgrep`(1F)

NAME

fmlexpr – evaluate arguments as an expression

SYNOPSIS

fmlexpr *arguments*

DESCRIPTION

The **fmlexpr** function evaluates its arguments as an expression. After evaluation, the result is written on the standard output. Terms of the expression must be separated by blanks. Characters special to FMLI must be escaped. Note that `0` is returned to indicate a zero value, rather than the null string. Strings containing blanks or other special characters should be quoted. Integer-valued arguments may be preceded by a unary minus sign. Internally, integers are treated as 32-bit, 2s complement numbers.

The operators and keywords are listed below. Characters that need to be escaped are preceded by `\`. The list is in order of increasing precedence, with equal precedence operators grouped within `{ }` symbols.

expr `\|` *expr*
: returns the first *expr* if it is neither null nor `0`, otherwise returns the second *expr*.

expr `\&` *expr*
: returns the first *expr* if neither *expr* is null or `0`, otherwise returns `0`.

expr { `=`, `\>`, `\>=`, `\<`, `\<=`, `!=` } *expr*
: returns the result of an integer comparison if both arguments are integers, otherwise returns the result of a lexical comparison.

expr { `+`, `-` } *expr*
: addition or subtraction of integer-valued arguments.

expr { `*`, `/`, `%` } *expr*
: multiplication, division, or remainder of the integer-valued arguments.

expr `:` *expr*
: The matching operator `:` compares the first argument with the second argument which must be a regular expression. Regular expression syntax is the same as that of **ed**(1), except that all patterns are "anchored" (that is, begin with ^) and, therefore, ^ is not a special character, in that context. Normally, the matching operator returns the number of bytes matched (`0` on failure). Alternatively, the `\( . . . \)` pattern symbols can be used to return a portion of the first argument.

EXAMPLES

1. Add 1 to the variable **a**:

```
'fmlexpr $a + 1 | set -l a'
```

2. For **$a** equal to either "**/usr/abc/***file*" or just "*file*":

```
fmlexpr  $a  :  .*/\(.*\)  \|  $a
```

returns the last segment of a path name (for example, *file*). Watch out for `/` alone as an argument: **fmlexpr** will take it as the division operator (see NOTES below).

3. A better representation of example 2.

```
fmlexpr //$a : .*/\(.*\)
```

The addition of the `//` characters eliminates any ambiguity about the division operator (because it makes it impossible for the left-hand expression to be interpreted as the division operator), and simplifies the whole expression.

4. Return the number of characters in **$VAR**.

```
fmlexpr $VAR : .*
```

DIAGNOSTICS

As a side effect of expression evaluation, **fmlexpr** returns the following exit values:

0	if the expression is neither null nor 0 (that is, TRUE)
1	if the expression is null or 0 (that is, FALSE)
2	for invalid expressions (that is, FALSE).

syntax error	for operator/operand errors
non-numeric argument	if arithmetic is attempted on such a string

In the case of syntax errors and non-numeric arguments, an error message will be printed at the current cursor position. Use **refresh** to redraw the screen.

NOTES

After argument processing by FMLI, **fmlexpr** cannot tell the difference between an operator and an operand except by the value. If **$a** is an `=`, the command:

```
fmlexpr $a = =
```

looks like:

```
fmlexpr = = =
```

as the arguments are passed to **fmlexpr** (and they will all be taken as the `=` operator). The following works, and returns TRUE:

```
fmlexpr X$a = X=
```

SEE ALSO

ed(1), **expr**(1), **set**(1F), **sh**(1)

NAME

fmlgrep – search a file for a pattern

SYNOPSIS

fmlgrep [*options*] *limited_regular_expression* [*file* . . .]

DESCRIPTION

fmlgrep searches *file* for a pattern and prints all lines that contain that pattern. The **fmlgrep** function uses limited regular expressions (expressions that have string values that use a subset of the possible alphanumeric and special characters) like those used with **ed**(1) to match the patterns. It uses a compact non-deterministic algorithm.

Be careful when using FMLI special characters (for example, **$, `, ´, "**) in *limited_regular_expression*. It is safest to enclose the entire *limited_regular_expression* in single quotes ´ . . . ´.

If *file* is not specified, **fmlgrep** assumes standard input. Normally, each line matched is copied to standard output. The file name is printed before each line matched if there is more than one input file.

Command line options are:

- `-b` Precede each line by the block number on which it was found. This can be useful in locating block numbers by context (first block is 0).
- `-c` Print only a count of the lines that contain the pattern.
- `-i` Ignore upper/lower case distinction during comparisons.
- `-l` Print only the names of files with matching lines, separated by new-lines. Does not repeat the names of files when the pattern is found more than once.
- `-n` Precede each line by its line number in the file (first line is 1).
- `-s` Suppress error messages about nonexistent or unreadable files.
- `-v` Print all lines except those that contain the pattern.

DIAGNOSTICS

fmlgrep returns the following exit values:

`0` if the pattern is found (that is, TRUE)
`1` if the pattern is not found (that is, FALSE)
`2` if an invalid expression was used or *file* is inaccessible

NOTES

Lines are limited to BUFSIZ characters; longer lines are truncated. BUFSIZ is defined in **/usr/include/stdio.h**.

If there is a line with embedded nulls, **fmlgrep** will only match up to the first null; if it matches, it will print the entire line.

SEE ALSO

ed(1), **egrep**(1), **fgrep**(1), **fmlcut**(1F), **grep**(1)

NAME

`fmli` – invoke FMLI

SYNOPSIS

`fmli` [`-a` *alias_file*] [`-c` *command_file*] [`-i` *initialization_file*] *file* . . .

DESCRIPTION

The `fmli` command invokes the Form and Menu Language Interpreter and opens the frame(s) specified by the *file* argument. The *file* argument is the pathname of the initial frame definition file(s), and must follow the naming convention `Menu.`*xxx*, `Form.`*xxx* or `Text.`*xxx* for a menu, form or text frame respectively, where *xxx* is any string that conforms to UNIX system file naming conventions. The FMLI descriptor `lifetime` will be ignored for all frames opened by argument to `fmli`. These frames have a lifetime of `immortal` by default.

The available options are as follows:

`-a` If `-a` is specified, *alias_file* is the name of a file which contains lines of the form *alias=pathname*. Thereafter, `$`*alias* can be used in definition files to simplify references to objects or devices with lengthy pathnames, or to define a search path (similar to `$PATH` in the UNIX system shell).

`-c` If `-c` is specified, *command_file* is the name of a file in which default FMLI commands can be disabled, and new application-specific commands can be defined. The contents of *command_file* are reflected in the FMLI Command Menu.

`-i` If `-i` is specified, *initialization_file* is the name of a file in which the following characteristics of the application as a whole can be specified:

A transient introductory frame displaying product information

A banner, its position, and other elements of the banner line

Color attributes for all elements of the screen

Screen Labeled Keys (SLKs) and their layout on the screen.

Environment Variables

`LOADPFK` When this variable is set to `yes`, `true`, or the null string, it directs FMLI to download alternative keystroke sequences into the function keys of terminals (such as the AT&T 5620 and 630) that do not have fixed, preset values for them. See the appendix titled "Keyboard and Mouse Support" of the for more information on automatic function key downloading.

`COLUMNS` Can be used to override the width of the logical screen defined for the terminal set in `TERM`. For terminals with a 132-column mode, for example, invoking FMLI with the line

`COLUMNS=132 fmli` *frame-file*

will allow this wider screen width to be used.

`LINES` Can be used to override the length of the logical screen defined for the terminal set in `TERM`.

LANG Can be used to obtain FMLI messages in a certain language. The default setting of **LANG** (**LANG=C**) makes FMLI output messages in English.

EXAMPLES

To invoke **fmli**:

```
fmli Menu.start
```

where **Menu.start** is an example of *file* named according to the file name conventions for menu definition files explained above.

To invoke **fmli** and name an initialization file:

```
fmli -i init.myapp Menu.start
```

where **init.myapp** is an example of *initialization_file*.

DIAGNOSTICS

If *file* is not supplied to the **fmli** command, **fmli** returns the message:

```
Initial object must be specified.
```

If *file* does not exist or is not readable, **fmli** returns an error message and exits. The example command line above returns the following message and exits:

```
Can't open object "Menu.start"
```

If *file* exists, but does not start with one of the three correct object names (**Menu.**, **Form.**, or **Text.**) or if it is named correctly but does not contain the proper data, **fmli** starts to build the screen by putting out the screen labels for function keys, after which it flashes the message:

```
I do not recognize that kind of object
```

and then exits.

FILES

/usr/bin/fmli

SEE ALSO

vsig(1F)

fmlmax (1F)

NAME

fmlmax – determine position or length of a field in a form

SYNOPSIS

fmlmax [-c *column*] [-l] *field1 . . .fieldn*

DESCRIPTION

The **fmlmax** command determines the position of a field on the screen after having determined the longest of the fields specified by the arguments *field1* to *fieldn*. Fields are input as strings between "". Normally, **fmlmax** would be used when re-designing forms that have been described with the autolayout descriptor set to **TRUE**. The **fmlmax** command can be alternatively used to determine the longest among a number of fields.

The available options are as follows:

-c If -c is specified, the column in which the fields start must be indicated in the variable **column**. The **fmlmax** utility would then calculate the beginning column on the basis of the following formula:

column + *length_of_longest_field* + 1.

-l If -l is specified, **fmlmax** is to calculate the length of the longest field among *field1* to *fieldn*.

EXAMPLES

To invoke **fmlmax**:

```
fmlmax -c 4 "abc" "abcdefgh" "a"
```

In this case **fmlmax** will return 13 as the beginning column of the input field after "abc", "abcdefgh" and "a".

To invoke **fmlmax** with the -l option:

```
fmlmax -l "abc"
```

the return value of fmlmax will be 3.

DIAGNOSTICS

The -c and -l options and cannot be used together.

If **fmlmax** is called without any option, the default for the beginning column of *field1* to *field* will be 1.

If **fmlmax** is used without arguments the **fmli** will flash the following message:

```
fmlmax: wrong number of arguments
```

and then will continue with the interpretation of the description file.

NAME

fmt – simple text formatters

SYNOPSIS

fmt [**-cs**] [**-w** *width*] [*file* . . .]

DESCRIPTION

fmt is a simple text formatter that fills and joins lines to produce output lines of (up to) the number of characters specified in the **-w** *width* option. The default *width* is 72. **fmt** concatenates the *inputfile*s listed as arguments. If none are given, **fmt** formats text from the standard input.

Blank lines are preserved in the output, as is the spacing between words. **fmt** does not fill lines beginning with a "**.**" (dot), for compatibility with **nroff**(1). Nor does it fill lines starting with "**From:**".

Indentation is preserved in the output, and input lines with differing indentation are not joined (unless **-c** is used).

fmt can also be used as an in-line text filter for **vi**(1); the **vi** command:

```
!}fmt
```

reformats the text between the cursor location and the end of the paragraph.

OPTIONS

-c Crown margin mode. Preserve the indentation of the first two lines within a paragraph, and align the left margin of each subsequent line with that of the second line. This is useful for tagged paragraphs.

-s Split lines only. Do not join short lines to form longer ones. This prevents sample lines of code, and other such formatted text, from being unduly combined.

-w *width* Fill output lines to up to *width* columns.

SEE ALSO

nroff(1), **vi**(1)

NOTES

The **-w** *width* option is acceptable for BSD compatibility, but it may go away in future releases.

fmtmsg (1)

NAME

fmtmsg – display a message on **stderr** or system console

SYNOPSIS

fmtmsg [**-c** *class*] [**-u** *subclass*] [**-l** *label*] [**-s** *severity*] [**-t** *tag*] [**-a** *action*] *text*

DESCRIPTION

Based on a message's classification component, **fmtmsg** either writes a formatted message to **stderr** or writes a formatted message to the console.

A formatted message consists of up to five standard components as defined below. The classification and subclass components are not displayed as part of the standard message, but rather define the source of the message and direct the display of the formatted message. The valid options are:

-c *class* — Describes the source of the message. Valid keywords are:

- **hard** — The source of the condition is hardware.
- **soft** — The source of the condition is software.
- **firm** — The source of the condition is firmware.

-u *subclass* — A list of keywords (separated by commas) that further defines the message and directs the display of the message. Valid keywords are:

- **appl** — The condition originated in an application. This keyword should not be used in combination with either **util** or **opsys**.
- **util** — The condition originated in a utility. This keyword should not be used in combination with either **appl** or **opsys**.
- **opsys** — The message originated in the kernel. This keyword should not be used in combination with either **appl** or **util**.
- **recov** — The application will recover from the condition. This keyword should not be used in combination with **nrecov**.
- **nrecov** — The application will not recover from the condition. This keyword should not be used in combination with **recov**.
- **print** — Print the message to the standard error stream **stderr**.
- **console** — Write the message to the system console. **print**, **console**, or both may be used.

-l *label* — Identifies the source of the message.

-s *severity* — Indicates the seriousness of the error. The keywords and definitions of the standard levels of *severity* are:

- **halt** — The application has encountered a severe fault and is halting.
- **error** — The application has detected a fault.
- **warn** — The application has detected a condition that is out of the ordinary and might be a problem.
- **info** — The application is providing information about a condition that is not in error.

`-t` *tag* — The string containing an identifier for the message.

`-a` *action* — A text string describing the first step in the error recovery process. This string must be written so that the entire *action* argument is interpreted as a single argument. **fmtmsg** precedes each action string with the **TO FIX:** prefix.

text — A text string describing the condition. Must be written so that the entire *text* argument is interpreted as a single argument.

The environment variables **MSGVERB** and **SEV_LEVEL** control the behavior of **fmtmsg**. **MSGVERB** is set by the administrator in the **/etc/profile** for the system. Users can override the value of **MSGVERB** set by the system by resetting **MSGVERB** in their own **.profile** files or by changing the value in their current shell session. **SEV_LEVEL** can be used in shell scripts.

MSGVERB tells **fmtmsg** which message components to select when writing messages to **stderr**. The value of **MSGVERB** is a colon separated list of optional keywords. **MSGVERB** can be set as follows:

> **MSGVERB=**[*keyword*[**:***keyword*[**:**. . .]]]
> **export MSGVERB**

Valid *keywords* are: **label**, **severity**, **text**, **action**, and **tag**. If **MSGVERB** contains a keyword for a component and the component's value is not the component's null value, **fmtmsg** includes that component in the message when writing the message to **stderr**. If **MSGVERB** does not include a keyword for a message component, that component is not included in the display of the message. The keywords may appear in any order. If **MSGVERB** is not defined, if its value is the null string, if its value is not of the correct format, or if it contains keywords other than the valid ones listed above, **fmtmsg** selects all components.

MSGVERB affects only which message components are selected for display. All message components are included in console messages.

SEV_LEVEL defines severity levels and associates print strings with them for use by **fmtmsg**. The standard severity levels shown below cannot be modified. Additional severity levels can be defined, redefined, and removed.

0	(no severity is used)
1	HALT
2	ERROR
3	WARNING
4	INFO

SEV_LEVEL is set as follows:

> **SEV_LEVEL=**[*description*[**:**description*[**:**. . .]]]
> **export SEV_LEVEL**

description is a comma-separated list containing three fields:

> *description***=***severity_keyword***,***level***,***printstring*

severity_keyword is a character string used as the keyword with the **-s** *severity* option to **fmtmsg**.

level is a character string that evaluates to a positive integer (other than `0`, `1`, `2`, `3`, or `4`, which are reserved for the standard severity levels). If the keyword *severity_keyword* is used, *level* is the severity value passed on to **fmtmsg**(3C).

printstring is the character string used by **fmtmsg** in the standard message format whenever the severity value *level* is used.

If **SEV_LEVEL** is not defined, or if its value is null, no severity levels other than the defaults are available. If a *description* in the colon separated list is not a comma separated list containing three fields, or if the second field of a comma separated list does not evaluate to a positive integer, that *description* in the colon separated list is ignored.

DIAGNOSTICS

The exit codes for **fmtmsg** are the following:

`0` All the requested functions were executed successfully.

`1` The command contains a syntax error, an invalid option, or an invalid argument to an option.

`2` The function executed with partial success, however the message was not displayed on **stderr**.

`4` The function executed with partial success, however the message was not displayed on the system console.

`32` No requested functions were executed successfully.

EXAMPLES

Example 1

The following example of **fmtmsg** produces a complete message in the standard message format and displays it to the standard error stream:

```
fmtmsg -c soft -u recov,print,appl -l UX:cat -s error -t
UX:cat:001 -a "refer to manual" "invalid syntax"
```

produces:

```
UX:cat: ERROR: invalid syntax
TO FIX: refer to manual   UX:cat:001
```

Example 2

When the environment variable **MSGVERB** is set as follows:

```
MSGVERB=severity:text:action
```

and Example 1 is used, **fmtmsg** produces:

```
ERROR: invalid syntax
TO FIX: refer to manual
```

Example 3

When the environment variable **SEV_LEVEL** is set as follows:

```
SEV_LEVEL=note,5,NOTE
```

the following **fmtmsg** command:

```
fmtmsg -c soft -u print -l UX:cat -s note -a "refer to
manual" "invalid syntax"
```

produces:

```
UX:cat: NOTE: invalid syntax
TO FIX: refer to manual
```

and displays the message on **stderr**.

NOTES

A slightly different standard error message format and a new developer interface, **pfmt**, is being introduced as the replacement for **fmtmsg**. A similar interface, **lfmt**, is also being introduced for producing a standard format message and forwarding messages to the console and/or to the system message logging and monitoring facilities.

fmtmsg will be removed and replaced by **pfmt** in a future release.

SEE ALSO

addseverity(3C), **fmtmsg**(3C)

fold(1)

NAME

`fold` – fold long lines

SYNOPSIS

`fold` [`-w` *width* | `-`*width*] [*filename* . . .]

DESCRIPTION

Fold the contents of the specified *filename*s, or the standard input if no files are specified, breaking the lines to have maximum width *width*. The default for *width* is 80. *width* should be a multiple of 8 if tabs are present, or the tabs should be expanded.

SEE ALSO

`pr`(1)

NOTES

Folding may not work correctly if underlining is present.

The `-w` *width* option is provided as a transition tool only. It will be removed in future releases.

NAME

`format` – format floppy disk tracks

SYNOPSIS

`/bin/format` [`-qvVE`] [`-f` *first*] [`-l` *last*] [`-i` *interleave*] *device*[`t`]

DESCRIPTION

The `format` command formats floppy disks. Unless otherwise specified, formatting starts at track 0 and continues until an error is returned at the end of a partition.

Options

The `-f` and `-l` options specify the first and last track to be formatted. The default interleave of 2 may be modified by using the `-i` option. *device* must specify a raw (character) floppy device. The `t` indicates the entire disk. Absence of this letter indicates that the first track of the diskette cannot be accessed.

`-q` Quiet mode. Perform the floppy disk format operation, but do not report status, inquiry, or error messages.

`-v` Verbose mode (always true).

`-V` Verify. After tracks are formatted, a random sector is chosen and a write of test data is done into it. The sector is then read back and a comparison is made.

`-E` exhaustive verify. Every sector is verified by write/read/compare.

Files

`/dev/rdsk/`* raw device for partition to be formatted

REFERENCES

`fd`(7)

NAME

fsadm (vxfs) – resize or reorganize a **vxfs** file system

SYNOPSIS

fsadm [**-F vxfs**] [**-D**] *mount_point*
fsadm [**-F vxfs**] [**-E**] *mount_point*
fsadm [**-F vxfs**] [**-e**] [**-E**] [**-s**] [**-v**] [**-l** *largesize*] [**-a** *days*] [**-t** *time*] [**-p** *passes*] [**-r** *rawdev*] *mount_point*
fsadm [**-F vxfs**] [**-d**] [**-D**] [**-s**] [**-v**] [**-a** *days*] [**-t** *time*] [**-p** *passes*] [**-r** *rawdev*] *mount_point*
fsadm [**-F vxfs**] [**-b** *newsize*] [**-r** *rawdev*] *mount_point*

DESCRIPTION

The **fsadm** utility is designed to perform file system administrative operations. The current version supports file system resizing, extent reorganization, and directory reorganization. The **fsadm** utility operates on file systems mounted for read/write access. Only a privileged user can resize or reorganize file systems.

The options are:

-F vxfs Specify the **vxfs** FSType.

-b *newsize* Resize the file system to *newsize* sectors.

-D Report on directory fragmentation. If specified in conjunction with the **-d** option, the fragmentation report is produced both before and after the directory reorganization.

-E Report on extent fragmentation. If specified in conjunction with the **-e** option, the fragmentation report is produced both before and after the extent reorganization.

-d Reorganize directories. Directory entries are reordered to place subdirectory entries first, then all other entries in order of time since last access. The directory is also compacted to remove free space.

-e Extent reorganization. Attempt to minimize fragmentation. Aged files are moved to the end of the allocation units to produce free space. Other files are reorganized to have the minimum number of extents possible.

-a *days* Consider files not accessed within the specified number of *days* as aged files. The default is 14 days. Aged files are moved to the end of the directory by the directory sort, and reorganized differently by the extent reorganization.

-l *largesize* Large file size in file system blocks. Indicates size of files to be considered as large files. The value must be between 8 and 2048 blocks. The default is 64 blocks.

-p *passes* Maximum number of *passes* to run. The default is five passes. Reorganizations are processed until reorganization is complete, or the specified number of passes have been run.

`-r` *rawdev* — Pathname of raw device to use. This option can be used when **fsadm** cannot determine what the raw device should be.

`-t` *time* — Maximum time to run. Reorganizations are processed until reorganization is complete, or the time limit has expired. The *time* is specified in seconds.

`-s` — Print a summary of activity at the end of each pass.

`-v` — Verbose. Report reorganization activity.

The `-b`, `-D`, `-E`, `-d`, and `-e` options determine what function will be performed. At least one of these options must be selected. The `-b` option can't be specified if any of the other options are specified. If both `-e` and `-d` are specified, the **fsadm** utility will do the directory reorganization first. It will do the extent reorganization after the directory reorganization has been completed.

For optimal performance, the kernel extent allocator must be able to find large extents when it wants them. To maintain the file system performance levels, the **fsadm** utility should be run periodically against all **vxfs** file systems to reduce fragmentation. The **fsadm** utility should be run somewhere between once a day and once a month against each file system. The frequency depends on file system usage and activity patterns, and the importance of performance. The `-v` option can be used to examine the amount of work performed by **fsadm**. The frequency of reorganization can be adjusted based on the rate of file system fragmentation.

There are two options that are available to control the amount of work done by the **fsadm** utility. The `-t` option is used to specify a maximum length of time to run. The `-p` option is used to specify a maximum number of passes to run. If both are specified, the utility exits if either of the terminating conditions is reached. By default, the **fsadm** utility will run two passes. If both the `-e` and `-d` options have been specified, the utility will run all the directory reorganization passes before any extent reorganization passes.

The **fsadm** utility uses the file **.fsadm** in the **lost+found** directory as a lock file. When **fsadm** is invoked, it opens the file **lost+found/.fsadm** in the root of the file system specified by *mount_point*. If the file doesn't exist, it is created. The **fcntl**(2) system call is used to obtain a write lock on the file. If the write lock fails, **fsadm** will assume that another **fsadm** is running and will fail. The **fsadm** utility will report the process ID of the process holding the write lock on the **.fsadm** file.

File System Resizing

If the `-b` option is specified, the **fsadm** utility will resize the file system whose mount point is *mount_point*. If *newsize* is larger than the current size of the file system, the file system will be expanded to *newsize* sectors. Similarly, if *newsize* is smaller than the current size of the file system, an attempt will be made to shrink the file system to *newsize* sectors.

Reducing the size of a file system can fail if there are file system resources currently in use within the sectors to be removed from the file system. In this case, a reorganization may help free those busy resources and allow a subsequent reduction in the file system size.

Directory Reorganization

If the **-d** option is specified, the **fsadm** utility will reorganize the directories on the file system whose mount point is *mount_point*. Directories are reorganized in two ways, compression and sorting.

For compression, the entries in the directory are moved to the front of the directory and the free space is grouped at the end of the directory. If there are no entries in the last block of the directory, the block is released and the directory size is lowered. If the directory entries are small enough, the directory will be placed in the inode immediate data area.

The entries in a directory are also sorted to improve pathname lookup performance. Entries are sorted based on the last access time of the entry. The **-a** option is used to specify a time interval, seven days is the default if **-a** isn't specified. The time interval is broken up into 128 buckets, and all times within the same bucket are considered equal. All access times older than the time interval are considered equal, and those entries are placed last. Subdirectory entries are placed at the front of the directory and symbolic links are placed after subdirectories, with the most recently accessed files.

The directory reorganization runs in one pass across the entire file system.

Extent Reorganization

If the **-e** option is specified, the **fsadm** utility will reorganize the data extents on the file system whose mount point is *mount_point*. The primary goal of extent reorganization is defragmentation of the file system.

To reduce fragmentation, the reorganization tries to place all small files in one contiguous extent. The **-l** option is used to specify the size of a file that is considered large. The default is 64 blocks. The reorganization also tries to group large files into large extents of at least 64 blocks. In addition to reducing fragmentation, these reorganizations can improve performance. Small files can be read or written in one I/O operation. Large files can approach raw disk performance for sequential I/O operations.

The extent reorganization also tries to improve locality of reference on the file system. Files are moved into the same allocation unit as their inode. Within the allocation unit, small files and directories are migrated to the front of the allocation unit. Large files and inactive files are migrated towards the back of the allocation unit. A file is considered inactive if the access time on the inode is more than 14 days old. The time interval can be varied using the **-a** option. This reorganization should reduce the average seek time by placing inodes and frequently used data closer together.

The **fsadm** utility will try to perform these reorganizations on all inodes on the file system. Each pass through the inodes will move the file system closer to the organization considered optimal by the **fsadm** utility. The first pass might place a file into one contiguous extent. The second pass might move the file into the same allocation unit at its inode. Then, since the first file has been moved, a third pass might move a file from another allocation unit into the space vacated by the first file during the second pass.

When the file system is more than 90% full, the **fsadm** utility shifts to a different reorganization scheme. Instead of attempting to make files contiguous, the reorganization tries to defragment the freelist into chunks of at least 64 blocks (*largesize*).

NOTES

`fsadm` is available with the VxFS Advanced package only.

FILES

`lost+found/.fsadm` lock file

SEE ALSO

`fcntl`(2), **vxfs**-specific `fs`(4), **vxfs**-specific **mkfs**(1M), **vxfsio**(7)

NAME

fsba – file system block analyzer

SYNOPSIS

/usr/sbin/fsba [**-b** *target_block_size*] *file-system1* [*file-system2* . . .]

DESCRIPTION

The **fsba** command determines the disk space required to store the data from an existing file system in a new file system with the specified logical block size. Each *file-system* listed on the command line refers to an existing file system and should be specified by device name (for example, **/dev/rdsk/***, where the value of * is machine dependent).

The *target_block_size* specifies the logical block size in bytes of the new file system. Valid target block sizes for the S5 file system are 512, 1024, and 2048. The default target block size for the S5 file system is 2048.

The **fsba** command prints information about how many 512-byte disk sectors are allocated to store the data in the old (existing) file system and how many would be required to store the same data in a new file system with the specified logical block size. It also prints the number of allocated and free i-nodes for the existing file system.

If the number of free sectors listed for the new file system is negative, the data will not fit in the new file system unless the new file system is larger than the existing file system. The new file system must be made at least as large as the number of sectors listed by **fsba** as allocated for the new file system. The maximum size of the new file system is limited by the size of the disk partition used for the new file system.

Note that it is possible to specify a *target_block_size* that is smaller than the logical block size of the existing file system. In this case the new file system would require fewer sectors to store the data.

SEE ALSO

mkfs(1M), **prtvtoc**(1M)

NAME

fscat – cat a **vxfs** file system

SYNOPSIS

fscat [**-F vxfs**] [**-o offset**] [**-l length**] [**-b block_size**] *special*

DESCRIPTION

The **fscat** utility provides an interface to a **vxfs** snapshot file system similar to that provided by the **dd** utility invoked on the special file of other **vxfs** file systems. On most **vxfs** file systems, the block or character special file for the file system provides access to a raw image of the file system for purposes such as backing up the file system to tape. On a snapshot file system, access to the corresponding block or character special provides little useful information. The **fscat** utility, however, provides a stream of bytes representing the file system snapshot. This stream can be processed in any of several ways, such as being processed in a pipeline, being written to a tape, and so on. **fscat** will work when executed on the special device of any **vxfs** file system.

By default, the output is a stream of bytes that starts at the beginning of the file system and goes to the end. On a snapshot file system, data is read from the file system using the **VX_SNAPREAD** ioctl on the mount point. On other **vxfs** file systems, data is read from the specified special file. Unless otherwise specified, data is written to standard output.

All numbers entered as options may have **0** prepended to indicate octal, or **0x** prepended to indicate hexadecimal. A **b** may be appended to indicate the value is in 512-byte blocks, a **k** to indicate the value is in kilobytes, or an **m** to indicate the value is in megabytes. An appended letter may be separated from the number by a space, in which case the letter and number should be enclosed in a set of quotes (for example, **"512 b"**).

The options are:

-F vxfs	Specify a **vxfs** FSType.
-o *offset*	Specify the starting offset, in bytes.
-l *length*	Specify the length, in bytes. A *length* of 0 goes to the end of the file system.
-b *block_size*	Specify the output block size, in bytes. *block_size* must be less than or equal to 1 megabyte.

NOTES

fscat is available with the VxFS Advanced package only.

A snapshot file system cannot be written to. A snapshot file system exists only as long as it is mounted; once unmounted, the special file no longer contains a snapshot file system.

SEE ALSO

dd(1M), **vxfs**-specific **fs**(4), **vxfsio**(7)

NAME

fsck (generic) – check and repair file systems

SYNOPSIS

fsck [**-F** *FSType*] [**-V**] [**-m**] [*special* . . .]
fsck [**-F** *FSType*] [**-V**] [*current_options*] [**-o** *specific_options*] [*special* . . .]

DESCRIPTION

fsck audits and interactively repairs inconsistent conditions for file systems. If the file system is inconsistent the user is prompted for concurrence before each correction is attempted. It should be noted that some corrective actions will result in some loss of data. The amount and severity of data loss may be determined from the diagnostic output. The default action for each correction is to wait for the user to respond **yes** or **no**.

The file system should be unmounted when **fsck** is used. If this is not possible, care should be taken that the system is quiescent and that it is rebooted immediately afterwards if the file system is a critical one, for example **root**.

current_options are options supported by the **s5**-specific module of **fsck**. Other *FSTypes* do not necessarily support these options. *specific_options* indicate suboptions specified in a comma-separated list of suboptions and/or keyword-attribute pairs for interpretation by the *FSType*-specific module of the command.

special represents a block or character special device (for example, **/dev/rdsk/***, where the value of * is machine dependent). It is preferable that a character special device be used. **fsck** will not work on a block device if it is mounted. If *special* is not supplied, **fsck** looks through **/etc/vfstab** and executes **fsck** for all character specials in the **fsckdev** field of **/etc/vfstab** for which there is a numeric entry in the **fsckpass** field.

The options are:

-F Specify the *FSType* on which to operate. If you are uncertain about the *FSType*, use the **fstyp** command to determine it, rather than looking it up in the **vfstab** file.

-V Echo the complete command line, but do not execute the command. The command line is generated by using the options and arguments provided by the user and adding to them information derived from **/etc/vfstab**. This option should be used to verify and validate the command line.

-m Check but don't repair. This option checks that the file system is suitable for mounting.

-o Specify *FSType*-specific options.

NOTE

This command may not be supported for all *FSTypes*.

FILES

/etc/vfstab list of default parameters for each file system

SEE ALSO

bfs-specific **fsck**(1M), **s5**-specific **fsck**(1M), **sfs**-specific **fsck**(1M), **ufs**-specific **fsck**(1M), **vxfs**-specific **fsck**(1M), **mkfs**(1M), **vfstab**(4)

NAME

fsck – (XENIX) check and repair XENIX filesystems

SYNOPSIS

fsck [*options*] [**filesystem**] . . .

DESCRIPTION

The **fsck** command audits and interactively repairs inconsistent conditions for XENIX System V filesystems. If the filesystem is consistent, then **fsck** reports number of files, number of blocks used, and number of blocks free. If the filesystem is inconsistent, the user is prompted whether or not **fsck** should proceed with each correction. It should be noted that most corrective actions result in some loss of data. The amount and severity of the loss can be determined from the diagnostic output. If the user does not have write permission, fsck defaults to the action of the **-n** option.

The **fsck** options are:

-y Assumes a response to all questions asked by **fsck**.

-n Assumes a response to all questions asked by **fsck**. This option does not open the filesystem for writing.

-s *b:c* Ignores the actual free list and unconditionally reconstructs a new one by rewriting the super-block of the filesystem. The filesystem must be unmounted while this is done.

This option allows for creating an optimal free-list organization. The following forms are supported:

-s

-sBlocks-per-cylinder:Blocks-to-skip (filesystem interleave)

If *b:c* is not given, then the values that were used when the filesystem was created are used again. If these values were not specified, then the default value is used.

-S Conditionally reconstructs the free list. This option is similar to **-s** *b:c* above, except that the free list is rebuilt only if there are no discrepancies discovered in the filesystem. The **-S** option forces a "no" response to all questions asked by **fsck**. This option is useful for forcing free-list reorganization on uncontaminated filesystems.

-t Causes **fsck** to use the next argument as the scratch file, if needed. A scratch file is used if **fsck** cannot obtain enough memory to keep its tables. Without the **-t** flag, **fsck** prompts the user for the name of the scratch file. The file chosen should not be on the filesystem being checked. In addition, if the scratch file is not a special file or did not already exist, it is removed when **fsck** completes. Note that if the system has a large hard disk, there may not be enough space on another filesystem for the scratch file. In such cases, if the system has a floppy disk drive, use a blank, formatted floppy disk in the floppy disk drive with (for example) **/dev/fd0** specified as the scratch file.

`-q` Causes **fsck** to perform a quiet check. Does not print size-check messages in Phase 1. Unreferenced **fifo5** files are selectively removed. If **fsck** requires it, counts in the superblock are automatically fixed and the free list salvaged.

`-D` Checks directories for bad blocks. Use this option after the system crashes.

`-f` Causes **fsck** to perform a fast check. **fsck** checks block and sizes (Phase 1) and checks the free list (Phase 5). The free list is reconstructed (Phase 6), if necessary.

`-c` Causes any supported filesystem to be converted to the current filesystem type. The user is prompted to verify the conversion of each filesystem, unless the **-y** option is specified. It is recommended that every filesystem be checked with this option *while unmounted* if it is to be used with the current version of XENIX. To update the active root filesystem, check it with the following command line:

```
fsck -c -rr /dev/root
```

If no *filesystems* are specified, **fsck** reads a list of default filesystems from the **/etc/checklist** file.

The following are some of the inconsistencies **fsck** checks for:

- Blocks claimed by more than one inode or the free list
- Blocks claimed by an inode or the free list outside the range of the filesystem
- Incorrect link counts
- Size checks:
  Incorrect number of blocks
  Directory size not 16-byte aligned
- Bad inode format
- Blocks not accounted for anywhere
- Directory checks:
  File pointing to unallocated inode
  Inode number out of range
- Super block checks:
  More than 65536 inodes
  More blocks for inodes than there are in the filesystem
- Bad free block list format
- Total free block or free inode count incorrect

With the user's consent, **fsck** reconnects orphaned (allocated, but unreferenced) files and directories by placing them in the *lost+found* directory. The file's (or directory's) inode number then becomes its name. Note that the *lost+found* directory must already exist in the root of the filesystem being checked and must have empty slots in which entries can be made. To create the *lost+found* directory, copy a few files to the directory, then remove them (before executing **fsck**).

FILES

`/etc/checklist`	Contains default list of filesystems to check
`/etc/default/boot`	Contains flags for automatic boot control

NOTES

fsck will not run on a mounted non-raw filesystem, unless the filesystem is the root filesystem, or the **-n** option is specified and no writing out of the filesystem will take place. If any such attempt is made, **fsck** displays a warning and no further processing of the filesystem is done for the specified device.

fsck does not support filesystems created under XENIX-86 version 3.0 because the word order in type *long* variables has changed. However, **fsck** is capable of auditing and repairing XENIX version 3.0 filesystems if the word ordering is correct.

Run **fsck /dev/??** on the *unmounted* block device for all other filesystems.

It is not recommended that users use **fsck** on raw devices. Although checking a raw device is almost always faster, there is no way to tell if the filesystem is mounted. If the filesystem is mounted, cleaning it will almost certainly result in an inconsistent superblock.

NAME

fsck (bfs) - check and repair **bfs** file systems

SYNOPSIS

fsck [-F bfs] [*generic_options*] [*special* . . .]
fsck [-F bfs] [*generic_options*] **[-y | -n]** [*special* . . .]

DESCRIPTION

generic_options are options supported by the generic **fsck** command.

fsck checks to see if compaction was in process but was not completed, perhaps as a result of a system crash. If it was, **fsck** completes the compaction of the file [see **bfs**-specific **fs**(4)].

The options are:

- **-y** Assume a yes response to all questions asked by **fsck**.
- **-n** Assume a no response to all questions asked by **fsck**.

SEE ALSO

generic **fsck**(1M), **bfs**-specific **fs**(4), **mkfs**(1M)

NAME

fsck (s5) – check and repair **s5** file systems

SYNOPSIS

fsck [**-F s5**] [*generic_options*] [*special...*]
fsck -F s5 [*generic_options*] [**-y**] [**-n**] [**-p**] [**-s***X*] [**-S***X*] [**-t***file*] [**-l**] [**-q**] [**-D**] [**-f**] [*special . . .*]

DESCRIPTION

generic_options are options supported by the generic **fsck** command.

The options are:

-F s5 Specifies the **s5**-FSType.

-y Assume a **yes** response to all questions asked by **fsck**.

-n Assume a **no** response to all questions asked by **fsck**; do not open the file system for writing.

-p Correct inconsistencies that can be fixed automatically, that is, inconsistencies that are deemed harmless and can be fixed without confirmation by the administrator. Examples of such inconsistencies are unreferenced i-nodes, incorrect counts in the superblocks, and missing blocks in the free list.

-s*X* Ignore the actual free list and (unconditionally) reconstruct a new one by rewriting the super-block of the file system. The file system should be unmounted while this is done; if this is not possible, care should be taken that the system is quiescent and that it is rebooted immediately afterwards. This precaution is necessary so that the old, bad, in-core copy of the superblock will not continue to be used, or written on the file system.

The **-s***X* suboption allows for creating an optimal free-list organization.

If *X* is not given, the values used when the file system was created are used. The format of *X* is *cylinder size:gap size.*

-S*X* Conditionally reconstruct the free list. This suboption is like **-s***X* above except that the free list is rebuilt only if there were no discrepancies discovered in the file system. Using **S** will force a **no** response to all questions asked by **fsck**. This suboption is useful for forcing free list reorganization on uncontaminated file systems.

-t*file* If **fsck** cannot obtain enough memory to keep its tables, it uses a scratch file. If the **t** option is specified, the *file* named is used as the scratch file, if needed. Without the **t** option, **fsck** will prompt the user for the name of the scratch file. The file chosen should not be on the file system being checked, and if it is not a special file or did not already exist, it is removed when **fsck** completes.

-l Identify damaged files by their logical names.

-q Quiet **fsck**. Unreferenced **fifos** will silently be removed. If **fsck** requires it, counts in the superblock will be automatically fixed and the free list salvaged.

-D Directories are checked for bad blocks. Useful after system crashes.

-f Fast check. Check block and sizes and check the free list. The free list will be reconstructed if it is necessary.

Inconsistencies checked are as follows:

1. Blocks claimed by more than one i-node or the free list.
2. Blocks claimed by an i-node or the free list outside the range of the file system.
3. Incorrect link counts.
4. Size checks:
   - Incorrect number of blocks.
   - Directory size not 16-byte aligned.
5. Bad i-node format.
6. Blocks not accounted for anywhere.
7. Directory checks:
   - File pointing to unallocated i-node.
   - I-node number out of range.
8. Super Block checks:
   - More than 65536 i-nodes.
   - More blocks for i-nodes than there are in the file system.
9. Bad free block list format.
10. Total free block and/or free i-node count incorrect.

Orphaned files and directories (allocated but unreferenced) are, with the user's concurrence, reconnected by placing them in the **lost+found** directory, if the files are nonempty. The user will be notified if the file or directory is empty or not. Empty files or directories are removed, as long as the **n** suboption is not specified. **fsck** will force the reconnection of nonempty directories. The name assigned is the i-node number.

NOTE

Checking the raw device is almost always faster.

I-node numbers for **.** and **..** in each directory are not checked for validity.

When **fsck** detects an incorrect file size, it prompts you to choose whether you want the file truncated or expanded to match the number of blocks allocated. Increasing the file size may produce unwanted data at the end of your file; truncating the file may destroy data in the last few blocks.

SEE ALSO

crash(1M), **s5**-specific version of **fs**(4), generic **fsck**(1M), **mkfs**(1M), **ncheck**(1M)

NAME

fsck (sfs) – file system consistency check and interactive repair

SYNOPSIS

fsck [**-F sfs**] [*generic_options*] [*special* . . .]
fsck [**-F sfs**] [*generic_options*] [**(-y|-Y)|(-n|-N)**] [**-o p,b=#,w**] [*special* . . .]

DESCRIPTION

generic_options are options supported by the generic **fsck** command. *current_options* are options supported by the **s5**-specific module of the **fsck** command.

fsck audits and interactively repairs inconsistent conditions on file systems. In this case, it asks for confirmation before attempting any corrections. Inconsistencies other than those mentioned above can often result in some loss of data. The amount and severity of data lost can be determined from the diagnostic output.

fsck corrects innocuous inconsistencies such as: unreferenced inodes, too-large link counts in inodes, missing blocks in the free list, blocks appearing in the free list and also in files, or incorrect counts in the super block, automatically. It displays a message for each inconsistency corrected that identifies the nature of, and file system on which, the correction is to take place. After successfully correcting a file system, **fsck** prints the number of files on that file system, the number of used and free blocks, and the percentage of fragmentation.

The default action for each correction is to wait for the operator to respond either **yes** or **no**. If the operator does not have write permission on the file system, **fsck** will default to a **-n** (no corrections) action.

The **sfs** file system is based on the **ufs** file system, but uses only the even-numbered inodes for conventional purposes. The odd-numbered inodes are used to store security information. When this manual page uses the term inode, it refers to an even-numbered inode. An odd-numbered inode will be called a secure inode.

Inconsistencies checked are as follows:

> Blocks claimed by more than one inode, secure inode, ACL, or the free list.
>
> Blocks claimed by an inode, secure inode, ACL, or the free list outside the range of the file system.
>
> Incorrect link counts.
>
> Incorrect directory sizes.
>
> Bad inode format.
>
> Blocks not accounted for anywhere.
>
> Directory checks, file pointing to unallocated inode, inode number out of range, absence of '**.**' and '**. .**' as the first two entries in each directory.
>
> Super Block checks: more blocks for inodes than there are in the file system.
>
> Bad free block list format.
>
> Total free block and/or free inode count incorrect.

Orphaned files and directories (allocated but unreferenced) are, with the operator's concurrence, reconnected by placing them in the **lost+found** directory. The name assigned is the inode number. If the **lost+found** directory does not exist, it is created. If there is insufficient space its size is increased.

A file system may be specified by giving the name of the block or character special device on which it resides, or by giving the name of its mount point.

The options are:

-F sfs Specifies the **sfs**-FSType.

-y | -Y Assume a yes response to all questions asked by **fsck**.

-n | -N Assume a no response to all questions asked by **fsck**; do not open the file system for writing.

-o Specify **sfs** file system specific suboptions. These suboptions can be any combination of the following:

- **p** Check the filesystem non-interactively. Exit if there is a problem requiring intervention.
- **b=#** Use the block specified as the super block for the file system. Block 32 is always an alternate super block.

NOTES

Checking the character special device is almost always faster.

SEE ALSO

crash(1M), **sfs**-specific **fs**(4), generic **fsck**(1M), **mkfs**(1M)

NAME

fsck (ufs) – file system consistency check and interactive repair

SYNOPSIS

fsck [**-F ufs**] [*generic_options*] [*special* ...]
fsck [**-F ufs**] [*generic_options*] [**(-y|-Y)|(-n|-N)**] [**-o p,b=***blkno*,w]
[*special* . . .]

DESCRIPTION

generic_options are options supported by the generic **fsck** command.

fsck audits and interactively repairs inconsistent conditions on file systems. In this case, it asks for confirmation before attempting any corrections. Inconsistencies other than those mentioned above can often result in some loss of data. The amount and severity of data lost can be determined from the diagnostic output.

fsck corrects innocuous inconsistencies such as: unreferenced inodes, too-large link counts in inodes, missing blocks in the free list, blocks appearing in the free list and also in files, or incorrect counts in the super block, automatically. It displays a message for each inconsistency corrected that identifies the nature of, and file system on which, the correction is to take place. After successfully correcting a file system, **fsck** prints the number of files on that file system, the number of used and free blocks, and the percentage of fragmentation.

The default action for each correction is to wait for the operator to respond either **yes** or **no**. If the operator does not have write permission on the file system, **fsck** will default to a **-n** (no corrections) action.

Inconsistencies checked are as follows:

- Blocks claimed by more than one inode or the free list.
- Blocks claimed by an inode or the free list outside the range of the file system.
- Incorrect link counts.
- Incorrect directory sizes.
- Bad inode format.
- Blocks not accounted for anywhere.
- Directory checks, file pointing to unallocated inode, inode number out of range, absence of '**.**' and '**..**' as the first two entries in each directory.
- Super Block checks: more blocks for inodes than there are in the file system.
- Bad free block list format.
- Total free block and/or free inode count incorrect.

Orphaned files and directories (allocated but unreferenced) are, with the operator's concurrence, reconnected by placing them in the **lost+found** directory. The name assigned is the inode number. If the **lost+found** directory does not exist, it is created. If there is insufficient space its size is increased.

A file system may be specified by giving the name of the block or character special device on which it resides, or by giving the name of its mount point.

The options are:

-F ufs Specifies the **ufs**-FSType.

-y | -Y Assume a yes response to all questions asked by **fsck**.

-n | -N Assume a no response to all questions asked by **fsck**; do not open the file system for writing.

-o Specify the options specific to the **ufs** file system. These options can be any combination of the following:

- **p** Check the filesystem non-interactively. Exit if there is a problem requiring intervention.
- **b=***blkno* Use *blkno* as the super block for the file system. Block 32 is always an alternate super block.

NOTES

Checking the character special device is almost always faster.

SEE ALSO

crash(1M), generic **fsck**(1M), **mkfs**(1M)

NAME

fsck (vxfs) – check and repair **vxfs** file systems

SYNOPSIS

fsck [**-F vxfs**] [*generic_options*] [**-y**] [**-n**] [**-o full,nolog**] *special* . . .

DESCRIPTION

generic_options are options supported by the generic **fsck** command.

The options are:

-F vxfs Specify the **vxfs** FSType.

-y Assume a **yes** response to all questions asked by **fsck**. Additionally, if the file system requires a full file system check after the log replay, or if the **nolog** suboption causes the log replay to be skipped and the file system is not clean, then a full file system check is performed.

-n Assume a **no** response to all questions asked by **fsck**; do not open the file system for writing. Log replay is not performed. A full file system check is performed.

-o Specify **vxfs** file system specific options. These options can be a combination of the following in a comma-separated list:

- **full** Perform a full file system check. The default is to perform an intent log replay only. Since the **vxfs** file system maintains an intent log, a complete check is generally not required. If the file system detects damage or the log replay operation detects damage, an indication that a complete check is required is placed in the super-block, and a full check is performed.
- **nolog** Do not perform log replay. This option may be used if the log area was physically damaged.

When a full check is performed, the following inconsistencies are checked:

- Blocks claimed by more than one inode or the free list.
- Blocks claimed by an inode outside the range of the file system.
- Incorrect link counts.
- Size checks:
  - Incorrect number of blocks.
  - Directory entry format.
- Bad inode format.
- Blocks not accounted for anywhere.
- Directory checks:
  - File pointing to unallocated inode.
  - Inode number out of range.
  - Linkage to parent directory.
  - Hash chain linkage.
  - Free space count.
- Super-block checks:
  - Checksum mismatch.
  - More blocks for inodes than there are in the file system.

— Bad free block list format.
— Total free block and/or free inode count incorrect.

Orphaned files and directories (allocated but unreferenced) are, with the user's concurrence, reconnected by placing them in the **lost+found** directory. The name assigned is the inode number. The only restriction is that the directory **lost+found** must already exist in the root of the file system being checked.

OUTPUT

Structural errors discovered during a full check are displayed on standard output. Responses required during a full check are read from standard input.

The following return codes are used for the **-m** (generic) option for all devices other than the one used by the root file system:

- 0 The file system is unmounted and clean.
- 32 The file system is unmounted and needs checking.
- 33 The file system is mounted.
- 34 The **stat** of the device failed.
- Other The state could not be determined because of an error.

The following return codes are used for the **-m** (generic) option for the device used by the root file system:

- 0 The root file system is mounted read-only and is clean, or the root file system is mounted read/write and therefore doesn't need checking.
- 32 The root file system is mounted read-only and needs checking.
- 34 The **stat** of the device failed.
- Other The state could not be determined because of an error.

ERROR/DIAGNOSTICS

All error messages that relate to the contents of a file system produced during a log replay are displayed on standard output. All I/O failures and exit messages are displayed on standard error output.

NOTES

Checking the raw device is almost always faster.

A full file system check will always perform any pending extended inode operations without operator interaction. If a structural flaw is detected, the full **fsck** flag will be set on the file system, without operator interaction.

SEE ALSO

crash(1M), **vxfs**-specific **fs**(4), generic **fsck**(1M), **mkfs**(1M), **ncheck**(1M), **uadmin**(2)

fsdb (1M)

NAME

fsdb (generic) – file system debugger

SYNOPSIS

fsdb [**-F** *FSType*] [**-V**] [*current_options*] [**-o** *specific_options*] *special*

DESCRIPTION

fsdb is a file system debugger which allows for the manual repair of a file system after a crash. *special* is a special device used to indicate the file system to be debugged. **fsdb** is intended for experienced users only. *FSType* is the file system type to be debugged. Since different *FSTypes* have different structures and hence different debugging capabilities the manual pages for the *FSType*-specific **fsdb** should be consulted for a more detailed description of the debugging capabilities.

fsdb processes supplementary code set characters according to the locale specified in the **LC_CTYPE** environment variable [see **LANG** on **environ**(5)], except that the **f** or **="** symbols do not display multibyte characters correctly.

current_options are options supported by the **s5**-specific module of **fsdb**. Other *FSTypes* do not necessarily support these options. *specific_options* indicate suboptions specified in a comma-separated list of suboptions and/or keyword-attribute pairs for interpretation by the *FSType*-specific module of the command.

The options are:

-F Specify the *FSType* on which to operate. The *FSType* should either be specified here or be determinable from **/etc/vfstab** by matching the *special* with an entry in the table.

-V Echo the complete command line, but do not execute the command. The command line is generated by using the options and arguments provided by the user and adding to them information derived from **/etc/vfstab**. This option should be used to verify and validate the command line.

-o Specify *FSType*-specific options.

FILES

/etc/vfstab list of default parameters for each file system

SEE ALSO

s5-specific **fsdb**(1M), **sfs**-specific **fsdb**(1M), **ufs**-specific **fsdb**(1M), **vxfs**-specific **fsdb**(1M), **mkfs**(1M), **vfstab**(4)

NOTES

This command may not be supported for all *FSTypes*.

NAME

fsdb (s5) – **s5** file system debugger

SYNOPSIS

fsdb [**-F s5**] [*generic_options*] [**-z** *i-number*] *special* [–]

DESCRIPTION

generic_options are options supported by the generic **fsdb** command.

fsdb can be used to patch up a damaged **s5** file system after a crash. *special* is a special device used to indicate the file system to be debugged. It has conversions to translate block and i-numbers into their corresponding disk addresses. Also included are mnemonic offsets to access different parts of an i-node. These greatly simplify the process of correcting control block entries or descending the file system tree.

fsdb contains several error-checking routines to verify i-node and block addresses. These can be disabled if necessary by invoking **fsdb** with the optional - argument or by the use of the **O** symbol. (**fsdb** reads the i-size and f-size entries from the superblock of the file system as the basis for these checks.)

The options are:

-F s5 Specifies the **s5**-FSType.

-z *i-number* Clear the i-node identified by *i-number*. Non-interactive.

Numbers are considered decimal by default. Octal numbers must be prefixed with a zero. During any assignment operation, numbers are checked for a possible truncation error due to a size mismatch between source and destination.

fsdb reads a block at a time and will therefore work with raw as well as block I/O. A buffer management routine is used to retain commonly used blocks of data in order to reduce the number of read system calls. All assignment operations result in an immediate write-through of the corresponding block.

The symbols recognized by **fsdb** are:

#	absolute address
i	convert from i-number to i-node address
b	convert to block address
d	directory slot offset
+, -	address arithmetic
q	quit
>, <	save, restore an address
=	numerical assignment
=+	incremental assignment
=-	decremental assignment
="	character string assignment
O	error checking flip flop
p	general print facilities
f	file print facility
B	byte mode

`W`	word mode
`D`	double word mode
`!`	escape to shell

The print facilities generate a formatted output in various styles. The current address is normalized to an appropriate boundary before printing begins. It advances with the printing and is left at the address of the last item printed. The output can be terminated at any time by typing the delete character. If a number follows the `p` symbol, that many entries are printed. A check is made to detect block boundary overflows since logically sequential blocks are generally not physically sequential. If a count of zero is used, all entries to the end of the current block are printed. The print options available are:

`i`	print as i-nodes
`d`	print as directories
`o`	print as octal words
`e`	print as decimal words
`c`	print as characters
`b`	print as octal bytes

The `f` symbol is used to print data blocks associated with the current i-node. If followed by a number, that block of the file is printed. (Blocks are numbered from zero.) The desired print option letter follows the block number, if present, or the `f` symbol. This print facility works for small as well as large files. It checks for special devices and that the block pointers used to find the data are not zero.

Dots, tabs, and spaces may be used as function delimiters but are not necessary. A line with just a new-line character will increment the current address by the size of the data type last printed. That is, the address is set to the next byte, word, double word, directory entry or i-node, allowing the user to step through a region of a file system. Information is printed in a format appropriate to the data type. Bytes, words and double words are displayed with the octal address followed by the value in octal and decimal. A `.B` or `.D` is appended to the address for byte and double word values, respectively. Directories are printed as a directory slot offset followed by the decimal i-number and the character representation of the entry name. I-nodes are printed with labeled fields describing each element.

The following mnemonics are used for i-node examination and refer to the current working i-node:

`md`	mode
`ln`	link count
`uid`	user ID number
`gid`	group ID number
`sz`	file size
`a#`	data block numbers (0 – 12)
`at`	access time
`mt`	modification time
`maj`	major device number
`min`	minor device number

EXAMPLES

`386i` prints i-number 386 in an i-node format. This now becomes the current working i-node.

`ln=4` changes the link count for the working i-node to 4.

`ln=+1` increments the link count by 1.

`fc` prints, in ASCII, block zero of the file associated with the working i-node.

`2i.fd` prints the first 32 directory entries for the root i-node of this file system.

`d5i.fc` changes the current i-node to that associated with the 5th directory entry (numbered from zero) found from the above command. The first logical block of the file is then printed in ASCII.

`512B.p0o` prints the superblock of this file system in octal.

`2i.a0b.d7=3` changes the i-number for the seventh directory slot in the root directory to 3. This example also shows how several operations can be combined on one command line.

`d7.nm="`*name*`"` changes the name field in the directory slot to the given string. Quotes are optional when used with **nm** if the first character is alphabetic.

`a2b.p0d` prints the third block of the current i-node as directory entries.

SEE ALSO

dir(4), **s5**-specific **fs**(4), **fsck**(1M), generic **fsdb**(1M)

NAME

fsdb (sfs)– **sfs** file system debugger

SYNOPSIS

fsdb [**-F sfs**] [*generic_options*] [**-z** *i-number*] *special*

DESCRIPTION

generic_options are options supported by the generic **fsdb** command.

The options are:

-F sfs
: Specifies the **sfs**-FSType.

-z *i-number*
: Clear the i-node identified by *i-number*. Note that the *i-number* must be even. Non-interactive.

SEE ALSO

dirent(4), **sfs**-specific **fs**(4) **fsck**(1M), generic **fsdb**(1M)

NAME

fsdb (ufs) – **ufs** file system debugger

SYNOPSIS

fsdb [**-F ufs**] [*generic_options*] [**-z** *i-number*] *special*

DESCRIPTION

generic_options are options supported by the generic **fsdb** command.

The options are:

-F ufs Specifies the **ufs**-FSType.

-z *i-number* Clear the i-node identified by *i-number*. Non-interactive.

SEE ALSO

dir(4), **fsck**(1M), generic **fsdb**(1M)

NAME

fsdb (vxfs) – **vxfs** file system debugger

SYNOPSIS

fsdb [**-F vxfs**] [*generic_options*] [**-z** *inumber*] *special*

DESCRIPTION

generic_options are options supported by the generic **fsdb** command.

fsdb can be used to patch up a damaged **vxfs** file system. It has conversions to translate block and inumbers into their corresponding disk addresses. Also included are mnemonic offsets to access different parts of an inode. These greatly simplify the process of correcting control block entries or descending the file system tree.

The options are:

-F vxfs Specify the **vxfs** FSType.

-z *inumber* Clear the inode identified by *inumber* (non-interactive). Multiple **-z** options accumulate.

NOTE: After using the **fsdb -z** command, a full file system check should be performed (using **fsck -o full,nolog**).

By default, numbers are considered decimal. Octal numbers must be prefixed with a zero. Hexadecimal numbers must be prefixed with **0x**. When using hexadecimal numbers, it is preferable to follow the number with a space, since a number of commands are letters that are also hexadecimal digits. In this document a pound sign (#) is used to indicate that a number is to be specified.

fsdb reads a block at a time and works with raw and block I/O. All I/O is unbuffered, so changes made to the file system are immediate and changes made by other processes or by the kernel are immediately seen by **fsdb**.

The following symbols are recognized by **fsdb**:

? h help	Print command summary.
!	Escape to shell.
q	Quit.
"*string*"	A character string. Inside a character string, a NULL character may be specified with "\0"; a double quote may be specified with "\""; and a backslash may be specified with "\\".
- + * /	Add, subtract, multiply, and divide.
=	Assignment
i	An inode.
au	An allocation unit.
b	A block.
im	The immediate data area of an inode. Small directories and symbolic link files (96 bytes or less) are stored directly in the inode itself, in the area normally occupied by data block numbers and extent sizes.

`cdb`	Current directory block.
`d`	A directory entry.
`a`	An inode address entry.
`B`	A byte.
`H`	A half-word (2 bytes)
`W`	A word (4 bytes)
`D`	A double-word (8 bytes)
`p`	General print facility
`calc`	Simple calculator and base converter
`find`	Find a matching pattern in the file system

The print facility recognizes the following print formats:

`S`	Print as a super-block.
`A`	Print as an allocation unit header.
`L`	Print as intent log records.
`I`	Print as inodes.
`dent`	Print as directory entries.
`db`	Print as a directory block.
`dh`	Print as a directory header.
`o`	Print as octal words.
`oB oH oW oD`	Print as octal bytes, half-words, words, or double-words.
`x`	Print as hexadecimal words.
`xB xH xW xD`	Print as hexadecimal bytes, half-words, words, or double-words.
`e`	Print as decimal words.
`eB eH eW eD`	Print as decimal bytes, half-words, words, or double-words.
`c`	Print as characters.

Changes to inode fields may be made symbolically. The following symbols represent inode fields:

`md`	Inode mode field
`ln`	Inode link count field
`uid`	Inode user ID Number field
`gid`	Inode group ID Number field
`sz`	Inode file size field
`de` #	Inode direct extent data block numbers (0 – 9)
`des` #	Inode direct extent sizes (0 – 9)
`ie` #	Inode indirect extent data block numbers (0 – 1)
`ies`	Inode indirect extent size
`im`	Immediate data area. Small directories and symbolic link files (96 bytes or less) are stored directly in the inode itself, in the area normally occupied by data block numbers and extent sizes.
`at`	Inode access time field.

ct	Inode change time field.
mt	Inode modification time field.
af	Inode allocation flags field.
gen	Inode generation count field.
org	Inode mapping type field.
fe	Inode fixed extent size field.
bl	Inode blocks held field.
eopflg	Inode extended operation flag field.
eopdat	Inode extended operation data field.
maj	If device, inode major number.
min	If device, inode minor number.
pd	If directory, inode parent directory.
res	If regular file, inode reservation.
serhi	Inode high order word of serial number.
serlo	Inode low order word of serial number.

Changes to directory block fields may be made symbolically. The following symbols represent directory block fields:

tfree	Total free space (only if in a data block).
hash #	Hash chain start (0 through 31, only if in a data block).
d #	Directory entry (variable number of entries).
nhash	Number of hash chains.

Changes to directory entry fields may be made symbolically. The following symbols represent directory entry fields:

ino	Inode number
nm	Entry name
nmlen	Name length
reclen	Record length (only if in a data block)
hnext	Name hash next (only if in a data block)

It is preferable to separate each token on a command line with a space. Although the command parser does not insist on space separation, there is no ambiguity in the command language if each token is separated with a space. For example, the command **0x23b b** sets the current position to block 0x23b hexadecimal. The command **0x23bb** is invalid, since the command is parsed as simply a hexadecimal number. The command **23b** positions to block 23 decimal, since the command is not ambiguous.

Commands are separated by new lines or multiple commands may be placed on one line, separated by a period (.) or a semicolon (;). When multiple commands are placed on one line, generally only the last command displays results. This allows positioning commands to be followed by printing commands or change commands without intermediate printing. The following commands are supported:

#B | H | W | D Set current position in the file system to the specified offset in bytes, half-words, words, or double-words. If the last command on a line, print the byte, half-word, word, or double-words in hexadecimal.

+ | - # B | H | W | D
Set current position to specified relative offset in bytes, half-words, words, or double-words. If the last command on a

line, print the byte, calf-word, word, or double-words in hexadecimal.

`#b` Set current position in the file system to the specified offset in blocks. Set current block position to the resulting offset. The block size is the block size of the file system. If the last command on a line, print the first word in the block in hexadecimal.

`+|- # b` Set current position to specified relative offset in blocks. Set current block position to the resulting offset. If the last command on a line, print the first word in the block in hexadecimal.

b Set current position to current block position (the block specified by the last `[+|-] # b` operation). If the last command on a line, print the first word in the block in hexadecimal.

`# i` Set current position in the file system to the ilist entry for the specified inode. Set current inode position to the resulting offset. If the last command on a line, print the ilist entry for the inode.

`+|- # i` Set current position in the file system to the ilist entry for the specified relative inode. Set current inode position to the resulting offset. If the last command on a line, print the ilist entry for the inode.

`i` Set current position in the file system to the current inode position. If the last command on a line, print the ilist entry for the inode.

`a#` Set current position to specified offset in blocks specified by the inode address #. Addresses 0 through 9 are for direct extents (**de**). Addresses 10-11 are for indirect extents (**ie**). The addresses are displayed when printing an ilist entry. Set current block position to the resulting offset. If the last command on a line, print the first word in the block in hexadecimal.

`im` Set current position to immediate data area of the current inode. Set current block position to the resulting offset. If the last command on a line, print the first word in the block in hexadecimal.

`# B|H|W|D =# [#]`

Set the current position and change the number at the specified offset to the given number. If a double-word offset is specified, then two numbers separated by a space are required. The resulting value is printed in hexadecimal.

`+|-# B|H|W|D =# [#]`

Set the current position and change the number at the specified relative offset to the given number. If a double-word offset is specified, then two numbers separated by a space are required. The resulting value is printed in hexadecimal.

`# B|H|W|D = "`*string*`"`
: Set the current position and change the characters at the specified offset to the given string. The resulting value is printed as a character string.

`+|-# B|H|W|D = "`*string*`"`
: Set the current position and change the characters at the specified relative offset to the given string. The resulting value is printed as a character string.

`p [#]` *format*
: Print the contents of the file system at the current offset as the specified number of entries of a given format. The allowable print formats are specified above. If a number of entries to print is not specified, one entry is printed.

inode_field `= #`
: Set the contents of the given inode field to the specified number. The current inode specifies the inode list entry to be modified. The symbols representing inode fields are previously listed.

directory_block_field `= #`
: Set the contents of the given directory block field to the specified number. The current block is treated as a directory block and the offset in that block which is represented by the given field is changed. The symbols representing directory block fields are listed above.

`d #`
: Set the current directory entry to the specified number. The current block is treated as a directory block. If the current block is an immediate data area for an inode, then the block is treated as containing immediate directory entries. If the last command on a line, the directory entry at the resulting offset is printed.

directory_entry_field `= #`
: Set the contents of the given directory field to the specified number. The current directory entry specifies where the directory entry is located. The resulting value is printed in hexadecimal.

`nm = "`*string*`"`
: Set the directory name field of the current directory entry to the specified string. The resulting value is printed as a character string.

`calc # [+|-|*|/ #]`
: Take a number or the sum, difference, product or dividend of two numbers and print in decimal, octal, hexadecimal and character format.

`find # B|H|W|D [#]`
: Search for the given numeric pattern in the file system. The size of the object to match is specified. If a double-word is specified, then two numbers must be given. The search is performed forward from the current offset. A maximum

number of blocks to search may be specified. If found, the location and value are printed in hexadecimal.

`find "`*string*`" [#]`
: Search for the given character string in the file system. The search is performed forward from the current offset. A maximum number of blocks to search may be specified. If found the location and string are printed.

`fmtlog`
: Format all intent log entries. A completely formatted intent log can be quite lengthy. It is a good idea use **fsdb** as a filter and redirect the output to a file or pager to look at a complete log format.

EXAMPLES

`386i` Prints inumber 386 in an inode format. This now becomes the current working inode.

`ln=4` Changes the link count for the working inode to 4.

`1024B.pS` Prints the super-block of this file system symbolically

`1024B.p0o` Prints the super-block of this file system in octal.

`2i.a0b.d7.ino=3`
: Changes the inumber for the seventh directory slot in the root directory to 3. This example also shows how several operations can be combined on one command line.

`d7.nm="`*string*`"` Changes the name field in the directory slot to the given string.

`23i.im.pdb` Prints the immediate area of inode 23 as a directory block.

`23i.im.d5` Prints the sixth directory entry in the immediate area of inode 23.

SEE ALSO

vxfs-specific **fs**(4), **fsck**(1M), generic **fsdb**(1M)

NAME

fsirand – (BSD) install random inode generation numbers

SYNOPSIS

/usr/ucb/fsirand [**-p**] *special*

DESCRIPTION

fsirand installs random inode generation numbers on all the inodes on device *special*, and also installs a filesystem ID in the superblock. This helps increase the security of filesystems exported by NFS.

fsirand must be used only on an unmounted filesystem that has been checked with **fsck**(1M). The only exception is that it can be used on the root filesystem in single-user mode, if the system is immediately re-booted afterwards.

The **-p** option prints out the generation numbers for all the inodes, but does not change the generation numbers.

SEE ALSO

fsck(1M)

NAME

fstyp (generic) – determine file system type

SYNOPSIS

fstyp [**-v**] *special*

DESCRIPTION

fstyp allows the user to determine the file system type of unmounted file systems using heuristic programs.

An **fstyp** module for each file system type to be checked is executed; each of these modules applies some appropriate heuristic to determine whether the supplied *special* file is of the type for which it checks. If it is, the program prints on standard output the usual file-system identifier for that type and exits with a return code of 0; if none of the modules succeed, the error message **unknown_fstyp (no matches)** is returned and the exit status is 1. If more than one module succeeds the error message **unknown_fstyp (multiple matches)** is returned and the exit status is 2.

The options are:

-v Produce verbose output. This is usually information about the file systems superblock and varies across different *FSTypes*.

NOTES

The use of heuristics implies that the result of **fstyp** is not guaranteed to be accurate.

ftp(1)

NAME

`ftp` – file transfer program

SYNOPSIS

ftp [**-dgintv**] [*hostname*]

DESCRIPTION

The **ftp** command is the user interface to the ARPANET standard File Transfer Protocol (FTP). **ftp** transfers files to and from a remote network site.

The client host with which **ftp** is to communicate may be specified on the command line. If this is done, **ftp** immediately attempts to establish a connection to an FTP server on that host; otherwise, **ftp** enters its command interpreter and awaits instructions from the user. When **ftp** is awaiting commands from the user, it displays the prompt **ftp>**.

The following options may be specified at the command line, or to the command interpreter:

-d Enable debugging.

-g Disable filename globbing.

-i Turn off interactive prompting during multiple file transfers.

-n Do not attempt auto-login upon initial connection. If auto-login is not disabled, **ftp** checks the **.netrc** file in the user's home directory for an entry describing an account on the remote machine. If no entry exists, **ftp** will prompt for the login name of the account on the remote machine (the default is the login name on the local machine), and, if necessary, for a password and an account with which to log in.

-t Enable packet tracing (unimplemented).

-v Show all responses from the remote server, as well as report on data transfer statistics. This is turned on by default if **ftp** is running interactively with its input coming from the user's terminal.

The following commands can be specified to the command interpreter:

! [*command*]
: Run *command* as a shell command on the local machine. If no *command* is given, invoke an interactive shell.

$ *macro-name* [*args*]
: Execute the macro *macro-name* that was defined with the **macdef** command. Arguments are passed to the macro unglobbed.

account [*passwd*]
: Supply a supplemental password required by a remote system for access to resources once a login has been successfully completed. If no argument is included, the user will be prompted for an account password in a non-echoing input mode.

append *local-file* [*remote-file*]
Append a local file to a file on the remote machine. If *remote-file* is not specified, the local file name is used, subject to alteration by any **ntrans** or **nmap** settings. File transfer uses the current settings for representation type, file structure, and transfer mode.

ascii Set the representation type to network ASCII. This is the default type.

bell Sound a bell after each file transfer command is completed.

binary
Set the representation type to image.

bye Terminate the FTP session with the remote server and exit **ftp**. An EOF will also terminate the session and exit.

case Toggle remote computer file name case mapping during **mget** commands. When **case** is on (default is off), remote computer file names with all letters in upper case are written in the local directory with the letters mapped to lower case.

cd *remote-directory*
Change the working directory on the remote machine to *remote-directory*.

cdup Change the remote machine working directory to the parent of the current remote machine working directory.

close Terminate the FTP session with the remote server, and return to the command interpreter. Any defined macros are erased.

cr Toggle RETURN stripping during network ASCII type file retrieval. Records are denoted by a RETURN/LINEFEED sequence during network ASCII type file transfer. When **cr** is on (the default), RETURN characters are stripped from this sequence to conform with the UNIX system single LINEFEED record delimiter. Records on non-UNIX-system remote hosts may contain single LINEFEED characters; when an network ASCII type transfer is made, these LINEFEED characters may be distinguished from a record delimiter only when **cr** is off.

delete *remote-file*
Delete the file *remote-file* on the remote machine.

debug
Toggle debugging mode. When debugging is on, **ftp** prints each command sent to the remote machine, preceded by the string **-->**.

dir [*remote-directory*] [*local-file*]
Print a listing of the directory contents in the directory, *remote-directory*, and, optionally, placing the output in *local-file*. If no directory is specified, the current working directory on the remote machine is used. If no local file is specified, or *local-file* is **-**, output is sent to the terminal.

disconnect
A synonym for **close**.

form [*format-name*]
Set the carriage control format subtype of the representation type to *format-name*. The only valid *format-name* is **non-print**, which corresponds to the default non-print subtype.

get *remote-file* [*local-file*]
Retrieve the *remote-file* and store it on the local machine. If the local file name is not specified, it is given the same name it has on the remote machine, subject to alteration by the current **case**, **ntrans**, and **nmap** settings. The current settings for representation type, file structure, and transfer mode are used while transferring the file.

glob Toggle filename expansion, or globbing, for **mdelete**, **mget** and **mput**. If globbing is turned off, filenames are taken literally.

Globbing for **mput** is done as in **sh**(1). For **mdelete** and **mget**, each remote file name is expanded separately on the remote machine, and the lists are not merged.

Expansion of a directory name is likely to be radically different from expansion of the name of an ordinary file: the exact result depends on the remote operating system and FTP server, and can be previewed by doing **mls** *remote-files* **-**.

mget and **mput** are not meant to transfer entire directory subtrees of files. You can do this by transferring a **tar**(1) archive of the subtree (using a representation type of image as set by the **binary** command).

hash Toggle hash-sign (**#**) printing for each data block transferred. The size of a data block is 8192 bytes.

help [*command*]
Print an informative message about the meaning of *command*. If no argument is given, **ftp** prints a list of the known commands.

lcd [*directory*]
Change the working directory on the local machine. If no *directory* is specified, the user's home directory is used.

ls [*remote-directory*] [*local-file*]
Print an abbreviated listing of the contents of a directory on the remote machine. If *remote-directory* is left unspecified, the current working directory is used. If no local file is specified, or if *local-file* is **-**, the output is sent to the terminal.

macdef *macro-name*
Define a macro. Subsequent lines are stored as the macro *macro-name*; a null line (consecutive NEWLINE characters in a file or RETURN characters from the terminal) terminates macro input mode. There is a limit of 16 macros and 4096 total characters in all defined macros. Macros remain defined until a **close** command is executed.

The macro processor interprets **$** and \ as special characters. A **$** followed by a number (or numbers) is replaced by the corresponding argument on the macro invocation command line. A **$** followed by an **i** signals that macro processor that the executing macro is to be looped. On the first pass

`$i` is replaced by the first argument on the macro invocation command line, on the second pass it is replaced by the second argument, and so on. A \ followed by any character is replaced by that character. Use the \ to prevent special treatment of the **$**.

mdelete [*remote-files*]
Delete the *remote-files* on the remote machine.

mdir *remote-files local-file*
Like **dir**, except multiple remote files may be specified. If interactive prompting is on, **ftp** will prompt the user to verify that the last argument is indeed the target local file for receiving **mdir** output.

mget *remote-files*
Expand the *remote-files* on the remote machine and do a **get** for each file name thus produced. See **glob** for details on the filename expansion. Resulting file names will then be processed according to **case**, **ntrans**, and **nmap** settings. Files are transferred into the local working directory, which can be changed with **lcd** *directory*; new local directories can be created with **! mkdir** *directory*.

mkdir *directory-name*
Make a directory on the remote machine.

mls *remote-files local-file*
Like **ls**(1), except multiple remote files may be specified. If interactive prompting is on, **ftp** will prompt the user to verify that the last argument is indeed the target local file for receiving **mls** output.

mode [*mode-name*]
Set the transfer mode to *mode-name*. The only valid *mode-name* is **stream**, which corresponds to the default stream mode. This implementation only supports **stream**, and requires that it be specified.

mput *local-files*
Expand wild cards in the list of local files given as arguments and do a **put** for each file in the resulting list. See **glob** for details of filename expansion. Resulting file names will then be processed according to **ntrans** and **nmap** settings.

nmap [*inpattern outpattern*]
Set or unset the filename mapping mechanism. If no arguments are specified, the filename mapping mechanism is unset. If arguments are specified, remote filenames are mapped during **mput** commands and **put** commands issued without a specified remote target filename. If arguments are specified, local filenames are mapped during **mget** commands and **get** commands issued without a specified local target filename.

This command is useful when connecting to a non-UNIX-system remote host with different file naming conventions or practices. The mapping follows the pattern set by *inpattern* and *outpattern*. *inpattern* is a template for incoming filenames (which may have already been processed according to the **ntrans** and **case** settings). Variable templating is accomplished by including the sequences **$1**, **$2**, ..., **$9** in *inpattern*. Use \ to prevent this special treatment of the **$** character. All other characters are treated literally, and are used to determine the **nmap** *inpattern* variable values.

For example, given *inpattern* **$1.$2** and the remote file name **mydata.data**, **$1** would have the value **mydata**, and **$2** would have the value **data**.

The *outpattern* determines the resulting mapped filename. The sequences **$1**, **$2**, ..., **$9** are replaced by any value resulting from the *inpattern* template. The sequence **$0** is replaced by the original filename. Additionally, the sequence [*seq1* , *seq2*] is replaced by *seq1* if *seq1* is not a null string; otherwise it is replaced by *seq2*.

For example, the command **nmap $1.$2.$3 [$1,$2].[$2,file]** would yield the output filename **myfile.data** for input filenames **myfile.data** and **myfile.data.old**, **myfile.file** for the input filename **myfile**, and **myfile.myfile** for the input filename **myfile**. SPACE characters may be included in *outpattern*, as in the example **nmap $1 | sed "s/ *$//" > $1**. Use the **** character to prevent special treatment of the **$**, **[**, **]**, and **,**, characters.

ntrans [*inchars* [*outchars*]]

Set or unset the filename character translation mechanism. If no arguments are specified, the filename character translation mechanism is unset. If arguments are specified, characters in remote filenames are translated during **mput** commands and **put** commands issued without a specified remote target filename, and characters in local filenames are translated during **mget** commands and **get** commands issued without a specified local target filename.

This command is useful when connecting to a non-UNIX-system remote host with different file naming conventions or practices. Characters in a filename matching a character in *inchars* are replaced with the corresponding character in *outchars*. If the character's position in *inchars* is longer than the length of *outchars*, the character is deleted from the file name.

open *host* [*port*]

Establish a connection to the specified *host* FTP server. An optional port number may be supplied, in which case, **ftp** will attempt to contact an FTP server at that port. If the *auto-login* option is on (default setting), **ftp** will also attempt to automatically log the user in to the FTP server.

prompt

Toggle interactive prompting. Interactive prompting occurs during multiple file transfers to allow the user to selectively retrieve or store files. By default, prompting is turned on. If prompting is turned off, any **mget** or **mput** will transfer all files, and any **mdelete** will delete all files.

proxy *ftp-command*

Execute an FTP command on a secondary control connection. This command allows simultaneous connection to two remote FTP servers for transferring files between the two servers. The first **proxy** command should be an **open**, to establish the secondary control connection. Enter the command **proxy ?** to see other FTP commands executable on the secondary connection.

The following commands behave differently when prefaced by **proxy**: **open** will not define new macros during the auto-login process, **close** will not erase existing macro definitions, **get** and **mget** transfer files from the host on the primary control connection to the host on the secondary control connection, and **put**, **mputd**, and **append** transfer files from the host on the secondary control connection to the host on the primary control connection.

Third party file transfers depend upon support of the **PASV** command by the server on the secondary control connection.

put *local-file* [*remote-file*]
Store a local file on the remote machine. If *remote-file* is left unspecified, the local file name is used after processing according to any **ntrans** or **nmap** settings in naming the remote file. File transfer uses the current settings for representation type, file structure, and transfer mode.

pwd Print the name of the current working directory on the remote machine.

quit A synonym for **bye**.

quote *arg1 arg2 . . .*
Send the arguments specified, verbatim, to the remote FTP server. A single FTP reply code is expected in return. (The **remotehelp** command displays a list of valid arguments.)

quote should be used only by experienced users who are familiar with the FTP protocol.

recv *remote-file* [*local-file*]
A synonym for **get**.

remotehelp [*command-name*]
Request help from the remote FTP server. If a *command-name* is specified it is supplied to the server as well.

rename *from to*
Rename the file *from* on the remote machine to have the name *to*.

reset Clear reply queue. This command re-synchronizes command/reply sequencing with the remote FTP server. Resynchronization may be necessary following a violation of the FTP protocol by the remote server.

rmdir *directory-name*
Delete a directory on the remote machine.

runique
Toggle storing of files on the local system with unique filenames. If a file already exists with a name equal to the target local filename for a **get** or **mget** command, a **.1** is appended to the name. If the resulting name matches another existing file, a **.2** is appended to the original name. If this process continues up to **.99**, an error message is printed, and the transfer does not take place. The generated unique filename will be

reported. `runique` will not affect local files generated from a shell command. The default value is off.

`send` *local-file* [*remote-file*]
A synonym for `put`.

`sendport`
Toggle the use of **PORT** commands. By default, `ftp` will attempt to use a **PORT** command when establishing a connection for each data transfer. The use of **PORT** commands can prevent delays when performing multiple file transfers. If the **PORT** command fails, `ftp` will use the default data port. When the use of **PORT** commands is disabled, no attempt will be made to use **PORT** commands for each data transfer. This is useful when connected to certain FTP implementations that ignore **PORT** commands but incorrectly indicate they have been accepted.

`status`
Show the current status of `ftp`.

`struct` [*struct-name*]
Set the file structure to *struct-name*. The only valid *struct-name* is **`file`**, which corresponds to the default file structure. The implementation only supports **`file`**, and requires that it be specified.

`sunique`
Toggle storing of files on remote machine under unique file names. The remote FTP server must support the **STOU** command for successful completion. The remote server will report the unique name. Default value is off.

`tenex` Set the representation type to that needed to talk to TENEX machines.

`trace` Toggle packet tracing (unimplemented).

`type` [*type-name*]
Set the representation type to *type-name*. The valid *type-names* are **`ascii`** for network ASCII, **`binary`** or **`image`** for image, and **`tenex`** for local byte size with a byte size of 8 (used to talk to TENEX machines). If no type is specified, the current type is printed. The default type is network ASCII.

`user` *user-name* [*password*] [*account*]
Identify yourself to the remote FTP server. If the password is not specified and the server requires it, `ftp` will prompt the user for it (after disabling local echo). If an account field is not specified, and the FTP server requires it, the user will be prompted for it. If an account field is specified, an account command will be relayed to the remote server after the login sequence is completed if the remote server did not require it for logging in. Unless `ftp` is invoked with auto-login disabled, this process is done automatically on initial connection to the FTP server.

`verbose`
Toggle verbose mode. In verbose mode, all responses from the FTP server are displayed to the user. In addition, if verbose mode is on, when a file transfer completes, statistics regarding the efficiency of the transfer are

reported. By default, verbose mode is on if **ftp**'s commands are coming from a terminal, and off otherwise.

? [*command*]
A synonym for **help**.

Command arguments which have embedded spaces may be quoted with quote (") marks.

If any command argument which is not indicated as being optional is not specified, **ftp** will prompt for that argument.

ABORTING A FILE TRANSFER

To abort a file transfer, use the terminal interrupt key. Sending transfers will be immediately halted. Receiving transfers will be halted by sending an FTP protocol **ABOR** command to the remote server, and discarding any further data received. The speed at which this is accomplished depends upon the remote server's support for **ABOR** processing. If the remote server does not support the **ABOR** command, an **ftp>** prompt will not appear until the remote server has completed sending the requested file.

The terminal interrupt key sequence will be ignored when **ftp** has completed any local processing and is awaiting a reply from the remote server. A long delay in this mode may result from the **ABOR** processing described above, or from unexpected behavior by the remote server, including violations of the ftp protocol. If the delay results from unexpected remote server behavior, the local **ftp** program must be killed by hand.

FILE NAMING CONVENTIONS

Local files specified as arguments to **ftp** commands are processed according to the following rules.

1. If the file name **-** is specified, the standard input (for reading) or standard output (for writing) is used.
2. If the first character of the file name is **|**, the remainder of the argument is interpreted as a shell command. **ftp** then forks a shell, using **popen**(3S) with the argument supplied, and reads (writes) from the standard output (standard input) of that shell. If the shell command includes SPACE characters, the argument must be quoted; for example **"| ls -lt"**. A particularly useful example of this mechanism is: **"dir | more"**.
3. Failing the above checks, if globbing is enabled, local file names are expanded according to the rules used in the **sh**(1); see the **glob** command. If the **ftp** command expects a single local file (for example, **put**), only the first filename generated by the globbing operation is used.
4. For **mget** commands and **get** commands with unspecified local file names, the local filename is the remote filename, which may be altered by a **case**, **ntrans**, or **nmap** setting. The resulting filename may then be altered if **runique** is on.
5. For **mput** commands and **put** commands with unspecified remote file names, the remote filename is the local filename, which may be altered by a **ntrans** or **nmap** setting. The resulting filename may then be altered by the remote server if **sunique** is on.

FILE TRANSFER PARAMETERS

The FTP specification specifies many parameters which may affect a file transfer.

The representation type may be one of network ASCII, EBCDIC, image, or local byte size with a specified byte size (for PDP-10's and PDP-20's mostly). The network ASCII and EBCDIC types have a further subtype which specifies whether vertical format control (NEWLINE characters, form feeds, etc.) are to be passed through (non-print), provided in TELNET format (TELNET format controls), or provided in ASA (FORTRAN) (carriage control (ASA)) format. **ftp** supports the network ASCII (subtype non-print only) and image types, plus local byte size with a byte size of 8 for communicating with TENEX machines.

The file structure may be one of **file** (no record structure), **record**, or **page**. **ftp** supports only the default value, which is **file**.

The transfer mode may be one of **stream**, **block**, or **compressed**. **ftp** supports only the default value, which is **stream**.

SEE ALSO

ls(1), **rcp**(1), **tar**(1), **sh**(1), **ftpd**(1M), **popen**(3S), **netrc**(4)

NOTES

Correct execution of many commands depends upon proper behavior by the remote server.

An error in the treatment of carriage returns in the 4.2 BSD code handling transfers with a representation type of network ASCII has been corrected. This correction may result in incorrect transfers of binary files to and from 4.2 BSD servers using a representation type of network ASCII. Avoid this problem by using the image type.

NAME

ftpd – file transfer protocol server

SYNOPSIS

in.ftpd [**-dl**] [**-t***timeout*]

DESCRIPTION

ftpd is the Internet File Transfer Protocol (FTP) server process. The server is invoked by the Internet daemon **inetd**(1M) each time a connection to the FTP service [see **services**(4)] is made, with the connection available as descriptor 0.

Inactive connections are timed out after 90 seconds.

The following options are available:

-d Write debugging information into the system log.

-l Write each FTP session into the system log.

-t*timeout* Set the inactivity timeout period to *timeout*, in seconds. The FTP server will timeout an inactive session after 15 minutes.

Requests

The FTP server currently supports the following FTP requests; case is not distinguished.

Request	Description
ABOR	abort previous command
ACCT	specify account (ignored)
ALLO	allocate storage (vacuously)
APPE	append to a file
CDUP	change to parent of current working directory
CWD	change working directory
DELE	delete a file
HELP	give help information
LIST	give list files in a directory (**ls -lg**)
MKD	make a directory
MODE	specify data transfer *mode*
NLST	give name list of files in directory (**ls**)
NOOP	do nothing
PASS	specify password
PASV	prepare for server-to-server transfer
PORT	specify data connection port
PWD	print the current working directory

QUIT	terminate session
RETR	retrieve a file
RMD	remove a directory
RNFR	specify rename-from file name
RNTO	specify rename-to file name
STOR	store a file
STOU	store a file with a unique name
STRU	specify data transfer *structure*
TYPE	specify data transfer *type*
USER	specify user name
XCUP	change to parent of current working directory
XCWD	change working directory
XMKD	make a directory
XPWD	print the current working directory
XRMD	remove a directory

The remaining FTP requests specified in RFC 959 are recognized, but not implemented.

The FTP server will abort an active file transfer only when the **ABOR** command is preceded by a Telnet Interrupt Process (IP) signal and a Telnet Synch signal in the command Telnet stream, as described in RFC 959.

ftpd interprets file names according to the globbing conventions used by **sh**(1). This allows users to utilize the metacharacters: *** ? [ ] { } ~**

ftpd authenticates users according to four rules.

1. The user name must be in the password data base, **/etc/passwd**, and not have a null password. In this case a password must be provided by the client before any file operations may be performed.
2. If the user name appears in the file **/etc/ftpusers**, **ftp** access is denied.
3. **ftp** access is denied unless the user's shell (from **/etc/passwd**) is listed in the file **/etc/shells**, or the user's shell is one of the following:

   /bin/sh
   /bin/ksh
   /bin/csh
   /usr/bin/sh
   /usr/bin/ksh
   /usr/bin/csh

4. If the user name is **anonymous** or **ftp**, an anonymous account must be present in the password file (user **ftp**). In this case the user is allowed to log in by specifying any password (by convention this is given as the client host's name).

In the last case, **ftpd** takes special measures to restrict the client's access privileges. The server performs a **chroot**(2) command to the home directory of the **ftp** user. In order that system security is not breached, it is recommended that the **ftp** subtree be constructed with care; the following rules are recommended.

home_directory
: Make the home directory owned by **ftp** and unwritable by anyone.

home_directory/**usr/bin**
: Make this directory owned by a privileged user and unwritable by anyone. The program **ls**(1) must be present to support the list commands. This program should have mode 111.

home_directory/**etc**
: Make this directory owned by the super-user and unwritable by anyone. Copies of the files **passwd**(4), **group**(4), and **netconfig** must be present for the **ls** command to work properly. These files should be mode 444.

home_directory/**pub**
: Make this directory mode 777 and owned by **ftp**. Users should then place files which are to be accessible via the anonymous account in this directory.

home_directory/**dev**
: Make this directory owned by the super-user and unwritable by anyone. Change directories to this directory and do the following:

```
FTP="'grep ^ftp: /etc/passwd | cut -d: -f6'"
MAJORMINOR="'ls -l /dev/tcp | nawk '{ gsub(/,/, ""); print $5, $6}''
mknod $FTP/dev/tcp c $MAJORMINOR
chmod 666 $FTP/dev/tcp
```

SEE ALSO

ftp(1), **getsockopt**(3N), **passwd**(4), **services**(4)

Postel, Jon, and Joyce Reynolds, *File Transfer Protocol (FTP)*, RFC 959, Network Information Center, SRI International, Menlo Park, Calif., October 1985

NOTES

The anonymous account is inherently dangerous and should be avoided when possible.

The server must run as a privileged process to create sockets with privileged port numbers. It maintains an effective user ID of the logged in user, changing to user ID 0 only when binding addresses to sockets. The possible security holes have been extensively scrutinized, but are possibly incomplete.

/etc/ftpusers contains a list of users who cannot access the system; the format of the file is one username per line.

If a remote user does not have a home directory, the root directory (**/**) becomes the user's current directory.

fumount(1M)

NAME

fumount – forced unmount of advertised resources

SYNOPSIS

fumount [-w *sec*] *resource* [[-w *sec*] *resource*]. . .

DESCRIPTION

This command is obsolete and will not be supported after this release. **fumount** unadvertises each *resource* and disconnects remote access to the *resource*. The **-w** *sec* causes a delay of *sec* seconds prior to the disconnect from the *resource* specified immediately after the **-w**.

When the forced unmount occurs, an administrative shell script is started on each remote computer that has the resource mounted (**/etc/rfs/rfuadmin**). If a grace period of several seconds is specified with **-w**, **rfuadmin** is started with the **fuwarn** option. When the actual forced unmount is ready to occur, **rfuadmin** is started with the **fumount** option. See the **rfuadmin**(1M) manual page for information on the action taken in response to the forced unmount.

When used with no arguments, the usage message is displayed.

Only a privileged user can execute this command.

ERRORS

If *resource*

1. does not physically reside on the local machine,
2. is an invalid resource name,
3. is not currently advertised and is not remotely mounted, or
4. the command is not run with appropriate privilege,

an error message will be sent to standard error.

SEE ALSO

mount(1M), **rfuadmin**(1M), **rfudaemon**(1M), **rmount**(1M), **RFS**-specific **share**(1M), **RFS**-specific **unshare**(1M)

NAME

fusage – disk access profiler

SYNOPSIS

fusage [[*mount_point*] | [*advertised_resource*] | [*block_special_device*] [. . .]]

DESCRIPTION

When used with no options, **fusage** reports block I/O transfers, in kilobytes, to and from all locally mounted file systems and advertised Remote File Sharing resources on a per client basis. The count data are cumulative since the time of the mount. When used with an option, **fusage** reports on the named file system, advertised resource, or block special device.

The report includes one section for each file system and advertised resource and has one entry for each machine that has the directory remotely mounted, ordered by decreasing usage. Sections are ordered by device name; advertised resources that are not complete file systems will immediately follow the sections for the file systems they are in.

SEE ALSO

crash(1M), **df**(1M), **mount**(1M), **RFS**-specific **share**(1M)

NAME

`fuser` – identify processes using a file or file structure

SYNOPSIS

`/usr/sbin/fuser [-[c|f]ku]` *files* | *resources* `[[-] [-[c|f]ku]` *files* | *resources*] . . .

DESCRIPTION

This command is obsolete and will not be supported after this release. `fuser` outputs the process IDs of the processes that are using the *files* or remote *resources* specified as arguments. Each process ID is followed by one of these letter codes, which identify how the process is using the file:

`c` as its current directory.

`r` as its root directory, which was set up by the `chroot`(1M) command.

`o` as an open file.

`t` as its text file.

`a` as its trace file located in the `/proc` directory.

For block special devices with mounted file systems, processes using any file on that device are listed. For remote resource names, processes using any file associated with that remote resource (Remote File Sharing) are reported. For all other types of files (text files, executables, directories, devices, and so on) only the processes using that file are reported.

The following options may be used with `fuser`:

`-c` may be used with files that are mount points for file systems. With that option the report is for use of the mount point and any files within that mounted file system.

`-f` when this is used, the report is only for the named file, not for files within a mounted file system.

`-u` the user login name, in parentheses, also follows the process ID.

`-k` the `SIGKILL` signal is sent to each process. Since this option spawns kills for each process, the kill messages may not show up immediately [see `kill`(2)].

If more than one group of files are specified, the options may be respecified for each additional group of files. A lone dash cancels the options currently in force.

The process IDs are printed as a single line on the standard output, separated by spaces and terminated with a single new line. All other output is written on standard error.

Any user with permission to read `/dev/kmem` and `/dev/mem` can use `fuser`. Only a privileged user can terminate another user's process.

EXAMPLES

`fuser -ku /dev/dsk/1s?`

if typed by a user with appropriate privileges, terminates all processes that are preventing disk drive one from being unmounted, listing the process ID and login name of each as it is killed.

fuser -u /etc/passwd
lists process IDs and login names of processes that have the password file open.

fuser -ku /dev/dsk/1s? -u /etc/passwd
executes both of the above examples in a single command line.

fuser -cu /home
if the /dev/dsk/c1d0s9 device is mounted on /home, lists process IDs and login names of processes that are using /dev/dsk/c1d0s9.

FILES

`/stand/unix` for system namelist
`/dev/kmem` for system image
`/dev/mem` also for system image

NOTE

If an RFS resource from a pre System V Release 4 server is mounted, **fuser** can only report on use of the whole file system, not on individual files within it.

Because **fuser** works with a snapshot of the system image, it may miss processes that begin using a file while **fuser** is running. Also, processes reported as using a file may have stopped using it while **fuser** was running. These factors should discourage the use of the **-k** option.

fuser does not report all possible usages of a file (for example, a mapped file).

SEE ALSO

chroot(1M), **kill**(2), **mount**(1M), **proc**(4), **ps**(1), **signal**(2)

NAME

fwtmp, **wtmpfix** – manipulate connect accounting records

SYNOPSIS

/usr/lib/acct/fwtmp [**-ic**]
/usr/lib/acct/wtmpfix [*files*]

DESCRIPTION

fwtmp reads from the standard input and writes to the standard output, converting binary records of the type found in **/var/adm/wtmp** to formatted ASCII records. The ASCII version is useful when it is necessary to edit bad records.

The argument **-ic** is used to denote that input is in ASCII form, and output is to be written in binary form.

wtmpfix examines the standard input or named files in **utmp.h** format, corrects the time/date stamps to make the entries consistent, and writes to the standard output. A - can be used in place of *files* to indicate the standard input. If time/date corrections are not performed, **acctcon** will fault when it encounters certain date-change records.

Each time the date is set, a pair of date change records are written to **/var/adm/wtmp**. The first record is the old date denoted by the string "**old time**" placed in the **line** field and the flag **OLD_TIME** placed in the **type** field of the **utmp** structure. The second record specifies the new date and is denoted by the string **new time** placed in the **line** field and the flag **NEW_TIME** placed in the **type** field. **wtmpfix** uses these records to synchronize all time stamps in the file.

In addition to correcting time/date stamps, **wtmpfix** will check the validity of the **name** field to ensure that it consists solely of alphanumeric characters or spaces. If it encounters a name that is considered invalid, it will change the login name to **INVALID** and write a diagnostic to the standard error. In this way, **wtmpfix** reduces the chance that **acctcon** will fail when processing connect accounting records.

FILES

/var/adm/wtmp
/usr/include/utmp.h

SEE ALSO

acct(1M), **acct**(2), **acct**(4), **acctcms**(1M), **acctcom**(1), **acctcon**(1M), **acctmerg**(1M), **acctprc**(1M), **acctsh**(1M), **ed**(1), **runacct**(1M), **utmp**(4)

NAME

gcore – get core images of running processes

SYNOPSIS

gcore [**-o** *file*] *process-id* . . .

DESCRIPTION

gcore creates a core image of each specified process. Such an image may be used with debuggers such as **debug**. The name of the core image file for the process whose process ID is *process-id* will be **core.***process-id*.

The **-o** option substitutes *file* in place of **core** as the first part of the name of the core image files.

FILES

core.*process-id*   core images

SEE ALSO

core(4), **debug**(1), **kill**(1), **proc**(4), **sh**(1)

gencat (1)

NAME

gencat – generate a formatted message catalog

SYNOPSIS

gencat [-m] [-f *format*] *catfile msgfile . . .*

DESCRIPTION

The **gencat** utility merges the message text source file(s) *msgfile* into a formatted message database *catfile*. The database *catfile* will be created if it does not already exist. If *catfile* does exist its messages will be included in the new *catfile*. If set and message numbers collide, the new message-text defined in *msgfile* will replace the old message text currently contained in *catfile*. The message text source file (or set of files) input to **gencat** can contain either set and message numbers or simply message numbers, in which case the set **NL_SETD** [see **nl_types**(5)] is assumed.

The **-f** option allows different format message catalogs to be generated. Arguments that can be used with this option are:

SVR4 Produce the System V Release 4 format catalog. (This is the default if **-f** or **-m** are not specified.)

m This is equivalent to the **-m** option.

XENIX Produce message catalogs suitable for use with SCO UNIX/XENIX applications. If the **-m** or **-f** options are not used, the format of an existing message catalog will be retained. The **-f** option can be used to change the format of a catalog.

The format of a message text source file is defined as follows. Note that the fields of a message text source line are separated by a single ASCII space or tab character. Any other ASCII spaces or tabs are considered as being part of the subsequent field.

$set *n comment*

n specifies the set identifier of the following messages until the next **$set**, **$delset**, or end-of-file appears. *n* must be a number in the range (1–{**NL_SETMAX**}). Set identifiers within a single source file need not be contiguous. Any string following the set identifier is treated as a comment. If no **$set** directive is specified in a message text source file, all messages will be located in the default message set **NL_SETD**.

$delset *n comment*

Delete message set *n* from an existing message catalog. Any string following the set number is treated as a comment. (If *n* is not a valid set it is ignored.)

$ *comment*

A line beginning with a dollar symbol "**$**" followed by an ASCII space or tab character is treated as a comment.

m message-text

The *m* denotes the message identifier, which is a number in the range (1–{**NL_MSGMAX**}). The message-text is stored in the message catalog with the set identifier specified by the last **$set** directive, and with message identifier *m*. If the *message-text* is empty, and an ASCII space or tab field separator is present, an empty string is stored in the message catalog. If a message source line has a message number, but neither a field separator nor *message-text*, the existing message with that number (if any) is deleted from the catalog. Message identifiers need not be contiguous. The length of *message-text* must be in the range (0–{**NL_TEXTMAX**}).

`$quote` *c*

This line specifies an optional quote character *c*, which can be used to surround message-text so that trailing spaces or null (empty) messages are visible in a message source line. By default, or if an empty **$quote** directive is supplied, no quoting of message-text will be recognized.

Empty lines in a message text source file are ignored.

Text strings can contain the special characters and escape sequences defined in the following table:

Description	Symbol	Sequence
newline	NL(LF)	`\n`
horizontal tab	HT	`\t`
vertical tab	VT	`\v`
backspace	BS	`\b`
carriage return	CR	`\r`
form feed	FF	`\f`
backslash	\	`\\`
bit pattern	*ddd*	*ddd*

The escape sequence *ddd* consists of backslash followed by 1, 2 or 3 octal digits, which are taken to specify the value of the desired character. If the character following a backslash is not one of those specified, the backslash is ignored.

Backslash followed by an ASCII newline character is also used to continue a string on the following line. Thus, the following two lines describe a single message string:

```
1 This line continues \
to the next line
```

which is equivalent to:

```
1 This line continues to the next line
```

NOTES

This version of **gencat** is built on the **mkmsgs** utility. The **gencat** database comprises two files: *catfile*`.m`, which is a catalog in **mkmsgs** format and the file *catfile*, which contains the information required to translate a set and message number into a simple message number which can be used in a call to **gettxt**.

Using **gettxt** constrains the catalogs to be located in a subdirectory under **/usr/lib/locale**. This restriction is lifted by placing only a symbolic link to the catalog in the directory **/usr/lib/locale/Xopen/LC_MESSAGES** when the catalog is opened. It is this link that **gettxt** uses when attempting to access the catalog. The link is removed when the catalog is closed, but occasionally as applications exit abnormally without closing catalogs redundant symbolic links will be left in the directory.

For compatibility with previous version of **gencat** released in a number of specialized internationalization products, the **-m** option is supplied. This option causes **gencat** to build a single file *catfile* that is compatible with the format catalogs produced by the earlier versions. The retrieval routines detect the type of catalog they are using and act appropriately.

FILES

/usr/lib/locale/*locale***/LC_MESSAGES/uxmesg**
language-specific message file [See **LANG** on **environ**(5).]

SEE ALSO

catgets(3C), **catopen**(3C), **gettxt**(3C), **mkmsgs**(1), **nl_types**(5)

NAME

get – get a version of an SCCS file

SYNOPSIS

get [-a*seq-no.*] [-c*cutoff*] [-i*list*] [-r*SID*] [-w*string*] [-x*list*] [-l[p]] [-b] [-e] [-g] [-k] [-m] [-n] [-p] [-s] [-t] *file* . . .

DESCRIPTION

get extracts the contents of each named SCCS *file* based on the values of the keyletter arguments. The arguments may be specified in any order, but all keyletter arguments apply to all named SCCS *file*s. The file name specified must be in the form **s.***file* or be the name of a directory. If a directory is named, **get** behaves as though each file in the directory were specified as a named file, except that non-SCCS files (last component of the path name does not begin with **s.**) and unreadable files are silently ignored. If a name of **-** is given, the standard input is read; each line of the standard input is taken to be the name of an SCCS file to be processed.

The generated text is normally written into a file called the **g.***file* whose name is derived from the SCCS file name by simply removing the leading "**s.**" (see also the FILES section below).

Each of the keyletter arguments is explained below as though only one SCCS file is to be processed, but the effects of any keyletter argument apply independently to each named file.

-r*SID* The SCCS identification string (SID) of the version (delta) of an SCCS file to be retrieved. Table 1 below shows, for the most useful cases, what version of an SCCS file is retrieved (as well as the SID of the version to be eventually created by **delta**(1) if the **-e** keyletter is also used), as a function of the SID specified.

-c*cutoff* Cutoff date-time, in the form:

YY[*MM*[*DD*[*HH*[*MM*[*SS*]]]]]

No changes (deltas) to the SCCS file that were created after the specified *cutoff* date-time are included in the generated ASCII text file. Units omitted from the date-time default to their maximum possible values; that is, **-c7502** is equivalent to **-c750228235959**. Any number of non-numeric characters may separate the two-digit pieces of the *cutoff* date-time. This feature allows one to specify a *cutoff* date in the form:

-c"77/2/2 9:22:25".

-i*list* A *list* of deltas to be included (forced to be applied) in the creation of the generated file. The *list* has the following syntax:

<list> ::= *<range>* | *<list>* , *<range>*
<range> ::= *SID* | *SID* – *SID*

SID, the SCCS Identification of a delta, may be in any form shown in the "SID Specified" column of Table 1.

-x*list* A *list* of deltas to be excluded in the creation of the generated file. See the **-i** keyletter for the *list* format.

-e Indicates that the **get** is for the purpose of editing or making a change (delta) to the SCCS file via a subsequent use of **delta**(1). The **-e** keyletter used in a **get** for a particular version (SID) of the SCCS file prevents further **get**s for editing on the same SID until **delta** is executed or the **j** (joint edit) flag is set in the SCCS file [see **admin**(1)]. Concurrent use of **get -e** for different SIDs is always allowed.

If the **g.***file* generated by **get** with an **-e** keyletter is accidentally ruined in the process of editing it, it may be regenerated by re-executing the **get** command with the **-k** keyletter in place of the **-e** keyletter.

SCCS file protection specified via the ceiling, floor, and authorized user list stored in the SCCS file [see **admin**(1)] are enforced when the **-e** keyletter is used.

-b Used with the **-e** keyletter to indicate that the new delta should have an SID in a new branch as shown in Table 1. This keyletter is ignored if the **b** flag is not present in the file [see **admin**(1)] or if the retrieved **delta** is not a leaf **delta**. (A leaf **delta** is one that has no successors on the SCCS file tree.) A branch **delta** may always be created from a non-leaf **delta**. Partial SIDs are interpreted as shown in the "SID Retrieved" column of Table 1.

-k Suppresses replacement of identification keywords (see below) in the retrieved text by their value. The **-k** keyletter is implied by the **-e** keyletter.

-l[p] Causes a delta summary to be written into an **l.***file*. If **-lp** is used, then an **l.***file* is not created; the delta summary is written on the standard output instead. See the "Identification Keywords" section below for detailed information on the **l.***file*.

-p Causes the text retrieved from the SCCS file to be written on the standard output. No **g.***file* is created. All output that normally goes to the standard output goes to file descriptor 2 instead, unless the **-s** keyletter is used, in which case it disappears.

-s Suppresses all output normally written on the standard output. However, fatal error messages (which always go to file descriptor 2) remain unaffected.

-m Causes each text line retrieved from the SCCS file to be preceded by the SID of the delta that inserted the text line in the SCCS file. The format is: SID, followed by a horizontal tab, followed by the text line.

-n Causes each generated text line to be preceded with the **%M%** identification keyword value (see below). The format is: **%M%** value, followed by a horizontal tab, followed by the text line. When both the **-m** and **-n** keyletters are used, the format is: **%M%** value, followed by a horizontal tab, followed by the **-m** keyletter generated format.

`-g` Suppresses the actual retrieval of text from the SCCS file. It is primarily used to generate an `l.`*file*, or to verify the existence of a particular SID.

`-t` Used to access the most recently created delta in a given release (for example, `-r1`), or release and level (for example, `-r1.2`).

`-w` *string* Substitute *string* for all occurrences of `%W%` when getting the file. Substitution occurs prior to keyword expansion.

`-a`*seq-no.* The delta sequence number of the SCCS file delta (version) to be retrieved. This keyletter is used by the **`comb`** command; it is not a generally useful keyletter. If both the `-r` and `-a` keyletters are specified, only the `-a` keyletter is used. Care should be taken when using the `-a` keyletter in conjunction with the `-e` keyletter, as the SID of the delta to be created may not be what one expects. The `-r` keyletter can be used with the `-a` and `-e` keyletters to control the naming of the SID of the delta to be created.

For each file processed, `get` responds (on the standard output) with the SID being accessed and with the number of lines retrieved from the SCCS file.

If the `-e` keyletter is used, the SID of the delta to be made appears after the SID accessed and before the number of lines generated. If there is more than one named file or if a directory or standard input is named, each file name is printed (preceded by a new-line) before it is processed. If the `-i` keyletter is used, included deltas are listed following the notation "`Included`;" if the `-x` keyletter is used, excluded deltas are listed following the notation "`Excluded`."

TABLE 1. Determination of SCCS Identification String

SID* Specified	-b Keyletter Used†	Other Conditions	SID Retrieved	SID of Delta to be Created
none‡	no	R defaults to mR	mR.mL	mR.(mL+1)
none‡	yes	R defaults to mR	mR.mL	mR.mL.(mB+1).1
R	no	R > mR	mR.mL	R.1***
R	no	R = mR	mR.mL	mR.(mL+1)
R	yes	R > mR	mR.mL	mR.mL.(mB+1).1
R	yes	R = mR	mR.mL	mR.mL.(mB+1).1
R	–	R < mR and R does not exist	hR.mL**	hR.mL.(mB+1).1
R	–	Trunk succ.# in release > R and R exists	R.mL	R.mL.(mB+1).1
R.L	no	No trunk succ.	R.L	R.(L+1)
R.L	yes	No trunk succ.	R.L	R.L.(mB+1).1
R.L	–	Trunk succ. in release ≥ R	R.L	R.L.(mB+1).1
R.L.B	no	No branch succ.	R.L.B.mS	R.L.B.(mS+1)
R.L.B	yes	No branch succ.	R.L.B.mS	R.L.(mB+1).1
R.L.B.S	no	No branch succ.	R.L.B.S	R.L.B.(S+1)
R.L.B.S	yes	No branch succ.	R.L.B.S	R.L.(mB+1).1
R.L.B.S	–	Branch succ.	R.L.B.S	R.L.(mB+1).1

* "R," "L," "B," and "S" are the "release," "level," "branch," and "sequence" components of the SID, respectively; "m" means "maximum." Thus, for example, "R.mL" means "the maximum level number within release R;" "R.L.(mB+1).1" means "the first sequence number on the new branch (for example, maximum branch number plus one) of level L within release R." Note that if the SID specified is of the form "R.L", "R.L.B", or "R.L.B.S", each of the specified components must exist.

** "hR" is the highest existing release that is lower than the specified, nonexistent, release R.

*** This is used to force creation of the first delta in a new release.

\# Successor.

† The **-b** keyletter is effective only if the **b** flag [see **admin**(1)] is present in the file. An entry of – means "irrelevant."

‡ This case applies if the **d** (default SID) flag is not present in the file. If the **d** flag is present in the file, then the SID obtained from the **d** flag is interpreted as if it had been specified on the command line. Thus, one of the other cases in this table applies.

Identification Keywords

Identifying information is inserted into the text retrieved from the SCCS file by replacing identification keywords with their value wherever they occur. The following keywords may be used in the text stored in an SCCS file:

Keyword	Value
%M%	Module name: either the value of the **m** flag in the file [see **admin**(1)], or if absent, the name of the SCCS file with the leading **s.** removed.
%I%	SCCS identification (SID) (%R%.%L%.%B%.%S%) of the retrieved text.
%R%	Release.
%L%	Level.
%B%	Branch.
%S%	Sequence.
%D%	Current date (*YY/MM/DD*).
%H%	Current date (*MM/DD/YY*).
%T%	Current time (*HH:MM:SS*).
%E%	Date newest applied delta was created (*YY/MM/DD*).
%G%	Date newest applied delta was created (*MM/DD/YY*).
%U%	Time newest applied delta was created (*HH:MM:SS*).
%Y%	Module type: value of the **t** flag in the SCCS file [see **admin**(1)].
%F%	SCCS file name.
%P%	Fully qualified SCCS file name.
%Q%	The value of the **q** flag in the file [see **admin**(1)].
%C%	Current line number. This keyword is intended for identifying messages output by the program such as "this should not have happened" type errors. It is not intended to be used on every line to provide sequence numbers.
%Z%	The four-character string **@(#)** recognizable by the **what** command.
%W%	A shorthand notation for constructing **what** strings for UNIX System program files. %W% = %Z%%M%<tab>%I%
%A%	Another shorthand notation for constructing **what** strings for non-UNIX System program files: %A% = %Z%%Y% %M% %I%%Z%

Several auxiliary files may be created by **get**. These files are known generically as the **g.***file*, **l.***file*, **p.***file*, and **z.***file*. The letter before the dot is called the tag. An auxiliary file name is formed from the SCCS file name: the last component of all SCCS file names must be of the form **s.***module-name*, the auxiliary files are named by replacing the leading **s** with the tag. The **g.***file* is an exception to this scheme: the **g.***file* is named by removing the **s.** prefix. For example, **s.xyz.c**, the auxiliary file names would be **xyz.c**, **l.xyz.c**, **p.xyz.c**, and **z.xyz.c**, respectively.

A **g.***file*, containing the generated text, is created in the current directory. It is owned by the real user, and only the real user need have write permission in the current directory. The permissions of the **g.***file* depend on the permissions of the SCCS file, the options used when **get** was executed, and the **x** flag in the SCCS file [see **admin**(1)]. Users who have read permission to the SCCS file have read permission to the **g.***file*, and if the **x** flag has been set in the SCCS file, also have execute permission to the **g.***file*. Invoking **get** with the **-e** option enables write permission on the **g.***file* for the invoker.

The **l.***file* contains a table showing which deltas were applied in generating the retrieved text. The **l.***file* is created in the current directory if the **-l** keyletter is used; its mode is 444 and it is owned by the real user. Only the real user need have write permission in the current directory.

Lines in the **l.***file* have the following format:

a. A blank character if the delta was applied; * otherwise.

b. A blank character if the delta was applied or was not applied and ignored; * if the delta was not applied and was not ignored.

c. A code indicating a "special" reason why the delta was or was not applied: "**I**" (included), "**X**" (excluded), or "**C**" (cut off by a **-c** keyletter).

d. Blank.

e. SCCS identification (SID).

f. Tab character.

g. Date and time (in the form *YY/MM/DD HH:MM:SS*) of creation.

h. Blank.

i. Login name of person who created **delta**.

The comments and MR data follow on subsequent lines, indented one horizontal tab character. A blank line terminates each entry.

The **p.***file* is used to pass information resulting from a **get** with an **-e** keyletter along to **delta**. Its contents are also used to prevent a subsequent execution of **get** with an **-e** keyletter for the same SID until **delta** is executed or the joint edit flag, **j**, [see **admin**(1)] is set in the SCCS file. The **p.***file* is created in the directory containing the SCCS file and the effective user must have write permission in that directory. Its mode is 644 and it is owned by the effective user. The format of the **p.***file* is: the gotten SID, followed by a blank, followed by the SID that the new delta will have when it is made, followed by a blank, followed by the login name of the real user, followed by a blank, followed by the date-time the **get** was executed, followed by a blank and the **-i** keyletter argument if it was present, followed by a blank and the **-x** keyletter argument if it was present, followed by a new-line. There can be an arbitrary number of lines in the **p.***file* at any time; no two lines can have the same new delta SID.

The **z.***file* serves as a lock-out mechanism against simultaneous updates. Its contents are the binary (2 bytes) process ID of the command (that is, **get**) that created it. The **z.***file* is created in the directory containing the SCCS file for the duration of **get**. The same protection restrictions as those for the **p.***file* apply for the **z.***file*. The **z.***file* is created with mode 444.

FILES

g.*file* created by the execution of **get**.
l.*file* created by **-l** option; contains delta summary
p.*file* [see **delta**(1)]
q.*file* [see **delta**(1)]
z.*file* [see **delta**(1)]
bdiff Program to compute differences between the "gotten" file and the **g.***file*.

SEE ALSO

admin(1), **bdiff**(1), **delta**(1), **help**(1), **prs**(1), **what**(1)

DIAGNOSTICS

Use **help**(1) for explanations.

NOTES

If the effective user has write permission (either explicitly or implicitly) in the directory containing the SCCS files, but the real user does not, then only one file may be named when the **-e** keyletter is used.

getdev (1M)

NAME

getdev – list devices defined in the Device Database based on criteria

SYNOPSIS

getdev [**-ae**] [*criteria* [. . .]] [*device* [. . .]]

DESCRIPTION

getdev generates a list of devices that match certain criteria. These criteria include a list of attributes (given in expressions) and a list of devices. If no criteria are given, all devices are included in the generated list.

Devices must satisfy at least one of the criteria in the list unless the **-a** option is used. Then, only those devices that match all the criteria in a list will be included in the generated list.

Devices that are defined on the command line and that match the criteria are included in the generated list. However, if the **-e** flag is used, the list of devices defined on the command line becomes a set of devices to be excluded from the list.

Criteria

The *criteria* argument may be specified with any of the following four expression types:

attribute=*value*
: Select all devices for which *attribute* is defined and is equal to *value*

attribute!=*value*
: Select all devices for which *attribute* is defined and does not equal *value*

attribute:*
: Select all devices for which *attribute* is defined

attribute!:*
: Select all devices that do not have *attribute* defined

See the **putdev**(1M) manual page for a complete listing and description of available attributes.

Options and Arguments

The options and arguments for this command are:

-a Specifies that the list of devices that follows on the command line must match all criteria to be included in the list generated by this command. The flag has no effect if no criteria are defined.

-e Specifies that the list of devices following on the command line should be excluded from the list generated by this command. The flag has no effect if no devices are defined.

criteria
: Defines the criteria that a device must match to be included in the generated list. The criteria should be given in expressions.

device Defines the devices that should be included or excluded (based on the command options) in the generated list. This can be the pathname of the device or the device alias.

Return Values

If successful, **getdev** exits with a code of zero (0). If there are errors, the command exits with one of the following values and prints the corresponding error message:

1 `usage:getdev [-ae] [criterion[...]] [device[...]]`

2 `Device Database in inconsistent state - notify administrator`

2 `Device Database could not be opened for reading`

Files

`/etc/device.tab`

REFERENCES

devattr(1M), **getdgrp**(1M), **putdev**(1M), **putdgrp**(1M)

NAME

getdgrp – lists device groups which contain devices that match criteria

SYNOPSIS

getdgrp [**-ael**] [*criteria* [. . .]] [*dgroup* [. . .]]

DESCRIPTION

getdgrp generates a list of device groups that contain devices matching the given criteria. The criteria is given in the form of expressions.

criteria can be one expression or a list of expressions which a device must meet for its group to be included in the list generated by **getdgrp**. If you do not provide a criteria, all device groups are included in the list.

Devices must satisfy at least one of the criteria in the list. However, the **-a** flag can be used to define that a "logical and" operation should be performed. Then, only those groups containing devices which match all of the criteria in a list will be included.

dgroup defines a set of device groups to be included in the list. Device groups that are defined and which contain devices matching the criteria are included. However, if the **-e** flag is used, this list defines a set of device groups to be excluded. When the **-e** option is used and criteria is also defined, the generated list will include device groups containing devices which match the criteria and are not in the command line list.

Criteria

There are four possible criteria expression types:

attribute=value
: Selects all device groups with a member whose attribute *attribute* is defined and is equal to *value*.

attribute!=*value*
: Selects all device groups with a member whose attribute *attribute* is defined and does not equal *value*.

attribute:*
: Selects all device groups with a member which has the attribute *attribute* defined.

attribute!:*
: Selects all device groups with a member which does not have the attribute *attribute* defined.

See the **putdev**(1M) manual page for a complete listing and description of available attributes.

Options and Arguments

getdgrp takes the following options and arguments:

-a Specifies that a device must match all criteria before a device group to which it belongs can be included in the list generated by this command. The flag has no effect if no criteria are defined.

`-e` Specifies that the list of device groups on the command line should be excluded from the list generated by this command. (Without the `-e` the named device groups are the only ones which can be included in the generated list.) The flag has no effect if no device groups are defined.

`-l` Specifies that all device groups (subject to the `-e` option and the *dgroup* list) should be listed, even if they contain no valid device members. This option has no affect if *criteria* is specified on the command line.

criteria
Defines criteria that a device must match before a device group to which it belongs can be included in the generated list.

dgroup
Defines device groups which should be included in or excluded from the generated list.

Return Values

getdgrp returns with one of the following values:

`0` Successful completion of the task

`1` Command syntax incorrect, invalid option used, or internal error occurred

`2` Device table or device group table could not be opened for reading

Files

`/etc/device.tab`
`/etc/dgroup.tab`

REFERENCES

devattr(1M), **getdev**(1M), **putdev**(1M), **putdgrp**(1M)

NAME

getext (vxfs) – get extent attributes

SYNOPSIS

getext [**-e** *extent_size*] [**-f**] [**-s**] *file* . . .

DESCRIPTION

getext displays extent attribute information associated with a set of files.

The options are:

-f Do not print the filename.

-s Do not print output for files that do not have fixed extent sizes or reservation.

OUTPUT

```
file1:   Bsize   1024   Reserve   36   Extent Size   3   align
noextend
```

The above line indicates a file with 36 blocks of reservation, a fixed extent size of 3 blocks, all extents aligned to 3 block boundaries, and the file unable to be grown once the current reservation is exhausted. The file system block size is 1024. Reservation and fixed extent sizes are allocated in multiples of the file system block size.

NOTES

getext is available with the VxFS Advanced package only.

SEE ALSO

setext(1), **vxfsio**(7)

NAME

`getfrm` – returns the current frameID number

SYNOPSIS

`getfrm`

DESCRIPTION

`getfrm` returns the current frameID number. The frameID number is a number assigned to the frame by FMLI and displayed flush left in the frame's title bar. If a frame is closed its frameID number may be reused when a new frame is opened. `getfrm` takes no arguments.

EXAMPLES

If a menu whose frameID is `3` defines an item to have this **`action`** descriptor:

```
action=open text stdtext `getfrm`
```

the text frame defined in the definition file **`stdtext`** would be passed the argument `3` when it is opened.

NOTES

It is not a good idea to use **`getfrm`** in a backquoted expression coded on a line by itself. Stand-alone backquoted expressions are evaluated before any descriptors are parsed, thus the frame is not yet fully current, and may not have been assigned a frameID number.

getitems (1F)

NAME

getitems – return a list of currently marked menu items

SYNOPSIS

getitems [*delimiter_string*]

DESCRIPTION

The **getitems** function returns the value of **lininfo** if defined, else it returns the value of the **name** descriptor, for all currently marked menu items. Each value in the list is delimited by *delimiter_string*. The default value of *delimiter_string* is newline.

EXAMPLE

The **done** descriptor in the following menu definition file executes **getitems** when the user presses ENTER (note that the menu is multiselect):

```
Menu="Example"
multiselect=TRUE
done=`getitems ":" | message`

name="Item 1"
action=`message "You selected item 1"`

name="Item 2"
lininfo="This is item 2"
action=`message "You selected item 2"`

name="Item 3"
action=`message "You selected item 3"`
```

If a user marked all three items in this menu, pressing ENTER would cause the following string to be displayed on the message line:

```
Item 1:This is item 2:Item 3
```

Note that because **lininfo** is defined for the second menu item, its value is displayed instead of the value of the **name** descriptor.

NAME

getopt – parse command options

SYNOPSIS

set -- getopt *optstring* **$***

DESCRIPTION

The **getopts**(1) command supersedes **getopt**. For more information, see the section NOTES which follows.

getopt is used to break up options in command lines for easy parsing by shell procedures and to check for valid options. It recognizes supplementary code set characters in the argument given to *optstring* according to the locale specified in the **LC_CTYPE** environment variable [see **LANG** on **environ**(5)].

optstring is a string of recognized option letters; see **getopt**(3C). If a letter is followed by a colon, the option is expected to have an argument that may or may not be separated from it by white space. The special option **--** is used to delimit the end of the options. If it is used explicitly, **getopt** recognizes it; otherwise, **getopt** generates it; in either case, **getopt** places it at the end of the options. The positional parameters (**$1 $2** . . .) of the shell are reset so that each option is preceded by a – and is in its own positional parameter; each option argument is also parsed into its own positional parameter.

Files

/usr/lib/locale/*locale***/LC_MESSAGES/uxcore**
language-specific message file [See **LANG** on **environ**(5).]

Diagnostics

getopt prints an error message on the standard error when it encounters an option letter not included in *optstring*.

USAGE

Reset **OPTIND** to 1 when rescanning the options.

getopt does not support the part of Rule 8 of the command syntax standard [see **intro**(1)] that permits groups of option-arguments following an option to be separated by white space and quoted. For example,

```
cmd -a -b -o "xxx z yy" file
```

is not handled correctly. To correct this deficiency, use the **getopts** command instead of **getopt**.

If an option that takes an option-argument is followed by a value that is the same as an option listed in **optstring** (referring to the earlier "Examples" section, but using the following command line: **cmd -o -a file**), **getopt** always treats **-a** as an option-argument to **-o**; it never recognizes **-a** as an option. For this case, the **for** loop in the example shifts past the *file* argument.

Examples

The following code fragment shows how you might process the arguments for a command that can take the options **a** or **b**, as well as the option **o** that requires an argument:

```
set -- getopt abo: $*
if [ $? != 0 ]
then
        echo $USAGE
        exit 2
fi
for i in $*
do
        case $i in
        -a | -b)        FLAG=$i; shift;;
        -o)             OARG=$2; shift 2;;
        --)             shift; break;;
        esac
done
```

This code accepts any of the following as equivalent:

```
cmd -aoarg file file
cmd -a -o arg file file
cmd -oarg -a file file
cmd -a -oarg -- file file
```

NOTES

Future Directions

getopt will not be supported in the next major release. For this release a conversion tool has been provided, **getoptcvt**. For more information about **getopts** and getoptcvt, see getopts(1).

REFERENCES

getopt(3C), getopts(1), **sh**(1)

NAME

getopts, (**getoptcvt**) – parse command options

SYNOPSIS

getopts *optstring name* [*arg* . . .]

/usr/lib/getoptcvt [**-b**] *file*

DESCRIPTION

getopts is used by shell procedures to parse positional parameters and to check for valid options. It supports all applicable rules of the command syntax standard [see Rules 3-10, **intro**(1), and the NOTES section below]. It should be used in place of the **getopt**(1) command. **getopts** recognizes supplementary code set characters in the argument given to *optstring* according to the locale specified in the **LC_CTYPE** environment variable [see **LANG** on **environ**(5)].

USAGE

optstring must contain the option letters that the command using **getopts** will recognize. If a letter is followed by a colon, the option is expected to have an argument, or group of arguments, which must be separated from it by white space.

Each time it is invoked, **getopts** places the next option in the shell variable *name* and the index of the next argument to be processed in the shell variable **OPTIND**. Whenever the shell or a shell procedure is invoked, **OPTIND** is initialized to **1**. (**OPTIND** is not initialized to **1** when a shell function is called.)

When an option requires an option-argument, **getopts** places it in the shell variable **OPTARG**.

If an illegal option is encountered, **?** will be placed in *name*.

When the end of options is encountered, **getopts** exits with a non-zero exit status. The special option **--** may be used to delimit the end of the options.

By default, **getopts** parses the positional parameters. If arguments *arg* . . . are given on the **getopts** command line, **getopts** parses them instead.

/usr/lib/getoptcvt reads the shell script in *file*, converts it to use **getopts** instead of **getopt**, and writes the results on the standard output.

-b Make the converted script portable to earlier releases of the UNIX system. **/usr/lib/getoptcvt** modifies the shell script in *file* so that when the resulting shell script is executed, it determines at run time whether to invoke **getopts** or **getopt**.

So all new commands will adhere to the command syntax standard described in **intro**(1), they should use **getopts** or **getopt**(3C) to parse positional parameters and check for options that are valid for that command (see the NOTES section below).

Example

The following fragment of a shell program shows how one might process the arguments for a command that can take the options **a** or **b**, as well as the option **o**, which requires an option-argument:

```
while getopts 'abo:?' c
do
        case $c in
        a | b)          FLAG=$c;;
        o)              OARG=$OPTARG;;
        \?)             echo $USAGE
                        exit 2;;
        esac
done
shift expr $OPTIND - 1
```

This code accepts any of the following as equivalent:

```
cmd -a -b -o "xxx z yy" file
cmd -a -b -o "xxx z yy" -- file
cmd -ab -o xxx,z,yy file
cmd -ab -o "xxx z yy" file
cmd -o xxx,z,yy -b -a file
```

Files

`/usr/lib/locale/`*locale*`/LC_MESSAGES/uxcore.abi`
language-specific message file [See **LANG** on **environ** (5).]

Output

getopts prints an error message on the standard error when it encounters an option letter not included in *optstring*.

NOTES

Although the following command syntax rule [see **intro**(1)] relaxations are permitted under the current implementation, they should not be used because they may not be supported in future releases of the system. As in the EXAMPLE section above, **a** and **b** are options, and the option **o** requires an option-argument. The following example violates Rule 5: options with option-arguments must not be grouped with other options:

```
cmd -aboxxx file
```

The following example violates Rule 6: there must be white space after an option that takes an option-argument:

```
cmd -ab -oxxx file
```

Changing the value of the shell variable **OPTIND** or parsing different sets of arguments may lead to unexpected results.

REFERENCES

getopt(1), **getopt**(3C), **intro**(1), **sh**(1)

NAME

gettable – get DoD Internet format host table from a host

SYNOPSIS

gettable [-v] *host* **[***file***]**

DESCRIPTION

gettable is a simple program used to obtain the DoD Internet host table from a hostname server. The indicated *host* is queried for the table. The table, if retrieved, is placed in the file *file*, or, by default in the file **hosts.txt**.

The **-v** option will only get the version number instead of the complete host table, and put the output in the file *file*, or, by default in the file **hosts.ver**.

gettable operates by opening a TCP connection to the port indicated in the service specification for hostname. A request is then made for all names and the resultant information is placed in the output file.

gettable is best used in conjunction with the **htable**(1M) program which converts the DoD Internet host table format to that used by the network library lookup routines.

SEE ALSO

htable(1M)

Harrenstien, Ken, Mary Stahl, and Elizabeth Feinler, *HOSTNAME Server,* RFC 953, Network Information Center, SRI International, Menlo Park, Calif., October 1985

NOTES

Should allow requests for only part of the database.

gettxt (1)

NAME

gettxt – retrieve a text string from a message database

SYNOPSIS

gettxt *msgfile*:*msgnum* [*dflt_msg*]

DESCRIPTION

gettxt retrieves a text string from a message file in the directory **/usr/lib/locale/***locale***/LC_MESSAGES**. The directory name *locale* corresponds to the language in which the text strings are written; see **setlocale**(3C) and **environ**(5).

msgfile Name of the file from which to retrieve *msgnum*. The name can be up to 14 characters in length, but may not contain either \ 0 (**NULL**) or the characters **/** (slash) or **:** (colon).

msgnum Sequence number of the string to retrieve from *msgfile*. The strings in *msgfile* are numbered sequentially from 1 to *n*, where *n* is the number of strings in the file.

dflt_msg Default string to be displayed if **gettxt** fails to retrieve *msgnum* from *msgfile*. Nongraphic characters must be represented as alphabetic escape sequences.

The text string to be retrieved is in the file *msgfile*, created by the **mkmsgs**(1) utility and installed under the directory **/usr/lib/locale/***locale***/LC_MESSAGES**. The directory searched is specified by the environment variable **LC_MESSAGES**. If **LC_MESSAGES** is not set, the environment variable **LANG** will be used. If **LANG** is not set, the files containing the strings are under the directory **/usr/lib/locale/C/LC_MESSAGES**.

If **gettxt** fails to retrieve a message in the requested language, it will try to retrieve the same message from **/usr/lib/locale/C/LC_MESSAGES/***msgfile*. If this also fails, and if *dflt_msg* is present and non-empty, then it will display the value of *dflt_msg*; if *dflt_msg* is not present or is empty, then it will display the string **Message not found!!\n**. If the environment variables **LANG** or **LC_MESSAGES** have not been set to other than their default values,

```
gettxt UX:10 "hello world\n"
```

will try to retrieve the 10th message from **/usr/lib/locale/C/LC_MESSAGES/UX**. If the retrieval fails, the message **hello world**, followed by a newline, will be displayed.

FILES

/usr/lib/locale/C/LC_MESSAGES/*
    default message files created by **mkmsgs**(1)

/usr/lib/locale/*locale***/LC_MESSAGES/***
    language-specific message files created by **mkmsgs**(1)

/usr/lib/locale/*locale***/LC_MESSAGES/uxcore.abi**
    language-specific message file for **gettxt**

SEE ALSO

exstr(1), **gettxt**(3C), **mkmsgs**(1), **setlocale**(3C), **srchtxt**(1)

NAME

`getty` – set terminal type, modes, speed, and line discipline

SYNOPSIS

`getty` [`-h`] [`-t` *timeout*] *line* [*speed* [*terminal* [*linedisc*]]]

`getty -c` *file*

DESCRIPTION

`getty` is included for compatibility with previous releases for the few applications that still call `getty` directly. `getty` can only be executed by a process with the appropriate privileges. Initially `getty` prints the login prompt, waits for the user's login name, and then invokes the **`login`** command. `getty` attempts to adapt the system to the terminal speed by using the options and arguments specified on the command line.

line The name of a TTY line in `/dev` to which `getty` is to attach itself. `getty` uses this string as the name of a file in the `/dev` directory to open for reading and writing.

`-h` If the `-h` flag is not set, a hangup will be forced by setting the speed to zero before setting the speed to the default or specified speed.

`-t` *timeout*
specifies that `getty` should exit if the open on the line succeeds and no one types anything in *timeout* seconds.

speed The *speed* argument is a label to a speed and TTY definition in the file `/etc/ttydefs`. This definition tells `getty` at what speed to run initially, what the initial TTY settings are, and what speed to try next, should the user indicate, by pressing the BREAK key, that the speed is inappropriate. If not specified on the command line, *speed* defaults to the first entry in `/etc/ttydefs`.

terminal
The *terminal* option is the name of the terminal type.

linedisc
The *linedisc* option is the name of the line discipline.

`-c` *file* The `-c` option performs a check on the `gettydefs` file.

When given no optional arguments, `getty` specifies the following: The *speed* of the interface is set to the speed defined in the first entry in `/etc/gettydefs`, either parity is allowed, new-line characters are converted to carriage return-line feed, and tab expansion is performed on the standard output. `getty` types the login prompt before reading the user's name a character at a time. If a null character (or framing error) is received, it is assumed to be the result of the user pressing the BREAK key. This will cause `getty` to attempt the next *speed* in the series. The series that `getty` tries is determined by what it finds in `/etc/ttydefs`.

NOTES

Administrators and developers are encouraged to use **`ttymon`**(1M) as support for `getty` may be dropped in the future.

FILES

`/etc/ttydefs`

SEE ALSO

`ct`(1C), **`ioctl`**(2), **`login`**(1), **`sttydefs`**(1M), **`tty`**(7), **`ttymon`**(1M)

NAME

`getvol` – verifies device accessibility

SYNOPSIS

`getvol -n` [`-l` *label*] *device*
`getvol` [`-f` | `-F`] [`-wo`] [`-l` *label* | `-x` *label*] *device*

DESCRIPTION

`getvol` verifies that the specified device is accessible and that a volume of the appropriate medium has been inserted. The command is interactive and displays instructional prompts, describes errors, and shows required label information. `getvol` uses the device table, **`/etc/device.tab`**, to determine the characteristics of the device when performing the volume label checking.

Options and Arguments

`getvol` has the following options and arguments:

`-n` Runs the command in non-interactive mode. The volume is assumed to be inserted upon command invocation.

`-l` *label*
Specifies that the label *label* must exist on the inserted volume (can be overridden by the `-o` option).

`-f` Formats the volume after insertion, using the format command defined for this device in the device table.

`-F` Formats the volume after insertion and places a file system on the device. Also uses the format command defined for this device in the device table.

`-w` Allows administrator to write a new label on the device. User is prompted to supply the label text. This option is ineffective if the `-n` option is enabled.

`-o` Allows the administrator to override a label check.

`-x` *label*
Specifies that the label *label* must exist on the device. This option should be used instead of the `-l` option when the label can only be verified by visual means. Use of the option causes a message to be displayed asking the administrator to visually verify that the label is indeed *label*.

device Names the device which should be verified for accessibility.

Return Values

`getvol` returns with one of the following values:

0 Successful completion of the task

1 Command syntax incorrect, invalid option used, or internal error occurred

3 Device table could not be opened for reading

Files

`/etc/device.tab`

grep(1)

NAME

grep – search a file for a pattern

SYNOPSIS

grep [*options*] *limited_regular_expression* [*file* . . .]

DESCRIPTION

grep searches files for a pattern and prints all lines that contain that pattern. **grep** uses limited regular expressions (expressions that have string values that use a subset of the possible alphanumeric and special characters) like those used with **ed**(1) to match the patterns. It uses a compact non-deterministic algorithm.

Be careful using the characters **$**, *, **[**, ^, |, (,), and \ in the *limited_regular_expression* because they are also meaningful to the shell. It is safest to enclose the entire *limited_regular_expression* in single quotes ' . . . '.

grep processes supplementary code set characters according to the locale specified in the **LC_CTYPE** environment variable [see **LANG** on **environ**(5)], except as noted under the **-i** option below. In regular expressions, pattern searches are performed on characters, not bytes, as described on **ed**(1).

If no files are specified, **grep** assumes standard input. Normally, each line found is copied to standard output. The filename is printed before each line found if there is more than one input file.

Command line options are:

-b Precede each line by the block number on which it was found. This can be useful in locating block numbers by context (first block is 0).

-c Print only a count of the lines that contain the pattern.

-i Ignore uppercase/lowercase distinction during comparisons. Valid for single-byte characters only.

-h Prevents the name of the file containing the matching line from being appended to that line. Used when searching multiple files.

-l Print the names of files with matching lines once, separated by newlines. Does not repeat the names of files when the pattern is found more than once.

-n Precede each line by its line number in the file (first line is 1).

-s Suppress error messages about nonexistent or unreadable files

-v Print all lines except those that contain the pattern.

-e *special_expression*
Search for a *special_expression* (*full_regular_expression* that begins with a -).

-f *file*
Take the list of *full_regular_expressions* from *file*.

FILES

/usr/lib/locale/*locale***/LC_MESSAGES/uxcore.abi**
language-specific message file [See **LANG** on **environ** (5).]

SEE ALSO

ed(1), **egrep**(1), **fgrep**(1), **sed**(1), **sh**(1)

DIAGNOSTICS

Exit status is 0 if any matches are found, 1 if none, 2 for syntax errors or inaccessible files (even if matches were found).

NOTES

Lines are limited to **BUFSIZ** bytes; longer lines are truncated. **BUFSIZ** is defined in **/usr/include/stdio.h**.

If there is a line with embedded nulls, **grep** will only match up to the first null; if it matches, it will print the entire line.

groupadd (1M)

NAME

groupadd – add (create) a new group definition on the system

SYNOPSIS

`groupadd [-g` *gid* `[-o]]` *group*

DESCRIPTION

The **groupadd** command creates a new group definition on the system by adding the appropriate entry to the **/etc/group** file.

The following options are available:

`-g` *gid* The group ID for the new group. This group ID must be a non-negative decimal integer below **MAXUID** as defined in the <**param.h**> header file. By default, a unique group ID is allocated in the valid range. Group IDs from 0-99 are reserved.

`-o` This option allows the *gid* to be duplicated (non-unique).

group A string of printable characters that specifies the name of the new group. It may not include a colon (:) or newline (\\n).

FILES

`/etc/group`

SEE ALSO

groupdel(1M), **groupmod**(1M), **logins**(1M), **useradd**(1M), **userdel**(1M), **usermod**(1M), **users**(1)

DIAGNOSTICS

The **groupadd** command exits with `0` on success, or displays error messages under the following conditions:

Invalid command syntax.

An invalid argument was provided to an option.

gid is not unique (when the `-o` option is not used).

group is not unique.

Cannot update the **/etc/group** file.

NAME

groupdel – delete a group definition from the system

SYNOPSIS

groupdel *group*

DESCRIPTION

The **groupdel** command removes a group definition from the system by deleting the entry for the relevant group from the **/etc/group** file. It does not, however, remove the group ID (GID) from the password file; the deleted GID remains in effect for any directories and files that have it.

The following options are available:

group A string of printable characters that specifies the group to be deleted.

FILES

/etc/group

SEE ALSO

groupadd(1M), **groupmod**(1M), **logins**(1M), **useradd**(1M), **userdel**(1M), **usermod**(1M), **users**(1)

DIAGNOSTICS

The **groupdel** command exits with 0 on success, or displays error messages under the following conditions:

group does not exist.

Cannot update the **/etc/group** file.

groupmod (1M)

NAME

groupmod – modify a group definition on the system

SYNOPSIS

groupmod [**-g** *gid* [**-o**]] [**-n** *name*] *group*

DESCRIPTION

The **groupmod** command modifies the definition of the specified group by modifying the appropriate entry in the **/etc/group** file.

The following options are available:

-g *gid* The group ID for the new group. This group ID must be a non-negative decimal integer below **MAXUID** as defined in <**param.h**>. The group ID defaults to the next available (unique) number above 99. (Group IDs from 0-99 are reserved.)

-o This option allows the *gid* to be duplicated (non-unique).

-n *name*
A string of printable characters that specifies a new name for the group. It may not include a colon (:) or newline (\n).

group The current name of the group to be modified.

FILES

/etc/group

SEE ALSO

groupadd(1M), **groupdel**(1M), **logins**(1M), **useradd**(1M), **userdel**(1M), **usermod**(1M), **users**(1)

DIAGNOSTICS

The **groupmod** command exits with **0** on success, or displays error messages for the following conditions:

Invalid command syntax.

An invalid argument was provided to an option.

gid is not unique (when the **-o** option is not used).

group does not exist.

name already exists as a group name.

Cannot update the **/etc/group** file.

NAME

groups – print group membership of user

SYNOPSIS

groups [*user* . . .]

DESCRIPTION

The command **groups** prints on standard output the groups to which you or the optionally specified user belong. Each user belongs to a group specified in **/etc/passwd** and possibly to other groups as specified in **/etc/group**.

SEE ALSO

group(4), **passwd**(4)

FILES

/etc/passwd
/etc/group

NAME

groups – (BSD) display a user's group memberships

SYNOPSIS

/usr/ucb/groups [*user* . . .]

DESCRIPTION

With no arguments, **groups** displays the groups to which you belong; otherwise it displays the groups to which the **user** belongs. Each user belongs to a group specified in the password file **/etc/passwd** and possibly to other groups as specified in the file **/etc/group**. If you do not own a file but belong to the group by which it is owned, you are granted group access to the file.

FILES

/etc/passwd

/etc/group

SEE ALSO

getgroups(2)

NOTES

This command is obsolescent.

NAME

grpck – (BSD) check group database entries

SYNOPSIS

/usr/ucb/grpck [*file*]

DESCRIPTION

grpck checks that a file in **group**(4) does not contain any errors; it checks the **/etc/group** file by default.

This command differs from **/usr/sbin/grpck** in its ability to correctly parse YP entries in **/etc/passwd.**

FILES

/etc/group

SEE ALSO

group(4), passwd(4)

DIAGNOSTICS

Too many/few fields
: An entry in the group file does not have the proper number of fields.

No group name
: The group name field of an entry is empty.

Bad character(s) in group name
: The group name in an entry contains characters other than lowercase letters and digits.

Invalid GID
: The group ID field in an entry is not numeric or is greater than 65535.

Null login name
: A login name in the list of login names in an entry is null.

Login name not found in password file
: A login name in the list of login names in an entry is not in the password file.

NAME

halt – (BSD) stop the processor

SYNOPSIS

/usr/ucb/halt [**-lnqy**]

DESCRIPTION

halt writes out any information pending to the disks and then stops the processor.

halt -l logs the system shutdown to the system log daemon, **syslogd**(1M), and places a shutdown record in the login accounting file **/var/adm/wtmp**. These actions are inhibited if the **-n** or **-q** options are present.

The following options are available:

-l Logs a message to the system log indicating who halted the system.

-n Prevent the *sync* before stopping.

-q Quick halt. No graceful shutdown is attempted.

-y Halt the system, even from a dialup terminal.

FILES

/var/adm/wtmp login accounting file

SEE ALSO

init(1M), **reboot**(1M), **shutdown**(1M), **syslogd**(1M)

NOTES

This command is equivalent to **init 0**.

NAME

`hd` – (XENIX) display files in hexadecimal format

SYNOPSIS

`hd` [*-format* [`-s` *offset*] [`-n` *count*] [*file*]

DESCRIPTION

The `hd` command displays the contents of files in hexadecimal octal, decimal and character formats. Control over the specification of ranges of characters is also available. The default behavior is with the following flags set: "**`-abx -A`**". This says that addresses (file offsets) and bytes are printed in hexadecimal and that characters are also printed. If no *file* argument is given, the standard input is read.

Options

Options for `hd` include:

`-s` *offset*
: Specify the beginning offset in the file where printing is to begin. If no 'file' argument is given, or if a seek fails because the input is a pipe, 'offset' bytes are read from the input and discarded. Otherwise, a seek error will terminate processing of the current file.

  The *offset* may be given in decimal, hexadecimal (preceded by '`0x`'), or octal (preceded by a '0'). It is optionally followed by one of the following multipliers: `w, l, b,` or `k`; for words (2 bytes), long words (4 bytes), blocks (512 bytes), or `K` bytes (1024 bytes). Note that this is the one case where "`b`" does not stand for bytes. Since specifying a hexadecimal offset in blocks would result in an ambiguous trailing '`b`', any offset and multiplier may be separated by an asterisk (*).

`-n` *count*
: Specify the number of bytes to process. The *count* is in the same format as *offset*, above.

Format Flags

Format flags may specify addresses, characters, bytes, words (2 bytes), or longs (4 bytes) to be printed in hexadecimal, decimal, or octal. Two special formats may also be indicated: test or `ASCII`. Format and base specifiers may be freely combined and repeated as desired in order to specify different bases (hexadecimal, decimal or octal) for different output formats (addresses, characters, etc.). All format flags appearing in a single argument are applied as appropriate to all other flags in that argument.

`acbwlA`
: Output format specifiers for address, characters, bytes, words, longs and ASCII, respectively. Only one base specifier will be used for addresses; the address will appear on the first line of output that begins each new offset in the input.

  The character format prints printable characters unchanged, special C escapes as defined in the language, and remaining values in the specified base.

The ASCII format prints all printable characters unchanged, and all others as a period (.). This format appears to the right of the first of other specified output formats. A base specifier has no meaning with the ASCII format. If no other output format (other than addresses) is given, **bx** is assumed. If no base specifier is given, all of **xdo** are used.

xdo Output base specifiers for hexadecimal, decimal and octal. If no format specifier is given, all of **acbwl** are used.

t Print a test file, each line preceded by the address in the file. Normally, lines should be terminated by a **\n** character; but long lines will be broken up. Control characters in the range 0x00 to 0x1f are rpinted as **'^@'** to '^_'. Bytes with the high bit set are preceded by a tilde (~) and printed as if the high bit were not set. The special characters (^,~,\) are preceded by a backslash (\) to escape their special meaning. As special cases, two values are represented numerically as '\177' and '\377'. This flag will override all output format specifiers except addresses.

NAME

head – display first few lines of files

SYNOPSIS

head [-*n*] [*file* . . .]

DESCRIPTION

head copies the first *n* lines of each *file* to the standard output. If no *file* is given, **head** copies lines from the standard input. The default value of *n* is 10 lines.

When more than one file is specified, the start of each file will look like:

==>*file*<==

Thus, a common way to display a set of short files, identifying each one, is:

head -9999 *file1 file2* . . .

SEE ALSO

cat(1), **more**(1), **pg**(1), **tail**(1)

help (1)

NAME

help – ask for help with message numbers or SCCS commands

SYNOPSIS

help [*args***]**

DESCRIPTION

help finds information to explain a message from a command or explain the use of a SCCS command. Zero or more arguments may be supplied. If no arguments are given, **help** will prompt for one.

The arguments may be either information within the parentheses following a message or SCCS command names.

The response of the program will be the explanatory information related to the argument, if there is any.

When all else fails, try **help stuck**.

FILES

LIBDIR/**help**	directory containing files of message text.
LIBDIR/**help/helploc**	file containing locations of help files not in *LIBDIR*/**help**.
LIBDIR	usually **/usr/ccs/lib**

NAME

hostid – print the numeric identifier of the current host

SYNOPSIS

/usr/ucb/hostid

DESCRIPTION

The **hostid** command prints the identifier of the current host in hexadecimal. This numeric value is likely to differ when **hostid** is run on a different machine.

SEE ALSO

gethostid(3), **sysinfo**(2)

NAME

hostname – (BSD) set or print name of current host system

SYNOPSIS

/usr/ucb/hostname [*name-of-host*]

DESCRIPTION

The **hostname** command prints the name of the current host, as given before the **login** prompt. The super-user can set the hostname by giving an argument.

SEE ALSO

uname(1)

NAME

`htable` – convert DoD Internet format host table

SYNOPSIS

`htable [-c` *connected-nets*`] [-l` *local-nets*`] [`*input-file*`]`

DESCRIPTION

htable converts a host table in the format specified by RFC 952 to the format used by the network library routines. Three files are created as a result of running **htable**: **hosts**, **networks**, and **gateways**. The **hosts** file is used by the **gethostent**(3N) routines in mapping host names to addresses. The **networks** file is used by the **getnetent**(3N) routines in mapping network names to numbers. The **gateways** file is used by the routing daemon in identifying passive Internet gateways; see **routed**(1M) for an explanation.

If any of the files **localhosts**, **localnetworks**, or **localgateways** are present in the current directory, the file's contents are prepended to the output file without interpretation. This allows sites to maintain local aliases and entries which are not normally present in the master database.

If the **gateways** file is to be used, a list of networks to which the host is directly connected is specified with the **-c** option. The networks, separated by commas, may be given by name, or the Internet-standard "." (dot) notation. **htable** only includes gateways which are directly connected to one of the specified networks, or which can be reached from another gateway on a connected network.

If the **-l** option is given with a list of networks (in the same format as the networks specified with the **-c** option), these networks will be treated as "local," and information about hosts on local networks is taken only from the **localhosts** file. Entries for local hosts from the main database will be omitted. This allows the **localhosts** file to completely overrid any entries in the input file.

htable is best used in conjunction with the **gettable**(1M) program which retrieves the DoD Internet host table from a host.

FILES

`localhosts`
`localnetworks`
`localgateways`

SEE ALSO

gethostent(3N), **getnetent**(3N), **gettable**(1M), **routed**(1M)

Harrenstien, Ken, Mary Stahl, and Elizabeth Feinler, *DoD Internet Host Table Specification*, RFC 952, Network Information Center, SRI International, Menlo Park, Calif., October 1985

NOTES

Does not properly calculate the **gateways** file.

iconv(1)

NAME

iconv – code set conversion utility

SYNOPSIS

iconv -f *fromcode* **-t** *tocode* [*file*]

DESCRIPTION

iconv converts the characters or sequences of characters in *file* from one code set to another and writes the results to standard output. Should no conversion exist for a particular character then it is converted to the underscore '_' in the target code set.

The required arguments *fromcode* and *tocode* identify the input and output code sets, respectively. If no *file* argument is specified on the command line, **iconv** reads the standard input.

iconv will always convert to or from the ISO 8859-1 Latin alphabet No.1, from or to an ISO 646 ASCII variant code set for a particular language. The ISO 8859-1 code set will support the majority of 8-bit code sets. The conversions attempted by **iconv** accommodate the most commonly used languages.

The following table lists the supported conversions.

Code Set Conversions Supported				
Code	Symbol	Target Code	Symbol	comment
ISO 646	646	ISO 8859-1	8859	US ASCII
ISO 646de	646de	ISO 8859-1	8859	German
ISO 646da	646da	ISO 8859-1	8859	Danish
ISO 646en	646en	ISO 8859-1	8859	English ASCII
ISO 646es	646es	ISO 8859-1	8859	Spanish
ISO 646fr	646fr	ISO 8859-1	8859	French
ISO 646it	646it	ISO 8859-1	8859	Italian
ISO 646sv	646sv	ISO 8859-1	8859	Swedish
ISO 8859-1	8859	ISO 646	646	7 bit ASCII
ISO 8859-1	8859	ISO 646de	646de	German
ISO 8859-1	8859	ISO 646da	646da	Danish
ISO 8859-1	8859	ISO 646en	646en	English ASCII
ISO 8859-1	8859	ISO 646es	646es	Spanish
ISO 8859-1	8859	ISO 646fr	646fr	French
ISO 8859-1	8859	ISO 646it	646it	Italian
ISO 8859-1	8859	ISO 646sv	646sv	Swedish

The conversions are performed according to the tables found on the **iconv**(5) manual page.

EXAMPLES

The following converts the contents of file **mail1** from code set 8859 to 646fr and stores the results in file **mail.local**.

```
iconv -f 8859 -t 646fr mail1 > mail.local
```

FILES

/usr/lib/iconv/iconv_data
lists the conversions supported

/usr/lib/iconv/*
conversion tables

/usr/lib/locale/*locale*/LC_MESSAGES/uxmesg
language-specific message file [See **LANG** on **environ**(5).]

SEE ALSO

iconv(5)

DIAGNOSTICS

iconv returns 0 upon successful completion, 1 otherwise.

id(1M)

NAME

id – print the user name and ID, and group name and ID

SYNOPSIS

id [-a]

DESCRIPTION

id displays the calling process's **ID** and name. It also displays the group **ID** and name. If the real effective **ID**s do not match, both are printed.

The **-a** option reports all the groups to which the invoking process belongs. ID, and your username. If your real and effective IDs do not match, both are printed.

The **-a** option reports all the groups to which the invoking user belongs.

SEE ALSO

getuid(2)

NAME

idadmin – ID map database administration

SYNOPSIS

idadmin [-S *scheme* **[-l** *logname***]]**
idadmin -S *scheme* **-a -r** *g_name* **-l** *logname*
idadmin -S *scheme* **-d [-r** *g_name***] -l** *logname*
idadmin -S *scheme* **-I** *descr*
idadmin -S *scheme* **[-Duscf]**

DESCRIPTION

The **idadmin** command displays and updates entries in the system ID mapping database. The system ID mapping database consists of one or more system map files, where each map has a different record descriptor. Maps with different record descriptors support different authentication schemes. **idadmin** also provides an administrator with a mechanism to enable and disable user-controlled mapping [see **uidadmin**].

ID mapping databases are used by **namemap** to map remote lognames to local ones. If an ID mapping scheme is enabled for user-controlled mapping, **namemap** looks at the user ID map before the system ID map.

Only a privileged user can execute this command.

The options to **idadmin** have the following meanings:

-S *scheme*
: Specify the name of the ID mapping scheme.

-l *logname*
: Specify a local name (*logname*) into which the remote name maps. *logname* must be a valid logname on the local server. To be valid, *logname* must appear in **/etc/passwd**. The *logname* may take the form **%***n* or **%***i*, where **%***n* is used for transparent mapping and **%i** forces remote names to be rejected.

-a
: Add a map entry. The local and remote names must be specified.

-r *g_name*
: Specify the remote (global) name. The format of *g_name* is scheme-dependent; generally, it includes a login name and a machine name.

-d
: Delete a map entry. The scheme name and the local name must be specified. Specifying the remote name is optional. If only the local name is specified, all entries mapping to that local name are deleted. If a remote name is also specified, only that particular map entry is deleted.

-I *descr*
: Install a new scheme. A remote name format descriptor *descr* must be specified for the new scheme. The remote name file descriptor is a string that indicates the format of the remote name; it includes field numbers, the letter M to indicate the field is mandatory, and field separators.

-D
: Delete a scheme. The scheme name must be specified.

-u Enable user-controlled ID mapping (**USER** mode). The scheme name must be specified.

-s Disable user-controlled ID mapping (**SECURE** mode). The scheme name must be specified.

-c Check the consistency of a map file. The scheme name must be specified. Map entries containing syntax errors and unknown users are displayed. Users are unknown if they do not exist in **/etc/passwd**.

-f Fix an inconsistent mapping file. Entries that are out of order are sorted; mapping entries containing syntax errors and unknown users are displayed, and the system administrator is given the opportunity to change or delete them.

When no options are specified, **idadmin** lists all installed schemes and the mode of each, **USER** or **SECURE**. If only a *scheme* is specified, **idadmin** displays the contents of the system map file. When a *scheme* and a *logname* are entered, **idadmin** lists all entries in the scheme's system map file that map into the logname.

Transparent mapping may be achieved by specifying the metacharacter ***** in the remote name and **%***n* for the local logname, where *n* is the number of the field that **namemap** will extract from the remote name and return as the local name. An asterisk may appear in any field in *g_name* and matches any string of characters in the corresponding field of a remote name. If **%i** is used for *logname*, **namemap** will reject all remote names that match the *g_name*.

When **namemap** searches for a remote name in the system map file, it sequentially scans the file. Therefore, the ordering of remote names in this file is critical.

Remote names are sorted on the highest numbered field first. Entries with explicit values in this field appear first in the file. Entries which include regular expressions in this field are sorted from the most specific to the least specific based on the position of metacharacters in the pattern. The more a metacharacter is to the left in the pattern the less specific the pattern is. For example, **s*** is less specific than **sf***.

If two or more entries have patterns which are equally specific, the specificity of the next lower numbered field is examined. Fields are examined from highest to lowest until the remote names can be differentiated.

EXAMPLES

The following command line installs a new scheme, called **myscheme**:

```
idadmin -S myscheme -I M2!M1
```

In the remote name format descriptor **M2!M1**, **M** indicates that the field is mandatory. The numbers indicate the order of significance of the fields, where higher numbered fields are more significant; in this example, the first field (**M2**) is meant to contain a system name, and the second field (**M1**) is meant to contain a user name. Because the first field indicates the entity of greater significance, it is assigned the higher field number. The character **!** is used as the field separator.

Given the ID Mapping scheme **myscheme**, the following command line creates an entry in the database that maps user **foo** on machine **comunix** into user **foo** on the local host.

```
idadmin -S myscheme -a -r comunix!foo -l foo
```

The following command line creates an entry in the database that provides transparent mapping from any logname on any remote machine to a local user identity with the same logname:

```
idadmin -S myscheme -a -r "*!*" -l %1
```

FILES

/etc/idmap/*scheme_name***/idata**	system map file for scheme *scheme_name*
/etc/idmap/*scheme_name***/uidata**	user map file for scheme *scheme_name*
/var/adm/log/idmap.log	log file
/etc/passwd	password file

SEE ALSO

attradmin(1M), **attrmap**(3I), **namemap**(3I), **uidadmin**(1)

NOTES

All update operations are logged (whether successful or not) in the file **/var/adm/log/idmap.log**.

idbuild (1M)

NAME

idbuild – build new UNIX system base kernel and/or configure loadable modules

SYNOPSIS

/etc/conf/bin/idbuild [–**B**] [-**#**] [–**K**] [–**Q**] [[–**I** *include-path*] . . .] [–**O** *output-file*] [–**S**] [[-**M** *module-name*] . . .] [–**l** *symbol-list*] [[–**D** *symbol*] . . .] [[–**U** *symbol*] . . .]

DESCRIPTION

One of the ID/TP kernel configuration tools, **idbuild** builds a UNIX system base kernel and/or configures loadable kernel modules using the current system configuration in *$ROOT*/*$MACH*/**etc/conf**.

idbuild uses the environment variables *$ROOT* and *$MACH* from the user's environment to compose its starting path as *$ROOT*/*$MACH*. Except for the special case of kernel development in a non-root source tree, the shell variable *$ROOT* should always be set to null or to "/"; if *$ROOT* is null or "/", *$MACH* is ignored (treated as null).

Options

idbuild takes the following options:

–**B** Rebuild the kernel immediately. If any of the other options is used, it is not necessary to specify this one.

–**#** Print debugging information.

–**K** Keep the temporary configuration files and object modules created by **idbuild**. This can allow you to perform a quick rebuild using the –**Q** option.

–**Q** Perform a quick build, where the normal processing and compilation of configuration-dependent files is skipped. To use the quick build option, you must have the temporary configuration files and object modules from the last rebuild of the kernel, which are kept when you use the –**K** option for a normal build.

Use the quick build option with caution. The use of this option precludes the use of the other configuration options, except for **-#**, **-K**, **-O**, **-l**.

–**I** *include-path* Search the specified directory for **#include** files before searching the default directory, *$ROOT*/**usr/include**. This option can be repeated on the command line as many times as needed to list all the directories to be searched.

–**O** *output-file* Place the kernel in *output-file* rather than placing it in the default file *$ROOT*/*$MACH*/**etc/conf/cf.d/unix**.

–**S** Statically link all the configured kernel modules into the base kernel.

–**M** *module-name* Configure the specified loadable kernel module and put it into the *$ROOT*/*$MACH*/**etc/conf/mod.d** directory, using a file named the same as the module. The –**M** option can be repeated on the command line as many times as needed to include all the required modules. More details about using this option are listed below.

–l *symbol-list* — Limit the symbol table information attached to the newly generated kernel to the symbols listed in the file *symbol-list*.

–D *symbol* — In addition to the standard symbols, **#define** the specified symbol when configuration-dependent files are compiled. This option can be repeated on the command line as many times as needed to specify all the required symbols.

–U *symbol* — **#undef** for the specified symbol when the configuration-dependent files are compiled, even if the symbol normally would be defined. The **–U** option overrides any **–D** option specified for the same symbol, and can be repeated on the command line as many times as needed to specify all the undefined symbols.

Files

The configuration data files needed as input for each module are described in:

- **Init**(4)
- **Master**(4)
- **Mtune**(4)
- **Node**(4)
- **Rc**(4)
- **Sassign**(4)
- **Sd**(4)
- **System**(4)
- **Space.c**(4)
- **Stubs.c**(4)

These files must be installed in *$ROOT*/*$MACH*/**etc/conf** using **idinstall**(1M) prior to invoking **idbuild**. In addition, **idbuild** expects the following files to be in *$ROOT*/*$MACH*/**etc/conf/cf.d**:

deflist — This file contains a list of extra **cc**(1) arguments to use when compiling configuration-dependent files (including **Space.c** files); these should be of the form "**-D***xxxxxxx*" or "**-U***xxxxxxx*", where *xxxxxxx* is used to define or undefine platform-specific preprocessor symbols (for example, **-Dat386** or **-Dhector**). This file is provided as part of the base system and should not be modified.

kernmap — This platform-specific mapfile is passed to **ld**(1) to control the kernel linking. This file is provided as part of the base system and should not be modified.

stune — This file contains site-specific tunable parameter values. You should access the **stune** file using **idtune**(1M).

Errors

Since **idbuild** calls other system commands to perform the system reconfiguration, link editing, and symbol table set up, it will report all errors encountered by those commands. In general, the exit value 1 indicates an error was encountered by **idbuild** and the exit value 0 indicates success.

The errors encountered fall into the following categories:

Configuration data file error messages from **idbuild**(1M).

Compiler and link-editor error messages from **cc**(1) and **ld**(1).

If when loading a module using the **-M** option, if a driver module is already loaded at a different major device range, the **idbuild** command will fail with the error **ENXIO**. A description of what to do if this happens follows in the next section of this manual page.

USAGE

Building a UNIX system kernel consists of three steps. First, configuration tables and symbols, and module lists are generated from the configuration data files. Second, configuration-dependent files are compiled, and then these are linked together with all of the configured kernel and device driver object modules. Third, if the loadable kernel module feature or a kernel debugger is enabled, kernel symbol table information is attached to the kernel.

The kernel is, by default, placed in *$ROOT*/*$MACH*/**etc/conf/cf.d/unix**.

If the kernel build is successful and *$ROOT* is null or "/", **idbuild** sets a flag to instruct the system shutdown/reboot sequence to replace the standard kernel in **/stand/unix** with the new kernel. Then, another flag will be set to cause the environment (device special files, **/etc/inittab**, and so on) to be reconfigured accordingly.

If one or more loadable kernel modules are specified with the **-M** option, **idbuild** will configure only the specified loadable kernel modules and put them into the *$ROOT*/*$MACH*/**etc/conf/mod.d** directory. Otherwise a UNIX system base kernel is rebuilt with all the loadable modules reconfigured into the *$ROOT*/*$MACH*/**etc/conf/modnew.d** directory, which will be changed to **/etc/conf/mod.d** at the next system reboot if *$ROOT* is null or "/" [see **modadmin**(1M)].

If a loadable module has already been loaded, but to another major device range, you can either unload the module and then use **idbuild** with the **-M** option, or use **idbuild** without the **-M** option and reboot the system. If you attempt to use the **-M** option for a module already loaded at another major device range, **idbuild** will fail with error **ENXIO**.

When loadable kernel modules are configured with the **-M** option, **idbuild** also creates the necessary nodes in the **/dev** directory, adding and activating **/etc/inittab** entries if any **Init** file is associated with the modules, and registering the modules to the running kernel [see **idmodreg**(1M)]. This makes them available for dynamic loading without requiring a system reboot.

Base kernel rebuilds are usually needed after a statically linked kernel module is installed, when any static module is removed, or when system tunable parameters are modified. If you execute **idbuild** without any options and if the environment variable *$ROOT* is null or "/", a flag is set and the kernel rebuild is deferred to next system reboot.

SEE ALSO

`idinstall`(1M), `idmkinit`(1M), `idmknod`(1M), `idmodreg`(1M), `idtune`(1M), `Init`(4), `Master`(4), `Mtune`(4), `Node`(4), `Rc`(4), `Sassign`(4), `Sd`(4), `Space.c`(4), `Stubs.c`(4), `stune`(4), `System`(4)

idcheck (1M)

NAME

idcheck – return selected information about the system configuration

SYNOPSIS

/etc/conf/bin/idcheck –p *module-name* [**-R** *dir*]

/etc/conf/bin/idcheck –y *module-name* [**-R** *dir*]

/etc/conf/bin/idcheck –v *vector* [**–R** *dir*] [**–r**]

/etc/conf/bin/idcheck –d *dma-channel* [**-R** *dir*] [**–r**]

/etc/conf/bin/idcheck –a –l *lower-address* **–u** *upper-address* [**–R** *dir*] [**–r**]

/etc/conf/bin/idcheck –c –l *lower-address* **–u** *upper-address* [**–R** *dir*] [**–r**]

DESCRIPTION

One of the ID/TP kernel configuration tools, **idcheck** returns selected information about the system configuration. It is useful in add-on Driver Software Package (DSP) installation scripts to determine if a particular device driver has already been installed, or to verify that a particular interrupt vector, I/O address or other selectable parameter is in fact available for use.

Options

idcheck takes the following options:

–r Report the device name of the first conflicting device, if any, on **stdout**.

–p *module-name* Check for the existence of selected components of the DSP, as well as the DSP directory under **/etc/conf/pack.d**. The exit code is created by adding the return codes, resulting in a unique exit code for any combination of existing components.

Add 1 to the exit code if the DSP directory under **/etc/conf/pack.d** exists.

Add 2 to the exit code if the **Master** file for the module has been installed.

Add 4 to the exit code if the **System** file for the module has been installed.

Add 8 to the exit code if the last kernel was built with the specified module.

Add 16 to the exit code if a **Driver.o** is part of the DSP (as opposed to a **stubs.c** file).

–y *module-name* Return 1 if the DSP has been configured. The DSP is considered to be configured if it has a "Y" in any of its controller entries in the **System** file.

–v *vector* Return the *itype* field of the device using the specified vector (that is, when another DSP is already using the vector). Return 0 if the vector is not in use.

–d *dma-channel* Return 1 if the DMA channel specified is being used.

–a Determine whether the IOA range bounded by *lower-address* and *upper-address* (inclusive) conflicts with another DSP. Specify the *lower-address* and *upper-address* using the **–l** and **–u** options. The return value will be one of the following:

0 if the IOA range does not overlap with any currently-installed device.

1 if the IOA range overlaps with one or more devices, and at least one of these does not have the "O" option specified in the *characteristics* field of its **Master** entry. The "O" option permits a driver to overlap the IOA region of another driver.

2 if the IOA range overlaps with one or more devices, which all have the "O" option specified in the *characteristics* field of their **Master** entries.

–c Return 1 if the CMA range bounded by *lower-address* and *upper-address* (inclusive) conflicts with another DSP. Specify the *lower-address* and *upper-address* by using the **–l** and **–u** options.

–l *lower-address* Specify the lower bound of an address range, specified in hex (without a leading **0x**).

–u *upper-address* Specify the upper bound of an address range, specified in hex (without a leading **0x**).

–R *dir* Specify the directory in which the configuration files and directories reside. The default directory is **/etc/conf**. The old "**–i** *dir*" option, which gives the location of the **/etc/conf/cf.d** directory, is supported for compatibility, but is discouraged, because the needed files no longer all reside in this subdirectory.

Return Values

idcheck returns the following values:

100 if an error occurs

0 if no conflict exists

A positive number greater than 0 and less than 100 if a conflict exists

Refer to the "Options" subsection for more information on the possible return values.

Errors

There are no error messages or checks for valid arguments to options. **idcheck** interprets these arguments using the rules of **scanf**(3S). For example, if a letter is used in the place of a digit, **scanf**(3S) translates the letter to 0. **idcheck** then uses this value in its query.

SEE ALSO

idbuild(1M), **idinstall**(1M), **Master**(4), **System**(4)

NAME

idinstall – add, delete, update, or get kernel configuration data

SYNOPSIS

/etc/conf/bin/idinstall –[**adugGM**] [–**ek**] [–**msoptnirhATb**] [–**R** *rootdir*]
[–**f** *major-list*] *module-name*

DESCRIPTION

One of the ID/TP kernel configuration tools, **idinstall** is called by a Driver Software Package (DSP) installation script or removal script to add (–**a**), delete (–**d**), update (–**u**), or get (–**g** or –**G**) device driver/kernel module configuration data. It can also be run from a kernel source makefile to make (–**M**) driver/module configuration data.

idinstall expects to find driver/module component files in the current directory. When components are installed or updated with **-a** or **-u** option, they are copied into subdirectories of the **/etc/conf** directory and then deleted from the current directory, unless the **-k** flag is used.

Options

The options for **idinstall** are:

Action Specifiers

–**a** Add the DSP components.

–**u** Update the DSP components.

–**d** Remove the DSP components.

–**g** or –**G** Get the DSP components (print to **stdout**). If you use the –**g** option, the component configuration file specified is output using the configuration file's original format, unconverted by **idinstall**. If you use the –**G** option, **idinstall** converts the file output to appear in the most current configuration file format. If the component configuration is already in the most current format at the time it is installed, these two options provide identical output.

–**M** Add or update any DSP components which are out-of-date (that is, modified more recently than the installed copy, if any).

Component Specifiers

If no component is specified, the default is all components present in the current directory. However, when using the –**g** or –**G** option, a single component must be specified explicitly.

The **Mfsys** (–**c**) and **Sfsys** (–**l**) component files are obsolete, but are supported for compatibility. If the –**a** or –**u** option is used, they are converted to **Master** and **System** components, respectively (using the **F** characteristic to indicate a file system module).

–**m** **Master** component

-s	**System** component
-o	**Driver**.o component
-p	**Space**.c component
-t	**Stubs**.c component
-n	**Node** (special file) component
-i	**inittab** component (**Init**)
-r	System startup script (**Rc**)
-h	System shutdown script (**Sd**)
-A	**Sassign** component
-T	**Mtune** component
-b	**Modstub.o** component

Miscellaneous

-e	Disable free disk space check on add or update
-k	Keep files (do not remove from current directory) on add or update
-R *rootdir*	Use *rootdir* as the root of the configuration directory structure instead of **/etc/conf**
-f *major_list*	Use *major_list* file as the reserved major numbers list instead of **/etc/conf/cf.d/res_major**

Errors

An exit value of zero indicates success. If an error occurs, **idinstall** exits with a non-zero value and reports an error message. The error messages are designed to be self-explanatory. Typical error messages reported by **idinstall** can include:

```
Device package already exists
Cannot make the driver package directory
Cannot remove driver package directory
Local directory does not contain a Driver object (Driver.o) file
Local directory does not contain a Master file
Local directory does not contain a System file
Cannot remove driver entry
```

USAGE

In the simplest case of installing a new DSP, the command syntax used by the DSP's Install script should be **/etc/conf/bin/idinstall -a** *module-name*. In this case the command requires and installs the DSP **Driver.o**, **Master**, and **System** components, and optionally installs the **Space.c**, **Stubs.c**, **Node**, **Init**, **Rc**, **Sd**, **Sassign**, and **Mtune** components if those files are present in the current directory.

The **Driver.o**, **Modstub.o**, **Space.c**, and **Stubs.c** components are moved to a directory named **/etc/conf/pack.d/***module-name*. The remaining components are stored in directories under **/etc/conf**, which are organized by component type, in files named *module-name*. For example, the **Node** file would be moved to **/etc/conf/node.d/***module-name*.

idinstall –a requires that the module specified is not currently installed.

idinstall –u *module-name* allows an Update DSP (that is, one that replaces an existing device driver component) to be installed. It overlays the files of the old DSP with the files of the new DSP. **idinstall -u** requires that the module specified is currently installed.

idinstall –M *module-name* works whether or not the module is currently installed. It copies into the configuration directories any component files which are not yet installed or are newer than the installed versions. In any case, the files in the current directory are not removed.

When the **-a** or **-u** options are used, unless the **-e** option is used as well, **idinstall** attempts to verify that enough free disk space is available to start the reconfiguration process. This is done by calling the **idspace**(1M) command. **idinstall** will fail if there is not enough space and will exit with a non-zero return code.

SEE ALSO

idbuild(1M), **idcheck**(1M), **idspace**(1M), **Init**(4), **installf**(1M), **Master**(4), **Mtune**(4), **Node**(4), **Rc**(4), **removef**(1M), **res_major**(4), **Sassign**(4), **Sd**(4), **Space.c**(4), **Stubs.c**(4), **stune**(4), **System**(4)

NAME

`idload` – Remote File Sharing user and group mapping

SYNOPSIS

idload [-n] [-g *gid_rules*] [**-u** *uid_rules*] [**directory**]
idload -k

DESCRIPTION

This command is obsolete and will not be supported after this release. **idload** is used on Remote File Sharing server machines to build translation tables for user and group ids. It takes your **/etc/passwd** and **/etc/group** files and produces translation tables for user and group ids from remote machines, according to the rules set down in the *uid_rules* and *gid_rules* files. If you are mapping by user and group name, you will need copies of remote **/etc/passwd** and **/etc/group** files. If no rules files are specified, remote user and group ids are mapped to **MAXUID+1** (this is an id number that is one higher than the highest number you could assign on your system.)

By default, the remote password and group files are assumed to reside in **/etc/rfs/auth.info/***domain*/*nodename*/[**passwd** | **group**]. The **directory** argument indicates that some directory structure other than **/etc/rfs/auth.info** contains the *domain*/*nodename* **passwd** and **group** files. (*nodename* is the name of the computer the files are from and *domain* is the domain that computer is a member of.)

You must run **idload** to put the mapping into place. Global mapping will take effect immediately for machines that have one of your resources currently mounted. Mapping for other specific machines will take effect when each machine mounts one of your resources.

-n This is used to do a trial run of the id mapping. No translation table will be produced. However, a display of the mapping is output to the terminal (*stdout*).

-k This is used to print the id mapping that is currently in use. (Specific mapping for remote machines will not be shown until that machine mounts one of your resources.)

-u *uid_rules* The *uid_rules* file contains the rules for user id translation. The default rules file is **/etc/rfs/auth.info/uid.rules**.

-g *gid_rules* The *gid_rules* file contains the rules for group id translation. The default rules file is **/etc/rfs/auth.info/gid.rules**.

Only a privileged user can execute this command.

Rules

The rules files have two types of sections (both optional): **global** and **host**. There can be only one global section, though there can be one host section for each computer you want to map.

The **global** section describes the default conditions for translation for any machines that are not explicitly referenced in a **host** section. If the global section is missing, the default action is to map all remote user and group ids from undefined computers to **MAXUID+1**. The syntax of the first line of the **global** section is:

```
global
```

A **host** section is used for each machine or group of machines that you want to map differently from the global definitions. The syntax of the first line of each **host** section is:

host *name . . .*

where *name* is replaced by the full name of a computer (*domain.nodename*).

The format of a rules file is described below. (All lines are optional, but must appear in the order shown.)

global
default *local* | **transparent**
exclude *remote_id-remote_id* | *remote_id*
map *remote_id:local*

host *domain.nodename* [*domain.nodename . . .*]
default *local* | **transparent**
exclude *remote_id-remote_id* | *remote_id* | *remote_name*
map *remote:local* | *remote* | **all**

Each of these instruction types is described below.

The line

default *local* | **transparent**

defines the mode of mapping for remote users that are not specifically mapped in instructions in other lines. **transparent** means that each remote user and group id will have the same numeric value locally unless it appears in the **exclude** instruction. *local* can be replaced by a local user name or id to map all users into a particular local name or id number. If the default line is omitted, all users that are not specifically mapped are mapped into a "special guest" login id. The value of *local* is not allowed to be **root** or id number **0**. This would give users that are not specifically mapped **root** privilege.

The line

exclude *remote_id-remote_id* | *remote_id* | *remote_name*

defines remote ids that will be excluded from the **default** mapping. The **exclude** instruction must precede any **map** instructions in a block. You can use a range of id numbers, a single id number, or a single name. (*remote_name* cannot be used in a **global** block.)

The line

map *remote:local* | *remote* | **all**

defines the local ids and names that remote ids and names will be mapped into. *remote* is either a remote id number or remote name; *local* is either a local id number or local name. Placing a colon between a *remote* and a *local* will give the value on the left the permissions of the value on the right. A single *remote* name or id will assign the user or group permissions of the same local name or id. **all** is a predefined alias for the set of all user and group ids found in the local **/etc/passwd** and **/etc/group** files. (You cannot map by remote name in **global** blocks.)

Note: **idload** will always output warning messages for **map all**, since password files always contain multiple administrative user names with the same id number. The first mapping attempt on the id number will succeed, each subsequent attempts will produce a warning.

Remote File Sharing doesn't need to be running to use **idload**.

EXIT STATUS

On successful completion, **idload** will produce one or more translation tables and return a successful exit status. If **idload** fails, the command will return an exit status of zero and not produce a translation table.

ERRORS

If (1) either rules file cannot be found or opened, (2) there are syntax errors in the rules file, (3) there are semantic errors in the rules file, (4) **host** password or group information could not be found, or (5) the command is not run with appropriate privilege, an error message will be sent to standard error. Partial failures will cause a warning message to appear, though the process will continue.

FILES

/etc/passwd
/etc/group
/etc/rfs/auth.info/*domain*/*nodename*/[**passwd** | **group**]
/etc/rfs/auth.info/uid.rules
/etc/rfs/auth.info/gid.rules

SEE ALSO

mount(1M), RFS-specific **mount**(1M)

idmkinit (1M)

NAME

idmkinit – construct inittab file from configuration data

SYNOPSIS

/etc/conf/bin/idmkinit [**–o** *directory*] [**–e** *directory*] [[**–M** *module-name*] ...] [**–#**]

DESCRIPTION

One of the ID/TP kernel configuration tools, **idmkinit** reconstructs **/etc/inittab** from the **Init**(4) files in **/etc/conf/init.d**. The new **inittab** is normally placed in the **/etc/conf/cf.d** directory, although this can be changed through the **–o** option.

Options

The command line options are:

–o *directory* Create **inittab** in the directory specified, instead of the default, **/etc/conf/cf.d**.

–e *directory* Use the **init** files in the directory specified, instead of the default location, **/etc/conf/init.d**.

–M *module-name* Append the **inittab** lines generated from the **Init** file, if there is one, of the loadable kernel module specified to **/etc/inittab** so it can take effect.

–# Print debugging information.

Return Values

idmkinit returns 0 on success and a positive number on error.

Errors

An exit value of zero indicates success. If an error is encountered, **idmkinit** will exit with a non-zero value and report an error message.

USAGE

In the **sysinit** state during the next system reboot after a kernel reconfiguration, the **idmkinit** command is called automatically (by **idmkenv**) to establish the correct **/etc/inittab** for the running (newly-built) kernel. **idmkinit** is also called by **idbuild** when loadable kernel module configuration is requested. **idmkinit** can be executed as a user level command to test a modification of **inittab** before a Driver Software Package (DSP) is actually built. It is also useful in installation scripts that do not reconfigure the kernel, but which need to create **inittab** entries. In this case, the **inittab** generated by **idmkinit** must be copied to **/etc/inittab**, and an **init q** command must be run for the new entry to take effect.

SEE ALSO

idbuild(1M), **idinstall**(1M), **idmknod**(1M), **init**(1M), **Init**(4), **inittab**(4)

NAME

/etc/conf/bin/idmknod – update device nodes to reflect kernel configuration

SYNOPSIS

idmknod [**–o** *device-dir*] [**–r** *config-dir*] [[**–M** *module-name*] . . .] [**–s**] [**–d** *sdev*] [**–#**]

DESCRIPTION

One of the ID/TP configuration tools, **idmknod** reconstructs nodes (block and character special device files) in **/dev** and its subdirectories, based on the **Node** files for currently configured modules (those with at least one **Y** in their **System** files). Any nodes for devices with an **r** flag set in the *characteristics* fields of their **Master** file are left unchanged. All other nodes will be removed or created as needed to exactly match the configured **Node** files.

Any needed subdirectories are created automatically. Subdirectories which become empty as a result of node removal are removed as well.

All other files in the **/dev** directory tree are left unchanged, including symbolic links.

Options

idmknod takes the following options:

–o *device-dir* Install nodes in (or remove them from) the directory specified rather than the default, **/dev**.

–r *config-dir* Use the directory specified, instead of **/etc/conf**, as the root of the configuration data directories.

–s Suppress removing nodes; just add new nodes.

–M *module-name* Make new nodes in **/dev**, as specified in the **node** file for the specified loadable kernel module.

–d *sdev* Use the *sdev* file instead of **/etc/conf/cf.d/sdevice** for current configuration information.

–# Print debugging information.

Return Values

idmknod returns 0 on success and a positive number on error.

Errors

An exit value of zero indicates success. If an error was encountered due to a syntax or format error in a **node** entry, an advisory message is printed to **stdout** and the command execution continues. If a serious error is encountered (for example, a required file cannot be found), **idmknod** exits with a non-zero value and reports an error message.

USAGE

On the next system reboot after a kernel reconfiguration, in **sysinit** state, the **idmknod** command is run automatically (by **idmkenv**) to establish the correct representation of device nodes in the **/dev** directory tree for the running kernel. **idmknod** (with the **–M** option) is also called by **idbuild** when loadable kernel module configuration is requested. **idmknod** can be executed as a user level command to test modification of the **/dev** directory before a Driver Software Package (DSP) is actually built. It is also useful in installation scripts that do not reconfigure the kernel, but which need to create **/dev** entries.

SEE ALSO

`idbuild`(1M), `idinstall`(1M), `idmkinit`(1M), `Master`(4), `mknod`(2), `Node`(4), `System`(4)

NAME

idmodload – load configured loadable kernel modules

SYNOPSIS

/etc/conf/bin/idmodload [**–r** *root*] [**–f** *modlist*] [**–#**]

DESCRIPTION

One of the Installable Driver Tools (idtools) for kernel configuration, **idmodload** loads all the configured loadable kernel modules listed in **/etc/loadmods**, or in another file as specified with the **–f** option. A kernel module is considered to be configured if one or more entries in the module's **sdevice** file contains the value **Y** in the *configure* field. The **/etc/loadmods** file has the same format as **/etc/mod_register** file [see **idmodreg**(1M)].

The **idmodload** command is executed automatically [by **init**(1M)] on every system reboot in **sysinit** state. This command is not intended to be executed directly and may be changed or eliminated in a future release.

Options

idmodload takes the following options:

–f *modlist* — Load all the configured loadable kernel modules listed in *modlist*, instead of the default file, **/etc/loadmods**.

–r *root* — Use all the configuration information under the *root* directory, instead of the default directory, **/etc/conf**.

–# — Print debugging information.

Errors

An exit value of zero indicates success. If an error occurs, an error message is reported for each error, and the command exits with a return value of 1. If the error is a failure in loading a module, an error message with the module name and module type is included with the error message, then the command continues processing the other modules listed in **/etc/loadmods**.

SEE ALSO

idmodreg(1M), **init**(1M), **modadmin**(1M), **modload**(2), **System**(4)

idmodreg (1M)

NAME

idmodreg – register loadable kernel modules with the running kernel

SYNOPSIS

/etc/conf/bin/idmodreg [**-r** *root*] [**-f** *modreglist*] [[**-M** *module-name*] . . .] [**-#**]

DESCRIPTION

One of the Installable Driver Tools (idtools) for kernel configuration, **idmodreg** registers all the loadable kernel modules listed in **/etc/mod_register**, or in another file if specified by the **-f** option. All loadable kernel modules need to be registered by **idmodreg** before they can be auto-loaded by the running kernel or demand-loaded using the **modadmin**(1M) command.

The file **/etc/mod_register** is generated and updated by **idbuild**(1M). A new **mod_register** file is generated for every kernel rebuild, and will be copied to **/etc/mod_register** the next time the system is rebooted. When configuring a loadable kernel module with the **-M** option of **idbuild**, the entries for the module are appended to **/etc/mod_register**. You should not modify the file manually.

This command is not intended to be executed directly, and may be changed or eliminated in a future release.

Options

idmodreg takes the following options:

-f *modreglist* — Register all the loadable kernel modules listed in *modreglist* instead of the default file **/etc/mod_register**.

-r *root* — Use the configuration information under the *root* directory instead of **/etc/conf**.

-M *module-name* — Register the specified loadable kernel module, and append an entry (or entries) for the module to **/etc/mod_register**, so it will be registered every time the system is rebooted. **idbuild** uses this option when a loadable kernel module configuration is requested.

-# — Print debugging information.

Files

Each **mod_register** file entry provides information about a single module, specified on a line of the form:

module-type:command:module-name:module-data

All fields are positional and are separated by colons.

The **mod_register** file fields are:

module-type — Contains an integer representing the module type. If a module has more than one type, separate entries will be generated for each type.

command — Currently contains the value **1** to indicate "registration."

module-name — Identifies the module using the name specified in the *module-name* field of the module's **Master** file.

module-data If the module is a device driver, this field contains a major number specified in the module's **Master** file. If the driver has multiple major numbers, there must be a separate **mod_register** entry for each major number.

If the module is a not a filesystem type name, this field contains the module's *module-name*.

Errors

An exit value of zero indicates successful completion of the command. If errors occur, **idmodreg** reports error messages for each error and exits with the return value 1. If the error is a failure to register a module, an error message is reported, but the command continues processing the remaining modules listed in **/etc/mod_register**.

USAGE

The **idmodreg** command is executed automatically [by **init**(1M)] on every system reboot. **idbuild** also calls **idmodreg**, with the **–M** option, when a loadable kernel module configuration is requested [see **idbuild**(1M)]. **idmodreg** can also be invoked as a user-level command to register all the loadable kernel modules again.

SEE ALSO

idbuild(1M), **init**(1M), **modadmin**(1M)

idspace (1M)

NAME

idspace – determine if there is enough file system free space

SYNOPSIS

/etc/conf/bin/idspace [**–i** *inodes*] [**–r** *blocks* | **–u** *blocks* | **–t** *blocks*]

DESCRIPTION

One of the ID/TP kernel configuration tools, **idspace** checks whether sufficient free space exists to perform a kernel reconfiguration [see **idbuild**(1M)]. By default, **idspace** checks the number of available disk blocks and inodes in three file systems: **/** (and, if they exist) **/usr**, and **/tmp**.

The default tests performed by **idspace** are:

> Verify that the root file system (**/**) has 400 blocks more than the size of the current **/stand/unix**. This verifies that a device driver being added to the current **/stand/unix** can be built and placed in the root filesystem. **idspace** also checks to ensure that 100 inodes exist in the root directory.
>
> Determine whether a **/usr** file system exists. If it does exist, **idspace** checks whether 400 free blocks and 100 inodes are available in the **/usr** file system. If the file system does not exist, **idspace** does not report an error, however, because files created in **/usr** by the reconfiguration process will be created in the parent root file system, and space requirements are covered by the **idspace** test of the root file system.
>
> Determine whether a **/tmp** file system exists. If it does exist, **idspace** checks whether 400 free blocks and 100 inodes are available in the **/tmp** file system. As with the test for the **/usr** file system, if the **/tmp** file system does not exist, **idspace** does not report an error, because files created in **/tmp** by the reconfiguration process will be created in the root file system, and space requirements are covered by the **idspace** test of the root file system.

Options

idspace takes the following options:

–i *inodes* Override the default test for 100 inodes for all three of the **idspace** file system space checks, and test for the specified number of inodes instead.

–r *blocks* Override the default test for **/stand/unix** size + 400 blocks when checking the root (**/**) file system, and test for the specified number of blocks instead. When the **–r** option is used, the **/usr** and **/tmp** file systems are not tested.

–u *blocks* Override the default test for 400 blocks when checking the **/usr** file system, and test for the specified number of blocks instead. When the **–u** option is used, the root (**/**) and **/tmp** file systems are not tested. If **/usr** is not a separate file system, an error is reported.

–t *blocks* Override the default test for 400 blocks when checking the **/tmp** file system, and test for the specified number of blocks instead. When the **–t** option is used, the root (**/**) and **/usr** file systems are not tested. If **/tmp** is not a separate file system, an error is reported.

Errors

An exit value of zero indicates success. If insufficient space exists in a file system or an error was encountered due to a syntax or format error, **idspace** reports the error in a message. The specific exit values are as follows:

0 Successful completion

1 Command syntax error, or needed file does not exist

2 File system has insufficient space or inodes

3 Requested file system does not exist (–**u** and –**t** options only).

SEE ALSO

idbuild(1M), **idinstall**(1M)

idtune (1M)

NAME

idtune – set or get the value of a tunable parameter

SYNOPSIS

/etc/conf/bin/idtune [**–f** | **–m**] [**–c**] *parm value*
/etc/conf/bin/idtune –g [**–c**] *parm*
/etc/conf/bin/idtune –d [**–c**] *parm*

DESCRIPTION

One of the ID/TP kernel configuration tools, **idtune** sets or gets the value of an existing tunable parameter. **idtune** is called by a Driver Software Package (DSP) installation or removal script; it can also be invoked directly as a user-level command. New tunable parameters must be installed using **idinstall**(1M) and a DSP **Mtune** file before they can be accessed using **idtune**.

Note that existing tunable parameter values must be modified using the **idtune** command.

There are three different ways to use the **idtune** command, which are explained in the USAGE section.

Options

–f Force the change of the tunable parameter *parm* to *value* and suppress all confirmation messages. If the **–c** option is used with the **–f** option, the values in both **stune.current** and **stune** are changed; otherwise, only the tunable parameter value in **stune** is changed.

–m Change the value of *parm*, but only if the existing value is smaller than the *value* specified by this **idtune** command. If the **–c** option is used with the **–m** option, the values in both **stune.current** and **stune** are changed; otherwise, only the tunable parameter value in **stune** is changed.

–c Apply the change to the tunable parameter in both **stune** and **stune.current**. Note that all changes made to **stune.current** will affect any loadable kernel modules configured thereafter, and can potentially create inconsistencies between the running kernel and the new loadable kernel modules. For this reason, the **–c** option should be used with caution.

–g Print the following sequence of four values (separated by white space) to **stdout**:

The current value of the tunable parameter

The default value, from the **Mtune** entry

The minimum valid value, from the **Mtune** entry

The maximum valid value, from the **Mtune** entry

If the **–c** option is used with the **–g** option, the current value in **stune.current** is displayed; otherwise, the current value in **stune** is displayed.

–d *parm*

Reset the tunable parameter to its default value. If the **–c** option is used with the **–d** option, the values in both **stune.current** and **stune** are reset; otherwise, only the tunable parameter value in **stune** is reset. All confirmation messages are suppressed.

Errors

The exit status will be non-zero if errors are encountered.

USAGE

The first form of the **idtune** command, with no options or with **-f** or **-m**, is used to change the value of a parameter. The tunable parameter to be changed is indicated by *parm*, and the desired value for the tunable parameter is *value*.

By default, if the parameter in the **stune** file has a value, you are asked to confirm the change with the following message:

> **Tunable Parameter** *parm* **is currently set to** *old_value* **in /etc/conf/cf.d/stune**
> **Is it OK to change it to** *value*? **(y/n)**

If you answer "**y**", the change is made. Otherwise, the tunable parameter will not be changed, and the following message is displayed:

> *parm* **left at** *old_value*.

However, if you use the **-f** (force) option, the change is always made and no messages are reported.

If you use the **-m** (minimum) option, and there is an existing value which is greater than the desired value, no change is made and no messages are reported.

If you use the **-c** (current) option with the first form of the **idtune** command, the change applies to both **stune** and **stune.current**; otherwise, only the tunable parameter in **stune** is affected. Since any change made to the **stune.current** file will affect all the loadable kernel modules configured thereafter, it is very easy to introduce inconsistencies between the currently running kernel and the new loadable kernel modules. Therefore, you should be extremely careful when using the **-c** option.

If you are modifying system tunable parameters as part of a device driver or application add-on package, you may want to change parameter values without prompting the user for confirmation. Your add-on package **Install** script could override the existing value using the **-f** or **-m** options. However, you must be careful not to invalidate a tunable parameter modified earlier by the user or another add-on package.

Any attempt to set a parameter to a value outside the valid minimum/maximum (as given in the **Mtune** file) range will be reported as an error, even when using the **-f** or **-m** options.

The UNIX system kernel must be rebuilt [using **idbuild**(1M)] and the system rebooted for any changes to tunable parameter values in **stune** to take effect.

SEE ALSO

idbuild(1M), **idinstall**(1M), **Mtune**(4), **stune**(4)

ifconfig (1M)

NAME

ifconfig – configure network interface parameters

SYNOPSIS

ifconfig {-a | *interface*} [*parameters*]
ifconfig {-a | *interface*} [*protocol_family*]

DESCRIPTION

ifconfig is used to assign an address to a network interface and/or to configure network interface parameters. **ifconfig** requires a valid network device (*interface*) or **-a** for its first argument. When the **-a** argument is used, all initialized network boards are selected. **ifconfig** must be used at boot time to define the network address of each interface present on a machine; it may also be used at a later time to redefine an interface's address or other operating parameters. Used without options, **ifconfig** displays the usage message. If a *protocol_family* is specified (for example: **inet**), **ifconfig** will report only the details specific to that *protocol_family*. Only the super-user may modify the configuration of a network interface.

The *interface* parameter is a string of the form *PrefixUnit#*, for example **lo0** or **wd0**. See **interface**(4) for more information on the *PrefixUnit#* parameter.

Since an interface may receive transmissions in differing protocols, each of which may require separate naming schemes, the parameters and addresses are interpreted according to the rules of some address family, specified by the *af* parameter. The address families currently supported are **ether** and **inet**. If no address family is specified, **inet** is assumed.

For the DARPA Internet family (**inet**), the address is either a host name present in the host name data base [see **hosts**(4)], or a DARPA Internet address expressed in the Internet standard dot notation. Typically, an Internet address specified in dot notation will consist of your system's network number and the machine's unique host number. A typical Internet address is **192.9.200.44**, where **192.9.200** is the network number and **44** is the machine's host number.

For the **ether** address family, the address is an Ethernet address represented as *x*:*x*:*x*:*x*:*x*:*x* where *x* is a hexadecimal number between 0 and ff. Only the super-user may use the **ether** address family.

If the *dest_address* parameter is supplied in addition to the *address* parameter, it specifies the address of the correspondent on the other end of a point to point link.

OPTIONS

-a This option affects all initialized network interfaces on the system. When used by itself, the **-a** option displays information for all of the network interfaces installed on the system. When the **-a** option is used with any of the valid **ifconfig** options the change(s) will be applied to all of the initialized interfaces. Using **-a** with some *parameters*, such as **up** and **down** are useful if you want to bring all of the initialized network interfaces **up** or **down**. However, you would not want to use the **-a** option with **broadcast** *address*. This would effectively set the **broadcast** parameter for all of the initialized interfaces to the same address, and cause unpredictable results to your networked machine.

The following *parameters* may be set with **ifconfig**:

up Mark an interface up. This may be used to enable an interface after an ifconfig down. It happens automatically when setting the first address on an interface. If the interface was reset when previously marked down, the hardware will be re-initialized.

down Mark an interface down. When an interface is marked down, the system will not attempt to transmit messages through that interface. If possible, the interface will be reset to disable reception as well. This action does not automatically disable routes using the interface.

trailers (**inet** only) Enable the use of a trailer link level encapsulation when sending. If a network interface supports trailer encapsulation, the system will, when possible, encapsulate outgoing messages in a manner which minimizes the number of memory to memory copy operations performed by the receiver. This feature is machine-dependent, and therefore not recommended. On networks that support the Address Resolution Protocol [see **arp**(7)]; currently, only 10 Mb/s Ethernet), this flag indicates that the system should request that other systems use trailer encapsulation when sending to this host. Similarly, trailer encapsulations will be used when sending to other hosts that have made such requests.

-trailers Disable the use of a trailer link level encapsulation.

arp Enable the use of the Address Resolution Protocol in mapping between network level addresses and link level addresses (default). This is currently implemented for mapping between DARPA Internet addresses and 10Mb/s Ethernet addresses.

-arp Disable the use of the Address Resolution Protocol.

metric *n* Set the routing metric of the interface to *n*, default 0. The routing metric is used by the routing protocol [**routed**(1M)]. Higher metrics have the effect of making a route less favorable; metrics are counted as additional hops to the destination network or host.

netmask *mask*

(**inet** only) Specify how much of the address to reserve for subdividing networks into sub-networks. The mask includes the network part of the local address and the subnet part, which is taken from the host field of the address. The mask can be specified as a single hexadecimal number with a leading 0x, with a dot-notation Internet address, or with a pseudo-network name listed in the network table **networks**(4). The mask contains 1's for the bit positions in the 32-bit address which are to be used for the network and subnet parts, and 0's for the host part. The mask should contain at least the standard network portion, and the subnet field should be contiguous with the network portion. For example, to create a netmask that has an 8 bit host ID portion for a Class B address, such as 157.2.123.100, use

netmask 255.255.255.0

or

netmask 0xffffff00

broadcast *address*

(**inet** only) Specify the address to use to represent broadcasts to the network. The default broadcast address is the address with a host part of all 1's.

EXAMPLES

If your workstation is not attached to an Ethernet, the **wd0** interface should be marked down as follows:

```
ifconfig wd0 down
```

FILES

/dev/ip

SEE ALSO

interface(4), **netstat**(1M)

DIAGNOSTICS

Messages indicating the specified interface does not exist, the requested address is unknown, or the user is not privileged and tried to alter an interface's configuration.

NAME

indicator – display application specific alarms and/or the ''working'' indicator

SYNOPSIS

indicator [**-b** [*n*]] [**-c** *column*] [**-l** *length*] [**-o**] [**-w**] [*string* ...]

DESCRIPTION

The **indicator** function displays application specific alarms or the ''working'' indicator, or both, on the FMLI banner line. By default, **indicator** ???? The argument *string* is a string to be displayed on the banner line, and should always be the last argument given. Note that *string* is not automatically cleared from the banner line.

The following options are available:

-b *n* — The **-b** option rings the terminal bell *n* times, where *n* is an integer from 1 to 10. The default value is 1. If the terminal has no bell, the screen is flashed instead, if possible.

-c *column* — The **-c** option defines the column of the banner line at which to start the indicator string. The argument *column* must be an integer from **0** to **DISPLAYW-1**. If the **-c** option is not used, *column* defaults to **0**.

-l *length* — The **-l** option defines the maximum length of the string displayed. If *string* is longer than *length* characters, it will be truncated. The argument *length* must be an integer from **1** to **DISPLAYW**. If the **-l** option is not used, *length* defaults to **DISPLAYW**. NOTE: if *string* doesn't fit it will be truncated.

-o — The **-o** option causes **indicator** to duplicate its output to *stdout*.

-w — The **-w** option turns on the working indicator.

EXAMPLES

When the value entered in a form field is invalid, the following use of **indicator** will ring the bell three times and display the word **WRONG** starting at column 1 of the banner line.

```
invalidmsg=`indicator -b 3 -c 1 "WRONG"`
```

To clear the indicator after telling the user the entry is wrong:

```
invalidmsg=`indicator -b 9 -c 1 "WRONG"; sleep(3);
      indicator -c 1 "      "`
```

In this example the value of **invalidmsg** (in this case the default value **Input is not valid**), still appears on the FMLI message line.

NAME

indxbib – (BSD) create an inverted index to a bibliographic database

SYNOPSIS

/usr/ucb/indxbib *database-file* . . .

DESCRIPTION

indxbib makes an inverted index to the named *database-file* (which must reside within the current directory), typically for use by **lookbib** and **refer**. A *database* contains bibliographic references (or other kinds of information) separated by blank lines.

A bibliographic reference is a set of lines, constituting fields of bibliographic information. Each field starts on a line beginning with a '%', followed by a key-letter, then a blank, and finally the contents of the field, which may continue until the next line starting with '%' (see **addbib**).

indxbib is a shell script that calls two programs: **mkey** and **inv**. **mkey** truncates words to 6 characters, and maps upper case to lower case. It also discards words shorter than 3 characters, words among the 100 most common English words, and numbers (dates) < 1900 or > 2000. These parameters can be changed.

indxbib creates an entry file (with a **.ia** suffix), a posting file (**.ib**), and a tag file (**.ic**), in the working directory.

FILES

/usr/ucblib/reftools/mkey	
/usr/ucblib/reftools/inv	
*.ia	entry file
*.ib	posting file
*.ic	tag file

SEE ALSO

addbib(1), **lookbib**(1), **refer**(1), **roffbib**(1), **sortbib**(1)

NOTES

All dates should probably be indexed, since many disciplines refer to literature written in the 1800s or earlier.

indxbib does not recognize pathnames.

NAME

inetd – Internet services daemon

SYNOPSIS

inetd [-d] [-s] [-t] [*configuration-file*]

DESCRIPTION

inetd, the Internet services daemon, is normally run at boot time by the Service Access Facility (SAF). When started, **inetd** reads its configuration information from *configuration-file* , the default being **/etc/inetd.conf**. See **inetd.conf**(4) for more information on the format of this file. It listens for connections on the Internet addresses of the services that its configuration file specifies. When a connection is found, it invokes the server daemon specified by that configuration file for the service requested. Once a server process exits, **inetd** continues to listen on the socket.

The **-s** option allows you to run **inetd** "stand-alone," outside the Service Access Facility (SAF). When the **-s** is not used, **inetd** must be running under SAF via the **sacadm**(1M) command.

The **-d** option puts **inetd** into debug mode, and is usually used with the **-s** option to print debug messages to **stderr** (standard error). In debug mode, TCP connections will have the **SO_DEBUG** option enabled via **setsockopt** [see **getsockopt**(3N)]; **SO_DEBUG** is needed for **trpt**(1M). Note that when **-d** option is used, **inetd** is running in the foreground.

The **-t** option puts **inetd** into calltrace mode, which produces additional **syslog**(3) entries.

Rather than having several daemon processes with sparsely distributed requests each running concurrently, **inetd** reduces the load on the system by invoking Internet servers only as they are needed.

inetd itself provides a number of simple TCP-based services. These include **echo**, **discard**, **chargen** (character generator), **daytime** (human readable time), and **time** (machine readable time, in the form of the number of seconds since midnight, January 1, 1900). For details of these services, consult the appropriate RFC, as listed below, from the Network Information Center.

inetd rereads its configuration file whenever it receives a hangup signal, **SIGHUP**. New services can be activated, and existing services deleted or modified in between whenever the file is reread.

SEE ALSO

comsat(1M), **ftpd**(1M), **getsockopt**(3N), **inetd.conf**(4), **rexecd**(1M), **rlogind**(1M), **rshd**(1M), **sacadm**(1M), **telnetd**(1M), **tftpd**(1M), **trpt**(1M)

Postel, Jon, "Echo Protocol," RFC 862, Network Information Center, SRI International, Menlo Park, Calif., May 1983

Postel, Jon, "Discard Protocol," RFC 863, Network Information Center, SRI International, Menlo Park, Calif., May 1983

Postel, Jon, "Character Generator Protocol," RFC 864, Network Information Center, SRI International, Menlo Park, Calif., May 1983

Postel, Jon, "Daytime Protocol," RFC 867, Network Information Center, SRI International, Menlo Park, Calif., May 1983

Postel, Jon, and Ken Harrenstien, "Time Protocol," RFC 868, Network Information Center, SRI International, Menlo Park, Calif., May 1983

NAME

`infocmp` – compare or print out *terminfo* descriptions

SYNOPSIS

`infocmp` [`-d`] [`-c`] [`-n`] [`-I`] [`-L`] [`-C`] [`-r`] [`-u`] [`-s d` | `i` | `l` | `c`] [`-v`] [`-V`]
[`-1`] [`-w` *width*] [`-A` *directory*] [`-B` *directory*] [*termname . . .*]

DESCRIPTION

`infocmp` can be used to compare a binary **terminfo** entry with other terminfo entries, rewrite a **terminfo** description to take advantage of the **use=** terminfo field, or print out a **terminfo** description from the binary file (**term**) in a variety of formats. In all cases, the boolean fields will be printed first, followed by the numeric fields, followed by the string fields.

Default Options

If no options are specified and zero or one *termnames* are specified, the **-I** option will be assumed. If more than one *termname* is specified, the **-d** option will be assumed.

Comparison Options [–d] [–c] [–n]

`infocmp` compares the **terminfo** description of the first terminal *termname* with each of the descriptions given by the entries for the other terminal's *termnames*. If a capability is defined for only one of the terminals, the value returned will depend on the type of the capability: **F** for boolean variables, **-1** for integer variables, and **NULL** for string variables.

-d produces a list of each capability that is different between two entries. This option is useful to show the difference between two entries, created by different people, for the same or similar terminals.

-c produces a list of each capability that is common between two entries. Capabilities that are not set are ignored. This option can be used as a quick check to see if the **-u** option is worth using.

-n produces a list of each capability that is in neither entry. If no *termnames* are given, the environment variable **TERM** will be used for both of the *termnames*. This can be used as a quick check to see if anything was left out of a description.

Source Listing Options [–I] [–L] [–C] [–r]

The **-I**, **-L**, and **-C** options will produce a source listing for each terminal named.

-I use the **terminfo** names

-L use the long C variable name listed in <**term.h**>

-C use the **termcap** names

-r when using **-C**, put out all capabilities in **termcap** form

If no *termnames* are given, the environment variable **TERM** will be used for the terminal name.

The source produced by the **-C** option may be used directly as a **termcap** entry, but not all of the parameterized strings may be changed to the **termcap** format. `infocmp` will attempt to convert most of the parameterized information, but anything not converted will be plainly marked in the output and commented out. These should be edited by hand.

All padding information for strings will be collected together and placed at the beginning of the string where **termcap** expects it. Mandatory padding (padding information with a trailing '/') will become optional.

All **termcap** variables no longer supported by **terminfo**, but which are derivable from other **terminfo** variables, will be output. Not all **terminfo** capabilities will be translated; only those variables which were part of **termcap** will normally be output. Specifying the **-r** option will take off this restriction, allowing all capabilities to be output in *termcap* form.

Note that because padding is collected to the beginning of the capability, not all capabilities are output. Mandatory padding is not supported. Because **termcap** strings are not as flexible, it is not always possible to convert a **terminfo** string capability into an equivalent **termcap** format. A subsequent conversion of the **termcap** file back into **terminfo** format will not necessarily reproduce the original **terminfo** source.

Some common **terminfo** parameter sequences, their **termcap** equivalents, and some terminal types which commonly have such sequences, are:

terminfo	termcap	Representative Terminals
%p1%c	%.	adm
%p1%d	%d	hp, ANSI standard, vt100
%p1%'x'%+%c	%+x	concept
%i	%i	ANSI standard, vt100
%p1%?%'x'%>%t%p1%'y'%+%;	%>xy	concept
%p2 is printed before %p1	%r	hp

Use= Option [–u]

-u produces a **terminfo** source description of the first terminal *termname* which is relative to the sum of the descriptions given by the entries for the other terminals *termnames*. It does this by analyzing the differences between the first *termname* and the other *termnames* and producing a description with **use=** fields for the other terminals. In this manner, it is possible to retrofit generic terminfo entries into a terminal's description. Or, if two similar terminals exist, but were coded at different times or by different people so that each description is a full description, using **infocmp** will show what can be done to change one description to be relative to the other.

A capability will get printed with an at-sign (@) if it no longer exists in the first *termname*, but one of the other *termname* entries contains a value for it. A capability's value gets printed if the value in the first *termname* is not found in any of the other *termname* entries, or if the first of the other *termname* entries that has this capability gives a different value for the capability than that in the first *termname*.

The order of the other *termname* entries is significant. Since the terminfo compiler **tic** does a left-to-right scan of the capabilities, specifying two **use=** entries that contain differing entries for the same capabilities will produce different results depending on the order that the entries are given in. **infocmp** will flag any such inconsistencies between the other *termname* entries as they are found.

Alternatively, specifying a capability *after* a **use=** entry that contains that capability will cause the second specification to be ignored. Using **infocmp** to recreate a description can be a useful check to make sure that everything was specified correctly in the original source description.

Another error that does not cause incorrect compiled files, but will slow down the compilation time, is specifying extra **use=** fields that are superfluous. **infocmp** will flag any other *termname* **use=** fields that were not needed.

Other Options [–s d | i | l | c] [–v] [–V] [–1] [–w *width*]

`-s` sorts the fields within each type according to the argument below:

- `d` leave fields in the order that they are stored in the *terminfo* database.
- `i` sort by *terminfo* name.
- `l` sort by the long C variable name.
- `c` sort by the *termcap* name.

If the `-s` option is not given, the fields printed out will be sorted alphabetically by the **terminfo** name within each type, except in the case of the `-C` or the `-L` options, which cause the sorting to be done by the **termcap** name or the long C variable name, respectively.

`-v` prints out tracing information on standard error as the program runs.

`-V` prints out the version of the program in use on standard error and exit.

`-1` causes the fields to be printed out one to a line. Otherwise, the fields will be printed several to a line to a maximum width of 60 characters.

`-w` changes the output to *width* characters.

Changing Databases [–A *directory*] [–B *directory*]

The location of the compiled **terminfo** database is taken from the environment variable **TERMINFO** . If the variable is not defined, or the terminal is not found in that location, the system **terminfo** database, usually in `/usr/share/lib/terminfo`, will be used. The options `-A` and `-B` may be used to override this location. The `-A` option will set **TERMINFO** for the first *termname* and the `-B` option will set **TERMINFO** for the other *termnames*. With this, it is possible to compare descriptions for a terminal with the same name located in two different databases. This is useful for comparing descriptions for the same terminal created by different people.

FILES

`/usr/share/lib/terminfo/?/*` Compiled terminal description database.

SEE ALSO

curses(3curses), **captoinfo**(1M), **terminfo**(4), **tic**(1M)

NAME

initprivs – set the system privilege information

SYNOPSIS

initprivs

DESCRIPTION

The **initprivs** command initializes the system with privilege information. It reads this information from **/etc/security/tcb/privs**. Invalid entries in this file are ignored. If the validity information for the entry does not match the validity information stored on disk, the file specified by the entry is not privileged. In either case, a warning is issued if the command is run at the shell level. Otherwise, **initprivs** operates silently.

initprivs must have the **P_SETSPRIV** or **P_SETUPRIV** privilege. Otherwise permission is denied. In addition, the maximum privilege set of **initprivs** must be a super–set of the privileges to be set. If not, only those privileges in the maximum set of **initprivs** that can be set for the file are in effect.

Defaults

The file **/etc/default/privcmds** contains the following parameter:

VAL_CKSUM If the value of this parameter is **No**, then the **initprivs** command will not validate the check sum value stored in the Privilege Data File (PDF) located in **/etc/security/tcb/privs**; this results in faster performance compared to validating the check sum value each time the command is run. If the value of this parameter is anything other than **No** (including **NULL**, the default), then the **initprivs** command validates the check sum for each file each time it is run.

FILES

/etc/security/tcb/privs Privilege Data File (PDF).
/etc/default/privcmds Default file.

SEE ALSO

intro(2), **priv**(4), **filepriv**(1M)

DIAGNOSTICS

initprivs exits with a return code of 0 upon successful completion.

If **initprivs** detects errors, the following messages may be displayed:

Cannot clear file privileges on ''*file*''

File ''*file*'' **fails validation; entry ignored.**

1 entry ignored in ''/etc/security/tcb/privs''

 # entries ignored in ''/etc/security/tcb/privs''

NAME

install – install commands

SYNOPSIS

/usr/sbin/install [**-c** *dira*] [**-f** *dirb*] [**-i**] [**-n** *dirc*] [**-m** *mode*] [**-u** *user*] [**-g** *group*] [**-o**] [**-s**] *file* [*dirx* . . .]

DESCRIPTION

The **install** command is most commonly used in "makefiles" [see **make**(1)] to install a *file* (updated target file) in a specific place within a file system. Each *file* is installed by copying it into the appropriate directory, thereby retaining the mode and owner of the original command. The program prints messages telling the user exactly what files it is replacing or creating and where they are going.

If no options or directories (*dirx* . . .) are given, **install** will search a set of default directories (**/bin**, **/usr/bin**, **/etc**, **/lib**, and **/usr/lib**, in that order) for a file with the same name as *file*. When the first occurrence is found, **install** issues a message saying that it is overwriting that file with *file*, and proceeds to do so. If the file is not found, the program states this and exits without further action.

If one or more directories (*dirx* ...) are specified after *file*, those directories will be searched before the directories specified in the default list.

The meanings of the options are:

-c *dira* Installs a new command (*file*) in the directory specified by *dira*, only if it is not found. If it is found, **install** issues a message saying that the file already exists, and exits without overwriting it. May be used alone or with the **-s** option.

-f *dirb* Forces *file* to be installed in given directory, whether or not one already exists. If the file being installed does not already exist, the mode and owner of the new file will be set to **755** and **bin**, respectively. If the file already exists, the mode and owner will be that of the already existing file. May be used alone or with the **-o** or **-s** options.

-i Ignores default directory list, searching only through the given directories (*dirx* ...). May be used alone or with any other options except **-c** and **-f**.

-n *dirc* If *file* is not found in any of the searched directories, it is put in the directory specified in *dirc*. The mode and owner of the new file will be set to **755** and **bin**, respectively. May be used alone or with any other options except **-c** and **-f**.

-m *mode* The mode of the new file is set to *mode*.

-u *user* The owner of the new file is set to *user*.

-g *group* The group id of the new file is set to *group*. Only available to the superuser.

-o If *file* is found, this option saves the "found" file by copying it to OLD*file* in the directory in which it was found. This option is useful when installing a frequently used file such as **/bin/sh** or **/lib/saf/ttymon**, where the existing file cannot be removed.

May be used alone or with any other options except `-c`.

`-s` Suppresses printing of messages other than error messages. May be used alone or with any other options.

SEE ALSO

`make`(1)

NAME

`install` – (BSD) install files

SYNOPSIS

/usr/ucb/install [**-cs**] [**-g** *group*] [**-m** *mode*] [**-o** *owner*] *file1 file2*

/usr/ucb/install [**-cs**] [**-g** *group*] [**-m** *mode*] [**-o** *owner*] *file . . . directory*

/usr/ucb/install -d [**-g** *group*] [**-m** *mode*] [**-o** *owner*] *directory*

DESCRIPTION

Install is used within makefiles to copy new versions of files into a destination directory and to create the destination directory itself.

The first two forms are similar to the **cp**(1) command with the addition that executable files can be stripped during the copy and the owner, group, and mode of the installed file(s) can be given.

The third form can be used to create a destination directory with the required owner, group and permissions.

Note: **install** uses no special privileges to copy files from one place to another. The implications of this are:

> You must have permission to read the files to be installed.
>
> You must have permission to copy into the destination file or directory.
>
> You must have permission to change the modes on the final copy of the file if you want to use the **-m** option to change modes.
>
> You must be superuser if you want to specify the ownership of the installed file with **-o**. If you are not the super-user, or if **-o** is not in effect, the installed file will be owned by you, regardless of who owns the original.

OPTIONS

-g *group* Set the group ownership of the installed file or directory. (staff by default)

-m *mode* Set the mode for the installed file or directory. (0755 by default)

-o *owner* If run as root, set the ownership of the installed file to the user-ID of *owner*.

-c Copy files. In fact **install** *always* copies files, but the **-c** option is retained for backwards compatibility with old shell scripts that might otherwise break.

-s Strip executable files as they are copied.

-d Create a directory. Missing parent directories are created as required as in **mkdir -p**. If the directory already exists, the owner, group and mode will be set to the values given on the command line.

SEE ALSO

chgrp(1), chmod(1), chown(1), cp(1), install(1M), mkdir(1), strip(1)

NAME

installf – add a file to the software installation database

SYNOPSIS

installf [**-c** *class*] *pkginst pathname* [*ftype* [[*major minor*] [*mode owner group*]

installf [**-c** *class*] *pkginst* **-**

installf -f [**-c** *class*] *pkginst*

installf [[-c *class] pkginst path1=path2* **[l|s]**

DESCRIPTION

installf is a tool available for use from within custom procedure scripts such as **preinstall**, **postinstall**, **preremove**, and **postremove**. When these scripts create or modify files, **installf** should be used to register the addition or change into the system's contents database.

When the second synopsis is used, the pathname descriptions will be read from standard input. These descriptions are the same as would be given in the first synopsis but the information is given in the form of a list. (The descriptions should be in the form: *pathname* [*ftype* [[*major minor*] [*mode owner group*]].)

When the last synopsis is invoked, the pathname argument is used to specify a link, where *path1* indicates the link and *path2* the file being linked to. The **ftypes l** and **s** are used to specify a hard link or symbolic link, respectively. If *ftype* is not specified, **installf** defaults to type 1.

After all files have been appropriately created and/or modified, **installf** should be invoked with the **-f** synopsis to indicate that installation is final. Links will be created at this time and, if attribute information for a pathname was not specified during the original invocation of **installf** or was not already stored on the system, the current attribute values for the pathname will be stored. Otherwise, **installf** verifies that attribute values match those given on the command line, making corrections as necessary. In all cases, the current content information is calculated and stored appropriately.

-c *class* — Class to which installed objects should be associated. Default class is **none**.

pkginst — Name of package instance with which the pathname should be associated.

pathname — Pathname that is being created or modified. Special characters, such as an equal sign (**=**), are included in pathnames by surrounding the entire pathname in single quotes (as in, for example, **'/usr/lib/~='**). When a pathname is specified on a shell command line, the single quotes must be preceded by backslashes so they're not interpreted by the shell.

ftype — A one-character field that indicates the file type. Possible file types include:

`f`	a standard executable or data file
`e`	a file to be edited upon installation or removal
`v`	volatile file (one whose contents are expected to change)
`d`	directory
`x`	an exclusive directory
`l`	linked file
`p`	named pipe
`c`	character special device
`b`	block special device
`s`	symbolic link

Once a file has the file type attribute **v**, it will always be volatile. For example, if a file being installed already exists and has the file type attribute **v**, then even if the version of the file being installed is not specified as volatile, the file type attribute will remain volatile.

major The major device number. The field is only specified for block or character special devices.

minor The minor device number. The field is only specified for block or character special devices.

mode The octal mode of the file (for example, 0664). A question mark (?) indicates that the mode will be left unchanged, implying that the file already exists on the target machine. If the directory doesn't exist, the default is 0755. If it's a file, the default is 0644. This field is not used for linked or symbolically linked files.

owner The owner of the file (for example, **bin** or **root**). The field is limited to 14 characters in length. A question mark (?) indicates that the owner will be left unchanged, implying that the file already exists on the target machine. If it doesn't exist, *owner* defaults to **root**. This field is not used for linked or symbolically linked files.

group The group to which the file belongs (for example, **bin** or **sys**). The field is limited to 14 characters in length. A question mark (?) indicates that the group will be left unchanged, implying that the file already exists on the target machine. If it doesn't exist, *group* defaults to **other**. This field is not used for linked or symbolically linked files.

-f Indicates that installation is complete. This option is used with the final invocation of **installf** (for all files of a given class).

NOTES

When *ftype* is specified, all applicable fields, as shown below, must be defined:

ftype	*Required Fields*
p x d f v or **e**	**mode owner group**
c or **b**	**major minor mode owner group**

The **installf** command will create directories, named pipes and special devices on the original invocation. Links are created when **installf** is invoked with the **-f** option to indicate installation is complete.

For symbolically linked files, *path2* can be a relative pathname, such as `./` or `../`. For example, if you enter a line such as

```
installf -c none pkgx /foo/bar/etc/mount=../usr/sbin/mount s
```

path2 (`/foo/bar/etc/mount`) will be a symbolic link to `../usr/sbin/mount`.

When a link is specified, the directory in which the link is to reside must exist, otherwise **installf -f** will fail for that entry.

Files installed with **installf** will be placed in the class *none*, unless a class is defined with the command. Subsequently, they will be removed when the associated package is deleted. If this file should not be deleted at the same time as the package, be certain to assign it to a class which is ignored at removal time. To do this, associate the file to a class which will be handled by a removal class action script delivered with the package.

When classes are used, **installf** must be used as follows:

```
installf -c class1
installf -c class2
installf -f
```

Using multiple invocations is discouraged if standard input style invocations can be used with a list of files. This will be much faster because the **contents** file must be sought

EXAMPLE

The following example shows the use of **installf** invoked from an optional preinstall or postinstall script:

```
#create /dev/xt directory
#(needs to be done before drvinstall)
installf $PKGINST /dev/xt d 755 root sys ||
             exit 2
majno='/usr/sbin/drvinstall -m /etc/master.d/xt
     -d $BASEDIR/data/xt.o -v1.0' ||
             exit 2
i=00
while [ $i -lt $limit ]
do
  for j in 0 1 2 3 4 5 6 7
  do
    echo /dev/xt$i$j c $majno 'expr $i * 8 + $j' 644 root sys
    echo /dev/xt$i$j=/dev/xt/$i$j
  done
  i='expr $i + 1'
  [ $i -le 9 ] && i="0$i" #add leading zero
done | installf $PKGINST - || exit 2
# finalized installation, create links
installf -f $PKGINST || exit 2
for each entry.
```

SEE ALSO

pkgadd(1M), pkgask(1M), pkgchk(1M), pkginfo(1), pkgmk(1), pkgparam(1), pkgproto(1), pkgrm(1M), pkgtrans(1), removef(1M)

NAME

ipcrm – remove a message queue, semaphore set, or shared memory ID

SYNOPSIS

ipcrm [*options*]

DESCRIPTION

ipcrm removes one or more messages, semaphores, or shared memory identifiers. The identifiers are specified by the following *options*:

-q *msqid* Remove the message queue identifier *msqid* from the system and destroy the message queue and data structure associated with it.

-m *shmid* Remove the shared memory identifier *shmid* from the system. The shared memory segment and data structure associated with it are destroyed after the last detach.

-s *semid* Remove the semaphore identifier *semid* from the system and destroy the set of semaphores and data structure associated with it.

-Q *msgkey* Remove the message queue identifier, created with key *msgkey*, from the system and destroy the message queue and data structure associated with it.

-M *shmkey* Removes the shared memory identifier, created with key *shmkey*, from the system. The shared memory segment and data structure associated with it are destroyed after the last detach.

-S *semkey* Remove the semaphore identifier, created with key *semkey*, from the system and destroy the set of semaphores and data structure associated with it.

The details of the removes are described in **msgctl**(2), **shmctl**(2), and **semctl**(2). Use the **ipcs** command to find the identifiers and keys.

SEE ALSO

ipcs(1), **msgctl**(2), **msgget**(2), **msgop**(2), **semctl**(2), **semget**(2), **semop**(2), **shmctl**(2), **shmget**(2), **shmop**(2)

NAME

ipcs – report inter-process communication facilities status

SYNOPSIS

ipcs [*options*]

DESCRIPTION

ipcs prints information about active inter-process communication facilities.

Note that information is displayed only for objects to which the user has read access.

A user with the appropriate privileges is able to override the read access restriction and display information on all objects.

Without *options*, information is printed in short format for message queues, shared memory, and semaphores that are currently active in the system. Otherwise, the information that is displayed is controlled by the following *options*:

-q Print information about active message queues.

-m Print information about active shared memory segments.

-s Print information about active semaphores.

If **-q**, **-m**, or **-s** are specified, information about only those indicated is printed. If none of these three are specified, information about all three is printed subject to these options:

-b Print information on maximum allowable size. (Maximum number of bytes in messages on queue for message queues, size of segments for shared memory, and number of semaphores in each set for semaphores.) See below for meaning of columns in a listing.

-c Print creator's login name and group name. See below.

-o Print information on outstanding usage. (Number of messages on queue and total number of bytes in messages on queue for message queues and number of processes attached to shared memory segments.)

-p Print process number information. (Process ID of last process to send a message, process ID of last process to receive a message on message queues, process ID of creating process, and process ID of last process to attach or detach on shared memory segments.) See below.

-t Print time information. (Time of the last control operation that changed the access permissions for all facilities, time of last **msgsnd** and **msgrcv** operations on message queues, time of last **shmat** and **shmdt** operations on shared memory, and time of last **semop** operation on semaphores.) See below.

-a Use all print options. (This is a shorthand notation for **-b**, **-c**, **-o**, **-p**, **-t**.)

-C *corefile*
Use the file *corefile* in place of **/dev/kmem**.

-N *namelist*
Use the file *namelist* in place of **/stand/unix**.

-X Print information about XENIX interprocess communication, in addition to the standard interprocess communication status. The XENIX process information describes a second set of semaphores and shared memory.

Note that the **-p** option does not print process number information for XENIX shared memory, and the **-t** option does not print time information about XENIX semaphores and shared memory.

The column headings and the meaning of the columns in an **ipcs** listing are given below; the letters in parentheses indicate the *options* that cause the corresponding heading to appear; "all" means that the heading always appears. Note that these *options* only determine what information is provided for each facility; they do not determine which facilities are listed.

T (all) Type of facility:

- **q** message queue
- **m** shared memory segment
- **s** semaphore

ID (all) The identifier for the facility entry.

KEY (all) The key used as an argument to **msgget**, **semget**, or **shmget** to create the facility entry. (Note:The key of a shared memory segment is changed to **IPC_PRIVATE** when the segment has been removed until all processes attached to the segment detach it.).TP **MODE** (all) The facility access modes and flags. The mode consists of 11 characters that are interpreted as follows:

The first character is:

- **S** if a process is waiting on a **msgsnd** operation.
- **D** if the associated shared memory segment has been removed. It will disappear when the last process attached to the segment detaches it.
- **-** if neither of the above is true.

The second character is:

- **R** if a process is waiting on a **msgrcv** operation.
- **C** if the associated shared memory segment is to be cleared when the first attach operation is executed.
- **-** if neither of the above is true.

The next nine characters are interpreted as three sets of three bits each. The first set refers to the owner's permissions; the next to permissions of others in the user-group of the facility entry; and the last to all others. Within each set, the first character indicates permission to read, the second character indicates permission to write or alter the facility entry, and the last character is currently unused.

The permissions are indicated as follows:

- `r` if read permission is granted.
- `w` if write permission is granted.
- `a` if alter permission is granted.
- `-` if the indicated permission is not granted.

`OWNER`	(all)	The login name of the owner of the facility entry.
`GROUP`	(all)	The group name of the owner of the facility entry.
`CREATOR`	(a,c)	The login name of the creator of the facility entry.
`CGROUP`	(a,c)	The group name of the creator of the facility entry.
`CBYTES`	(a,o)	The number of bytes in messages currently outstanding on the associated message queue.
`QNUM`	(a,o)	The number of messages currently outstanding on the associated message queue.
`QBYTES`	(a,b)	The maximum number of bytes allowed in messages outstanding on the associated message queue.
`LSPID`	(a,p)	The process ID of the last process to send a message to the associated queue.
`LRPID`	(a,p)	The process ID of the last process to receive a message from the associated queue.
`STIME`	(a,t)	The time the last message was sent to the associated queue.
`RTIME`	(a,t)	The time the last message was received from the associated queue.
`CTIME`	(a,t)	The time the associated entry was created or changed.
`NATTCH`	(a,o)	The number of processes attached to the associated shared memory segment.
`SEGSZ`	(a,b)	The size of the associated shared memory segment.
`CPID`	(a,p)	The process ID of the creator of the shared memory entry.
`LPID`	(a,p)	The process ID of the last process to attach or detach the shared memory segment.
`ATIME`	(a,t)	The time the last attach on the associated shared memory segment was completed.
`DTIME`	(a,t)	The time the last detach on the associated shared memory segment was completed.
`NSEMS`	(a,b)	The number of semaphores in the set associated with the semaphore entry.
`OTIME`	(a,t)	The time the last semaphore operation on the set associated with the semaphore entry was completed.

FILES

`/stand/unix`	system namelist
`/dev/kmem`	memory
`/etc/passwd`	user names
`/etc/group`	group names

NOTES

If the user specifies the **-N** flag, the real and effective UID/GID is set to the real UID/GID of the user invoking **ipcs**.

Things can change while **ipcs** is running; the information it gives is guaranteed to be accurate only when it was retrieved.

SEE ALSO

msgop(2), **semop**(2), **shmop**(2)

NAME

join – relational database operator

SYNOPSIS

join [*options*] *file1 file2*

DESCRIPTION

join forms, on the standard output, a join of the two relations specified by the lines of *file1* and *file2*. If *file1* is **-**, the standard input is used. *file1* and *file2* must be sorted in increasing code set collating sequence on the fields on which they are to be joined, normally the first in each line [see **sort**(1)]. **join** processes supplementary code set characters in files, and recognizes supplementary code set characters given to the **-e** and **-t** options (see below) according to the locale specified in the **LC_CTYPE** environment variable [see **LANG** on **environ**(5)].

There is one line in the output for each pair of lines in *file1* and *file2* that have identical join fields. The output line normally consists of the common field, then the rest of the line from *file1*, then the rest of the line from *file2*.

The default input field separators are blank, tab, or new-line. In this case, multiple separators count as one field separator, and leading separators are ignored. The default output field separator is a blank.

Some of the options below use the argument *n*. This argument should be a **1** or a **2** referring to either *file1* or *file2*, respectively. The following options are recognized:

-a*n* In addition to the normal output, produce a line for each unpairable line in file *n*, where *n* is 1 or 2.

-e *s* Replace empty output fields with string *s*. *s* may contain supplementary code set characters.

-j*n m* Join on the *m*th field of file *n*. If *n* is missing, use the *m*th field in each file. Fields are numbered starting with **1**.

-o *list* Each output line includes the fields specified in *list*, each element of which has the form *n*.*m*, where *n* is a file number and *m* is a field number. The common field is not printed unless specifically requested.

-t*c* Use character *c* as a separator (tab character). Every appearance of *c* in a line is significant. The character *c* is used as the field separator for both input and output. *c* may be a supplementary code set character.

EXAMPLE

The following command line will join the password file and the group file, matching on the numeric group ID, and outputting the login name, the group name, and the login directory. It is assumed that the files have been sorted in code set collating sequence on the group ID fields.

```
join -j1 4 -j2 3 -o 1.1 2.1 1.6 -t: /etc/passwd /etc/group
```

FILES

/usr/lib/locale/*locale***/LC_MESSAGES/uxdfm**
language-specific message file [See **LANG** on **environ**(5).]

SEE ALSO

`awk`(1), `comm`(1), `sort`(1), `uniq`(1)

NOTES

With default field separation, the collating sequence is that of `sort -b`; with `-t`, the sequence is that of a plain sort.

The conventions of the `join`, `sort`, `comm`, `uniq`, and `awk` commands are wildly incongruous.

Filenames that are numeric may cause conflict when the `-o` option is used just before listing filenames.

kdb(1)

NAME

kdb – kernel debugger

SYNOPSIS

kdb

DESCRIPTION

KDB is a kernel debugger that works like a Reverse Polish Notation (RPN) calculator. KDB can set breakpoints, display kernel stack traces and various kernel structures, and modify the contents of memory, I/O, and registers. The debugger supports basic arithmetic operations, conditional execution, variables, and macros. KDB does conversions from a kernel symbol name to its virtual address, from a virtual address to the value at that address, and from a virtual address to the name of the nearest kernel symbol. You have a choice of different numeric bases, address spaces, and operand sizes.

This is an advanced tool, only for those who are thoroughly familiar with the UNIX kernel. Because UNIX systems differ, you could possibly damage your system by following some of the examples in this discussion.

You can invoke the debugger by using the **kdb** command or the **sysi86(SI86TODEMON)** system call on all systems, CTRL-ALT-d (from the console only) on an AT-bus system, or the interrupt character (from the console only) on a Multibus system. In addition, KDB is entered automatically under various conditions, such as panics and breakpoint traps. Any time the **kdb>>** prompt appears, you are in the debugger. I/O is done via the console (kd), or a serial terminal.

To exit the debugger, type CTRL-d or q.

When you exit and re-enter the debugger, its state is preserved, including the contents of the value stack.

USING KDB AS A CALCULATOR

KDB operates as an RPN calculator, similar to **dc**(1). This calculator has a 32-level value stack for storing results and intermediate values. Commands and values you enter operate on the value stack, which is an internal data structure in KDB. It has no connection with the kernel stack or any other stack in the system.

To use KDB, at the **kdb>>** prompt type one or more items (values or commands) on a line. Separate items with spaces or tabs. Press ENTER to end a line and send its contents to KDB for processing. Each item is processed separately, from left to right.

The values can be:

Numbers
: Use positive or negative integers. Numbers must begin with a digit, or a minus sign for negative numbers. Begin octal numbers with "0o" and hex numbers with "0x." Otherwise, numbers are assumed to be in the default base — the default is hex, unless you change it. (See "Resetting the Numeric Base" for instructions.)

Character constants
: You can have KDB convert characters to a number by entering one to four characters inside single quotes. C-style escapes are supported in character constants.

strings   Use C-style strings, enclosed in double quotes.

Kernel symbol names
When you type a kernel symbol name, its address is pushed onto the value stack.

When you enter a number or a string, it is pushed onto the value stack, becoming the new TOS (Top Of Stack). Values remain on the value stack until they are popped off as a result of a command.

In the descriptions below, [TOS] means the value on the top of the stack and [TOS-1] means the value just below it (pushed previously).

Stack Operations

KDB provides these commands for examining or changing the value stack:

`stk`	print all values on the stack
`p`	print [TOS]
`dup`	push [TOS]
`pop`	pop 1 value
`clrstk`	pop all values

`stk`   For example, starting with an empty value stack, this input:

```
5 "xyzzy" 7 stk
```

displays the entire stack:

```
5
"xyzzy"
7
```

`p`   At this point, the input:

```
p
```

displays the top value on the stack, which is:

```
7
```

The next example uses the `p` command to display the address of a kernel symbol. The input:

```
lbolt p
```

produces an address something like this:

```
D01821BC
```

`dup`   This command is useful when you want to use a value twice in a calculation. For example:

```
5 3 * dup 2 + * p
```

would produce the output:

```
FF
```

which is the value of `(((5 * 3) + 2) * (5 * 3))`.

pop This command removes the top value from the value stack. For example, if this is the stack:

```
5
"xyzzy"
7
```

the input:

```
pop stk
```

removes the top value from the stack and displays the resulting stack:

```
5
"xyzzy"
```

clrstk

This command clears the value stack. Remember that the contents of the stack are saved when you exit and re-enter KDB.

Arithmetic Operations

You can perform arithmetic operations on the top values on the stack:

`+`	compute [TOS-1] + [TOS]; pop 2; push result
`-`	compute [TOS-1] - [TOS]; pop 2; push result
`*`	compute [TOS-1] * [TOS]; pop 2; push result
`/`	compute [TOS-1] / [TOS]; pop 2; push result
`%`	compute [TOS-1] % [TOS]; pop 2; push result
`>>`	compute [TOS-1] >> [TOS]; pop 2; push result
`<<`	compute [TOS-1] << [TOS]; pop 2; push result
`<`	compute [TOS-1] < [TOS]; pop 2; push result
`>`	compute [TOS-1] > [TOS]; pop 2; push result
`==`	compute [TOS-1] == [TOS]; pop 2; push result
`!=`	compute [TOS-1] != [TOS]; pop 2; push result
`&`	compute [TOS-1] & [TOS]; pop 2; push result
`|`	compute [TOS-1] | [TOS]; pop 2; push result
`^`	compute [TOS-1] ^ [TOS]; pop 2; push result
`&&`	compute [TOS-1] && [TOS]; pop 2; push result
`||`	compute [TOS-1] || [TOS]; pop 2; push result
`!`	replace [TOS] with ![TOS]
`++`	replace [TOS] with [TOS] + 1
`--`	replace [TOS] with [TOS] - 1

For example, this input (subtracting 5 from 7):

```
7 5 - p
```

would produce this output:

```
2
```

The power of KDB's calculator feature lies in its ability to evaluate expressions like this:

```
callout 16 +
```

This pushes the address of the callout table on the stack and adds 16 to it. If the size of a callout table entry is 16 bytes, the result of the calculation is the address of the second entry in the callout table. (Use the **size** command of **crash**(1M) to find the sizes of common system tables.)

Be careful: Make sure the divide operator (slash character) is both preceded and followed by spaces. If any other character appears next to the slash, it indicates a suffix instead of division.

READING AND WRITING TO MEMORY

These commands still operate like an RPN calculator, but they perform specific debugging operations instead of calculations. To examine and set the contents of memory (and I/O) use the commands:

`r`	replace [TOS] with the value at virtual address [TOS]
`w`	write [TOS-1] into virtual address [TOS]; pop 2
`dump`	show [TOS] bytes starting at virtual address [TOS-1]; pop 2

`r` For example, you can find the value of the (long) kernel variable, `lbolt`, by typing:

```
lbolt r p
```

This puts the virtual address of `lbolt` on the stack, replaces it with the value found at that address, and prints the result.

`w` To change the value of `lbolt` to 2000, type:

```
2000 lbolt w
```

This writes 2000 at `lbolt's` virtual address.

You could increment `lbolt` by typing:

```
lbolt r ++ lbolt w
```

This puts the virtual address of `lbolt` on the stack, replaces it with the value found at that address, adds 1 to the value, and writes the result at `lbolt's` virtual address.

`dump` This command displays a range of memory, both in hex and ASCII. For example, if you typed:

```
putbuf 10 dump
```

which shows 10 bytes, starting at the virtual address of `putbuf`, you would see something like:

```
........ ........ ........ 61746F74  D0108C50  ............tota
6572206C 6D206C61 726F6D65 ........  D0108C60  l real memor....
```

In each line, the block of four values on the left shows the values of 16 bytes, displayed as four 4-byte longwords in hex. The dots represent values outside of the requested range. (`dump` may also display question marks here; that means the address is invalid). The next column is the address of the first of the 16 bytes. The last column is the same 16 bytes displayed in ASCII. Dots here represent values outside the requested range or unprintable characters.

Suffixes

Suffixes can be appended to many KDB commands. They always begin with the slash character (`/`).

Be careful: Don't leave spaces before or after the slash character. When the slash is preceded and followed by a space, it indicates division instead of a suffix.

Operand-size suffixes

The `r`, `w` and **`dump`** commands can also work with units of bytes and words, as well as the default longs. To do this, append one of these suffixes to the command:

`/b`	byte
`/w`	word (2 bytes)
`/l`	long (4 bytes)—this is the default.

For example, to display the value of a short (2-byte) variable at address `0xD0008120`, type:

```
0xD0008120 r/w p
```

Entering the **`dump`** command with `/b` displays 16 1-byte values per line, with `/w` displays eight 2-byte values per line, and with `/l` (or nothing) displays four 4-byte values per line.

Address-space suffixes

The `r`, `w` and **`dump`** commands, by default, work with kernel virtual addresses. You can change to physical addresses, I/O addresses, or user process virtual addresses by appending one of these suffixes to the command:

`/k`	kernel virtual — the default
`/p`	physical
`/io`	I/O port
`/u#`	user process number # virtual (# is a process slot number in hex)

`/p` For example, to dump 40 (hex) bytes in longword format from physical address 2000, type:

```
2000 40 dump/p
```

The default address is kernel virtual, so the `/p` suffix is required for the physical address. Note that an operand-size suffix is not required, because long is the default.

`/io` For example, to read from port 300 (in bytes) and display the result, type:

```
300 r/io/b p
```

`/u#` For example, to dump 20 longwords from process 16's u area at an offset of 1000, type:

```
1000 u + 20 dump/u16
```

Suffix formats

Address-space suffixes can be combined with operand-size suffixes; only the first slash is required. For example, to do the read from I/O port 300 shown above, any of these command lines is acceptable:

```
300 r/io/b
300 r/b/io
300 r/iob
300 r/bio
```

Suffixes can also be attached directly to an address as shorthand for "read and print." Thus, **2000 r/p p** can be shortened to **2000/p**.

Since the default address-space is kernel virtual, the common operation of "read and print from kernel virtual" can be even further shortened. Type **lbolt/** to read and print the value of the (long) kernel variable, **lbolt**.

DISPLAYING AND WRITING TO REGISTERS

You can examine the CPU's general registers (and some pseudo-registers) with these commands:

%eax	push the contents of 32-bit register **eax**
%ebx	push the contents of 32-bit register **ebx**
%ecx	push the contents of 32-bit register **ecx**
%edx	push the contents of 32-bit register **edx**
%esi	push the contents of 32-bit register **esi**
%edi	push the contents of 32-bit register **edi**
%ebp	push the contents of 32-bit register **ebp**
%esp	push the contents of 32-bit register **esp**
%eip	push the contents of 32-bit register **eip**
%efl	push the contents of 32-bit register **efl**
%cs	push the contents of 16-bit register **cs**
%ds	push the contents of 16-bit register **ds**
%es	push the contents of 16-bit register **es**
%fs	push the contents of 16-bit register **fs**
%gs	push the contents of 16-bit register **gs**
%err	push the error number
%trap	push the trap number
%ax	push the contents of 16-bit register **ax**
%bx	push the contents of 16-bit register **bx**
%cx	push the contents of 16-bit register **cx**
%dx	push the contents of 16-bit register **dx**
%si	push the contents of 16-bit register **si**
%di	push the contents of 16-bit register **di**
%bp	push the contents of 16-bit register **bp**
%sp	push the contents of 16-bit register **sp**
%ip	push the contents of 16-bit register **ip**
%fl	push the contents of 16-bit register **fl**
%al	push the contents of 8-bit register **al**
%ah	push the contents of 8-bit register **ah**
%bl	push the contents of 8-bit register **bl**
%bh	push the contents of 8-bit register **bh**
%cl	push the contents of 8-bit register **cl**
%ch	push the contents of 8-bit register **ch**
%dl	push the contents of 8-bit register **dl**
%dh	push the contents of 8-bit register **dh**

You can modify the values of general-purpose registers with these commands:

w%eax	write [TOS] into 32-bit register **eax**; pop 1
w%ebx	write [TOS] into 32-bit register **ebx**; pop 1
w%ecx	write [TOS] into 32-bit register **ecx**; pop 1
w%edx	write [TOS] into 32-bit register **edx**; pop 1
w%esi	write [TOS] into 32-bit register **esi**; pop 1
w%edi	write [TOS] into 32-bit register **edi**; pop 1
w%ebp	write [TOS] into 32-bit register **ebp**; pop 1
w%esp	write [TOS] into 32-bit register **esp**; pop 1
w%eip	write [TOS] into 32-bit register **eip**; pop 1
w%efl	write [TOS] into 32-bit register **efl**; pop 1
w%cs	write [TOS] into 16-bit register **cs**; pop 1
w%ds	write [TOS] into 16-bit register **ds**; pop 1
w%es	write [TOS] into 16-bit register **es**; pop 1
w%fs	write [TOS] into 16-bit register **fs**; pop 1
w%gs	write [TOS] into 16-bit register **gs**; pop 1
w%err	write [TOS] into the error number pseudo-register; pop 1
w%trap	write [TOS] into the trap number pseudo-register; pop 1
w%ax	write [TOS] into 16-bit register **ax**; pop 1
w%bx	write [TOS] into 16-bit register **bx**; pop 1
w%cx	write [TOS] into 16-bit register **cx**; pop 1
w%dx	write [TOS] into 16-bit register **dx**; pop 1
w%si	write [TOS] into 16-bit register **si**; pop 1
w%di	write [TOS] into 16-bit register **di**; pop 1
w%bp	write [TOS] into 16-bit register **bp**; pop 1
w%sp	write [TOS] into 16-bit register **sp**; pop 1
w%ip	write [TOS] into 16-bit register **ip**; pop 1
w%fl	write [TOS] into 16-bit register **fl**; pop 1
w%al	write [TOS] into 8-bit register **al**; pop 1
w%ah	write [TOS] into 8-bit register **ah**; pop 1
w%bl	write [TOS] into 8-bit register **bl**; pop 1
w%bh	write [TOS] into 8-bit register **bh**; pop 1
w%cl	write [TOS] into 8-bit register **cl**; pop 1
w%ch	write [TOS] into 8-bit register **ch**; pop 1
w%dl	write [TOS] into 8-bit register **dl**; pop 1
w%dh	write [TOS] into 8-bit register **dh**; pop 1

Register Sets

The commands listed above can also be used to access specific register sets. Multiple sets of general registers may have been saved on the kernel stack (one for each interrupt, trap, and so on.). For more information see "Printing Kernel Stack Traces."

Register sets are numbered from 0 to 19, with 0 being the current (most recent) set. By default, the general-register commands use register set 0, but you can override this with a *register-set suffix:*

/rs#	register set number #

Note that by combining suffixes, you can access any register of any process. For example, you can get the **eax** register from process 5's register set 1 by typing:

```
%eax/u5rs1
```

to push the contents of that register (**%eax**) in register set 1 (**/rs1**) of user process 5 (**/u5**).

CPU Control Registers

In addition to the general registers, you can examine the values of CPU control registers with these commands:

`cr0`	push the contents of register **cr0**
`cr2`	push the contents of register **cr2**
`cr3`	push the contents of register **cr3**

CREATING DEBUGGER VARIABLES

KDB allows you to create named variables that are stored in the debugger and hold debugger values (numbers or strings). Two KDB commands apply to variables:

= *variable*	store [TOS] in [variable]; pop 1
vars	show values of debugger variables

= variable

This command assigns a value to a debugger variable. For example:

```
5 = abc
```

creates the variable **abc** if it does not exist, and sets the variable equal to 5. Now whenever you use the variable name, its value is pushed onto the stack. For example:

```
abc abc + 2 - p
```

(5 + 5 - 2) will yield **8**.

Note that variable names share the same namespace as debugger macros and kernel global symbols.

vars To look at all the existing variables, use the **vars** command. Variables are shown in the following format:

name = *value*

The **vars** command also lists macros, in this format:

name **::** *value*

SETTING BREAKPOINTS

Set and modify breakpoints with these commands:

`B`	set breakpoint #[TOS] at address [TOS-1]; pop 2, or set breakpoint #[TOS] at address [TOS-2] with command string [TOS-1]; pop 3
`b`	set first free breakpoint address [TOS]; pop 1, or set first free breakpoint at address [TOS-1] with command string [TOS]; pop 2

brkoff	disable breakpoint #[TOS]; pop 1
brkon	re-enable breakpoint #[TOS]; pop 1
brksoff	disable all breakpoints
brkson	re-enable all (disabled) breakpoints
trace	set breakpoint #[TOS] trace count to [TOS-1]; pop 2
clrbrk	clear breakpoint #[TOS]; pop 1
clrbrks	clear all breakpoints
curbrk	push the current breakpoint number, or -1 if not entered from a breakpoint
?brk	show current breakpoint settings

You can have up to 20 breakpoints, numbered 0 through 19, set at one time.

B and b The **B** command lets you set specific breakpoints, while the **b** command automatically picks the first un-set breakpoint.

This example sets breakpoint 3 at a specific address:

```
0xD0125098 3 B
```

Normally, you'll just set a breakpoint at a certain address. For example:

```
read b
```

This sets an instruction breakpoint at the beginning of the kernel **read** routine, using the next available breakpoint number. When the specified address is executed (after exiting from the debugger), you enter the debugger again, with a message indicating which breakpoint was triggered.

Debugger command strings can be added to the breakpoint commands. Enter a quoted string of commands after the address:

```
read "stack" b
```

which is used as a series of debugger commands that are executed when the breakpoint is triggered. If there are several items in the string, separate them with spaces:

```
ie6unitdata_req "300 r/bio p" b
```

After these commands are executed, you are prompted for debugger commands, as usual, unless the **q** (quit) command is executed in the command string.

You can append breakpoint-type suffixes to the breakpoint commands (**B** and **b**). By default, breakpoints are "instruction" breakpoints, which trigger when the specified address is executed. The suffixes cause breakpoints to trigger on data accesses instead. The breakpoint-type suffixes are:

`/a`	data access breakpoint
`/m`	data modify breakpoint
`/i`	instruction execution breakpoint—this is the default

With access and modify breakpoints, you can also use operand-size suffixes to control the size of the address range that will trigger the breakpoint. The default is **/l** (4 bytes); you can also use **/w** (word) and **/b** (byte). (See the earlier discussion of suffixes under "Reading and Writing to Memory" for more information.)

brkoff and brkon
These commands let you temporarily disable and re-enable a breakpoint, instead of clearing it with **clrbrk** and then re-entering it later. This is especially handy for breakpoints with command strings.

trace This command sets a trace count for a breakpoint. This causes the debugger to just print a message and decrement the count when the breakpoint is triggered, instead of entering the debugger, until the count reaches zero. Commands attached to the breakpoint are not executed.

?brk Use this command to determine the current breakpoint settings. Each set breakpoint is displayed, with (1) the breakpoint number, the address (both (2) in hex and (3) symbolic), (4) the current state, and (5) the type:

```
0: 0xD003907C(read) ON /i
1       2         3  4  5
```

The possible states are:

ON	set and enabled
DISABLED	set, but currently disabled
OFF	un-set (these breakpoints are not displayed by **?brk**)

The possible types (in this example **/i**) are the same as the breakpoint-type suffixes described earlier.

If a breakpoint has a non-zero trace count, that is displayed after the breakpoint state. If a breakpoint has a command string, it is displayed at the end of the line. For example, with a count of 5 and a **stack** command, the above breakpoint would display as:

```
0: 0xD003907C(read) ON  0x5 /i "stack"
```

SINGLE-STEPPING THROUGH INSTRUCTIONS

You can use these commands for single-stepping:

s	single step 1 instruction
ss	single step [TOS] instructions; pop 1
S	single step 1 instruction (passing calls)
SS	single step [TOS] instructions (passing calls); pop 1

s and **ss** single-step all instructions. **S** and **SS** single-step all instructions except call instructions. They don't step down into the called routine, but instead skip ahead to the return from the call, treating the whole subroutine sequence as a single instruction.

EXAMINING KERNEL DATA STRUCTURES

KDB provides commands for looking at certain kernel structures:

ps	show process information
sleeping	show list of sleeping processes
pinode	print s5 inode at address [TOS]; pop 1
puinode	print ufs inode at address [TOS]; pop 1
pprnode	print /proc inode at address [TOS]; pop 1
psnode	print snode at address [TOS]; pop 1
pvfs	print vfs struct at address [TOS]; pop 1
pvnode	print vnode at address [TOS]; pop 1

The **sleeping** command shows sleeping processes with their process table slot numbers and the channels on which they are waiting. This information can be used with the **call** and **pstack** commands.

The **ps** command shows information about each active process in the system. This information includes process IDs, flags, states, and command names. The current process is marked with an asterisk (*) after its state code.

PRINTING KERNEL STACK TRACES

KDB provides the following commands to look at kernel stack traces:

stack	kernel stack trace for the current process
pstack	kernel stack trace for process [TOS]; pop 1
stackargs	set max # arguments in stack trace to [TOS]; pop 1
stackdump	show contents of kernel stack in hex

Note that the argument to **pstack** can be specified either as a process table slot number, the address of the process structure, or **-1** for the current process. (**-1 pstack** is equivalent to the **stack** command.)

The output of **stack** and **pstack** have the same format. A typical stack trace (for the current process, entered via CTRL-ALT-d) looks like this:

```
DEBUGGER ENTERED FROM USER REQUEST
 kdcksysrq(D101FD40 D00DE624 81)...........ebp:E0000D30  ret:D008F592
*kdintr+0x186(1 0).........................ebp:E0000D74  ret:D0011A3A
INTERRUPT 0x1 from 158:D001218A (ebp:E0000D84)
  eax:      8 ebx:       0 ecx:FFFFFFFF edx:        8 efl: 246 ds:160
  esi:D00EDDD0 edi:D106BC00 esp:E0000DC8 ebp:E0000DE0 regset:0 es:160
 idle(0 D00EDDD0 D106BC00)................(ebp:E0000DC4) ret:D006F11F
 pswtch(D002464C 0 D00F9090)...............ebp:E0000DE0  ret:D00122ED
 swtch(0 D00F9090 D101A160)...............(ebp:E0000DE4) ret:D002464C
 sleep(D0038B0C 14 D00BCA3C)...............ebp:E0000DFC  ret:D0038D6F
 fsflush(0 E0000002 E0000002)..............ebp:E0000E38  ret:D001E24B
 main+0x5FB()..............................ebp:E0000E70
```

The stack trace shows a history of which routine called which other routine, up until the point the debugger was entered (or in the case of a non-current process, until the process was context-switched out).

The most-recently-entered routine is shown on the first line. In the example, the debugger was entered from **kdcksysrq**, which, in turn, was called by **kdintr**; **idle** was called from **pswtch**, and so on. The stack trace ends at the point the kernel was entered from user mode. In the case of a system process (as shown here) where there is no user mode, the stack trace ends at the call from **main**.

Routine Trace Format

The trace for each routine has four parts: (1) its address, (2) the arguments passed to it, (3) the value of its **ebp** register, and (4) its return address. For example:

```
fsflush(0 E0000002 E0000002)............ebp:E0000E38  ret:D001E24B
   1    ----------2---------                ------3-----  ------4-----
```

Address

The address that was called usually appears in symbolic form. A routine name may also include:

An offset (a plus sign (`+`) and a hex number): `*kdintr+0x186`

The offset may mean that the actual address called was somewhere past the start of the indicated routine. This will most likely happen if a subroutine was declared "static." Since the debugger only has access to global symbols, it finds the nearest preceding global symbol.

The offset may also mean that the exact address called cannot be determined. The address displayed in this case is the return address into this routine from the routine it called. This will most likely happen if this routine was called indirectly via a function pointer.

An asterisk (`*`): `*kdintr+0x186`

This means the routine was called indirectly. There is insufficient information in the stack format to be 100% sure of the correctness of indirect call traces.

A tilde (~)

This is used where there is some uncertainty in the stack trace that did not arise from indirect calls.

Whenever you see an asterisk or a tilde in a stack trace, there is a small chance that some part of the stack trace from that point on is incorrect.

Arguments

The arguments passed to the routine appear as a list of hex numbers, enclosed in parentheses. Since the actual number of arguments passed cannot be determined, KDB assumes that each routine has no more than a certain maximum number of arguments. The default is three, but you can change it with the **`stackargs`** command. If a routine actually has:

Fewer arguments than displayed:

Only the first ones are real. In rare cases when the debugger can deduce that a routine could not have been called with the maximum number of arguments (because there isn't enough room on the stack), it displays only the maximum possible number of arguments. In the above stack trace, the call to **`kdintr`** is shown with only two arguments `(1 0)`.

More arguments than displayed:

Increase the number with **`stackargs`** and then display the stack trace again, or dump out a portion of the stack directly in order to see all the arguments (continue to the next section for details).

`ebp` register

The value of the **`ebp`** register inside the routine is shown as a hex number following **`ebp:`**. This value can be used as a "frame pointer" to access arguments and local variables for the routine. The following diagram illustrates the stack layout.

```
               |          . . .           |
               +--------------------------+
[EBP] + 0xC    | argument 2               |
               +--------------------------+
[EBP] + 8      | argument 1               |
               +--------------------------+
[EBP] + 4      | return address           |
               +--------------------------+
[EBP] --->     | saved EBP from caller    |
               +--------------------------+
[EBP] - 4      | local or saved register  |
               +--------------------------+
[EBP] - 8      | local or saved register  |
               +--------------------------+
               |          . . .           |
```

For example, if you want to see all the arguments to a routine that takes five arguments, find its **ebp** value from the stack trace — **0xE0000E0C**, for example — and enter these commands:

```
0xE0000E0C 8 + 5 4 * dump
```

or, more succinctly:

```
0xE0000E14 14 dump
```

Any **ebp** value in parentheses is a computed value (see the **ebp** values for **idle** and **switch** in the example). In these cases, due to code optimization or partial execution, the **ebp** value has not been set up for one or more routines. KDB computes the value **ebp** ought to have had and displays it in parentheses.

Return address

This is the address this routine returns to in its caller. It is shown as a hex number following **ret:**.

Trap Frames

In addition to lines for each routine, stack traces will often include "trap frames" created when an event causes suspension of current processing, saving all register values on the stack. Typical events are interrupts, hardware exceptions, and system calls. Trap frames are three lines each, starting with an upper-case, non-indented keyword (like INTERRUPT in the example). The next two lines contain the values of the registers at the time the event occurred. The first line of a trap frame is in one of these formats:

```
INTERRUPT 0x1 from 158:D001218A (ebp:E0000D84)
TRAP 0x1(err 0x0)from 158:D001218A (ebp:E0000D94,ss:esp:1F:80468E8)
SYSTEM CALL from 158:D001218A (ebp: E0000D94, ss:esp: 1F:80468E8)
SIGNAL RETURN from 158:D001218A (ebp: E0000D94, ss:esp: 1F:80468E8)
```

These represent interrupts, hardware exception traps, system calls, and returns from old-style signal handlers, respectively. The number after **INTERRUPT** is the interrupt vector number (IRQ). The number after **TRAP** is the hardware exception number; the most common are **0x1** for breakpoint traps and **0xE** for page faults.

The colon-separated numbers after the word **from** are the segment and offset (**cs** and **eip**) at the time the event occurred. The values in parentheses show the **ebp** value for the beginning of the trap frame, and the user stack pointer segment and offset at the time the event occurred. The user stack information is only displayed if the trap frame is for an entry into the kernel from user mode.

RESETTING THE NUMERIC BASE

If you don't start numbers with "0o" (for octal) or "0x" (for hex), KDB assumes they are in the default numeric base. Initially, the defaults for both input and output are set to 16 (hex), but you can use these commands to change them:

ibase	set default input base to [TOS]; pop 1
ibinary	set default input base to 2
ioctal	set default input base to 8
idecimal	set default input base to 10
ihex	set default input base to 16
obase	set output base to [TOS]; pop 1
ooctal	set output base to 8
odecimal	set output base to 10
ohex	set output base to 16

CONVERTING ADDRESS SPACES

Use these commands to convert a virtual address to a physical address:

kvtop	convert kernel virtual address [TOS] to physical
uvtop	convert user proc #[TOS] address [TOS-1] to physical; pop 1

PERFORMING CONDITIONAL EXECUTION

KDB provides two commands for conditional execution:

then	if [TOS] = 0, skip to **endif**; pop 1
endif	end scope of **then** command

In other words, a sequence like:

```
<condition> then <commands> endif
```

executes **<commands>** if and only if the **<condition>** is true (non-zero).

These are mostly useful for macros and breakpoint command strings. For example, imagine you wish to set a breakpoint for when the function **inb** is called with **2E** as its first argument. Use the following command:

```
inb "%esp 4 + r 2E != then q" b
```

This says to set a breakpoint at **inb**, but enter the debugger only if the contents of **(%esp+4)** are equal to **2E**. This works because **esp** points to the return address on the stack, and the longword after that is the first argument. For the second argument, you would add 8 instead of 4 (see the "Printing Kernel Stack Traces" section for details of the stack layout).

If you do a **?brk** command, the display for that breakpoint includes the string of debugger commands:

```
0: 0xD003907C(inb) ON  /i "%esp 4 + r 2E != then q"
```

CALLING A KERNEL FUNCTION

Use this command to call an arbitrary kernel function:

call call the function at address [TOS-1] with [TOS] arguments, given by [TOS-([TOS]+1)], ... [TOS-2]; pop [TOS]+2

To call **psignal**(3) with two arguments, the current process and **9**, type:

```
curproc r 9 psignal 2 call
```

curproc r gives the value of the current process, the first argument, and **9** is the second argument. **psignal** is converted into the address at which that function can be called, and **2** specifies the number of arguments to pass to **psignal**(3).

PERFORMING A SYSTEM DUMP

This command causes a system dump and forces a reboot:

sysdump cause a system dump

All of memory and the current state is dumped to the dump partition on the disk, so you can use **crash**(1M) to do a postmortem.

MISCELLANEOUS COMMANDS

Some miscellaneous KDB commands are:

findsym	print kernel symbol with address closest to [TOS]; pop 1
dis	disassemble [TOS] instructions starting at address [TOS-1]; pop 2
nonverbose	turn verbose mode off
verbose	turn verbose mode on
newdebug	switch to another debugger on next debugger entry
help	print a help message
?	print a help message (same as **help**)
cmds	print a list of all debugger commands

WRITING MACROS

KDB provides the ability to assign a string of commands to a single new command name, called a macro. When a debugging task involves repeating the same set of commands many times (possibly doing other things in between), it is easier to define a macro and use it in place of the whole set of commands.

These commands are used for macros:

`::` *macro*	`define [macro] as command string [TOS]; pop 1`
`P`	`print [TOS] in raw form; pop 1`
`PP`	`print [TOS] values in raw form,` `from [TOS-[TOS]], ... [TOS-1]; pop [TOS]+1`
`vars`	`show values of debugger macros and variables`

:: macro

Use this command to define macros. For example:

```
"curproc r 16 - p" :: newaddr
```

Note that macro names share the same namespace as debugger variables and kernel global symbols.

P and **PP**

These commands are provided to aid in writing macros. **P** and **PP** print values in raw form, without the embellishments provided by the **p** command, such as quotes around strings and automatic newlines after each value. This allows complete control over formatting. For example, the input:

```
"The value of curproc is " curproc r ".\n" 3 PP
```

might produce the output:

```
The value of curproc is 0xD1011E80.
```

To put something like this into a macro means putting strings inside strings, so you'll have to escape the inner quotes:

```
"\"The value of curproc is \" curproc r \".\n\" 3 PP" :: pcurproc
```

vars Use this command to show the macro definitions. Macros are shown in this format:

name **::** *value*

Note that the **vars** command also shows the values of variables, in this format:

name = *value*

EXECUTING DEBUGGER COMMANDS AT BOOT TIME

KDB allows you to specify an arbitrary command sequence to be executed at boot time, when the system is coming up (specifically, from **main()** at the time of the **io_start** routines, or as early as just before the mlsetup() routine). You can do this by writing the commands into the files **$ROOT/etc/conf/cf.d/kdb.rc** and/or **$ROOT/etc/conf/cf.d/kdb.early**, then rebuilding the kernel with **idbuild**. The file **kdb.rc** contains commands to be executed after initialization; **kdb.early** is used for commands to be executed before initialization is complete, a capability useful for debugging problems early in system startup. Note, however, that KDB breakpoint and single-step commands cannot be used with **kdb.early**, because the capabilities are not yet available in the system at that point in the startup process. All other KDB commands are available, though.

Instead of rebuilding the kernel with **idbuild**, you can modify the KDB information in an already-built kernel by typing the command:

```
unixsyms -i /etc/conf/cf.d/kdb.rc /unix
```

or

```
unixsyms -e /etc/conf/cf.d/kdb.early /unix
```

At boot time, after the (possibly blank) strings in **kdb.rc** and **kdb.early** are executed, the system enters KDB at the **kdb>>** prompt, unless a **q** command was executed as part of the string — just like conditional breakpoints. (A non-existent or zero-length **kdb.rc** or **kdb.early** file acts as a single **q** command, so KDB is not entered.)

If using the `-i` option, the KDB string is executed after the init routines, and provides full-featured KDB command access. The `-e` option tells KDB to execute the string at an early access point in the system initialization process. However, as mentioned previously, because the string is executed before KDB is fully initialized, breakpoint and single-step commands are disabled; although all other KDB commands are available. You can use either or both of the `-i` and the `-e` options.

USING A SERIAL TERMINAL

KDB can be used from a serial terminal as well as the console. This is particularly useful if you are trying to debug a scenario that involves graphics or multiple virtual terminals on the console.

Before you attempt to use the debugger from a serial terminal, make sure there is a **getty** or **ttymon** running on it. It may be either logged in or waiting at the login prompt. This ensures that the baud rate and other parameters are properly set.

You can switch from the console to a terminal, and vice-versa, with the **newterm** command. This immediately switches you to the new terminal. The debugger continues to use this terminal until you give it the **newterm** command again, even if you exit and re-enter KDB.

The **newterm** command does not take an argument. On a 386, the serial terminal is assumed to be `tty00`, the terminal on the com1 port. You can change the device used by editing the **/etc/conf/pack.d/kdb-util/space.c** file, rebuilding the kernel and rebooting. If the terminal is attached to the com2 port, set the device to `tty01` by changing all occurrences of **asyputchar** and **asygetchar** to **asyputchar2** and **asygetchar2**, respectively, and changing the minor number of the device from 0 to 1. The first lines of 386-specific code should look like this:

```
#ifdef AT386
int asyputchar2(), asygetchar2();
static struct conssw asysw = {
        asyputchar2,    1,      asygetchar2
};
#endif
```

To use terminals on both com1 and com2 ports, you can set up **newterm** to cycle from the console to `tty00` to `tty01` and back to the console. Edit all the 386-specific code in the **space.c** file to look like this:

```
#ifdef AT386
int asyputchar(), asygetchar();
int asyputchar2(), asygetchar2();
static struct conssw asysw = {
        asyputchar,     0,      asygetchar
};
static struct conssw asysw2 = {
        asyputchar2,    1,      asygetchar2
};
#endif
        .
        .
        .
```

```
#ifdef AT386
                &asysw,
                &asysw2,
#endif
```

Once you exit from KDB, you can invoke it again from either the console or a serial terminal. Use the **kdb** command to invoke the debugger from a terminal; CTRL-ALT-d only works from the console. Regardless of where you invoke KDB, its I/O appears where you directed it during the last KDB session.

ENTERING THE DEBUGGER FROM A DRIVER

If you are debugging a device driver or another part of the kernel, you can directly invoke the kernel debugger by including this code in your driver:

```
#include <sys/xdebug.h>
(*cdebugger) (DR_OTHER, NO_FRAME);
```

DR_OTHER tells the debugger that the reason for entering is "other." See **sys/xdebug.h** for a list of other reason codes.

Note that this mechanism cannot be used for debugging early kernel startup code or driver **init** routines, since the debugger cannot be used until its **init** routine (**kdb_init**) has been called.

DISABLING THE CTRL-ALT-d SEQUENCE

As a security feature, KDB can only be called from the console using CTRL-ALT-d if the **kdb_security** flag was set to 0 when the kernel was built. To disable the CTRL-ALT-d key sequence, reset the **kdb_security** flag by using **/etc/conf/bin/idtune** to change the **KDBSECURITY** tunable to 1. Note that the flag setting does not affect the **kdb** command.

COMMAND SUMMARY

+	compute [TOS-1] + [TOS]; pop 2; push result
-	compute [TOS-1] - [TOS]; pop 2; push result
*	compute [TOS-1] * [TOS]; pop 2; push result
/	compute [TOS-1] / [TOS]; pop 2; push result
%	compute [TOS-1] % [TOS]; pop 2; push result
>>	compute [TOS-1] >> [TOS]; pop 2; push result
<<	compute [TOS-1] << [TOS]; pop 2; push result
<	compute [TOS-1] < [TOS]; pop 2; push result
>	compute [TOS-1] > [TOS]; pop 2; push result
==	compute [TOS-1] == [TOS]; pop 2; push result
!=	compute [TOS-1] != [TOS]; pop 2; push result
&	compute [TOS-1] & [TOS]; pop 2; push result
|	compute [TOS-1] | [TOS]; pop 2; push result
^	compute [TOS-1] ^ [TOS]; pop 2; push result
&&	compute [TOS-1] && [TOS]; pop 2; push result
||	compute [TOS-1] || [TOS]; pop 2; push result
!	replace [TOS] with ![TOS]
++	replace [TOS] with [TOS] + 1

`--`	replace [TOS] with [TOS] - 1
`%eax`	push the contents of 32-bit register **eax**
`%ebx`	push the contents of 32-bit register **ebx**
`%ecx`	push the contents of 32-bit register **ecx**
`%edx`	push the contents of 32-bit register **edx**
`%esi`	push the contents of 32-bit register **esi**
`%edi`	push the contents of 32-bit register **edi**
`%ebp`	push the contents of 32-bit register **ebp**
`%esp`	push the contents of 32-bit register **esp**
`%eip`	push the contents of 32-bit register **eip**
`%efl`	push the contents of 32-bit register **efl**
`%cs`	push the contents of 16-bit register **cs**
`%ds`	push the contents of 16-bit register **ds**
`%es`	push the contents of 16-bit register **es**
`%fs`	push the contents of 16-bit register **fs**
`%gs`	push the contents of 16-bit register **gs**
`%err`	push the error number
`%trap`	push the trap number
`%ax`	push the contents of 16-bit register **ax**
`%bx`	push the contents of 16-bit register **bx**
`%cx`	push the contents of 16-bit register **cx**
`%dx`	push the contents of 16-bit register **dx**
`%si`	push the contents of 16-bit register **si**
`%di`	push the contents of 16-bit register **di**
`%bp`	push the contents of 16-bit register **bp**
`%sp`	push the contents of 16-bit register **sp**
`%ip`	push the contents of 16-bit register **ip**
`%fl`	push the contents of 16-bit register **fl**
`%al`	push the contents of 8-bit register **al**
`%ah`	push the contents of 8-bit register **ah**
`%bl`	push the contents of 8-bit register **bl**
`%bh`	push the contents of 8-bit register **bh**
`%cl`	push the contents of 8-bit register **cl**
`%ch`	push the contents of 8-bit register **ch**
`%dl`	push the contents of 8-bit register **dl**
`%dh`	push the contents of 8-bit register **dh**
`= variable`	store [TOS] in [variable]; pop 1
`:: macro`	define [macro] as command string [TOS]; pop 1
`?`	print a help message (same as **help**)
`?brk`	show current breakpoint settings
`B`	set breakpoint #[TOS] at address [TOS-1]; pop 2 -or- set brkpoint #[TOS] at address [TOS-2] w/command string [TOS-1]; pop 3
`b`	set 1st free breakpoint address [TOS]; pop 1 -or- set 1st free brkpoint at address [TOS-1] w/command string [TOS]; pop 2
`brkoff`	disable breakpoint #[TOS]; pop 1
`brkon`	re-enable breakpoint #[TOS]; pop 1

`brksoff`	disable all breakpoints
`brkson`	re-enable all (disabled) breakpoints
`call`	call the function at address [TOS-1] with [TOS] arguments, given by [TOS-([TOS]+1)], ... [TOS-2]; pop [TOS]+2
`clrbrk`	clear breakpoint #[TOS]; pop 1
`clrbrks`	clear all breakpoints
`clrstk`	pop all values
`cmds`	print a list of all debugger commands
`cr0`	push the contents of register **cr0**
`cr2`	push the contents of register **cr2**
`cr3`	push the contents of register **cr3**
`curbrk`	push the current breakpoint number, or -1 if not entered from a breakpoint
`dis`	disassemble [TOS] instructions starting at address [TOS-1]; pop 2
`dump`	show [TOS] bytes starting at virtual address [TOS-1]; pop 2
`dup`	push [TOS]
`endif`	end scope of **then** command
`findsym`	print kernel symbol with address closest to [TOS]; pop 1
`help`	print a help message
`ibase`	set default input base to [TOS]; pop 1
`ibinary`	set default input base to 2
`ioctal`	set default input base to 8
`idecimal`	set default input base to 10
`ihex`	set default input base to 16
`kvtop`	convert kernel virtual addr [TOS] to physical
`newterm`	alternate debugger I/O between console and tty00
`newdebug`	switch to another debugger on next debugger entry
`nonverbose`	turn verbose mode off
`obase`	set output base to [TOS]; pop 1
`odecimal`	set output base to 10
`ohex`	set output base to 16
`ooctal`	set output base to 8
`P`	print [TOS] in raw form; pop 1
`p`	print [TOS]
`PP`	print [TOS] values in raw form, from [TOS-[TOS]], ... [TOS-1]; pop [TOS]+1
`pinode`	print s5 inode at address [TOS]; pop 1
`pop`	pop 1 value
`pprnode`	print /proc inode at address [TOS]; pop 1
`psnode`	print snode at address [TOS]; pop 1
`ps`	show process information
`pstack`	kernel stack trace for process [TOS]; pop 1
`pvfs`	print vfs struct at address [TOS]; pop 1
`pvnode`	print vnode at address [TOS]; pop 1
`puinode`	print ufs inode at address [TOS]; pop 1
`q`	quit—exit from the debugger

`r`	replace [TOS] with the value at virtual address [TOS]
`S`	single step 1 instruction (passing calls)
`s`	single step 1 instruction
`sleeping`	show list of sleeping processes
`SS`	single step [TOS] instructions (passing calls); pop 1
`ss`	single step [TOS] instructions; pop 1
`stack`	kernel stack trace for the current process
`stackargs`	set max # arguments in stack trace to [TOS]; pop 1
`stackdump`	show contents of kernel stack in hex
`stk`	print all values on the stack
`sysdump`	cause a system dump
`then`	if [TOS] = 0, skip to **endif**; pop 1
`trace`	set breakpoint #[TOS] trace count to [TOS-1]; pop 2
`uvtop`	convert user process #[TOS] address [TOS-1] to physical; pop 1
`vars`	show values of debugger variables
`verbose`	turn verbose mode on
`w`	write [TOS-1] into virtual address [TOS]; pop 2
`w%eax`	write [TOS] into 32-bit register **eax**; pop 1
`w%ebx`	write [TOS] into 32-bit register **ebx**; pop 1
`w%ecx`	write [TOS] into 32-bit register **ecx**; pop 1
`w%edx`	write [TOS] into 32-bit register **edx**; pop 1
`w%esi`	write [TOS] into 32-bit register **esi**; pop 1
`w%edi`	write [TOS] into 32-bit register **edi**; pop 1
`w%ebp`	write [TOS] into 32-bit register **ebp**; pop 1
`w%esp`	write [TOS] into 32-bit register **esp**; pop 1
`w%eip`	write [TOS] into 32-bit register **eip**; pop 1
`w%efl`	write [TOS] into 32-bit register **efl**; pop 1
`w%cs`	write [TOS] into 16-bit register **cs**; pop 1
`w%ds`	write [TOS] into 16-bit register **ds**; pop 1
`w%es`	write [TOS] into 16-bit register **es**; pop 1
`w%fs`	write [TOS] into 16-bit register **fs**; pop 1
`w%gs`	write [TOS] into 16-bit register **gs**; pop 1
`w%err`	write [TOS] into the error number pseudo-register; pop 1
`w%trap`	write [TOS] into the trap number pseudo-register; pop 1
`w%ax`	write [TOS] into 16-bit register **ax**; pop 1
`w%bx`	write [TOS] into 16-bit register **bx**; pop 1
`w%cx`	write [TOS] into 16-bit register **cx**; pop 1
`w%dx`	write [TOS] into 16-bit register **dx**; pop 1
`w%si`	write [TOS] into 16-bit register **si**; pop 1
`w%di`	write [TOS] into 16-bit register **di**; pop 1
`w%bp`	write [TOS] into 16-bit register **bp**; pop 1
`w%sp`	write [TOS] into 16-bit register **sp**; pop 1
`w%ip`	write [TOS] into 16-bit register **ip**; pop 1
`w%fl`	write [TOS] into 16-bit register **fl**; pop 1
`w%al`	write [TOS] into 8-bit register **al**; pop 1
`w%ah`	write [TOS] into 8-bit register **ah**; pop 1

`w%bl`	write [TOS] into 8-bit register **bl**; pop 1
`w%bh`	write [TOS] into 8-bit register **bh**; pop 1
`w%cl`	write [TOS] into 8-bit register **cl**; pop 1
`w%ch`	write [TOS] into 8-bit register **ch**; pop 1
`w%dl`	write [TOS] into 8-bit register **dl**; pop 1
`w%dh`	write [TOS] into 8-bit register **dh**; pop 1

Command Suffixes

Operand size

`/b`	byte
`/w`	word (2 bytes)
`/l`	long (4 bytes)—this is the default

Address space

`/k`	kernel virtual—this is the default
`/p`	physical
`/io`	I/O port
`/u#`	user process number **#** virtual

Register set

`/rs#`	register set number **#**

Breakpoint type

`/a`	data access breakpoint
`/m`	data modify breakpoint
`/i`	instruction execution breakpoint—this is the default

Old Commands

These commands from previous versions are supported as aliases to new commands:

Old Command	New Equivalent
`r1`	r/b
`r2`	r/w
`r4`	r/l
`w1`	w/b
`w2`	w/w
`w4`	w/l
`rp1`	r/b/p
`rp2`	r/w/p
`rp4`	r/l/p
`wp1`	w/b/p
`wp2`	w/w/p
`wp4`	w/l/p
`rio1`	r/b/io
`rio2`	r/w/io
`rio4`	r/l/io

`wio1`	w/b/io
`wio2`	w/w/io
`wio4`	w/l/io
`.trap`	%trap
`trc0`	0 trace
`trc1`	1 trace
`trc2`	2 trace
`trc3`	3 trace
`db?`	?brk

These old commands are supported:

`.i`	push breakpoint type: instruction
`.a`	push breakpoint type: access byte
`.m`	push breakpoint type: modify byte
`.aw`	push breakpoint type: access word
`.mw`	push breakpoint type: modify word
`.al`	push breakpoint type: access long
`.ml`	push breakpoint type: modify long
`.clr`	push breakpoint type: clear breakpoint
`brk0`	set breakpoint 0 to type [TOS] at address [TOS-1]; pop 2
`brk1`	set breakpoint 1 to type [TOS] at address [TOS-1]; pop 2
`brk2`	set breakpoint 2 to type [TOS] at address [TOS-1]; pop 2
`brk3`	set breakpoint 3 to type [TOS] at address [TOS-1]; pop 2

REFERENCES

`crash`(1M), `dc`(1)

NAME

kbdcomp – compile code set and keyboard map tables

SYNOPSIS

kbdcomp [-vrR] [-o *outfile***] [***infile***]**

DESCRIPTION

The **kbdcomp** command compiles tables for use with the **iconv** utility and with the **kbd** [see **kbd**(7)] STREAMS module, a programmable string-translation module. Both the **iconv** utility and the **kbd** STREAMS module have two separate functions, each of which may be used alone or in combination.

The lookup function is that of performing simple substitution of bytes in an input stream. This function is based on a simple 256-entry lookup table (as there are 256 possible bit combinations for a byte). As input is received, each byte is looked up in the translation table, and the table value for that byte is substituted in place of the original byte. The process is quick, and can be performed on each STREAMS message with no message copying or duplication.

The second function, mapping, provides searching for occurrences of specified strings of bytes (or individual bytes) in an input stream, and substituting other strings (or bytes) for them as they are recognized. There are three kinds of mapping that are differentiated by the relationship between the number of bytes in the input and the number of bytes in the output. One to many mapping is substituting many bytes for a given byte in the input. Many to one mapping is substituting many bytes for a given input byte. Many to many mapping includes the other two types as a proper subset, but also includes substitution of many bytes in the input with many bytes of output. Both **iconv** and **kbd** can perform all three types of mapping. The lookup function (that is, one to one mapping) is a common special case useful enough to be included separately. By using combinations of both lookup and mapping instead of either one alone, a larger class of input translation and conversion problems can be solved.

During operation, processing occurs in two major passes: the lookup table pass always precedes string mapping. The string mapping procedure is non-recursive for a given table and there is no feedback mechanism (that is, input is scanned in order received and output is not re-scanned for occurrences of recognizable input strings). As an example of mapping, suppose you want to translate all occurrences of the string **this** in an input stream into the string **there**. Both utility and module recognize and buffer occurrences of the string **th** (as each byte is received); if the following character is **i**, it will also be buffered, but if **x** is then received, a mismatch is recognized and no translation occurs. Assuming **thi** has been buffered, if the next character seen is **s**, a match is recognized, the buffer containing **this** is discarded, and the string **there** replaces it.

Both input and output strings can be of any non-zero length (see below for limitations). Each string to be recognized and translated must be unique, and no complete input string may constitute the leading substring of any other (for example, one may not define **abc** and **ab** simultaneously, but may so define **abc**, **abd**, and **abxy**).

Given a filename (or standard input if no name is supplied), **kbdcomp** will compile tables into the output file specified by the **-o** option. If the **-o** option is not supplied, output is to the file **kbd.out**.

The **-v** option causes parsing and verification, that is, no output file is produced. If no error messages are printed, then the input file is syntactically correct. The **-r** option causes the compiler to check for and report on byte values that cannot be generated in a table (see the description below). The option **-R** is equivalent to the option **-r** but it tries to print printable characters as themselves rather than in octal format.

Input Language

Source files for **kbdcomp** are a series of table declarations. Within each table declaration there are a number of definitions and functions. A table declaration can be the **map**, **link**, or **extern** form:

> **map** *type* (*name*) { *expressions* }
>
> **link** (*string*)
>
> **extern** (*string*)

First the **map** form is described, then the **link** and **extern** forms. The *name* of a **map** must be a simple token not containing any colons, commas, quotes, or spaces. (For our purposes, a simple token is a sequence of alphabetic or numeric characters with no embedded punctuation, white space, or special symbols.) The *type* field is an optional field that may be either of the keywords **full** or **sparse**. If omitted, the type defaults to **sparse**. The effect of this field is described in more detail below. The expressions contained in the **map** declaration are one of the following forms. Reserved keywords are printed in **constant width**, variables in *italics*:

> **keylist** (*string string*)
> **define** (*word value*)
> *word* (*extension result*)
> **string** (*word word*)
> **strlist** (*string string*)
> **error** (*string*)
> **timed**

The **keylist** form is for defining lookup table entries while the remaining forms are the separate string functions.

The definition form (**define**) allows a mnemonic word (the first argument) to be associated with a string (the second argument). It is useful for replacing complicated sequences (for example, those containing special symbols or control characters) with mnemonic words to facilitate the design and readability of tables.

Using the *word* form (where *word* must be a previously defined sequence) in a way similar to a **C** function call results in the *value* of *word* being concatenated with *extension*; when the combination is recognized, it is mapped to *result*. The *value* may be a string of characters or a single byte. The following is an illustration (not intended to be complete):

```
map (some_accents) {
        define(acute '\047')
        define(grave '`' )
        acute(a '\341')         # same as string("\047a" "\341")
        grave(a '\340')
        # ...et cetera...
        keylist("zyZY" "yzYZ")
    }
```

This **map** defines the single quote and reverse quote keys as dead-keys that when followed by **a** produce a character from the ISO 8859-1 code set. It is not necessary for the definition, extension, or result to be a single byte; they can be arbitrary strings.

Strings in definitions and arguments can be entered between double quotes or without the quotes. Byte constants can be entered without quotes or between single quotes. Double quotes are required when a string contains parentheses, spaces, tab characters, or other special symbols. The language makes no distinction between byte constants and string constants; both are treated as null-terminated strings. You can choose to use a one-character string or a byte constant; it is your preference. Most quoting conventions of C are recognized, except that octal constants must be three digits. Octal constants may be used in strings, also. In the example above, the arguments to **keylist** need not be quoted, since they contain no special symbols. The following example shows where strings must be quoted:

```
string(abc "two words")     # literal space
keylist("[{}]" "(())")      # brackets/parentheses
define(esc_seq "\033\t(")   # tab and parenthesis
define(space ' ')           # literal space
string(abc "keylist")       # keyword used as argument
```

Comments in files (inside or outside of map declarations) may be entered in the same way as for **sh**(1); that is, after a **#** at the end of a line, or on a line beginning with **#**, as shown in the above examples.

The **keylist** form allows single bytes to be mapped to other single bytes; it defines actions that are treated in the lookup table (that is, are performed before mapping). Any byte value that is not explicitly changed by being included in a **keylist** form will be unchanged; if no **keylist** forms appear in a map definition, then **kbdcomp** does not generate a lookup table for the map, and the lookup phase is skipped during module operation. Each byte in the first string argument to **keylist** is mapped to the byte at the same position in the second string argument. That is, given two strings X and Y as arguments: X_i maps to Y_i, X_j maps to Y_j, and so forth. The two arguments must, after evaluation, be found to contain the same number of bytes.

The **string** form has a function similar to mnemonic forms defined with **define** and may be used for any type of many to many mapping. The first argument to **string** is mapped to the second argument (see the comment in the sample map above).

Mappings using both **keylist** and **string** or any **define** forms may be combined: if **i** is mapped to **a** with a **keylist** form, and **a** is used in the sequence **`a**, then when the user types **`i**, the sequence **`a** is seen by the string mapping process (because lookup is done first) and translated accordingly.

The **keylist** form is intended mainly for use in simple keyboard re-arrangement and case-conversion applications; **string** is for one to many mapping or for isolated instances of many to many mapping; the **define** form and words defined with it are intended for more general use in groups of related sequences. Sometimes, while a one to one mapping with **keylist** may be an obvious choice, the same effect may be achieved with **string** forms to avoid having a contradictory mapping. For example, suppose one wants, simultaneously, to translate **x** into **y** and **y** into **abc**. If **x** is mapped to **y** via a **keylist** form and **y** is mapped to **abc** via a **string** form, then it may be impossible to obtain **y** itself (unless defined in another sequence), even though that was not the intention—the intention was to obtain **y** whenever the user enters **x**. This is a contradictory mapping:

```
keylist(x y)
string(y abc)     # "y" itself cannot be generated
```

There are cases where the intention is that **y** not be generated, but most often the intention is to generate it. This problem (a common one in code set mapping) can be solved by using a **string** form to map **x** to **y** initially rather than using a **keylist** form. This allows both **y** and **abc** to be generated:

```
string(x y)
string(y abc)
```

Entering a large number of one to one mappings with **string** can be somewhat tedious. To make things easier, the **strlist** form is provided. The two string arguments to **strlist** are interpreted similar to arguments to the **keylist** form (that is, they are one to one mappings), except that they are processed as string mappings rather than with the lookup table. In the following example, the first three **string** definitions can be reduced to the **strlist** form that follows:

```
string(a b)
string(c d)
string(e f)

strlist(ace bdf)
```

It is important to recognize the difference between **string** and **strlist**. With **string**, the two arguments are a single mapping definition (that can be of any type) whereas with **strlist**, one or more one to one string mappings are defined simultaneously. A set of mappings defined with a combination of **string** and **strlist** do not exhibit the same type of incompatibility described above between **keylist** and **string**.

Some further aspects of module processing can now be presented. When a partial match in an input sequence is detected during string processing, it is buffered. If at some point the match no longer succeeds, the first byte of the matched buffer is normally sent to the neighboring module. The rest of the input is left in the buffer and scanned again to see if it matches the beginning of another sequence. The **error** entry allows you to send a string (or byte) constant (called a fallback character) instead of the byte that began the previous sequence; this is particularly useful in code set mapping and conversion applications where the character that failed to be translated might be one that does not occur or has some other meaning in the target code set. The following (somewhat contrived) example illustrates use of the **error** form:

```
# turn arrow keys into vi commands
map (vi_map) {
      string("\033[A" k) # up
      string("\033[B" j) # down
      error("!")
}
```

Given input of the *escape* character followed by `[A` or `[B`, a single character (`j` or `k`) is generated. If presented with the sequence *escape*-`[Q`, the module will produce the sequence `![Q`. The error string `!` replaces *escape* because the sequence failed to match when `Q` was received. The remaining characters are re-scanned, and neither `[` nor `Q` is found to begin a recognized sequence.

One to one mapping with strings or other defined forms (rather than via a **keylist** lookup table) is generally done with a linear search operation when looking for bytes that begin sequences. However, if the table is specified as a **full** table, it is initially indexed rather than searched linearly, and thus processed much more quickly when there are a large number of entries. This should be kept in mind in code set mapping applications where nearly all characters are mapped, and many (or most) are one to one mappings. If only a few characters are mapped with string functions, you must decide whether to trade a small gain in processing speed for the space needed to store the index if a table is made **full**.

The **link** form, is used to produce a composite table. A composite table is really a form of linkage that allows several tables to be used together in sequence as if the sequence were a single table. The string argument to **link** is of the following form:

`composite:component`*1*`,component`*2*`,component`*n*

The target composite name is followed by a colon, and the ordered component list is comma-separated. If the string argument contains spaces or special characters, it must be quoted. (This string is not interpreted by **kbdcomp**, but is left intact in the output file; it is interpreted by the module at run time.) When a composite table is used, the effect is similar to pushing more than one instance of the **kbd** module in the sense that the component tables function sequentially. However, it is done within a single instance of the module. As output is produced by processing with one table in the composite, the data is subsequently processed by the next component and so on until the final result emerges at the end of the sequence. (There is no restriction on the use of any combination of **full** and **sparse** tables in a composite.)

Composite tables are useful for simplifying complex mappings by modularizing the processing and for increasing the re-usability of tables for different mapping applications. Tables primarily implementing code set mappings can be linked to other tables primarily implementing compose- or dead-key sequences. With a single table implementing a common code set mapping, several different tables implementing combinations of code set mapping and compose-key layouts may be built.

A typical configuration might use one table for mapping from an external to internal code set, then use one or more separate tables working in the internal code set to provide compose- or dead-key functionality, as in the following example. One table, **646Sp-8859** maps from an ISO 646 variant (Spanish) external code set to ISO 8859-1; this is combined with two other tables respectively implementing 8859-1 by compose-sequences, and by dead-key sequences:

```
link("composed:646Sp-8859,8859-1-cmp")
link("deadkey:646Sp-8859,8859-1-dk")
```

Composite tables can also be built while the module is running from the **kbdload** command line; details are in the **kbdload**(1M) manual page. The component tables are linked and processed in the given order (left-to-right). Because the **link** argument is actually parsed at run time by **kbd** module, it is not an error to refer to tables that are not contained in the file currently being compiled. An error will be generated when the file is loaded if any component of a link is not present in memory at that time.

The **extern** form can be used to declare an external function managed by the **alp** module. External functions are managed in a list by that module, and are available for use as if they were simple tables in **kbd**. External functions are not downloaded, but are resident in the kernel and merely accessed by the **kbd** module [see **alp**(7) for more information]. Such functions also can be declared dynamically when required [see **kbdload**(1M)].

The directive **timed** may appear any place within a **map** declaration. If used, it causes the table within which it is defined to be interpreted in timeout mode. In this mode, string mappings are considered not to match if more than a specified amount of time elapses after receipt of the first byte of a sequence without its being fully received and mapped. For example, suppose that **abc** is to be mapped to **xyz** and the timeout value is **30**; if the user types **ab** and then waits for longer than **30** time units before typing **c**, the entire sequence will not be translated. Then the sequence is treated as any other mismatch would be: **a** is passed to the neighboring module, and **b** is checked to see if it begins a sequence. The timer is reset when a mismatch occurs, so that if **bc** is defined and **c** has just been received, it will be mapped as expected. The default timeout is typically 1/5 to 1/3 of a second [see **kbd**(7) for details].

Timeout mode is generally useful in cases where terminal function keys are being interpreted, to distinguish between a string typed by the user and a function key string sent by the terminal; it is not intended for use with batch applications such as the **iconv** command [see **iconv**(1)], nor generally in pipelines [see **pipe**(2)]. In a composite table, some components may be timed and some not, making the mode useful for combinations of code set mapping and function key mapping.

Timing depends on several factors, including terminal baud-rate, system load, and the user's typing speed. If the timeout value is too long, then typed sequences that happen to be the same as function keys will be erroneously mapped; if the value is too short, then function keys may be missed under a heavy system load or with low speed devices. See **kbdset**(1) for information on how to change the timeout value, and **kbd**(7) for information on how an administrator may change the default timeout value. This directive should never be used in tables that implement code set mapping, as it makes the results unpredictable. Long timeouts, on the order of seconds, may be useful in some contexts.

Building & Debugging

Users who intend to build their own tables may study the source tables supplied with the distribution in the directory `/usr/lib/kbd`.

If characters other than alphanumerics are to be used, quoted strings are preferred to unquoted strings; quotation is required for some characters, as mentioned above. Map names and the first arguments of **define** should be alphanumeric tokens.

The report generated by the **-r** option may be useful for debugging complex tables. The report (produced on standard error) consists of two octal lists. One list contains byte values that cannot be generated from the lookup table (if **keylist** forms are used). The other list contains byte values that cannot be generated in any way, that is, values that are neither parts of "result text" (products of string mappings) nor generated by the lookup table (if there is one), but are used in other sequences. The report does not exhaustively list unreachable paths, but may show whether they exist and help locate them.

Output Files

The files produced by **kbdcomp** begin with a header. The magic string is **kbd!map** with a version number. This header is immediately followed by one or more tables. The lines below can be added to the **/etc/magic** file for the **file**(1) command to recognize **kbd** files.

```
0       string      kbd!map       kbd map file
>8      byte        >0            Ver %d:
>10     short       >0            with %d table(s)
```

Limitations

The maximum length for input strings is 128 bytes, and 256 bytes for output strings. The total amount of space consumed by a single table is limited to about 65,000 bytes. Versions are incompatible; object tables are machine-dependent in their byte order and structure size. Thus, while source files are portable, the output of **kbdcomp** is not. This implies that when using remote devices across a network between heterogeneous machines, tables must be loaded on the machine where the module is actually pushed (that is, the remote side).

FILES

`/usr/lib/kbd` - directory containing system standard map files.
`/usr/lib/kbd/*.map` - source for some system map files.

SEE ALSO

alp(7), **iconv**(1), **kbd**(7), **kbdload**(1M), **kbdset**(1)

NAME

kbdload – load or link **kbd** tables

SYNOPSIS

kbdload [-p] *filename*

kbdload -u *table*

kbdload -l *string*

kbdload -L *string*

kbdload -e *string*

DESCRIPTION

Tables included in *file* are loaded into the **kbd** STREAMS module that must already have been pushed into the standard input stream. (In this context loaded means copied from a disk file into main memory within the operating system.) This program is intended both to provide for loading and linking of both shared or public tables and private tables implementing user-specific functionality. New users should refer to **kbdcomp**(1M) and **kbd**(7) for a general description of the module's capabilities.

Files are searched for only by the name specified on the command line; no search path is implied. Tables loaded by a privileged user with the **-p** option from an absolute path beginning at **/usr/lib/kbd** are made publicly available and permanently resident. Otherwise the loaded tables are available only to the caller, and are automatically unloaded when the **kbd** module is popped from the stream.

The **-u** option can be used to unload private tables and by a privileged user to remove public tables. Tables may be unloaded only if they are not currently in use. (Tables that are members of composite tables always have non-zero reference counts since they are "used" in the composite; all composites that refer to them must be unloaded first.)

The **-L** and **-l** options are used for making composite tables on the fly. The **-L** option, when executed by a privileged user causes the composite to be made publicly available; otherwise, it is private and equivalent to **-l**. The *string* argument is constructed in the same way as the **link** statement [see **kbdcomp**(1M)] in the compiler. If any component of the intended composite is not presently loaded in memory or if a component of a public table is not also public, an error message is printed and the linkage fails. More than one composite may be created in a single invocation by using either option sequentially.

The **-e** option with a string argument causes **kbdload** to declare to the **kbd** module a subroutine called *string*, which is assumed to be a subroutine managed by and registered with the **alp** module [see **alp**(7)]. These "external" subroutines may be used exactly as any other loaded table; they may participate as members of composite tables, and so on.

Security Issues

Allowing users other than a privileged user to load public tables is a security risk and is thus disallowed. (In general, any manipulation of a module instance by a user who is neither a privileged user nor the user who originally pushed it is disallowed.) The library directory and all files contained in it should be protected by being unwritable. Administrators are encouraged to remember that the **kbd** system can be used to arbitrarily re-map the entire keyboard of a terminal, as well as the entire output stream; thus in extremely hostile environments, it might be prudent to remove execution permissions from **kbdload** for non-administrative users (for example, setting the owner to **bin** or **root** and giving it a mode of 0500).

The **kbdload** command checks to insure that the real uid of the invoker is the same as the owner of both standard input and standard output files, unless the real uid of the invoking user is the privileged user. Paths to public tables are scrutinized for legitimacy. The **kbdload** command refuses to work as a **setuid** program.

DIAGNOSTICS

Exit status is 0 if all tables can be loaded and all operations succeeded. If there is an I/O error (for example, attempting to load a table with the same name as one already loaded and accessible to the caller) or failure to load a table, exit status is 1 and a message is printed showing the error.

FILES

/usr/lib/kbd – directory containing system standard map files.

SEE ALSO

alp(7), **kbd**(7), **kbdcomp**(1M), **kbdset**(1)

NOTES

Composite tables may be unloaded while they are actually in use without affecting current users. New users may no longer attach to the tables, since composite tables are copied and expanded when they are attached. This is done to keep state information related to the attaching user. The original composite always has a zero reference count, and is never itself attached. This is an anomaly; the effect on the user is that a composite table may be attached and functional, yet not appear in the output of a **kbdset**(1) query.

kbdpipe(1)

NAME

kbdpipe – use the **kbd** module in a pipeline

SYNOPSIS

kbdpipe -t *table* [**-f** *tablefile*] [**-F**] [**-o** *outfile*] [*infile(s)*]

DESCRIPTION

The **kbdpipe** command allows the use of **kbd** tables as pipeline elements between user programs. [See **kbdcomp**(1M) and **kbd**(7) for descriptions of the module and its capabilities.] **kbdpipe** is useful in code set conversion applications. If an output file is specified, then all *infiles* are piped to that output file. With no arguments other than **-t**, standard input is converted and sent to standard output.

The required option argument **-t** identifies the table to be used for conversion. If the table has already been loaded as a shared table [see **kbdload**(1M)] it is attached. If, however, the table has not been loaded, an attempt is made to load it. If the specified table name is not an absolute pathname then the name of the system mapping library is prepended to the argument, and an attempt is made to load the table from the resulting pathname (that is, it becomes an argument to the loader, **kbdload**). Assuming the table can be loaded, it is attached.

The argument to **-f** defines the file from which the table will be loaded, overriding the default action described above. The file is loaded (in its entirety), and the named table attached. This option should be used if the default action would fail.

The output file specified by **-o** must not already exist (a safety feature). The option **-F** may be used to override the check for existence of the output file; in this case, any existing *outfile* will be truncated before being written.

EXAMPLES

The following example converts two input files into relative nonsense by mapping ASCII into Dvorak keyboard equivalents using the **Dvorak** table. The table is assumed to reside in the file **/usr/lib/kbd/Dvorak**. The existing output file is overwritten:

```
kbdpipe -F -t Dvorak -o iapxai.vj file1 file2
```

The following example loads the **Dvorak** table from a different file, then converts standard input to standard output. The **Dvorak** table (assumed to be non-resident) is explicitly loaded from an absolute path beginning at the user's home directory:

```
kbdpipe -t Dvorak -f $HOME/tables/Dvorak.tab
```

FILES

/usr/lib/kbd – directory containing system standard table files.

SEE ALSO

kbd(7), **kbdload**(1M), **kbdset**(1)

NOTES

Because **kbdpipe** uses **kbdload**(1M) to load tables, it cannot resolve link references. Therefore, if a composite table is used, the relevant portions must either be already loaded and public, or be contained in the file used (via the **-f** option) on the command line. In the latter case, the composite elements must be loaded earlier than the link entry.

Users may use `kbd` tables in programs at user level by opening a pipe, pushing the module, and setting via related commands. Therefore, there is no need to use the `kbdpipe` command. `kbdpipe` may not be supported in future releases.

kbdset(1)

NAME

kbdset – attach to **kbd** mapping tables, set modes

SYNOPSIS

kbdset [**-o**] [**-a** *table*] [**-v** *string*] [**-k** *hotkey*] [**-m** *x*] [**-t** *ticks*]

kbdset [**-o**] [**-d** *table*] [**-v** *string*] [**-k** *hotkey*] [**-m** *x*] [**-t** *ticks*]

kbdset [**-q**]

DESCRIPTION

The **kbdset** command is the normal user interface to the **kbd** STREAMS module. [See **kbdcomp**(1M) and **kbd**(7) for a general description of the module's capabilities.] **kbdset** allows users to attach to pre-loaded tables, detach from tables, and set options. Options are provided for setting hot-keys to toggle tables and for controlling modes of the module.

Arguments and options are scanned and acted on in command line order. If the **-o** option is given, subsequent options affect the output side of the stream, otherwise the input side is assumed.

The **-q** option causes the **kbdset** command to list modules that can be accessed by the invoking user. In this case, all subsequent options are ignored. The output from the **-q** option lists the user's current hot-key settings, current timer value, and for each available table: an identifier, the name, size, attachments (input and/or output sides), reference count, number of components, and type (private or public). In the following example, there is one composite table, two tables are attached on the input side, and one on the output side.

```
In Hot Key = ^_
  Timers: In = 20 ; Out = 20
  ID        Name              Size I/O Ref Cmp Type
  4039f300  Ucase               56 - o  1   -   ext
  403a0480  Case/Dvorak         68 - -  0   2   pri
              [4039f300]  [4037e400]
  4036ce00  Deutsche           332 i -  4   -   pub
  4037e400  Dvorak             312 i -  2   -   pri
```

The **ID** field is an identifier unique to a given table; it is its address in memory Currently attached tables are marked **i** or **o**; otherwise, the **I/O** fields are marked with a dash. **Ref** is a reference count of attached users (including composites that refer to simple tables) and if non-zero, indicates that the table is in use. **Size** is the total size in bytes of the table and associated overhead in memory. If the table is a composite table, the **Cmp** field contains a number instead of a dash, and the following line lists an identifier for each component, in order of processing (allowing identification of the components in a composite table). Publicly available tables are marked with the type **pub** and private tables with **pri**. Private tables are available only to the invoking user and within the current stream. Tables which are really external functions [see **kbd**(7)] are marked **ext**; they are always of type **pub**. Tables that are interpreted in timeout [see **kbdcomp**(1M)] mode have an asterisk (*) preceding the **Type** field; members of composite tables that are interpreted in timeout mode have an asterisk after their bracketed identifier (on the second output line).

External functions are never time-sensitive, unless by their own internal specifications.

The option `-a` accompanied by an argument attaches to the named table. A table may not be multiply attached by a single user. When a table is attached and no other table is already attached, then the table is automatically made current. The option `-d` detaches from the named table. [See **kbdload**(1M) for a description of how tables are loaded.]

The `-k` option sets the user's hot-key. Setting a hot-key with only a single active table allows mapping to be toggled on and off, depending on the hot-key mode. A hot-key is a single byte, typically set to a relatively unused control character, that is caught by the **kbd** module and used for module control rather than being translated in any way. The key used as a hot-key becomes unavailable for other uses (unless it is generated by mapping). The hot-key may be reset at any time, independently from other options. Note that **kbdset** does not interpret ^X-type sequences; it expects a literal hot-key character.

The `-m` option with an integer argument controls the hot-key mode. Valid modes are 0, 1 (the default), and 2. Mode 0 allows one to toggle through the list of attached tables. Upon reaching the end of the list, the cycle returns to the beginning of the list. Use of Mode 0 with only one table loaded does not allow mapping to be turned off. Mode 1 toggles to the unmapped state upon reaching the end of the list (for example, given two tables, the sequence is table1, table2, off, table1, and so on). Mode 2 toggles to the unmapped (or off) state between every table in the list of attached tables (for example, given two tables, the sequence is table1, off, table2, off, table1, and so on).

The `-v` option turns on verbose mode, which can be useful when multiple tables are used in interactive sessions. In verbose mode, the name of the table can be output to the terminal whenever the user changes to a new table with the hot-key. The string associated with the option can be any short string. If the character sequence `%n` appears in the string, the name of the current table (or a null string) will be substituted for the `%n`. (A null argument to `-v` is equivalent to terse mode.) One useful sequence for this mode is *save-cursor goto-status-line clear-to-end-of-line* `%n` *restore-cursor*. This causes output of the current table name on the terminal's status line; in absence of a status-line, a simple sequence is to print the table name and RETURN [see **terminfo**(4) for the appropriate escape sequences.] Verbose mode is only available to show input table status to the output side of the stream. The output string for verbose mode is not itself passed through the mapping process, but is transmitted directly downstream with no other interpretation (it should thus be a string of ASCII characters or in some other externally available code set).

The `-t` option with an argument is used to change the timer for tables in the stream that are interpreted in timeout mode. Values (in clock ticks) between 5 and 400 are acceptable. (Depending on the hardware, the clock is usually either 60Hz or 100Hz, thus one tick is either 1/60 or 1/100 of a second; with a bit of experimentation, a suitable value for one's own system and typing speed can be found.) When a table that uses timeout mode is attached, it is assigned the current timer value. All tables that are attached after setting the timer value will take on the new value, but tables currently attached are unaffected (this allows one to set different values for different tables). The option does not affect other users' values. The timer value may be set independently for input and output sides by using `-t` in conjunction with `-o`. The value for a currently attached table may be reset by detaching the table, setting the value, then re-attaching the table.

In the query output, the line beginning with **`Timers:`** shows the timer values for input and output sides of the module.

FILES

`/usr/lib/kbd` – directory containing system standard map files.

SEE ALSO

`alp`(7), `alpq`(1), `kbd`(7), `kbdcomp`(1M), `kbdload`(1M)

NOTES

A table may be detached while it is current. However, in this case, it is first made non-current to allow error recovery under adverse circumstances. Detachment of a current table is not affected by the current hot-key mode, but always toggles to a state where no table is current.

It is not possible with the `-q` option to see the timer values assigned to currently attached tables, nor to reset the value for a table that is currently attached.

NAME

keylogin – decrypt and store secret key

SYNOPSIS

keylogin

DESCRIPTION

The **keylogin** command prompts for a password, and uses it to decrypt the user's secret key stored in the **publickey**(4) database. Once decrypted, the user's key is stored by the local key server process, **keyserv**(1M), to be used by any secure network service, such as NFS.

SEE ALSO

chkey(1), **keylogout(1),** **keyserv**(1M), **newkey**(1M), **publickey**(4)

keylogout (1)

NAME

keylogout – unsets a user's secret key on a local machine

SYNOPSIS

`keylogout [ -f ]`

DESCRIPTION

The **keylogout** command unsets the user's secret key, which is stored in the **publickey**(4) database.

If you are logged in as **root**, use **keylogout -f** to unset your (**root**) secret key. Note that using **keylogout -f** by **root** will break all servers that use the secure Remote Procedure Call (RPC).

SEE ALSO

chkey(1), **keylogin(1),** **keyserv**(1M), **newkey**(1M), **publickey**(4)

NAME

keymaster – cr1 key database administration

SYNOPSIS

keymaster [-k | -cn] [-s *scheme***]**

DESCRIPTION

keymaster starts the **cr1** key management daemon and sets the master key that is used to encrypt and decrypt the shared keys stored in the **keys** file [see **cr1**(1M)]. Use of **keymaster** is restricted to the privileged user. The privileged user is the owner of the **keys** file.

A shared key is a bit string, known only to the parties in an exchange, that is used to authenticate a connection. When shared keys are entered, they are stored in a **keys** file by a daemon process. If a master key exists, the shared keys in the file are encrypted.

When **keymaster** is first entered, it forks a process that continues as the key management daemon.

The options to **keymaster** have the following meanings:

-c Indicates that the master key is to be changed. When the **-c** option is entered, the command first prompts the user to enter the old master key, then a new master key.

-n Indicates that the **keys** file is not encrypted. When the **-n** option is used, the **keymaster** command does not prompt for a master key.

-k Indicates that the key management daemon is to be stopped. No key is required to stop the key management daemon. This option takes precedence over both **-c** and **-n**.

-s *scheme*
Specifies the name of the scheme to be used. The default for *scheme* is **cr1**, which uses DES encryption, and requires that the Encryption Utilities package be installed. If this package is not available, ENIGMA encryption can be used by specifying **cr1.enigma** as the *scheme*.

When no options are specified, **keymaster** prompts for the current master key. If the master key is entered correctly, the **keymaster** daemon is started.

keymaster does not echo keys as they are typed. It confirms a new master key by requiring the user to enter the key a second time. If the second entry does not match the first, the operation is not executed.

FILES

/etc/iaf/cr1/keys cr1 key database

SEE ALSO

cr1(1M), **cryptkey**(1), **getkey**(3N)

DIAGNOSTICS

keymaster passes a request to the key management daemon either by becoming the daemon, or by writing to the current daemon's pipe. If the daemon returns success, **keymaster** exits with a value of 0; otherwise, it prints an error message and exits with a non-zero value.

NOTES

If **keymaster** successfully starts the key management daemon, it indicates success to the user, even though the daemon may subsequently fail.

NAME

keyserv – server for storing public and private keys

SYNOPSIS

keyserv [**-dDn**]

DESCRIPTION

keyserv is a daemon that is used for storing the private encryption keys of each user logged into the system. These encryption keys are used for accessing secure network services such as secure NFS.

Normally, root's key is read from the file **/etc/.rootkey** when the daemon is started. This is useful during power-fail reboots when no one is around to type a password.

OPTIONS

The options are:

-d Disables the use of default keys

-D Used for debugging

-n root's key is not read from **/etc/.rootkey**, instead, **keyserv** prompts the user for the password to decrypt root's key stored in the **publickey**(4) database and then stores the decrypted key in **/etc/.rootkey** for future use. This option is useful if the **/etc/.rootkey** file ever gets out of date or corrupted.

To start **keyserv** manually, you must be **root** with the appropriate privileges.

FILES

/etc/.rootkey

SEE ALSO

publickey(4)

kill(1)

NAME

kill – terminate a process by default

SYNOPSIS

kill [-*signal*] **pid**. . .
kill -*signal* **-pgid**. . .
kill -l

DESCRIPTION

kill sends a signal to the specified processes. The value of *signal* may be numeric or symbolic [see **signal**(5)]. The symbolic signal name is the name as it appears in **/usr/include/sys/signal.h**, with the **SIG** prefix stripped off. Signal 15 (**SIGTERM**) is sent by default; this will normally kill processes that do not catch or ignore the signal.

pid and *pgid* are unsigned numeric strings that identify which process(es) should receive the signal. If *pid* is used, the process with process ID *pid* is selected. If *pgid* is used, all processes with process group ID *pgid* are selected.

The process number of each asynchronous process started with **&** is reported by the shell (unless more than one process is started in a pipeline, in which case the number of the last process in the pipeline is reported). Process numbers can also be found by using **ps**(1).

When invoked with the **-l** option, **kill** will print a list of symbolic signal names. The details of the kill are described in **kill**(2). For example, if process number 0 is specified, all processes in the process group are signaled.

The signaled process must belong to the current user unless the user is a privileged user.

FILES

/usr/lib/locale/*locale***/LC_MESSAGES/uxcore.abi**
language-specific message file [see **LANG** on **environ**(5).]

SEE ALSO

kill(2), **ps**(1), **sh**(1), **signal**(2), **signal**(5)

NAME

killall – kill all active processes

SYNOPSIS

/usr/sbin/killall [*signal*]

DESCRIPTION

killall is used by **/usr/sbin/shutdown** to kill all active processes not directly related to the shutdown procedure.

killall terminates all processes with open files so that the mounted file systems will be unbusied and can be unmounted.

killall sends *signal* [see **kill**(1)] to all processes not belonging to the above group of exclusions. If no *signal* is specified, a default of 9 (**SIGTERM**) is used.

FILES

/usr/sbin/shutdown

SEE ALSO

fuser(1M), **kill**(1), **ps**(1), **shutdown**(1M), **signal**(2), **signal**(5)

NOTES

The **killall** command can be run only by a privileged user.

If the **killall** command is issued in an environment where a mouse is used, the mousemgr itself will be terminated. Subsequently, any process which uses a mouse (such as X Windows) will wait for the mousemgr indefinitely, since it no longer exists at this point. Therefore, it is advisable to terminate any process that uses a mouse before issuing the **killall** command.

ksh (1)

NAME

ksh, **rksh** – KornShell, a standard/restricted command and programming language

SYNOPSIS

ksh [**±aefhikmnprstuvx**] [**±o** *option*] . . . [**-c** *string*] [*arg* . . .]
rksh [**±aefhikmnprstuvx**] [**±o** *option*] . . . [**-c** *string*] [*arg* . . .]

DESCRIPTION

ksh is a command and programming language that executes commands read from a terminal or a file. **rksh** is a restricted version of the command interpreter **ksh**; it is used to set up login names and execution environments whose capabilities are more controlled than those of the standard shell. See Invocation below for the meaning of arguments to the shell.

Definitions.

A *metacharacter* is one of the following characters:

; **&** **(** **)** **|** **<** **>** new-line space tab

A *blank* is a tab or a space. An *identifier* is a sequence of letters, digits, or underscores starting with a letter or underscore. Identifiers are used as names for *functions* and *variables*. A *word* is a sequence of *characters* separated by one or more non-quoted *metacharacters*.

A *command* is a sequence of characters in the syntax of the shell language. The shell reads each command and carries out the desired action either directly or by invoking separate utilities. A special command is a command that is carried out by the shell without creating a separate process. Except for documented side effects, most special commands can be implemented as separate utilities.

Commands.

A *simple-command* is a sequence of *blank* separated words which may be preceded by a variable assignment list (see Environment below). The first word specifies the name of the command to be executed. Except as specified below, the remaining words are passed as arguments to the invoked command. The command name is passed as argument 0 [see **exec**(2)]. The *value* of a simple-command is its exit status if it terminates normally, or (octal) 200+*status* if it terminates abnormally [see **signal**(2) for a list of *status* values].

A *pipeline* is a sequence of one or more *commands* separated by **|**. The standard output of each command but the last is connected by a **pipe**(2) to the standard input of the next command. Each command is run as a separate process; the shell waits for the last command to terminate. The exit status of a pipeline is the exit status of the last command.

A *list* is a sequence of one or more pipelines separated by **;**, **&**, **&&**, or **||**, and optionally terminated by **;**, **&**, or **|&**. Of these five symbols, **;**, **&**, and **|&** have equal precedence, which is lower than that of **&&** and **||**. The symbols **&&** and **||** also have equal precedence. A semicolon (**;**) causes sequential execution of the preceding pipeline; an ampersand (**&**) causes asynchronous execution of the preceding pipeline (that is, the shell does not wait for that pipeline to finish). The symbol **|&** causes asynchronous execution of the preceding command or pipeline with a two-way pipe established to the parent shell. The standard input and output of the spawned command can be written to and read from by the parent shell using the **-p** option of the special commands **read** and **print** described later. The symbol **&&**

(**||**) causes the *list* following it to be executed only if the preceding pipeline returns a zero (non-zero) value. An arbitrary number of new-lines may appear in a *list*, instead of a semicolon, to delimit a command.

A *command* is either a simple-command or one of the following. Unless otherwise stated, the value returned by a command is that of the last simple-command executed in the command.

for *identifier* [**in** *word* ...] **;do** *list* **;done**
: Each time a **for** command is executed, *identifier* is set to the next *word* taken from the **in** *word* list. If **in** *word* ... is omitted, then the **for** command executes the **do** *list* once for each positional parameter that is set (see Parameter Substitution below). Execution ends when there are no more words in the list.

select *identifier* [**in** *word* ...] **;do** *list* **;done**
: A **select** command prints on standard error (file descriptor 2), the set of *word*s, each preceded by a number. If **in** *word* ... is omitted, then the positional parameters are used instead (see Parameter Substitution below). The **PS3** prompt is printed and a line is read from the standard input. If this line consists of the number of one of the listed *word*s, then the value of the parameter *identifier* is set to the *word* corresponding to this number. If this line is empty the selection list is printed again. Otherwise the value of the parameter *identifier* is set to **null**. The contents of the line read from standard input is saved in the variable **REPLY.** The *list* is executed for each selection until a **break** or end-of-file is encountered.

case *word* **in** [[**(**]*pattern* [| *pattern*] ... **)** *list* **;;**] ... **esac**
: A **case** command executes the *list* associated with the first *pattern* that matches *word*. The form of the patterns is the same as that used for file-name generation (see File Name Generation below).

if *list* **;then** *list* [**elif** *list* **;then** *list*] ... [**;else** *list*] **;fi**
: The *list* following **if** is executed and, if it returns a zero exit status, the *list* following the first **then** is executed. Otherwise, the *list* following **elif** is executed and, if its value is zero, the *list* following the next **then** is executed. Failing that, the **else** *list* is executed. If no **else** *list* or **then** *list* is executed, then the **if** command returns a zero exit status.

while *list* **;do** *list* **;done**
until *list* **;do** *list* **;done**
: A **while** command repeatedly executes the **while** *list* and, if the exit status of the last command in the list is zero, executes the **do** *list*; otherwise the loop terminates. If no commands in the **do** *list* are executed, then the **while** command returns a zero exit status; **until** may be used in place of **while** to negate the loop termination test.

(*list***)**
: Execute *list* in a separate environment. Note, that if two adjacent open parentheses are needed for nesting, a space must be inserted to avoid arithmetic evaluation as described below.

`{` *list* `;}`
list is simply executed. The `{` must be followed by a space. Note that unlike the metacharacters `(` and `)`, `{` and `}` are *reserved words* and must be typed at the beginning of a line or after a `;` in order to be recognized.

`[[`*expression*`]]`
Evaluates *expression* and returns a zero exit status when *expression* is true. See Conditional Expressions below, for a description of *expression*.

function *identifier* `{` *list* `;}`
identifier `()` `{` *list* `;}`
Define a function which is referenced by *identifier*. The body of the function is the *list* of commands between `{` and `}`. (see Functions below). The `{` must be followed by a space.

time *pipeline*
The *pipeline* is executed and the elapsed time as well as the user and system time are printed on standard error.

The following reserved words are only recognized as the first word of a command and when not quoted:

if	then	else	elif	fi	case	esac	for	while
until	do	done	{	}	function	select	time	[[ ]]

Comments.

A word beginning with **#** causes that word and all the following characters up to a new-line to be ignored.

Aliasing.

The first word of each command is replaced by the text of an **alias** if an **alias** for this word has been defined. An alias name consists of any number of characters excluding meta-characters, quoting characters, file expansion characters, parameter and command substitution characters and **=**. The replacement string can contain any valid shell script including the metacharacters listed above. The first word of each command in the replaced text, other than any that are in the process of being replaced, will be tested for aliases. If the last character of the alias value is a *blank* then the word following the alias will also be checked for alias substitution. Aliases can be used to redefine special builtin commands but cannot be used to redefine the reserved words listed above. Aliases can be created, listed, and exported with the **alias** command and can be removed with the **unalias** command. Exported aliases remain in effect for scripts invoked by name, but must be reinitialized for separate invocations of the shell (see Invocation below).

Aliasing is performed when scripts are read, not while they are executed. Therefore, for an alias to take effect the **alias** definition command has to be executed before the command which references the alias is read.

Aliases are frequently used as a short hand for full path names. An option to the aliasing facility allows the value of the alias to be automatically set to the full pathname of the corresponding command. These aliases are called tracked aliases. The value of a tracked alias is defined the first time the corresponding command is looked up and becomes undefined each time the **PATH** variable is reset. These aliases remain tracked so that the next subsequent reference will redefine the value.

Several tracked aliases are compiled into the shell. The **-h** option of the **set** command makes each referenced command name into a tracked alias.

The following *exported aliases* are compiled into the shell but can be unset or redefined:

```
autoload='typeset -fu'
false='let 0'
functions='typeset -f'
hash='alias -t'
history='fc -l'
integer='typeset -i'
nohup='nohup '
r='fc -e -'
true=':'
type='whence -v'
```

Tilde Substitution.

After alias substitution is performed, each word is checked to see if it begins with an unquoted ~. If it does, then the word up to a **/** is checked to see if it matches a user name in the **/etc/passwd** file. If a match is found, the ~ and the matched login name is replaced by the login directory of the matched user. This is called a *tilde* substitution. If no match is found, the original text is left unchanged. A ~ by itself, or in front of a **/**, is replaced by **$HOME**. A ~ followed by a **+** or **-** is replaced by **$PWD** and **$OLDPWD** respectively.

In addition, *tilde* substitution is attempted when the value of a *variable assignment* begins with a ~.

Command Substitution.

The standard output from a command enclosed in parentheses preceded by a dollar sign (**$()**) or a pair of grave accents (**``**) may be used as part or all of a word; trailing new-lines are removed. In the second (archaic) form, the string between the quotes is processed for special quoting characters before the command is executed (see Quoting below). The command substitution **$(cat file)** can be replaced by the equivalent but faster **$(<file)**. Command substitution of most special commands that do not perform input/output redirection are carried out without creating a separate process.

An arithmetic expression enclosed in double parentheses and preceded by a dollar sign [**$(())**] is replaced by the value of the arithmetic expression within the double parentheses.

Parameter Substitution.

A *parameter* is an *identifier*, one or more digits, or any of the characters *, **@**, **#**, **?**, **-**, **$**, and **!**. A *variable* (a parameter denoted by an identifier) has a *value* and zero or more *attributes*. *Variables* can be assigned **values** and *attributes* by using the **typeset** special command. The attributes supported by the shell are described later with the **typeset** special command. Exported parameters pass values and attributes to the environment.

The shell supports a one-dimensional array facility. An element of an array variable is referenced by a *subscript*. A *subscript* is denoted by a **[**, followed by an *arithmetic expression* (see Arithmetic Evaluation below) followed by a **]**. To assign values to an array, use **set -A** *name value* .... The value of all subscripts must be in the range of 0 through 1023. Arrays need not be declared. Any reference to a variable with a valid subscript is legal and an array will be created if necessary. Referencing an array without a subscript is equivalent to referencing the element zero.

The *value* of a *variable* may also be assigned by writing:

name=*value* [*name*=*value*] ...

If the integer attribute, **-i**, is set for *name* the *value* is subject to arithmetic evaluation as described below.

Positional parameters, parameters denoted by a number, may be assigned values with the **set** special command. Parameter **$0** is set from argument zero when the shell is invoked.

The character **$** is used to introduce substitutable *parameters*.

${*parameter***}**
: The shell reads all the characters from **${** to the matching **}** as part of the same word even if it contains braces or metacharacters. The value, if any, of the parameter is substituted. The braces are required when *parameter* is followed by a letter, digit, or underscore that is not to be interpreted as part of its name or when a variable is subscripted. If *parameter* is one or more digits then it is a positional parameter. A positional parameter of more than one digit must be enclosed in braces. If *parameter* is * or **@**, then all the positional parameters, starting with **$1**, are substituted (separated by a field separator character). If an array *identifier* with subscript * or **@** is used, then the value for each of the elements is substituted (separated by a field separator character).

${#*parameter***}**
: If *parameter* is * or **@**, the number of positional parameters is substituted. Otherwise, the length of the value of the *parameter* is substituted.

${#*identifier***[*]}**
: The number of elements in the array *identifier* is substituted.

${*parameter***:-***word***}**
: If *parameter* is set and is non-null then substitute its value; otherwise substitute *word*.

${*parameter***:=***word***}**
: If *parameter* is not set or is null then set it to *word*; the value of the parameter is then substituted. Positional parameters may not be assigned to in this way.

${*parameter***:?***word***}**
: If *parameter* is set and is non-null then substitute its value; otherwise, print *word* and exit from the shell. If *word* is omitted then a standard message is printed.

${*parameter***:+***word***}**
: If *parameter* is set and is non-null then substitute *word*; otherwise substitute nothing.

`${`*parameter*`#`*pattern*`}`
`${`*parameter*`##`*pattern*`}`
If the shell *pattern* matches the beginning of the value of *parameter*, then the value of this substitution is the value of the *parameter* with the matched portion deleted; otherwise the value of this *parameter* is substituted. In the first form the smallest matching pattern is deleted and in the second form the largest matching pattern is deleted.

`${`*parameter*`%`*pattern*`}`
`${`*parameter*`%%`*pattern*`}`
If the shell *pattern* matches the end of the value of *parameter*, then the value of this substitution is the value of the *parameter* with the matched part deleted; otherwise substitute the value of *parameter*. In the first form the smallest matching pattern is deleted and in the second form the largest matching pattern is deleted.

In the above, *word* is not evaluated unless it is to be used as the substituted string, so that, in the following example, **pwd** is executed only if **d** is not set or is null:

echo ${d:–$(pwd)}

If the colon (**:**) is omitted from the above expressions, then the shell only checks whether *parameter* is set or not.

The following parameters are automatically set by the shell:

- `#` The number of positional parameters in decimal.
- `-` Flags supplied to the shell on invocation or by the **set** command.
- `?` The decimal value returned by the last executed command.
- `$` The process number of this shell.
- `_` Initially, the value _ is an absolute pathname of the shell or script being executed as passed in the *environment*. Subsequently it is assigned the last argument of the previous command. This parameter is not set for commands which are asynchronous. This parameter is also used to hold the name of the matching **MAIL** file when checking for mail.
- `!` The process number of the last background command invoked.
- `ERRNO` The value of **errno** as set by the most recently failed system call. This value is system dependent and is intended for debugging purposes.
- `LINENO` The line number of the current line within the script or function being executed.
- `OLDPWD` The previous working directory set by the **cd** command.
- `OPTARG` The value of the last option argument processed by the **getopts** special command.
- `OPTIND` The index of the last option argument processed by the **getopts** special command.
- `PPID` The process number of the parent of the shell.
- `PWD` The present working directory set by the **cd** command.
- `RANDOM` Each time this variable is referenced, a random integer, uniformly distributed between 0 and 32767, is generated. The sequence of random numbers can be initialized by assigning a numeric value to **RANDOM**.

REPLY This variable is set by the **select** statement and by the **read** special command when no arguments are supplied.

SECONDS
Each time this variable is referenced, the number of seconds since shell invocation is returned. If this variable is assigned a value, then the value returned upon reference will be the value that was assigned plus the number of seconds since the assignment.

The following variables are used by the shell:

CDPATH The search path for the **cd** command.

COLUMNS
If this variable is set, the value is used to define the width of the edit window for the shell edit modes and for printing **select** lists.

EDITOR If the value of this variable ends in *emacs*, *gmacs*, or **vi** and the **VISUAL** variable is not set, then the corresponding option (see Special Command **set** below) will be turned on.

ENV If this variable is set, then parameter substitution is performed on the value to generate the pathname of the script that will be executed when the *shell* is invoked (see Invocation below). This file is typically used for *alias* and *function* definitions.

FCEDIT The default editor name for the **fc** command.

FPATH The search path for function definitions. This path is searched when a function with the **-u** attribute is referenced and when a command is not found. If an executable file is found, then it is read and executed in the current environment.

IFS Internal field separators— normally space, tab, and new-line—used to separate command words that result from command or parameter substitution and for separating words with the special command **read**. The first character of the **IFS** variable is used to separate arguments for the **"$*"** substitution (see Quoting below).

HISTFILE
If this variable is set when the shell is invoked, then the value is the pathname of the file that will be used to store the command history (see Command re-entry below).

HISTSIZE
If this variable is set when the shell is invoked, then the number of previously entered commands that are accessible by this shell will be greater than or equal to this number. The default is 128.

HOME The default argument (home directory) for the **cd** command.

LINES If this variable is set, the value is used to determine the column length for printing **select** lists. Select lists will print vertically until about two-thirds of **LINES** lines are filled.

MAIL If this variable is set to the name of a mail file *and* the **MAILPATH** variable is not set, then the shell informs the user of arrival of mail in the specified file.

MAILCHECK
This variable specifies how often (in seconds) the shell will check for changes in the modification time of any of the files specified by the **MAILPATH** or **MAIL** variables. The default value is 600 seconds.

When the time has elapsed the shell will check before issuing the next prompt.

MAILPATH
A colon (**:**) separated list of file names. If this variable is set then the shell informs the user of any modifications to the specified files that have occurred within the last **MAILCHECK** seconds. Each file name can be followed by a **?** and a message that will be printed. The message will undergo parameter substitution with the variable, **$_** defined as the name of the file that has changed. The default message is **you have mail in $_**.

PATH The search path for commands (see Execution below). The user may not change **PATH** if executing under **rksh** (except in **.profile**).

PS1 The value of this variable is expanded for parameter substitution to define the primary prompt string which by default is "**$** ". The character **!** in the primary prompt string is replaced by the *command* number (see Command Re-entry below).

PS2 Secondary prompt string, by default "**>** ".

PS3 Selection prompt string used within a **select** loop, by default "**#?** ".

PS4 The value of this variable is expanded for parameter substitution and precedes each line of an execution trace. If omitted, the execution trace prompt is "**+** ".

SHELL The pathname of the *shell* is kept in the environment. At invocation, if the basename of this variable matches the pattern ***r*sh**, then the shell becomes restricted.

TMOUT If set to a value greater than zero, the shell will terminate if a command is not entered within the prescribed number of seconds after issuing the **PS1** prompt. (Note that the shell can be compiled with a maximum bound for this value which cannot be exceeded.)

VISUAL If the value of this variable ends in *emacs*, *gmacs*, or **vi** then the corresponding option (see Special Command **set** below) will be turned on.

The shell gives default values to **PATH**, **PS1**, **PS2**, **MAILCHECK**, **TMOUT** and **IFS**. **HOME**, **MAIL** and **SHELL** are set by **login**(1).

Blank Interpretation.

After parameter and command substitution, the results of substitutions are scanned for the field separator characters (those found in **IFS**) and split into distinct arguments where such characters are found. Explicit null arguments (**""** or **''**) are retained. Implicit null arguments (those resulting from *parameters* that have no values) are removed.

File Name Generation.

Following substitution, each command *word* is scanned for the characters *, **?**, and **[** unless the **-f** option has been **set**. If one of these characters appears then the word is regarded as a *pattern*. The word is replaced with lexicographically sorted file names that match the pattern. If no file name is found that matches the pattern, then the word is left unchanged. When a *pattern* is used for file name generation, the character **.** at the start of a file name or immediately following a **/**, as well as the character / itself, must be matched explicitly. In other instances of pattern matching the / and . are not treated specially.

- `*` Matches any string, including the null string.
- `?` Matches any single character.
- `[...]` Matches any one of the enclosed characters. A pair of characters separated by - matches any character lexically between the pair, inclusive. If the first character following the opening "[" is a "! " then any character not enclosed is matched. A - can be included in the character set by putting it as the first or last character.

A *pattern-list* is a list of one or more patterns separated from each other with a |. Composite patterns can be formed with one or more of the following:

?(*pattern-list*)
: Optionally matches any one of the given patterns.

*(*pattern-list*)
: Matches zero or more occurrences of the given patterns.

+(*pattern-list*)
: Matches one or more occurrences of the given patterns.

@(*pattern-list*)
: Matches exactly one of the given patterns.

!(*pattern-list*)
: Matches anything, except one of the given patterns.

Quoting.

Each of the *metacharacters* listed above (see Definitions above) has a special meaning to the shell and causes termination of a word unless quoted. A character may be *quoted* (that is, made to stand for itself) by preceding it with a \. The pair **\new-line** is removed. All characters enclosed between a pair of single quote marks (' '), are quoted. A single quote cannot appear within single quotes. Inside double quote marks (""), parameter and command substitution occurs and \ quotes the characters \, ‘, ", and $. The meaning of $* and $@ is identical when not quoted or when used as a variable assignment value or as a file name. However, when used as a command argument, "$*" is equivalent to "$1*d* $2*d*...", where *d* is the first character of the **IFS** variable, whereas "$@" is equivalent to "$1"*d*"$2"*d*... Inside grave quote marks (‘ ‘) \ quotes the characters \, ‘, and $. If the grave quotes occur within double quotes then \ also quotes the character ".

The special meaning of reserved words or aliases can be removed by quoting any character of the reserved word. The recognition of function names or special command names listed below cannot be altered by quoting them.

Arithmetic Evaluation.

An ability to perform integer arithmetic is provided with the special command **let**. Evaluations are performed using *long* arithmetic. Constants are of the form [*base*#]*n* where *base* is a decimal number between two and thirty-six representing the arithmetic base and *n* is a number in that base. If *base*# is omitted then base 10 is used.

An arithmetic expression uses the same syntax, precedence, and associativity of expression of the C language. All the integral operators, other than `++`, `--`, `?:`, and `,` are supported. Variables can be referenced by name within an arithmetic expression without using the parameter substitution syntax. When a variable is referenced, its value is evaluated as an arithmetic expression.

An internal integer representation of a *variable* can be specified with the `-i` option of the **`typeset`** special command. Arithmetic evaluation is performed on the value of each assignment to a variable with the `-i` attribute. If you do not specify an arithmetic base, the first assignment to the variable determines the arithmetic base. This base is used when parameter substitution occurs.

Since many of the arithmetic operators require quoting, an alternative form of the `let` command is provided. For any command which begins with a `((`, all the characters until a matching `))` are treated as a quoted expression. More precisely, `((...))` is equivalent to `let "..."`.

Prompting.

When used interactively, the shell prompts with the parameter expanded value of `PS1` before reading a command. If at any time a new-line is typed and further input is needed to complete a command, then the secondary prompt (that is, the value of `PS2`) is issued.

Conditional Expressions.

A *conditional expression* is used with the `[[` compound command to test attributes of files and to compare strings. Word splitting and file name generation are not performed on the words between `[[` and `]]`. Each expression can be constructed from one or more of the following unary or binary expressions:

`-a` *file*	True, if *file* exists.
`-b` *file*	True, if *file* exists and is a block special file.
`-c` *file*	True, if *file* exists and is a character special file.
`-d` *file*	True, if *file* exists and is a directory.
`-f` *file*	True, if *file* exists and is an ordinary file.
`-g` *file*	True, if *file* exists and is has its setgid bit set.
`-k` *file*	True, if *file* exists and is has its sticky bit set.
`-n` *string*	True, if length of *string* is non-zero.
`-o` *option*	True, if option named *option* is on.
`-p` *file*	True, if *file* exists and is a fifo special file or a pipe.
`-r` *file*	True, if *file* exists and is readable by current process.
`-s` *file*	True, if *file* exists and has size greater than zero.
`-t` *fildes*	True, if file descriptor number *fildes* is open and associated with a terminal device.
`-u` *file*	True, if *file* exists and is has its setuid bit set.
`-w` *file*	True, if *file* exists and is writable by current process.
`-x` *file*	True, if *file* exists and is executable by current process. If *file* exists and is a directory, then the current process has permission to search in the directory.
`-z` *string*	True, if length of *string* is zero.
`-L` *file*	True, if *file* exists and is a symbolic link.

-O *file*	True, if *file* exists and is owned by the effective user id of this process.
-G *file*	True, if *file* exists and its group matches the effective group id of this process.
-S *file*	True, if *file* exists and is a socket.
file1 **-nt** *file2*	True, if *file1* exists and is newer than *file2*.
file1 **-ot** *file2*	True, if *file1* exists and is older than *file2*.
file1 **-ef** *file2*	True, if *file1* and *file2* exist and refer to the same file.
string **=** *pattern*	True, if *string* matches *pattern*.
string **!=** *pattern*	True, if *string* does not match *pattern*.
string1 **<** *string2*	True, if *string1* comes before *string2* based on ASCII value of their characters.
string1 **>** *string2*	True, if *string1* comes after *string2* based on ASCII value of their characters.
exp1 **-eq** *exp2*	True, if *exp1* is equal to *exp2*.
exp1 **-ne** *exp2*	True, if *exp1* is not equal to *exp2*.
exp1 **-lt** *exp2*	True, if *exp1* is less than *exp2*.
exp1 **-gt** *exp2*	True, if *exp1* is greater than *exp2*.
exp1 **-le** *exp2*	True, if *exp1* is less than or equal to *exp2*.
exp1 **-ge** *exp2*	True, if *exp1* is greater than or equal to *exp2*.

In each of the above expressions, if *file* is of the form **/dev/fd/***n*, where *n* is an integer, then the test applied to the open file whose descriptor number is *n*.

A compound expression can be constructed from these primitives by using any of the following, listed in decreasing order of precedence.

(*expression***)**	True, if *expression* is true. Used to group expressions.
! *expression*	True if *expression* is false.
expression1 **&&** *expression2*	True, if *expression1* and *expression2* are both true.
expression1 **||** *expression2*	True, if either *expression1* or *expression2* is true.

Input/Output.

Before a command is executed, its input and output may be redirected using a special notation interpreted by the shell. The following may appear anywhere in a simple-command or may precede or follow a *command* and are not passed on to the invoked command. Command and parameter substitution occurs before *word* or *digit* is used except as noted below. File name generation occurs only if the pattern matches a single file and blank interpretation is not performed.

<*word*	Use file *word* as standard input (file descriptor 0).
>*word*	Use file *word* as standard output (file descriptor 1). If the file does not exist then it is created. If the file exists, is a regular file, and the **noclobber** option is on, this causes an error; otherwise, it is truncated to zero length.
>|*word*	Sames as **>**, except that it overrides the **noclobber** option.
>>*word*	Use file *word* as standard output. If the file exists then output is appended to it (by first seeking to the end-of-file); otherwise, the file is created.

<>*word* Open file *word* for reading and writing as standard input.

<<[-]*word* The shell input is read up to a line that is the same as *word*, or to an end-of-file. No parameter substitution, command substitution or file name generation is performed on *word*. The resulting document, called a *here-document*, becomes the standard input. If any character of *word* is quoted, then no interpretation is placed upon the characters of the document; otherwise, parameter and command substitution occurs, **\new-line** is ignored, and \ must be used to quote the characters \, $, ', and the first character of *word*. If - is appended to <<, then all leading tabs are stripped from *word* and from the document.

<&*digit* The standard input is duplicated from file descriptor *digit* [see **dup**(2)]. Similarly for the standard output using >& *digit*.

<&- The standard input is closed. Similarly for the standard output using >&-.

<&p The input from the co-process is moved to standard input.

>&p The output to the co-process is moved to standard output.

If one of the above is preceded by a digit, then the file descriptor number referred to is that specified by the digit (instead of the default 0 or 1). For example:

... 2>&1

means file descriptor 2 is to be opened for writing as a duplicate of file descriptor 1.

The order in which redirections are specified is significant. The shell evaluates each redirection in terms of the (*file descriptor*, *file*) association at the time of evaluation. For example:

... 1>*fname* 2>&1

first associates file descriptor 1 with file *fname*. It then associates file descriptor 2 with the file associated with file descriptor 1 (that is, *fname*). If the order of redirections were reversed, file descriptor 2 would be associated with the terminal (assuming file descriptor 1 had been) and then file descriptor 1 would be associated with file *fname*.

If a command is followed by & and job control is not active, then the default standard input for the command is the empty file **/dev/null**. Otherwise, the environment for the execution of a command contains the file descriptors of the invoking shell as modified by input/output specifications.

Environment.

The *environment* [see **environ**(5)] is a list of name-value pairs that is passed to an executed program in the same way as a normal argument list. The names must be *identifiers* and the values are character strings. The shell interacts with the environment in several ways. On invocation, the shell scans the environment and creates a variable for each name found, giving it the corresponding value and marking it *export* . Executed commands inherit the environment. If the user modifies the values of these variables or creates new ones, using the **export** or **typeset -x** commands they become part of the environment. The environment seen by any executed command is thus composed of any name-value pairs originally inherited by the shell, whose values may be modified by the current shell, plus any additions which must be noted in **export** or **typeset -x** commands.

The environment for any *simple-command* or function may be augmented by prefixing it with one or more variable assignments. A variable assignment argument is a word of the form *identifier=value*. Thus:

```
TERM=450 cmd args
```

and

```
(export TERM; TERM=450; cmd args)
```

are equivalent (as far as the above execution of *cmd* is concerned except for commands listed with one or two daggers, †, in the Special Commands section).

If the **-k** flag is set, *all* variable assignment arguments are placed in the environment, even if they occur after the command name. The following first prints **a=b c** and then **c:**

```
echo a=b c
set -k
echo a=b c
```

This feature is intended for use with scripts written for early versions of the shell and its use in new scripts is strongly discouraged. It is likely to disappear someday.

Functions.

The **function** reserved word, described in the Commands section above, is used to define shell functions. Shell functions are read in and stored internally. Alias names are resolved when the function is read. Functions are executed like commands with the arguments passed as positional parameters (see Execution below).

Functions execute in the same process as the caller and share all files and present working directory with the caller. Traps caught by the caller are reset to their default action inside the function. A trap condition that is not caught or ignored by the function causes the function to terminate and the condition to be passed on to the caller. A trap on **EXIT** set inside a function is executed after the function completes in the environment of the caller. Ordinarily, variables are shared between the calling program and the function. However, the **typeset** special command used within a function defines local variables whose scope includes the current function and all functions it calls.

The special command **return** is used to return from function calls. Errors within functions return control to the caller.

Function identifiers can be listed with the **-f** or **+f** option of the **typeset** special command. The text of functions may also be listed with **-f**. Function can be undefined with the **-f** option of the **unset** special command.

Ordinarily, functions are unset when the shell executes a shell script. The **-xf** option of the **typeset** command allows a function to be exported to scripts that are executed without a separate invocation of the shell. Functions that need to be defined across separate invocations of the shell should be specified in the **ENV** file with the **-xf** option of **typeset**.

Jobs.

If the **monitor** option of the **set** command is turned on, an interactive shell associates a *job* with each pipeline. It keeps a table of current jobs, printed by the **jobs** command, and assigns them small integer numbers. When a job is started asynchronously with **&**, the shell prints a line which looks like:

[1] 1234

indicating that the job which was started asynchronously was job number 1 and had one (top-level) process, whose process id was 1234.

If you are running a job and wish to do something else you may hit the key **^Z** (CTRL-z) which sends a STOP signal to the current job. The shell will then normally indicate that the job has been 'Stopped', and print another prompt. You can then manipulate the state of this job, putting it in the background with the **bg** command, or run some other commands and then eventually bring the job back into the foreground with the foreground command **fg**. A **^Z** takes effect immediately and is like an interrupt in that pending output and unread input are discarded when it is typed.

A job being run in the background will stop if it tries to read from the terminal. Background jobs are normally allowed to produce output, but this can be disabled by giving the command "stty tostop". If you set this tty option, then background jobs will stop when they try to produce output like they do when they try to read input.

There are several ways to refer to jobs in the shell. A job can be referred to by the process id of any process of the job or by one of the following:

%*number*	The job with the given number.
%*string*	Any job whose command line begins with *string*.
%?*string*	Any job whose command line contains *string*.
%%	Current job.
%+	Equivalent to %%.
%–	Previous job.

This shell learns immediately whenever a process changes state. It normally informs you whenever a job becomes blocked so that no further progress is possible, but only just before it prints a prompt. This is done so that it does not otherwise disturb your work.

When the monitor mode is on, each background job that completes triggers any trap set for **CHLD**.

When you try to leave the shell while jobs are running or stopped, you will be warned that 'You have stopped(running) jobs.' You may use the **jobs** command to see what they are. If you do this or immediately try to exit again, the shell will not warn you a second time, and the stopped jobs will be terminated.

Signals.

When a command is run in the background (that it, when it is followed by **&**) and the job **monitor** option is active, the command does not receive INTERRUPT or QUIT signals. When a command is run in the background (that it, when it is followed by **&**) and the job **monitor** option is not active, the command receives INTERRUPT or QUIT signals but ignores them. Otherwise, signals have the values inherited by the shell from its parent (but see also the **trap** command below).

Execution.

Each time a command is executed, the above substitutions are carried out. If the command name matches one of the Special Commands listed below, it is executed within the current shell process. Next, the command name is checked to see if it matches one of the user defined functions. If it does, the positional parameters are saved and then reset to the arguments of the *function* call. When the *function* completes or issues a **return**, the positional parameter list is restored and any trap set on **EXIT** within the function is executed. The value of a *function* is the value of the last command executed. A function is also executed in the current shell process. If a command name is not a *special command* or a user defined *function*, a process is created and an attempt is made to execute the command via **exec**(2).

The shell variable **PATH** defines the search path for the directory containing the command. Alternative directory names are separated by a colon (**:**). The default path is **/usr/bin:** (specifying **/usr/bin** and the current directory in that order). The current directory can be specified by two or more adjacent colons, or by a colon at the beginning or end of the path list. If the command name contains a **/** then the search path is not used. Otherwise, each directory in the path is searched for an executable file. If the file has execute permission but is not a directory or an **a.out** file, it is assumed to be a file containing shell commands. A sub-shell is spawned to read it. All non-exported aliases, functions, and variables, are removed in this case. A parenthesized command is executed in a sub-shell without removing non-exported quantities.

Command Re-entry.

The text of the last **HISTSIZE** (default 128) commands entered from a terminal device is saved in a *history* file. The file **$HOME/.sh_history** is used if the file denoted by the **HISTFILE** variable is not set or is not writable. A shell can access the commands of all *interactive* shells which use the same named **HISTFILE**. The special command **fc** is used to list or edit a portion of this file. The portion of the file to be edited or listed can be selected by number or by giving the first character or characters of the command. A single command or range of commands can be specified. If you do not specify an editor program as an argument to **fc** then the value of the variable **FCEDIT** is used. If **FCEDIT** is not defined then **/usr/bin/ed** is used. The edited command(s) is printed and re-executed upon leaving the editor. The editor name **-** is used to skip the editing phase and to re-execute the command. In this case a substitution variable of the form *old=new* can be used to modify the command before execution. For example, if **r** is aliased to **'fc -e -'** then typing **'r bad=good c'** will re-execute the most recent command which starts with the letter **c**, replacing the first occurrence of the string **bad** with the string **good**.

In-line Editing Options

Normally, each command line entered from a terminal device is simply typed followed by a new-line ('RETURN' or 'LINE FEED'). If either the **emacs**, **gmacs**, or **vi** option is active, the user can edit the command line. To be in either of these edit modes **set** the corresponding option. An editing option is automatically selected each time the **VISUAL** or **EDITOR** variable is assigned a value ending in either of these option names.

The editing features require that the user's terminal accept 'RETURN' as carriage return without line feed and that a space (' ') must overwrite the current character on the screen.

The editing modes implement a concept where the user is looking through a window at the current line. The window width is the value of **COLUMNS** if it is defined, otherwise 80. If the line is longer than the window width minus two, a mark is displayed at the end of the window to notify the user. As the cursor moves and reaches the window boundaries the window will be centered about the cursor. The mark is a **>** (**<**, *****) if the line extends on the right (left, both) side(s) of the window.

The search commands in each edit mode provide access to the history file. Only strings are matched, not patterns, although a leading ^ in the string restricts the match to begin at the first character in the line.

vi Editing Mode

There are two typing modes. Initially, when you enter a command you are in the *input* mode. To edit, the user enters *control* mode by typing ESC (`\033`) and moves the cursor to the point needing correction and then inserts or deletes characters or words as needed. Most control commands accept an optional repeat *count* prior to the command.

When in **vi** mode on most systems, canonical processing is initially enabled and the command will be echoed again if the speed is 1200 baud or greater and it contains any control characters or less than one second has elapsed since the prompt was printed. The ESC character terminates canonical processing for the remainder of the command and the user can then modify the command line. This scheme has the advantages of canonical processing with the type-ahead echoing of raw mode.

If the option **viraw** is also set, the terminal will always have canonical processing disabled.

Input Edit Commands

By default the editor is in input mode.

erase — (User defined erase character as defined by the stty command, usually **^H** or **#**.) Delete previous character.

^W — Delete the previous blank separated word.

^D — Terminate the shell.

^V — Escape next character. Editing characters, the user's erase or kill characters may be entered in a command line or in a search string if preceded by a **^V**. The **^V** removes the next character's editing features (if any).

\ — Escape the next *erase* or **kill** character.

Motion Edit Commands

These commands will move the cursor.

[*count*]**l** — Cursor forward (right) one character.

[*count*]**w** — Cursor forward one alpha-numeric word.

[*count*]**W** — Cursor to the beginning of the next word that follows a blank.

[*count*]`e` Cursor to end of word.

[*count*]`E` Cursor to end of the current blank delimited word.

[*count*]`h` Cursor backward (left) one character.

[*count*]`b` Cursor backward one word.

[*count*]`B` Cursor to preceding blank separated word.

[*count*]`|` Cursor to column *count*.

[*count*]`f`*c* Find the next character *c* in the current line.

[*count*]`F`*c* Find the previous character *c* in the current line.

[*count*]`t`*c* Equivalent to `f` followed by `h`.

[*count*]`T`*c* Equivalent to `F` followed by `l`.

[*count*]`;` Repeats *count* times, the last single character find command, `f`, `F`, `t`, or `T`.

[*count*]`,` Reverses the last single character find command *count* times.

`0` Cursor to start of line.

`^` Cursor to first non-blank character in line.

`$` Cursor to end of line.

Search Edit Commands

These commands access your command history.

[*count*]`k` Fetch previous command. Each time `k` is entered the previous command back in time is accessed.

[*count*]`-` Equivalent to `k`.

[*count*]`j` Fetch next command. Each time `j` is entered the next command forward in time is accessed.

[*count*]`+` Equivalent to `j`.

[*count*]`G` The command number *count* is fetched. The default is the least recent history command.

`/`*string* Search backward through history for a previous command containing *string*. *String* is terminated by a "RETURN" or "NEW LINE". If string is preceded by a ^, the matched line must begin with *string*. If *string* is null the previous string will be used.

`?`*string* Same as `/` except that search will be in the forward direction.

`n` Search for next match of the last pattern to `/` or `?` commands.

`N` Search for next match of the last pattern to `/` or `?`, but in reverse direction. Search history for the *string* entered by the previous `/` command.

Text Modification Edit Commands

These commands will modify the line.

`a` Enter input mode and enter text after the current character.

`A` Append text to the end of the line. Equivalent to `$a`.

[*count*]`c`*motion*

`c`[*count*]*motion*
Delete current character through the character that *motion* would move the cursor to and enter input mode. If *motion* is `c`, the entire line will be deleted and input mode entered.

`C` Delete the current character through the end of line and enter input mode. Equivalent to `c$`.

`S` Equivalent to `cc`.

`D` Delete the current character through the end of line. Equivalent to `d$`.

[*count*]`d`*motion*

`d`[*count*]*motion*
Delete current character through the character that *motion* would move to. If *motion* is `d`, the entire line will be deleted.

`i` Enter input mode and insert text before the current character.

`I` Insert text before the beginning of the line. Equivalent to `0i`.

[*count*]`P` Place the previous text modification before the cursor.

[*count*]`p` Place the previous text modification after the cursor.

`R` Enter input mode and replace characters on the screen with characters you type overlay fashion.

[*count*]`r`*c* Replace the *count* character(s) starting at the current cursor position with *c*, and advance the cursor.

[*count*]`x` Delete current character.

[*count*]`X` Delete preceding character.

[*count*]`.` Repeat the previous text modification command.

[*count*]~ Invert the case of the *count* character(s) starting at the current cursor position and advance the cursor.

[*count*]_ Causes the *count* word of the previous command to be appended and input mode entered. The last word is used if *count* is omitted.

`*` Causes an `*` to be appended to the current word and file name generation attempted. If no match is found, it rings the bell. Otherwise, the word is replaced by the matching pattern and input mode is entered.

`\` Filename completion. Replaces the current word with the longest common prefix of all filenames matching the current word with an asterisk appended. If the match is unique, a **/** is appended if the file is a directory and a space is appended if the file is not a directory.

Other Edit Commands

Miscellaneous commands.

[*count*]**y***motion*

y[*count*]*motion*
: Yank current character through character that *motion* would move the cursor to and puts them into the delete buffer. The text and cursor are unchanged.

Y Yanks from current position to end of line. Equivalent to **y$**.

u Undo the last text modifying command.

U Undo all the text modifying commands performed on the line.

[*count*]**v** Returns the command **fc -e ${VISUAL:-${EDITOR:-vi}}** *count* in the input buffer. If *count* is omitted, then the current line is used.

^L Line feed and print current line. Has effect only in control mode.

^J (New line) Execute the current line, regardless of mode.

^M (Return) Execute the current line, regardless of mode.

Sends the line after inserting a **#** in front of the line. Useful for causing the current line to be inserted in the history without being executed.

= List the file names that match the current word if an asterisk were appended it.

@*letter* Your alias list is searched for an alias by the name *_letter* and if an alias of this name is defined, its value will be inserted on the input queue for processing.

Emacs Editing Mode

This mode is entered by enabling either the *emacs* or *gmacs* option. The only difference between these two modes is the way they handle **^T**. To edit, the user moves the cursor to the point needing correction and then inserts or deletes characters or words as needed. All the editing commands are control characters or escape sequences. The notation for control characters is caret (^) followed by the character. For example, **^F** is the notation for CTRL-**f**. This is entered by depressing 'f' while holding down the 'CTRL' (control) key. (The notation **^?** indicates the DEL (delete) key.)

The notation for escape sequences is **M-** followed by a character. For example, **M-f** (pronounced Meta f) is entered by depressing ESC (ascii **\033**) followed by 'f'. (**M-F** would be the notation for ESC followed by 'SHIFT' (capital) 'F'.)

All edit commands operate from any place on the line (not just at the beginning). Neither the "RETURN" nor the "LINE FEED" key is entered after edit commands except when noted.

`^F`	Move cursor forward (right) one character.
`M-f`	Move cursor forward one word. (The emacs editor's idea of a word is a string of characters consisting of only letters, digits and underscores.)
`^B`	Move cursor backward (left) one character.
`M-b`	Move cursor backward one word.
`^A`	Move cursor to start of line.
`^E`	Move cursor to end of line.
`^]`*char*	Move cursor forward to character *char* on current line.
`M-^]`*char*	Move cursor back to character *char* on current line.
`^X^X`	Interchange the cursor and mark.
erase	(User defined erase character as defined by the **stty**(1) command, usually `^H` or `#`.) Delete previous character.
`^D`	Delete current character.
`M-d`	Delete current word.
`M-^H`	(Meta-backspace) Delete previous word.
`M-h`	Delete previous word.
`M-^?`	(Meta-DEL) Delete previous word (if your interrupt character is `^?` (DEL, the default) then this command will not work).
`^T`	Transpose current character with next character in *emacs* mode. Transpose two previous characters in *gmacs* mode.
`^C`	Capitalize current character.
`M-c`	Capitalize current word.
`M-l`	Change the current word to lower case.
`^K`	Delete from the cursor to the end of the line. If preceded by a numerical parameter whose value is less than the current cursor position, then delete from given position up to the cursor. If preceded by a numerical parameter whose value is greater than the current cursor position, then delete from cursor up to given cursor position.
`^W`	Kill from the cursor to the mark.
`M-p`	Push the region from the cursor to the mark on the stack.
`kill`	(User defined kill character as defined by the stty command, usually `^G` or `@`.) Kill the entire current line. If two **kill** characters are entered in succession, all kill characters from then on cause a line feed (useful when using paper terminals).
`^Y`	Restore last item removed from line. (Yank item back to the line.)
`^L`	Line feed and print current line.
`^@`	(Null character) Set mark.
`M-space`	(Meta space) Set mark.
`^J`	(New line) Execute the current line.
`^M`	(Return) Execute the current line.
eof	End-of-file character, normally `^D`, is processed as an End-of-file only if the current line is null.
`^P`	Fetch previous command. Each time `^P` is entered the previous command back in time is accessed. Moves back one line when not on the first line of a multi-line command.

M-< Fetch the least recent (oldest) history line.

M-> Fetch the most recent (youngest) history line.

^N Fetch next command line. Each time **^N** is entered the next command line forward in time is accessed.

^R*string* Reverse search history for a previous command line containing *string*. If a parameter of zero is given, the search is forward. *String* is terminated by a "RETURN" or "NEW LINE". If string is preceded by a ^, the matched line must begin with *string*. If *string* is omitted, then the next command line containing the most recent *string* is accessed. In this case a parameter of zero reverses the direction of the search.

^O Operate – Execute the current line and fetch the next line relative to current line from the history file.

M-*digits* (Escape) Define numeric parameter, the digits are taken as a parameter to the next command. The commands that accept a parameter are **^F**, **^B**, *erase*, **^C**, **^D**, **^K**, **^R**, **^P**, **^N**, **^]**, **M-.**, **M-^]**, **M-_**, **M-b**, **M-c**, **M-d**, **M-f**, **M-h** **M-l** and **M-^H**.

M-*letter* Soft-key – Your alias list is searched for an alias by the name *_letter* and if an alias of this name is defined, its value will be inserted on the input queue. The *letter* must not be one of the above meta-functions. **M-]***letter* Soft-key – Your alias list is searched for an alias by the name *__letter* and if an alias of this name is defined, its value will be inserted on the input queue. The can be used to program functions keys on many terminals.

M-. The last word of the previous command is inserted on the line. If preceded by a numeric parameter, the value of this parameter determines which word to insert rather than the last word.

M-_ Same as **M-.**.

M-* Attempt file name generation on the current word. An asterisk is appended if the word doesn't match any file or contain any special pattern characters.

M-ESC File name completion. Replaces the current word with the longest common prefix of all filenames matching the current word with an asterisk appended. If the match is unique, a / is appended if the file is a directory and a space is appended if the file is not a directory.

M-= List files matching current word pattern if an asterisk were appended.

^U Multiply parameter of next command by 4.

**** Escape next character. Editing characters, the user's erase, kill and interrupt (normally **^?**) characters may be entered in a command line or in a search string if preceded by a \. The \ removes the next character's editing features (if any).

^V Display version of the shell.

M-# Insert a **#** at the beginning of the line and execute it. This causes a comment to be inserted in the history file.

Special Commands.

The following simple-commands are executed in the shell process. Input/Output redirection is permitted. Unless otherwise indicated, the output is written on file descriptor 1 and the exit status, when there is no syntax error, is zero. Commands that are preceded by one or two † are treated specially in the following ways:

1. Variable assignment lists preceding the command remain in effect when the command completes.
2. I/O redirections are processed after variable assignments.
3. Errors cause a script that contains them to abort.
4. Words, following a command preceded by †† that are in the format of a variable assignment, are expanded with the same rules as a variable assignment. This means that tilde substitution is performed after the = sign and word splitting and file name generation are not performed.

† **:** [*arg* ...]
: The command only expands parameters.

† **.** *file* [*arg* ...]
: Read the complete *file* then execute the commands. The commands are executed in the current shell environment. The search path specified by **PATH** is used to find the directory containing *file*. If any arguments *arg* are given, they become the positional parameters. Otherwise the positional parameters are unchanged. The exit status is the exit status of the last command executed.

†† **alias** [**-tx**] [*name*[=*value*]] ...
: *Alias* with no arguments prints the list of aliases in the form *name=value* on standard output. An *alias* is defined for each name whose *value* is given. A trailing space in *value* causes the next word to be checked for alias substitution. The **-t** flag is used to set and list tracked aliases. The value of a tracked alias is the full pathname corresponding to the given *name*. The value becomes undefined when the value of **PATH** is reset but the aliases remain tracked. Without the **-t** flag, for each *name* in the argument list for which no *value* is given, the name and value of the alias is printed. The **-x** flag is used to set or print exported aliases. An exported alias is defined for scripts invoked by name. The exit status is non-zero if a *name* is given, but no value, for which no alias has been defined.

bg [*job*...]
: This command is only on systems that support job control. Puts each specified *job* into the background. The current job is put in the background if *job* is not specified. See *Jobs* for a description of the format of *job*.

† **break** [*n*]
: Exit from the enclosing **for**, **while**, **until** or **select** loop, if any. If *n* is specified then break *n* levels.

† **continue** [*n*]
: Resume the next iteration of the enclosing **for**, **while**, **until** or **select** loop. If *n* is specified then resume at the *n*-th enclosing loop.

cd [*arg*]
cd *old new*
: This command can be in either of two forms. In the first form it changes the current directory to *arg*. If *arg* is - the directory is changed to the previous directory. The shell variable **HOME** is the default *arg*. The variable **PWD** is set to the current directory. The shell variable **CDPATH** defines the search path for the directory containing *arg*. Alternative directory names are separated

by a colon (**:**). The default path is **<null>** (specifying the current directory). Note that the current directory is specified by a null path name, which can appear immediately after the equal sign or between the colon delimiters anywhere else in the path list. If *arg* begins with a **/** then the search path is not used. Otherwise, each directory in the path is searched for *arg*.

The second form of **cd** substitutes the string *new* for the string *old* in the current directory name, **PWD** and tries to change to this new directory.

The **cd** command may not be executed by **rksh**.

echo [*arg* ...]
See **echo**(1) for usage and description.

† **eval** [*arg* ...]
The arguments are read as input to the shell and the resulting command(s) executed.

† **exec** [*arg* ...]
If *arg* is given, the command specified by the arguments is executed in place of this shell without creating a new process. Input/output arguments may appear and affect the current process. If no arguments are given the effect of this command is to modify file descriptors as prescribed by the input/output redirection list. In this case, any file descriptor numbers greater than 2 that are opened with this mechanism are closed when invoking another program.

† **exit** [*n*]
Causes the shell to exit with the exit status specified by *n*. If *n* is omitted then the exit status is that of the last command executed. An end-of-file will also cause the shell to exit except for a shell which has the *ignoreeof* option (see **set** below) turned on.

†† **export** [*name*[=*value*]] ...
The given *name*s are marked for automatic export to the *environment* of subsequently-executed commands.

fc [**-e** *ename*] [**-nlr**] [*first* [*last*]]
fc -e - [*old*=*new*] [*command*]
In the first form, a range of commands from *first* to *last* is selected from the last **HISTSIZE** commands that were typed at the terminal. The arguments *first* and *last* may be specified as a number or as a string. A string is used to locate the most recent command starting with the given string. A negative number is used as an offset to the current command number. If the flag **-l**, is selected, the commands are listed on standard output. Otherwise, the editor program *ename* is invoked on a file containing these keyboard commands. If *ename* is not supplied, then the value of the variable **FCEDIT** (default /usr/bin/ed) is used as the editor. When editing is complete, the edited command(s) is executed. If *last* is not specified then it will be set to *first*. If *first* is not specified the default is the previous command for editing and –16 for listing. The flag **-r** reverses the order of the commands and the flag **-n** suppresses command numbers when listing. In the second form the *command* is re-executed after the substitution *old*=*new* is performed.

fg [*job*...]
This command is only on systems that support job control. Each *job* specified is brought to the foreground. Otherwise, the current job is brought into the foreground. See *Jobs* for a description of the format of *job*.

getopts *optstring name* [*arg* ...]
Checks *arg* for legal options. If *arg* is omitted, the positional parameters are used. An option argument begins with a **+** or a **-**. An option not beginning with **+** or **-** or the argument **--** ends the options. *optstring* contains the letters that **getopts** recognizes. If a letter is followed by a **:**, that option is expected to have an argument. The options can be separated from the argument by blanks.

getopts places the next option letter it finds inside variable *name* each time it is invoked with a **+** prepended when *arg* begins with a **+**. The index of the next *arg* is stored in **OPTIND**. The option argument, if any, gets stored in **OPTARG**.

A leading **:** in *optstring* causes **getopts** to store the letter of an invalid option in **OPTARG**, and to set *name* to **?** for an unknown option and to **:** when a required option is missing. Otherwise, **getopts** prints an error message. The exit status is non-zero when there are no more options.

jobs [**-lnp**] [*job* ...]
Lists information about each given job; or all active jobs if *job* is omitted. The **-l** flag lists process ids in addition to the normal information. The **-n** flag only displays jobs that have stopped or exited since last notified. The **-p** flag causes only the process group to be listed. See *Jobs* for a description of the format of *job*.

kill [-*sig*] *job* ...
kill -l
Sends either the TERM (terminate) signal or the specified signal to the specified jobs or processes. Signals are either given by number or by names (as given in **/usr/include/signal.h**, stripped of the prefix "SIG"). If the signal being sent is TERM (terminate) or HUP (hangup), then the job or process will be sent a CONT (continue) signal if it is stopped. The argument *job* can the process id of a process that is not a member of one of the active jobs. See *Jobs* for a description of the format of *job*. In the second form, **kill -l**, the signal numbers and names are listed.

let *arg* ...
Each *arg* is a separate *arithmetic expression* to be evaluated. See Arithmetic Evaluation above, for a description of arithmetic expression evaluation.

The exit status is 0 if the value of the last expression is non-zero, and 1 otherwise.

† **newgrp** [*arg* ...]
Equivalent to **exec /usr/bin/newgrp** *arg* ....

print [**-Rnprsu**[*n*]] [*arg* ...]
The shell output mechanism. With no flags or with flag **-** or **--** the arguments are printed on standard output as described by **echo**(1). In raw mode, **-R** or **-r**, the escape conventions of **echo** are ignored. The **-R** option

will print all subsequent arguments and options other than **-n**. The **-p** option causes the arguments to be written onto the pipe of the process spawned with **|&** instead of standard output. The **-s** option causes the arguments to be written onto the history file instead of standard output. The **-u** flag can be used to specify a one digit file descriptor unit number **n** on which the output will be placed. The default is 1. If the flag **-n** is used, no new-line is added to the output.

pwd Equivalent to **print -r - $PWD**

read [**-prsu**[*n*]] [*name***?***prompt*] [*name* ...]
The shell input mechanism. One line is read and is broken up into fields using the characters in **IFS** as separators. In raw mode, **-r**, a \ at the end of a line does not signify line continuation. The first field is assigned to the first *name*, the second field to the second *name*, and so on, with leftover fields assigned to the last *name*. The **-p** option causes the input line to be taken from the input pipe of a process spawned by the shell using **|&**. If the **-s** flag is present, the input will be saved as a command in the history file. The flag **-u** can be used to specify a one digit file descriptor unit to read from. The file descriptor can be opened with the **exec** special command. The default value of *n* is 0. If *name* is omitted then **REPLY** is used as the default *name*. The exit status is 0 unless an end-of-file is encountered. An end-of-file with the **-p** option causes cleanup for this process so that another can be spawned. If the first argument contains a **?**, the remainder of this word is used as a *prompt* on standard error when the shell is interactive. The exit status is 0 unless an end-of-file is encountered.

†† **readonly** [*name*[=*value*]] ...
The given *names* are marked readonly and these names cannot be changed by subsequent assignment.

† **return** [*n*]
Causes a shell *function* to return to the invoking script with the return status specified by *n*. If *n* is omitted then the return status is that of the last command executed. If **return** is invoked while not in a *function* or a **.** script, then it is the same as an **exit**.

set [±**aefhkmnpstuvx**] [±**o** *option*]... [±**A** *name*] [*arg* ...]
The flags for this command have meaning as follows:

- **-A** Array assignment. Unset the variable *name* and assign values sequentially from the list *arg*. If **+A** is used, the variable *name* is not unset first.
- **-a** All subsequent variables that are defined are automatically exported.
- **-e** If a command has a non-zero exit status, execute the **ERR** trap, if set, and exit. This mode is disabled while reading profiles.
- **-f** Disables file name generation.
- **-h** Each command becomes a tracked alias when first encountered.
- **-k** All variable assignment arguments are placed in the environment for a command, not just those that precede the command name.

-m Background jobs will run in a separate process group and a line will print upon completion. The exit status of background jobs is reported in a completion message. On systems with job control, this flag is turned on automatically for interactive shells.

-n Read commands and check them for syntax errors, but do not execute them. Ignored for interactive shells.

-o The following argument can be one of the following option names:

allexport	Same as **-a**.
errexit	Same as **-e**.
bgnice	All background jobs are run at a lower priority. This is the default mode.
emacs	Puts you in an *emacs* style in-line editor for command entry.
gmacs	Puts you in a *gmacs* style in-line editor for command entry.
ignoreeof	The shell will not exit on end-of-file. The command **exit** must be used.
keyword	Same as **-k**.
markdirs	All directory names resulting from file name generation have a trailing **/** appended.
monitor	Same as **-m**.
noclobber	Prevents redirection **>** from truncating existing files. Require **>|** to truncate a file when turned on.
noexec	Same as **-n**.
noglob	Same as **-f**.
nolog	Do not save function definitions in history file.
nounset	Same as **-u**.
privileged	Same as **-p**.
verbose	Same as **-v**.
trackall	Same as **-h**.
vi	Puts you in insert mode of a **vi** style in-line editor until you hit escape character **033**. This puts you in move mode. A return sends the line.
viraw	Each character is processed as it is typed in **vi** mode.
xtrace	Same as **-x**.

If no option name is supplied then the current option settings are printed.

-p Disables processing of the **$HOME/.profile** file and uses the file **/etc/suid_profile** instead of the **ENV** file. This mode is on whenever the effective uid (gid) is not equal to the real uid (gid). Turning this off causes the effective uid and gid to be set to the real uid and gid.

-s Sort the positional parameters lexicographically.

-t Exit after reading and executing one command.

-u Treat unset parameters as an error when substituting.

-v Print shell input lines as they are read.

-x Print commands and their arguments as they are executed.

- Turns off **-x** and **-v** flags and stops examining arguments for flags.

-- Do not change any of the flags; useful in setting **$1** to a value beginning with **-**. If no arguments follow this flag then the positional parameters are unset.

Using **+** rather than **-** causes these flags to be turned off. These flags can also be used upon invocation of the shell. The current set of flags may be found in **$-**. Unless **-A** is specified, the remaining arguments are positional parameters and are assigned, in order, to **$1 $2** .... If no arguments are given then the names and values of all variables are printed on the standard output.

† **shift** [*n*]
The positional parameters from **$***n***+1** ... are renamed **$1** ... , default *n* is 1. The parameter *n* can be any arithmetic expression that evaluates to a non-negative number less than or equal to **$#**.

† **times** Print the accumulated user and system times for the shell and for processes run from the shell.

† **trap** [*arg*] [*sig*] ...
arg is a command to be read and executed when the shell receives signal(s) *sig*. (Note that *arg* is scanned once when the trap is set and once when the trap is taken.) Each *sig* can be given as a number or as the name of the signal. Trap commands are executed in order of signal number. Any attempt to set a trap on a signal that was ignored on entry to the current shell is ineffective. If *arg* is omitted or is **-**, then all trap(s) *sig* are reset to their original values. If *arg* is the null string then this signal is ignored by the shell and by the commands it invokes. If *sig* is **ERR** then *arg* will be executed whenever a command has a non-zero exit status. *sig* is **DEBUG** then *arg* will be executed after each command. If *sig* is **0** or **EXIT** and the **trap** statement is executed inside the body of a function, then the command *arg* is executed after the function completes. If *sig* is **0** or **EXIT** for a **trap** set outside any function then the command *arg* is executed on exit from the shell. The **trap** command with no arguments prints a list of commands associated with each signal number.

†† **typeset** [±**HLRZfilrtux**[*n*]] [*name*[**=***value*]] ...
Sets attributes and values for shell variables. When invoked inside a function, a new instance of the variable *name* is created. The parameter value and type are restored when the function completes. The following list of attributes may be specified:

-H This flag provides UNIX to host-name file mapping on non-UNIX machines.

-L Left justify and remove leading blanks from *value*. If *n* is nonzero it defines the width of the field, otherwise it is determined by the width of the value of first assignment. When the variable is assigned to, it is filled on the right with blanks or truncated, if necessary, to fit into the field. Leading zeros are removed if the **-Z** flag is also set. The **-R** flag is turned off.

- **-R** Right justify and fill with leading blanks. If *n* is non-zero it defines the width of the field, otherwise it is determined by the width of the value of first assignment. The field is left filled with blanks or truncated from the end if the variable is reassigned. The **L** flag is turned off.
- **-Z** Right justify and fill with leading zeros if the first non-blank character is a digit and the **-L** flag has not been set. If *n* is non-zero it defines the width of the field, otherwise it is determined by the width of the value of first assignment.
- **-f** The names refer to function names rather than variable names. No assignments can be made and the only other valid flags are **-t**, **-u** and **-x**. The flag **-t** turns on execution tracing for this function. The flag **-u** causes this function to be marked undefined. The **FPATH** variable will be searched to find the function definition when the function is referenced. The flag **-x** allows the function definition to remain in effect across shell procedures invoked by name.
- **-i** Variable is an integer. This makes arithmetic faster. If *n* is non-zero it defines the output arithmetic base, otherwise the first assignment determines the output base.
- **-l** All upper-case characters converted to lower-case. The upper-case flag, **-u** is turned off.
- **-r** The given *names* are marked readonly and these names cannot be changed by subsequent assignment.
- **-t** Tags the variables. Tags are user definable and have no special meaning to the shell.
- **-u** All lower-case characters are converted to upper-case characters. The lower-case flag, **-l** is turned off.
- **-x** The given *names* are marked for automatic export to the *environment* of subsequently-executed commands.

Using **+** rather than **-** causes these flags to be turned off. If no *name* arguments are given but flags are specified, a list of *names* (and optionally the **values**) of the *variables* which have these flags set is printed. (Using **+** rather than **-** keeps the values from being printed.) If no *names* and flags are given, the *names* and *attributes* of all *variables* are printed.

ulimit [–[**HS**][**a** | **cdfnstv**]]

ulimit [–[**HS**][**c** | **d** | **f** | **n** | **s** | **t** | **v**]] *limit*

ulimit prints or sets hard or soft resource limits. These limits are described in **getrlimit**(2).

If *limit* is not present, **ulimit** prints the specified limits. Any number of limits may be printed at one time. The **-a** option prints all limits.

If *limit* is present, **ulimit** sets the specified limit to *limit*. The string **unlimited** requests the largest valid limit. Limits may be set for only one resource at a time. Any user may set a soft limit to any value below the hard limit. Any user may lower a hard limit. Only a privileged user may raise a hard limit; see **su**(1M).

The **-H** option specifies a hard limit. The **-S** option specifies a soft limit. If neither option is specified, **ulimit** will set both limits and print the soft limit.

The following options specify the resource whose limits are to be printed or set. If no option is specified, the file size limit is printed or set.

-c maximum core file size (in 512-byte blocks)

-d maximum size of data segment or heap (in kbytes)

-f maximum file size (in 512-byte blocks)

-n maximum file descriptor plus 1

-s maximum size of stack segment (in kbytes)

-t maximum CPU time (in seconds)

-v maximum size of virtual memory (in kbytes)

If no option is given, **-f** is assumed.

umask [*mask*]
The user file-creation mask is set to *mask* [see **umask**(2)]. *mask* can either be an octal number or a symbolic value as described in **chmod**(1). If a symbolic value is given, the new umask value is the complement of the result of applying *mask* to the complement of the previous umask value. If *mask* is omitted, the current value of the mask is printed.

unalias *name* ...
The variables given by the list of *name*s are removed from the *alias* list.

unset [**-f**] *name* ...
The variables given by the list of *name*s are unassigned, i. e., their values and attributes are erased. Read-only variables cannot be unset. If the flag, **-f**, is set, then the names refer to *function* names. Unsetting **ERRNO**, **LINENO**, **MAILCHECK**, **OPTARG**, **OPTIND**, **RANDOM**, **SECONDS**, **TMOUT**, and _ causes removes their special meaning even if they are subsequently assigned to.

† **wait** [*job*]
Wait for the specified *job* and report its termination status. If *job* is not given then all currently active child processes are waited for. The exit status from this command is that of the process waited for. See *Jobs* for a description of the format of *job*.

whence [**-pv**] *name* ...
For each *name*, indicate how it would be interpreted if used as a command name.

-v produces a more verbose report.

-p does a path search for *name* even if name is an alias, a function, or a reserved word.

Invocation.

If the shell is invoked by **exec**(2), and the first character of argument zero (**$0**) is **-**, then the shell is assumed to be a **login** shell and commands are read from **/etc/profile** and then from either **.profile** in the current directory or **$HOME/.profile**, if either file exists. Next, commands are read from the file named by performing parameter substitution on the value of the environment variable **ENV** if the file exists. If the **-s** flag is not present and *arg* is, then a path search is performed on the first *arg* to determine the name of the script to execute. The script *arg* must have read permission and any **setuid** and **setgid** settings will be ignored. Commands are then read as described below; the following flags are interpreted by the shell when it is invoked:

-c *string* If the **-c** flag is present then commands are read from *string*.

-s If the **-s** flag is present or if no arguments remain then commands are read from the standard input. Shell output, except for the output of the Special commands listed above, is written to file descriptor 2.

-i If the **-i** flag is present or if the shell input and output are attached to a terminal (as told by **ioctl**(2)) then this shell is *interactive*. In this case TERM is ignored (so that **kill 0** does not kill an interactive shell) and INTR is caught and ignored (so that **wait** is interruptible). In all cases, QUIT is ignored by the shell.

-r If the **-r** flag is present the shell is a restricted shell.

The remaining flags and arguments are described under the **set** command above.

rksh Only.

rksh is used to set up login names and execution environments whose capabilities are more controlled than those of the standard shell. The actions of **rksh** are identical to those of **sh**, except that the following are disallowed:

changing directory [see **cd**(1)],
setting the value of **SHELL**, **ENV**, or **PATH**,
specifying path or command names containing **/**,
redirecting output (**>**, **>|** , **<>** , and **>>**).

The restrictions above are enforced after **.profile** and the **ENV** files are interpreted.

When a command to be executed is found to be a shell procedure, **rksh** invokes **ksh** to execute it. Thus, it is possible to provide to the end-user shell procedures that have access to the full power of the standard shell, while imposing a limited menu of commands; this scheme assumes that the end-user does not have write and execute permissions in the same directory.

The net effect of these rules is that the writer of the **.profile** has complete control over user actions, by performing guaranteed setup actions and leaving the user in an appropriate directory (probably not the login directory).

The system administrator often sets up a directory of commands (that is, **/usr/rbin**) that can be safely invoked by **rksh**.

EXIT STATUS

Errors detected by the shell, such as syntax errors, cause the shell to return a non-zero exit status. Otherwise, the shell returns the exit status of the last command executed (see also the **exit** command above). If the shell is being used non-interactively then execution of the shell file is abandoned. Run time errors detected by the shell are reported by printing the command or function name and the error condition. If the line number that the error occurred on is greater than one, then the line number is also printed in square brackets (**[]**) after the command or function name.

FILES

/etc/passwd
/etc/profile
/etc/suid_profile
$HOME/.profile
/tmp/sh*
/dev/null

SEE ALSO

a.out(4), **cat**(1), **cd**(1), **chmod**(1), **cut**(1), **dup**(2), **echo**(1), **env**(1), **environ**(4), **exec**(2), **fork**(2), **ioctl**(2), **lseek**(2), **newgrp**(1M), **paste**(1), **pipe**(2), **profile**(4), **rand**(3C), **signal**(2), **stty**(1), **test**(1), **ulimit**(2), **umask**(1), **umask**(2), **vi**(1), **wait**(2)

Morris I. Bolsky and David G. Korn, *The KornShell Command and Programming Language*, Prentice Hall, 1989

NOTES

If a command which is a *tracked alias* is executed, and then a command with the same name is installed in a directory in the search path before the directory where the original command was found, the shell will continue to **exec** the original command. Use the **-t** option of the **alias** command to correct this situation.

Some very old shell scripts contain a ^ as a synonym for the pipe character. |.

Using the **fc** built-in command within a compound command will cause the whole command to disappear from the history file.

The built-in command **.** *file* reads the whole file before any commands are executed. Therefore, **alias** and **unalias** commands in the file will not apply to any functions defined in the file.

Traps are not processed while a job is waiting for a foreground process. Thus, a trap on **CHLD** won't be executed until the foreground job terminates.

NAME

labelit (generic) – provide labels for file systems

SYNOPSIS

labelit [**-F** *FSType*] [**-V**] [*current_options*] [**-o** *specific_options*] *special* [*operands*]

DESCRIPTION

labelit can be used to provide labels for unmounted disk file systems or file systems being copied to tape.

The *special* name should be the disk partition (for example, **/dev/rdsk/***, where the value of * is machine specific), or the cartridge tape (for example, **/dev/rmt/***). The device may not be on a remote machine. *operands* are *FSType*-specific and the manual page of the *FSType*-specific **labelit** command should be consulted for a detailed description.

current_options are options supported by the **s5**-specific module of **labelit**. Other *FSTypes* do not necessarily support these options. *specific_options* indicate suboptions specified in a comma-separated list of suboptions and/or keyword-attribute pairs for interpretation by the *FSType*-specific module of the command.

The options are:

-F specify the *FSType* on which to operate. The *FSType* should either be specified here or be determinable from **/etc/vfstab** by matching *special* with an entry in the table.

-V echo complete command line. This option is used to verify and validate the command line. Additional information obtained via a **/etc/vfstab** lookup is included in the output. The command is not executed.

-o Specify *FSType*-specific options.

NOTES

This command may not be supported for all FSTypes.

FILES

/etc/vfstab list of default parameters for each file system

SEE ALSO

s5-specific **labelit**(1M), **sfs**-specific **labelit**(1M), **ufs**-specific **labelit**(1M), **vxfs**-specific **labelit**(1M), **vfstab**(4)

NAME

labelit (s5) – provide labels for **s5** file systems

SYNOPSIS

labelit [**-F s5**] [*generic_options*] [**-n**] *special* [*fsname volume*]

DESCRIPTION

generic_options are options supported by the generic **labelit** command.

labelit can be used to provide labels for unmounted **s5** disk file systems or **s5** file systems being copied to tape.

With the optional arguments omitted, **labelit** prints current label values.

The *special* name should be the disk partition (for example, **/dev/rdsk/***), or the cartridge tape (for example, **/dev/rmt/***, where the value of * is machine dependent.) The device may not be on a remote machine.

The *fsname* argument represents the mounted name (for example, **root**, **usr**, and so on) of the file system. *fsname* must be less than seven characters long.

Volume may be used to equate an internal name to a volume name applied externally to the hard disk, diskette or tape. *volume* must be less than seven characters long.

For file systems on disk, *fsname* and *volume* are recorded in the superblock.

The options are:

-F s5 Specifies the **s5**-FSType. Used to ensure that an **s5** file system is labelled.

-n Provides for initial tape labeling only. (This destroys the previous contents of the tape.)

SEE ALSO

s5-specific **fs**(4), generic **labelit**(1M)

NAME

labelit (sfs) – provide labels for **sfs** file systems

SYNOPSIS

labelit [**-F sfs**] [*generic_options*] [**-n**] *special* [*fsname volume*]

DESCRIPTION

labelit can be used to provide labels for unmounted disk file systems or file systems being copied to tape.

generic_options are options supported by the generic **labelit** command.

If neither *fsname* nor *volume* is specified, **labelit** prints the current values.

The *special* name should be the physical disk section (for example, **/dev/dsk/c0t0d0s6**), or the cartridge tape (for example, **/dev/dsk/c0s0**). The device may not be on a remote machine.

The *fsname* argument represents the mounted name (for example, **root**, **home**, and so on) of the file system. *fsname* must be less than seven characters long.

Volume may be used to equate an internal name to a volume name applied externally to the disk pack, diskette, or tape. *volume* must be less than seven characters long.

The options are:

-F sfs Specifies the **sfs**-FSType.

-n For initial tape labeling only (to prepare for **volcopy**(1M).) This destroys the previous contents of the tape.

SEE ALSO

sfs-specific **fs**(4) generic **labelit**(1M)

NAME

labelit (ufs) – provide labels for **ufs** file systems

SYNOPSIS

labelit [**-F ufs**] [*generic_options*] [**-n**] *special* [*fsname volume*]

DESCRIPTION

labelit can be used to provide labels for unmounted disk file systems or file systems being copied to tape.

generic_options are options supported by the generic **labelit** command.

If neither *fsname* nor *volume* is specified, **labelit** prints the current values.

The *special* name should be the physical disk section (for example, **/dev/rdsk/***, where the value of * is machine specific), or the cartridge tape (for example, **/dev/rmt/***). The device may not be on a remote machine.

The *fsname* argument represents the mounted name (for example, **root**, **usr**, and so on) of the file system. *fsname* must be less than seven characters long.

Volume may be used to equate an internal name to a volume name applied externally to the disk pack, diskette, or tape. *volume* must be less than seven characters long.

The options are:

-F ufs Specifies the **ufs**-FSType.

-n For initial tape labeling only (to prepare for **volcopy**(1M).) This destroys the previous contents of the tape.

NOTES

Labeling a tape that already has a label will destroy the tape's contents.

SEE ALSO

ufs-specific **fs**(4), generic **labelit**(1M)

NAME

labelit (vxfs) – provide labels for **vxfs** file systems

SYNOPSIS

labelit [**-F vxfs**] [*generic_options*] [**-n**] *special* [*fsname volume*]

DESCRIPTION

generic_options are options supported by the generic **labelit** command.

labelit can be used to provide labels for unmounted **vxfs** disk file systems or for tapes being used to copy **vxfs** file systems.

With the optional arguments omitted, **labelit** prints current label values.

The *special* name should be the disk partition (for example, **/dev/rdsk/c0t1d0s5**) or the tape device (for example, **/dev/rmt/c0s0**). The device may not be on a remote machine.

The *fsname* argument represents the mounted name (for example, **root**, **usr**, and so on) of the file system.

volume may be used to equate an internal name to a volume name applied externally to the disk pack, diskette, or tape.

For file systems on disk, *fsname* and *volume* are recorded in the super-block.

The options are:

-F vxfs Specify the **vxfs** FSType. Used to ensure that a **vxfs** file system is labeled.

-n For initial tape labeling only (to prepare tapes for **volcopy**). This destroys the previous contents of the tape.

SEE ALSO

vxfs-specific **fs**(4), generic **labelit**(1M), generic **volcopy**(1M), **vxfs**-specific **volcopy**(1M)

last (1)

NAME

last – indicate last user or terminal logins

SYNOPSIS

last [**-n** *number* | *-number*] [**-f** *file*] [*name* | tty] . . .

DESCRIPTION

The **last** command looks in the **/var/adm/wtmpx**, file which records all logins and logouts, for information about a user, a terminal or any group of users and terminals. Arguments specify names of users or terminals of interest. Names of terminals may be given fully or abbreviated. For example **last 10** is the same as **last term/10**. If multiple arguments are given, the information which applies to any of the arguments is printed. For example **last root console** lists all of root's sessions as well as all sessions on the console terminal. **last** displays the sessions of the specified users and terminals, most recent first, indicating the times at which the session began, the duration of the session, and the terminal which the session took place on. If the session is still continuing or was cut short by a reboot, **last** so indicates.

The pseudo-user **reboot** logs in at reboots of the system, thus

```
last reboot
```

will give an indication of mean time between reboot.

last with no arguments displays a record of all logins and logouts, in reverse order.

If **last** is interrupted, it indicates how far the search has progressed in **/var/adm/wtmpx**. If interrupted with a quit signal (generated by a CTRL-\) **last** indicates how far the search has progressed so far, and the search continues.

The following options are available:

-n *number* | *-number* Limit the number of entries displayed to that specified by *number*. These options are identical; the *-number* option is provided as a transition tool only and will be removed in future releases.

-f *file* Use *file* as the name of the accounting file instead of **/var/adm/wtmpx**.

FILES

/var/adm/wtmpx accounting file

SEE ALSO

utmpx(4)

NAME

`lastcomm` – (BSD) show the last commands executed, in reverse order

SYNOPSIS

`/usr/ucb/lastcomm` [*command-name*] . . . [*user-name*] . . . [*terminal-name*] . . .

DESCRIPTION

The `lastcomm` command gives information on previously executed commands. `lastcomm` with no arguments displays information about all the commands recorded during the current accounting file's lifetime. If called with arguments, `lastcomm` only displays accounting entries with a matching *command-name*, *user-name*, or *terminal-name*.

EXAMPLE

The command:

```
lastcomm a.out root term/01
```

would produce a listing of all the executions of commands named **a.out**, by user **root** while using the terminal **term/01**. and

```
lastcomm root
```

would produce a listing of all the commands executed by user **root**.

For each process entry, `lastcomm` displays the following items of information:

the command name under which the process was called

one or more flags indicating special information about the process. The flags have the following meanings:

`F` The process performed a **fork** but not an **exec**.

`S` The process ran as a set-user-id program.

the name of the user who ran the process

the terminal which the user was logged in on at the time (if applicable)

the amount of CPU time used by the process (in seconds)

the date and time the process exited

FILES

`/var/adm/pacct` accounting file

NOTES

`lastcomm` looks for the file **/var/adm/pacct**, and will fail if it does not find it. Accounting must be turned on, by executing **/usr/lib/acct/startup**, which creates the **pacct** file.

SEE ALSO

acct(4), **acctsh**(1M), **core**(4), **last**(1), **sigvec**(3)

NAME

`ld` – link editor for object files

SYNOPSIS

`ld` [*options*] *file* . . .

DESCRIPTION

The `ld` command combines relocatable object files, performs relocation, and resolves external symbols. `ld` operates in two modes, static or dynamic, as governed by the `-d` option. In static mode, `-dn`, relocatable object files given as arguments are combined to produce an executable object file; if the `-r` option is specified, relocatable object files are combined to produce one relocatable object file. In dynamic mode, `-dy`, the default, relocatable object files given as arguments are combined to produce an executable object file that will be linked at execution with any shared object files given as arguments; if the `-G` option is specified, relocatable object files are combined to produce a shared object. In all cases, the output of `ld` is left in `a.out` by default.

If any argument is a library, it is searched exactly once at the point it is encountered in the argument list. The library may be either a relocatable archive or a shared object. For an archive library, only those routines defining an unresolved external reference are loaded. The archive library symbol table [see `ar`(4)] is searched sequentially with as many passes as are necessary to resolve external references that can be satisfied by library members. Thus, the ordering of members in the library is functionally unimportant, unless there exist multiple library members defining the same external symbol. A shared object consists of a single entity all of whose references must be resolved within the executable being built or within other shared objects with which it is linked.

The following options are recognized by `ld`:

`-a` In static mode only, produce an executable object file; give errors for undefined references. This is the default behavior for static mode. `-a` may not be used with the `-r` option.

`-b` In dynamic mode only, when creating an executable, do not do special processing for relocations that reference symbols in shared objects. Without the `-b` option, the link editor will create special position-independent relocations for references to functions defined in shared objects and will arrange for data objects defined in shared objects to be copied into the memory image of the executable by the dynamic linker at run time. With the `-b` option, the output code may be more efficient, but it will be less sharable.

`-d` *yn* `ld` uses static linking only when *yn* is `n`; otherwise, by default, or when *yn* is `y`, `ld` uses dynamic linking.

`-e` *epsym* Set the entry point address for the output file to be that of the symbol *epsym*.

`-h` *name* In dynamic mode only, when building a shared object, record *name* in the object's dynamic section. *name* will be recorded in executables that are linked with this object rather than the object's UNIX System file name. Accordingly, *name* will be used by the dynamic linker as the name of the shared object to search for at run time.

`-l`*x* — Search a library `lib`*x*`.so` or `lib`*x*`.a`, the conventional names for shared object and archive libraries, respectively. In dynamic mode, unless the `-Bstatic` option is in effect, `ld` searches each directory specified in the library search path for a file `lib`*x*`.so` or `lib`*x*`.a`. The directory search stops at the first directory containing either. `ld` chooses the file ending in `.so` if `-l`*x* expands to two files whose names are of the form `lib`*x*`.so` and `lib`*x*`.a`. If no `lib`*x*`.so` is found, then `ld` accepts `lib`*x*`.a`. In static mode, or when the `-Bstatic` option is in effect, `ld` selects only the file ending in `.a`. A library is searched when its name is encountered, so the placement of `-l` is significant.

`-m` — Produce a memory map or listing of the input/output sections on the standard output.

`-o` *outfile* — Produce an output object file named *outfile*. The name of the default object file is `a.out`.

`-r` — Combine relocatable object files to produce one relocatable object file. `ld` will not complain about unresolved references. This option cannot be used in dynamic mode or with `-a`.

`-s` — Strip symbolic information from the output file. The debug and line sections and their associated relocation entries will be removed. Except for relocatable files or shared objects, the symbol table and string table sections will also be removed from the output object file.

`-t` — Turn off the warning about multiply defined symbols that are not the same size.

`-u` *symname* — Enter *symname* as an undefined symbol in the symbol table. This is useful for loading entirely from an archive library, since initially the symbol table is empty and an unresolved reference is needed to force the loading of the first routine. The placement of this option on the command line is significant; it must be placed before the library that will define the symbol.

`-z defs` — Force a fatal error if any undefined symbols remain at the end of the link. This is the default when building an executable. It is also useful when building a shared object to assure that the object is self-contained, that is, that all its symbolic references are resolved internally.

`-z nodefs` — Allow undefined symbols. This is the default when building a shared object. It may be used when building an executable in dynamic mode and linking with a shared object that has unresolved references in routines not used by that executable. This option should be used with caution.

`-z text` — In dynamic mode only, force a fatal error if any relocations against non-writable, allocatable sections remain.

-B *arg* — *arg* can be any one of the following: *dynsat*, *symb*, **sortbss**

dynstat — *dynstat* can be either **dynamic** or **static**. These options govern library inclusion. **dynamic** is valid in dynamic mode only. These options may be specified any number of times on the command line as toggles: if **-Bstatic** is given, no shared objects will be accepted until **-Bdynamic** is seen. See also the **-l** option.

symb — *symb* takes the form **symbolic**[=*symbol*, . . .]
When building a shared object, if a definition for *symbol* exists, bind all references to *symbol* to that definition. If no list of symbols is provided, bind all references to symbols to definitions that are available; **ld** will issue warnings for undefined symbols unless **-z defs** overrides. Normally, references to global symbols within shared objects are not bound until run time, even if definitions are available, so that definitions of the same symbol in an executable or other shared objects can override the object's own definition.

sortbss — All uninitialized global variables within a module will be assigned contiguous addresses. This is the way these variables were assigned by the COFF version of the link editor.

-G — In dynamic mode only, produce a shared object. Undefined symbols are allowed.

-I *name* — When building an executable, use *name* as the path name of the interpreter to be written into the program header. The default in static mode is no interpreter; in dynamic mode, the default is the name of the dynamic linker, **/usr/lib/libc.so.1**. Either case may be overridden by **-I**. **exec** will load this interpreter when it loads the **a.out** and will pass control to the interpreter rather than to the **a.out** directly.

-L *path* — Add *path* to the library search directories. **ld** searches for libraries first in any directories specified with **-L** options, then in the standard directories. This option is effective only if it precedes the **-l** option on the command line.

-M *mapfile* — In *static* mode only, read *mapfile* as a text file of directives to **ld**. Because these directives change the shape of the output file created by **ld**, use of this option is strongly discouraged.

-Q *yn* — If *yn* is **y**, an **ident** string is added to the **.comment** section of the output file to identify the version of the link editor used to create the file. This will result in multiple **ld idents** when there have been multiple linking steps, such as when using **ld -r**. This is identical with the default action of the **cc** command. If *yn* is **n**, the version information is suppressed. The default is **n**.

`-V` Output a message giving information about the version of `ld` being used.

`-YP,` *dirlist* Change the default directories used for finding libraries. *dirlist* is a colon-separated path list.

The environment variable **LD_LIBRARY_PATH** may be used to specify library search directories. In the most general case, it will contain two directory lists separated by a semicolon:

dirlist1`;`*dirlist2*

If `ld` is called with any number of occurrences of `-L`, as in

`ld` . . . `-L`*path1* . . . `-L`*pathn* . . .

then the search path ordering is

dirlist1 path1 . . . pathn dirlist2 LIBPATH

LD_LIBRARY_PATH is also used to specify library search directories to the dynamic linker at run time. That is, if **LD_LIBRARY_PATH** exists in the environment, the dynamic linker will search the directories named in it, before its default directory, for shared objects to be linked with the program at execution.

The environment variable **LD_RUN_PATH**, containing a directory list, may also be used to specify library search directories to the dynamic linker. If present and not null, it is passed to the dynamic linker by `ld` via data stored in the output object file.

FILES

`lib`*x*`.so`	libraries
`lib`*x*.a	libraries
`a.out`	output file
LIBPATH	usually **/usr/ccs/lib:/usr/lib**

SEE ALSO

`a.out`(4), **ar**(4), **as**(1), **cc**(1), **end**(3C), **exec**(2), **exit**(2)

NOTES

Through its options, the link editor gives users great flexibility; however, those who use the **-M** *mapfile* option must assume some added responsibilities. Use of this feature is strongly discouraged.

NAME

`ld` – (BSD) link editor, dynamic link editor

SYNOPSIS

`/usr/ucb/ld` [*options*]

DESCRIPTION

`/usr/ucb/ld` is the link editor for the BSD Compatibility Package. `/usr/ucb/ld` is identical to `/usr/bin/ld` [see `ld`(1)] except that BSD libraries and routines are included *before* System V libraries and routines.

`/usr/ucb/ld` accepts the same options as `/usr/bin/ld`, with the following exceptions:

`-L` *dir* Add *dir* to the list of directories searched for libraries by `/usr/bin/ld`. Directories specified with this option are searched before `/usr/ucblib` and `/usr/lib`.

`-Y LU,` *dir* Change the default directory used for finding libraries. Warning: this option may have unexpected results, and should not be used.

FILES

`/usr/ucblib`
`/usr/lib`
`/usr/ucblib/libx.a`
`/usr/lib/libx.a`

SEE ALSO

`ar`(1), `as`(1), `cc`(1), `ld`(1), `lorder`(1), `strip`(1), `tsort`(1)

NAME

ldd – list dynamic dependencies

SYNOPSIS

ldd [-d | -r] *file*

DESCRIPTION

The **ldd** command lists the path names of all shared objects that would be loaded as a result of executing *file*. If *file* is a valid executable but does not require any shared objects, **ldd** will succeed, producing no output.

ldd may also be used to check the compatibility of *file* with the shared objects it uses. It does this by optionally printing warnings for any unresolved symbol references that would occur if *file* were executed. Two options govern this mode of **ldd**:

-d Causes **ldd** to check all references to data objects.

-r Causes **ldd** to check references to both data objects and functions.

Only one of the above options may be given during any single invocation of **ldd**.

SEE ALSO

cc(1), **dlopen**(3X), **ld**(1)

DIAGNOSTICS

ldd prints its record of shared object path names to **stdout**. The optional list of symbol resolution problems are printed to **stderr**. If *file* is not an executable file or cannot be opened for reading, a non-zero exit status is returned.

NOTES

ldd doesn't list shared objects explicitly attached via **dlopen**(3X).

ldd uses the same algorithm as the dynamic linker to locate shared objects.

ldsysdump(1M)

NAME

ldsysdump – load system dump from floppy diskettes or cartridge tape

SYNOPSIS

/usr/sbin/ldsysdump *destination_file*

DESCRIPTION

The **ldsysdump** command loads the memory image files from the floppy diskettes or cartridge tape used to take a system dump and recombines them into a single file on the hard disk suitable for use by the **crash** command. The *destination_file* is the name of the hard disk file into which the data from the diskettes will be loaded.

When executed, **ldsysdump** begins an interactive procedure that prompts the user to insert the diskettes or tape to be loaded. The user has the option of quitting the session at any time. This allows only the portion of the system image needed to be dumped.

USAGE

Errors

If a floppy diskette is inserted out of sequence a message is printed. The user is allowed to insert a new one and continue the session.

NOTES

The file size limit must be set large enough to hold the dump.

REFERENCES

crash(1M), **ulimit**(2)

NAME

lex – generate programs for simple lexical tasks

SYNOPSIS

lex [-ctvn -V -Q[y|n]] [*file*]

DESCRIPTION

The **lex** command generates programs to be used in simple lexical analysis of text. The input *file*s (standard input default) contain strings and expressions to be searched for and C text to be executed when these strings are found. **lex** processes supplementary code set characters in program comments and strings, and single-byte supplementary code set characters in tokens, according to the locale specified in the **LC_CTYPE** environment variable [see **LANG** on **environ**(5)].

lex generates a file named **lex.yy.c**. When **lex.yy.c** is compiled and linked with the lex library, it copies the input to the output except when a string specified in the file is found. When a specified string is found, then the corresponding program text is executed. The actual string matched is left in **yytext**, an external character array. Matching is done in order of the patterns in the *file*. The patterns may contain square brackets to indicate character classes, as in **[abx-z]** to indicate **a**, **b**, **x**, **y**, and **z**; and the operators *, **+**, and **?** mean, respectively, any non-negative number of, any positive number of, and either zero or one occurrence of, the previous character or character class. Thus, **[a-zA-Z]+** matches a string of letters. The character **.** is the class of all characters except new-line. Parentheses for grouping and vertical bar for alternation are also supported. The notation *r*{*d*,*e*} in a rule indicates between *d* and *e* instances of regular expression *r*. It has higher precedence than |, but lower than *, ?, +, and concatenation. The character ^ at the beginning of an expression permits a successful match only immediately after a new-line, and the character **$** at the end of an expression requires a trailing new-line. The character **/** in an expression indicates trailing context; only the part of the expression up to the slash is returned in **yytext**, but the remainder of the expression must follow in the input stream. An operator character may be used as an ordinary symbol if it is within **"** symbols or preceded by \.

Three macros are expected: **input** to read a character; **unput**(*c*) to replace a character read; and **output**(*c*) to place an output character. They are defined in terms of the standard streams, but you can override them. The program generated is named **yylex**, and the lex library contains a **main** that calls it. The macros **input** and **output** read from and write to **stdin** and **stdout**, respectively.

The function **yymore** accumulates additional characters into the same **yytext**. The function **yyless**(*n*) pushes back **yyleng** –*n* characters into the input stream. (**yyleng** is an external **int** variable giving the length in bytes of **yytext**.) The function **yywrap** is called whenever the scanner reaches end of file and indicates whether normal wrapup should continue. The action **REJECT** on the right side of the rule causes the match to be rejected and the next suitable match executed. The action **ECHO** on the right side of the rule is equivalent to **printf("%s", yytext)**.

Any line beginning with a blank is assumed to contain only C text and is copied; if it precedes **%%**, it is copied into the external definition area of the **lex.yy.c** file. All rules should follow a **%%**, as in **yacc**. Lines preceding **%%** that begin with a non-blank character define the string on the left to be the remainder of the line; it can be called out later by surrounding it with **{}**. In this section, C code (and preprocessor statements) can also be included between `%{` and `%}`. Note that curly brackets do not imply parentheses; only string substitution is done.

The external names generated by **lex** all begin with the prefix **yy** or **YY**.

The flags must appear before any files.

- `-c` Indicates C actions and is the default.
- `-t` Causes the **lex.yy.c** program to be written instead to standard output.
- `-v` Provides a two-line summary of statistics.
- `-n` Will not print out the **-v** summary.
- `-V` Print out version information on standard error.
- `-Q[y|n]` Print out version information to output file **lex.yy.c** by using **-Qy**. The **-Qn** option does not print out version information and is the default.

Multiple files are treated as a single file. If no files are specified, standard input is used.

Certain default table sizes are too small for some users. The table sizes for the resulting finite state machine can be set in the definitions section:

- **%p** *n* number of positions is *n* (default 20000)
- **%n** *n* number of states is *n* (4000)
- **%e** *n* number of parse tree nodes is *n* (8000)
- **%a** *n* number of transitions is *n* (16000)
- **%k** *n* number of packed character classes is *n* (20000)
- **%o** *n* size of output array is *n* (24000)

The use of one or more of the above automatically implies the **-v** option, unless the **-n** option is used.

EXAMPLES

```
D       [0-9]
O       [0-7]
%{
void
skipcommnts(void)
{
        for(;;)
        {
                while(input()!='*')
                        ;
                if(input()=='/')
                        return;
                else

                        unput(yytext[yyleng-1]);
        }
}
%}
```

```
%%
        if      printf("IF statement\n");
        [a-z]+  printf("tag, value %s\n",yytext);
        0{O}+   printf("octal number %s\n",yytext);
        {D}+    printf("decimal number %s\n",yytext);
        "++"    printf("unary op\n");
        "+"     printf("binary op\n");
        "\n"    ;/*no action */
        "/*"      skipcommnts();
        %%
```

SEE ALSO

yacc(1)

lidload (1M)

NAME

lidload - load distributed file system security database

SYNOPSIS

lidload

DESCRIPTION

The **lidload** command updates the RFS and NFS internal representations of the **lid_and_priv** database from the current information in the corresponding file **/etc/dfs/lid_and_priv** and copies that information to the kernel. The **lidload** command should be run every time **lid_and_priv** is edited. Changes to the database do not take effect until **lidload** has been run.

On running the **lidload** command, changes to **lid_and_priv** immediately affect all mounted and unmounted resources. Mounted resources do not need to be unmounted in order for **lidload** to take effect.

Only a privileged user can execute this command.

FILES

/etc/dfs/lid_and_priv

SEE ALSO

fumount(1M), **lid_and_priv**(4)

NOTES

Changes made to the **lid_and_priv** database do not affect RFS files that are open at the time **lidload** is executed until the files are closed and re-opened. To ensure that changes immediately affect RFS resources, including open files, an administrator should use the **fumount**(1M) command to force clients to unmount RFS resources.

NFS open files are affected immediately by changes to **lid_and_priv** once **lidload** is executed.

NAME

`line` – read one line

SYNOPSIS

`line`

DESCRIPTION

`line` copies one line (up to a new-line) from the standard input and writes it on the standard output. It returns an exit code of 1 on EOF and always prints at least a new-line. It is often used within shell files to read from the user's terminal.

SEE ALSO

read(2), **sh**(1)

NAME

link, **unlink** – link and unlink files and directories

SYNOPSIS

/usr/sbin/link *file1 file2*
/usr/sbin/unlink *file*

DESCRIPTION

The **link** command is used to create a file name that points to another file. Linked files and directories can be removed by the **unlink** command; however, it is strongly recommended that the **rm** and **rmdir** commands be used instead of the **unlink** command.

The only difference between **ln** and **link** and **unlink** is that the latter do exactly what they are told to do, abandoning all error checking. This is because they directly invoke the **link** and **unlink** system calls.

SEE ALSO

link(2), **rm**(1), **unlink**(2)

NOTES

These commands can be run only by the super-user.

NAME

`lint` – a C program checker

SYNOPSIS

`lint` [*options*] *file* . . .

DESCRIPTION

`lint` detects features of C program files which are likely to be bugs, non-portable, or wasteful. It also checks type usage more strictly than the compiler. `lint` issues error and warning messages. Among the things it detects are unreachable statements, loops not entered at the top, automatic variables declared and not used, and logical expressions whose value is constant. `lint` checks for functions that return values in some places and not in others, functions called with varying numbers or types of arguments, and functions whose values are not used or whose values are used but not returned.

Arguments that end with `.c` are taken to be C source files. Arguments whose names end with `.ln` are taken to be the result of an earlier invocation of `lint` with either the `-c` or the `-o` option used. The `.ln` files are analogous to `.o` (object) files that are produced by the `cc`(1) command when given a `.c` file as input. Files with other suffixes are warned about and ignored.

`lint` takes all the `.c`, `.ln`, and `llib-l`*x*`.ln` (specified by `-l`*x*) files and processes them in their command line order. By default, `lint` appends the standard C lint library (`llib-lc.ln`) to the end of the list of files. When the `-c` option is used, the `.ln` and the `llib-l`*x*`.ln` files are ignored. When the `-c` option is not used, the second pass of `lint` checks the `.ln` and the `llib-l`*x*`.ln` list of files for mutual compatibility.

The following options are used to suppress certain kinds of complaints:

`-a` Suppress complaints about assignments of long values to variables that are not long.

`-b` Suppress complaints about **`break`** statements that cannot be reached.

`-h` Do not apply heuristic tests that attempt to intuit bugs, improve style, and reduce waste.

`-m` Suppress complaints about external symbols that could be declared static.

`-u` Suppress complaints about functions and external variables used and not defined, or defined and not used. (This option is suitable for running `lint` on a subset of files of a larger program).

`-v` Suppress complaints about unused arguments in functions.

`-x` Do not report variables referred to by external declarations but never used.

The following arguments alter **lint**'s behavior:

-I*dir* Search for included header files in the directory *dir* before searching the current directory and/or the standard place.

-l*x* Include the lint library **llib-l***x***.ln**. For example, you can include a lint version of the math library **llib-lm.ln** by inserting **-lm** on the command line. This argument does not suppress the default use of **llib-lc.ln**. These lint libraries must be in the assumed directory. This option can be used to reference local lint libraries and is useful in the development of multi-file projects.

-L*dir* Search for lint libraries in *dir* before searching the standard place.

-n Do not check compatibility against the standard C lint library.

-p Attempt to check portability to other machines. Along with stricter checking, this option causes all non-external names to be truncated to eight characters and all external names to be truncated to six characters and one case.

-s Produce one-line diagnostics only. **lint** occasionally buffers messages to produce a compound report.

-k Alter the behavior of /***LINTED** [*message*]*/ directives. Normally, **lint** will suppress warning messages for the code following these directives. Instead of suppressing the messages, **lint** prints an additional message containing the comment inside the directive.

-y Specify that the file being linted will be treated as if the /***LINTLIBRARY***/ directive had been used. A lint library is normally created by using the /***LINTLIBRARY***/ directive.

-F Print pathnames of files. **lint** normally prints the filename without the path.

-c Cause **lint** to produce a **.ln** file for every **.c** file on the command line. These **.ln** files are the product of **lint**'s first pass only, and are not checked for inter-function compatibility.

-o*x* Cause **lint** to create a lint library with the name **llib-l***x***.ln**. The **-c** option nullifies any use of the **-o** option. The lint library produced is the input that is given to **lint**'s second pass. The **-o** option simply causes this file to be saved in the named lint library. To produce a **llib-l***x***.ln** without extraneous messages, use of the **-x** option is suggested. The **-v** option is useful if the source file(s) for the lint library are just external interfaces.

Some of the above settings are also available through the use of "lint comments" (see below).

-V Write to standard error the product name and release.

-W*file* Write a **.ln** file to *file*, for use by **cflow**(1).

-R*file* Write a **.ln** file to *file*, for use by **cxref**(1).

lint recognizes many **cc**(1) command line options, including **-D**, **-U**, **-g**, **-O**, **-Xt**, **-Xa**, and **-Xc**, although **-g** and **-O** are ignored. Unrecognized options are warned about and ignored. The predefined macro **lint** is defined to allow certain questionable code to be altered or removed for **lint**. Thus, the symbol **lint** should be thought of as a reserved word for all code that is planned to be checked by **lint**.

Certain conventional comments in the C source will change the behavior of **lint**:

/***ARGSUSED***n**/
: makes **lint** check only the first *n* arguments for usage; a missing *n* is taken to be 0 (this option acts like the **-v** option for the next function).

/***CONSTCOND***/ or /***CONSTANTCOND***/ or /***CONSTANTCONDITION***/
: suppresses complaints about constant operands for the next expression.

/***EMPTY***/
: suppresses complaints about a null statement consequent on an if statement. This directive should be placed after the test expression, and before the semicolon. This directive is supplied to support empty if statements when a valid else statement follows. It suppresses messages on an empty **else** consequent.

/***FALLTHRU***/ or /***FALLTHROUGH***/
: suppresses complaints about fall through to a **case** or **default** labeled statement. This directive should be placed immediately preceding the label.

/***LINTLIBRARY***/
: at the beginning of a file shuts off complaints about unused functions and function arguments in this file. This is equivalent to using the **-v** and **-x** options.

/***LINTED** [*message*]*/
: suppresses any intra-file warning except those dealing with unused variables or functions. This directive should be placed on the line immediately preceding where the lint warning occurred. The **-k** option alters the way in which **lint** handles this directive. Instead of suppressing messages, **lint** will print an additional message, if any, contained in the comment. This directive is useful in conjunction with the **-s** option for post-lint filtering.

/***NOTREACHED***/
: at appropriate points stops comments about unreachable code. [This comment is typically placed just after calls to functions like **exit**(2)].

/***PRINTFLIKE***n**/
: makes **lint** check the first *(n-1)* arguments as usual. The *nth* argument is interpreted as a **printf** format string that is used to check the remaining arguments.

/***PROTOLIB***n**/
: causes **lint** to treat function declaration prototypes as function definitions if *n* is non-zero. This directive can only be used in conjunction with the /* **LINTLIBRARY** */ directive. If *n* is zero, function prototypes will be treated normally.

/***SCANFLIKE***n**/
: makes **lint** check the first *(n-1)* arguments as usual. The *nth* argument is interpreted as a **scanf** format string that is used to check the remaining arguments.

/***VARARGS***_n_*/

suppresses the usual checking for variable numbers of arguments in the following function declaration. The data types of the first *n* arguments are checked; a missing *n* is taken to be 0. The use of the ellipsis terminator (. . .) in the definition is suggested in new or updated code.

lint produces its first output on a per-source-file basis. Complaints regarding included files are collected and printed after all source files have been processed, if **-s** is not specified. Finally, if the **-c** option is not used, information gathered from all input files is collected and checked for consistency. At this point, if it is not clear whether a complaint stems from a given source file or from one of its included files, the source filename will be printed followed by a question mark.

The behavior of the **-c** and the **-o** options allows for incremental use of **lint** on a set of C source files. Generally, one invokes **lint** once for each source file with the **-c** option. Each of these invocations produces a **.ln** file that corresponds to the **.c** file, and prints all messages that are about just that source file. After all the source files have been separately run through **lint**, it is invoked once more (without the **-c** option), listing all the **.ln** files with the needed **-l**_x_ options. This will print all the inter-file inconsistencies. This scheme works well with **make**; it allows **make** to be used to **lint** only the source files that have been modified since the last time the set of source files were **lint**ed.

FILES

LIBDIR	the directory where the lint libraries specified by the **-l**_x_ option must exist
LIBDIR/**lint[12]**	first and second passes
LIBDIR/**llib-lc.ln**	declarations for C Library functions (binary format; source is in *LIBDIR*/**llib-lc)**
LIBPATH/**llib-lm.ln**	declarations for Math Library functions (binary format; source is in *LIBDIR*/llib-lm)
TMPDIR/*__lint__*	temporaries
TMPDIR	usually **/var/tmp** but can be redefined by setting the environment variable **TMPDIR** [see **tempnam** in **tmpnam**(3S)].
LIBDIR	usually **/ccs/lib**
LIBPATH	usually **/usr/ccs/lib:/usr/lib**

SEE ALSO

cc(1), **make**(1)

NAME

`listdgrp` – lists members of a device group

SYNOPSIS

`listdgrp` *dgroup*

DESCRIPTION

`listdgrp` displays the members of the device group specified by *dgroup*.

Return Values

`listdgrp` exits with one of the following values:

0 Successful completion of the task

1 Command syntax incorrect, invalid option used, or internal error occurred

2 Device group table could not be opened for reading

3 Device group *dgroup* could not be found in the device group table.

USAGE

Example

To list the devices that belong to the hypothetical group **`partitions`**:

```
$ listdgrp partitions
root
swap
usr
```

Files

`/etc/dgroup.tab`

REFERENCES

`putdgrp`(1M)

listen (1M)

NAME

listen – network listener port monitor

SYNOPSIS

/usr/lib/saf/listen [**-m** *devstem*] *net_spec*

DESCRIPTION

The **listen** port monitor "listens" to a network for service requests, accepts requests when they arrive, and invokes servers in response to those service requests. The network listener process may be used with any connection-oriented network (more precisely, with any connection-oriented transport provider) that conforms to the Transport Interface (TLI) specification.

The listener internally generates a pathname for the minor device for each connection; it is this pathname that is used in the **utmp** entry for a service, if one is created. By default, this pathname is the concatenation of the prefix **/dev/***netspec* with the decimal representation of the minor device number. When the **-m** *devstem* option is specified, the listener will use *devstem* as the prefix for the pathname. In either case, the representation of the minor device number will be at least two digits (for example, 05 or 27), but will be longer when necessary to accommodate minor device numbers larger than 99.

SERVER INVOCATION

When a connection indication is received, the listener creates a new transport endpoint and accepts the connection on that endpoint. Before giving the file descriptor for this new connection to the server, any designated STREAMS modules are pushed and the configuration script is executed, if one exists. This file descriptor is appropriate for use with either TLI (see especially **t_sync**(3N)) or the sockets interface library.

By default, a new instance of the server is invoked for each connection. When the server is invoked, file descriptor 0 refers to the transport endpoint, and is open for reading and writing. File descriptors 1 and 2 are copies of file descriptor 0; no other file descriptors are open. The service is invoked either with the user ID under which the service was registered with the listener, or as an authenticated ID if an authentication scheme was specified instead. If both an ID and authentication scheme are specified for the service in the listener's administrative file, the listener does the authentication, but then runs the service under the specified ID.

Alternatively, a service may be registered so that the listener will pass connections to a standing server process through a FIFO or a named STREAM, instead of invoking the server anew for each connection. In this case, the connection is passed in the form of a file descriptor that refers to the new transport endpoint. Before the file descriptor is sent to the server, the listener interprets any configuration script registered for that service using **doconfig**(3N), although **doconfig** is invoked with both the NORUN and NOASSIGN flags. The server receives the file descriptor for the connection in a **strrecvfd** structure via an I_RECVFD **ioctl**(2).

For more details about the listener and its administration, see **nlsadmin**(1M).

FILES

/etc/saf/*pmtag***/***

SEE ALSO

`doconfig`(3N), `nlsadmin`(1M), `nlsgetcall`(3N), `nlsprovider`(3N), `pmadm`(1M), `sac`(1M), `sacadm`(1M), `streamio`(7)

NOTES

When passing a connection to a standing server, the user and group IDs contained in the **`strrecvfd`** structure will be those for the listener; the user name under which the service was registered with the listener or the authenticated ID is not reflected in these IDs.

When operating multiple instances of the listener on a single transport provider, there is a potential race condition in the binding of addresses during initialization of the listeners if any of their services have dynamically assigned addresses. This condition would appear as an inability of the listener to bind a static-address service to its otherwise valid address, and would result from a dynamic-address service having been bound to that address by a different instance of the listener.

listusers (1)

NAME

`listusers` – list user login information

SYNOPSIS

`listusers` [`-g` *groups*] [`-l` *logins*]

DESCRIPTION

Executed without any options, this command lists all user logins sorted by login. The output shows the login ID and the account field value in `/etc/passwd`.

`-g` Lists all user logins belonging to `group`, sorted by login. Multiple groups can be specified as a comma-separated list.

`-l` Lists the user login or logins specified by `logins`, sorted by login. Multiple logins can be specified as a comma-separated list.

NOTES

A user login is defined as having a UID of 100 or greater.

The `-l` and `-g` options can be combined. User logins will only be listed once, even if they belong to more than one of the selected groups.

NAME

ln – (BSD) make hard or symbolic links to files

SYNOPSIS

/usr/ucb/ln [**-fs**] *filename* [*linkname*]
/usr/ucb/ln [**-fs**] *pathname* . . . *directory*

DESCRIPTION

/usr/ucb/ln creates an additional directory entry, called a link, to a file or directory. Any number of links can be assigned to a file. The number of links does not affect other file attributes such as size, protections, data, and so on.

filename is the name of the original file or directory. *linkname* is the new name to associate with the file or filename. If *linkname* is omitted, the last component of *filename* is used as the name of the link.

If the last argument is the name of a directory, symbolic links are made in that directory for each *pathname* argument; **/usr/ucb/ln** uses the last component of each *pathname* as the name of each link in the named *directory*.

A hard link (the default) is a standard directory entry just like the one made when the file was created. Hard links can only be made to existing files. Hard links cannot be made across file systems (disk partitions, mounted file systems). To remove a file, all hard links to it must be removed, including the name by which it was first created; removing the last hard link releases the inode associated with the file.

A symbolic link, made with the **-s** option, is a special directory entry that points to another named file. Symbolic links can span file systems and point to directories. In fact, you can create a symbolic link that points to a file that is currently absent from the file system; removing the file that it points to does not affect or alter the symbolic link itself.

A symbolic link to a directory behaves differently than you might expect in certain cases. While an **/usr/ucb/ls**(1) on such a link displays the files in the pointed-to directory, an '**/usr/ucb/ls -l**' displays information about the link itself:

```
example% /usr/ucb/ln -s dir link
example% /usr/ucb/ls link
file1 file2 file3 file4
example% /usr/ucb/ls -l link
lrwxrwxrwx  1 user           7 Jan 11 23:27 link -> dir
```

When you **cd**(1) to a directory through a symbolic link, you wind up in the pointed-to location within the file system. This means that the parent of the new working directory is not the parent of the symbolic link, but rather, the parent of the pointed-to directory. For instance, in the following case the final working directory is **/var** and not **/home/user/linktest**.

```
example% pwd
/home/var/linktest
example% /usr/ucb/ln -s /var/tmp symlink
example% cd symlink
example% cd ..
example% pwd
/usr
```

C shell user's can avoid any resulting navigation problems by using the **pushd** and **popd** built-in commands instead of **cd**.

OPTIONS

`-f` Force a hard link to a directory — this option is only available to the superuser.

`-s` Create a symbolic link or links.

EXAMPLE

The commands below illustrate the effects of the different forms of the `/usr/ucb/ln` command:

```
example% /usr/ucb/ln file link
example% /usr/ucb/ls -F file link
file   link
example% /usr/ucb/ln -s file symlink
example% /usr/ucb/ls -F file symlink
file   symlink@
example% /usr/ucb/ls -li file link symlink
 10606 -rw-r--r--  2 user          0 Jan 12 00:06 file
 10606 -rw-r--r--  2 user          0 Jan 12 00:06 link
 10607 lrwxrwxrwx  1 user          4 Jan 12 00:06 symlink -> file
example% /usr/ucb/ln -s nonesuch devoid
example% /usr/ucb/ls -F devoid
devoid@
example% cat devoid
ux:cat: ERROR: Cannot open deviod: No such file or directory
example% /usr/ucb/ln -s /proto/bin/* /tmp/bin
example% /usr/ucb/ls -F /proto/bin /tmp/bin
/proto/bin:
x*      y*      z*

/tmp/bin:
x@      y@      z@
```

SEE ALSO

`cp`(1), `link`(2), `ls`(1), `mv`(1), `readlink`(2), `rm`(1) `stat`(2), `symlink`(2)

NOTES

When the last argument is a directory, simple basenames should not be used for *pathname* arguments. If a basename is used, the resulting symbolic link points to itself:

```
example% /usr/ucb/ln -s file /tmp
example% ls -l /tmp/file
lrwxrwxrwx  1 user    4 Jan 12 00:16 /tmp/file -> file
example% cat /tmp/file
ux:cat:ERROR:Cannot open /tmp/file:
Too many symbolic links in pathname traversal.
```

To avoid this problem, use full pathnames, or prepend a reference to the PWD variable to files in the working directory:

```
example% rm /tmp/file
example% /usr/ucb/ln -s $PWD/file /tmp
example% /usr/ucb/ls -l /tmp/file
lrwxrwxrwx  1 user
    4  Jan 12 00:16 /tmp/file -> /home/user/subdir/file
```

ln(1)

NAME

`ln` – link files

SYNOPSIS

`ln` [`-s`] [`-f`] [`-n`] *file1* [*file2* . . .] *target*

DESCRIPTION

The `ln` command links *filen* to *target* by creating a directory entry that refers to *target*. By using `ln` with one or more file names, the user may create one or more links to *target*.

The `ln` command may be used to create both hard links and symbolic links; by default it creates hard links. A hard link to a file is indistinguishable from the original directory entry. Any changes to a file are effective independent of the name used to reference the file. Hard links may not span file systems and may not refer to directories.

Without the `-s` option, `ln` is used to create hard links. *filen* is linked to *target*. If *target* is a directory, another file named *filen* is created in *target* and linked to the original *filen*. If *target* is a file, its contents are overwritten.

If `ln` determines that the mode of *target* forbids writing, it will print the mode [see **chmod**(2)], ask for a response, and read the standard input for one line. If the line begins with `y`, the link occurs, if permissible; otherwise, the command exits.

There are three options to `ln`. If multiple options are specified, the one with the highest priority is used and the remainder are ignored. The options, in descending order of priority, are:

`-s` `ln` will create a symbolic link. A symbolic link contains the name of the file to which it is linked. Symbolic links may span file systems and may refer to directories. If the linkname exists, then do not overwrite the contents of the file. A symbolic link's permissions are always set to read, write, and execute permission for owner, group, and world (`777`).

`-f` `ln` will link files without questioning the user, even if the mode of *target* forbids writing. Note that this is the default if the standard input is not a terminal.

`-n` If the linkname is an existing file, do not overwrite the contents of the file. The `-f` option overrides this option.

If the `-s` option is used with two arguments, *target* may be an existing directory or a non-existent file. If *target* already exists and is not a directory, an error is returned. *filen* may be any path name and need not exist. If it exists, it may be a file or directory and may reside on a different file system from *target*. If *target* is an existing directory, a file is created in directory *target* whose name is *filen* or the last component of *filen*. This file is a symbolic link that references *filen*. If *target* does not exist, a file with name *target* is created and it is a symbolic link that references *filen*.

If the `-s` option is used with more than two arguments, *target* must be an existing directory or an error will be returned. For each *filen*, a file is created in *target* whose name is *filen* or its last component; each new *filen* is a symbolic link to the original *filen*. The *files* and *target* may reside on different file systems.

FILES

`/usr/lib/locale/`*locale*`/LC_MESSAGES/uxcore.abi`
language-specific message file [See **LANG** on **environ** (5).]

SEE ALSO

chmod(1), **cp**(1), **link**(2), **mv**(1), **rm**(1), **readlink**(2), **stat**(2), **symlink**(2)

NOTES

Doing operations that involve ". ." (such as "**cd ..**") in a directory that is symbolically linked will reference the original directory not the target.

The **-s** option does not use the current working directory. In the command

ln -s *path target*

path is taken literally without being evaluated against the current working directory.

loadpci (1M)

NAME

loadpci – starts the PC-Interface map server and connection server

SYNOPSIS

/usr/pci/bin/loadpci [**-BbDINnPS**] <program>

DESCRIPTION

The **loadpci** program initializes the **pcimapsvr.ip** and **pciconsvr.ip** daemons. It is invoked by **pcistart**.

The following options can be entered from the command line:

-B Uses BSD43 **ioctls** to read interface list, broadcast addresses, and subnet masks.

-D Specifies the debug level for **loadpci**. 0 means no debugging and –Dffff means full debugging. This option is also sent to the program.

-I Use interface list supplied by the user. Specifying this option causes the local host not to be interrogated for its interface list. This option is passed through.

-N Use specified device name for net opens. If name doesn't start with a / (slash), a **/dev/** is prepended. This option is also sent through to the program.

-P Specifies port number. It should be specified as **CONSVR** or **MAPSVR** to use our defined ports.

-S Subnets should be used as read from the system. If this option is not specified, the subnet masks will be set to the network portion only.

-b Broadcasts are not received locally. This option adds an interface of the local host so that the local **mapsvr** will see its "consvr here" packets.

-n Network descriptor. This option must not be specified.

Any other option specified is sent directly to the underlying program. The specified program is **exec**'d after **loadpci** opens the network and reads the interface list.

NAME

`localmail` – look up local mail names

SYNOPSIS

`localmail` [–p] [–P prefix] [–S suffix] user-name . . .

DESCRIPTION

`/usr/lib/mail/surrcmd/localmail` looks up the given user names in /etc/passwd and in /var/mail. If they are not local mail names or user names, then output *prefix*`user-name`*suffix*, where *prefix* and *suffix* are specified by the `-P` and `-S` options, respectively. If `-p` is specified, the original user name is printed first. For example,

```
localmail -p -S @system.domain bin unknown-user
```

would print

```
bin bin unknown-user unknown-user@system.domain
```

because `sysb` can only talk with one `sysa`. Similarly,

```
sysa!sysa!user
```

is collapsed down to to

```
sysa!user
```

This program is intended to be used from the `/etc/mail/mailsurr` file. If you have a flat user name space across multiple machines, but user names only exist on disjoint machines, this command can be used to cause any user name not known locally to be forwarded off to another system.

SEE ALSO

`mail`(1), `mailsurr`(4).

lockd (1M)

NAME

lockd – network lock daemon

SYNOPSIS

/usr/lib/nfs/lockd [-t *timeout*] **[-g** *graceperiod*]

DESCRIPTION

lockd processes lock requests that are either sent locally by the kernel or remotely by another lock daemon. **lockd** forwards lock requests for remote data to the server site's lock daemon through RPC/XDR. **lockd** then requests the status monitor daemon, **statd**(1M), for monitor service. The reply to the lock request will not be sent to the kernel until the status daemon and the server site's lock daemon have replied.

If either the status monitor or server site's lock daemon is unavailable, the reply to a lock request for remote data is delayed until all daemons become available.

When a server recovers, it waits for a grace period for all client-site lock daemons to submit reclaim requests. Client-site lock daemons, on the other hand, are notified by the status monitor daemon of the server recovery and promptly resubmit previously granted lock requests. If a lock daemon fails to secure a previously granted lock at the server site, then it sends SIGLOST to a process.

The **lockd** daemon is automatically invoked in run level 3.

Only a privileged user can execute this command.

OPTIONS

-t *timeout*
: Use *timeout* **seconds** as the interval instead of the default value (25 seconds) to retransmit lock request to the remote server.

-g *graceperiod*
: Use *graceperiod* **seconds** as the grace period duration instead of the default value (25 seconds).

SEE ALSO

fcntl(2), **lockf**(3C), **nfsping**(1M), **signal**(2), **statd**(1M)

NAME

`logger` – (BSD) add entries to the system log

SYNOPSIS

`/usr/ucb/logger` [`-t` *tag*] [`-p` *priority*] [`-i`] [`-f` *filename*] [*message*] . . .

DESCRIPTION

`logger` provides a method for adding one-line entries to the system log file from the command line. One or more *message* arguments can be given on the command line, in which case each is logged immediately. Otherwise, a *filename* can be specified, in which case each line in the file is logged. If neither is specified, `logger` reads and logs messages on a line-by-line basis from the standard input.

The following options are available:

`-t` *tag* Mark each line added to the log with the specified *tag*.

`-p` *priority* Enter the message with the specified *priority*. The message priority can be specified numerically, or as a *facility*.*level* pair. For example, '`-p local3.info`' assigns the message priority to the `info` level in the `local3` facility. The default priority is `user.notice`.

`-i` Log the process ID of the `logger` process with each line.

`-f` *filename* Use the contents of *filename* as the message to log.

message If this is unspecified, either the file indicated with `-f` or the standard input is added to the log.

EXAMPLE

```
logger System rebooted
```

will log the message '`System rebooted`' to the facility at priority `notice` to be treated by `syslogd` as other messages to the facility `notice` are.

```
logger -p local0.notice -t HOSTIDM -f /dev/idmc
```

will read from the file `/dev/idmc` and will log each line in that file as a message with the tag '`HOSTIDM`' at priority `notice` to be treated by `syslogd` as other messages to the facility `local0` are.

SEE ALSO

`syslog`(3), `syslogd`(1M)

NAME

login – sign on

SYNOPSIS

[-p] *name* [*environ* . . .]

DESCRIPTION

login is an identification and authentication mechanism that is invoked by a port monitor, typically **ttymon**, at the beginning of each terminal session. It provides a means of identifying users to the system and authenticating user identity. As the last step in the login procedure, a service, usually **sh**, is invoked.

login cannot be invoked from a shell. Instead, it is placed in a port monitor's administrative file by the system administrator and is invoked by the port monitor, typically **ttymon**. [See **ttymon**(1M) and **pmadm**(1M).]

When **login** is invoked by the port monitor, a prompt appears. The minimum response is a login name. Other possible options and parameters are outlined below.

If appropriate, **login** may ask for a password. Where possible, echoing is turned off while the password is typed so the password does not appear on the written record of the session. If the **-p** option has been included, **login** invokes the **passwd** command. [See **passwd**(1).] If the **LOGIN_ONLY** keyword is set in the password default file, this use of the **-p** option is the only way a user can change passwords.

At some installations, you may be required to enter a dialup password for dialup connections, as well as a login password. In this case, the prompt for the dialup password will be:

```
Dialup Password:
```

If you do not complete the login successfully within a certain period of time [see **defadm**(1M)], you are likely to be silently disconnected.

The following arguments and options may be entered in response to the login prompt.

name — The user's login name.

-p — Changes the user's password. The system prompts for the old password and a new password, and then asks for the new password again as a check against typing errors.

environ — Sets environment variable(s).

The basic environment is initialized to:

HOME=*your_login_directory*
LOGNAME=*your_login_name*
MAIL=/var/mail/*your_login_name*
PATH=/usr/bin
SHELL=*last_field_of_passwd_entry* or **/bin/sh** if the field is empty
TZ=*timezone_specification*

The environment may be expanded or modified by supplying additional arguments when **login** prints the prompt requesting the user's login name. The arguments may take either of two forms: *xxx* or *xxx*=*yyy*. Arguments without an equal sign are placed in the environment as

L*n*=*xxx*

where *n* is a number that starts at 0 and is incremented each time a new variable name is required. Variables containing = are placed in the environment without modification. If such a variable is already defined, the new value replaces the old value. To prevent users who log in to restricted shell environments from spawning secondary shells that are not restricted, the following environment variables cannot be changed:

HOME
IFS
LOGNAME
PATH
SHELL

login understands simple, single-character quoting conventions. Typing a backslash in front of a character quotes it and allows the inclusion of such characters as spaces and tabs.

If the authentication performed by the **login** authentication scheme, **/usr/lib/iaf/login/scheme**, is successful, the **scheme** pushes the following information onto a STREAMS module and returns control to the port monitor:

- AUDITMASK
- GID
- GIDCNT (group count)
- HOME
- HZ
- LOGNAME
- PATH
- SGID (supplementary group list)
- SHELL
- TTY
- TZ
- UID
- ULIMIT

The port monitor then calls **set_id()** and **set_env()**, which use this information to set the user's identity and environment.

After a successful login, accounting files are updated, the time you last logged in is printed, and (if appropriate) your current level is printed.

FILES

`/etc/default/login`	login default file
`/etc/dialups`	
`/etc/d_passwd`	
`/etc/motd`	message of the day
`/etc/passwd`	password file
`/etc/profile`	system profile
`$HOME/.profile`	user's login profile
`/etc/security/ia/index`	index into **/etc/security/ia/master**
`/etc/security/ia/master`	contains all INA information about users
`/usr/lib/iaf/login/scheme`	**login** authentication scheme
`/var/adm/lastlog`	time of last login
`/var/adm/loginlog`	record of failed login attempts
`/var/adm/utmp`	accounting
`/var/adm/wtmp`	accounting
/var/mail/*your_name*	mailbox for user *your_name*
/usr/lib/locale/*locale***/LC_MESSAGES/uxcore**	language-specific message file [See **LANG** on **environ**(5).]

SEE ALSO

defadm(1M), **environ**(5) **login**(4), **loginlog**(4), **mail**(1), **newgrp**(1M), **passwd**(4), **profile**(4), **sh**(1), **su**(1M), **ttymon**(1M)

DIAGNOSTICS

The message:

```
UX:login: ERROR: Login incorrect
```

is printed if the user name or the password cannot be matched or if the user's login account has expired or remained inactive for a period greater than the system threshold.

NAME

`logins` – list user and system login information

SYNOPSIS

`logins` [`-dmopstuxab`] [`-g groups`] [`-l` *logins*]

DESCRIPTION

This command displays information on user and system logins. Contents of the output is controlled by the command options and can include the following: user or system login, user id number, `/etc/passwd` account field value (user name or other information), primary group name, primary group id, multiple group names, multiple group ids, home directory, login shell, and four password aging parameters. The default information is the following: login id, user id, primary group name, primary group id and the account field value from `/etc/passwd`. Output is sorted by user id, displaying system logins followed by user logins.

`-d` Selects logins with duplicate uids.

`-m` Displays multiple group membership information.

`-o` Formats output into one line of colon-separated fields.

`-p` Selects logins with no passwords.

`-s` Selects all system logins.

`-t` Sorts output by login instead of by uid.

`-u` Selects all user logins.

`-x` Prints an extended set of information about each selected user. The extended information includes home directory, login shell and password aging information, each displayed on a separate line. The password information consists of password status (PS for passworded, NP for no password or LK for locked), the date the password was last changed, the number of days required between changes, the number of days allowed before a change is required, and the number of days that the user will receive a password expiration warning message (when logging on) before the password expires.

`-a` Adds two password expiration fields to the display. The fields show how many days a password can remain unused before it automatically becomes inactive and the date that the password will expire.

`-b` Print's the user's audit event mask. This option is valid only if the Auditing Utilities are installed.

`-g` Selects all users belonging to `group`, sorted by user id. Multiple groups can be specified as a comma-separated list.

`-l` Selects the requested login. Multiple logins can be specified as a comma-separated list.

NOTES

Options may be used together. If so, any login matching any criteria will be displayed. When the `-l` and `-g` options are combined, a user will only be listed once, even if they belong to more than one of the selected groups.

logname (1)

NAME

`logname` – get login name

SYNOPSIS

`logname`

DESCRIPTION

`logname` returns the name of the user running the process.

FILES

`/etc/profile`

SEE ALSO

`cuserid`(3S) `env`(1), `environ`(5) `login`(1)

NAME

`look` – (BSD) find words in the system dictionary or lines in a sorted list

SYNOPSIS

`/usr/ucb/look` [`-d`] [`-f`] [`-t`*c*] *string* [*file*]

DESCRIPTION

The **`look`** command consults a sorted *file* and prints all lines that begin with *string*.

If no *file* is specified, **`look`** uses **`/usr/ucblib/dict/words`** with collating sequence **`-df`**.

The following options are available:

`-d` Dictionary order. Only letters, digits, TAB and SPACE characters are used in comparisons.

`-f` Fold case. Upper case letters are not distinguished from lower case in comparisons.

`-t`*c* Set termination character. All characters to the right of *c* in *string* are ignored.

FILES

`/usr/ucblib/dict/words`

SEE ALSO

`grep`(1), `sort`(1)

NAME

lookbib – (BSD) find references in a bibliographic database

SYNOPSIS

/usr/ucb/lookbib *database*

DESCRIPTION

A bibliographic reference is a set of lines, constituting fields of bibliographic information. Each field starts on a line beginning with a '%', followed by a key-letter, then a blank, and finally the contents of the field, which may continue until the next line starting with '%'. [See **addbib**(1)].

lookbib uses an inverted index made by **indxbib** to find sets of bibliographic references. It reads keywords typed after the '>' prompt on the terminal, and retrieves records containing all these keywords. If nothing matches, nothing is returned except another '>' prompt.

It is possible to search multiple databases, as long as they have a common index made by **indxbib**. In that case, only the first argument given to **indxbib** is specified to **lookbib**.

If **lookbib** does not find the index files (the **.i[abc]** files), it looks for a reference file with the same name as the argument, without the suffixes. It creates a file with a **.ig** suffix, suitable for use with **fgrep** [see **grep**(1)]. **lookbib** then uses this **fgrep** file to find references. This method is simpler to use, but the **.ig** file is slower to use than the **.i[abc]** files, and does not allow the use of multiple reference files.

FILES

*.ia
*.ib   index files
*.ic

*.ig   reference file

SEE ALSO

addbib(1), **grep**(1), **indxbib**(1), **refer**(1), **roffbib**(1), **sortbib**(1)

NOTES

Probably all dates should be indexed, since many disciplines refer to literature written in the 1800s or earlier.

NAME

`lorder` – find ordering relation for an object library

SYNOPSIS

`lorder` *file* . . .

DESCRIPTION

The input is one or more object or library archive *files* [see **ar**(1)]. The standard output is a list of pairs of object file or archive member names; the first file of the pair refers to external identifiers defined in the second. The output may be processed by **tsort**(1) to find an ordering of a library suitable for one-pass access by **ld**. Note that the link editor **ld** is capable of multiple passes over an archive in the portable archive format [see **ar**(4)] and does not require that **lorder** be used when building an archive. The usage of the **lorder** command may, however, allow for a more efficient access of the archive during the link edit process.

The following example builds a new library from existing `.o` files.

```
ar -cr library ´lorder *.o | tsort´
```

FILES

TMPDIR/*`symref`	temporary files
TMPDIR/*`symdef`	temporary files
TMPDIR	usually `/var/tmp` but can be redefined by setting the environment variable **TMPDIR** [see **tempnam** in **tmpnam**(3S)].

SEE ALSO

ar(1), **ar**(4), **ld**(1), **tmpnam**(3S), **tsort**(1)

NOTES

lorder will accept as input any object or archive file, regardless of its suffix, provided there is more than one input file. If there is but a single input file, its suffix must be `.o`.

NAME

lp, **cancel** – send/cancel print requests

SYNOPSIS

lp [*print-options*] [*files*]

lp -i *request-ID print-options*

cancel [*request-IDs*] [*printers*]

cancel -u *login-names* [*printers*]

DESCRIPTION

The first form of the **lp** command arranges for the named *files* and associated information (collectively called a request) to be printed. If filenames are not specified on the command line, the standard input is assumed. The standard input may be specified along with named *files* on the command line by listing the filenames and specifying **-** for the standard input. The *files* will be printed in the order in which they appear on the command line. **lp** processes supplementary code set characters according to the locale specified in the **LC_CTYPE** environment variable [see **LANG** on **environ**(5)], except as noted under the **-t** option below.

The LP print service associates a unique *request-ID* with each request and displays it on the standard output. This *request-ID* can be used later when canceling or changing a request, or when determining its status. See the section on **cancel** for details about canceling a request, and **lpstat**(1) for information about checking the status of a print request.

The second form of **lp** is used to change the options for a request submitted previously. The print request identified by the *request-ID* is changed according to the *print-options* specified with this command. The *print-options* available are the same as those with the first form of the **lp** command. If the request has finished printing, the change is rejected. If the request is already printing, it will be stopped and restarted from the beginning (unless the **-P** option has been given).

If a print job fails because of level range restrictions, the job will be canceled, and you will be notified by **mail**. In that case, you will need to submit the job to a different printer (one with the appropriate security level range). Ask your system administrator for information on printer security level ranges. For information on levels, see the *Programmer's Guide: System Services and Application Packaging Tools.*

For printers configured to use the **B2** interface, unless you use the **-o nolabels** option, all paginated output will have a single line of security level information printed at the top and bottom of each page of the output. (The security level name is truncated if it is longer than one line.) In addition, the banner and trailer pages for the print job will contain complete security level information.

The **cancel** command allows users to cancel print requests previously sent with the **lp** command. The first form of **cancel** permits cancellation of requests based on their *request-ID*. The second form of **cancel** permits cancellation of requests based on the *login-name* of their owner.

Sending a Print Request

The first form of the **lp** command is used to send a print request either to a particular printer or to any printer capable of meeting all requirements of the print request.

Options to `lp` must always precede filenames, but may be specified in any order. The following options are available for `lp`:

`-c` Make copies of the *files* to be printed immediately when `lp` is invoked. Normally *files* will not be copied, but will be linked whenever possible. If the `-c` option is not specified, the user should be careful not to remove any of the *files* before the request has been printed in its entirety. It should also be noted that if the `-c` option is not specified, any changes made to the named *files* after the request is made but before it is printed will be reflected in the printed output.

`-d` *dest* Choose *dest* as the printer or class of printers that is to do the printing. If *dest* is a printer, then the request will be printed only on that specific printer. If *dest* is a class of printers, then the request will be printed on the first available printer that is a member of the class. If *dest* is **any**, then the request will be printed on any printer that can handle it. Under certain conditions (unavailability of printers, file space limitations, and so on) requests for specific destinations may not be accepted [see **lpstat**(1)]. By default, *dest* is taken from the environment variable **LPDEST** (if it is set). Otherwise, a default destination (if one exists) for the computer system is used. Destination names vary between systems [see **lpstat**(1)].

`-f` *form-name* [`-d` **any**]

Print the request on the form *form-name*. The LP print service ensures that the form is mounted on the printer. If *form-name* is requested with a printer destination that cannot support the form, the request is rejected. If *form-name* has not been defined for the system, or if the user is not allowed to use the form, the request is rejected [see **lpforms**(1M)]. When the **-d any** option is given, the request is printed on any printer that has the requested form mounted and can handle all other needs of the print request.

`-H` *special-handling*

Print the request according to the value of *special-handling*. Acceptable values for *special-handling* are defined below:

hold Don't print the request until notified. If printing has already begun, stop it. Other print requests will go ahead of a held request until it is resumed. If the Auditing Utilities are installed, the use of this option is an auditable event.

resume Resume a held request. If it had been printing when held, it will be the next request printed, unless subsequently bumped by an **immediate** request. If the Auditing Utilities are installed, the use of this option is an auditable event. The **-i** option (followed by a *request-ID*) must be used whenever this argument is specified.

immediate (Available only to LP administrators)
Print the request next. If more than one request is assigned **immediate**, the most recent request will be printed first. If another request is currently printing, it must be put on hold to allow this immediate request to print.

-m Send mail [see **mail**(1)] after the files have been printed. By default, mail is not sent upon normal completion of the print request.

-n *number* Print *number* copies of the output. The default is one copy.

-o *options* Specify printer-dependent *options*. Several such *options* may be collected by specifying the **-o** keyletter more than once (that is, **-o** $option_1$ **-o** $option_2$ . . . **-o** $option_n$), or by specifying a list of options with one **-o** keyletter enclosed in double quotes and separated by spaces (that is, **-o "**$option_1$ $option_2$ . . . $option_n$**"**).

nobanner Do not print a banner page with this request. The administrator can disallow this option at any time. This option is not supported by printers configured to use the **B2** interface.

nofilebreak
Do not insert a form feed between the files given, if submitting a job to print more than one file. This option is not supported by printers configured to use the **PS** (PostScript) interface.

nolabels Do not print security level information at the top and bottom of each page of the output. If the Auditing Utilities are installed, the use of this option is an auditable event. This option is not supported by printers configured to use the **standard** or **PS** (PostScript) interface.

length=*scaled-decimal-number*
Print this request with pages *scaled-decimal-number* long. A *scaled-decimal-number* is an optionally scaled decimal number that gives a size in lines, characters, inches, or centimeters, as appropriate. The scale is indicated by appending the letter **i** for inches, or the letter **c** for centimeters. For length or width settings, an unscaled number indicates lines or characters; for line pitch or character pitch settings, an unscaled number indicates lines per inch or characters per inch (the same as a number scaled with **i**). For example, **length=66** indicates a page length of 66 lines, **length=11i** indicates a page length of 11 inches, and **length=27.94c** indicates a page length of 27.94 centimeters. This option may not be used with the **-f** option and is not supported by the **PS** (PostScript) or B2 interface.

width=*scaled-decimal-number*

Print this request with pages *scaled-decimal-number* wide. (See the explanation of *scaled-decimal-numbers* in the discussion of **length**, above.) This option may not be used with the **-f** option and is not supported by the **PS** (PostScript) or B2 interface.

lpi=*scaled-decimal-number*

Print this request with the line pitch set to *scaled-decimal-number*. (See the explanation of *scaled-decimal-numbers* in the discussion of **length**, above.) This option may not be used with the **-f** option and is not supported by the **PS** (PostScript) or B2 interface.

cpi=pica | elite | compressed

Print this request with the character pitch set to **pica** (representing 10 characters per inch), **elite** (representing 12 characters per inch), or **compressed** (representing as many characters per inch as a printer can handle). There is not a standard number of characters per inch for all printers; see the Terminfo database [**terminfo**(4)] for the default character pitch for your printer. This option may not be used with the **-f** option and is not supported by the **PS** (PostScript) or B2 interface.

stty=*stty-option-list*

A list of options valid for the **stty** command; enclose the list with single quotes if it contains blanks.

-P *page-list* Print the pages specified in *page-list*. This option can be used only if there is a filter available to handle it; otherwise, the print request will be rejected. The *page-list* may consist of ranges of numbers, single page numbers, or a combination of both. The pages will be printed in ascending order.

-q *priority-level*

Assign this request *priority-level* in the printing queue. The values of *priority-level* range from 0 (highest priority) to 39 (lowest priority). If a priority is not specified, the default for the print service is used, as assigned by the system administrator. A priority limit may be assigned to individual users by the system administrator. If the Auditing Utilities are installed, the use of this option is an auditable event.

-r See "**-T** *content-type* [**-r**]" below.

-s Suppress the **request id is** . . . message.

-S *character-set* [**-d any**]
-S *print-wheel* [**-d any**]

Print this request using the specified *character-set* or *print-wheel*. If a form was requested and it requires a character set or print wheel other than the one specified with the **-S** option, the request is rejected.

For printers that take print wheels: if the print wheel specified is not one listed by the administrator as acceptable for the printer specified in this request, the request is rejected unless the print wheel is already mounted on the printer.

For printers that use selectable or programmable character sets: if the *character-set* specified is not one defined in the Terminfo database for the printer [see **terminfo**(4)], or is not an alias defined by the administrator, the request is rejected.

When the **-d any** option is used, the request is printed on any printer that has the print wheel mounted or any printer that can select the character set, and that can handle all other needs of the request.

-t *title* Print *title* on the banner page of the output. The default is no title. Enclose *title* in quotes if it contains blanks. Supplementary code set characters specified in *title* are not printed correctly [see **banner**(1)].

-T *content-type* **[-r]**
Print the request on a printer that can support the specified *content-type*. If no printer accepts this type directly, a filter will be used to convert the content into an acceptable type. If the **-r** option is specified, a filter will not be used. If **-r** is specified but no printer accepts the *content-type* directly, the request is rejected. If the *content-type* is not acceptable to any printer, either directly or with a filter, the request is rejected.

In addition to ensuring that no filters will be used, the **-r** option will force the equivalent of the **-o 'stty=-opost'** option.

-w Write a message on the user's terminal after the *files* have been printed. If the user is not logged in, or if the printer resides on a remote system, then mail will be sent instead. Be aware that messages may be sent to a window other than the one in which the command was originally entered.

-y *mode-list* Print this request according to the printing modes listed in *mode-list*. The allowed values for *mode-list* are locally defined. This option may be used only if there is a filter available to handle it; otherwise, the print request will be rejected.

The following list describes the *mode-list* options:

"**-y reverse**"
Reverse the order in which pages are printed.

"**-y landscape**"
Change the orientation of a physical page from portrait to landscape.

"**-y x=***number***,y=***number*"
Change the default position of a logical page on a physical page by moving the origin.

"**-y group=***number*"
Group multiple logical pages on a single physical page.

"**-y magnify=***number*"
Change the logical size of each page in a document.

"**-o length=***number*"
Select the number of lines in each page of the document.

"**-P** *number*" Select, by page numbers, a subset of a document to be printed.

"**-n** *number*" Print multiple copies of a document.

Canceling a Print Request

The **cancel** command cancels requests for print jobs made with the **lp** command. The first form allows a user to specify one or more *request-IDs* of print jobs to be canceled. Alternatively, the user can specify one or more *printers*, on which only the currently printing job will be canceled if it is the user's job.

The second form of **cancel** cancels all jobs for users specified in *login-names*. In this form the *printers* option can be used to restrict the printers on which the users' jobs will be canceled. Note that in this form, when the *printers* option is used, all jobs queued by the users for those printers will be canceled. A printer class is not a valid argument.

Users without special privileges can cancel only requests that are associated with their own login names; To cancel a request, a user issues the following command:

cancel -u *login-name* [*printer*]

This command cancels all print requests associated with the *login-name* of the user making the request, either on all printers (by default) or on the printer specified.

Administrative users with the appropriate privileges can cancel jobs submitted by any user by issuing the following types of commands:

cancel -u "*login-name-list***"**
Cancels all requests (on all relevant printers) by the specified users, including those jobs currently being printed. Double quotes must be used around *login-name-list* if the list contains blanks. The argument *login-name-list* may include any or all of the following constructs:

login-name	a user on the local system
*system-name***!***login-name*	a user on system *system-name*
*system-name***!all**	all users on system *system-name*
all!*login-name*	a user on all systems
all	all users on the local system
all!all	all users on all systems

Note that a remote job can be canceled only if it originated on the client system; that is, a server system can cancel jobs that came from a client, and a client system can cancel jobs it sent to a server.

cancel -u "*login-name-list***"** *printer-1 printer-2 printer-n*
Cancels all requests by the specified users for the specified printers, including those jobs currently being printed. (For a complete list of printers available on your system, execute the **lpstat -p** command.)

In any of these cases, the cancellation of a request that is currently printing frees the printer to print the next request.

If the Auditing Utilities are installed, the use of this command is an auditable event.

Downloading Type 1 PostScript Fonts to PostScript Printers

The desktop metaphor has a feature allowing the installation of retail Type 1 fonts for use with applications running under the metaphor. These fonts may be downloaded to PostScript printers if the application generates PostScript output that uses them. The **lp** command handles this automatically using the filter named **download**. For more information, see **download**(1M).

FILES

/var/spool/lp/*

/usr/lib/locale/*locale***/LC_MESSAGES/uxlp**
language-specific message file [See **LANG** on **environ**(5).]

SEE ALSO

desktop(1), **download**(1), **lpstat**(1), **mail**(1), **mkfontscale**(1)

NOTES

Printers for which requests are not being accepted will not be considered when the destination is **any**. (Use the **lpstat -a** command to see which printers are accepting requests.) However, if a request is destined for a class of printers and the class itself is accepting requests, then all printers in the class will be considered, regardless of their acceptance status.

For printers that take mountable print wheels or font cartridges, if you do not specify a particular print wheel or font with the **-S** option, whichever one happens to be mounted at the time your request is printed will be used. The **lpstat -p** *printer* **-l** command is used to see which print wheels are available on a particular printer. The **lpstat -S -l** command is used to see what print wheels are available and on which printers. Without the **-S** option, the standard character set is used for printers that have selectable character sets.

If you experience problems with jobs that usually print but on occasion do not print, check the physical connections between the printer and your computer. If you are using an automatic data switch or an A/B switch, try removing it and see if the problem clears.

NAME

lpadmin – configure the LP print service

SYNOPSIS

lpadmin -p *printer options*

lpadmin -x *dest*

lpadmin -d [*dest*]

lpadmin -S *print-wheel* **-A** *alert-type* [**-W** *minutes*] [**-Q** *requests*]

DESCRIPTION

lpadmin configures the LP print service by defining printers and devices. It is used to add and change printers, to remove printers from the service, to set or change the system default destination, to define alerts for printer faults, to mount print wheels, and, when the LP Networking Service is installed, to define printers for remote printing services. [For details about network printers, see the **lpsystem**(1M) page.]

Adding or Changing a Printer

The first form of the **lpadmin** command (**lpadmin -p** *printer options*) is used to configure a new printer or to change the configuration of an existing printer. The following *options* may appear in any order.

-A *alert-type* [**-W** *minutes*]

The **-A** option is used to define an alert to inform the administrator when a printer fault is detected, and periodically thereafter, until the printer fault is cleared by the administrator. If an alert is not defined for a particular printer, mail will be sent to user **lp** by default. The *alert-types* are:

mail Send the alert message via mail [see **mail**(1)] to the administrator.

write Write the message to the terminal on which the administrator is logged in. If the administrator is logged in on several terminals, one is chosen arbitrarily.

quiet Do not send messages for the current condition. An administrator can use this option to temporarily stop receiving further messages about a known problem. Once the fault has been cleared and printing resumes, messages will again be sent when another fault occurs with the printer.

none Do not send messages; any existing alert definition for the printer will be removed. No alert will be sent when the printer faults until a different alert-type (except **quiet**) is used.

shell-command

Run the *shell-command* each time the alert needs to be sent. The shell command should expect the message in standard input. If there are blanks embedded in the command, enclose the command in quotes. Note that the **mail** and **write** values for this option are equivalent to the values **mail** *login-name* and **write** *login-name* respectively, where *login-name* is the current name for the administrator. This will be the login name of the person submitting this command unless he or she has used the **su** command to change to another login name. If the **su** command has been used to change the login name, then the *login-name* for the new login is used.

`list` Display the type of the alert for the printer fault. No change is made to the alert.

The message sent appears as follows:

> **The printer** *printer* **has stopped printing for the reason given below. Fix the problem and bring the printer back on line. Printing has stopped, but will be restarted in a few minutes; issue an enable command if you want to restart sooner. Unless someone issues a change request**
>
> **lp -i** *request-id* **-P . . .**
>
> **to change the page list to print, the current request will be reprinted from the beginning.**
>
> **The reason(s) it stopped (multiple reasons indicate reprinted attempts):**
>
> *reason*

The LP print service can detect printer faults only through an adequate fast filter and only when the standard interface program or a suitable customized interface program is used. Furthermore, the level of recovery after a fault depends on the capabilities of the filter.

If the *printer* is **all**, the alerting defined in this command applies to all existing printers.

If the **-W** option is not used to arrange fault alerting for *printer*, the default procedure is to mail one message to the administrator of *printer* per fault. This is equivalent to specifying **-W once** or **-W 0**. If *minutes* is a number greater than zero, an alert will be sent at intervals specified by *minutes*.

-c *class*
Insert *printer* into the specified *class*. *Class* will be created if it does not already exist.

-D *comment*
Save this *comment* for display whenever a user asks for a full description of *printer* [see **lpstat**(1)]. The LP print service does not interpret this comment.

-e $printer_1$
Copy the interface program of an existing $printer_1$ to be the interface program for *printer*. (Options **-i** and **-m** may not be specified with this option.)

-F *fault-recovery*
This option specifies the recovery to be used for any print request that is stopped because of a printer fault, according to the value of *fault-recovery*:

continue
Continue printing on the top of the page where printing stopped. This requires a filter to wait for the fault to clear before automatically continuing.

beginning
Start printing the request again from the beginning.

wait Disable printing on *printer* and wait for the administrator or a user to enable printing again.

During the wait the administrator or the user who submitted the stopped print request can issue a change request that specifies where printing should resume. (See the **-i** option of the **lp** command.) If no change request is made before printing is enabled, printing will resume at the top of the page where stopped, if the filter allows; otherwise, the request will be printed from the beginning.

The default value of *fault-recovery* is **beginning**.

-f allow:*form-list*
-f deny:*form-list*
Allow or deny the forms in *form-list* to be printed on *printer*. By default no forms are allowed on a new printer.

For each printer, the LP print service keeps two lists of forms: an "allow-list" of forms that may be used with the printer, and a "deny-list" of forms that may not be used with the printer. With the **-f allow** option, the forms listed are added to the allow-list and removed from the deny-list. With the **-f deny** option, the forms listed are added to the deny-list and removed from the allow-list.

If the allow-list is not empty, only the forms in the list may be used on the printer, regardless of the contents of the deny-list. If the allow-list is empty, but the deny-list is not, the forms in the deny-list may not be used with the printer. All forms can be excluded from a printer by specifying **-f deny:all**. All forms can be used on a printer (provided the printer can handle all the characteristics of each form) by specifying **-f allow:all**.

The LP print service uses this information as a set of guidelines for determining where a form can be mounted. Administrators, however, are not restricted from mounting a form on any printer. If mounting a form on a particular printer is in disagreement with the information in the allow-list or deny-list, the administrator is warned but the mount is accepted. Nonetheless, if a user attempts to issue a print or change request for a form and printer combination that is in disagreement with the information, the request is accepted only if the form is currently mounted on the printer. If the form is later unmounted before the request can print, the request is canceled and the user is notified by mail.

If the administrator tries to specify a form as acceptable for use on a printer that doesn't have the capabilities needed by the form, the command is rejected.

The **lpadmin** command will issue a warning when an invalid (nonexistent) form name is submitted with the "**-f deny:**" option.

Note the other use of **-f**, with the **-M** option, below.

-h Indicate that the device associated with the printer is hardwired. If neither of the mutually exclusive options, **-h** and **-l**, is specified, this option is assumed.

-I *content-type-list*
Allow *printer* to handle print requests with the content types listed in a *content-type-list*. If the list includes names of more than one type, the names must be separated by commas or blank spaces. (If they are separated by blank spaces, the entire list must be enclosed in double quotes.)

The type **simple** is recognized as the default content type for files in the UNIX system. A **simple** type of file is a data stream containing only printable ASCII characters and the following control characters.

Control Character	Octal Value	Meaning
backspace	10_8	move back one character, except at beginning of line
tab	11_8	move to next tab stop
linefeed (newline)	12_8	move to beginning of next line
form feed	14_8	move to beginning of next page
carriage return	15_8	move to beginning of current line

To prevent the print service from considering **simple** a valid type for the printer, specify either an explicit value (such as the printer type) in the *content-type-list*, or an empty list. If you do want **simple** included along with other types, you must include **simple** in the *content-type-list*.

Except for **simple**, each *content-type* name is freely determined by the administrator. If the printer type is specified by the **-T** option, then the printer type is implicitly considered to be also a valid content type.

-i *interface*
Establish a new interface program for *printer*. *Interface* is the pathname of the new program. (The **-e** and **-m** options may not be specified with this option.)

-l Indicate that the device associated with *printer* is a login terminal. The LP scheduler (**lpsched**) disables all login terminals automatically each time it is started. (The **-h** option may not be specified with this option.)

-M -f *form-name* [**-a** [**-o filebreak**]]
Mount the form *form-name* on *printer*. Print requests that need the pre-printed form *form-name* will be printed on *printer*. If more than one printer has the form mounted and the user has specified **any** (with the **-d** option of the **lp** command) as the printer destination, then the print request will be printed on the one printer that also meets the other needs of the request.

The page length and width, and character and line pitches needed by the form are compared with those allowed for the printer, by checking the capabilities in the **terminfo** database for the type of printer. If the form requires attributes that are not available with the printer, the administrator is warned but the mount is accepted. If the form lists a print wheel as mandatory, but the print wheel mounted on the printer is different, the administrator is also warned but the mount is accepted.

If the **-a** option is given, an alignment pattern is printed, preceded by the same initialization of the physical printer that precedes a normal print request. Printing is assumed to start at the top of the first page of the form. After the pattern is printed, the administrator can adjust the mounted form in the printer and press return for another alignment pattern (no initialization this time), and can continue printing as many alignment patterns as desired. The administrator can quit the printing of alignment patterns by typing **q**.

If the **-o filebreak** option is given, a formfeed is inserted between each copy of the alignment pattern. By default, the alignment pattern is assumed to correctly fill a form, so no formfeed is added.

A form is "unmounted" either by mounting a new form in its place or by using the **-f none** option. By default, a new printer has no form mounted.

Note the other use of **-f** without the **-M** option above.

-M -S *print-wheel*
Mount the *print-wheel* on *printer*. Print requests that need the *print-wheel* will be printed on *printer*. If more than one printer has *print-wheel* mounted and the user has specified **any** (with the **-d** option of the **lp** command) as the printer destination, then the print request will be printed on the one printer that also meets the other needs of the request.

If the *print-wheel* is not listed as acceptable for the printer, the administrator is warned but the mount is accepted. If the printer does not take print wheels, the command is rejected.

A print wheel is "unmounted" either by mounting a new print wheel in its place or by using the option **-S none**. By default, a new printer has no print wheel mounted.

Note the other uses of the **-S** option without the **-M** option described below.

-m *model*
Select *model* interface program, provided with the LP print service, for the printer. (Options **-e** and **-i** may not be specified with this option.) The following interface programs are available:

standard generic printer interface

PS interface for PostScript printers only

By default, the **standard** interface is used.

-O *copy-option*
The **-O** controls whether or not **lp** will make a copy of the user's file(s) when a print job is submitted. The *copy-option* can be either **copy** or **nocopy**. If **-O copy** is specified, the LP system will always copy the user's source files to the spool area when a print job is submitted. If **-O nocopy** is specified, the files are copied only if the user specifies the **-c** option of **lp** when submitting the job.

This option sets the value of the **copy-files** parameter in the **/etc/lp/defaults** file. The value, which can be either **on** or **off**, is checked every time a print job is submitted.

-o *printing-option*

Each **-o** option in the list below is the default given to an interface program if the option is not taken from a preprinted form description or is not explicitly given by the user submitting a request [see **lp**(1)]. The only **-o** options that can have defaults defined are listed below.

length=*scaled-decimal-number*
width=*scaled-decimal-number*
cpi=*scaled-decimal-number*
lpi=*scaled-decimal-number*
stty=*'stty-option-list'*

The term "scaled-decimal-number" refers to a non-negative number used to indicate a unit of size. The type of unit is shown by a "trailing" letter attached to the number. Three types of scaled decimal numbers can be used with the LP print service: numbers that show sizes in centimeters (marked with a trailing **c**); numbers that show sizes in inches (marked with a trailing **i**); and numbers that show sizes in units appropriate to use (without a trailing letter), that is, lines, characters, lines per inch, or characters per inch.

The first four default option values must agree with the capabilities of the type of physical printer, as defined in the **terminfo** database for the printer type. If they do not, the command is rejected.

The *stty-option-list* is not checked for allowed values, but is passed directly to the **stty** program by the standard interface program. Any error messages produced by **stty** when a request is processed (by the standard interface program) are mailed to the user submitting the request.

For each printing option not specified, the defaults for the following attributes are defined in the **terminfo** entry for the specified printer type.

length
width
cpi
lpi

The default for **stty** is

```
stty='9600 cs8 -cstopb -parenb ixon
     -ixany opost -olcuc onlcr -ocrnl -onocr
     -onlret -ofill nl0 cr0 tab0 bs0 vt0 ff0'
```

You can set any of the **-o** options to the default values (which vary for different types of printers), by typing them without assigned values, as follows:

length=
width=
cpi=
lpi=
stty=

`-o nobanner`
Allow a user to submit a print request specifying that no banner page be printed.

`-o banner`
Force a banner page to be printed with every print request, even when a user asks for no banner page. This is the default; you must specify `-o nobanner` if you want to allow users to be able to specify `-o nobanner` with the `lp` command.

`-R` *high*[`,` *low*]
The `-R` option allows you to define the range of device levels used for the initial screening of requests to a network printer. You define such a range by specifying its high and low ends (with the arguments *high* and *low*) on a local system. (`lpadmin` stores the range of device levels you specify in a file called `/etc/lp/printers/`*printer*`/configuration`, where *printer* is the name of the relevant device.) The default values of *high* and *low* are `SYS_RANGE_MAX` and `SYS_RANGE_MIN`, respectively (the same values assigned to a local printer).

This option is available only if the LP Networking Service is installed and running on the system. This option is valid only if you use the `-s` *system* option or the `-R` option for an existing network printer. (If you don't specify the value of *low* after the `-R` option, it is assigned the same value as *high* by default.)

`-r` *class* Remove *printer* from the specified *class*. If *printer* is the last member of *class*, then *class* will be removed.

`-S` *list* Allow either the print wheels or aliases for character sets named in *list* to be used on the printer. The `-S` option doesn't let you add items to a *list* specified with an earlier invocation of `-S`; instead, it replaces an existing *list* with a new one. (Thus `-S` differs from the `-f`, `-u`, `allow`, and `deny` options, which allow you to modify existing lists of available filters and authorized users.) Once you've run the `-S` option, the print wheels and character sets specified (in *list*) on the current command line will be the only ones available.

If the printer is a type that takes print wheels, then *list* is a comma or space separated list of print wheel names. (Enclose the list with quotes if it contains blanks.) These will be the only print wheels considered mountable on the printer. (You can always force a different print wheel to be mounted, however.) Until the option is used to specify a list, no print wheels will be considered mountable on the printer, and print requests that ask for a particular print wheel with this printer will be rejected.

If the printer is a type that has selectable character sets, then *list* is a comma or blank separated list of character set name "mappings" or aliases. (Enclose the list with quotes if it contains blanks.) Each "mapping" is of the form

known-name=alias

The *known-name* is a character set number preceded by **cs** (such as **cs3** for character set three) or a character set name from the **Terminfo** database entry **csnm**. [See **terminfo**(4).] If this option is not used to specify a list, only the names already known from the Terminfo database or numbers with a prefix of **cs** will be acceptable for the printer.

If *list* is the word **none**, any existing print wheel lists or character set aliases will be removed.

Note the other uses of the **-S** with the **-M** option described above.

-s *server-name*[**!***server-printer-name*]

Make a server printer accessible to users on your system. *Server-name* is the name of the system on which the printer is located. It must be listed in the LP systems table. [See **lpsystem**(1M)]. *Server-printer-name* is the name used on the *server* system for that printer. For example, if you want to access $printer_1$ on $server_1$ and you want it called $printer_2$ on your system, enter **-p** $printer_2$ **-s** $server_1$**!**$printer_1$.

If the **-R** option is not also specified, the default values of **SYS_RANGE_MAX** and **SYS_RANGE_MIN** are assigned to the *high* and *low* parameters, respectively. These parameters define the range of device levels for a server printer. If you use this option (either to define a new server printer or to redefine a formerly local printer as a server printer) without also using the **-R** option, then, by default, *high* will be set to **SYS_RANGE_MAX**, and *low* will be set to **SYS_RANGE_MIN**.

This option is available only if the LP Networking Service is installed and running on your system.

-T *printer-type-list*

Identify the printer as being of one or more *printer-types*. Each *printer-type* is used to extract data from the **terminfo** database; this information is used to initialize the printer before printing each user's request. Some filters may also use a *printer-type* to convert content for the printer. If this option is not used, the default *printer-type* will be **unknown**; no information will be extracted from **terminfo** so each user request will be printed without first initializing the printer. Also, this option must be used if the following are to work: **-o cpi**, **-o lpi**, **-o width**, and **-o length** options of the **lpadmin** and **lp** commands, and the **-S** and **-f** options of the **lpadmin** command.

If the *printer-type-list* contains more than one type, then the *content-type-list* of the **-I** option must either be specified as **simple**, as empty (**-I ""**), or not specified at all.

-u allow:*login-name-list*
-u deny:*login-name-list*

Allow or deny the users in *login-name-list* access to the printer. By default all users are allowed on a new printer. The *login-ID-list* argument may include any or all of the following constructs:

login-name	a user on the local system
system-name!*login-name*	a user on system *system-name*
system-name!**all**	all users on system *system-name*
all!*login-name*	a user on all systems
all	all users on the local system
all!all	all users on all systems

For each printer the LP print service keeps two lists of users: an "allow-list" of people allowed to use the printer, and a "deny-list" of people denied access to the printer. With the **-u allow** option, the users listed are added to the allow-list and removed from the deny-list. With the **-u deny** option, the users listed are added to the deny-list and removed from the allow-list.

If the allow-list is not empty, only the users in the list may use the printer, regardless of the contents of the deny-list. If the allow-list is empty, but the deny-list is not, the users in the deny-list may not use the printer. All users can be denied access to the printer by specifying **-u deny:all**. All users may use the printer by specifying **-u allow:all**.

-U *dial-info*

The **-U** option allows your print service to access a remote printer. (It does not enable your print service to access a remote printer service.) Specifically, **-U** assigns the "dialing" information *dial-info* to the printer. *Dial-info* is used with the **dial** routine to call the printer. Any network connection supported by the Basic Networking Utilities will work. *Dial-info* can be either a phone number for a modem connection, or a system name for other kinds of connections. Or, if **-U direct** is given, no dialing will take place, because the name **direct** is reserved for a printer that is directly connected. If a system name is given, it is used to search for connection details from the file **/etc/uucp/Systems** or related files. This option is available only if the LP Networking Service and the Basic Networking Utilities are installed and running on the system. By default, **-U direct** is assumed.

-v *device*

Associate a *device* with *printer*. *Device* is the pathname of a file that is writable by **lp**. Note that the same *device* can be associated with more than one printer.

Restrictions

When creating a new printer, one of three options (**-v**, **-U**, or **-s**) must be supplied. In addition, only one of the following may be supplied: **-e**, **-i**, or **-m**; if none of these three options is supplied, the model standard is used. The **-h** and **-l** options are mutually exclusive. Printer and class names may be no longer than 14 characters and must consist entirely of the characters **A-Z**, **a-z**, **0-9** and

_ (underscore). If `-s` and/or `-R` is specified, the following options are invalid: `-A`, `-e`, `-F`, `-h`, `-i`, `-l`, `-M`, `-m`, `-o`, `-U`, `-v`, and `-W`.

Removing a Printer Destination

The `-x` *dest* option removes the destination *dest* (a printer or a class), from the LP print service. If *dest* is a printer and is the only member of a class, then the class will be deleted, too. If *dest* is `all`, all printers and classes are removed. No other *options* are allowed with `-x`.

Setting/Changing the System Default Destination

The `-d` [*dest*] option makes *dest*, an existing printer or class, the new system default destination. If *dest* is not supplied, then there is no system default destination. No other *options* are allowed with `-d`. To unset the system default printer, the user can enter the keyword "none."

Setting an Alert for a Print Wheel

`-S` *print-wheel* `-A` *alert-type* [`-W` *minutes*] [`-Q` *requests*]

The `-S` *print-wheel* option is used with the `-A` *alert-type* option to define an alert to mount the print wheel when there are jobs queued for it. If this command is not used to arrange alerting for a print wheel, no alert will be sent for the print wheel. Note the other use of `-A`, with the `-p` option, above.

The *alert-types* are the same as those available with the `-A` option: `mail`, `write`, `quiet`, `none`, *shell-command*, and `list`. See the description of `-A`, above, for details about each.

The message sent appears as follows:

The print wheel *print-wheel* **needs to be mounted**
on the printer(s):
printer (*integer*$_1$ **requests)**
integer$_2$ **print requests await this print wheel.**

The printers listed are those that the administrator had earlier specified were candidates for this print wheel. The number *integer*$_1$ listed next to each printer is the number of requests eligible for the printer. The number *integer*$_2$ shown after the printer list is the total number of requests awaiting the print wheel. It will be less than the sum of the other numbers if some requests can be handled by more than one printer.

If the *print-wheel* is `all`, the alerting defined in this command applies to all print wheels already defined to have an alert.

If the `-W` option is not given, the default procedure is that only one message will be sent per need to mount the print wheel. Not specifying the `-W` option is equivalent to specifying `-W once` or `-W 0`. If *minutes* is a number greater than zero, an alert will be sent at intervals specified by *minutes*.

If the `-Q` option is also given, the alert will be sent when a certain number (specified by the argument *requests*) of print requests that need the print wheel are waiting. If the `-Q` option is not given, or *requests* is 1 or the word `any` (which are both the default), a message is sent as soon as anyone submits a print request for the print wheel when it is not mounted.

FILES

`/var/spool/lp/*`

`/etc/lp`

`/usr/lib/locale/`*locale*`/LC_MESSAGES/uxlp`

language-specific message file [See **LANG** on **environ**(5).]

SEE ALSO

accept(1M), **admalloc**(1M), **enable**(1M), **lpsched**(1M), **lpsystem**(1M), **putdev**(1M)

NAME

`lpc` – (BSD) line printer control program

SYNOPSIS

`/usr/ucb/lpc` [*command* [*parameter...*]]

DESCRIPTION

`lpc` controls the operation of the printer, or of multiple printers. `lpc` commands can be used to start or stop a printer, disable or enable a printer's spooling queue, rearrange the order of jobs in a queue, or display the status of each printer—along with its spooling queue and printer daemon.

With no arguments, `lpc` runs interactively, prompting with '`lpc>`'. If arguments are supplied, `lpc` interprets the first as a *command* to execute; each subsequent argument is taken as a *parameter* for that command. The standard input can be redirected so that `lpc` reads commands from a file.

Commands may be abbreviated to an unambiguous substring. Note: the *printer* parameter is specified just by the name of the printer (as `lw`), not as you would specify it to `lpr`(1) or `lpq`(1) (not as `-Plw`).

`?` [*command*]...

`help` [*command*]...

Display a short description of each command specified in the argument list, or, if no arguments are given, a list of the recognized commands.

`abort` [`all` | [*printer* ...]]

Terminate an active spooling daemon on the local host immediately and then disable printing (preventing new daemons from being started by `lpr`(1)) for the specified printers. The `abort` command can only be used by the privileged user.

`clean` [`all` | [*printer* ...]]

Remove all files created in the spool directory by the daemon from the specified printer queue(s) on the local machine. The `clean` command can only be used by the privileged user.

`disable` [`all` | [*printer* ...]]

Turn the specified printer queues off. This prevents new printer jobs from being entered into the queue by `lpr`(1). The `disable` command can only be used by the privileged user.

`down` [`all` | [*printer* ...]] [*message*]

Turn the specified printer queue off, disable printing and put *message* in the printer status file. The message does not need to be quoted, the remaining arguments are treated like `echo`(1). This is normally used to take a printer down and let others know why (`lpq`(1) indicates that the printer is down, as does the `status` command).

`enable` [`all` | [*printer* ...]]

Enable spooling on the local queue for the listed printers, so that `lpr`(1) can put new jobs in the spool queue. The `enable` command can only be used by the privileged user.

exit
quit Exit from **lpc**.

restart [**all** | [*printer* ...]]
Attempt to start a new printer daemon. This is useful when some abnormal condition causes the daemon to die unexpectedly leaving jobs in the queue. This command can be run by any user.

start [**all** | [*printer* ...]]
Enable printing and start a spooling daemon for the listed printers. The **start** command can only be used by the privileged user.

status [**all** | [*printer* ...]]
Display the status of daemons and queues on the local machine. This command can be run by any user.

stop [**all** | [*printer* ...]]
Stop a spooling daemon after the current job completes and disable printing. The **stop** command can only be used by the privileged user.

topq *printer* [*job#* ...] [*user* ...]
Move the print job(s) specified by *job#* or those job(s) belonging to *user* to the top (head) of the printer queue. The **topq** command can only be used by the privileged user.

up [**all** | [*printer* ...]] Enable everything and start a new printer daemon. Undoes the effects of **down**.

FILES

/var/spool/lp/*
/var/spool/lp/system/pstatus

SEE ALSO

lpq(1), **lpr**(1), **lprm**(1), **lpsched**(1M)

DIAGNOSTICS

?Ambiguous command
The abbreviation you typed matches more than one command.

?Invalid command
You typed a command or abbreviation that was not recognized.

?Privileged command
You used a command can be executed only by the privileged user.

lpc: *printer* **: unknown printer to the print service**
The **printer** was not found in the System V LP database. Usually this is a typing mistake; however, it may indicate that the printer does not exist on the system. Use '**lptstat -p**' to find the reason.

lpc: error on opening queue to spooler
The connection to **lpsched** on the local machine failed. This usually means the printer server started at boot time has died or is hung. Check if the printer spooler daemon **/usr/lib/lp/lpsched** is running.

`lpc: Can't send message to LP print service`

`lpc: Can't receive message from LP print service`
These indicate that the LP print service has been stopped. Get help from the system administrator.

`lpc: Received unexpected message from LP print service`
It is likely there is an error in this software. Get help from system administrator.

NAME

`lpfilter` – administer filters used with the LP print service

SYNOPSIS

`lpfilter -f` *filter-name* `-F` *pathname*

`lpfilter -f` *filter-name* `-`

`lpfilter -f` *filter-name* `-i`

`lpfilter -f` *filter-name* `-x`

`lpfilter -f` *filter-name* `-l`

DESCRIPTION

The `lpfilter` command is used to add, change, delete, and list a filter used with the LP print service. These filters are used to convert the content type of a file to a content type acceptable to a printer. One of the following options must be used with the `lpfilter` command: `-F` *pathname* (or `-` for standard input) to add or change a filter; `-i` to reset an original filter to its factory setting; `-x` to delete a filter; or `-l` to list a filter description.

The argument `all` can be used instead of a *filter-name* with any of these options. When `all` is specified with the `-F` or `-` option, the requested change is made to all filters. Using `all` with the `-i` option has the effect of restoring to their original settings all filters for which predefined settings were initially available. Using the `all` argument with the `-x` option results in all filters being deleted, and using it with the `-l` option produces a list of all filters.

Adding or Changing a Filter

The filter named in the `-f` option is added to the filter table. If the filter already exists, its description is changed to reflect the new information in the input.

The filter description is taken from the *pathname* if the `-F` option is given, or from the standard input if the `-` option is given. One of the two must be given to define or change a filter. If the filter named is one originally delivered with the LP print service, the `-i` option will restore the original filter description.

When an existing filter is changed with the `-F` or `-` option, items that are not specified in the new information are left as they were. When a new filter is added with this command, unspecified items are given default values. (See below.)

Filters are used to convert the content of a request into a data stream acceptable to a printer. For a given print request, the LP print service will know the following: the type of content in the request, the name of the printer, the type of the printer, the types of content acceptable to the printer, and the modes of printing asked for by the originator of the request. It will use this information to find a filter or a pipeline of filters that will convert the content into a type acceptable to the printer.

Below is a list of items that provide input to this command, and a description of each item. All lists are comma or space separated.

`Input types:` *content-type-list*
`Output types:` *content-type-list*
`Printer types:` *printer-type-list*
`Printers:` *printer-list*
`Filter type:` *filter-type*

```
Command: shell-command
Options: template-list
```

`Input types` This gives the types of content that can be accepted by the filter. (The default is **any**.)

`Output types` This gives the types of content that the filter can produce from any of the input content types. (The default is **any**.)

`Printer types` This gives the type of printers for which the filter can be used. The LP print service will restrict the use of the filter to these types of printers. (The default is **any**.)

`Printers` This gives the names of the printers for which the filter can be used. The LP print service will restrict the use of the filter to just the printers named. (The default is **any**.)

`Filter type` This marks the filter as a **slow** filter or a **fast** filter. Slow filters are generally those that take a long time to convert their input. They are run unconnected to a printer, to keep the printers from being tied up while the filter is running. If a listed printer is on a remote system, the filter type for it must have the value **slow**. Fast filters are generally those that convert their input quickly, or those that must be connected to the printer when run. These will be given to the interface program to run connected to the physical printer.

`Command` This specifies the program to run to invoke the filter. The full program pathname as well as fixed options must be included in the *shell-command*; additional options are constructed, based on the characteristics of each print request and on the **Options** field. A command must be given for each filter.

The command must accept a data stream as standard input and produce the converted data stream on its standard output. This allows filter pipelines to be constructed to convert data not handled by a single filter.

`Options` This is a comma separated list of templates used by the LP print service to construct options to the filter from the characteristics of each print request listed in the table later.

In general, each template is of the following form:

keyword-pattern=*replacement*

The *keyword* names the characteristic that the template attempts to map into a filter specific option; each valid *keyword* is listed in the table below. A *pattern* is one of the following: a literal pattern of one of the forms listed in the table, a single asterisk (*), or a regular expression. If *pattern* matches the value of the characteristic, the template fits and is used to generate a filter specific option. The *replacement* is what will be used as the option.

Regular expressions are the same as those found in the **ed** or **vi** commands. This includes the `\( . . . \)` and `\`*n* constructions, which can be used to extract portions of the *pattern* for copying into the *replacement*, and the **&**, which can be used to copy the entire *pattern* into the *replacement*.

The *replacement* can also contain a *; it too, is replaced with the entire *pattern*, just like the **&** of **ed**(1).

`lp` Option	Characteristic	*keyword*	Possible *patterns*
-T	Content type (input)	**INPUT**	*content-type*
N/A	Content type (output)	**OUTPUT**	*content-type*
N/A	Printer type	**TERM**	*printer-type*
-d	Printer name	**PRINTER**	*printer-name*
-f, -o cpi=	Character pitch	**CPI**	*integer*
-f, -o lpi=	Line pitch	**LPI**	*integer*
-f, -o length=	Page length	**LENGTH**	*integer*
-f, -o width=	Page width	**WIDTH**	*integer*
-P	Pages to print	**PAGES**	*page-list*
-S	Character set	**CHARSET**	*character-set-name*
	Print wheel	**CHARSET**	*print-wheel-name*
-f	Form name	**FORM**	*form-name*
-y	Modes	**MODES**	*mode*
-n	Number of copies	**COPIES**	*integer*

For example, the template

```
MODES landscape = -l
```

shows that if a print request is submitted with the **-y landscape** option, the filter will be given the option **-l**. As another example, the template

```
TERM * = -T *
```

shows that the filter will be given the option **-T** *printer-type* for whichever *printer-type* is associated with a print request using the filter.

As a last example, consider the template

```
MODES prwidth\=\(.*\) = -w\1
```

Suppose a user gives the command

```
lp -y prwidth=10
```

From the table above, the LP print service determines that the **-y** option is handled by a **MODES** template. The **MODES** template here works because the *pattern* **prwidth\=\(.*\)** matches the **prwidth=10** given by the user. The *replacement* **-w\1** causes the LP print service to generate the filter option **-w10**.

If necessary, the LP print service will construct a filter pipeline by concatenating several filters to handle the user's file and all the print options. [See **sh**(1) for a description of a pipeline.] If the print service constructs a filter pipeline, the **INPUT** and **OUTPUT** values used for each filter in the pipeline are the types of the input and output for that filter, not for the entire pipeline.

Deleting a Filter

The **-x** option is used to delete the filter specified in *filter-name* from the LP filter table.

Listing a Filter Description

The **-l** option is used to list the description of the filter named in *filter-name*. If the command is successful, the following message is sent to standard output:

Input types: *content-type-list*
Output types: *content-type-list*
Printer types: *printer-type-list*
Printers: *printer-list*
Filter type: *filter-type*
Command: *shell-command*
Options: *template-list*

If the command fails, an error message is sent to standard error.

FILES

/usr/lib/locale/*locale***/LC_MESSAGES/uxlp**
language-specific message file [See **LANG** on **environ**(5).]

SEE ALSO

lpadmin(1M)

NAME

lpforms – administer forms used with the LP print service

SYNOPSIS

lpforms -f *form-name options*
lpforms -f *form-name* **-A** *alert-type* [**-Q** *minutes*] [**-W** *requests*]

DESCRIPTION

The **lpforms** command is used to administer the use of preprinted forms, such as company letterhead paper, with the LP print service. A form is specified by its *form-name*. Users may specify a form when submitting a print request [see **lp**(1)]. The argument **all** can be used instead of *form-name* with either of the command lines shown above. The first command line allows the administrator to add, change, and delete forms, to list the attributes of an existing form, and to allow and deny users access to particular forms. The second command line is used to establish the method by which the administrator is alerted that the form *form-name* must be mounted on a printer.

With the first **lpforms** command line, one of the following options must be used:

-F *pathname*	to add or change form *form-name*, as specified by the information in *pathname*
-	to add or change form *form-name*, as specified by the information from standard input
-x	to delete form *form-name* (this option must be used separately; it may not be used with any other option)
-l	to list the attributes of form *form-name*

Adding or Changing a Form

The **-F** *pathname* option is used to add a new form, *form-name*, to the LP print service, or to change the attributes of an existing form. The form description is taken from *pathname* if the **-F** option is given, or from the standard input if the **-** option is used. One of these two options must be used to define or change a form. *Pathname* is the pathname of a file that contains all or any subset of the following information about the form.

Page length: *scaled – decimal – number* $_1$
Page width: *scaled – decimal – number* $_2$
Number of pages: *integer*
Line pitch: *scaled – decimal – number* $_3$
Character pitch: *scaled – decimal – number* $_4$
Character set choice: *character-set/print-wheel* [**mandatory**]
Ribbon color: *ribbon-color*
Comment:
comment
Alignment pattern: [*content-type*]
content

The term "scaled-decimal-number" refers to a non-negative number used to indicate a unit of size. The type of unit is shown by a "trailing" letter attached to the number. Three types of scaled decimal numbers can be used with the LP print service: numbers that show sizes in centimeters (marked with a trailing **c**); numbers that show sizes in inches (marked with a trailing **i**); and numbers that show sizes in units appropriate to use (without a trailing letter), that is, lines, characters, lines per inch, or characters per inch.

Except for the last two lines, the above lines may appear in any order. The **Comment:** and *comment* items must appear in consecutive order but may appear before the other items, and the **Alignment pattern:** and the *content* items must appear in consecutive order at the end of the file. Also, the *comment* item may not contain a line that begins with any of the key phrases above, unless the key phrase is preceded with a **>** sign. Any leading > sign found in the *comment* will be removed when the comment is displayed. Case distinctions in the key phrases are ignored.

When this command is issued, the form specified by *form-name* is added to the list of forms. If the form already exists, its description is changed to reflect the new information. Once added, a form is available for use in a print request, except where access to the form has been restricted, as described under the **-u** option. A form may also be allowed to be used on certain printers only.

A description of each form attribute is below:

Page length and Page Width

Before printing the content of a print request needing this form, the generic interface program provided with the LP print service will initialize the physical printer to handle pages $scaled-decimal-number_1$ long, and $scaled-decimal-number_2$ wide using the printer type as a key into the **terminfo** database.

The page length and page width will also be passed, if possible, to each filter used in a request needing this form.

Number of pages

Each time the alignment pattern is printed, the LP print service will attempt to truncate the *content* to a single form by, if possible, passing to each filter the page subset of 1-*integer*.

Line pitch and **Character pitch**

Before printing the content of a print request needing this form, the interface programs provided with the LP print service will initialize the physical printer to handle these pitches, using the printer type as a key into the **terminfo** database. Also, the pitches will be passed, if possible, to each filter used in a request needing this form. $Scaled\text{-}decimal\text{-}number_3$ is in lines per centimeter if a **c** is appended, and lines per inch otherwise; similarly, $scaled-decimal-number_4$ is in characters per centimeter if a **c** is appended, and characters per inch otherwise. The character pitch can also be given as **elite** (12 characters per inch), **pica** (10 characters per inch), or **compressed** (as many characters per inch as possible).

Character set choice

When the LP print service alerts an administrator to mount this form, it will also mention that the print wheel *print-wheel* should be used on those printers that take print wheels. If printing with this form is to be done on a printer that has selectable or loadable character sets instead of print wheels, the interface programs provided with the LP print service will automatically select or load the correct character set. If **mandatory** is appended, a user is not allowed to select a different character set for use with the form; otherwise, the character set or print wheel named is a suggestion and a default only.

`Ribbon color`
: When the LP print service alerts an administrator to mount this form, it will also mention that the color of the ribbon should be *ribbon-color*.

`Comment`
: The LP print service will display the *comment* unaltered when a user asks about this form [see **`lpstat`**(1)].

`Alignment pattern`
: When mounting this form an administrator can ask for the *content* to be printed repeatedly, as an aid in correctly positioning the preprinted form. The optional *content-type* defines the type of printer for which *content* had been generated. If *content-type* is not given, **`simple`** is assumed. Note that the *content* is stored as given, and will be readable only by the user **`lp`**.

When an existing form is changed with this command, items missing in the new information are left as they were. When a new form is added with this command, missing items will get the following defaults:

```
Page Length: 66
Page Width: 80
Number of Pages: 1
Line Pitch: 6
Character Pitch: 10
Character Set Choice: any
Ribbon Color: any
```

Deleting a Form

The **`-x`** option is used to delete the form *form-name* from the LP print service.

Listing Form Attributes

The **`-l`** option is used to list the attributes of the existing form *form-name*. The attributes listed are those described under **Adding or Changing a Form,** above. Because of the potentially sensitive nature of the alignment pattern, only the administrator can examine the form with this command. Other people may use the **`lpstat`** command to examine the non-sensitive part of the form description.

Allowing and Denying Access to a Form

The **`-u`** option, followed by the argument **`allow:`***login-name-list* or **`-u deny:`***login-name-list* lets you determine which users will be allowed to specify a particular form with a print request. This option can be used with the **`-F`** or **`-`** option, each of which is described above under **Adding or Changing a Form.**

The *login-name-list* argument may include any or all of the following constructs:

login-name	a user on the local system
system-name!*login-name*	a user on system *system-name*
system-name!**all**	all users on system *system-name*
all!*login-name*	a user on all systems
all	all users on the local system
all!all	all users on all systems

The default value of *login-name-list* is **all**.

The LP print service keeps two lists of users for each form: an "allow-list" of people allowed to use the form, and a "deny-list" of people that may not use the form.

- if *allow-list* is present and *login-name* is in it, access is allowed
- if only *deny-list* is present and *login-name* is not in it, access is allowed
- if *login-name* is in *deny-list*, access is denied
- if neither *allow-list* or *deny-list* are present, access is denied
- if both lists are present, and *login-name* is in neither, access is denied
- if only *allow-list* is present and *login-name* is not in it, access is denied

If the allow-list is not empty, only the users in the list are allowed access to the form, regardless of the contents of the deny-list. If the allow-list is empty but the deny-list is not, the users in the deny-list may not use the form (but all others may use it).

All users can be denied access to a form by specifying **-f deny:all**. All users can be allowed access to a form by specifying **-f allow:all**. (This is the default.)

Setting an Alert to Mount a Form

The **-f** *form-name* option is used with the **-A** *alert-type* option to define an alert to mount the form when there are queued jobs which need it. If this option is not used to arrange alerting for a form, no alert will be sent for that form.

The method by which the alert is sent depends on the value of the *alert-type* argument specified with the **-A** option. The *alert-types* are the same as those available with the **-A** option to **lpadmin**: **mail**, **write**, **quiet**, **none**, *shell-command*, and **list**. See the description of **-A** on **lpadmin**(1M) for details about each.

The message sent appears as follows:

The form *form-name* **needs to be mounted**
on the printer(s):
printer (*integer*$_1$ **requests).**
integer$_2$ **print requests await this form.**
Use the *ribbon-color* **ribbon.**
Use the *print-wheel* **print wheel, if appropriate.**

The printers listed are those that the administrator had earlier specified were candidates for this form. The number *integer*$_1$ listed next to each printer is the number of requests eligible for the printer. The number *integer*$_2$ shown after the list of printers is the total number of requests awaiting the form. It will be less than the sum of the other numbers if some requests can be handled by more than one printer. The *ribbon-color* and *print-wheel* are those specified in the form description. The last line in the message is always sent, even if none of the printers listed use print wheels, because the administrator may choose to mount the form on a printer that does use a print wheel.

Where any color ribbon or any print wheel can be used, the statements above will read:

```
Use any ribbon.

Use any print-wheel.
```

If *form-name* is **any**, the alerting defined in this command applies to any form for which an alert has not yet been defined. If *form-name* is **all**, the alerting defined in this command applies to all forms.

If the **-W** option is not given, the default procedure is that only one message will be sent per need to mount the form. Not specifying the **-W** option is equivalent to specifying **-W once** or **-W 0**. If *minutes* is a number greater than 0, an alert will be sent at intervals specified by *minutes*.

If the **-Q** option is also given, the alert will be sent when a certain number (specified by the argument *requests*) of print requests that need the form are waiting. If the **-Q** option is not given, or the value of *requests* is **1** or **any** (which are both the default), a message is sent as soon as anyone submits a print request for the form when it is not mounted.

Listing the Current Alert

The **-f** option, followed by the **-A** option and the argument **list** is used to list the type of alert that has been defined for the specified form *form-name*. No change is made to the alert. If *form-name* is recognized by the LP print service, one of the following lines is sent to the standard output, depending on the type of alert for the form.

- **When** *requests* **requests are queued:**
  alert with *shell-command* **every** *minutes* **minutes**
- **When** *requests* **requests are queued:**
  write to *user-name* **every** *minutes* **minutes**
- **When** *requests* **requests are queued:**
  mail to *user-name* **every** *minutes* **minutes**
- **No alert**

The phrase **every** *minutes* **minutes** is replaced with **once** if *minutes* (**-W** *minutes)* is 0.

Terminating an Active Alert

The **-A quiet** option is used to stop messages for the current condition. An administrator can use this option to temporarily stop receiving further messages about a known problem. Once the form has been mounted and then unmounted, messages will again be sent when the number of print requests reaches the threshold *requests*.

Removing an Alert Definition

No messages will be sent after the **-A none** option is used until the **-A** option is given again with a different *alert-type*. This can be used to permanently stop further messages from being sent as any existing alert definition for the form will be removed.

FILES

/usr/lib/locale/*locale***/LC_MESSAGES/uxlp**
language-specific message file [See **LANG** on **environ**(5).]

SEE ALSO

lpadmin(1M), **terminfo**(4)

NAME

lpmove – move print requests

SYNOPSIS

lpmove *requests dest*
lpmove $dest_1$ $dest_2$

DESCRIPTION

lpmove moves requests that were queued by **lp** between LP destinations. The first form of the **lpmove** command shown above (under SYNOPSIS) moves the named *requests* to the LP destination *dest*. Requests are request-IDs as returned by **lp**. The second form of the **lpmove** command attempts to move all requests for destination $dest_1$ to destination $dest_2$; **lp** then rejects any new requests for $dest_1$.

Note that when moving requests, **lpmove** never checks the acceptance status [see **accept**(1M)] of the new destination. Also, the request-IDs of the moved requests are not changed, so users can still find their requests. The **lpmove** command does not move requests that have options (such as content type and form required) that cannot be handled by the new destination.

If a request was originally queued for a class or the special destination **any**, and the first form of **lpmove** was used, the destination of the request is changed to *new-destination*. A request thus affected is printable only on *new-destination* and not on other members of the **class** or other acceptable printers if the original destination was **any**.

FILES

/var/spool/lp/*
/usr/lib/locale/*locale***/LC_MESSAGES/uxlp**
language-specific message file [See **LANG** on **environ**(5).]

SEE ALSO

accept(1M), **enable**(1M), **lp**(1), **lpadmin**(1M), **lpstat**(1)

NAME

lpq – (BSD) display the queue of printer jobs

SYNOPSIS

/usr/ucb/lpq [**-P***printer*] [**-l**] [**+** [*interval*]] [*job#* . . .] [*username* . . .]

DESCRIPTION

lpq displays the contents of a printer queue. It reports the status of jobs specified by *job#*, or all jobs owned by the user specified by *username*. **lpq** reports on all jobs in the default printer queue when invoked with no arguments.

For each print job in the queue, **lpq** reports the user's name, current position, the names of input files comprising the job, the job number (by which it is referred to when using **lprm**(1)) and the total size in bytes. Normally, only as much information as will fit on one line is displayed. Jobs are normally queued on a first-in-first-out basis. Filenames comprising a job may be unavailable, such as when **lpr** is used at the end of a pipeline; in such cases the filename field indicates the standard input.

If **lpq** warns that there is no daemon present (that is, due to some malfunction), the **lpc**(1M) command can be used to restart a printer daemon.

OPTIONS

-P *printer* — Display information about the queue for the specified *printer*. In the absence of the **-P** option, the queue to the printer specified by the **PRINTER** variable in the environment is used. If the **PRINTER** variable is not set, the queue for the default printer is used.

-l — Display queue information in long format; includes the name of the host from which the job originated.

+[*interval*] — Display the spool queue periodically until it empties. This option clears the terminal screen before reporting on the queue. If an *interval* is supplied, **lpq** sleeps that number of seconds in between reports.

FILES

/var/spool/lp	spooling directory.
/var/spool/lp/tmp/*system_name***/*-0**	request files specifying jobs

DIAGNOSTICS

lpq: *printer* **is printing**

The **lpq** program queries the spooler **LPSCHED** about the status of the printer. If the printer is disabled, the system administrator can restart the spooler using **lpc**(1M).

lpq: *printer* **waiting for auto-retry (offline ?)**

The daemon could not open the printer device. The printer may be turned off-line. This message can also occur if a printer is out of paper, the paper is jammed, and so on. Another possible cause is that a process, such as an output filter, has exclusive use of the device. The only recourse in this case is to kill the offending process and restart the printer with **lpc**.

lpq: waiting for *host* **to come up**
A daemon is trying to connect to the remote machine named *host*, in order to send the files in the local queue. If the remote machine is up, **lpd** on the remote machine is probably dead or hung and should be restarted using **lpc**.

lpq: sending to *host*
The files are being transferred to the remote *host*, or else the local daemon has hung while trying to transfer the files.

lpq: printer disabled reason:
The printer has been marked as being unavailable with **lpc**.

lpq: The LP print service isn't running or can't be reached.
The **lpsched** process overseeing the spooling queue does not exist. This normally occurs only when the daemon has unexpectedly died. You can restart the printer daemon with **lpc**.

lpq: *printer* **: unknown printer**
The **printer** was not found in the System V LP database. Usually this is a typing mistake; however, it may indicate that the printer does not exist on the system. Use '**lptstat -p**' to find the reason.

lpq: error on opening queue to spooler
The connection to **lpsched** on the local machine failed. This usually means the printer server started at boot time has died or is hung. Check if the printer spooler daemon **/usr/lib/lp/lpsched** is running.

lpq: Can't send message to LP print service

lpq: Can't establish contact with LP print service
These indicate that the LP print service has been stopped. Get help from the system administrator.

lpq: Received unexpected message from LP print service
It is likely there is an error in this software. Get help from system administrator.

SEE ALSO

lpc(1M), **lpr**(1), **lprm**(1)

NOTES

Output formatting is sensitive to the line length of the terminal; this can result in widely-spaced columns.

NAME

lpr – (BSD) send a job to the printer

SYNOPSIS

/usr/ucb/lpr [**-P** *printer*] [**-#** *copies*] [**-C** *class*] [**-J** *job*] [**-T** *title*]
[**-i** [*indent*]] [**-w** *cols*] [**-B**] [**-r**] [**-m**] [**-h**] [**-s**]
[*-filter_option*] [*filename* . . .]

DESCRIPTION

lpr forwards printer jobs to a spooling area for subsequent printing as facilities become available. Each printer job consists of copies of, or, with **-s** , complete pathnames of each *filename* you specify. The spool area is managed by the line printer spooler, **lpsched**. **lpr** reads from the standard input if no files are specified.

OPTIONS

-P *printer* — Send output to the named *printer*. Otherwise send output to the printer named in the **PRINTER** environment variable, or to the default printer, **lp**.

-# *copies* — Produce the number of *copies* indicated for each named file. For example:

```
lpr -#3 index.c lookup.c
```

produces three copies of **index.c**, followed by three copies of **lookup.c**. On the other hand,

```
cat index.c lookup.c | lpr -#3
```

generates three copies of the concatenation of the files.

-C *class* — Print *class* as the job classification on the burst page. For example,

```
lpr -C Operations new.index.c
```

replaces the system name (the name returned by *hostname*) with **Operations** on the burst page, and prints the file **new.index.c**.

-J *job* — Print *job* as the job name on the burst page. Normally, **lpr** uses the first file's name.

-T *title* — Use *title* instead of the file name for the title used by **pr**(1).

-i[*indent*] — Indent output *indent* SPACE characters. Eight SPACE characters is the default.

-w *cols* — Use *cols* as the page width for **pr**.

-r — Remove the file upon completion of spooling, or upon completion of printing with the **-s** option. This is not supported in the SunOS compatibility package. However if the job is submitted to a remote SunOS system, these options will be sent to the remote system for processing.

-m — Send mail upon completion.

-h Suppress printing the burst page.

-s Use the full pathnames (not symbolic links) of the files to be printed rather than trying to copy them. This means the data files should not be modified or removed until they have been printed. **-s** only prevents copies of local files from being made. Jobs from remote hosts are copied anyway. **-s** only works with named data files; if the **lpr** command is at the end of a pipeline, the data is copied to the spool.

filter_option The following single letter options notify the line printer spooler that the files are not standard text files. The spooling daemon will use the appropriate filters to print the data accordingly.

- **-p** Use **pr** to format the files (**lpr -p** is very much like **pr | lpr**).
- **-l** Print control characters and suppress page breaks.
- **-t** The files contain **troff**(1) (cat phototypesetter) binary data.
- **-n** The files contain data from **ditroff** (device independent troff).
- **-d** The files contain data from **tex** (DVI format from Stanford).
- **-g** The files contain standard plot data as produced by the routine **plot**(1) for the filters used by the printer spooler.
- **-v** The files contain a raster image. The printer must support an appropriate imaging model such as PostScript® in order to print the image.
- **-c** The files contain data produced by *cifplot*.
- **-f** Interpret the first character of each line as a standard FORTRAN carriage control character.

If no *filter_option* is given (and the printer can interpret PostScript), the string '%!' as the first two characters of a file indicates that it contains PostScript commands.

These filter options offer a standard user interface, and all options may not be available for, nor applicable to, all printers.

FILES

/etc/passwd	personal identification
/usr/lib/lp/lpsched	System V line printer spooler
/var/spool/lp/tmp/*	directories used for spooling
/var/spool/lp/tmp/*system***/*-0**	spooler control files
/var/spool/lp/tmp/*system***/*-***N*	(*N* is an integer and > 0) data files specified in '*-0' files

DIAGNOSTICS

lpr: *printer* **: unknown printer**

The **printer** was not found in the LP database. Usually this is a typing mistake; however, it may indicate that the printer does not exist on the system. Use '**lptstat -p**' to find the reason.

lpr: error on opening queue to spooler
The connection to **lpsched** on the local machine failed. This usually means the printer server started at boot time has died or is hung. Check if the printer spooler daemon **/usr/lib/lpsched** is running.

lpr: *printer* **: printer queue is disabled**
This means the queue was turned off with

/usr/etc/lpc disable *printer*

to prevent **lpr** from putting files in the queue. This is normally done by the system manager when a printer is going to be down for a long time. The printer can be turned back on by a privileged user with **lpc**.

lpr: Can't send message to the LP print service

lpr: Can't establish contact with the LP print service
These indicate that the LP print service has been stopped. Get help from the system administrator.

lpr: Received unexpected message from LP print service
It is likely there is an error in this software. Get help from system administrator.

lpr: There is no filter to convert the file content
Use the '**lpstat -p -l**' command to find a printer that can handle the file type directly, or consult with your system administrator.

lpr: cannot access the file
Make sure file names are valid.

SEE ALSO

lpc(1M), **lpq**(1), **lprm**(1), **plot**(1), **troff**(1)

NOTES

lp is the preferred interface.

Command-line options cannot be combined into a single argument as with some other commands. The command:

```
lpr -fs
```

is not equivalent to

```
lpr -f -s
```

Placing the **-s** flag first, or writing each option as a separate argument, makes a link as expected.

lpr -p is not precisely equivalent to **pr | lpr**. **lpr -p** puts the current date at the top of each page, rather than the date last modified.

Fonts for **troff**(1) and T_EX® reside on the printer host. It is currently not possible to use local font libraries.

lpr objects to printing binary files.

The **-s** option, intended to use symbolic links in SunOS, does not use symbolic links in the compatibility package. Instead, the complete path names are used. Also, the copying is avoided only for print jobs that are run from the printer host itself. Jobs added to the queue from a remote host are always copied into the spool area. That is, if the printer does not reside on the host that **lpr** is run from, the spooling system makes a copy the file to print, and places it in the spool area of the printer host, regardless of **-s**.

If userA uses **su** to become userB on a windowing interface (SVR4.2) and uses **/usr/ucb/lpr**, then the printer request will be entered as userB, not userA

NAME

lprm – (BSD) remove jobs from the printer queue

SYNOPSIS

/usr/ucb/lprm [**-P***printer*] [**-**] [*job #* . . .] [*username* . . .]

DESCRIPTION

lprm removes a job or jobs from a printer's spooling queue. Since the spool directory is protected from users, using **lprm** is normally the only method by which a user can remove a job.

Without any arguments, **lprm** deletes the job that is currently active, provided that the user who invoked **lprm** owns that job.

When the privileged user specifies a *username*, **lprm** removes all jobs belonging to that user.

You can remove a specific job by supplying its job number as an argument, which you can obtain using **lpq**(1). For example:

```
lpq  -Phost
host is ready and printing
Rank Owner    Job      Files    Total Size
active        wendy    385      standard input  35501 bytes
lprm -Phost 385
```

lprm reports the names of any files it removes, and is silent if there are no applicable jobs to remove.

lprm Sends the request to cancel a job to the print spooler, **LPSCHED**.

OPTIONS

-P*printer* Specify the queue associated with a specific printer. Otherwise the value of the **PRINTER** variable in the environment is used. If this variable is unset, the queue for the default printer is used.

– Remove all jobs owned by you. If invoked by the privileged user, all jobs in the spool are removed. Job ownership is determined by the user's login name and host name on the machine where the **lpr** command was executed.

FILES

/var/spool/lp/* spooling directories

SEE ALSO

lp(1), **lpq**(1), **lpr**(1), **lpsched**(1M)

DIAGNOSTICS

lprm: *printer* **: unknown printer**

The **printer** was not found in the System V LP database. Usually this is a typing mistake; however, it may indicate that the printer does not exist on the system. Use '**lpstat -p**' to get the status of printers.

lprm: error on opening queue to spooler

The connection to **lpsched** on the local machine failed. This usually means the printer server started at boot time has died or is hung. Check if the printer spooler daemon **/usr/lib/lp/lpsched** is running.

lprm: Can't send message to the LP print service

lprm: Can't receive message from the LP print service
These indicate that the LP print service has been stopped. Get help from the system administrator.

lprm: Received unexpected message from the LP print service
It is likely there is an error in this software. Get help from system administrator.

lprm: Can't cancel request
You are not allowed to remove another user's print request.

NOTES

An active job may be incorrectly identified for removal by an **lprm** command issued with no arguments. During the interval between an **lpq**(1) command and the execution of **lprm**, the next job in queue may have become active; that job may be removed unintentionally if it is owned by you. To avoid this, supply **lprm** with the job number to remove when a critical job that you own is next in line.

Only the privileged user can remove print jobs submitted from another host.

lp is the preferred interface.

lprof(1)

NAME

lprof – display line-by-line execution count profile data

SYNOPSIS

lprof [**-p**] [**-P**] [**-s**] [**-x**] [**-I** *incdir*] [**-r** *srcfile*] [**-c** *cntfile*] [**-o** *prog*] [**-V**]

lprof -m *file1*.**cnt** *file2*.**cnt** *filen*.**cnt** [**-T**] **-d** *destfile*.**cnt**

DESCRIPTION

lprof reports the execution characteristics of a program on a (source) line by line basis. This is useful as a means to determine which and how often portions of the code were executed.

lprof interprets a profile file (*prog*.**cnt** by default) produced by the profiled program *prog* (**a.out** by default). *prog* creates a profile file if it has been loaded with the **-ql** option of **cc(1)**. The profile information is computed for functions in a source file if the **-ql** option was used when the source file was compiled.

A shared object may also be profiled by specifying **-ql** when the shared object is created. When a dynamically linked executable is run, one profile file is produced for each profiled shared object linked to the executable. This feature is useful in building a single report covering multiple and disparate executions of a common library. For example, if programs **prog1** and **prog2** both use the archive library **libx.a**, running these profiled programs will produce two profile files, **prog1.cnt** and **prog2.cnt**, which cannot be combined. However, if **libx** is built as a profiled shared object, **libx.so**, and **prog1** and **prog2** are built as profiled dynamically linked executables, then running these programs with the merge option will produce three profile files; one of them, **libx.so.cnt**, will contain the **libx** profile information from both runs.

By default, **lprof** prints a listing of source files (the names of which are stored in the symbol table of the executable file), with each line preceded by its line number (in the source file) and the number of times the line was executed.

The following options may appear singly or be combined in any order:

-p Print listing, each line preceded by the line number and the number of times it was executed (default). This option can be used together with the **-s** option to print both the source listing and summary information.

-P Print a different form of the listing where the file names appear in the leftmost column, followed by function names indented one space, and indented three spaces is a list of the line numbers of the executable lines in the function and the corresponding execution count. This option cannot be used with the **-s**, **-x**, or **-m** options.

-s Print summary information of percentage of lines of code executed per function.

-x Instead of printing the execution count numbers for each line, print each line preceded by its line number and a **[U]** if the line was not executed. If the line was executed, print only the line number.

`-I` *incdir* — Look for source or header files in the directory *incdir* in addition to the current directory and the standard place for **#include** files (usually **/usr/include**). The user can specify more than one directory by using multiple **-I** options.

`-r` *srcfile* — Instead of printing all source files, print only those files named in **-r** options (to be used with the **-p** option only). The user can specify multiple files with a single **-r** option.

`-c` *cntfile* — Use the file *cntfile* instead of *prog*.**cnt** as the input profile file.

`-o` *prog* — Use the name of the program *prog* instead of the name used when creating the profile file. Because the program name stored in the profile file contains the relative path, this option is necessary if the executable file or profile file has been moved.

`-V` — Print, on standard error, the version number of **lprof**.

Merging Data Files

lprof can also be used to merge profile files. The **-m** option must be accompanied by the **-d** option:

-m *file1*.**cnt** *file2*.**cnt** *filen*.**cnt** **-d** *destfile*.**cnt**
Merge the data files *file1*.**cnt** through *filen*.**cnt** by summing the execution counts per line, so that data from several runs can be accumulated. The result is written to *destfile*.**cnt**. The data files must contain profiling data for the same *prog* (see the **-T** option below).

`-T` — Time stamp override. Normally, the time stamps of the executable files being profiled are checked, and data files will not be merged if the time stamps do not match. If **-T** is specified, this check is skipped.

CONTROLLING THE RUN-TIME PROFILING ENVIRONMENT

The environment variable **PROFOPTS** provides run-time control over profiling. When a profiled program (or shared object) is about to terminate, it examines the value of **PROFOPTS** to determine how the profiling data are to be handled. A terminating shared object will honor every **PROFOPTS** option except **file=***filename*.

The environment variable **PROFOPTS** is a comma-separated list of options interpreted by the program being profiled. If **PROFOPTS** is not defined in the environment, then the default action is taken: The profiling data are saved in a file (with the default name, *prog*.**cnt**) in the current directory. If **PROFOPTS** is set to the null string, no profiling data are saved. The following are the available options:

msg=[y|n] — If **msg=y** is specified, a message stating that profile data are being saved is printed to **stderr**. If **msg=n** is specified, only the profiling error messages are printed. The default is **msg=y**.

merge=[y|n] — If **merge=y** is specified, the data files will be merged after successive runs. If **merge=n** is specified, the data files are not merged after successive runs, and the data file is overwritten after each execution. The merge will fail if the program has been recompiled, and the data file will be left in **TMPDIR**. The default is **merge=n**.

pid=[**y**|**n**] If **pid=y** is specified, the name of the data file will include the process ID of the profiled program. Inclusion of the process ID allows for the creation of different data files for programs calling **fork**. If **pid=n** is specified, the default name is used. The default is **pid=n**. For **lprof** to generate its profiling report, the **-c** option must be specified with **lprof** otherwise the default will fail.

dir=*dirname* The data file is placed in the directory *dirname* if this option is specified. Otherwise, the data file is created in the directory that is current at the end of execution.

file=*filename* *filename* is used as the name of the data file in *dir* created by the profiled program if this option is specified. Otherwise, the default name is used. For **lprof** to generate its profiling report, the **-c** option must be specified with **lprof** if the file option has been used at execution time; otherwise the default will fail.

FILES

prog.**cnt**	profile data
TMPDIR	usually **/var/tmp** but can be redefined by setting the environment variable **TMPDIR** [see **tempnam** in **tmpnam**(3S)].

NOTES

The full pathname of *prog*.**cnt** must not exceed 60 characters.

For the **-m** option, if *destfile*.**cnt** exists, its previous contents are destroyed.

Optimized code cannot be profiled; if both optimization and line profiling are requested, profiling has precedence.

Including header files that contain code (such as **stat.h** or **utsname.h**) will cause erroneous data.

Different parts of one line of a source file may be executed different numbers of times (for example, the **for** loop below); the count corresponds to the first part of the line.

For example, in the following **for** loop

```
                main()
   1   [2]      {
                    int j;

   1   [5]          for (j = 0; j < 5; j++)
   5   [6]          sub(j);

   1   [8]      }

                sub(a)
                int a;
   5   [12]         {
   5   [13]         printf("a is %d\n", a);
   5   [14]         }
```

line 5 consists of three parts. The line count listed, however, is for the initialization part, that is, `j = 0`.

SEE ALSO

cc(1), fork(2), prof(1), tmpnam(3S)

NAME

lpsched, **lpshut** – start/stop the LP print service

SYNOPSIS

/usr/lib/lp/lpsched
lpshut

DESCRIPTION

lpsched allows you to start the LP print service.

lpshut shuts down the print service. All printers that are printing at the time **lpshut** is invoked will stop printing. When **lpsched** is started again, requests that were printing at the time a printer was shut down will be reprinted from the beginning.

NOTES

If the scheduler fails to run, check the **lpsched** log file which contains all failed attempts to load print requests, printer descriptions, forms, filters, classes, alerts, and systems. The log files are located in **/var/lp/logs**. Useful information on the LP Networking Service can also be found in the log file **/var/lp/logs/lpNet**.

FILES

/var/spool/lp/*
/usr/lib/locale/*locale***/LC_MESSAGES/uxlp**
language-specific message file [See **LANG** on **environ**(5).]

SEE ALSO

accept(1M), **enable**(1M), **lpadmin**(1M)

NAME

lpstat – print information about the status of the LP print service

SYNOPSIS

lpstat [*options*] [*request-ID-list*]

DESCRIPTION

The **lpstat** command displays information about the current status of the LP print service. If no *options* are given, **lpstat** displays the status of all print requests made by you. [See **lp**(1) for details.] If the command is issued on a system running the LP Networking Service, **lpstat** displays the status of requests made to both local and remote printers. Status messages containing supplementary code set characters are displayed according to the locale specified in the **LC_CTYPE** environment variable [see **LANG** on **environ**(5)].

Any arguments that are not *options* are assumed to be *request-IDs* as returned by **lp**. The **lpstat** command displays the status of such requests. The *options* may appear in any order and may be repeated and intermixed with other arguments. Some of the keyletters below may be followed by an optional *list* that can be in one of two forms: a list of items separated by commas or a list of items separated by spaces and enclosed in quotes. For example:

> **-p** *printer1*,*printer2*
> **-u** "*user1 user2 user3*"

Administrative users with the appropriate privileges may override these restrictions and report information on all jobs.

Specifying **all** after any keyletter that takes *list* as an argument causes all information relevant to the keyletter to be displayed. For example, the command

```
lpstat -o all
```

displays the status of all output requests.

The omission of a *list* following such keyletters causes all information relevant to the keyletter to be displayed. For example, the command

```
lpstat -o
```

displays the status of all output requests.

The following options and arguments may be used with **lpstat**:

-a [*list*] — Report whether print destinations are accepting requests. *list* is a list of intermixed printer names and class names.

-c [*list*] — Report names of all classes and their members. *list* is a list of class names.

-d — Report what the system default destination is (if any).

-f [*list*] [**-l**] — Verify that the forms in *list* are recognized by the LP print service. *list* is a list of forms; the default is **all**. The **-l** option will list the form parameters.

`-o` [*list*] [`-l`]
: Report the status of print requests. *list* is a list of intermixed printer names, class names, and *request-IDs*. The keyletter `-o` may be omitted. The `-l` option lists for each request whether it is queued for, assigned to, or being printed on a printer, the form required (if any), and the character set or print wheel required (if any).

`-p` [*list*] [`-D`] [`-l`]
: If the `-D` option is given, a brief description is printed for each printer in *list*. If the `-l` option is given, a full description of each printer's configuration is given, including the form mounted, the acceptable content and printer types, a printer description, the interface used, and so on.

In order to maintain system security access information, the information needed to produce the printer status given by **`lpstat -p`** is available only if the LP scheduler is running.

`-r`
: Report the status of the LP request scheduler (whether it is running).

`-R`
: Report a number showing the rank order of jobs in the print queue for each printer.

`-s` [`-l`]
: Display a status summary, including the status of the LP scheduler, the system default destination, a list of class names and their members, a list of printers and their associated devices, a list of the systems sharing print services, a list of all forms and their availability, and a list of all recognized character sets and print wheels. The `-l` option displays all parameters for each form and the printer name where each character set or print wheel is available.

`-S` [*list*] [`-l`]
: Verify that the character sets or the print wheels specified in *list* are recognized by the LP print service. Items in *list* can be character sets or print wheels; the default for *list* is **`all`**. If the `-l` option is given, each line is appended by a list of printers that can handle the print wheel or character set. The list also shows whether the print wheel or character set is mounted or specifies the built-in character set into which it maps.

`-t` [`-l`]
: Display all status information: all the information obtained with the `-s` option, plus the acceptance and idle/busy status of all printers and status of all requests. The `-l` option displays more detail as described for the `-f`, `-o`, `-p`, and `-s` options. Supplementary code set characters specified are not printed correctly.

`-u` [*login-name-list*]
: Display the status of output requests for users. The *login-name-list* argument may include any or all of the following constructs:

login-name	a user on the local system
system-name!*login-name*	a user on system *system-name*
system-name!**all**	all users on system *system-name*
all!*login-name*	a user on all systems
all	all users on the local system
all!all	all users on all systems

The default value of *login-name-list* is **all**.

FILES

/etc/lp/*
/var/spool/lp/*
/usr/lib/locale/*locale*/LC_MESSAGES/uxlp
language-specific message file [See **LANG** on **environ**(5).]

SEE ALSO

lp(1)

lpsystem (1M)

NAME

lpsystem – register remote systems with the print service

SYNOPSIS

lpsystem [**-t** *type*] [**-T** *timeout*] [**-R** *retry*] [**-y** **"***comment***"**] *system-name* [*system-name* . . .]

lpsystem -l [*system-name* . . .]

lpsystem -r *system-name* [*system-name* . . .]

lpsystem -A

DESCRIPTION

The **lpsystem** command is used to define parameters for the LP print service, with respect to communication (via a high-speed network such as STARLAN or TCP/IP) with remote systems. Only a privileged user (that is, the owner of the login **root**) may execute the **lpsystem** command.

Specifically, the **lpsystem** command is used to define remote systems with which the local LP print service can exchange print requests. These remote systems are described to the local LP print service in terms of several parameters that control communication: type, retry and timeout. These parameters are defined in **/etc/lp/Systems**. You can edit this file with a text editor (such as **vi**) but editing is not recommended. By using **lpsystem**, you can ensure that **lpsched** is notified of any changes to the **Systems** file.

The *type* parameter defines the remote system as one of two types: **s5** (System V Release 4) or **bsd** (SunOS). The default type is **s5**.

The *timeout* parameter specifies the length of time (in minutes) that the print service should allow a network connection to be idle. If the connection to the remote system is idle (that is, there is no network traffic) for *N* minutes, then drop the connection. (When there is more work the connection will be reestablished.) Legal values are **n**, **0**, and *N*, where *N* is an integer greater than 0. The value **n** means "never time out"; **0** means "as soon as the connection is idle, drop it." The default is **n**.

The *retry* parameter specifies the length of time to wait before trying to re-establish a connection to the remote system, when the connection was dropped abnormally (that is, a network error). Legal values are **n**, **0**, and *N*, where *N* is an integer greater than 0 and it means "wait *N* minutes before trying to reconnect. (The default is 10 minutes.) The value **n** means "do not retry dropped connections until there is more work"; **0** means "try to reconnect immediately."

The *comment* argument allows you to associate a free form comment with the system entry. This is visible when **lpsystem -l** is used.

System-name is the name of the remote system from which you want to be able to receive jobs, and to which you want to be able to send jobs.

The command **lpsystem -l** [*system-name*] will print out a description of the parameters associated with *system-name* (if a system has been specified), or with all the systems in its database (if *system-name* has not been specified).

The command **lpsystem -r** *system-name* will remove the entry associated with *system-name*. The print service will no longer accept jobs from that system or send jobs to it, even if the remote printer is still defined on the local system. The scheduler must be running when the removal of a systems file entry occurs, because the scheduler checks whether the system entry is currently used by a printer destination. If currently used, the system entry cannot be removed.

If you use **lpsystem -r** *system-name* to remove a system and you have active printers for that system, you will not be allowed to remove the system from the system file. **lpsystem -r** *system-name* will only work if no printers for that system exist.

The command **lpsystem -A** will print out the TCP/IP address of the local machine in a format to be used when configuring the local port monitor to accept requests from a SunOS system.

NOTES

Network addresses and services are handled by the Name-to-Address Mapping facilities. (See the "Network Services" chapter in the *Network Administration* for a discussion of network addresses and services.) Port monitors handle listening for remote service requests and routing the connection to the print service. (See the "Managing Ports" chapter in the *Advanced System Administration* for a discussion of port monitors.)

If the Name-to-Address Mapping facilities are not set up properly, out-bound remote print service probably will not work. Similarly, if the local port monitors are not set up to route remote print requests to the print service, then service for remote systems will not be provided. (See "Configuring a Network Printer" in the "Advanced Print Service" chapter of the *Basic System Administration* to find out how to do this.)

With respect to the semantics of the *timeout* and *retry* values, the print service uses one process for each remote system with which it communicates, and it communicates with a remote system only when there is work to be done on that system or work is being sent from that system.

The system initiating the connection is the "master" process and the system accepting the connection is the "slave" process. This designation serves only to determine which process dies (the slave) when a connection is dropped. This helps prevent there from being more than one process communicating with a remote system. Furthermore, all connections are bi-directional, regardless of the master/slave designation. You cannot control a system's master/slave designation. Typically, a client machine has the master child and the server machine has the slave child. Now, keeping all this information in mind, if a master process times out, then both the slave and master will exit. If a slave times out, then it is possible that the master may still live and retry the connection after the retry interval. Therefore, one system's resource management strategy can affect another system's strategy.

With respect to **lpsystem -A**: a SunOS system (described with **-t bsd**) can be connected to your system only via TCP/IP, and print requests from a SunOS system can come in to your machine only via a special port (515). The address given to you from **lpsystem** will be the address of your system and port 515. This address is used by your TCP/IP port monitor to "listen" on that address and port, and to route connections to the print service. [See **sacadm**(1M), **nlsadmin**(1M), and the "Managing Ports" chapter of the *Advanced System Administration*.] The important point here is that this is where you get the address referred to in that procedure.

The command **lpsystem -A** will not work if your system name and IP address are not listed in **/etc/inet/hosts** and the printer service is not listed in **/etc/inet/services**.

FILES

/etc/lp/*

/usr/lib/locale/*locale***/LC_MESSAGES/uxlp**

language-specific message file [See **LANG** on **environ**(5).]

/var/spool/lp/*

SEE ALSO

netconfig(4)

NAME

`lptest` – (BSD) generate lineprinter ripple pattern

SYNOPSIS

`/usr/ucb/lptest` [*length* [*count*]]

DESCRIPTION

`lptest` writes the traditional "ripple test" pattern on standard output. In 96 lines, this pattern will print all 96 printable ASCII characters in each position. While originally created to test printers, it is quite useful for testing terminals, driving terminal ports for debugging purposes, or any other task where a quick supply of random data is needed.

The *length* argument specifies the output line length if the the default length of 79 is inappropriate.

The *count* argument specifies the number of output lines to be generated if the default count of 200 is inappropriate.

NOTES

If *count* is to be specified, *length* must be also be specified.

This command is obsolescent.

NAME

lpusers – set printing queue priorities

SYNOPSIS

lpusers -d *priority-level*
lpusers -q *priority-level* **-u** *login-name-list*
lpusers -u *login-name-list*
lpusers -q *priority-level*
lpusers -l

DESCRIPTION

The **lpusers** command is used to set limits to the queue priority level that can be assigned to jobs submitted by users of the LP print service.

The first form of the command (with **-d**) sets the system-wide priority default to *priority-level*, where *priority-level* is a value of 0 to 39, with 0 being the highest priority. If a user does not specify a priority level with a print request [see **lp**(1)], the default priority is used. Initially, the default priority level is 20.

The second form of the command (with **-q** and **-u**) sets the default highest *priority-level* (0-39) that the users in *login-name-list* can request when submitting a print request. The *login-name-list* argument may include any or all of the following constructs:

login-name	a user on the local system
system_name!*login-name*	a user on the system *system_name*
system_name!**all**	all users on system *system_name*
all!*login-name*	a user on all systems
all	all users on the local system

Users that have been given a limit cannot submit a print request with a higher priority level than the one assigned, nor can they change a request already submitted to have a higher priority. Any print requests submitted with priority levels higher than allowed will be given the highest priority allowed.

The third form of the command (with **-u**) removes any explicit priority level for the specified users.

The fourth form of the command (with **-q**) sets the default highest priority level for all users not explicitly covered by the use of the second form of this command.

The last form of the command (with **-l**) lists the default priority level and the priority limits assigned to users.

FILES

/usr/lib/locale/*locale***/LC_MESSAGES/uxlp**
language-specific message file [See **LANG** on **environ**(5).]

NAME

ls, **lc** – list contents of directory

SYNOPSIS

ls [**-RadLCxmlenogrtucpFbqisf1**] [*file* . . .]
lc [**-1CFLRabcfgilmnopqrstux**] [*name*. . .]

DESCRIPTION

For each directory argument, **ls** lists the contents of the directory; for each *file* argument, **ls** repeats its name and any other information requested. The output is sorted alphabetically by default. When arguments are not given, the current directory is listed. When several arguments are given, the arguments are first sorted appropriately, but file arguments appear before directories and their contents. **ls** processes supplementary code set characters according to the locale specified in the **LC_CTYPE** and **LC_COLLATE** environment variables [see **LANG** on **environ**(5)], except as noted under the **-b** and **-q** options below.

If the Application Compatibility Package is installed, the XENIX command **lc** functions the same as **ls** except that the **lc** default output format is columnar, even if the output is redirected.

There are three major listing formats. The default format for output directed to a terminal is multi-column with entries sorted down the columns. The options **-C** and **-x** enable multi-column formats; and the **-m** option enables stream output format, in which files are listed across the page, separated by commas.

To determine output formats for the **-C**, **-x**, and **-m** options, **ls** uses an environment variable, **COLUMNS**, to determine the number of positions available on one output line. If this variable is not set, the **terminfo**(4) database is used to determine the number of columns, based on the environment variable **TERM**. If this information cannot be obtained, 80 columns are assumed.

The **ls** command has the following options:

-R Recursively list subdirectories encountered.

-a List all entries, including those that begin with a period (**.**), which are normally not listed.

-d If an argument is a directory, list only its name (not its contents); often used with **-l** to get the status of a directory.

-L When listing status, if an argument is a symbolic link, list the status of the file or directory referenced by the link rather than that of the link itself.

-C Multi-column output with entries sorted down the columns. This is the default output format.

-x Multi-column output with entries sorted across rather than down the page.

-m Stream output format; files are listed across the page, separated by commas.

-l List in long format, giving mode, number of links, owner, group, size in bytes, and time of last modification for each file (see below). If the file is a special file, the size field contains the major and minor device numbers rather than a size. If the file is a symbolic link, the filename is printed followed by "`->`" and the pathname of the referenced file.

`-e` *extent_opt*
: Specify how to handle a **`vxfs`** file that has extent attribute information. Extent attributes include reserved space, a fixed extent size, and extent alignment. It may not be possible to preserve the information if the destination file system does not support extent attributes, has a different block size than the source file system, or lacks free extents appropriate to satisfy the extent attribute requirements. Valid values for *extent_opt* are:

  `warn` Issue a warning message if extent attribute information cannot be kept (default).

  `force` Fail the copy if extent attribute information cannot be kept.

  `ignore` Ignore extent attribute information entirely.

  When used with `-l`, `-e` displays extent attribute information for files with reserved space or fixed extent sizes.

`-n` The same as `-l`, except that the owner's **`UID`** and group's **`GID`** numbers are printed, rather than the associated character strings.

`-o` The same as `-l`, except that the group is not printed.

`-g` The same as `-l`, except that the owner is not printed.

`-r` Reverse the order of sort to get reverse alphabetic or oldest first as appropriate.

`-t` Sort by time stamp (latest first) instead of by name. The default is the last modification time. (See `-n` and `-c`.)

`-u` Use time of last access instead of last modification for sorting (with the `-t` option) or printing (with the `-l` option).

`-c` Use time of last modification of the i-node (file created, mode changed, and so on) for sorting (`-t`) or printing (`-l`).

`-p` Put a slash (`/`) after each filename if the file is a directory.

`-F` Put a slash (`/`) after each filename if the file is a directory, an asterisk (*) if the file is executable, and an ampersand (`@`) if the file is a symbolic link.

`-b` Force printing of non-printable characters to be in the octal *ddd* notation. All multibyte characters are considered printable.

`-q` Force printing of non-printable characters in file names as the character question mark (`?`). All multibyte characters are considered printable.

`-i` For each file, print the i-node number in the first column of the report.

`-s` Give size in blocks, including indirect blocks, for each entry.

`-f` Force each argument to be interpreted as a directory and list the name found in each slot. This option turns off `-l`, `-t`, `-s`, and `-r`, and turns on `-a`; the order is the order in which entries appear in the directory.

`-1` Print one entry per line of output.

The mode printed under the `-l` option consists of eleven possible characters. The first character may be one of the following:

- `d` if the entry is a directory;
- `l` if the entry is a symbolic link;
- `b` if the entry is a block special file;
- `c` if the entry is a character special file;
- `m` the entry is XENIX shared data (memory) file;
- `p` if the entry is a fifo (named pipe) special file;
- `s` the entry is a XENIX semaphore;
- `-` if the entry is a regular file.

The next 9 characters are interpreted as three sets of three bits each. The first set refers to the owner's permissions; the next to permissions of others in the user-group of the file; and the last to all others. Within each set, the three characters indicate permission to read, write, and execute the file as a program, respectively. For a directory, "execute" permission is interpreted to mean permission to search the directory for a specified file.

`ls -l` (the long list) prints its output as follows:

```
-rwxrwxrwx  1 smith  dev     10876  May 16 9:42 part2
```

Reading from right to left, you see that the current directory holds one file, named **part2**. Next, the last time that file's contents were modified was 9:42 A.M. on May 16. The file contains 10,876 bytes. The owner of the file, or the user, belongs to the group **dev** (perhaps indicating "development"), and their login name is **smith**. The number, in this case `1`, indicates the number of links to file **part2** [see **cp**(1)]. Finally, the dash and letters tell you that user, group, and others have permissions to read, write, and execute **part2**.

The execute (**x**) symbol here occupies the third position of the three-character sequence. A - in the third position would have indicated a denial of execution permissions.

The permissions are indicated as follows:

- `r` the file is readable
- `w` the file is writable
- `x` the file is executable
- `-` the indicated permission is not granted
- `l` mandatory locking occurs during access (the set-group-ID bit is on and the group execution bit is off)
- `s` the set-user-ID or set-group-ID bit is on, and the corresponding user or group execution bit is also on
- `S` undefined bit-state (the set-user-ID bit is on and the user execution bit is off)
- `t` the 1000 (octal) bit, or sticky bit, is on [see **chmod**(1)], and execution is on
- `T` the 1000 bit is turned on, and execution is off (undefined bit-state)

For user and group permissions, the third position is sometimes occupied by a character other than **x** or **-**. **s** also may occupy this position, referring to the state of the set-ID bit, whether it be the user's or the group's. The ability to assume the same ID as the user during execution is, for example, used during login when you begin as root but need to assume the identity of the user you login as.

In the case of the sequence of group permissions, **l** may occupy the third position. **l** refers to mandatory file and record locking. This permission describes a file's ability to allow other files to lock its reading or writing permissions during access.

For other permissions, the third position may be occupied by **t** or **T**. These refer to the state of the sticky bit and execution permissions.

The **-e** option (used with **-l**) displays extent attribute information as follows:

```
-rwxrwxrwx 1 smith dev  10876  May 16 9:42 part2 :res 36 ext
3 align noextend
```

This output line indicates a file with 36 blocks of reservation, a fixed extent size of 3 blocks, all extents aligned to 3 block boundaries, and the file unable to be grown once the current reservation is exhausted.

EXAMPLES

An example of a file's permissions is:

```
-rwxr--r--
```

This describes a file that is readable, writable, and executable by the user and readable by the group and others.

Another example of a file's permissions is:

```
-rwsr-xr-x
```

This describes a file that is readable, writable, and executable by the user, readable and executable by the group and others, and allows its user-ID to be assumed, during execution, by the user presently executing it.

Another example of a file's permissions is:

```
-rw-rwl---
```

This describes a file that is readable and writable only by the user and the group and can be locked during access.

An example of a command line:

```
ls -a
```

This command prints the names of all files in the current directory, including those that begin with a dot (**.**), which normally do not print.

Another example of a command line:

```
ls -aisn
```

This command provides information on all files, including those that begin with a dot (**a**), the i-number—the memory address of the i-node associated with the file—printed in the left-hand column (**i**); the size (in blocks) of the files, printed in the column to the right of the i-numbers (**s**); finally, the report is displayed in the numeric version of the long list, printing the UID (instead of user name) and GID (instead of group name) numbers associated with the files.

When the sizes of the files in a directory are listed, a total count of blocks, including indirect blocks, is printed.

FILES

/etc/passwd
: user IDs for **ls -l** and **ls -o**

/etc/group
: group IDs for **ls -l** and **ls -g**

/usr/share/lib/terminfo/?/*
: terminal information database

/usr/lib/locale/*locale***/LC_MESSAGES/uxcore.abi**
: language-specific message file [See **LANG** on **environ** (5).]

SEE ALSO

chmod(1), **find**(1)

NOTES

In a Remote File Sharing environment, you may not have the permissions that the output of the **ls -l** command leads you to believe.

Unprintable characters in file names may confuse the columnar output options.

The total block count will be incorrect if there are hard links among the files.

NAME

`ls` – (BSD) list the contents of a directory

SYNOPSIS

`/usr/ucb/ls` [`-aAcCdfFgilLqrRstul`] *filename* . . .

DESCRIPTION

For each *filename* which is a directory, `ls` lists the contents of the directory; for each *filename* which is a file, `ls` repeats its name and any other information requested. By default, the output is sorted alphabetically. When no argument is given, the current directory is listed. When several arguments are given, the arguments are first sorted appropriately, but file arguments are processed before directories and their contents.

Permissions Field

The mode printed under the `-l` option contains 10 characters interpreted as follows. If the first character is:

- `d` entry is a directory;
- `b` entry is a block-type special file;
- `c` entry is a character-type special file;
- `l` entry is a symbolic link;
- `p` entry is a FIFO (also known as named pipe) special file, or
- `-` entry is a plain file.

The next 9 characters are interpreted as three sets of three bits each. The first set refers to owner permissions; the next refers to permissions to others in the same user-group; and the last refers to all others. Within each set the three characters indicate permission respectively to read, to write, or to execute the file as a program. For a directory, execute permission is interpreted to mean permission to search the directory. The permissions are indicated as follows:

- `r` the file is readable;
- `w` the file is writable;
- `x` the file is executable;
- `-` the indicated permission is not granted.

The group-execute permission character is given as `s` if the file has the set-group-id bit set; likewise the owner-execute permission character is given as `s` if the file has the set-user-id bit set.

The last character of the mode (normally `x` or '`-`') is `true` if the 1000 bit of the mode is on. See **chmod**(1) for the meaning of this mode. The indications of set-ID and 1000 bits of the mode are capitalized (`S` and `T` respectively) if the corresponding execute permission is *not* set.

When the sizes of the files in a directory are listed, a total count of blocks, including indirect blocks is printed. The following options are available:

`-a` List all entries; in the absence of this option, entries whose names begin with a '`.`' are *not* listed (except for the privileged user, for whom `ls` normally prints even files that begin with a '`.`').

-A Same as **-a**, except that '.' and '..' are not listed.

-c Use time of last edit (or last mode change) for sorting or printing.

-C Force multi-column output, with entries sorted down the columns; for **ls**, this is the default when output is to a terminal.

-d If argument is a directory, list only its name (not its contents); often used with **-l** to get the status of a directory.

-f Force each argument to be interpreted as a directory and list the name found in each slot. This option turns off **-l**, **-t**, **-s**, and **-r**, and turns on **-a**; the order is the order in which entries appear in the directory.

-F Mark directories with a trailing slash ('/'), executable files with a trailing asterisk ('*'), symbolic links with a trailing at-sign ('@').

-g For **ls**, show the group ownership of the file in a long output.

-i For each file, print the i-node number in the first column of the report.

-l List in long format, giving mode, number of links, owner, size in bytes, and time of last modification for each file. If the file is a special file the size field will instead contain the major and minor device numbers. If the time of last modification is greater than six months ago, it is shown in the format '*month date year*'; files modified within six months show '*month date time*'. If the file is a symbolic link the pathname of the linked-to file is printed preceded by '->'.

-L If argument is a symbolic link, list the file or directory the link references rather than the link itself.

-q Display non-graphic characters in filenames as the character **?**; for **ls**, this is the default when output is to a terminal.

-r Reverse the order of sort to get reverse alphabetic or oldest first as appropriate.

-R Recursively list subdirectories encountered.

-s Give size of each file, including any indirect blocks used to map the file, in kilobytes.

-t Sort by time modified (latest first) instead of by name.

-u Use time of last access instead of last modification for sorting (with the **-t** option) and/or printing (with the **-l** option).

-1 Force one entry per line output format; this is the default when output is not to a terminal.

FILES

/etc/passwd to get user ID's for '**ls -l**' and '**ls -o**'.
/etc/group to get group ID for '**ls -g**'

NOTES

NEWLINE and TAB are considered printing characters in filenames.

The output device is assumed to be 80 columns wide.

The option setting based on whether the output is a teletype is undesirable as '**ls -s**' is much different than '**ls -s | lpr**'. On the other hand, not doing this setting would make old shell scripts which used **ls** almost certain losers.

Unprintable characters in file names may confuse the columnar output options.

The identification of sockets made possible by **-l** or using the **-F** option on a BSD system is not supported.

Reference Manual Index

The Permuted Index that follows is a list of keywords, alphabetized in the second of three columns, together with the context in which each keyword is found. The manual page that produced an entry is listed in the right column.

Entries are identified with their section numbers shown in parentheses. This is important because there is considerable duplication of names among the sections, arising principally from commands and functions that exist only to exercise a particular system call.

The index is produced by rotating the NAME section of each manual page to alphabetize each keyword in it. Words that cannot fit in the middle column are rotated into the left column. If the entry is still too long, some words are omitted, and their omission is indicated with a slash ("/").

How the Permuted Index Is Created

Many users find that understanding a few things about how the permuted index is created helps them to read it more effectively and clarifies what kind of information can and cannot be obtained from it.

The basic building block for the index is the one-line description given in the NAME line on the top of each manual page. For example, this is what the top of the `mountall`(1M) manual page looks like:

---

mountall(1M) **mountall(1M)**

NAME

`mountall, umountall` – mount, unmount multiple file systems

Each NAME line includes:

- the command, file format, system call or other utility for which the manual page is named (this is the primary utility; `mountall` is the primary utility in the example)
- secondary utilities, which are also described on that manual page and do not have a separate manual page of their own (`umountall` is a secondary utility in the example)

- a brief description of the utility function(s)

For each manual page NAME line, the indexing software generates several index entries, generally one entry for each keyword in the phrase. The middle column of the index is alphabetized on these keywords.

For:

NAME

`mountall, umountall` – mount, unmount multiple file systems

This is generated:

mount, unmount multiple	file systems. /umountall:	mountall(1M)
systems. mountall, umountall:	mount, unmount multiple file	mountall(1M)
unmount multiple file systems.	mountall, umountall: mount, ...	mountall(1M)
/umountall: mount, unmount	multiple file systems.	mountall(1M)
mount, unmount multiple file	systems. mountall, umountall:	mountall(1M)
multiple file/ mountall,	umountall: mount, unmount	mountall(1M)
mountall, umountall: mount,	unmount multiple file systems.	mountall(1M)

How to Use the Index

Look in the middle column of the index for the word of interest. Then read the complete phrase by starting with the utility name, which may appear in the left or middle column. Utility names are followed by a colon.

The NAME line phrase is contained in the two columns, with long phrases wrapping around to the beginning of the left column. The right column of the index provides the manual page name and section number.

A slash (/) sometimes appears in the index entry to indicate that space limitations were exceeded and one or more words from the phrase were deleted.

Permuted Index

PERMUTED INDEX

blocks and inodes for vxfs file/ df	(vxfs) report number of free disk	df(1M)
file system fsadm	(vxfs) resize or reorganize a vxfs	fsadm(1M)
setext	(vxfs) set extent attributes	setext(1)
fsdb	(vxfs) vxfs file system debugger	fsdb(1M)
restore	vxrestore incremental file system	vxrestore(1M)
are they doing	w (BSD) who is logged in, and what	w(1)
	wait await completion of process	wait(1)
	wall write to all users	wall(1M)
	wc word count	wc(1)
and supplementary code sets	wchrtbl generate tables for ASCII	wchrtbl(1M)
summary about a keyword	whatis (BSD) display a one-line	whatis(1)
binary/ ckbinarsys determine	whether remote system can accept	ckbinarsys(1M)
current username	whoami display the effective	whoami(1)
	whodo who is doing what	whodo(1M)
service	whois Internet user name directory	whois(1)
rusers	who's logged in on local machines	rusers(1)
rwho	who's logged in on local machines	rwho(1)
xpr print an X	window dump	xpr(1)
olwm	Window Manager	olwm(1)
for X xsetroot root	window parameter setting utility	xsetroot(1)
to set terminal settings to current	window size resize utility	resize(1)
X X	Window System server	X(1)
extensions to ksh wksh	Windowing KornShell, graphical	wksh(1)
/(BSD) reboot/halt the system	without checking the disks	fastboot(1M)
extensions to ksh	wksh Windowing KornShell, graphical	wksh(1)
wc	word count	wc(1)
lines in a sorted/ look (BSD) find	words in the system dictionary or	look(1)
cd change	working directory	cd(1)
pwd	working directory name	pwd(1)
specific alarms and/or the	"working" indicator /application	indicator(1F)
auditmap create and	write audit map files	auditmap(1M)
rwall	write to all users over a network	rwall(1M)
wall	write to all users	wall(1M)
write	write to another user	write(1)
	write write to another user	write(1)
accounting records fwtmp,	wtmpfix manipulate connect	fwtmp(1M)
xdm	X Display Manager	xdm(1M)
xpr print an	X window dump	xpr(1)
X	X Window System server	X(1)
	X X Window System server	X(1)
xhost server access control for	X	xhost(1)
parameter setting utility for	X xsetroot root window	xsetroot(1)
xterm terminal emulator for	X	xterm(1)
BDF to SNF font compiler for	X11 bdftosnf	bdftosnf(1)
systems	x286emul emulate 80286 XENIX	x286emul(1)
CD-ROM Extended Attribute Record	(XAR) cdxar read	cdxar(1M)
and execute command	xargs construct argument list(s)	xargs(1)
	xdm X Display Manager	xdm(1M)
SCO UNIX System V/386/ fixshlib	(XENIX) alters executables to call	fixshlib(1M)
modification dates of/ settime	(XENIX) change the access and	settime(1)
filesystems fsck	(XENIX) check and repair XENIX	fsck(1M)
information to different/ maplocale	(XENIX) convert Release 4 locale	maplocale(1M)